Mass Media Law

Don R. Pember

University of Washington

Boston   Burr Ridge, IL   Dubuque, IA   Madison, WI   New York   San Francisco   St. Louis
Bangkok   Bogotá   Caracas   Lisbon   London   Madrid
Mexico City   Milan   New Delhi   Seoul   Singapore   Sydney   Taipei   Toronto

McGraw-Hill Higher Education

A Division of The **McGraw-Hill** *Companies*

MASS MEDIA LAW 2001–2002 Edition

Published by McGraw-Hill, an imprint of the The McGraw-Hill Companies, Inc. 1221 Avenue
of the Americas, New York, NY, 10020. Copyright © 2001, by The McGraw-Hill Companies, Inc.
All rights reserved. No part of this publication may be reproduced or distributed in any form or
by any means, or stored in a data base or retrieval system, without the prior written consent of
The McGraw-Hill Companies, Inc., including, but not limited to, in any network or other
electronic storage or transmission, or broadcast for distance learning. Some ancillaries, including
electronic and print components, may not be available to customers outside the United States.

This book is printed on acid-free paper.

2 3 4 5 6 7 8 9 0 DOC/DOC 0 9 8 7 6 5 4 3 2 1

ISBN 007237053X
ISSN 1088-9973

Editorial director: *Phillip A. Butcher*
Sponsoring editor: *Valerie Raymond*
Marketing manager: *Kelly M. May*
Project editor: *Karen J. Nelson*
Senior production supervisor: *Lori Koetters*
Freelance design coordinator: *Gino Cieslik*
Supplement coordinator: *Mark Sienicki*
Media technology producer: *Kimberly Stark*
Cover design: *Gino Cieslik*
Cover photos: *© PhotoDisc*
Compositor: *Electronic Publishing Services, Inc., TN*
Typeface: *10/12 Times Roman*
Printer: *R. R. Donnelley & Sons Company*

www.mhhe.com

The McGraw-Hill Series in Mass Communication and Journalism

Adams
Introduction to Radio: Production and Programming

Arnold
Media Writer's Handbook

Baskin, Aronoff, and Lattimore
Public Relations: The Profession and The Practice

Black, Bryant, and Thompson
Introduction to Media Communication

Bridges
An Internet Guide for Mass Communication Students

Brown and Quaal
Telecommunications Management: Radio-Television-Cable Mangement

Burrows, Gross, and Wood
Video Production: Disciplines and Techniques

Cremer, Keirstead, and Yoakam
ENG: Television News

Dominick
The Dynamics of Mass Communication

Dominick, Sherman, and Messere
Broadcasting, Cable, the Internet and Beyond

Frazell and Tuck
Principles of Editing: A Comprehensive Guide for Students and Journalists

Gross
Telecommunications: An Introduction to Electronic Media and *The International World of Electronic Media*

Harrower
The Newspaper Designer's Handbook

Holsinger and Dilts
Media Law

Itule and Anderson
News Writing and Reporting for Today's Media

Lewis
Photojournalism: Content and Technique

Lieb
Editing for Clear Communication

Mencher
News Reporting and Writing Basic Media Media Writing

Patterson and Wilkins
Media Ethics: Issues and Cases

Pember
Mass Media Law

Rich
Creating Online Media

Sherman
Telecommunications Management: Broadcasting/Cable and the New Technologies

Tuggle, Carr, Huffman
Broadcast News Handbook: Writing, Reporting, and Producing

Wilson and Wilson
Mass Media/Mass Culture: An Introduction

CONTENTS

12 Free Press/Fair Trial: Closed Judicial Proceedings ——— 433

13 Regulation of Obscene and Other Erotic Material ——— 459

14 Copyright ——— 497

Contents

PREFACE

No single theme has emerged in the past 12 months to describe the changing and growing body of mass media law in America. The Supreme Court handed down two rulings which related directly to mass communications law and a couple of others that related peripherally to the topic, but none of these cases are landmark decisions. The high court rebuffed the challenges of several states and said that the Congress can adopt a law requiring the states to limit access to drivers license records they maintain, an important victory for privacy advocates, but a disappointment to many journalists who argue that the records are useful in developing important news stories. But the high court rejected a congressional attempt to require most cable television system operators to funnel their adult movie and entertainment channels into the late night and early morning hours. The so-called signal-bleed provisions of the Telecommunications Act of 1996 were declared to be unconstitutional. Both these rulings are discussed in the text.

Congress continued to channel most of its legislative energy toward protecting the nation's youth from indecent or adult material on the Internet, but got little support from the nation's courts. Three days before this preface was prepared a three-judge panel of the 3rd U.S. Court of Appeals ruled that the Child Online Protection Act, the 1998 successor to the Communications Decency Act, ran seriously afoul of the First Amendment. Most observers argued that the Congress could serve the country in a more useful fashion if it focused its attention on other more important Internet problems related to the protection of privacy and copyright. But no legislation appeared to be forthcoming. The Federal Trade Commission became an active advocate for statutory privacy protection in the wake of inaction by both the administration and the Congress.

The growth of the Internet forced more and more courts to confront new issues in libel law, privacy, copyright, obscenity, access to information and general First Amendment areas like prior restraint. New terminology entered the legal domain with names like RioMP3, RioMP3.com and Napster turning up in lawsuits. Surprisingly, perhaps, the matter of downloading recorded music became one of the most complicated and interesting copyright issues as the year 2000 began.

A lot of people besides the author generate this text. The continued support of McGraw-Hill, and especially Valerie Raymond, Karen Nelson, and Karen Dorman, are especially important. Several of my colleagues who teach communications law offered valuable suggestions for this revision. I want to thank Dr. Herb Strentz, Drake University; Professor Glenn Cragwall, Carson-Newman College; Dr. Lynne Flocke, Syracuse University; Dr. Carol S. Lomicky, University of Nebraska at Kearney; Dr. George E. Whitehouse, University of South Dakota; Dr. Janet McMullen, University of North Alabama; Dr. Jack Lule, Lehigh University; Dr. S. L. Alexander, Loyola University; Dr. Emmanuel U. Onyedike, Hampton University; Dr. Mick Mulcrone, University of Portland; and Dr. Eddith A. Dashiell, Ohio University. I have taken many of their suggestions in preparing this edition of the book. My warmest regards go to Michelle Johnson, who, despite teaching at a school about 4,000 miles from the author, manages to generate a well-prepared and highly useful Student Study Guide for each edition. Clay Calvert at The Pennsylvania State University has made the Legal Resources Guide (found at www.mhhe.com/pember) even more useful this year with the addition of a new collection of sites on the United States Supreme Court. Continued support from my colleagues at the University of Washington, especially Jerry Baldasty and Richard Kielbowicz, is greatly appreciated as well. Finally, I want to thank my wife Diann for all her support and help during a particularly difficult year. The date at the end of this preface might be August or September rather than June without her willingness to pitch in.

Don R. Pember
Seattle, Washington,
June 25, 2000

NEW MATERIAL AND REVISIONS IN THIS EDITION

There were Substantial Cuts Made in the Material On:

University speech codes.

FOIA exemption.

Contempt.

Obscenity and indecency.

Fairness doctrine.

BILL OF RIGHTS
FIRST 10 AMENDMENTS TO THE CONSTITUTION

Article I

Congress shall make no law respecting an establishment of religion, or prohibiting the free exercise thereof; or abridging the freedom of speech, or of the press; or the right of the people peaceably to assemble, and to petition the government for a redress of grievances.

Article II

A well-regulated militia being necessary to the security of a free State, the right of the people to keep and bear arms shall not be infringed.

Article III

No soldier shall, in time of peace, be quartered in any house without the consent of the owner, nor in time of war, but in a manner to be prescribed by law.

Article IV

The right of the people to be secure in their persons, houses, papers, and effects, against unreasonable searches and seizures, shall not be violated, and no warrants shall issue but upon probable cause, supported by oath or affirmation, and particularly describing the place to be searched, and the persons or things to be seized.

Article V

No person shall be held to answer for a capital, or otherwise infamous crime, unless on a presentment or indictment of a grand jury, except in cases arising in the land or naval forces, or in the militia, when in actual service in time of war or public danger; nor shall any person be subject for the same offense to be twice put in jeopardy of life or limb; nor shall be compelled in any criminal case to be a witness against himself, nor be deprived of life, liberty, or property, without due process of law; nor shall private property be taken for public use without just compensation.

Article VI

In all criminal prosecutions, the accused shall enjoy the right to a speedy and public trial, by an impartial jury of the State and district wherein the crime shall have been committed, which district shall have been previously ascertained by law, and to be informed of the nature and cause of the accusation; to be confronted with the witnesses against him; to have compulsory process for obtaining witnesses in his favor, and to have the assistance of counsel for his defense.

Article VII

In suits at common law, where the value in controversy shall exceed twenty dollars, the right of trial by jury shall be preserved, and no fact tried by a jury shall be otherwise reexamined in any court of the United States, than according to the rules of the common law.

Article VIII

Excessive bail shall not be required, nor excessive fines imposed, nor cruel and unusual punishments inflicted.

Article IX

The enumeration in the Constitution, of certain rights, shall not be construed to deny or disparage others retained by the people.

Article X

The powers not delegated to the United States by the Constitution, nor prohibited by it to the States, are reserved to the States respectively, or to the people.

The first 10 Amendments (Bill of Rights) were adopted in 1791.

The American Legal System

Before a physician can study surgery, he or she needs to study anatomy. So it is with the study of mass media law. Before a study of this narrow aspect of American law is undertaken, a student must first have a general background in the law and in the operation of the judicial system. That is the purpose of this short chapter.

Probably no nation is more closely tied to the law than is the American Republic. From the 1770s, when at the beginning of a war of revolution we attempted to legally justify our separation from the motherland, to the 21st century, when citizens of the nation attempt to resolve weighty moral, political, social, and environmental problems through the judicial process, and during the more than 200 years between, the American people have showed a remarkable faith in the law. One could write a surprisingly accurate history of this nation using reports of court decisions as the only source. Not that what happens in the courts reflects everything that happens in the nation; but as has been observed by 19th-century British historian Alexis de Tocqueville and others, political and sometimes moral issues in the United States often end up as legal disputes. Beginning with the sedition cases in the late 1790s, which reflected the political turmoil of that era, one could chart the history of the United States from adolescence to maturity. As the frontier expanded in the 19th century, citizens used the courts to argue land claims and boundary problems. Civil rights litigation in both the mid-19th and mid-20th centuries reflects a people attempting to cope with racial and ethnic diversity. Industrialization brought labor unions, workers' compensation laws, and child labor laws, all of which resulted in controversies that found their way into the courts. As mass production developed and large manufacturers began to create most of the consumer goods used, judges and juries had to cope with new laws on product safety, honesty in advertising, and consumer complaints. In the late 20th century Americans went to court in disputes over abortion, gay rights, and sexually explicit books and films.

Americans have protested nearly every war the nation has fought—including the Revolutionary War. The record of these protests is contained in scores of court decisions. The prohibition and crime of the '20s and the economic woes of the '30s both left residue in the law. In the United States, as in most other societies, law is a basic part of existence, as necessary for the survival of civilization as are economic systems, political systems, mass communication systems, cultural achievement, and the family.

This chapter has two purposes: to acquaint readers with the law and to present a brief outline of the legal system in the United States. While this is not designed to be a comprehensive course in law and the judicial system—such material can better be studied in depth in an undergraduate political science course—it does provide sufficient introduction to understand the remaining 16 chapters of the book.

The chapter opens with a discussion of the law, giving consideration to the five most important sources of the law in the United States, and moves on to the judicial system, including both the federal and state court systems. A summary of judicial review and a brief outline of how both criminal and civil lawsuits are started and proceed through the courts are included in the discussion of the judicial system.

SOURCES OF THE LAW

There are almost as many definitions of law as there are people who study the law. Some people say that law is any social norm or any organized or ritualized method of settling disputes. Most writers on the subject insist that it is a bit more complex, that some system of sanctions is required before law exists. John Austin, a 19th-century English jurist, defined law as definite rules of human conduct with appropriate sanctions for their enforcement. He added that both the rules and the sanctions must be prescribed by duly constituted human authority.[1] Roscoe Pound, an American legal scholar, has suggested that law is really social engineering—the attempt to order the way people behave. For the purposes of this book, it is probably more helpful to consider the law to be a set of rules that attempt to guide human conduct and a set of formal, governmental sanctions that are applied when those rules are violated.

Scholars still debate the genesis of "the law." A question that is more meaningful and easier to answer is: What is the source of American law? There are really five major sources of the law in the United States: the Constitution, the common law, the law of equity, the statutory law, and the rulings of various executive and administrative bodies and agencies. Historically, we can trace American law to Great Britain. As colonizers of much of the North American continent, the British supplied Americans with an outline for both a legal system and a judicial system. In fact, because of the many similarities between British and American law, many people consider the Anglo-American legal system to be a single entity. Today in the United States, our federal Constitution is the supreme law of the land. Yet when each of these five sources of law is considered separately, it is more useful to begin with the earliest source of Anglo-American law, the common law.

THE COMMON LAW

The **common law,** which developed in England during the 200 years after the Norman Conquest in the 11th century, is one of the great legacies of the British people to colonial America. During those two centuries, the crude mosaic of Anglo-Saxon customs was replaced by a single system of law worked out by jurists and judges. The system of law became common throughout England; it became the common law. It was also called the common law to distinguish it from the ecclesiastical (church) law prevalent at the time. Initially, the customs of the people were used by the king's courts as the foundation of the law, disputes were resolved according to community custom, and governmental sanction was applied to enforce the resolution. As such, the common law was, and still is, considered "discovered law." When a problem arises, the court's task is to find or discover the proper solution, to seek the common custom of the people. The judge doesn't create the law; he or she merely finds it, much like a miner finds gold or silver.

This, at least, is the theory of the common law. Perhaps at one point judges themselves believed that they were merely discovering the law when they handed down decisions. As legal problems became more complex and as the law began to be professionally administered (the first lawyers appeared during this era, and eventually professional judges), it became clear that the common law reflected not so much the custom of the land as the custom of the court—or more properly, the custom of the judges. While judges continued to look to the past to discover how other courts decided a case when given similar facts (precedent is discussed in a moment), many times judges were forced to create the law themselves.

1. Abraham, *Judicial Process.*

This common-law system was the perfect system for the American colonies. Like most Anglo-Saxon institutions, it was a very pragmatic system aimed at settling real problems, not at expounding abstract and intellectually satisfying theories. The common law is an inductive system of law in which a legal rule is arrived at after consideration of a great number of cases. (In a deductive system the rules are expounded first and then the court decides the legal situation under the existing rule.) Colonial America was a land of new problems for British and other settlers. The old law frequently did not work. But the common law easily accommodated the new environment. The ability of the common law to adapt to change is directly responsible for its longevity.

Fundamental to the common law is the concept that judges should look to the past and follow court precedents. The Latin expression for the concept is this: "Stare decisis et non quieta movere" (to stand by past decisions and not disturb things at rest). **Stare decisis** is the key phrase: Let the decision stand. A judge should resolve current problems in the same manner as similar problems were resolved in the past. When high school wrestling coach Mike Milkovich sued the Lorain (Ohio) Journal Company in the mid-1970s for publishing the claim that Milkovich had lied during a hearing, the judge most certainly looked to past decisions to discover whether in previous cases such a charge had been considered defamatory or libelous. There are ample precedents for ruling that a published charge that a person lied is libelous, and Milkovich won his lawsuit.[2]

Stare decisis is the key phrase: Let the decision stand.

The Role of Precedent

At first glance one would think that the law can never change in a system that continually looks to the past. What if the first few rulings in a line of cases were bad decisions? Are we saddled with bad law forever? Fortunately, the law does not operate quite in this way. While following **precedent** is the desired state of affairs (many people say that certainty in the law is more important than justice), it is not always the proper way to proceed. To protect the integrity of the common law, judges have developed several means of coping with bad law and with new situations in which the application of old law would result in injustice.

Imagine for a moment that the newspaper in your hometown publishes a picture and story about a 12-year-old girl who gave birth to a 7-pound son in a local hospital. The mother and father do not like the publicity and sue the newspaper for invasion of privacy. The attorney for the parents finds a precedent, *Barber* v. *Time*,[3] in which a Missouri court ruled that to photograph a patient in a hospital room against her will and then to publish that picture in a newsmagazine is an **invasion of privacy.**

Does the existence of this precedent mean that the young couple will automatically win this lawsuit? that the court will follow the decision? No, it does not. For one thing, there may be other cases in which courts have ruled that publishing such a picture is not an invasion of privacy. In fact in 1956 in the case of *Meetze* v. *AP*,[4] a South Carolina court made just such a

---

2. *Milkovich* v. *Lorain Journal Co.,* 110 S. Ct. 2695 (1991).
3. 159 S.W. 2d 291 (1942).
4. 95 S.E. 2d 606 (1956).

ruling. But for the moment assume that *Barber* v. *Time* is the only precedent. Is the court bound by this precedent? No. The court has several options concerning the 1942 decision.

First, it can *accept* the precedent as law and rule that the newspaper has invaded the privacy of the couple by publishing the picture and story about the birth of their child. Second, the court can *modify*, or change, the 1942 precedent by arguing that *Barber* v. *Time* was decided nearly 60 years ago when people were more sensitive about going to a hospital, since a stay in the hospital was often considered to reflect badly on a patient, but that hospitalization is no longer a sensitive matter to most people. Therefore, a rule of law restricting the publication of a picture of a hospital patient is unrealistic, unless the picture is in bad taste or needlessly embarrasses the patient. Then the publication is an invasion of privacy. If not, the publication of such a picture is permissible. In our imaginary case, then, the decision turns on what kind of picture and story the newspaper published: a pleasant picture that flattered the couple? or one that mocked and embarrassed them? If the court rules in this manner, it *modifies* the 1942 precedent, making it correspond to what the judge perceives to be contemporary life.

As a third option the court can decide that *Barber* v. *Time* provides an important precedent for a plaintiff hospitalized because of disease—as Dorothy Barber was—but that in the case before the court, the plaintiff was hospitalized to give birth to a baby, a different situation: giving birth is a voluntary status; catching a disease is not. Because the two cases present different problems, they are really different cases. Hence, the *Barber* v. *Time* precedent does not apply. This practice is called *distinguishing the precedent from the current case,* a very common action.

Finally, the court can *overrule* the precedent. In 1941 the Supreme Court of the United States overruled a decision made by the Supreme Court in 1918 regarding the right of a judge to use what is called the **summary contempt power** (*Toledo Newspaper Co.* v. *U.S.* [5]). This is the power of a judge to charge someone with being in contempt of court, to find that person guilty of contempt, and then to punish him or her for the contempt—all without a jury trial. In *Nye* v. *U.S.*[6] the high court said that in 1918 it had been improperly informed as to the intent of a measure passed by Congress in 1831 that authorized the use of the summary power by federal judges. The 1918 ruling was therefore bad, was wrong, and was reversed. (Fuller explanation of summary contempt as it applies to the mass media is given in Chapter 10.) The only courts that can overrule the 1942 decision by the Missouri Supreme Court in *Barber* v. *Time* are the Missouri Supreme Court and the U.S. Supreme Court.

Obviously, the preceding discussion oversimplifies the judicial process. Rarely is a court confronted with only a single precedent. And whether or not precedent is binding on a court is often an issue. For example, decisions by the Supreme Court of the United States regarding the U.S. Constitution and federal laws are binding on all federal and state courts. Decisions by the U.S. Court of Appeals on federal matters are binding only on other lower federal and state courts in that circuit or region. (See pages 23–25 for a discussion of the circuits.) The supreme court of any state is the final authority on the meaning of the constitution and laws of that state, and its rulings on these matters are binding on all state and *federal*

5. 242 U.S. 402 (1918).
6. 313 U.S. 33 (1941).

courts in that state. Matters are more complicated when federal courts interpret state laws. State courts can accept or reject these interpretations in most instances. Because mass media law is so heavily affected by the First Amendment, state judges are frequently forced to look outside their borders to precedents developed by the federal courts. A state court ruling on a question involving the First Amendment guarantees of freedom of speech and freedom of the press is necessarily governed by federal court precedents on the same subject.

Lawyers and law professors often debate just how important precedent really is when a court makes a decision. Some persons have suggested what is called the "hunch theory" of jurisprudence. Under this theory a judge or justice decides a case based on instinct or a feeling of what is right and wrong and then seeks out precedents to support the decision.

The imaginary invasion-of-privacy case just discussed demonstrates that the common law can have vitality, that despite the rule of precedent a judge is rarely bound tightly by the past. There is a saying: Every age should be the mistress of its own law. This saying applies to the common law as well as to all other aspects of the legal system.

It must be clear at this point that the common law is not specifically written down someplace for all to see and use. It is instead contained in the hundreds of thousands of decisions handed down by courts over the centuries. Many attempts have been made to summarize the law. Sir Edward Coke compiled and analyzed the precedents of common law in the early 17th century. Sir William Blackstone later expanded Coke's work in the monumental "Commentaries on the Law of England." More recently, in such works as the massive "Restatement of Torts," the task was again undertaken, but on a narrower scale.

Courts began to keep records of their decisions centuries ago. In the 13th century unofficial reports of cases began to appear in yearbooks, but they were records of court proceedings in which procedural points were clarified for the benefit of legal practitioners rather than collections of court decisions. The modern concept of fully reporting the written decisions of all courts probably began in 1785 with the publication of the first British Term Reports.

While scholars and lawyers still uncover the common law using the case-by-case method, it is fairly easy today to locate the appropriate cases through a simple system of citation. The cases of a single court (such as the U.S. Supreme Court or the federal district courts) are collected in a single **case reporter** (such as the "United States Reports" or the "Federal Supplement"). The cases are collected chronologically and fill many volumes. Each case collected has its individual **citation,** or identification number, which reflects the name of the reporter in which the case can be found, the volume of that reporter, and the page on which the case begins (figure 1.1). For example, the citation for the decision in *Adderly* v. *Florida* (a freedom-of-speech case) is 385 U.S. 39 (1966). The letters in the middle (U.S.) indicate that the case is in the "United States Reports," the official government reporter for cases decided by the Supreme Court of the United States. The number 385 refers to the specific volume of the "United States Reports" in which the case is found. The last number (39) gives the page on which the case appears. Finally, 1966 provides the year in which the case was decided. So, *Adderly* v. *Florida* can be found on page 39 of volume 385 of the "United States Reports."

The coming of the computer age has affected the legal community in many ways. Court opinions are now available to lawyers and others via a variety of computer-mediated communication systems. In some jurisdictions, lawyers are permitted to file documents electronically

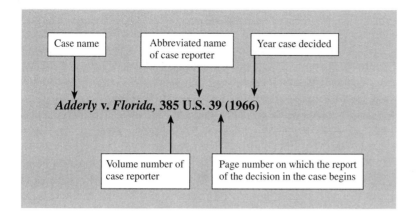

Reading a case citation.

with the court so long as they back these documents up with hard copies soon thereafter. Some legal authorities have argued that a new system of citations is needed, one that is suitable for printed case reporters—which will remain the standard in the judicial system at least in the early years of the 21st century—and for cases transmitted electronically. In August of 1996 the House of Delegates of the American Bar Association recommended that courts across the United States adopt a new system of citations. The citation for each case would be medium-neutral; that is, the citation would no longer be tied to a specific publisher or mode of transmission. (Currently, for example, the case citations for decisions of the Supreme Court of the United States published in the official government reports of the case are different from the citations for the same case in reporters that are privately published.) Each case would be assigned a sequential decision number and internal paragraphs in the case would also be numbered. The citation would include the name of the case, the year, the court decision number, a paragraph number if specific material is cited, and the traditional reporter volume number and page number. A citation for a decision by a U.S. court of appeals would look like this: *Smith* v. *Jones,* 1996 5 Cir 15, ¶18, 22 F. 3d 955. Translated, this would be the case of *Smith* v. *Jones,* the 15th decision by the 5th U.S. Circuit Court of Appeals during 1996. The material cited is in paragraph 18 and the case can be found in volume 22 of the "Federal Reporter 3d" at page 955. A survey by the U.S. Judicial Conference in early 1997 polled nearly 1,000 judges, lawyers, law librarians, and others who work in the legal system. Judges and others who work in the courts overwhelmingly opposed the new scheme, claiming it will result in more work and added costs. Lawyers and librarians said they like the idea. The states of Louisiana, Oklahoma, and South Dakota have already adopted similar citation systems, but universal acceptance by all state and federal courts is needed before the scheme can be universally applied.

If you have the correct citation, you can easily find any case you seek. Locating all citations of the cases apropos to a particular problem—such as a libel suit—is a different matter and is a technique taught in law schools. A great many legal encyclopedias, digests, compilations of the common law, books, and articles are used by lawyers to track down the names and citations of the appropriate cases.

There is no better way to sum up the common law than to quote Oliver Wendell Holmes ("The Common Law," published in 1881):[7]

> The life of the law has not been logic; it has been experience. The felt necessities of the time, the prevalent moral and political theories, intuitions of public policy, avowed or unconscious, even the prejudices which judges share with their fellow-men, have had a good deal more to do than syllogism in determining the rules by which men should be governed. The law embodies the story of a nation's development through many centuries, and it cannot be dealt with as if it contained only the axioms and corollaries of a book of mathematics. In order to know what it is, we must know what it has been, and what it tends to become. . . . The very considerations which judges most rarely mention, and always with an apology, are the secret root from which the law draws all the juices of life. I mean, of course, considerations of what is expedient for the community concerned.

"The life of the law has not been logic; it has been experience."

THE LAW OF EQUITY

The law of **equity** is another kind of judge-made law. The distinction today between the common law and equity law has blurred. The cases are heard by the same judges in the same courtrooms. Differences in procedures and remedies are all that is left to distinguish these two categories of the law. Separate consideration of the common law and equity leads to a better understanding of both, however. The law of equity, as developed in Britain beginning in the 14th and 15th centuries, is the second basic source of the law in the United States. Equity was originally a supplement to the common law and developed side by side with the common law. During the 1300s and 1400s rulings from the king's courts often became rigid and narrow. Many persons seeking relief under the common law for very real grievances were often turned away because the law did not provide a suitable remedy for their problems. In such instances the disappointed litigant could take the problem to the king for resolution, petitioning the king to "do right for the love of God and by way of charity." According to legal scholar Henry Abraham, "The king was empowered to mold the law for the sake of 'justice,' to grant the relief prayed for as an act of grace."[8] Soon the chancellor, the king's secretary or assistant, set up a special office or court to resolve the problems that the king's common-law courts could not handle. At the outset of the hearing, the aggrieved party had to establish that there was no adequate remedy under the common law and that a special court was needed to hear the case. The office of the chancellor soon became known as the Court of Chancery. Decisions were made on the basis of conscience or fairness or "equity."

British common law and equity law were American law until the Revolution in 1776. After independence was won, the basic principles of common law in existence before the Revolution were kept because the cases remained acceptable precedent. After some hesitation, equity was accepted in much the same way.

The rules and procedures under equity are far more flexible than those under the common law. Equity really begins where the common law leaves off. Equity suits are never tried

7. Holmes, *Common Law.*
8. Abraham, *Judicial Process.*

before a jury. Rulings come in the form of **judicial decrees,** not in judgments of yes or no. Decisions in equity are (and were) discretionary on the part of judges. And despite the fact that precedents are also relied upon in the law of equity, judges are free to do what they think is right and fair in a specific case.

Equity provides another advantage for troubled litigants—the restraining order. A judge sitting in equity can order preventive measures as well as remedial ones. Individuals who can demonstrate that they are in peril or are about to suffer a serious irremediable wrong can usually gain a legal writ such as an injunction or a restraining order to stop someone from doing something. Generally, a court issues a temporary restraining order until it can hear arguments from both parties in the dispute and decide whether an injunction should be made permanent. Under the common law the court can only provide a remedy (usually money damages) after the harm has occurred.

In 1971 the federal government asked the federal courts to restrain The New York Times and the Washington Post from publishing what have now become known as the Pentagon Papers (this case is discussed in greater detail in Chapter 2). This case is a good example of equity law in action. The government argued that if the purloined documents were published by the two newspapers the nation would suffer irremediable damage; that foreign governments would be reluctant to entrust the United States with their secrets if those secrets might someday be published in the public press; that the enemy would gain valuable defense secrets. The federal government argued further that it would do little good to punish the newspapers after the material had been published since there would be no way to repair the damage. The federal district court temporarily restrained both newspapers from publishing the material while the case was argued—all the way to the Supreme Court of the United States. After two weeks of hearings, the high court finally ruled that publication could continue, that the government had failed to prove that the nation would be damaged.[9]

STATUTORY LAW

Statutory law, or legislation, is the third great source of United States law. Today there are legislative bodies of all shapes and sizes. The common traits they share are that they are popularly elected and that they have the authority to pass laws. In the beginning of our nation, legislation, or statutory law, really did not play a very significant role in the legal system. Certainly many laws were passed, but the bulk of our legal rules were developed from the common law and from equity law. After 1825 statutory law began to play an important role in our legal system, and it was between 1850 and 1900 that a greater percentage of law began to come from legislative acts than from common-law court decisions.

Several important characteristics of statutory law can best be understood by contrasting them with common law. First, **statutes** tend to deal with problems affecting society or large groups of people, in contrast to common law, which usually deals with smaller, individual problems. (Some common-law rulings affect large groups of persons, but this occurrence is rare.) It should also be noted in this connection the importance of not confusing common law

---

9. *New York Times Co. v. United States,* 403 U.S. 713 (1971).

with constitutional law. Certainly when judges interpret a constitution, they make policy that affects us all. However, it should be kept in mind that a constitution is a legislative document voted on by the people and is not "discovered law" or "judge-made law."

Second, statutory law can anticipate problems, and common law cannot. For example, a state legislature can pass a statute that prohibits publication of the school records of a student without prior consent of the student. Under the common law the problem cannot be resolved until a student's record has been published in a newspaper or broadcast on television and the student brings action against the medium to recover damages for the injury incurred.

Third, the criminal laws in the United States are all statutory laws—common-law crimes no longer exist in this country and have not since 1812. Common-law rules are not precise enough to provide the kind of notice needed to protect a criminal defendant's right to due process of law.

The criminal laws in the United States are all statutory laws.

Fourth, statutory law is collected in codes and law books, instead of in reports as is the common law. When a proposal or bill is adopted by the legislative branch and approved by the executive branch, it becomes law and is integrated into the proper section of a municipal code, a state code, or whatever. However, this does not mean that some very important statutory law cannot be found in the case reporters.

Passage of a law is rarely the final word on the subject. Courts become involved in the process of determining what that law means. While a properly constructed statute sometimes needs little interpretation by the courts, judges are frequently called upon to rule on the exact meaning of ambiguous phrases and words. The resulting process is called **statutory construction** and is a very important part of the law. Even the simplest kind of statement often needs interpretation. For example, a prohibition stating "it is illegal to distribute an obscene newspaper" is filled with ambiguity. What does *distribution* mean? Can an obscene document be sent through the mail? distributed from house to house? passed out on street corners? transmitted on the Internet? Are all of these actions prohibited? What constitutes a newspaper? Is any printed matter a newspaper? Is any printed matter published regularly a newspaper? Are mimeographed sheets and photocopied newsletters considered newspapers? Of course, implicit is the classic question with which courts have wrestled in this country for nearly a century: What is obscenity?

Usually a legislature tries to leave some kind of trail to help a judge find out what the law means. For when judges rule on the meaning of a statute, they are supposed to determine what the legislature meant when it passed the law (the legislative intent), not what they think the law should mean. Minutes of committee hearings in which the law was discussed, legislative staff reports, and reports of debate on the floor can all be used to help a judge determine the legislative intent. Therefore, when lawyers deal with statutes, they frequently are forced to search the case reporters to find out how the courts interpreted a law in which they are interested.

CONSTITUTIONAL LAW

Great Britain does not have a written **constitution.** The United States does have a written constitution, and it is an important source of our law. In fact, there are many constitutions in this country: the federal Constitution, state constitutions, city charters, and so forth. All these documents accomplish the same ends. First, they provide the plan for the establishment and organization of the government. Next, they outline the duties, responsibilities, and powers of the various elements of government. Finally, they usually guarantee certain basic rights to the people, such as freedom of speech and freedom to peaceably assemble.

Legislative bodies may enact statutes rather easily by a majority vote. It is far more difficult to adopt or change a constitution. State constitutions are approved or changed by a direct vote of the people. It is even more difficult to change the federal Constitution. An amendment may be proposed by a vote of two-thirds of the members of both the U.S. House of Representatives and the Senate. Alternatively, two-thirds of the state legislatures can call for a constitutional convention for proposing amendments. Once proposed, the amendments must be approved either by three-fourths of the state legislatures or by three-fourths of the constitutional conventions called in all the states. Congress decides which method of ratification or approval is to be used. Because the people have an unusually direct voice in the approval and change of a constitution, constitutions are considered the most important source of U.S. law.

One Supreme Court justice described a constitution as a kind of yardstick against which all the other actions of government must be measured to determine whether the actions are permissible. The U.S. Constitution is the supreme law of the land. Any law or other constitution that conflicts with the U.S. Constitution is unenforceable. A state constitution plays the same role for a state: A statute passed by the Michigan legislature and signed by the governor of that state is clearly unenforceable if it conflicts with the Michigan Constitution. And so it goes for all levels of constitutions.

While constitutions tend to be short and infrequently amended, determining what these documents mean and whether a specific law or government action violates a certain constitutional provision is a laborious process. Consequently, with the exception of the bare-bones documents themselves, the case reporters are once again the repository for the constitutional law that governs the United States.

Twenty-seven amendments are appended to the U.S. Constitution. The first 10 of these are known as the Bill of Rights and provide a guarantee of certain basic human rights to all citizens. Included are freedom of speech and freedom of the press, rights you will come to understand more fully in future chapters.

The federal Constitution and the 50 state constitutions are very important when considering mass-media law problems. All 51 of these charters contain provisions, in one form or another, that guarantee freedom of speech and freedom of the press. Consequently, any government action that affects in any way the freedom of individuals or mass media to speak or publish or broadcast must be measured against the constitutional guarantees of freedom of expression. There are several reasons why a law limiting speaking or publishing might be declared unconstitutional. The law might be a direct restriction on speech or press that is protected by the First Amendment. For example, an order by a Nebraska judge that prohibited the press from publishing certain information about a pending murder trial was considered a direct restriction on freedom of the press (see *Nebraska Press Association* v. *Stuart*,[10] Chapter 11).

---

10. 427 U.S. 539 (1976).

A criminal obscenity statute or another kind of criminal law might be declared unconstitutional because it is too vague. A law must provide adequate notice to a person of ordinary intelligence that his or her contemplated conduct is prohibited by the law. An Indianapolis pornography ordinance that made it a crime to publish pornographic material was declared void, at least in part, because the law's definition of pornography was not specific enough. The law defined pornography as including depictions of "the subordination of women." It is almost impossible to settle in one's own mind upon a single meaning or understanding of that term, noted Judge Sarah Barker (see *American Booksellers Association* v. *Hudnut,*[11] Chapter 13). A statute might also be declared to be unconstitutional because it violates what is known as the overbreadth doctrine. A law is overbroad, the Supreme Court said many years ago, if it does not aim specifically at evils within the allowable area of government control but sweeps within its ambit other activities that constitute an exercise of protected expression. Struthers, Ohio, an industrial community where many people worked at night and slept during the day, passed an ordinance that forbade knocking on the door or ringing the doorbell at a residence in order to deliver a handbill. The Supreme Court ruled that the ordinance was overbroad, that the city's objective could be obtained by passing an ordinance making it an offense for any person to ring a doorbell of a householder who had, through a sign or some other means, indicated that he or she did not wish to be disturbed. As written, however, the law prohibited persons from distributing handbills to all persons—to those who wanted to see and read them as well as those who did not (see *Martin* v. *City of Struthers,*[12] Chapter 3). So there are many reasons why a court might declare a law to be an unconstitutional infringement upon the guarantees of freedom of speech and press.

ADMINISTRATIVE RULES

By the latter part of the 19th century in the United States, the job of governing had become much more complex. Congress was being asked to resolve questions going far beyond such simple matters as budgets, wars, treaties, and the like. Technology created new kinds of problems for the Congress to resolve. Many such issues were complex and required specialized knowledge and expertise that the representatives and senators lacked and could not easily acquire, had they wanted to. Federal administrative agencies were therefore created to deal with these problems.

For example, regulation of the railroads that traversed the nation created numerous problems in the late 19th century. Since questions concerning use of these railroads fell within the commerce power of the Congress, that deliberative body was given the task of resolving this complex issue. To deal with these problems, Congress created the first **administrative agency,** the Interstate Commerce Commission (ICC). This agency was established by legislation and funded by Congress. Its members were appointed by the president and approved by

---

11. 598 F. Supp. 1316 (1985).
12. 319 U.S. 141 (1943).

the Congress. Each member served a fixed term in office. The agency was independent of the Congress, the president, and the courts. Its task was (and is) to regulate commerce between the states, a matter that concerned pipelines, shipping, and transportation. The members of the board presumably were somewhat expert in the area before appointment and of course became more so during the course of their term.

Hundreds of such agencies now exist at both federal and state levels. In fact, many people speculate that the rules generated by these agencies comprise the bulk of American law today. Each agency undertakes to deal with a specific set of problems too technical or too large for the legislative branch to handle. Typical is the Federal Communications Commission (FCC), which was created by Congress in 1934. Its task is to regulate broadcasting and other electronic communication in the United States, a job that Congress has really never attempted. Its members must be citizens of the United States and are appointed by the president. The single stipulation is that at any one time no more than three of the five individuals on the commission can be from the same political party. The Senate must confirm the appointments.

Congress sketched the broad framework for the regulation of broadcasting in the Federal Communications Act of 1934, and this act is used by the agency as its basic regulatory guidelines. The agency also creates much law itself in administration of the 1934 act. In interpreting provisions, handing down rulings, developing specific guidelines, and the like, the FCC has developed a sizable body of regulations that bind broadcasters.

Persons dissatisfied with rulings by an agency can go to court and seek a reversal of the action. But courts have limited power to review decisions made by administrative agencies, and can overturn such a ruling in only these limited circumstances: (1) if the original act that established the commission or agency is unconstitutional, (2) if the commission or agency exceeds its authority, (3) if the commission or agency violates its own rules, or (4) if there is no evidentiary basis whatsoever to support the ruling. The reason for these limitations is simple: These agencies were created to bring expert knowledge to bear on complex problems, and the entire purpose for their creation would be defeated if judges with no special expertise in a given area could reverse an agency ruling merely because they had a different solution to a problem.

But courts have limited power to review decisions made by administrative agencies.

The case reporters contain some law created by the administrative agencies, but the reports that these agencies themselves publish contain much more such law. These reports are also arranged on a case-by-case basis in chronological order. A citation system similar to that used for the case reporters is used in these reports.

There are other sources of American law. Executives—a governor, a president, a mayor—have the power to make law, in some circumstances, through executive order. The five sources just discussed—common law, law of equity, statutory law, constitutional law, and rules and regulations by administrative agencies—are the most important, however, and are of most concern in this book. First Amendment problems fall under the purview of constitutional law. Libel and invasion of privacy are matters generally dealt with by the common law and the law of equity. Obscenity laws in this country are statutory provisions (although this fact is frequently obscured by the hundreds of court cases in which judges attempt to define the meaning of obscenity). And of course the regulation of broadcasting and advertising falls primarily under the jurisdiction of administrative agencies.

While this section provides a basic outline of the law and is not comprehensive, the information is sufficient to make upcoming material on mass media law understandable.

SUMMARY

There are five important sources of American law. The common law is the oldest source of our law, having developed in England more than 700 years ago. The law became common throughout Great Britain and reflected the customs of the people. It was easily transported to the New World, and its pragmatic philosophy was highly useful on the rapidly developing North American continent. Fundamental to the common law is the concept that judges should look to the past and follow earlier court rulings, called precedents. Stare decisis (let the decision stand) is a key concept. But judges have developed the means to change or adapt the common law by modifying, distinguishing, or overruling precedent case law. The common law is not written down in a law book but is collected in volumes that contain the reports of legal decisions. Each case is given its own legal identity through a system of numbered citations.

Equity law, the second source of American law, developed because in some instances the common law was simply too rigid to fairly resolve the real grievances of British subjects. The rules and procedures of equity are far more flexible than those of the common law and permit a judge (equity cases are never heard before a jury) to fashion a solution to unique or unusual problems. A court is permitted under equity law to restrain an individual or a corporation or even a government from taking an action. Under the common law a court can only attempt to compensate the injured party for the damage that results from the action.

Today a great volume of American law is generated by Congress, legislatures, city and county councils, and myriad other legislative bodies. This legislation, called statutory law, is the third important source of American law. All criminal laws are statutes. Statutes usually deal with problems that affect great numbers of people, and statutes can anticipate problems, whereas the common law cannot. All statutes are collected in codes or statute books. Courts become involved in the development of statutes when they are called on to interpret the meaning of the words and phrases contained in a statute.

Constitutions, the fourth source of our law, take precedence over all other American law. The U.S. Constitution is the supreme law of the land. Other laws, whether they spring from common law, equity, legislative bodies, or administrative agencies, cannot conflict with the provisions of the Constitution. Courts are often called upon to interpret the meaning of the provisions of our constitutions (one federal and 50 state constitutions) and through this process can often make these seemingly rigid legal prescriptions adaptable to contemporary problems.

There are thousands of administrative agencies, boards, and commissions in the nation that produce rules and regulations. This administrative law, the fifth source of American law, usually deals with technical and complicated matters requiring levels of expertise that members of traditional legislative bodies do not normally possess. Members of these agencies and commissions are usually appointed by presidents or by governors or mayors, and the agencies are supervised and funded by legislative bodies. Their tasks are narrowly defined and their rulings, while they carry the force of law, can always be appealed.

THE JUDICIAL SYSTEM

This section gives an introduction to the court system in the United States. Since the judicial branch of our three-part government is the field on which most of the battles involving communications law are fought, an understanding of the judicial system is essential.

It is technically improper to talk about the American judicial system. There are 52 different judicial systems in the United States, one for the federal government and one for each of the 50 states, plus the District of Columbia. While each of these systems is somewhat different from all the others, the similarities among the 52 systems are much more important than the differences. Each of the systems is divided into two distinct sets of courts—trial courts and appellate courts. Each judicial system is established by a constitution, federal or state. In each system the courts act as the third branch of a common triumvirate of government: a legislative branch, which makes the law; an executive branch, which enforces the law; and a judicial branch, which interprets the law.

FACTS VERSUS THE LAW

Common to all judicial systems is the distinction between trial courts and appellate courts, and it is important to understand this distinction. Each level of court has its own function: basically, **trial courts** are fact-finding courts and **appellate courts** are law-reviewing courts. Trial courts are the courts of first instance, the place where nearly all cases begin. Juries sit in trial courts, but never in appellate courts. Trial courts are empowered to consider both the facts and the law in a case. Appellate courts normally consider only the law. The difference between facts and law is significant. The facts are what happened. The law is what should be done because of the facts.

The facts are what happened. The law is what should be done because of the facts.

The difference between facts and law can be emphasized by looking at an imaginary libel suit that might result when the River City Sentinel published a story about costs at the Sandridge Hospital.

Ineffective Medications Given to Ill, Injured
SANDRIDGE HOSPITAL OVERCHARGING PATIENTS ON PHARMACY COSTS

Scores of patients at the Sandridge Hospital have been given ineffective medications, a three-week investigation at the hospital has revealed. In addition, many of those patients were overcharged for the medicine they received.

The Sentinel has learned that many of the prescription drugs sold to patients at the hospital had been kept beyond the manufacturer's recommended storage period.

Many drugs stored in the pharmacy (as late as Friday) had expiration dates as old as six months ago. Drug manufacturers have told the Sentinel that medication used beyond the expiration date, which is stamped clearly on most packages, may not have the potency or curative effects that fresher pharmaceuticals have.

Hospital representatives deny giving patients any of the expired drugs, but sources at the hospital say it is impossible for administrators to guarantee that none of the dated drugs were sold to patients.

In addition, the investigation by the Sentinel revealed that patients who were sold medications manufactured by Chaos Pharmaceuticals were charged on the basis of 1999 price lists despite the fact that the company lowered prices significantly in 2000.

The Sandridge Hospital sues the newspaper for libel. When the case gets to court, the first thing that has to be done is to establish what the facts are—what happened. The hospital and the newspaper each will present evidence, witnesses, and arguments to support its version of the facts. Several issues have to be resolved. In addition to the general questions of whether the story has been published and whether the hospital has been identified in the story, the hospital will have to supply evidence that its reputation has been injured, that the story is false, and that the newspaper staff has been extremely careless or negligent in the publication of the report. The newspaper will seek to defend itself by attempting to document the story or raise the defense that the report was privileged in some way. Or the newspaper may argue that even if the story is mistaken, it was the result of an innocent error, not negligence on the part of the staff.

All this testimony and evidence establishes the factual record—what actually took place at the hospital and in preparation of the story. When there is conflicting evidence, the jury decides whom to believe (in the absence of a jury, the judge makes the decision). Suppose the hospital is able to prove by documents that pharmacists in fact had removed the dated medicine from their shelves and simply stored it to return to the manufacturers. Further, the hospital can show that while it did accidentally overcharge some patients for Chaos products, it quickly refunded the excess charge to these patients. Finally, attorneys for the hospital demonstrate that the story was prepared by an untrained stringer for the newspaper who used but a single source—a pharmacist who had been fired by Sandridge for using drugs while on the job—to prepare the story and failed to relate to readers the substance of the evidence (which the reporter had when the story was published) presented by the hospital in court. In such a case, a court would likely rule that the hospital had carried its burden of proof and that no legitimate defense exists for the newspaper. Therefore, the hospital wins the suit. If the newspaper is unhappy with the verdict, it can appeal.

In an appeal, the appellate court does not establish a new factual record. No more testimony is taken. No more witnesses are called. The factual record established by the jury or judge at the trial stands. The appellate court has the power in some kinds of cases (libel suits that involve constitutional issues, for example) to examine whether the trial court properly considered the facts in the case. But normally it is the task of the appellate court to determine whether the law has been applied properly in light of the facts established at the trial. Perhaps the appellate court might rule that even with the documentary evidence it presented, the hospital failed to prove that the newspaper story was false. Perhaps the judge erred in allowing certain testimony into evidence or refused to allow a certain witness to testify. Nevertheless, in reaching an opinion the appellate court considers only the law; the factual record established at the trial stands.

What if new evidence is found or a previously unknown witness comes forth to testify? If the appellate court believes that the new evidence is important, it can order a new trial. However, the court itself does not hear the evidence. These facts are developed at a new trial.

There are other differences between the roles and procedures of trial and appellate courts. Juries are never used by appellate courts; a jury may be used in a trial court proceeding. The judge normally sits alone at a trial; appeals are heard by a panel of judges, usually three or more. Cases always begin at the trial level and then proceed to the appellate level. Although the appellate courts appear to have the last word in a legal dispute, that is not always the case. Usually cases are returned to the trial court for resolution with instructions from the appeals court to the trial judge to decide the case, keeping this or that factor in mind. In such a case the trial judge can frequently do what he or she wants.

In the discussion that follows, the federal court system and its methods of operating are considered first, and then some general observations about state court systems are given, based on the discussion of the federal system.

THE FEDERAL COURT SYSTEM

The Congress has the authority to abolish every federal court in the land, save the Supreme Court of the United States. The U.S. Constitution calls for but a single federal court, the Supreme Court. Article III, Section 1 states: "The judicial power of the United States shall be vested in one Supreme Court." The Constitution also gives Congress the right to establish inferior courts if it deems these courts to be necessary. And Congress has, of course, established a fairly complex system of courts to complement the Supreme Court.

The jurisdiction of the federal courts is also outlined in Article III of the Constitution. The jurisdiction of a court is its legal right to exercise its authority. Briefly, federal courts can hear the following cases:

1. Cases that arise under the U.S. Constitution, U.S. law, and U.S. treaties
2. Cases that involve ambassadors and ministers, duly accredited, of foreign countries
3. Cases that involve admiralty and maritime law
4. Cases that involve controversies when the United States is a party to the suit
5. Cases that involve controversies between two or more states
6. Cases that involve controversies between a state and a citizen of another state (we must remember that the 11th Amendment to the Constitution requires that a state give its permission before it can be sued)
7. Cases that involve controversies between citizens of different states

While special federal courts have jurisdiction that goes beyond this broad outline, these are the circumstances in which a federal court may normally exercise its authority. Of the seven categories of cases just listed, Categories 1 and 7 account for most of the cases tried in federal court. For example, disputes that involve violations of the myriad federal laws and disputes that involve constitutional rights such as the First Amendment are heard in federal courts. Also, disputes between citizens of different states—what is known as a diversity of citizenship matter—are heard in federal courts. It is very common, for example, for libel suits and invasion-of-privacy suits against publishing companies to start in federal courts rather than in state courts. If a citizen of Arizona is libeled by Time magazine, the case will very likely be tried in a federal court in the state of Arizona, rather than in a state court. Arizona law will be applied. The case will most often be heard where the legal wrong, in this case the injury to reputation by libel, occurs. In 1988 Congress limited federal trial courts to hearing only those diversity cases in which the damages sought exceeded $75,000.

The Supreme Court

The Supreme Court of the United States is the oldest federal court, having been in operation since 1789. The Constitution does not establish the number of justices who sit on the high court. That task is left to the Congress. In 1789 the Congress passed the first judiciary act and established the membership of the high court at six: a chief justice and five associate justices. This number was increased to seven in 1807, to nine in 1837, and to 10 in 1863. The Supreme Court had 10 members until 1866, when Congress ruled that only seven justices would sit on the high tribunal. Since 1869 the Supreme Court has comprised the chief justice of the United States and eight associate justices. (Note the title: not chief justice of the Supreme Court, but chief justice of the United States.)

Since 1869 the Supreme Court has comprised the chief justice of the United States and eight associate justices.

The Supreme Court exercises both original and appellate jurisdictions. Under its **original jurisdiction,** which is established in the Constitution, the Supreme Court is the first court to hear a case and acts much like a trial court. Sometimes the justices will hold a hearing to ascertain the facts; more commonly they will appoint what is called a special master to discern the facts and make recommendations. For example, in 1995 the high court was called on to decide whether a seven-mile stretch of Mississippi River frontage belonged to Mississippi or Louisiana. The property was once an island in the river, but beginning in 1954 migrated to become a part of the Louisiana riverbank. The court appointed the former Chief Justice of the Supreme Judicial Court of Maine as the special master; he concluded that the property, known as Stack Island, belonged to Mississippi. The Justices affirmed this conclusion in October.[13] But such jurisdiction is rarely exercised. The Stack Island ruling is one of fewer than 200 decisions the court has made in exercising its original jurisdiction since 1789. Because the high court is strictly limited by the Constitution to exercise its original jurisdiction in a few specific instances, and because Congress has given the lower federal courts concurrent jurisdiction with the Supreme Court in those specific instances, few persons begin their lawsuits at the Supreme Court.

The primary task of the Supreme Court is as an appellate tribunal, hearing cases already decided by lower federal courts and state courts of last resort. The appellate jurisdiction of the Supreme Court is established by the Congress, not by the Constitution. A case will come before the Supreme Court of the United States for review in one of two principal ways: on a direct appeal or by way of a writ of certiorari. The certification process is a third way for a case to get to the high court, but this process is rarely used today.

13. Greenhouse, "Supreme Court Awards," C18.

In some instances a litigant has an apparent right, guaranteed by federal statute, to appeal a case to the Supreme Court. This is called **direct appeal.** For example, if a federal appeals court declares that a state statute violates the U.S. Constitution or conflicts with a federal law, the state has a right to appeal this decision to the Supreme Court. But this is only an apparent right, because since 1928 the Supreme Court has had the right to reject such an appeal "for want of a substantial federal question." This is another way of the court saying, "We think this is a trivial matter." Almost 90 percent of all appeals that come to the Supreme Court via the direct appeal process are rejected.

The much more common way for a case to reach the nation's high court is via a **writ of certiorari.** No one has the right to such a writ. It is a discretionary order issued by the court when it feels that an important legal question has been raised. Litigants using both the federal court system and the various state court systems can seek a writ of certiorari. The most important requirement that must be met before the court will even consider issuing a writ is that a petitioner first exhaust all other legal remedies. While there are a few exceptions, this generally means that if a case begins in a federal district court (the trial level court) the **petitioner** must first seek a review by a U.S. court of appeals before bidding for a writ of certiorari. The writ can be sought if the court of appeals refuses to hear the case or sustains the verdict against the petitioner. All other legal remedies have then been exhausted. In state court systems every legal appeal possible must be made within the state before seeking a review by the U.S. Supreme Court. This usually means going through a trial court, an intermediate appeals court, and finally the state Supreme Court.

When the Supreme Court grants a writ of certiorari, it is ordering the lower court to send the records to the high court for review. Each request for a writ is considered by the entire nine-member court, and an affirmative vote of four justices is required before the writ can be

The U.S. Supreme Court. Back row, l. to r., Associate Justices Ruth Bader Ginsburg, David Souter, Clarence Thomas, and Stephen Breyer. Front row, l. to r., Associate Justices Antonin Scalia and John Paul Stevens, Chief Justice William Rehnquist, Associate Justices Sandra Day O'Connor and Anthony Kennedy.
Source: Collection, The Supreme Court of the United States, courtesy of The Supreme Court Historical Society. Photographed by Richard Strauss, Smithsonian Institution.

granted. The high court rejects most of the petitions it receives. It hears arguments in and decides only about 100 cases each year. Workload is the key factor. Certain important issues must be decided each term, and the justices do not have the time to consider thoroughly most cases for which an appeal is sought. Term after term, suggestions to reduce the court's workload are made, but most are not popular with the Congress or the people in the nation. All citizens believe that they should have the right to appeal to the Supreme Court, even if the appeal will probably be rejected, even if the court may never hear the case.

Hearing a Case

While the operation of state and federal appellate courts varies from state to state and court to court, these courts have a good deal in common in the way in which they hear and decide a case. So by examining here how the Supreme Court operates, we can also learn quite a bit about how other appellate courts operate.

The first thing the court does is to decide whether it will hear a case, either on appeal or via a writ of certiorari. Once a case is accepted, the attorneys for both sides have the greatest burden of work during the next few months. Oral argument on the case is scheduled, and both sides are expected to submit **legal briefs**—their legal arguments—for the court to study before the hearing. The greatest burden at this point is on the party seeking appeal, since he or she must provide the court with a complete record of the lower-court proceedings in the case. Included are trial transcripts, lower-court rulings, and all sorts of other materials.

Arguing a matter all the way to the Supreme Court takes a long time, often as long as five years (sometimes longer) from initiation of the suit until the court gives its ruling. James Hill brought suit in New York in 1953 against Time, Inc., for invasion of privacy. The U.S. Supreme Court made the final ruling in the case in 1967 (*Time, Inc.* v. *Hill*[14]). Even at that the matter would not have ended had Hill decided to go back to trial, which the Supreme Court said he must if he wanted to collect damages. He chose not to.

After the nine justices study the briefs (or at least the summaries provided by their law clerks), the **oral argument** is held. For a generation schooled on "Law and Order" and "Matlock," oral argument before the Supreme Court (or indeed before any court) must certainly seem strange. For one thing, the attorneys are strictly limited as to how much they may say. Each side is given a brief amount of time, usually no more than 30 minutes to an hour, to present its arguments. In important cases, "friends of the court" (**amici curiae**) are allowed to present briefs and to participate for 30 minutes in the oral arguments. For example, the American Civil Liberties Union often seeks the friend status in important civil rights cases.

Deciding a Case

After the oral argument (which of course is given in open court with visitors welcome) is over, the members of the high court move behind closed doors to undertake their deliberations. No one is allowed in the discussion room except members of the court itself—no clerks, no

---

14. 385 U.S. 374 (1967).

bailiffs, no secretaries. The discussion, which often is held several days after the arguments are completed, is opened by the chief justice. Discussion time is limited, and by being the first speaker the chief justice is in a position to set the agenda, so to speak, for each case—to raise what he or she thinks are the key issues. Next to speak is the justice with the most seniority, and after him or her, the next most senior justice. The court may have as many as 75 items or cases to dispose of during one conference or discussion day; consequently, brevity is valued. Each justice has just a few moments to state his or her thoughts on the matter. After discussion a tentative vote is taken and recorded by each justice in a small, hinged, lockable docket book. In the voting procedure the junior justice votes first; the chief justice, last.

Under the United States legal system, which is based so heavily on the concept of court participation in developing and interpreting the law, a simple yes-or-no answer to any legal question is hardly sufficient. More important than the vote, for the law if not for the **litigant,** are the reasons for the decision. Therefore the Supreme Court and all courts that deal with questions of law prepare what are called **opinions,** in which the reasons, or rationale, for the decision are given. One of the justices voting in the majority is asked to write what is called the **court's opinion.** If the chief justice is in the majority, he or she selects the author of the opinion. If not, the senior associate justice in the majority makes the assignment. Self-selection is always an option.

Opinion writing is a difficult task. Getting five or six or seven people to agree to yes or no is one thing; getting them to agree on why they say yes or no is something else. The opinion must therefore be carefully constructed. After it is drafted, it is circulated among all court members, who make suggestions or even draft their own opinions. The opinion writer incorporates as many of these ideas as possible into the opinion to retain its majority backing. Although all this is done in secret, historians have learned that rarely do court opinions reflect solely the work of the writer. They are more often a conglomeration of paragraphs and pages and sentences from the opinions of several justices.

A justice in agreement with the majority who cannot be convinced to join in backing the court's opinion has the option of writing what is called a **concurring opinion.** A justice who writes a concurring opinion may agree with the outcome of the decision, but does so for reasons different from those expressed in the majority opinion. Or the concurring justice may want to emphasize a specific point not addressed in the majority opinion.

Justices who disagree with the majority can also write an opinion, either individually or as a group, called a **dissenting opinion.** Dissenting opinions are very important. Sometimes, after the court has made a decision, it becomes clear that the decision was not the proper one. The issue is often litigated again by other parties who use the arguments in the dissenting opinion as the basis for a legal claim. If enough time passes, if the composition of the court changes sufficiently, or if the court members change their minds, the high court can swing to the views of the original dissenters. This is what happened in the case of *Nye* v. *U.S.*[15] (noted earlier) when the high court repudiated a stand it had taken in 1918 and supported instead the opinion of Justice Oliver Wendell Holmes, who had vigorously dissented in the earlier decision.

---

15. 313 U.S. 33 (1941).

Finally, it is possible for a justice to concur with the majority in part and to dissent in part as well. That is, the justice may agree with some of the things the majority says but disagree with other aspects of the ruling. This kind of stand by a justice, as well as an ordinary concurrence, frequently fractures the court in such a way that in a six-to-three ruling only three persons subscribe to the court's opinion, two others concur, the sixth concurs in part and dissents in part, and three others dissent. Such splits by the members of the court have become more common in recent years. While these kinds of decisions give each justice the satisfaction of knowing that he or she has put his or her own thoughts on paper for posterity, such splits thwart the orderly development of the law. They often leave lawyers and other interested parties at a loss when trying to predict how the court might respond in the next similar case that comes along. Some chief justices, such as William Howard Taft and Earl Warren, aggressively plied their colleagues to try to gain consensus for a single opinion.

The Supreme Court can dispose of a case in two other ways. A **per curiam** (by the court) **opinion** can be prepared. This is an unsigned opinion drafted by one or more members of the majority and published as the court's opinion. Per curiam opinions are not common, but neither are they rare.

Finally, the high court can dispose of a case with a **memorandum order**—that is, it just announces the vote without giving an opinion. Or the order cites an earlier Supreme Court decision as the reason for affirming or reversing a lower-court ruling. This device is quite common today as the workload of the high court increases. In cases with little legal importance and in cases in which the issues were really resolved earlier, the court saves a good deal of time by just announcing its decision.

One final matter in regard to voting remains for consideration: What happens in case of a tie vote? When all nine members of the court are present, a tie vote is technically impossible. However, if there is a vacancy on the court, only eight justices hear a case. Even when the court is full, a particular justice may disqualify himself or herself from hearing a case. When a vote ends in a tie, the decision of the lower court is affirmed. No opinion is written. It is as if the Supreme Court had never heard the case.

During the circulation of an opinion, justices have the opportunity to change their vote. The number and membership in the majority may shift. It is not impossible for the majority to become the minority if one of the dissenters writes a particularly powerful dissent that attracts support from members originally opposed to his or her opinion. This event is probably very rare. Nevertheless, a vote of the court is not final until it is announced on decision day, or opinion day. The authors of the various opinions—court opinions, concurrences, and dissents—publicly read or summarize their views. Printed copies of these documents are handed out to the parties involved and to the press.

Courts have no real way to enforce decisions and must depend on other government agencies for enforcement of their rulings. The job normally falls to the executive branch. If perchance the president decides not to enforce a Supreme Court ruling, no legal force exists to compel the president to do so. If former President Nixon, for example, had chosen to refuse to turn over the infamous Watergate tapes after the court ruled against his arguments of executive privilege, no other agency could have forced him to give up those tapes.

At the same time, there is one force that usually works to see that court decisions are carried out: It is that vague force called public opinion or what political scientists call "legitimacy." People believe in the judicial process; they have faith that what the courts do is probably right. This does not mean that they always agree with court decisions, but they do agree that the proper way to settle disputes is through the judicial process. Jurists help engender this spirit or philosophy by acting in a temperate manner. The Supreme Court, for example, has developed means that permit it to avoid having to answer highly controversial questions in which an unpopular decision could weaken its perceived legitimacy. The justices might call the dispute a political question, a **nonjusticiable matter,** or they may refuse to hear a case on other grounds. When the members of the court sense that the public is ready to accept a ruling, they may take on a controversial issue. School desegregation is a good example. In 1954 the Supreme Court ruled in *Brown* v. *Board of Education*[16] that segregated public schools violated the U.S. Constitution. The foundation for this ruling had been laid by a decade of less momentous desegregation decisions and executive actions. By 1954 the nation was prepared for the ruling, and it was generally accepted, even in most parts of the South. The legitimacy of a court's decisions, then, often rests upon prudent use of the judicial power.

People believe in the judicial process; they have faith that what the courts do is probably right.

Other Federal Courts

The Supreme Court of the United States is the most visible, perhaps the most glamorous (if that word is appropriate), of the federal courts. But it is not the only federal court nor even the busiest. There are two lower echelons of federal courts, plus various special courts, within the federal system. These special courts, such as the U.S. Court of Military Appeals, U.S. Tax Court, and so forth, were created by the Congress to handle special kinds of problems.

Most business in the federal system begins and ends in a district court. This court was created by Congress in the Federal Judiciary Act of 1789, and today in the United States there are 94 such courts staffed by 650 judges. Every state has at least one U.S. district court. Some states are divided into two districts or more: an eastern and western district or a northern, central, and southern district. Individual districts often have more than one judge, sometimes many more than one. The southern district of the U.S. District Court in New York has 28 judges.

When there is a jury trial, the case is heard in a district court. It has been estimated that about half the cases in U.S. district courts are heard by a jury.

At the intermediate level in the federal judiciary are the 13 circuits of the U.S. Court of Appeals. These courts were also created by the Federal Judiciary Act of 1789. Until 1948 these courts were called Circuit Courts of Appeal, a reflection of the early years of the republic when the justices of the Supreme Court "rode the circuit" and presided at the courts-of-appeal hearings. While the title Circuit Courts of Appeal is gone, the nation is still divided into circuits, each of which is served by one court (see figure 1.2).

16. 347 U.S. 483 (1954).

Fourth Circuit: Maryland, North Carolina, South Carolina, Virginia, and West Virginia
Fifth Circuit: Texas, Mississippi, and Louisiana
Sixth Circuit: Kentucky, Michigan, Ohio, and Tennessee
Seventh Circuit: Illinois, Indiana, and Wisconsin
Eighth Circuit: Arkansas, Iowa, Minnesota, Missouri, Nebraska, North Dakota, and South Dakota
Ninth Circuit: Alaska, Arizona, California, Hawaii, Idaho, Montana, Nevada, Oregon, Washington, Guam, and Northern Mariana Islands
Tenth Circuit: Colorado, Kansas, New Mexico, Utah, Oklahoma, and Wyoming
Eleventh Circuit: Alabama, Florida, Georgia, and the Canal Zone

First Circuit: Maine, Massachusetts, New Hampshire, Rhode Island, and Puerto Rico
Second Circuit: Connecticut, New York, and Vermont
Third Circuit: Delaware, New Jersey, Pennsylvania, and Virgin Islands

▶ FIGURE 1.2

Circuits 1–11 comprise the 50 states and the multiple U.S. territories.

The 12th and 13th circuits are unnumbered. One is the Court of Appeals for the District of Columbia. This is a very busy court because it hears most of the appeals from decisions made by federal administrative agencies. The 13th is the Court of Appeals for the Federal Circuit, a court created by the Congress in 1982 to handle special kinds of appeals. This court is specially empowered to hear appeals from patent and trademark decisions of U.S. district courts and other federal agencies such as the Board of Patent Appeals. It also hears appeals from rulings by the U.S. Claims Court, the U.S. Court of International Trade, the U.S. International Trade Commission, the Merit Systems Protection Board, and from a handful of other special kinds of rulings. Congress established this court to try to develop a uniform, reliable, and predictable body of law in each of these very special fields.

The circuit courts are appellate courts, which means that they only hear appeals from lower courts and other agencies. These courts are the last stop for 95 percent of all cases in the federal system. Each circuit has nine or more judges. Typically, a panel of three judges hears a case. In a case of great importance a larger panel of judges will hear the case. When a court hears a case in such a manner it is said to be sitting **en banc.** At one time this panel consisted of all the members of the court, usually 11 judges. Today the size of this panel varies. For example, the 9th U.S. Circuit Court of Appeals has 28 judges. Eleven judges are selected to hear an en banc appeal. In circuits with fewer judges, all the members of the court hear the case.

Federal Judges

All federal judges are appointed by the president and must be confirmed by the Senate. The appointment is for life. The only way a federal judge can be removed is by **impeachment.** Nine federal judges have been impeached: Four were found guilty by the Senate, and the other five were acquitted. Impeachment and trial is a long process and one rarely undertaken.

Political affiliation plays a distinct part in the appointment of federal judges. Democratic presidents usually appoint Democratic judges, and Republican presidents appoint Republican judges. Nevertheless, it is expected that nominees to the federal bench be competent jurists. This is especially true for appointees to the Court of Appeals and to the Supreme Court. The Senate must confirm all appointments to the federal courts, a normally perfunctory act in the case of lower-court judges. More careful scrutiny is given nominees to the appellate courts. The Senate has rejected 22 men nominated for the Supreme Court either by adverse vote or by delaying the vote so long that the appointment was withdrawn by the president or the president left office and the new chief executive nominated a different individual. Most recently, President Ronald Reagan's nomination of Judge Robert Bork to the Supreme Court was rejected.

The appointment of associate justices to the Supreme Court of the United States became a topic of substantial public interest during the last few decades. The high court had manifested a distinctly liberal political philosophy from the late 1930s through the 1960s, and the history of the court during this era is marked by substantial enlargement of both civil rights and civil liberties via constitutional interpretation. But the presidency of Richard Nixon marked the beginning of the end of this era. A steady stream of conservative Republican presidents filled the court with justices who appeared to be much more moderate or even conservative. Many persons feared the loss of some court-given liberties if and when the members of the high court reconsidered these critical issues.

The president appoints the members of the high court with the "advice and consent" of the U.S. Senate. When the White House and the Senate are both in the hands of the same party, Republicans or Democrats, this appointment process will usually proceed smoothly. President Clinton had few problems in winning the appointment of Ruth Bader Ginsburg and Stephen Breyer while Democrats controlled the Congress. On the other hand, Richard Nixon and Ronald Reagan, both conservative Republicans, had more difficulty getting their nominees on the court when the Senate was controlled by Democrats. Some argue that the Senate's only function is to ensure that competent jurists sit on the Supreme Court. Others take a more expansive view of the term "advice and consent" and argue that the Senate is obliged to consider judicial and political philosophy as well when evaluating the presidential nominees.

Presidents and senators alike have discovered that the individual who is nominated is not always the one who spends the remainder of his or her lifetime on the court. Justices and judges appointed to the bench for life sometimes change. Perhaps they are affected by their colleagues. Or maybe it is because they are largely removed from the pressures faced by others in public life. For whatever reasons, men and women appointed to the bench sometimes drastically modify their philosophy. It is doubtful that President Herbert Hoover expected the man he appointed chief justice, Charles Evans Hughes, to become the leader of the court that sustained much of the liberal and even radical legislation of the New Deal. Republican Dwight Eisenhower appointed

Chief Justice Earl Warren and Associate Justice William Brennan, two of the great liberal members of the court during the past 100 years. Liberal president John Kennedy's appointment to the high court, Justice Byron White, developed strong conservative leanings after he was confirmed. It is surely true, as writer Finley Peter Dunne's alter ego, Mr. Dooley, once remarked, "Th' Supreme Court follows th' iliction returns." But justices also sometimes follow a deeper set of beliefs as well, beliefs that aren't as obvious during the confirmation process.

THE STATE COURT SYSTEM

The constitution of every one of the 50 states either establishes a court system in that state or authorizes the legislature to do so. The court system in each of the 50 states is somewhat different from the court system in all the other states. There are, however, more similarities than differences among the 50 states.

The trial courts (or court) are the base of each judicial system. At the lowest level are usually what are called courts of limited jurisdiction. Some of these courts have special functions, like a traffic court, which is set up to hear cases involving violations of the motor-vehicle code. Some of these courts are limited to hearing cases of relative unimportance, such as trials of persons charged with misdemeanors, or minor crimes, or civil suits in which the damages sought fall below $1,000. The court may be a municipal court set up to hear cases involving violations of the city code. Whatever the court, the judges in these courts have limited jurisdiction and deal with a limited category of problems.

Above the lower-level courts normally exist trial courts of general jurisdiction similar to the federal district courts. These courts are sometimes county courts and sometimes state courts, but whichever they are, they handle nearly all criminal and civil matters. They are primarily courts of original jurisdiction; that is, they are the first courts to hear a case. However, on occasion they act as a kind of appellate court when the decisions of the courts of limited jurisdiction are challenged. When that happens, the case is retried in the trial court—the court does not simply review the law. This proceeding is called hearing a case **de novo.**

A **jury** is most likely to be found in the trial court of general jurisdiction. It is also the court in which most civil suits for libel and invasion of privacy are commenced (provided the state court has jurisdiction), in which prosecution for violating state obscenity laws starts, and in which many other media-related matters begin.

Above this court may be one or two levels of appellate courts. Every state has a supreme court, although some states do not call it that. In New York, for example, it is called the Court of Appeals, but it is the high court in the state, the court of last resort. Formerly, a supreme court was the only appellate court in most states. As legal business increased and the number of appeals mounted, the need for an intermediate appellate court became evident. Therefore, in most states there is an intermediate court, usually called the court of appeals. This is the court where most appeals end. In some states it is a single court with three or more judges. More often, numerous divisions within the appellate court serve various geographic regions, each division having three or more judges. Since every litigant is normally guaranteed at least one appeal, this intermediate court takes much of the pressure off the high court of the state. Rarely do individuals appeal beyond the intermediate level.

State courts of appeals tend to operate in much the same fashion as the U.S. Court of Appeals, with cases being heard by small groups of judges, usually three at a time.

Cases not involving federal questions go no further than the high court in a state, usually called the supreme court. This court—usually a seven- or nine-member body—is the final authority regarding the construction of state laws and interpretation of the state constitution. Not even the Supreme Court of the United States can tell a state supreme court what that state's constitution means. For example, in 1976 the U.S. Supreme Court ruled that the protection of the First Amendment did not include the right to distribute materials, demonstrate, or solicit petition signatures at privately owned shopping centers (*Hudgens* v. *NLRB*[17]—this case is discussed fully on pages 111–112). In 1980, however, the Supreme Court refused to overturn a decision by the California Supreme Court that declared that students had the right under the California constitution to solicit signatures for a pro-Israeli petition at a private shopping center in Campbell, California. Justice William Rehnquist wrote for the unanimous U.S. Supreme Court that perhaps the free-speech guarantee in the California constitution is broader than the First Amendment. In any case, the California high court was the final authority on the state's constitution (*Pruneyard Shopping Center* v. *Robins*[18]).

Not even the Supreme Court of the United States can tell a state supreme court what that state's constitution means.

State court judges are typically elected. Normally the process is nonpartisan, but because they are elected and must stand for reelection periodically, state court judges are generally a bit more politically active than their federal counterparts. Nearly half the states in the nation use a kind of compromise system that includes both appointment and election. The compromise is designed to minimize political influence and initially select qualified candidates, but still retain an element of popular control. The plans are named after the states that pioneered them, the **California Plan** and the **Missouri Plan.** Typically either the governor nominates a candidate to be approved by a judicial commission, or a judicial commission nominates a slate of candidates, one of which will be chosen by the governor. These jurists serve on the bench until the next general election, at which time the people of the state vote to retain or reject a particular judge. If retained, the judge serves until the next general election, when he or she again must attain voter approval. If the jurist is rejected, the appointment process begins again.

JUDICIAL REVIEW

One of the most important powers of courts (and at one time one of the most controversial) is the power of **judicial review**—that is, the right of any court to declare any law or official governmental action invalid because it violates a constitutional provision. We usually think of this right in terms of the U.S. Constitution. However, a state court can declare an act of its legislature to be invalid because the act conflicts with a provision of the state constitution. Theoretically, any court can exercise this power. The Circuit Court of Lapeer County, Michigan, can rule that the Environmental Protection Act of 1972 is unconstitutional because it deprives citizens of their property without due process of law, something guaranteed by the Fifth Amendment

17. 424 U.S. 507 (1976).
18. 447 U.S. 74 (1980).

to the federal Constitution. But this action isn't likely to happen, because a higher court would quickly overturn such a ruling. In fact, it is rather unusual for any court—even the U.S. Supreme Court—to invalidate a state or federal law on grounds that it violates the Constitution. Fewer than 200 federal statutes have been overturned by the courts in the 210-year history of the United States. During the same period, about 1,200 state laws and state constitutional provisions have been declared invalid. Judicial review is therefore not a power that the courts use excessively. In fact, a judicial maxim states: When a court has a choice of two or more ways in which to interpret a statute, the court should always interpret the statute in such a way that it is constitutional.

Judicial review is extremely important when matters concerning regulations of the mass media are considered. Because the First Amendment prohibits laws that abridge freedom of the press and freedom of speech, each new measure passed by the Congress, by state legislatures, and even by city councils and township boards must be measured by the yardstick of the First Amendment. Courts have the right, in fact have the duty, to nullify laws and executive actions and administrative rulings that do not meet the standards of the First Amendment. While many lawyers and legal scholars rarely consider constitutional principles in their work and rarely seek judicial review of a statute, attorneys who represent newspapers, magazines, broadcasting stations, and motion-picture theaters constantly deal with constitutional issues, primarily those of the First Amendment. The remainder of this book will illustrate the obvious fact that judicial review, a concept at the very heart of American democracy, plays an important role in maintaining the freedom of the American press, even though the power is not explicitly included in the Constitution.

LAWSUITS

The final topic that needs to be discussed is lawsuits. To the layman, and even those who work in the legal system, the United States appears to be awash in a sea of lawsuits. Lawyer bashing has become a popular leisure-time activity. The notion that there appears to be a lawsuit around every corner in every city can probably be blamed on the increased attention the press has given legal matters. Courts are fairly easy to cover and stories about lawsuits are more commonly published and broadcast. Also, some sensational cases are given saturation coverage, and this kind of coverage leaves the impression in the mind of the casual media consumer that the country is being swamped in a sea of legal briefs and writs.

This is not to say that we are not a highly litigious people. The backlogs in the courts are evidence of this. Going to court today is no longer a novelty but a common business or personal practice for a growing number of Americans. And in the end, the public pays a substantial price for all this litigation, through higher federal and state taxes to build and maintain courthouses and money to pay the salaries of those who work in the judiciary, and through higher insurance costs on everything from automobiles to protection from libel suits.

The material that follows is a simplified description of how a lawsuit proceeds. The picture is stripped of a great deal of the procedural activity that so often lengthens the lawsuit and keeps attorneys busy.

The party who commences a civil action is called the **plaintiff,** the person who brings the suit. The party against whom the suit is brought is called the **defendant.** In a libel suit the person who has been libeled is the plaintiff and is the one who starts the suit against the defendant—the newspaper, the magazine, the television station, or whatever. A civil suit is usually a dispute between two private parties. The government offers its good offices—the courts—to settle the matter. A government can bring a civil suit such as an antitrust action against someone, and an individual can bring a civil action against the government. But normally a civil suit is between private parties. (In a criminal action, the government always initiates the action.)

To start a civil suit the plaintiff first picks the proper court, one that has jurisdiction in the case. Then the plaintiff files a **civil complaint** with the court clerk. This complaint, or **pleading,** is a statement of the charges against the defendant and the remedy that is sought, typically money damages. The plaintiff also summons the defendant to appear in court to answer these charges. While the plaintiff may later amend his or her pleadings in the case, usually the initial complaint is the only pleading filed. After the complaint is filed, a hearing is scheduled by the court.

If the defendant fails to answer the charges, he or she normally loses the suit by default. Usually, however, the defendant will answer the summons and prepare his or her own set of pleadings, which constitute an answer to the plaintiff's charges. If there is little disagreement at this point about the facts—what happened—and that a wrong has been committed, the plaintiff and the defendant might settle their differences out of court. The defendant might say, "I guess I did libel you in this article, and I really don't have a very good defense. You asked for $100,000 in damages; would you settle for $50,000 and keep this out of court?" The plaintiff might very well answer yes, because a court trial is costly and takes a long time, and the plaintiff can also end up losing the case. Smart lawyers try to keep their clients out of court and settle matters in somebody's office.

If there is disagreement, the case is likely to continue. A common move for the defendant to make at this point is to file a motion to dismiss, or a **demurrer.** In such a motion the defendant says this to the court: "I admit that I did everything the plaintiff says I did. On June 5, 1997, I did publish an article in which she was called a socialist. But, Your Honor, it is not libelous to call someone a socialist." The plea made then is that even if everything the plaintiff asserts is true, the plaintiff has not been legally wronged. The law cannot help the plaintiff. The court might grant the motion, in which case the plaintiff can appeal. Or the court might refuse to grant the motion, in which case the defendant can appeal. If the motion to dismiss is ultimately rejected by all the courts up and down the line, a trial is then held. It is fair play for the defendant at that time to dispute the plaintiff's statement of the facts; in other words to deny, for example, that his newspaper published the article containing the alleged libel.

Before the trial is held, the judge may schedule a conference between both parties in an effort to settle the matter or at least to narrow the issues so that the trial can be shorter and less costly. If the effort to settle the dispute fails, the trial goes forward. If the facts are agreed upon by both sides and the question is merely one of law, a judge without a jury hears the case. There are no witnesses and no testimony, only legal arguments before the court. If the facts are disputed, the case can be tried before either a jury or, again, only a judge. Note that both sides must waive the right to a jury trial. In this event, the judge becomes both the fact finder and the lawgiver. Now, suppose that the case is heard by a jury. After all the testimony is given, all the evidence is presented, and all the arguments are made, the judge instructs the jury in the

Smart lawyers try to keep their clients out of court and settle matters in somebody's office.

law. Instructions are often long and complex, despite attempts by judges to simplify them. **Judicial instructions** guide the jury in determining guilt or innocence if certain facts are found to be true. The judge will say that if the jury finds that X is true and Y is true and Z is true, then it must find for the plaintiff, but if the jury finds that X is not true, but that R is true, then it must find for the defendant.

After deliberation the jury presents its **verdict,** the action by the jury. The judge then announces the **judgment of the court.** This is the decision of the court. The judge is not always bound by the jury verdict. If he or she feels that the jury verdict is unfair or unreasonable, the judge can reverse it and rule for the other party. This rarely happens.

If either party is unhappy with the decision, an appeal can be taken. At that time the legal designations may change. The person seeking the appeal becomes the **appellant,** or petitioner. The other party becomes the **appellee,** or **respondent.** The name of the party initiating the action is usually listed first in the name of the case. For example: Smith sues Jones for libel. The case name is *Smith* v. *Jones.* Jones loses and takes an appeal. At that point Jones becomes the party initiating the action and the case becomes *Jones* v. *Smith.* This change in designations often confuses novices in their attempt to trace a case from trial to final appeal. If Jones wins the appeal and Smith decides to appeal to a higher court, the case again becomes *Smith* v. *Jones.* In more and more jurisdictions today, however, the case name remains the same throughout the appeal process. This is an effort by the judiciary to relieve some of the confusion wrought by this constant shifting of party names within the case name. In California, for example, the case of *Smith* v. *Jones* remains *Smith* v. *Jones* through the entire life of that case.

The end result of a successful civil suit is usually the awarding of money **damages.** Sometimes the amount of damages is guided by the law, as in a suit for infringement of copyright in which the law provides that a losing defendant pay the plaintiff the amount of money he or she might have made if the infringement had not occurred, or at least a set number of dollars. But most of the time the damages are determined by how much the plaintiff seeks, how much the plaintiff can prove he or she lost, and how much the jury thinks the plaintiff deserves. It is not a very scientific means of determining the dollar amount.

A **criminal prosecution,** or **criminal action,** is like a civil suit in many ways. The procedures are more formal, are more elaborate, and involve the machinery of the state to a greater extent. The state brings the charges, usually through the county or state prosecutor. The defendant can be apprehended either before or after the charges are brought. In the federal system persons must be **indicted** by a **grand jury,** a panel of 21 citizens, before they can be charged with a serious crime. But most states do not use grand juries in that fashion, and the law provides that it is sufficient that the prosecutor issue an **information,** a formal accusation. After being charged, the defendant is arraigned. An **arraignment** is the formal reading of the charge. It is at the arraignment that the defendant makes a formal plea of guilty or not guilty. If the plea is guilty, the judge gives the verdict of the court and passes sentence, but usually not immediately, for presentencing reports and other procedures must be undertaken. If the plea is not guilty, a trial is scheduled.

Some state judicial systems have an intermediate step called a preliminary hearing or preliminary examination. The preliminary hearing is held in a court below the trial court, such as a municipal court, and the state has the responsibility of presenting enough evidence to convince the court—only a judge—that a crime has been committed and that there is suffi-cient evidence to believe that the defendant might possibly be involved. Today it is also not uncommon that **pretrial hearings** on a variety of matters precede the trial.

In both a civil suit and a criminal case, the result of the trial is not enforced until the final appeal is exhausted. That is, a money judgment is not paid in civil suits until defendants exhaust all their appeals. The same is true in a criminal case. Imprisonment or payment of a fine is not required until the final appeal. However, if the defendant is dangerous or if there is some question that the defendant might not surrender when the final appeal is completed, bail can be required. Bail is money given to the court to ensure appearance in court.

SUMMARY

There are 52 different judicial systems in the nation: one federal system, one for the District of Columbia, and one for each of the 50 states. Courts within each of these systems are divided into two general classes—trial courts and appellate courts. In any lawsuit both the facts and the law must be considered. The facts or the factual record is an account of what hap-pened to prompt the dispute. The law is what should be done to resolve the dispute. Trial courts determine the facts in the case; then the judge applies the law. Appellate courts, using the factual record established by the trial court, determine whether the law was properly applied by the lower court and whether proper judicial procedures were followed. Trial courts exercise original jurisdiction almost exclusively; that is, they are the first courts to hear a case. Trial courts have very little discretion over which cases they will and will not hear. Appellate courts exercise appellate jurisdiction almost exclusively; that is, they review the work done by the lower courts when decisions are appealed. While the intermediate appellate courts (i.e., courts of appeals; the appellate division) have limited discretion in the selection of cases, the high courts (supreme courts) in the states and the nation generally have the power to select the cases they wish to review.

Federal courts include the Supreme Court of the United States, the U.S. Courts of Appeals, the U.S. District Courts, and several specialized tribunals. These courts have juris-diction in all cases that involve the U.S. Constitution, U.S. law, and U.S. treaties; in disputes between citizens of different states; and in several less important instances. In each state there are trial-level courts and a court of last resort, usually called the supreme court. In about half the states there are intermediate appellate courts as well. State courts generally have jurisdic-tion in all disputes between citizens of their state that involve the state constitution or state law.

Judicial review is the power of a court to declare a statute, regulation, or executive action to be a violation of the Constitution and thus invalid. Because the First Amendment to the U.S. Constitution guarantees the rights of freedom of speech and freedom of the press, all government actions that relate to the communication of ideas and information face potential scrutiny by the courts to determine their validity.

There are two basic kinds of lawsuits—civil suits and criminal prosecutions or actions. A civil suit is normally a dispute between two private parties in which the government offers its good offices (the courts) to resolve the dispute. The person who initiates the civil suit is called the plaintiff; the person at whom the suit is aimed is called the defendant. A plaintiff who wins a civil suit is normally awarded money damages.

A criminal case is normally an action in which the state brings charges against a private individual, who is called the defendant. A defendant who loses a criminal case can be assessed a fine, jailed, or, in extreme cases, executed. A jury can be used in both civil and criminal cases. The jury becomes the fact finder and renders a verdict in a case. But the judge issues the judgment in the case. In a civil suit a judge can reject any jury verdict and rule in exactly the opposite fashion, finding for either plaintiff or defendant if the judge feels the jury has made a serious error in judgment. Either side can appeal the judgment of the court. In a criminal case the judge can take the case away from the jury and order a dismissal, but nothing can be done about an acquittal, even an incredible acquittal. While a guilty defendant may appeal the judgment, the state is prohibited from appealing an acquittal.

As stated at the outset, this chapter is designed to provide a glimpse, only a glimpse, of both our legal system and our judicial system. The discussion is in no way comprehensive, but it provides enough information to make the remaining 16 chapters meaningful. This chapter is not intended to be a substitute for a good political science course in the legal process. Students of communications law are at a distinct disadvantage if they do not have some grasp of how the systems work and what their origins are.

The United States legal and judicial systems are old and tradition-bound. But they have worked fairly well for these last 215 years. In the final analysis the job of both the law and the men and women who administer it is to balance the competing interests of society. How this balancing act is undertaken comprises the remainder of this book. The process is not always easy, but it is usually interesting.

BIBLIOGRAPHY

Abraham, Henry J. *The Judicial Process.* 7th ed. New York: Oxford University Press, 1998.
————. *The Judiciary: The Supreme Court in the Government Process.* 3d ed. Boston: Allyn & Bacon, 1973.
Cohn, Bob. "The Lawsuit Cha-Cha." *Newsweek,* 26 August 1991, 58.
Franklin, Marc A. *The Dynamics of American Law.* Mineola, N.Y.: Foundation Press, 1969.
Greenhouse, Linda. "Supreme Court Awards Island to Mississippi." *The New York Times,* 1 November 1995, C18.
Holmes, Oliver Wendell. *The Common Law.* Boston: Little, Brown & Co., 1881.
Pound, Roscoe. *The Development of the Constitutional Guarantees of Liberty.* New Haven: Yale University Press, 1957.
Rembar, Charles. *The Law of the Land.* New York: Simon & Schuster, 1980.
Roche, John P. *Courts and Rights.* 2d ed. New York: Random House, 1966.

The First Amendment
The Meaning of Freedom

The First Amendment is the wellspring from which flows nearly all U.S. laws on freedom of speech and freedom of the press. The amendment, adopted in 1791 as a part of the Bill of Rights, comprises only 45 words. But court decisions during the past 200 years have added substantial meaning to this basic outline. In this chapter we explore the evolution of the centuries-old notion of freedom of expression, outline the adoption of the First Amendment, and examine the development of some elements of the fundamental meaning of freedom of speech and press.

HISTORICAL DEVELOPMENT

Freedom of expression is not, and was not, exclusively an American idea. We did not invent the concept—in fact, no one invented it; it just grew from crude beginnings that can be traced back to Plato and Socrates. The concept developed more fully during the past 400 years. The modern history of freedom of the press really began in England during the 16th and 17th centuries as printing developed and grew. Today the most indelible embodiment of the concept is the First Amendment to the U.S. Constitution, forged in the last half of the 18th century by the men who built upon their memory of earlier experiences. To understand the meaning of freedom of the press and freedom of speech, it is necessary to understand the meaning of censorship, for viewed from a negative position freedom of expression can be simply defined as the absence of censorship.

FREEDOM OF THE PRESS IN ENGLAND

When William Caxton set up the first British printing press in Westminster in 1476, his printing pursuits were restricted only by his imagination and ability. There were no laws governing what he could or could not print—he was completely free. For more than five centuries, the British and Americans have attempted to regain the freedom that Caxton enjoyed, for shortly after he started publishing, the British Crown began the control and regulation of printing presses in England. Printing developed during a period of great religious struggle in Europe, and it soon became an important tool in that struggle. Printing presses made communication with hundreds of persons fairly easy and in doing so gave considerable power to small groups or individuals who owned or could use a printing press.

The British government soon realized that unrestricted publication and printing could seriously dilute its own power. Information is a powerful tool in any society, and the individual or individuals controlling the flow and content of the information received by a people exercise considerable control over those people. The printing press broke the Crown's monopoly of the flow of information, and therefore control of printing was essential.

Between 1476 and 1776 the British devised and used several means to limit or restrict the press in England. **Seditious libel** laws were used to punish those who criticized the government or the Crown, and it did not matter whether the criticism was truthful or not. The press suffered under **licensing** laws as well, which required printers to get prior approval from the government or the church before printing their handbills or pamphlets or newspapers. Printers were also often required to deposit with the government large sums of money called **bonds.** This money was forfeited if material appeared that the government felt should not have been published. And the printer was forced to post another bond before printing could be resumed. The British also granted special patents and monopolies to certain printers in exchange for their cooperation in printing only acceptable works and in helping the Crown ferret out other printers who broke the publication laws.

British control of the press during these 300 years was generally successful, but did not go unchallenged. As ideas about democracy spread throughout Europe, it became harder and harder for the government to limit freedom of expression. The power of the printing press in spreading ideas quickly to masses of people greatly helped foster the democratic spirit. Although British law regulated American printers as well during the colonial era, regulation of the press in North America was never as successful as it was in Great Britain.

As ideas about democracy spread throughout Europe, it became harder and harder for the government to limit freedom of expression.

FREEDOM OF THE PRESS IN COLONIAL AMERICA

There were laws in the United States restricting freedom of the press for almost 30 years before the first newspaper was published. As early as 1662, statutes in Massachusetts made it a crime to publish anything without first getting prior approval from the government, 28 years before Benjamin Harris published the first—and last—edition of *Publick Occurrences*. The second and all subsequent issues of the paper were banned because Harris had failed to get permission to publish the first edition, which contained material construed to be criticism of British policy in the colonies as well as a report that scandalized the Massachusetts clergy because it said the French king took immoral liberties with a married woman (not his wife).

Despite this inauspicious beginning, American colonists had a much easier time getting their views into print (and staying out of jail) than their counterparts in England. There was censorship, but American juries were reluctant to convict printers prosecuted by the British colonial authorities. The colonial governments were less efficient than the government in England. Also, the British had only limited control over the administration of government in many of the colonies.

The British attempted to use licensing, taxes, and sedition laws to control American printers and publishers. Licensing, which ended in England in 1695, lasted until the mid-1720s in the American colonies. Benjamin Franklin's older brother James was jailed in 1722 for failing to get prior government approval for publishing his New England Courant. The unpopular government move failed to daunt the older Franklin, and licensing eventually ended in the colonies as well. The taxes levied against the press, most of which were genuine attempts to raise revenues, were nevertheless seen as censorship by American printers and resulted in growing hostility toward the Parliament and the Crown. Most publishers refused to buy the tax stamps, and there was little retribution by the British.

Undoubtedly, the most famous case of government censorship in the American colonies was the seditious libel trial of immigrant printer John Peter Zenger, who found himself involved in a vicious political battle between leading colonial politicians in New York. Zenger published the New York Weekly Journal, a newspaper sponsored by Lewis Morris and James Alexander, political opponents of the unpopular colonial governor, William Cosby. Zenger was jailed in November of 1734 after his newspaper published several stinging attacks on Cosby, who surmised that by jailing the printer—one of only two in New York—he could silence his critics. There is little doubt that Zenger was guilty under 18th-century British sedition law. But his attorneys, including the renowned criminal lawyer Andrew Hamilton, were able to convince the jury that no man should be imprisoned or fined for publishing criticism of the government that was both truthful and fair. Jurors simply ignored the law and acquitted the German printer.

Front page from the
November 5, 1733
New York Weekly
Journal.

THE
New-York Weekly JOURNAL.

Containing the freshest Advices, Foreign, and Domestick.

MONDAY November 5, 1733.

Mr. Zenger,

UNDERSTANDING you intend shortly to publish a Weekly Paper, I recommend to your disposal the inclosed Verses upon Wisdom ; which is so noble a Theme, that whoever takes the Pains seriously to reflect thereon, will find himself happily lost in the boundless Ocean of Benefits and Satisfaction attending it. It is without Dispute the chief Wood of Mankind ; the firm Bank that constantly secures us again the impetuous Raging of that turbulent Sea of Passions, which incessantly dash against the Frame of human Nature. It is a Fort impregnable by all Assaults of Vice, Folly, and Misfortunes, and a secure Rock against all the Casualties of Misery. It is a Guide and Security to Youth, Health, and Vigour to Old Age ; and a Remedy and Ease in Sickness and Infirmity. It is Comfort in Adversity, it is Plenty in Poverty, and a constant Source of true Joy and Delight. It is infinitely beyond all that the feigned *Fortunatus* ever could wish, or *Gyges's* Treasures purchase ; *For her Ways are Ways of Pleasantness, and all her Paths are Peace.* She is of easy access to all that diligently seek her ; and refuses none that with Sincerity apply to her, and is always a ready Help in Time of Need : Therefore pray continue to recommed the earnest Pursuit of Her to all Mankind ; and you will particularly oblige.

PHILO-SOPHIA.

On WISDOM.

Victorious Wisdom whose supreme Command
Extends beyond the Bounds of Sea and Land ;
'Tis thou alone that dost reward our Pains,
With Pleasures that endure, and solid Gains.

N.Y. P.L.

But Oh ! What art thou, and where dost thou dwell ?
Not with the Hermit in his lonely Cell ;
The sullen Fumes of whose distemper'd Brain,
Make the dull Wretch torment himself in vain :
Whilst of the World affectedly afraid,
He shuns the End for which Mankind was made.

Not with the Epicure in all his Pleasures,
Nor with the Miser in his Bank of Treasures,
The one's a Slave bound fast in golden Chains,
The other buys short Joys with lasting Pains.

Not in the vain Pursuit of partial Fame,
The gaudy Outside of an empty Name ;
Which is bestow'd by Chance, not Merit common Breath,
Or else Shadow sudden Life or Death.

Honour, when meritoriously assigned,
The noble Actions of a God like Mind,
Is then indeed a Blessing sent from Heaven,
A bright Reward for human Labour given.

But when 'tis Fame's mistaken Flattery,
A popular Applause of Vanity,
The worthless Idol ought to be abhor'd;
And is by none but Knaves and Fools ador'd.

Thus as I'm searching with the feeble Light
Of human Reason, in dark error's Night,
For what has oft escap'd the curious Eye,
Of lofty Wit, and deep Philosophy,
From the bright Regions of eternal Day,
Methinks I see a small but glorious Ray,
Dart swift as Lightning throug the yielding Air,
To an unspotted Breast, and enter there.

This is the Wisdom I so much adore ;
Grant me but this, kind Heaven, I ask no more,
This once obtain'd, how happy shall I be ?
Kings will be little Men, compar'd to me :
They in their own Dominions only great,
I Conquer of the World, my self and Fate.

Thus arm'd, let Fortune use me as she will,
I stand prepar'd to meet with Good or Ill,
If I am born for Happiness and Ease,
And prosp'rous Gales salute the smiling Seas ;
This Path I'll tread, (the Blessings to repay)
Where Virtue calls and Honour leads the Way,

But if the Weather of my Life prove foul,
Though Storms arise that makes whole Kingdoms
rowle.

Yet

The verdict in the Zenger case was a great political triumph but did nothing to change the law of seditious libel. In other words, the case did not set an important legal precedent. But the revolt of the American jurors did force colonial authorities to reconsider the use of sedition law as a means of controlling the press. While a few sedition prosecutions were initiated after 1735, there is no record of a successful prosecution in the colonial courts after the Zenger case. The case received widespread publicity both in North America and in England, and the outcome of the trial played an important role in galvanizing public sentiment against this kind of government censorship.

The Zenger trial has today become an accepted part of American journalism mythology. While the case is certainly worth remembering, it doesn't represent the end of British attempts to control the press in the American colonies. Other means were substituted for sedition. Rather than haul printers and editors before jurors who were often hostile to the state, the government instead hauled printers and editors before colonial legislatures and assemblies that were usually hostile to journalists. The charge was not sedition, but breach of parliamentary privilege or contempt of the assembly. There was no distinct separation of powers then, and the legislative body could order printers to appear, question them, convict them, and punish them. Printers and publishers were thus still being jailed and fined for publications previously considered sedition. Only the means of exacting this punishment had changed.

Yet despite these potent sanctions occasionally levied against publishers and printers, the press of this era was remarkably robust. Researchers who have painstakingly read the newspapers and pamphlets and handbills produced in the last half of the 18th century are struck by the seeming lack of concern for government censorship. Historian Leonard Levy notes in his book "Emergence of a Free Press" the seeming paradox uncovered by scholars who seek to understand the meaning of freedom of expression during that era.[1] "To one [a scholar] whose prime concern was law and theory, a legacy of suppression [of the press] came into focus; to one who looks at newspaper judgments on public men and measures, the revolutionary controversy spurred an expanding legacy of liberty," he wrote. What Levy suggests is that while the law and legal pronouncements from jurists and legislatures suggest a fairly rigid control of the press, in fact journalists and other publishers tended to ignore the law and suffered little retribution.

But the appearance of such freedom can be deceptive, as political scientist John Roche points out in his book "Shadow and Substance,"[2] for the community often exerted tremendous pressure on anyone who expressed an unpopular idea. The belief of many persons that freedom was the hallmark of society in America ignores history, Roche argues. In colonial America the people simply did not understand that freedom of thought and expression meant freedom for the other person also, particularly for the person with hated ideas. Roche points out that colonial America was an open society dotted with closed enclaves—villages and towns and cities—in which citizens generally shared similar beliefs about religion and government and so forth. Citizens could hold any belief they chose and could espouse that belief, but personal safety

The belief of many persons that freedom was the hallmark of society in America ignores history.

1. Levy, *Emergence of a Free Press.*
2. Roche, *Shadow and Substance.*

depended on the people in a community agreeing with a speaker or writer. If they didn't, the speaker then kept quiet or moved to another enclave where the people shared those ideas. While there was much diversity of thought in the colonies, there was often little diversity of belief within towns and cities, according to Roche.

The propaganda war that preceded the Revolution is a classic example of the situation. In Boston, the patriots argued vigorously for the right to print what they wanted in their newspapers, even criticism of the government. Freedom of expression was their right, a God-given right, a natural right, a right of all British subjects. Many persons, however, did not favor revolution or even separation from England. Yet it was extremely difficult for them to publish such pro-British sentiments in many American cities after 1770. Printers who published such ideas in newspapers and handbills did so at their peril. In cities like Boston the printers were attacked, their shops were wrecked, and their papers were destroyed. Freedom of the press was a concept with limited utility in many communities for colonists who opposed revolution once the patriots had moved the populace to their side.

The plight of the pro-British printer in Boston in the 1770s is not a unique chapter in American history. Today such community censorship still exists—and in some instances is growing. In recent years extreme pressure has been exerted on many retailers, for example, to exclude so-called men's magazines like Playboy from their newsstands. Students at some universities have attempted to block the appearances of extreme right-wing speakers with whom they disagree. Libraries continue to be the target of those who seek to ban books that they find objectionable. In many of these instances the general public, the masses on the sidelines, finds little cause for concern about such attempts at censorship. The public malaise about such conditions is dangerous. No individual's freedom is secure unless the freedom of all is ensured.

SUMMARY

Freedom of the press is part of the great Anglo-American legal tradition, but it is a right that has been won only through many hard-fought battles. The British discovered the power of the press in the early 16th century and devised numerous schemes to restrict publication. Criticism of the government, called seditious libel, was outlawed. Licensing or prior censorship was also common. In addition, the Crown for many years used an elaborate system of patents and monopolies to control printing in England.

While under British law for more than 100 years, American colonists enjoyed somewhat more freedom of expression than did their counterparts in England. Censorship laws existed before the first printing press arrived in North America, but they were enforced erratically or not at all. Licensing ended in the United States colonies in the 1720s. There were several trials for sedition in the colonies, but the acquittal of John Peter Zenger in 1735 by a recalcitrant jury ended that threat. Colonial legislatures and assemblies then attempted to punish dissident printers by using their contempt power. By the time the American colonists began to build their own governments in the 1770s and 1780s, they had the history of a 300-year struggle for freedom of expression on which to build.

THE FIRST AMENDMENT

In 1781, even before the end of the Revolutionary War, the new nation adopted its first constitution, the Articles of Confederation. The Articles provided for a loose-knit confederation of the 13 colonies, or states, in which the central or federal government had little power. The Articles of Confederation did not contain a guarantee of freedom of expression. In fact, it had no bill of rights of any kind. The men who drafted this constitution did not believe such guarantees were necessary. Under these articles states were the most powerful political entities; the national government had few prerogatives. Guarantees of freedom of expression were already a part of the constitutions of most of the 13 states. The citizens of Virginia, for example, had adopted a new constitution that contained a declaration of rights in June 1776, five years before the Articles of Confederation were written. Freedom of the press was guaranteed as a part of that declaration of rights. Other states soon followed Virginia's lead.

But the system of government created by the Articles of Confederation did not work very well. In the hot summer of 1787, 12 of the 13 states sent a total of 55 delegates to Philadelphia to revise or amend the Articles, to make fundamental changes in the structure of the government.

THE NEW CONSTITUTION

It was a remarkable group of men; perhaps no such group has gathered before or since. The members were merchants and planters and professionals, and none were full-time politicians. As a group these men were by fact or inclination members of the economic, social, and intellectual aristocracy of their respective states. They shared a common education centered around history, political philosophy, and science. Some of them spent months preparing for the meeting—studying the governments of past nations. While some members came to modify the Articles of Confederation, many others knew from the start that a new constitution was needed. In the end that is what they produced, a new governmental charter. The charter was far different from the Articles in that it gave vast powers to a central government. The states remained supreme in some matters, but in other matters they were forced to relinquish their sovereignty to the new federal government.

No official record of the convention was kept. The delegates deliberated behind closed doors as they drafted the new charter. However, some personal records remain. We do know, for example, that inclusion of a bill of rights in the new charter was not discussed until the last days of the convention. The Constitution was drafted in such a way as not to infringe on state bills of rights. When the meeting was in its final week, George Mason of Virginia indicated his desire that "the plan be prefaced with a Bill of Rights. . . . It would give great quiet to the people," he said, "and with the aid of the state declarations, a bill might be prepared in a few hours." Few joined Mason's call. Only one delegate, Roger Sherman of Connecticut, spoke against the suggestion. He said he favored protecting the rights of the people when it was necessary, but in this case there was no need. "The state declarations of rights are not repealed by this Constitution; and being in force are sufficient." He said that where the rights of the people are involved Congress could be trusted to preserve the rights. The states, voting as units, unanimously opposed Mason's plan. While the Virginian later attempted to add a bill of rights in a piecemeal fashion, the Constitution emerged from the convention and was placed before the people for ratification without a bill of rights.

The new Constitution was not without opposition. The struggle for its adoption was hard fought. The failure to include a bill of rights in the document was a telling complaint raised against the new document. Even Thomas Jefferson, who was in France, lamented, in a letter to his friend James Madison, the lack of a guarantee of political rights in the charter. When the states finally voted on the new Constitution, it was approved, but only after supporters in several states had promised to petition the First Congress to add a bill of rights.

James Madison was elected from Virginia to the House of Representatives, defeating James Monroe only after promising his constituents to work in the First Congress toward adoption of a declaration of human rights. When Congress convened, Madison worked to keep his promise. He first proposed that the new legislature incorporate a bill of rights into the body of the Constitution, but the idea was later dropped. That the Congress would adopt the declaration was not a foregone conclusion. There was much opposition, but after several months, 12 amendments were finally approved by both houses and sent to the states for ratification. Madison's original amendment dealing with freedom of expression states: "The people shall not be deprived or abridged of their right to speak, to write or to publish their sentiments and freedom of the press, as one of the great bulwarks of liberty, shall be inviolable." Congressional committees changed the wording several times, and the section guaranteeing freedom of expression was merged with the amendment guaranteeing freedom of religion and freedom of assembly. The final version is the version we know today:

> Congress shall make no law respecting an establishment of religion, or prohibit-
> ing the free exercise thereof; or abridging the freedom of speech, or of the press;
> or the right of the people peaceably to assemble, and to petition the Government
> for a redress of grievances.

The concept of the "first freedom" has been discussed often. Historical myth tells us that because the amendment occurs first in the Bill of Rights it was considered the most important right. In fact, in the Bill of Rights presented to the states for ratification, the amendment was listed third. Amendments one and two were defeated and did not become part of the Constitution. The original First Amendment called for a fixed schedule that apportioned seats in the House of Representatives on a ratio many persons thought unfair. The Second Amendment prohibited senators and representatives from altering their salaries until after a subsequent election of representatives. Both amendments were rejected, and amendment three became the First Amendment. In 1992, the economy-minded legislatures in three-fourths of the United States finally approved the original Second Amendment, and it became the 27th amendment to the Constitution.

Passage of the last 10 amendments did not occur without struggle. Not until two years after being transmitted to the states for approval did a sufficient number of states adopt the amendments for them to become part of the Constitution. Connecticut, Georgia, and Massachusetts did not ratify the Bill of Rights until 1941, a kind of token gesture on the 150th anniversary of its constitutional adoption. In 1791 approval by these states was not needed, since only three-fourths of the former colonies needed to agree to the measures.

FREEDOM OF EXPRESSION IN THE 18TH CENTURY

What did the First Amendment mean to the people who supported its ratification in 1790? This is not an idle question. The Bill of Rights was, after all, approved by a vote of the people in the several states. By their votes of approval, they enacted into the supreme law of the land their definitions of such rights as freedom of the press. Technically, the definition of freedom of the press approved by the nation when the First Amendment was ratified in 1791 is what is guaranteed today. To enlarge or narrow that definition requires another vote of the people, a constitutional amendment. This notion is referred to today as "original intent" of the Constitution.

But most people today consider this notion so much legalistic poppycock. The nation has changed dramatically in 210 years. Television, radio, film, and the Internet did not exist in 1790, for example. Does this mean that the guarantees of the First Amendment should not apply to these mass media? Of course not. Our Constitution has lasted for more than 210 years because it has been somewhat elastic. The Supreme Court of the United States, our final arbiter on the meaning of the Constitution, has helped adapt the document to changing times.

Still, it is important that we respect the document that was adopted 210 years ago. If we stray too far from its original meaning, the document may become meaningless; there will be no rules of government. The Constitution will mean only what those in power say it means.

What was the legal or judicial definition of the First Amendment in 1790? Surprisingly, that is not an easy question to answer. The records of the period carry mixed messages. There was really no authoritative definition of freedom of the press and freedom of speech rendered by a body like the Supreme Court. And even the words used by persons of that era may have meant something different in 1790 than they mean in the 21st century. Most everyone agrees that freedom of expression meant at least the right to be free from **prior restraint** or licensing. Sir William Blackstone, a British legal scholar, published a major four-volume summary of the common law between 1765 and 1769. In this summary, "Commentaries on the Law of England," Blackstone defined freedom of expression as "laying no previous restraints upon publication." Today we call this no prior censorship. Many scholars argue that freedom of expression surely meant more than simply no prior censorship, that it also protected persons from punishment *after publication* for such offenses as criticizing the government. In other words, the First Amendment also precluded prosecutions for seditious libel. After all, they argue, one of the reasons for the American Revolution was to rid the nation of the hated British sedition laws.

The truth is that we probably don't know what freedom of the press meant to American citizens 210 years ago. The written residue of the period reveals only a partial story. It's very likely that it meant something a little different to different people, just as it does today. Even those individuals who drafted the Bill of Rights probably held somewhat different views on the meaning of the First Amendment.

Has the meaning of freedom of expression changed over the past two centuries? Surely, in many small and fairly obvious ways. But some scholars today suggest that a more subtle but profound change has taken place as well. They argue persuasively that many persons see a difference in the values that should be protected by the First Amendment. In the late 18th

Most everyone agrees that freedom of expression meant at least the right to be free from prior restraint or licensing.

century freedom of expression was designed to protect the rights of the speaker; the value of the First Amendment was to allow individuals the fullest possible right to say or publish what they wished. Scholars like Steven Helle at the University of Illinois argue that it is the protection of the public's right to know, or society's right to be informed, that is the central value in the First Amendment.[3] This subtle shift in what is being protected manifests a different interpretation of what and how much speech is protected under the Constitution. Only serious harm to other individuals or to the community will justify an interference with First Amendment freedoms if the rights of the speaker or publisher are paramount. But when societal interests are put ahead of those of the speaker or publisher, substantially more censorship will be tolerated in order to preserve the wider rights of the community. Those who advocate tougher sanctions on obscenity because it demeans women, or stricter limits on racially or ethnically insulting speech because it denigrates members of racial or ethnic minority groups, do so from the position of this latter interpretation of the First Amendment. We will encounter instances of the advocacy of this new proposition throughout this book.

FREEDOM OF EXPRESSION TODAY

If we are not certain what the First Amendment meant in 1790, do we know what it means today? More or less. The First Amendment means today what the Supreme Court of the United States says it means. Certainly many people disagree with the definition of freedom of expression rendered by the high court. But from the standpoint of the law—and that is what this book is about—the Supreme Court and, occasionally, lower courts define the meaning of the First Amendment to the Constitution.

The Supreme Court is a collection of nine justices, not a single individual. Consequently, at any given time there can be nine different definitions of freedom of expression. This has never happened—at least, not on important issues. What has happened is that groups of justices have subscribed to various theoretical positions regarding the meaning of the First Amendment. These theories of the meaning of the First Amendment help justices shape their vote on a question regarding freedom of expression. These theories have changed during the past 90 years, the point at which the First Amendment first came under serious scrutiny by the Supreme Court. It is rare that the justices themselves develop such theories. Most theories are proposed by persons outside the court: legal scholars, lower-court judges, even philosophers. At some point a jurist finds a comfortable theory and uses it to assist in interpreting the First Amendment.

Legal theories are sometimes difficult to handle. Judge Learned Hand, a distinguished American jurist, referred to the propagation of legal theory as "shoveling smoke." With such cautions in mind, we will attempt to identify five important First Amendment theories or strategies that have been used or are used today to help judges develop a practical definition of freedom of expression.

---

3. Helle, "Public's Right," 1077.

FIRST AMENDMENT THEORIES

1. Absolutist theory
2. Ad hoc balancing theory
3. Preferred position balancing theory
4. Meiklejohnian theory
5. Access theory

Absolutist theory: The First Amendment declares that "no law" shall abridge the freedom of speech or of the press. "No law" means *no law.* Speech and press are absolutely protected from interference by the government. There are no exceptions. This is what was intended by the men who drafted the First Amendment.

No more than two Supreme Court justices—Hugo Black and William Douglas—have subscribed to this position. Critics of the **absolutist theory** argue that the key words in the First Amendment are *"freedom of speech and press,"* not "no law." The freedom to speak and publish was not an absolute freedom in 1790; limits to this freedom were accepted by the people. What the amendment means, then, is that "no law" may abridge the qualified protection given to individuals to speak and publish. If speech and press were to be protected absolutely, the First Amendment would have been written this way: "Congress shall pass no law abridging speech and press." The absolutist theory has received little judicial or public support because it fails to acknowledge that other important human rights often conflict with freedom of speech and press.

Ad hoc balancing theory: Freedom of speech and press are two of a number of important human rights we value in this nation. These rights often conflict. When conflict occurs, it is the responsibility of the court to balance the freedom of expression with other values. For example, the government must maintain the military to protect the security of the nation. To function, the military must maintain secrecy about many of its weapons, plans, and movements. Imagine that the press seeks to publish information about a secret weapons system. The right to freedom of expression must be balanced with the need for secrecy in the military.

This theory is called *ad hoc* balancing because the scales are erected anew in every case; the meaning of the freedom of expression is determined solely on a case-by-case basis. Freedom of the press might outweigh the need for the government to keep secret the design of its new rifle, but the need for secrecy about a new fighter plane might take precedence over freedom of expression.

Ad hoc balancing is really not a theory; it is a strategy. Developing a definition of freedom of expression on a case-by-case basis leads to uncertainty. Under ad hoc balancing we will never know what the First Amendment means except as it relates to a specific, narrow problem (e.g., the right to publish information about a new army rifle). If citizens cannot reasonably predict whether a particular kind of expression might be protected or prohibited, they will have the tendency to play it safe and keep silent. This will limit the rights of expression of all persons. Also, ad hoc balancing relies too heavily in its final determination on the personal biases of the judge or justices who decide a case. Ad hoc balancing is rarely invoked as a strategy these days except by judges unfamiliar with First Amendment law.

Preferred position balancing theory: The Supreme Court has held in numerous rulings that some constitutional freedoms, principally those guaranteed by the First Amendment, are fundamental to a free society and consequently are entitled to more judicial protection than other constitutional values are.[4] Freedom of expression is essential to permit the operation of the political process and to permit citizens to protest when government infringes on their constitutionally protected prerogatives. The Fourth Amendment guarantee of freedom from illegal search and seizure surely has diminished value if citizens who suffer from such unconstitutional searches cannot protest such actions. Freedom of expression does not trump all other rights. The courts, for example, have attempted to balance the rights of free speech and press with the constitutionally guaranteed right of a fair trial. On the other hand, courts have consistently ruled that freedom of expression takes precedence over the right to personal privacy and the right to reputation, neither of which is explicitly guaranteed by the Bill of Rights.

By giving freedom of expression a preferred position courts will **presume** that government action that limits free speech and free press in order to protect other interests is usually unconstitutional. This presumption forces the government to bear the burden of proof in any legal action challenging the censorship. The city, the county, the state, or the federal government must prove to the court that its censorship is in fact justified and is not a violation of the First Amendment. Were it not for this presumption, the persons whose expression was limited would be forced to convince a court that they had a constitutional right to speak or publish. This difference sounds like a minor matter, but in a lawsuit this presumption means a great deal. Today, courts use the preferred position balancing theory more than any other theory, which adds substantial certainty to our definition of freedom of expression.

While it retains some of the negative features of ad hoc balancing, by tilting the scales in favor of freedom of expression, it adds somewhat more certainty to our definition of freedom of expression. By basing this balancing strategy on a philosophical foundation (the maintenance of all rights is dependent on free exercise of speech and press), it becomes easier to build a case in favor of the broad interpretation of freedom of expression under the First Amendment.

Meiklejohnian theory: Philosopher Alexander Meiklejohn presented the legal community with a rather complex set of ideas about freedom of expression in the late 1940s.[5] Meiklejohn looked at the First Amendment in a pragmatic manner and argued that freedom of expression is worth little as an abstract concept; that its primary value is as a means to an end. That end is successful self-government. Freedom of speech and press are protected in the Constitution so that our system of democracy can function, and that is the only reason they are protected. Expression that relates to the self-governing process must be protected absolutely

Expression that relates to the self-governing process must be protected absolutely by the First Amendment.

---

4. See *United States* v. *Carolene Products,* 304 U.S. 144 (1938) and *Palko* v. *Connecticut,* 302 U.S. 319 (1937). See also Justice Holmes' opinions in both *Lochner* v. *New York,* 198 U.S. 45 (1905) and *Abrams* v. *United States,* 250 U.S. 616 (1919).

5. Meiklejohn, *Free Speech.*

by the First Amendment. There can be no government interference with such expression. Expression that does not relate to the self-governing process is not protected absolutely by the First Amendment. The value or worth of such speech must be balanced by the courts against other rights and values.

Critics of this theory argue in a telling fashion that it is not always clear whether expression pertains to self-government (public speech) or to other interests (private speech). While not providing the specific definition sought by critics, Meiklejohn argued that a broad range of speech is essential to successful self-government. He included speech-related education (history, political science, geography, etc.), science, literature, and many other topics. This theory has been embraced by some members of the Supreme Court of the United States, most notably former justice William Brennan. American libel law was radically changed when Brennan led the Supreme Court to give First Amendment protection to persons who have defamed government officials or others who attempt to lead public policy, a purely Meiklejohnian approach to the problem.

Access theory: In the mid-1960s some legal scholars suggested that the intent of the First Amendment to permit all citizens the right to speak out on important government issues and other matters had been thwarted by the growing concentration of ownership in the nation's mass media. With fewer and fewer individuals and businesses controlling the print and broadcast media, the average person had fewer and fewer opportunities to have his or her voice heard. Surely the First Amendment means more than simply the right of wealthy and powerful media moguls to express their views in the public press while the rest of the nation's citizens are limited to passing out handbills or publishing small newsletters. It is this ideological foundation that supports the access theory, the notion that every individual should have the right to express his or her ideas in a daily or weekly newspaper or on a radio or television broadcast. The First Amendment must be made meaningful for all citizens; so the owners of the public press must open up newspapers and broadcasting stations and allow persons with different ideas a chance to be heard. If the press will not do this voluntarily, then government must force the mass media to provide this access.

The Supreme Court unanimously rejected this notion in 1974 in *Miami Herald* v. *Tornillo*.[6] Chief Justice Warren Burger, writing for the court, said that the choice of material to go into a newspaper and the decisions made as to limitations on the size of the paper and to content and treatment of public issues and public officials are decisions that must be made by the editors. The First Amendment does not give the government the right to force a newspaper to publish the views or ideas of a citizen. The Tornillo case sounded the legal death knell for this access theory for print media. (See *South Wind Motel* v. *Lashutka*[7] for an example of how courts have rejected the access theory since the *Tornillo* ruling.)

However, the access theory was a potent justification for the regulation of broadcasting. The Federal Communications Commission has in the past justified its regulation of the content of broadcasting on the theory that the airwaves belong to the people and that all persons really have a right to see and hear programs that reflect a diverse range of ideas. As Justice Byron

6. 418 U.S. 241 (1974).
7. 9 M.L.R. 1661 (1983).

White said in the famous case of *Red Lion Broadcasting* v. *FCC*,[8] "It is the right of the public to receive suitable access to social, political, esthetic, moral, and other ideas and experiences, which is crucial here." Using this argument as a foundation, the government for nearly 40 years justified the application of the **Fairness Doctrine** and other rules that forced broadcasters to carry certain kinds of programming. As we will note in Chapter 16, this philosophy of broadcast regulation has been largely rejected by those who regulate broadcasting for the government.

The five theories or strategies just outlined guide jurists across the nation as they attempt to fathom the meaning of these seemingly simple 13 words: "Congress shall make no law abridging freedom of speech or of the press." In the remainder of this book, we will attempt to tell you what the courts—using these theories—say the First Amendment means.

SUMMARY

The nation's first constitution, the Articles of Confederation, did not contain a guarantee of freedom of speech and press, but nearly all state constitutions provided for a guarantee of such rights. Citizens insisted that a written declaration of rights be included in the Constitution of 1787, and a guarantee of freedom of expression was a part of the Bill of Rights that was added to the national charter in 1791.

There is a debate within the legal-historical community over the meaning of the First Amendment when it was drafted and approved in the late 18th century. Some persons argue that it was intended to block both prior censorship and prosecution for seditious libel. Others argue that it was intended to prohibit only prior censorship. We will probably never know what the guarantee of freedom of expression meant to the persons who drafted it, but it is a good bet that citizens had a wide variety of interpretations of the First Amendment when they voted to approve it.

The meaning of the First Amendment today is largely determined through interpretation by the Supreme Court of the United States. Jurists use legal theories to guide them in determining the meaning of the Constitutional guarantee that "Congress shall make no law abridging freedom of speech or of the press." Five such theories are (1) absolutist theory, (2) ad hoc balancing theory, (3) preferred position balancing theory, (4) Meiklejohnian theory, and (5) access theory. Theories 2, 3, and 4 have the most supporters on the Supreme Court, and all the theories have assisted members of the high court to shape the meaning of the First Amendment.

THE MEANING OF FREEDOM

The struggle during the past 210 years to define the meaning of freedom of expression has involved a variety of issues. But three topics, more than any others, were at the heart of this struggle: the power of the state to limit criticism or other verbal or published attacks on the government; the power of the state to use taxation to censor the press; and the power of the government to forbid the publication of ideas or information it believes to be harmful. Each of these classic battles will be considered in the remainder of this chapter.

8. 395 U.S. 367 (1969).

SEDITIOUS LIBEL AND THE RIGHT TO CRITICIZE THE GOVERNMENT

The essence of a democracy is the participation by citizens in the process of government. At its most basic level, this participation involves selecting leaders for the nation, the state, and the various local governments through the electoral process. Popular participation also includes examination of government and public officials to determine their fitness for serving the people. Discussion, criticism, and suggestion all play a part in the orderly transition of governments and elected leaders. The right to speak and print, then, is inherent in a nation governed by popularly elected rulers.

Whether or not the rights of free expression as defined in 1790 included a broad right to criticize the government, this kind of political speech has emerged as a central element of our modern understanding of the First Amendment.

The right to discuss the government, the right to criticize the government, the right to oppose the government, the right to advocate the change of the government—all of these dimensions of free speech and free press are at the center of our political philosophy today. This is certainly not the case everywhere in the world, even in so-called free countries. In late 1995 the New York Times Co. and the Washington Post Co., co-publishers of the Paris-based International Herald Tribune, were forced to pay nearly $700,000 in damages for publishing comments supposedly critical of the government of Singapore. The Asian printing plant for the Herald Tribune is located in this small independent republic located on the Malay Peninsula. Failure to pay the damages would have forced the relocation of this printing plant and eliminated the opportunity for the newspaper to continue to do business in Singapore.

Even in the United States it has not always been possible to criticize the government or advocate political change without suffering reprisals from the government. Many Americans remain troubled even today when asked to support a broad definition of freedom of expression in light of the growing militancy by right-wing hate groups and radical Islamic terrorists. Can the use of force or violence be advocated as a means of changing the government? Can a citizen use the essence of democracy, free expression, to advocate the violent abolition of democracy and the establishment of a repressive state in which the rights of free speech and free press would be denied? Americans familiar with the history of the past 200 years know that these are more than academic questions. Some of the fiercest First Amendment battles have been fought over exactly these issues.

CRITICAL DATES IN THE HISTORY OF SEDITION LAW IN THE UNITED STATES

1735	Acquittal of John Peter Zenger
1791	Adoption of First Amendment
1798	Alien and Sedition Acts of 1798
1917	Espionage Act
1918	Sedition Act
1919	Clear and present danger test enunciated

1927	Brandeis sedition test in *Whitney* v. *California*
1940	Smith Act adopted
1951	Smith Act ruled constitutional
1957	Scope of Smith Act greatly narrowed
1969	Sedition test in *Brandenburg* v. *Ohio* substantially curbs sedition prosecutions

ALIEN AND SEDITION ACTS

The United States wasn't even 10 years old when the nation's resolve in protecting freedom of expression was first tested. Intense rivalry between President John Adams' Federalist party and Thomas Jefferson's Republican* or Jeffersonian party, coupled with the fear of some that the growing violence in the French Revolution might spread to this country, led to the adoption by the Federalist-dominated Congress of a series of highly repressive measures known as the **Alien and Sedition Acts of 1798.**[9] Three laws dealt with aliens, extending the period of residence prior to naturalization and giving the president extraordinary powers to detain and deport these noncitizen residents of the United States. A sedition law forbade false, scandalous, and malicious publications against the U.S. government, the Congress, and the president. The new law also punished persons who sought to stir up sedition or urged resistance to federal laws. Punishment was a fine of as much as $2,000 and a term in jail of up to two years. This latter statute was aimed squarely at the Jeffersonian political newspapers, many of which were relentless in their attacks on President Adams and his government.

There were 15 prosecutions under this law. This doesn't sound like many, but among those prosecuted were editors of eight Jeffersonian newspapers, including some of the leading papers in the nation. Imagine the federal government bringing sedition charges today against the editors of The New York Times, Washington Post, Miami Herald, and Chicago Tribune. Also prosecuted was a Republican member of Congress, Matthew Lyon. The so-called seditious libel that was the basis for the criminal charges was usually petty at best and hardly threatened our admittedly youthful government. But Federalist judges heard most of the cases and convictions were common.

Far from inhibiting dissent, the laws succeeded only in generating dissension among many of President Adams' supporters. Many argue that Adams lost his bid for re-election in 1800 largely because of public dissatisfaction with his attempt to muzzle his critics. The constitutionality of the laws was never tested before the full Supreme Court, but three members of the court heard Sedition Act cases while they were on the circuit. The constitutionality of the provisions was sustained by these justices. The Sedition Act expired in 1801 and President

---

9. Smith, *Freedom's Fetters.*

*This Republican political party was not the forerunner of the contemporary Republican party, which was formed in 1854.

Thomas Jefferson pardoned all persons convicted under it, while Congress eventually repaid most of the fines. This was the nation's first peacetime sedition law and it left such a bad taste that another peacetime sedition law was not passed until 1940.

Most historians of freedom of expression in the United States focus on two eras in the 19th century during which censorship was not uncommon: the abolitionist period and the Civil War. A wide range of government actions, especially in the South, were aimed at shutting down the abolitionist press in the years between 1830 and 1860. And both the United States government and the Confederate States government censored the press during the Civil War. But in a new book, "Free Speech in Its Forgotten Years," author David M. Rabban argues that there were also extensive censorship efforts in the latter half of the 19th century against radical labor unionists, anarchists, birth control advocates, and other so-called freethinkers. And there was little meaningful public debate about such activities. "In the decades before World War I," Rabban wrote, "Americans generally needed to experience repression of views they shared before formulating a theory of free speech that extended to ideas they opposed."[10]

The issue of political dissent did not enter the national debate again until the end of the 1800s, when hundreds of thousands of Americans began to understand that democracy and capitalism were not going to bring them the prosperity promised as an American birthright. The advancing rush of the new industrial society left many Americans behind and unhappy. Tens of thousands sought solace and change in political movements such as socialism and anarchism, movements that were considered by most in the mainstream to be foreign to the United States. Labor unrest in the late 19th century often turned violent; radical protests turned bloody. President William McKinley was assassinated in 1901, shot by a man most historians describe as an anarchist. Revolution, clearly unlikely, nevertheless arose as a specter in the minds of millions of Americans. Hundreds of laws were passed by states and cities across the nation to try to limit this kind of political dissent. War broke out in Europe in 1914; the United States joined the conflict three years later. This pushed the nation over the edge and anything that remained of our national tolerance toward political dissent and criticism of the government and economic system vanished. At both the state and the federal level, government struck out at those who sought to criticize or suggest radical change.

SEDITION IN WORLD WAR I

World War I is probably the most unpopular war this nation has fought, rivaling the Vietnam conflict in terms of public protest. The war was a replay of the imperial wars of the 17th and 18th centuries in Europe, except that it was fought with deadly new weapons. Industrialists and farmers saw the opportunity for vast economic gains in supplying war goods, and super-patriots were thrilled that the United States was actually going to have the opportunity to fight in a real war on the Continent. But to millions of immigrants in this nation, the war was being fought in their homelands. Their families were dying; their relatives were now our enemies. The economically dispossessed rightly feared as well that the outbreak of war signaled the beginning of a period of internal political repression for those with little power.

---

10. Rabban, "Free Speech."

Suppression of freedom of expression reached a higher level during World War I than at any other time in our history.[11] Government prosecutions during the Vietnam War, for example, were minor compared with government action between 1918 and 1920. Vigilante groups were active as well, persecuting when the government failed to prosecute.

Two federal laws were passed to deal with persons who opposed the war and U.S. participation in it. In 1917 the **Espionage Act** was approved by the Congress and signed by President Woodrow Wilson. The measure dealt primarily with espionage problems, but some parts were aimed expressly at dissent and opposition to the war. The law provided that it was a crime to willfully convey a false report with the intent to interfere with the war effort. It was a crime to cause or attempt to cause insubordination, disloyalty, mutiny, or refusal of duty in the armed forces. It also was a crime to willfully obstruct the recruiting or enlistment service of the United States. Punishment was a fine of not more than $10,000 or a jail term of not more than 20 years. The law also provided that material violating the law could not be mailed.

In 1918 the **Sedition Act,** an amendment to the Espionage Act, was passed, making it a crime to attempt to obstruct the recruiting service. It was criminal to utter or print or write or publish disloyal or profane language that was intended to cause contempt of, or scorn for, the federal government, the Constitution, the flag, or the uniform of the armed forces. Penalties for violation of the law were imprisonment for as long as 20 years or a fine of $10,000 or both. Approximately 2,000 people were prosecuted under these espionage and sedition laws, and nearly 900 were convicted. Persons who found themselves in the government's dragnet were usually aliens, radicals, publishers of foreign-language publications, and other persons who opposed the war.

In addition the U.S. Post Office Department censored thousands of newspapers, books, and pamphlets. Some publications lost their right to the government-subsidized second-class mailing rates and were forced to use the costly first-class rates or find other means of distribution. Entire issues of magazines were held up and never delivered, on the grounds that they violated the law (or what the postmaster general believed to be the law). Finally, the states were not content with allowing the federal government to deal with dissenters, and most adopted sedition statutes, laws against **criminal syndicalism,** laws that prohibited the display of a red flag or a black flag, and so forth.

Political repression in the United States did not end with the termination of fighting in Europe. The government was still suspicious of the millions of European immigrants in the nation and frightened by the organized political efforts of socialist and communist groups. As the Depression hit the nation, first in the farm belt in the '20s, and then in the rest of the nation by the next decade, labor unrest mushroomed. Hundreds of so-called agitators were arrested and charged under state and federal laws. Demonstrations were broken up; aliens were detained and threatened with deportation.

But what about the First Amendment? What happened to the rights of freedom of expression? The constitutional guarantees of freedom of speech and freedom of the press were of limited value during this era. The important legal meaning of freedom of expression had developed little in the preceding 125 years. There had been few cases and almost no

Suppression of freedom of expression reached a higher level during World War I than at any other time in our history.

---

11. See Peterson and Fite, *Opponents of War.*

important rulings before 1920. You will note as we proceed through this book that the words of the First Amendment—"Congress shall make no law"—are not nearly as important as the meaning attached to those words. And that meaning was only then beginning to develop through court rulings that resulted from the thousands of prosecutions for sedition and other such crimes between 1917 and the mid-1930s.

THE SMITH ACT

Congress adopted the nation's second peacetime sedition law in 1940 when it ratified the **Smith Act,** a measure making it a crime to advocate the violent overthrow of the government, to conspire to advocate the violent overthrow of the government, to organize a group that advocated the violent overthrow of the government, or to be a member of a group that advocated the violent overthrow of the government.[12] The law was aimed directly at the Communist party of the United States. While a small group of Trotskyites (members of the Socialist Workers party) were prosecuted and convicted under the Smith Act in 1943, no Communist was indicted under the law until 1948 when the nation's top Communist party leaders were charged with advocating the violent overthrow of the government. All were convicted after a nine-month trial and their appeals were denied. In a 7–2 ruling in 1951, the Supreme Court of the United States rejected the defendants' arguments that the Smith Act violated the First Amendment.[13]

Government prosecutions persisted during the early '50s. But then, in a surprising reversal of its earlier position, the Supreme Court in 1957 overturned the convictions of West Coast Communist party leaders.[14] Justice John Marshall Harlan wrote for the 5–2 majority that government evidence showed the defendants had advocated the violent overthrow of the government but only as an abstract doctrine, and this was not sufficient to sustain a conviction. Instead there must be evidence that proves the defendants advocated actual *action* aimed at the forcible overthrow of the government. This enhanced burden of proof levied against the government prosecutors made it extremely difficult to use the Smith Act against the Communists, and prosecutions therefore dwindled. The prosecutions dwindled for other reasons as well, however. The times had changed. The cold war was not as intense. Americans looked at the Soviet Union and the Communists with a bit less fear. The Communist party of the United States had failed to generate any public support. Its membership had fallen precipitously. In fact, political scientist John Roche has remarked with only a slight wink that it was the dues paid to the party by FBI undercover agents that kept the organization afloat in the mid-to-late '50s.

With the practical demise of the Smith Act, sedition has not been a serious threat against dissent for more than 40 years. No sedition cases were filed against Vietnam War protesters, and the last time the Supreme Court heard an appeal in a sedition case was in 1969 when it overturned the conviction of a Ku Klux Klan leader (*Brandenburg* v. *Ohio*[15]). The federal government has filed sedition charges several times in recent years against alleged white supremacists, neo-Nazis, and others on the fringe of the right wing. While juries have been willing to

12. Pember, "The Smith Act," 1.
13. *Dennis* v. *U.S.,* 341 U.S. 494 (1951).
14. *Yates* v. *U.S.,* 354 U.S. 298 (1957).
15. 395 U.S. 444 (1969).

convict such individuals of bombing, bank robbery, and even racketeering, the defendants have been acquitted of sedition. The federal government had greater success in the 1990s using a Civil War–era sedition statute to prosecute 10 Muslim militants who bombed the World Trade Center in New York City in 1993. Sheikh Omar Abdel Rahman and nine of his followers were found guilty of violating a 140-year-old law that makes it a crime to plan to wage war against the government. Although the government could not prove that Abdel Rahman actually participated in the bombing, federal prosecutors argued that his exhortations to his followers amounted to directing a violent conspiracy. The sheikh's attorneys argued that his pronouncements were protected by the First Amendment. In August of 1999 the Second U.S. Circuit Court of Appeals disagreed, noting that the Bill of Rights does not protect an individual who uses a public speech to commit crimes. Abdel Rahman's speeches were not simply the expression of ideas; "in some instances they constituted the crime of conspiracy to wage war against the United States," the court ruled. "Words of this nature," the three-judge panel wrote, "ones that instruct, solicit, or persuade others to commit crimes of violence—violate the law and may be properly prosecuted regardless of whether they are uttered in private, or in a public place."[16]

This brief narrative of the past 200 years does not begin to tell the story of the struggle for political dissent in this nation. For further details students are urged to check out some of the books listed in the bibliography at the end of the chapter. Missing from the narrative is the struggle undertaken by the courts—especially the Supreme Court—to attempt to reconcile prosecutions for sedition with the nation's constitutional guarantee of freedom of expression. Let's look at those cases more closely.

DEFINING THE LIMITS OF FREEDOM OF EXPRESSION

Remarkable as it may seem, the first time the Supreme Court of the United States seriously considered whether a prosecution for sedition violated the First Amendment was in 1919, 130 years after the founding of the Republic. The Philadelphia Socialist party authorized Charles Schenck, the general secretary of the organization, to publish 15,000 leaflets protesting against the U.S. involvement in World War I. The pamphlet described the war as a cold-blooded and ruthless adventure propagated in the interest of the chosen few of Wall Street and urged young men to resist the draft. Schenck and other party members were arrested, tried, and convicted of violating the Espionage Act (see page 50). The case was appealed all the way to the Supreme Court, with the Socialists asserting that they had been denied their First Amendment rights of freedom of speech and press. Justice Oliver Wendell Holmes penned the opinion for the court and rejected the First Amendment argument. In ordinary times, he said, such pamphlets might have been harmless and protected by the First Amendment. "But the character of every act depends upon the circumstances in which it is done. . . . The question in every case is whether the words used, are used in such circumstances and are of such a nature as to create a clear and present danger that they will bring about the substantive evils that Congress has a right to prevent. It is a question of proximity and degree."[17]

"The question in every case is whether the words used . . . create a clear and present danger that they will bring about the substantive evils that Congress has a right to prevent."

16. Weiser, "Appellate Court Backs Convictions."
17. *Schenck* v. *U.S., 249 U.S. 47 (1919).*

How do we reconcile prosecutions for sedition with freedom of expression? According to the Holmes test, Congress has the right to outlaw certain kinds of conduct that might be harmful to the nation. In some instances words, through speeches or pamphlets, can push people toward violating the laws passed by Congress. In such cases publishers or speakers can be punished without infringing on their First Amendment freedoms. How close must the connection be between the advocacy of the speaker or publisher and the forbidden conduct? Holmes said that the words must create a "clear" (unmistakable? certain?) and "present" (immediate? close?) danger.

Holmes' test means less in the abstract than it does when connected to the facts of the *Schenck* case. In the abstract, an endless debate might be conducted over whether a speech or book presented the requisite clear and present danger. But in rejecting Schenck's appeal, the high court ruled that these 15,000 seemingly innocuous pamphlets posed a real threat to the legitimate right of Congress to successfully conduct the war. To many American liberals this notion seemed farfetched, and Holmes was publicly criticized for the ruling. Recently, scholars like Jeremy Cohen[18] and G. Edward White[19] have taken Justice Holmes to task for rendering a naive and uninformed opinion. But the magic words "clear and present danger" stuck like glue on American sedition law, and for more than 30 years American jurists had to work their way around this standard. Holmes changed his mind about his test in less than six months and broke with the majority of the high court to outline a somewhat more liberal definition of freedom of expression in a ruling on the Sedition Act in the fall of 1919.[20] But the majority of the court continued to use the Holmes test to reject First Amendment appeals.

Justice Louis Brandeis attempted to fashion a more useful application of the clear and present danger test in 1927, but his definition of "clear and present danger" was confined to a concurring opinion in the case of *Whitney* v. *California.*[21] The state of California prosecuted Anita Whitney, a 64-year-old philanthropist who was the niece of Justice Stephen J. Field, a member of the Supreme Court from 1863 to 1897. She was charged with violating the state's Criminal Syndicalism Act after she attended a meeting of the Communist Labor party. She was not an active member in the party and during the convention had worked against proposals made by others that the party dedicate itself to gaining power through revolution and general strikes in which workers would seize power by violent means. But the state contended that the Communist Labor party was formed to teach criminal syndicalism, and as a member to the party she participated in the crime. After her conviction she appealed to the Supreme Court.

Justice Edward Sanford wrote the court's opinion and ruled that California had not violated Miss Whitney's First Amendment rights. The jurist said it was inappropriate to even apply the clear and present danger test. He noted that in *Schenck* and other previous cases, the statutes under which prosecution occurred forbade specific actions, such as interference with the draft. The clear and present danger test was then used to judge whether the words used by the defendant presented a clear and present danger that the forbidden action might occur. In

18. Cohen, *Congress Shall Make No Law.*
19. White, *Justice Oliver Wendell Holmes.*
20. *Abrams* v. *U.S.,* 250 U.S. 616 (1919).
21. 274 U.S. 357 (1927).

this case, Sanford noted, the state of California law forbade specific words—the advocacy of violence to bring about political change. The Holmes test was therefore inapplicable. In addition, the California law was neither unreasonable nor unwarranted.

Justice Brandeis concurred with the majority, but only, he said, because the constitutional issue of freedom of expression had not been raised sufficiently at the trial to make it an issue in the appeal. (If a legal issue is not raised during a trial it is difficult for an appellate court to later consider the matter.) In his concurring opinion, Brandeis disagreed sharply with the majority regarding the limits of free expression. In doing so he added flesh and bones to Holmes' clear and present danger test. Looking to the *Schenck* decision, the justice noted that the court had agreed that there must be a clear and imminent danger of a substantive evil that the state has the right to prevent before an interference with speech can be allowed. Then he went on to describe what he believed to be the requisite danger:

> To justify suppression of free speech there must be reasonable ground to fear that serious evil will result if free speech is practiced. There must be reasonable ground to believe that the danger apprehended is imminent. There must be reasonable ground to believe that the evil to be prevented is a serious one. Every denunciation of existing law tends in some measure to increase the probability that there will be violation of it. Condonation of a breach enhances the probability. Expressions of approval add to the probability. Propagation of the criminal state of mind by teaching syndicalism increases it. Advocacy of law-breaking heightens it further. But even advocacy of violation, however reprehensible morally, is not a justification for denying free speech where the advocacy falls short of incitement, and there is nothing to indicate that the advocacy would be immediately acted on. The wide difference between advocacy and incitement, between preparation and attempt, between assembling and conspiracy, must be borne in mind. In order to support a finding of clear and present danger it must be shown either that immediate serious violence was to be expected or was advocated, or that the past conduct furnished reason to believe that such advocacy was then contemplated.[22]

Brandeis concluded that if there is time to expose through discussion the falsehoods and fallacies, to avert the evil by the process of education, the remedy to be applied is more speech, not enforced silence.

This truly is a clear and present danger test that even the most zealous civil libertarian can live with. And this is the test that many mistakenly confuse with Holmes' original pronouncement. Unfortunately, this version of the clear and present danger test has never found its way into a majority opinion in a sedition case.

The next major ruling in which the high court attempted to reconcile sedition law and the First Amendment came in 1951 in the case of *Dennis* v. *U.S.*[23] (see page 51). Eleven Communist party members had been convicted of advocating the violent overthrow of the government,

22. *Whitney v. California,* 274 U.S. 357 (1927).
23. 341 U.S. 494 (1951).

a violation of the Smith Act. The defendants raised the clear and present danger test as a barrier to their convictions; the actions of a small band of Communists surely did not constitute a clear and present danger to the nation, they argued. Chief Justice Vinson, who wrote the opinion for the court, used neither the clear and present danger test enunciated by Holmes nor the more expansive version written by Brandeis. He instead created a third test, a clear and probable danger test. Surely the Congress has a right to prevent the overthrow of the government, Vinson said. How likely is it that the words spoken or written by the defendants would lead even to an attempted overthrow? "In each case [courts] must ask whether the gravity of the 'evil' discounted by its improbability, justifies such invasion of free speech as is necessary to avoid the danger," Vinson wrote, quoting a lower-court opinion written by Judge Learned Hand.

The test went only slightly beyond the original Holmes test, and the court ruled that the defendants' First Amendment rights had not been violated. If the Brandeis test from *Whitney* had been applied, however, it is likely the convictions would have gone out the window.

Six years later in *Yates* v. *U.S.* (see page 51), in its next major ruling on the Smith Act, the high court ignored both clear and present danger and clear and probable danger. Justice John Marshall Harlan wrote for the court that it was necessary to distinguish between the advocacy of the forcible overthrow of the government as an abstract doctrine and the advocacy of action toward the forcible overthrow of the government. "The essential distinction," Harlan noted, "is that those to whom the advocacy is addressed must be urged to do something now or in the future, rather than merely believe in something."[24] Surely this was a better test, but questions still remained. How specific does this advocacy of action have to be? Contrast two exhortations by a revolutionary speaker. "We must take action, we have waited long enough, we must move to replace the government now." Or, "We must demonstrate our resolve by blowing up the federal court building." Obviously, the last statement is the advocacy of action. But what about the first statement?

It has been more than 30 years since the Supreme Court heard the case of *Brandenburg* v. *Ohio* (see page 51) and made its last and probably best attempt to resolve the apparent contradiction between sedition law and freedom of expression. A leader of the Ku Klux Klan was prosecuted and convicted of violating an Ohio sedition law for stating: "We're not a revengent [revengeful] organization, but if our President, our Congress, our Supreme Court, continues to suppress the white Caucasian race, it's possible there might have to be some revengeance [revenge] taken." In reversing the conviction, the high court said the law must distinguish between the advocacy of ideas and the incitement to unlawful conduct. "The constitutional guarantees of free speech and free press do not permit a state to forbid or proscribe advocacy of the use of force or of law violation except where such advocacy is directed to inciting or producing imminent lawless action and is likely to incite or produce such actions."[25] This test, which stands as the rule today, comes very close to the Brandeis test from the *Whitney* case. And it provides a fairly safe haven for those who seek to urge others to take action to change the government or to redistribute power in society.

24. 354 U.S. 298 (1957).
25. 395 U.S. 444 (1969).

"The constitutional guarantees of free speech and free press do not permit a state to forbid or proscribe advocacy of the use of force or of law violation except where such advocacy is directed to inciting or producing imminent lawless action and is likely to incite or produce such actions."

The Book Made Me Do It

In the late 1870s Boston police arrested what some believe to be America's first serial killer, a teenage boy who began torturing children when he was 11 and began killing kids three years later. After the arrest of Jesse Pomeroy many persons blamed his killings on the dime novels that were published at the time, graphically violent stories with titles like *Desperate Dan* and *The Pirates of Pecos,* even though the young killer testified that he never read such books.[26] This may have been the first time, but surely not the last, that books or movies or magazines or recordings were said to be responsible for someone's death or injury.

Courts are frequently asked to rule in wrongful death, negligence, and product liability lawsuits whether a mass medium like a film or recording played some part in inciting the actual perpetrator of the crime to commit illegal acts. To determine the liability in such cases the courts use the *Brandenburg* test for seditious libel outlined earlier in this chapter. For example, in 1997 a U.S. district court in Texas refused to hold Time Warner responsible for the death of a Texas state trooper who was murdered after he stopped a driver for a routine traffic violation. The automobile that Ronald Howard was driving was stolen. At the time that Howard shot trooper Bill Davidson he was listening to an audiotape recording of rapper Tupac Shakur's "2Pocalypse Now." The plaintiffs argued that the recording incited Howard to kill Davidson. The court disagreed, noting that the shooting was not a random act, that Howard was a gang member attempting to elude apprehension. The court said that the constitutional protection afforded a recording like Shakur's is not based on the naive belief that speech can do no harm, but on the confidence that society reaps important benefits from the free flow of ideas, benefits that outweigh the cost that society endures by receiving dangerous ideas. "At best, this recording reveals that weak-willed individuals may be influenced by Shakur's work." "Swaying the weak-willed does not remove constitutional protection for speech," the court added.[27] And in 1999 a California appellate court refused to hold a motion picture theater responsible for the shooting death of a young man by a 13-year-old who had just viewed the film "Dead Presidents" in the theater. The parents of the dead boy argued that the owners of the theater were negligent when they permitted the 13-year-old to view the R-rated film, a film only those 18 and older are normally allowed to see without parental permission. In upholding the trial court's decision to dismiss the complaint, the appellate court said the rating system was merely to advise parents about the content of films. "Basic to the program was and is the responsibility of the parents to make the decision," the court added.[28] Cases like those just outlined are typical of the way the courts have handled claims that the mass media have incited a criminal act by a reader or a viewer. But an unusual case that was ultimately resolved in 1999 has raised a caution flag for the mass media.

In 1996 the families of Mildred and Trevor Horn and Janice Saunders filed a wrongful death suit against Paladin Enterprises and its president, Peter Lund. The company published a book titled "Hit Man: A Technical Manual for Independent Contractors." Lawrence Horn

26. Schechter, "A Movie."
27. *Davidson* v. *Time Warner Inc.,* 25 M.L.R. 1705 (1997).
28. *Delgado* v. *American Multi-Cinema Inc.*, 85 Cal Rptr 2d 838 (1999).

hired James Perry to kill his ex-wife, their 8-year-old quadriplegic son, and the son's nurse to gain access to the proceeds of a medical malpractice settlement. Both Perry and Horn were arrested and convicted of the murders; Perry was sentenced to death, Horn to life in prison. The plaintiffs contended that Perry used the Paladin publication as an instruction manual for the killings. A U.S. district court in Maryland ruled in August of 1996 that the book was protected by the First Amendment. "However loathsome one characterizes the publication, 'Hit Man' simply does not fall within the parameters of any recognized exceptions to the First Amendment principles of freedom of speech." The book failed to cross the line between permissible advocacy and impermissible incitation to crime or violence, Judge Williams wrote.[29] He noted that although 13,000 copies of the book had been sold, only one person over the past 10 years had actually used the book to commit a crime.

Fifteen months later the 4th U.S. Circuit Court of Appeals reversed the lower-court ruling. The defendant had agreed to a stipulation in the case that stated Paladin provided its assistance to Perry with both the knowledge and the intent that the book would immediately be used by criminals and would-be criminals in the solicitation, planning, and commission of murder and murder for hire. The court said the book was not an example of abstract advocacy but a form of aiding and abetting a crime. The book "methodically and comprehensively prepares and steels its audience to specific criminal conduct through exhaustively detailed instructions on planning, commission, and concealment of criminal conduct," the panel ruled. There is no First Amendment protection for such a publication. The court noted that this case was unique and should not be read as expanding the potential liability of publishers and broadcasters when third parties copy or mimic a crime or other act contained in a news report or a film or a television program.[30] An appeal to the U.S. Supreme Court was denied and the case was returned to the U.S. district court for trial. In May of 1999 the Washington Post reported that Paladin Press had settled the case out of court, a decision that was apparently made by its insurance carrier. Details of the settlement were not released, but according to the Post, Paladin agreed to pay the families of the victims several million dollars. The publisher also agreed to stop distributing "Hit Man." The decision to settle, the newspaper reported, was influenced by contemporary events. Lawyers thought it would be difficult to impanel a jury sympathetic to the publisher in the wake of several school shooting incidents and a Michigan jury's award of $25 million to the family of a gay man who was shot and killed by a fellow guest on the "Jenny Jones" television program.[31]

In spite of this case, the stringent requirements of the *Brandenburg* test make it difficult, bordering on impossible, for a plaintiff to win a lawsuit that alleges a play or book or song or movie was responsible for causing someone's illegal acts. The case law is highly one-sided in this regard.[32]

The attempts by the judiciary to accommodate both freedom of expression and the right of the nation to protect itself from violent revolution appear to many to be nothing more than

---

29. *Rice* v. *Paladin Enterprises Inc.,* 940 F. Supp. 836 (1996).
30. *Rice* v. *Paladin Enterprises Inc.,* 128 F. 3d 233 (1997).
31. "Hit Man Publisher Settles Suit."
32. See *Yakubowicz* v. *Paramount Pictures Corp.,* 404 Mass. 624 (1989) and *Herceg* v. *Hustler,* 814 F. 2d 1017 (1987).

semantic games, moving a noun here, an adjective there. A waste of time at best, some have argued. But these attempts demonstrate three important points. First, the adoption of the First Amendment raised more questions than it answered. The job of answering these questions has fallen to the judiciary; it must define the meaning of this abstract concept. Second, the range of permissible defiance of the government varies with the times, the political climate, the national mood. Finally, in guaranteeing freedom of expression to all, the American people have put themselves at risk, since our system of government contains a Constitution that fosters those who seek to change the status quo.

The Gitlow *Ruling*

Before leaving the discussion of sedition, one additional case must be noted, not for its impact on the law of sedition but for its impact on the civil liberties enjoyed by all Americans. In 1925 Benjamin Gitlow, a small-time, left-wing agitator, asked the U.S. Supreme Court to reverse his conviction for violating the New York criminal anarchy statute. Gitlow was a member of a radical left-wing splinter group within the Socialist party. The group adopted a "Left Wing Manifesto" that condemned the dominant "moderate socialism" and advocated a far more militant posture that called for mass political strikes for the destruction of the existing government. Gitlow arranged for the printing and distribution of 16,000 copies of the "Manifesto." While the description of the publication sounds somewhat threatening, legal scholar Zechariah Chafee, one of Gitlow's contemporaries, said that any agitator who read the pamphlet to a mob would "not stir them to violence, except possibly against himself. This manifesto would disperse them faster than the Riot Act."[33] Gitlow was nevertheless convicted by the state.

In his appeal to the high court, he argued that the statute violated his freedom of expression guaranteed by the U.S. Constitution. In making this plea, Gitlow was asking the court to overturn a 92-year-old precedent.

In 1833 the Supreme Court of the United States ruled that the Bill of Rights, the first 10 amendments to the U.S. Constitution, were applicable only in protecting citizens from actions of the federal government.[34] Chief Justice John Marshall ruled that the people of the United States established the U.S. Constitution for their government, not for the government of the individual states. The limitations of power placed on government by the Constitution applied only to the government of the United States. In fact, while considering the adoption of the Bill of Rights in 1789, the U.S. Senate rejected a resolution that would have applied to the states as well as the federal government the limits on government action contained in the 10 amendments. Applying this rule to the First Amendment meant that neither Congress nor the federal government could abridge freedom of the press, but that the government of New York or the government of Detroit could interfere with freedom of expression without violating the guarantees of the U.S. Constitution. The citizens of the individual states or cities could erect their own constitutional guarantees in state constitutions or city charters. Indeed, such provisions existed in many places.

33. Chafee, *Free Speech.*
34. *Barron* v. *Baltimore,* 7 Pet. 243 (1833).

As applied to the case of Benjamin Gitlow, then, it seemed unlikely that the First Amendment (which prohibited interference by the federal government with freedom of speech and press) could be erected as a barrier to protect the radical from prosecution by the state of New York. Yet this is exactly what the young Socialist argued.

Gitlow's attorneys, especially Walter Heilprin Pollak, did not attack Chief Justice Marshall's ruling in *Barron* v. *Baltimore* directly; instead they went around it. Pollak based his argument on the 14th Amendment to the Constitution, which was adopted in 1868, 35 years after the decision in *Barron* v. *Baltimore*. The attorney argued that there was general agreement that the First Amendment protected a citizen's right to liberty of expression. The 14th Amendment says, in part, "No state shall . . . deprive any person of life, liberty, or property, without due process of law." Pollak asserted that included among the liberties guaranteed by the 14th Amendment is liberty of the press as guaranteed by the First Amendment. Therefore, a state cannot deprive a citizen of the freedom of the press that is guaranteed by the First Amendment without violating the 14th Amendment. By jailing Benjamin Gitlow for exercising his right of freedom of speech granted by the First Amendment, New York state denied him the liberty assured him by the 14th Amendment. Simply, then, the First Amendment, as applied through the 14th Amendment, prohibits states and cities and counties from denying an individual freedom of speech and press.

The high court had heard this argument before, but apparently not as persuasively as Mr. Pollak presented it. In rather casual terms, Justice Edward Sanford made a startlingly new

Benjamin Gitlow, the leader of a dissident faction of the Socialist party, was prosecuted by New York state for publishing thousands of copies of a "Left Wing Manifesto." While the Supreme Court of the United States upheld his conviction, the high court ruling nevertheless declared that the First Amendment protected individuals from prosecutions by the states as well as the federal government. Bettman/CORBIS

constitutional pronouncement: "For present purposes we may and do assume that freedom of speech and of the press—which are protected by the First Amendment from abridgment by Congress—are among the fundamental personal rights and 'liberties' protected by the due process clause of the Fourteenth Amendment from impairment by the states."[35]

The importance of the ruling in *Gitlow* v. *New York* is that the high court acknowledged that the Bill of Rights places limitations on the actions of states and local governments as well as on the federal government. The *Gitlow* case states that freedom of speech is protected by the 14th Amendment. In later cases the court placed freedom of the press, freedom of religion, freedom from self-incrimination, and freedom from illegal search and seizure under the same protection. Today, virtually all the rights outlined in the Bill of Rights are protected via the 14th Amendment from interference by states and cities as well as by the federal government. The importance of the *Gitlow* case cannot be underestimated. It truly marked the beginning of attainment of a full measure of civil liberties for the citizens of the nation. It was the key that unlocked an important door.

In the end Gitlow lost his case anyway. He had won a major constitutional victory but was unable to persuade the high court that his political agitation was harmless. Justice Sanford ruled that New York state had not violated Gitlow's First Amendment rights when it prosecuted him for publishing his "Left Wing Manifesto," which the state contended advocated the violent overthrow of the government.

SUMMARY

Within eight years of the passage of the First Amendment, the nation adopted its first (and most wide-ranging) sedition laws, the Alien and Sedition Acts of 1798. Many leading political editors and politicians were prosecuted under the laws, which made it a crime to criticize both the president and the national government. While the Supreme Court never did hear arguments regarding the constitutionality of the laws, several justices of the Supreme Court presided at sedition act trials and refused to sustain a constitutional objection to the laws. The public hated the measures. John Adams was voted out of office in 1800 and was replaced by his political opponent and target of the sedition laws, Thomas Jefferson. The laws left such a bad taste that the federal government did not pass another sedition law until World War I, 117 years later.

Sedition prosecutions in the period from 1915 to 1925 were the most vicious in the nation's history as war protestors, socialists, anarchists, and other political dissidents became the target of government repression. It was during this era that the Supreme Court began to interpret the meaning of the First Amendment. In a series of rulings stemming from the World War I cases, the high court fashioned what is known as the clear and present danger test to measure state and federal laws and protests and other expressions against the First Amendment. The test was rigid and was never used to overturn a lower-court conviction, although in 1927 Justice Louis D. Brandeis did fashion a broad and liberal interpretation of the clear and present danger test in his dissent in the case of *Whitney* v. *California*. In 1925 the court ruled that the guarantees of freedom of speech apply to actions taken by all governments, that freedom of

35. *Gitlow* v. *New York*, 268 U.S. 652 (1925).

speech under the First Amendment protects individuals from censorship by all levels of government, not just from actions by the federal government. This pronouncement in *Gitlow* v. *New York* opened the door to a much broader protection of freedom of expression in the nation.

The nation's most recent sedition law was adopted in 1940. The Smith Act, as it is known, prohibits the advocacy of the violent overthrow of the government. Following a series of trials and two Supreme Court rulings in the 1950s, the law has become a relatively benign prohibition. The high court ruled in 1957 in *Yates* v. *U.S.* that to sustain a conviction under the Smith Act, the government must prove that the defendants advocate specific violent or forcible action toward the overthrow of the government. The government found it impossible to do this in the 1950s, and the Smith Act has not been invoked to punish an act of expression for more than 40 years. The Supreme Court made its last important attempt to reconcile the First Amendment and the law of sedition in 1969 when it ruled in *Brandenburg* v. *Ohio* that advocacy of unlawful conduct is protected by the Constitution unless it is directed toward inciting or producing imminent lawless action and is likely to incite or produce such action.

TAXATION AND THE PRESS

The First Amendment guarantees that the press shall be free from unfair and discriminatory taxes that have an impact on circulation or distribution. In this area the classic case concerns a U.S. senator from a southern state and the daily press of that state.[36]

During the late 1920s and early 1930s, the political leader of Louisiana was Huey P. Long. Long was a demagogue by most accounts and in 1934 held his state in virtual dictatorship. He controlled the legislature and the statehouse and had a deep impact on the judicial branch as well. Long started his career by attacking big business—Standard Oil of California, to be exact. He became a folk hero among the rural people of Louisiana and was elected governor in 1928. In 1931 he was elected to the U.S. Senate, and many people believe that he would have attempted to win the presidency had he not been assassinated in 1935.[37]

In 1934 the Long political machine, which the majority of the big-city residents had never favored, became annoyed at the frequent attacks by the state's daily newspapers against the senator and his political machine. The legislature enacted a special 2 percent tax on the gross advertising income of newspapers with a circulation of more than 20,000. Of the 163 newspapers in the state, only 13 had more than 20,000 subscribers, and of the 13, 12 were outspoken in their opposition to Long. The newspapers went to court and argued that the tax violated the First Amendment as well as other constitutional guarantees. The press won at the circuit court level on other grounds, but the state appealed. Then in 1936 the Supreme Court ruled in favor of the newspapers squarely on First Amendment grounds.

The state of Louisiana argued that the English common law, which it claimed the American courts had adopted after the Revolution, conferred on the government the right to tax

---

36. *Grosjean* v. *American Press Co.,* 297 U.S. 233 (1936).
37. Gerald, *The Press and the Constitution.*

61

newspapers and license them if need be. Justice George Sutherland, who wrote the opinion in this unanimous Supreme Court decision, said, however, that such taxes on newspapers were the direct cause of much civil unrest in England and were one of the chief objections Americans had had to British policy—objections that ultimately forced independence.

The justice wrote:

> It is impossible to concede that by the words "freedom of the press" the framers of the amendment intended to adopt merely the narrow view then reflected by the law of England that such freedom consisted in immunity from previous censorship. . . . It is equally impossible to believe that it was not intended to bring within the reach of these words such modes of restraint as were embodied in . . . taxation.[38]

Sutherland asserted that the tax not only restricted the amount of revenue the paper earned but also restrained circulation. Newspapers with fewer than 20,000 readers would be reluctant to seek new subscribers for fear of increasing circulation to the point where they would have to pay the tax as well. The justice added that any action by the government that prevents free and general discussion of public matters is a kind of censorship. Sutherland said that in this case even the form in which the tax was imposed—levied against a distinct group of newspapers—was suspicious. He then wrote:

> The tax here involved is bad not because it takes money from the pockets of the appellees [the newspapers]. If that were all, a wholly different question would be presented. It is bad because, in the light of its history and of its present setting, it is seen to be a deliberate and calculated device in the guise of a tax to limit the circulation of information to which the public is entitled in virtue of the constitutional guaranties. A free press stands as one of the great interpreters between the government and the people. To allow it to be fettered is to fetter ourselves.[39]

"A free press stands as one of the great interpreters between the government and the people. To allow it to be fettered is to fetter ourselves."

Therefore, in *Grosjean* v. *American Press Co.*, the Supreme Court struck down a discriminatory tax against the press. An interesting footnote to the case concerns the opinion. Justice Sutherland's opinion is one of the most eloquent ever penned in defense of free expression. The justice was not normally such an articulate spokesman. What happened in this case? Speculation is that Sutherland's opinion incorporates a concurring opinion by Justice Benjamin Cardozo, perhaps the most fluent writer ever to serve on the court, and the eloquence of the *Grosjean* opinion is really Cardozo's, not Sutherland's.

Despite the fact that Justice Sutherland specifically noted in his opinion that the ruling in *Grosjean* did not mean that newspapers are immune from ordinary taxes, some newspaper publishers apparently did not read the opinion that way, but saw it instead as a means of escaping other kinds of taxes. After *Grosjean,* for example, unsuccessful attempts were made to have a sales tax in Arizona declared inapplicable to newspapers because it was a restriction on freedom of the press.[40] Since 1953, when the U.S. Supreme Court refused to hear an appeal

---

38. *Grosjean* v. *American Press Co., 297* U.S. 233 (1936).
39. *Grosjean* v. *American Press Co., 297* U.S. 233 (1936).
40. *Arizona Publishing Co.* v. *O'Neil,* 22 F. Supp. 117; aff'd. 304 U.S. 543 (1938).

from a California decision affirming the constitutionality of a general business tax on newspapers, the matter has been fairly well settled. The California case involved the Corona Daily Independent, which challenged a business tax imposed by the city of Corona. A license tax of $32 had been levied for many years against all businesses. In 1953 the newspaper refused to pay the levy on the grounds that the tax violated its First Amendment rights to freedom of expression. The *Grosjean* case prohibited such taxation, lawyers for the publication argued. The trial court ruled in favor of the newspaper, but the California Appellate Court disagreed and reversed the ruling. Justice Griffin wrote that there is ample authority to the effect that newspapers are not made exempt from ordinary forms of taxation. Justice Griffin said that the newspaper had not shown that the amount of the tax was harsh or arbitrary, that the tax was oppressive or confiscatory, or that the tax in any way curtailed or abridged the newspaper's right to disseminate news and comment:

> We conclude that a nondiscriminatory tax, levied upon the doing of business, for the sole purpose of maintaining the municipal government, without whose municipal services and protection the press could neither exist nor function, must be sustained as being within the purview and necessary implications of the Constitution and its amendments.[41]

The U.S. Supreme Court refused to review the ruling in *City of Corona* v. *Corona Daily Independent,* and most people believed the refusal signaled concurrence with the opinion of the California court.

But in 1983 the U.S. Supreme Court did review an unusual tax placed on a handful of Minnesota newspapers.[42] Since 1971 Minnesota had imposed a use tax on the cost of the paper and ink products consumed in the production of a publication. The law was amended in 1974 to exempt from the tax the first $100,000 worth of paper and ink used. After the exemption was adopted, only about 15 newspapers in the state were forced to pay the tax. And the Minneapolis Star and Tribune Company ended up paying about two-thirds of all the revenues collected under the tax. The Star and Tribune Company challenged the tax, and in March 1983 the high court ruled that the levy against the newspapers was invalid.

Justice Sandra Day O'Connor described the tax as a "special tax that applies only to certain publications protected by the First Amendment." She added: "A power to tax differentially, as opposed to a power to tax generally, gives a government a powerful weapon against the taxpayer selected." Such a tax could be used to censor the press, a clear violation of the First Amendment. The tax is also deficient because it ends up hitting only a few of the newspapers in the state. "Whatever the motive of the legislature in this case," Justice O'Connor wrote for the court's majority, "we think that recognizing a power in the State not only to single out the press but also to tailor the tax so it singles out a few members of the press presents such a potential for abuse that no interest suggested by Minnesota can justify the scheme."[43]

41. *City of Corona* v. *Corona Daily Independent,* 252 P. 2d 56 (1953).
42. *Minneapolis Star* v. *Minnesota Commissioner of Revenue,* 460 U.S. 575 (1983).
43. *Minneapolis Star* v. *Minnesota Commissioner of Revenue,* 460 U.S. 575 (1983).

The Supreme Court voided another tax scheme in 1987 because, Justice Thurgood Marshall said, "the taxing scheme was based solely on the content of the publication."[44] Arkansas had a sales tax on tangible personal property. Several items were exempt from the tax, including newspapers and "religious, professional, trade and sports journals and/or publications printed and published in the state." The publisher of a general interest magazine sued to be exempt from the tax. The publisher argued that his magazine was published in the state and therefore should be exempt. The Arkansas Supreme Court ruled that the publisher had read the statute incorrectly. The law only exempted religious, professional, trade and sports publications that were printed in the state, not all magazines printed in the state. This tax was unconstitutional because it was discriminatory, because its applicability depended solely on the content of the publication, the high court said. This is a violation of the First Amendment. The high court heard arguments in the autumn of 1988 in a similar case, *Texas Monthly, Inc. v. Bullock,*[45] in which a Texas statute exempted religious periodicals from the general state sales tax. The publisher of the Texas Monthly argued that the law not only discriminated against certain publications based on their content, but also violated the separation of church and state clause in the First Amendment. In February of 1989, by a 6–3 vote, the Supreme Court declared the Texas tax invalid. Justice William Brennan, writing the court's opinion, said the tax violated the establishment clause of the First Amendment. In 1999 a U.S. district court in California struck down a tax on cable and satellite broadcasters. The state had levied a 5 percent tax on the gross receipts of pay-per-view telecasts of boxing, wrestling, kickboxing, and similar contests. Telecasts of movies or concerts or other sporting events were not taxed. The court ruled that the tax violated the First Amendment because it imposed a financial burden on speakers because of the content of their speech.[46]

The basic rule of First Amendment law regarding taxes on the press is this: Newspapers, broadcasting stations, and other mass media must pay the same taxes as any other business. Taxes that are levied only against the press and tend to inhibit circulation or impose other kinds of prior restraints (such as very high taxes that keep all but very wealthy people from publishing newspapers) are unconstitutional. Also, decisions by the state to tax or not tax cannot be based solely on the content of the publication. In some circumstances, however, states can distinguish between different mass media when levying taxes. This was a ruling by the Supreme Court in 1991 in a case from Arkansas. The state levied a 4 percent sales tax on cable television receipts; magazines and newspapers were exempt from paying this tax.

Justice Sandra Day O'Connor, writing for a 7–2 majority, restated the high court's doctrine that the First Amendment prevents government from singling out the press as a whole for special tax burdens. "The press plays a unique role as a check on government abuse and a tax limited to the press raises concerns about censorship of critical information and opinion," she wrote.[47] Nor may states discriminate among categories of mass media when taxing, if that discrimination is based on content or for purposes of censorship, she added. But "differential

---

44. *Arkansas Writers' Project* v. *Ragland,* 107 S. Ct. 1722 (1987).
45. 109 S. Ct. 890 (1989).
46. *United States Satellite Broadcasting Co.* v. *Lynch,* 41 F. Supp. 2d 1113 (1999).
47. *Leathers* v. *Medlock,* 111 S. Ct. 1438 (1991).

taxation of speakers, even members of the press, does not implicate the First Amendment unless the tax is directed at, or presents the danger of suppressing particular ideas," O'Connor wrote. Almost 20 other states have taxes on cable television but do not tax the print media, according to The New York Times. In 1995 the Pennsylvania Supreme Court upheld the constitutionality of a state sales tax on magazines but not on newspapers. The court ruled that the tax was based not on content but on format and frequency of publication, a reasonable basis for distinguishing between the two media.[48]

SUMMARY

Governments have traditionally used taxation as a means of controlling the press. Since the 1930s and the U.S. Supreme Court ruling in *Grosjean* v. *American Press Co.*, the First Amendment has posed a substantial barrier to such efforts by governments in the United States. Newspapers, broadcasting stations, and other mass media must surely pay the same taxes imposed on other businesses. But taxes that are levied only against the press and tend to inhibit circulation or impose other kinds of restraints are unconstitutional. Also, taxes levied against mass media that are based solely on the content of the particular medium are generally regarded as unconstitutional.

PRIOR RESTRAINT

The great compiler of the British law, William Blackstone, defined freedom of the press in the 1760s as freedom from "previous restraint," or prior restraint. Regardless of the difference of opinion on whether the First Amendment is intended to protect political criticism or to protect the press from unfair taxation, most students of the constitutional period agree that the guarantees of freedom of speech and press were intended to bar the government from exercising prior restraint. Despite the weight of such authority, the media in the United States in the 2000s still face instances of prepublication censorship.

Instances of prior censorship are difficult to categorize, as scores of laws and government actions hold the potential for a kind of prior restraint. In privacy law, for example, it is possible under some statutes to stop the publication of material that illegally appropriates a person's name or likeness. In extreme cases the press can be stopped from publishing information it has learned about a criminal case. The two instances just mentioned, as well as others, will be discussed fully in later, more appropriate sections of this book. The purpose of this section is to outline those kinds of prior restraint that seem to fall outside the boundaries of other chapters in the book.

The Supreme Court did not consider the issue of prior restraint until more than a decade after it had decided its first major sedition case. In 1931, in *Near* v. *Minnesota*,[49] the court struck an important blow for freedom of expression.

48. *Magazine Publishers of America* v. *Pennsylvania*, 654 A. 2d 519 (1995).
49. 283 U.S. 697 (1931).

NEAR v. *MINNESOTA*

City and county officials in Minneapolis, Minn., brought a legal action against Jay M. Near and Howard Guilford, publishers of the Saturday Press, a small weekly newspaper. Near and Guilford were reformers whose purpose was to clean up city and county government in Minneapolis. In their attacks on corruption in city government, they used language that was far from temperate and defamed some of the town's leading government officials. Near and Guilford charged that Jewish gangsters were in control of gambling, bootlegging, and racketeering in the city and that city government and its law enforcement agencies did not perform their duties energetically. They repeated these charges over and over in a highly inflammatory manner.[50]

Minnesota had a statute that empowered a court to declare any obscene, lewd, lascivious, malicious, scandalous, or defamatory publication a public nuisance. When such a publication was deemed a public nuisance, the court issued an injunction against future publication or distribution. Violation of the injunction resulted in punishment for contempt of court.

In 1927 County Attorney Floyd Olson initiated an action against the Saturday Press. A district court declared the newspaper a public nuisance and "perpetually enjoined" publication of the Saturday Press. The only way either Near or Guilford would be able to publish the newspaper again was to convince the court that their newspaper would remain free of objectionable material. In 1928 the Minnesota Supreme Court upheld the constitutionality of the law, declaring that under its broad police power the state can regulate public nuisances, including defamatory and scandalous newspapers.

The case then went to the U.S. Supreme Court, which reversed the ruling by the state supreme court. The nuisance statute was declared unconstitutional. Chief Justice Charles Evans Hughes wrote the opinion for the court in the 5–4 ruling, saying that the statute in question was not designed to redress wrongs to individuals attacked by the newspaper.[51] Instead, the statute was directed at suppressing the Saturday Press once and for all. The object of the law, Hughes wrote, was not punishment but censorship—not only of a single issue, but also of all future issues—which is not consistent with the traditional concept of freedom of the press. That is, the statute constituted prior restraint, and prior restraint is clearly a violation of the First Amendment.

The object of the law, Hughes wrote, was not punishment but censorship—not only of a single issue, but also of all future issues—which is not consistent with the traditional concept of freedom of the press.

One maxim in the law holds that when a judge writes an opinion for a court, he or she should stick to the problem at hand and not wander off and talk about matters that do not really concern the issue before the court. Such remarks are considered **dicta,** or words that do not really apply to the case. These words, these dicta, are never really considered an important part of the ruling in the case. Chief Justice Hughes' opinion in *Near* v. *Minnesota* contains a good deal of dicta.

In this case Hughes wrote that the prior restraint of the Saturday Press was unconstitutional, but in some circumstances, he added, prior restraint might be permissible. In what

50. Friendly, *Minnesota Rag.*
51. *Near* v. *Minnesota,* 283 U.S. 697 (1931).

kinds of circumstances? The government can constitutionally stop publication of obscenity, the government can stop publication of material that incites people to acts of violence, and it may prohibit publication of certain kinds of materials during wartime. (It is entirely probable that the Chief Justice was forced to make these qualifying statements in order to hold his slim five-person majority in the ruling.) Hughes admitted, on the other hand, that defining freedom of the press as only the freedom from prior restraint is equally wrong, for in many cases punishment after publication imposes effective censorship upon the freedom of expression.

Near v. *Minnesota* stands for the proposition that under American law prior censorship is permitted only in very unusual circumstances; it is the exception, not the rule. Courts have reinforced this interpretation many times since 1931. Despite this considerable litigation, we still lack a complete understanding of the kinds of circumstances in which prior restraint might be acceptable under the First Amendment, as the following cases illustrate.

AUSTIN v. *KEEFE*

A case that to some extent reinforced the *Near* ruling involved the attempt of a real estate broker to stop a neighborhood community action group from distributing pamphlets about him. The Organization for a Better Austin was a community organization in the Austin neighborhood of Chicago. Its goal was to stabilize the population in the integrated community. Members were opposed to the tactics of certain real estate brokers who came into white neighborhoods, spread the word that blacks were moving in, bought up the white-owned homes cheaply in the ensuing panic, and then resold them at a good profit to blacks or other whites. The organization received pledges from most real estate firms in the area to stop these blockbusting tactics. But Jerome Keefe refused to make such an agreement. The community group then printed leaflets and flyers describing his activities and handed them out in Westchester, the community in which Keefe lived. Group members told the Westchester residents that Keefe was a "panic peddler" and said they would stop distributing the leaflets in Westchester as soon as Keefe agreed to stop his blockbusting real estate tactics. Keefe went to court and obtained an injunction that prohibited further distribution by the community club of pamphlets, leaflets, and literature of any kind in Westchester on the grounds that the material constituted an invasion of Keefe's privacy and caused him irreparable harm. The Organization for a Better Austin appealed the ruling to the U.S. Supreme Court. In May 1971, the high court dissolved the injunction. Chief Justice Warren Burger wrote, "The injunction, so far as it imposes prior restraint on speech and publication, constitutes an impermissible restraint on First Amendment rights." He said that the injunction, as in the *Near* case, did not seek to redress individual wrongs, but instead sought to suppress on the basis of one or two handbills the distribution of any kind of literature in a city of 18,000 inhabitants. Keefe argued that the purpose of the handbills was not to inform the community but to force him to sign an agreement. The chief justice said this argument was immaterial and was not sufficient cause to remove the leaflets and flyers from the protection of the First Amendment. Justice Burger added:

> Petitioners [the community group] were engaged openly and vigorously in making
> the public aware of respondent's [Keefe's] real estate practices. Those practices

were offensive to them, as the views and practices of the petitioners are no doubt offensive to others. But so long as the means are peaceful, the communication need not meet standards of acceptability.[52]

The *Keefe* case did a good job of reinforcing the high court's decision in *Near* v. *Minnesota*.

PENTAGON PAPERS CASE

While it is more famous, another 1971 decision is not as strong a statement in behalf of freedom of expression as either *Near* or *Keefe*. This is the famous Pentagon Papers decision.[53] The case began in the summer of 1971 when The New York Times, followed by the Washington Post and a handful of other newspapers, began publishing a series of articles based on a top secret 47-volume government study officially entitled "History of the United States Decision-Making Process on Vietnam Policy." The day after the initial article on the so-called Pentagon Papers appeared, Attorney General John Mitchell asked The New York Times to stop publication of the material. When The Times' publisher refused, the government went to court to get an injunction to force the newspaper to stop the series. A temporary restraining order was granted as the case wound its way to the Supreme Court. Such an order was also imposed on the Washington Post after it began to publish reports based on the same material.

At first the government argued that the publication of this material violated federal espionage statutes. When that assertion did not satisfy the lower federal courts, the government argued that the president had inherent power under his constitutional mandate to conduct foreign affairs to protect the national security, which includes the right to classify documents secret and top secret. Publication of this material by the newspapers was unauthorized disclosure of such material and should be stopped. This argument did not satisfy the courts either, and by the time the case came before the Supreme Court, the government argument was that publication of these papers might result in irreparable harm to the nation and its ability to conduct foreign affairs. The Times and the Post consistently made two arguments. First, they said that the classification system is a sham, that people in the government declassify documents almost at will when they want to sway public opinion or influence a reporter's story. Second, the press also argued that an injunction against the continued publication of this material violated the First Amendment. Interestingly, the newspapers did not argue that under all circumstances prior restraint is in conflict with the First Amendment. Defense attorney Professor Alexander Bickel argued that under some circumstances prior restraint is acceptable—for example, when the publication of a document has a direct link with a grave event that is immediate and visible. Former Justice William O. Douglas noted that this was a strange argument for newspapers to make—and it is. Apparently, both newspapers decided that a victory in that immediate case was far more important than to establish a definitive and long-lasting constitutional principle. They therefore concentrated on winning the case, acknowledging that in future cases prior restraint might be permissible.[54]

---

52. *Organization for a Better Austin* v. *Keefe,* 402 U.S. 415 (1971).
53. *New York Times* v. *U.S.; U.S.* v. *Washington Post,* 713 U.S. 403 (1971).
54. Pember, "The Pentagon Papers," 403.

Vietnam Archive: Pentagon Study Traces 3 Decades of Growing U. S. Involvement

By NEIL SHEEHAN

A massive study of how the United States went to war in Indochina, conducted by the Pentagon three years ago, demonstrates that four administrations progressively developed a sense of commitment to a non-Communist Vietnam, a readiness to fight the North to protect the South, and an ultimate frustration with this effort—to a much greater extent than their public statements acknowledged at the time.

The 3,000-page analysis, to which 4,000 pages of official documents are appended, was commissioned by Secretary of Defense Robert S. McNamara and covers the American involvement in Southeast Asia from World War II to mid-1968—the start of the peace talks in Paris after President Lyndon B. Johnson had set a limit on further military commitments and revealed his intention to retire. Most of the study and many of the appended documents have been obtained by The New York Times and will be described and presented in a series of articles beginning today.

> Three pages of documentary material from the Pentagon study begin on Page 35.

Though far from a complete history, even at 2.5 million words, the study forms a great archive of government decision-making on Indochina over three decades. The study led its 30 to 40 authors and researchers to many broad conclusions and specific findings, including the following:

¶That the Truman Administration's decision to give military aid to France in her colonial war against the Communist-led Vietminh "directly involved" the United States in Vietnam and "set" the course of American policy.

¶That the Eisenhower Administration's decision to rescue a fledgling South Vietnam from a Communist takeover and attempt to undermine the new Communist regime of North Vietnam gave the Administration a "direct role in the ultimate breakdown of the Geneva settlement" for Indochina in 1954.

¶That the Kennedy Administration, though ultimately spared from major escalation decisions by the death of its leader, transformed a policy of "limited-risk gamble," which it inherited, into a "broad commitment" that left President Johnson with a choice between more war and withdrawal.

¶That the Johnson Administration, though the President was reluctant and hesitant to take the final decisions, intensified the covert warfare against North Vietnam and began planning in the spring of 1964 to wage overt war, a full year before it publicly revealed the depth of its involvement and its fear of defeat.

¶That this campaign of growing clandestine military pressure through 1964 and the expanding program of bombing North Vietnam in 1965 were begun despite the judgment of the Government's intelligence community that the measures would not cause Hanoi to cease its support of the Vietcong insurgency in the South, and that the bombing was

Continued on Page 38, Col. 1

On June 30 the high court ruled 6–3 in favor of The New York Times and the Washington Post. The court did not grant a permanent injunction against the publication of the Pentagon Papers, but the ruling was hardly the kind that strengthened the First Amendment. In a very short per curiam opinion, the majority said that in a case involving the prior restraint of a publication, the government bears a heavy burden to justify such a restraint. In this case the government failed to show the court why such a restraint should be imposed on the two newspapers.[55] In other words, the government failed to justify its request for the permanent restraining order.

The decision in the case rested on the preferred position First Amendment theory or doctrine (see page 44). The ban on publication was *presumed* to be an unconstitutional infringement on the First Amendment. The government had to prove that the ban was needed to protect the nation in some manner. If such evidence could be adduced, the court would strike the balance in favor of the government and uphold the ban on the publication of the articles. But in this case the government simply failed to show why its request for an injunction

Front page from The New York Times, June 12, 1971. The so-called Pentagon Papers. Copyright © 2000 by The New York Times Company. Reprinted by permission.

---

55. *New York Times* v. *U.S.; U.S.* v. *Washington Post,* 713 U.S. 403 (1971).

was vital to the national interest. Consequently, the high court denied the government's request for a ban on the publication of the Pentagon Papers on the grounds that such a prohibition was a violation of the First Amendment. Note: The court did not say that in all similar cases an injunction would violate the First Amendment. It did not even say that in this case an injunction was a violation of the First Amendment. It merely said that the government had not shown why the injunction was needed, why it was not a violation of the freedom of the press. Such a decision is not what one would call a ringing defense of the right of free expression.

In addition to the brief unsigned opinion from the majority, all nine members of the court wrote short individual opinions. Justices Black and Douglas clung to the absolutist theory and argued that they could conceive of no circumstance under which the government might properly interfere with freedom of expression. Justice Brennan's opinion echoed the unsigned opinion; the government had failed to carry the necessary burden of proof. Justice Potter Stewart said he agreed with Brennan and noted that there was simply too much secrecy in government. Justice Byron White said he supported the court's decision to refrain from issuing the injunction, but suggested the newspapers might be in violation of an espionage statute and subject to criminal prosecution. And Justice Thurgood Marshall questioned the power of the executive branch to classify documents. All three dissenters, Chief Justice Warren Burger and Justices John Harlan and Harry Blackmun, complained that there had not been sufficient time to properly consider the legal questions. Both Blackmun and Harlan said they were also concerned about the damage to foreign relations and national security that might be caused by the publication of the documents.

What many people initially called the case of the century ended in a First Amendment fizzle. The press won the day; the Pentagon Papers were published. But thoughtful observers expressed concern over the ruling. A majority of the court had not ruled that such prior restraint was unconstitutional—only that the government had failed to meet the heavy burden of showing such restraint was necessary in this case.

What many people initially called the case of the century ended in a First Amendment fizzle.

PROGRESSIVE MAGAZINE CASE

The fragile nature of the court's holding became clear in early 1979 when the government again went to court to block the publication of material it claimed could endanger the national security.[56] Free-lance writer Howard Morland had prepared an article entitled, "The H-Bomb Secret: How We Got It, Why We're Telling It." The piece was scheduled to be published in the April edition of the Progressive magazine, a 70-year-old political digest founded by Robert M. LaFollette as a voice of the progressive movement.

Morland had gathered the material for the article from unclassified sources. After completing an early draft of the piece, he sought technical criticism from various scholars. Somehow a copy found its way to officials in the federal government. With the cat out of the bag, Progressive editor Erwin Knoll sent a final draft to the government for prepublication comments on technical accuracy. The government said the piece was too accurate and moved into federal court to stop the magazine from publishing the story.

---

56. *U.S.* v. *Progressive,* 467 F. Supp. 990 (1979).

The defendants in the case argued that all the information in the article was from public sources, that any citizen could have gotten the same material by going to the Department of Energy, federal libraries, and the like. Other nations already had this information or could easily get it. Experts testifying in behalf of the magazine argued that the article was a harmless exposition of some exotic nuclear technology.

The government disagreed. It said that while some of the material was from public sources, much of the data was not publicly available. Prosecutors and the government's battery of technical experts argued that the article contained a core of information that had never before been published. The United States also argued that it was immaterial where Morland had gotten his information and whether it had come from classified or public documents. Prosecutors argued that the nation's national security interest permitted the classification and censorship of even information originating in public if, when such information is drawn together, synthesized, and collated, it acquires the character "of presenting immediate, direct and irreparable harm to the interests of the United States." The United States was arguing, then, that some material is automatically classified as soon as it is created if it has the potential to cause harm to the nation. The information in Morland's article met this description, prosecutors argued.

It fell to U.S. District Judge Robert Warren to evaluate the conflicting claims and reach a decision on the government's request to enjoin the publication of the piece. In a thoughtful opinion in which Warren attempted to sort out the issues in the case, the judge said he agreed with the government that there were concepts in the article not found in the public realm—concepts vital to the operation of a thermonuclear bomb. Was the piece a do-it-yourself guide for a hydrogen bomb? No, Warren said, it was not. "A number of affidavits make quite clear that a sine qua non to thermonuclear capability is a large, sophisticated industrial capability coupled with a coterie of imaginative, resourceful scientists and technicians."[57] But the article could provide some nations with a ticket to bypass blind alleys and help a medium-sized nation to move faster in developing a hydrogen bomb.

To the Progressive's argument that the publication of the article would provide people with the information needed to make an informed decision on nuclear issues, Warren wrote, "This Court can find no plausible reason why the public needs to know the technical details about hydrogen bomb construction to carry on an informed debate on this issue."

Looking to the legal issues in the case, Warren said he saw three differences between this case and the Pentagon Papers ruling of 1971. The Pentagon Papers themselves were a historical study; the Morland article focused on contemporary matter. In the Pentagon Papers case there had been no cogent national security reasons advanced by the government when it sought to enjoin the publication of the study. The national security interest is considerably more apparent in the Progressive case, Warren noted. Finally, the government lacked substantial legal authority to stop the publication of the Pentagon Papers. The laws raised by the government were vague, not at all appropriate. But Section 2274 of the Atomic Energy Act of 1954 is quite specific in prohibiting anyone from communicating or disclosing any restricted data to any persons "with reasons to believe such data will be utilized to injure the United States or to

57. *U.S.* v. *Progressive,* 467 F. Supp. 990 (1979).

secure an advantage to any foreign nation." Section 2014 of the same act defined restricted data to include information on the design, manufacture, or utilization of atomic weapons.

Warren concluded that the government had met the heavy burden of showing justification for prior restraint. The judge added that he was not convinced that suppression of the objected-to technical portions of the article would impede the Progressive in its crusade to stimulate public debate on the issue of nuclear armament. "What is involved here," Warren concluded, "is information dealing with the most destructive weapon in the history of mankind, information of sufficient destructive potential to nullify the right to free speech and to endanger the right to life itself."[58]

When the injunction was issued, the editors of the Progressive and their supporters inside and outside the press vowed to appeal the ruling. In September of 1979, as the Progressive case began its slow ascent up the appellate ladder, a small newspaper in Madison, Wis., published a story containing much of the same information as was in the Morland article. When this occurred, the Department of Justice unhappily withdrew its suit against the Progressive. But the victory in the Progressive case was bittersweet at best. The publication of the article had been enjoined. A considerable body of legal opinion had supported the notion that the injunction would have been sustained by the Supreme Court, rightly or wrongly. It must be remembered that as a legal precedent the decision in the Progressive case has limited value. It was, after all, only a U.S. district court ruling and doesn't carry the weight of the *Near* decision, for example. From a political standpoint, however, the case had important implications. Prior restraint, which had seemed quite distant in the years succeeding *Near* v. *Minnesota* and in the afterglow of the press victory in the Pentagon Papers case, took on realistic and frightening new proportions.

SUMMARY

While virtually all American legal scholars agree that the adoption of the First Amendment in 1791 was designed to abolish prior restraint in this nation, prior restraint still exists. A reason it still exists is the 1931 Supreme Court ruling in *Near* v. *Minnesota* in which Chief Justice Charles Evans Hughes ruled that while prior restraint is unacceptable in most instances, there are times when it must be tolerated if the republic is to survive. Protecting the security of the nation is one of those instances cited by Hughes and in the past quarter century in two important cases, the press has been stopped from publishing material the courts believed to be too sensitive. While the Supreme Court finally permitted The New York Times and the Washington Post to publish the so-called Pentagon Papers, the newspapers were blocked for two weeks from printing this material. And in the end the high court merely ruled that the government had failed to make its case, not that the newspapers had a First Amendment right under any circumstance to publish this history of the Vietnam War. Eight years later the Progressive magazine was enjoined from publishing an article about thermonuclear weapons. Only the publication of the same material by a small newspaper in Wisconsin thwarted the government's efforts to permanently stop publication of this article in the Progressive.

58. *U.S.* v. *Progressive,* 467 F. Supp. 990 (1979).

BIBLIOGRAPHY ⟶

Alexander, James. *A Brief Narrative on the Case and Trial of John Peter Zenger.* Edited by Stanley N. Katz. Cambridge: Harvard University Press, 1963.

Brooke, James. "Lawsuit Tests Legal Power of Words." *The New York Times,* 14 February 1996, A12.

Carelli, Richard. "High Court Allows 'Killers' Lawsuit." *Seattle Post-Intelligencer,* 9 September 1998, A3.

Chafee, Zechariah. *Free Speech in the United States.* Cambridge: Harvard University Press, 1941.

Cohen, Jeremy. *Congress Shall Make No Law.* Ames, Iowa: Iowa State University Press, 1989.

Friendly, Fred. *Minnesota Rag.* New York: Random House, 1981.

Gerald, J. Edward. *The Press and the Constitution.* Minneapolis: University of Minnesota Press, 1948.

Helle, Steven. "Whither the Public's Right (Not) to Know? Milton, Malls and Multicultural Speech." *University of Illinois Law Review* 1991, no. 6 (1991):1077.

"Hit Man Publisher Settles Suit." *Washington Post,* 22 May 1999, A1.

Levy, Leonard. *Emergence of a Free Press.* New York: Oxford University Press, 1985.

Meiklejohn, Alexander. *Free Speech and Its Relation to Self-Government.* New York: Harper & Brothers, 1948.

Pember, Don R. "The Pentagon Papers: More Questions Than Answers." *Journalism Quarterly* 48 (1971):403.

———. "The Smith Act as a Restraint on the Press." *Journalism Monographs* 10 (1969):1.

Peterson, H. C., and Gilbert Fite. *Opponents of War, 1917–1918.* Seattle: University of Washington Press, 1957.

Rabban, David M. *Free Speech in Its Forgotten Years.* Cambridge, United Kingdom: Cambridge University Press, 1997.

Roche, John P. *Shadow and Substance.* New York: Macmillan, 1964.

Rutland, Robert. *The Birth of the Bill of Rights.* Chapel Hill: University of North Carolina Press, 1955.

Schechter, Harold. "A Movie Made Me Do It." *The New York Times,* 3 December 1995, A17.

Siebert, Fredrick. *Freedom of the Press in England, 1476–1776.* Urbana: University of Illinois Press, 1952.

Smith, James M. *Freedom's Fetters.* Ithaca, N.Y.: Cornell University Press, 1956.

Smith, Jeffrey A. "Prior Restraint: Original Intentions and Modern Interpretations." *William and Mary Law Review* 28 (1987):439.

Weiser, Benjamin. "Appellate Court Backs Convictions in '93 Terror Plot." *The New York Times,* 17 August 1999, A1.

White, G. Edward. *Justice Oliver Wendell Holmes: Law and the Inner Self.* New York: Oxford University Press, 1993.

The First Amendment
Contemporary Problems

While First Amendment battles over sedition and taxation have been fought and won, other important issues related to freedom of expression continue to be debated. Most prior restraints are unconstitutional. The use of prior restraint to protect the national security, however, continues to be regarded differently. Similarly, school authorities may censor school newspapers, magazines, and yearbooks without running afoul of the First Amendment. In addition, prior restraint is an essential part of an entire class of government regulations called time, place, and manner rules that frequently win judicial approval. Governments at all levels face the dilemma of what to do about so-called hate speech, given the constitutional guarantees of freedom of expression. These are some of the issues we explore in this second chapter on the First Amendment.

PRIOR RESTRAINT DURING WARTIME

Censorship of the press during wartime is not uncommon, even in the United States. There was censorship in every war in which the United States was involved, beginning with the Civil War. Censorship in both World War I and World War II was extensive. For example, the American people did not know the full extent of damage to the U.S. Pacific Fleet in the wake of the bombing of Pearl Harbor on December 7, 1941, until after the war was ended. During World War II reporters had few limits on where they could go or with whom they could talk, but all news reports were screened by military censors before they were allowed to be published or broadcast. The press accepted some kind of censorship as a given; something normal in time of war. Journalists supported the war effort and believed that truthful press reports about the military struggle could harm the national interest.

The war in Vietnam was different from earlier wars in a number of important ways. There was never the massive, unquestioning kind of public support for the war that had existed in World War II, for example. And this was reflected in the kinds of stories journalists filed from the war zone. Unlike previous wars, which began with an important event (e.g., the firing on Fort Sumter in 1861, the bombing of Pearl Harbor in 1941, or the North Korean attack on South Korea in 1950), the fighting in Vietnam seemed to sneak up on this nation. Small groups of U.S. advisors went to Southeast Asia to try to help the South Vietnamese pick up the pieces following the defeat of the French. A handful of reporters went along to cover this story. Slowly the American military presence increased. By 1968 when the United States had committed more than half a million personnel to the fighting, American reporters had gotten used to very loose controls. They could pretty much go where they wanted to go, talk to whomever they met, and report on most military matters. Security guidelines existed and, according to the government officials who administered them, reporters generally abided by the guidelines. Still, reporters enjoyed a freedom to report that their colleagues in earlier wars had not experienced. Since U.S. officials doubted they could get the genie back in the bottle and institute stricter controls, they chose instead to use propaganda to counter what journalists reported. Government efforts at propaganda included attempts to undermine the journalists who reported the bad news from Vietnam by denying the truth of these reports and complaining to editors and publishers about their correspondents in the field. Government officials went so far as to lie to the American people. Perhaps the greatest deception of the war was the Johnson administration's insistence in 1964 that North Vietnamese gunboats had attacked U.S. Navy vessels patrolling in the Gulf of Tonkin, which is adjacent to North Vietnam. There was one unsuccessful attack, but on the following night a tense and inexperienced sonar operator on a U.S. Navy ship mistakenly reported a second attack. Reports describing what officials thought was an attack were transmitted to Washington, D.C., but another U.S. Navy cable quickly followed reporting that it was highly doubtful that a second attack had occurred. President Johnson suppressed the second message and used the phantom attack as a justification for the bombing of North Vietnam and a means of convincing the Congress to give him a virtual blank check to escalate U.S. involvement in the war, the so-called Gulf of Tonkin Resolution.[1]

1. Cranberg, "The Gulf of Credibility."

When U.S. forces invaded the small Caribbean island of Grenada in 1983 American reporters were left at home. President Ronald Reagan had left to his military commanders the decision of whether journalists would accompany the soldiers and marines during the invasion, and they decided to keep the press away for 72 hours. A few U.S. reporters already on the island were isolated from the fighting by the military. The operation was ostensibly a success; but both the public and the press were dissatisfied with how journalists had been treated. Government officials cited a serious problem if they were to permit the press to accompany the troops in an invasion like the one in Grenada: They would have to announce publicly that a secret invasion was planned. A military and civilian commission was formed to try to resolve this difficulty. The panel, headed by retired Army major general Winant Sidle, proposed that a press pool be established; a group of 12 to 16 journalists who could be secretly notified when a secret military operation was pending. These journalists would accompany the military forces and be the eyes and ears of the public and the rest of the press during the initial stages of the fighting. The government promised to provide logistical and technical support for reporters. After 72 hours other journalists would be permitted to enter the war zone; the work of the pool would end.

The pool was activated three times prior to the war in the Persian Gulf. On two occasions, when U.S. planes bombed Libya and when the U.S. Navy escorted Kuwaiti tankers in the Persian Gulf during the Iraq-Iran War, the pool concept worked well. In December of 1989, however, when the United States invaded Panama, the press pool failed to function as it was intended. The 16 members of the pool arrived in Panama five hours late, and then were confined at a local military base until most of the fighting had ended. At first the Department of Defense blamed the problems on innocent errors. But a subsequent investigation by the Defense Department revealed that Defense Secretary Richard Cheney ordered the delay in activation of the press pool and later blocked the attempt by the U.S. Army to form a pool from reporters who were already in Panama when the fighting began.[2] Pool member Fred Francis of NBC television reportedly said, "We missed the war."

In December of 1989, however, when the United States invaded Panama, the press pool failed to function as it was intended.

Press dissatisfaction with the operation of the pool in Panama led to the formation of another panel, this one headed by Fred S. Hoffman, a Pentagon spokesman during the Reagan administration. The panel recommended that the military give the press more freedom to cover its operations. Nevertheless, many members of the press talked seriously about pulling out of the pool. "We shouldn't commit [ourselves] to a charade," said Jean H. Otto, chairperson of the American Society of Newspaper Editors. "Either you have observers or you don't." But events in the Middle East overtook attempts to resolve these problems. In August of 1990 U.S. forces once again were on the march, this time into the Kingdom of Saudi Arabia.

WAR IN THE PERSIAN GULF

U.S. censorship of the press during the war in the Persian Gulf was the most extensive of any war in our history, according to most observers. Once the fighting on the ground began, the huge numbers of reporters in the area simply overwhelmed government efforts to control the

2. Schmeisser, "Shooting Pool," 21.

press. But throughout most of the six-month military buildup and air war, control of the American press was tight and effective.

The intensive censorship was the result of many factors, but three stand out as more important than the others. First, civilian authorities deferred important decisions regarding press coverage to senior military officers, many of whom came to the Persian Gulf with the anti-press prejudice they had accumulated in Vietnam some 25 years before. Next, the U.S. officials said they were bound to respect the wishes of the government of Saudi Arabia, a nation that has never seriously entertained concepts of freedom of expression. Finally, President George Bush sought to avoid what had happened to one of his predecessors, Lyndon B. Johnson, when press coverage helped generate strong public opposition to U.S. policies in Vietnam and ultimately cost Johnson a second full term in office.

At the peak of the military action as many as 800 journalists were in Saudi Arabia. But only a small percentage ever saw the fighting or even combat troops. Reporters who attempted to leave the rear areas in Dhahran and Riyadh were encumbered by a three-pronged censorship:

Reporters who left the rear area were confined to press pools. This policy was enforced throughout the duration of the buildup and fighting, not just the first 72 hours as proposed by the Sidle Commission. Some military units welcomed reporters in the pools, but others did not, so journalists only viewed what occurred in those areas in which they were welcome.

Members of the press pools were constantly escorted by military public affairs officers. These officers guided reporters to their destinations, accompanied them back to the rear areas, and stayed with journalists as they interviewed U.S. military personnel. Reporters who ventured off by themselves without escorts faced losing their press credentials if they were caught by U.S. or Saudi military police.

All print and broadcast reports had to be reviewed before they could be released for publication or broadcast. While most reporters said the guidelines used by the military censors were reasonable, many complained that the review process seriously delayed the transmission of important news. Some reporters said that to avoid additional delay in the transmission of their report, they would agree to make changes in a story rather than appeal a field censor's decision. Censors also often went beyond the guidelines and rejected material that posed no security problem but was embarrassing to the military.

Because of the censorship there was frequently little important news coming from reporters in the field. To fill this vacuum and satisfy the American appetite for news, the press reported information handed out at military news briefings in both Saudi Arabia and the United States. These reports carried the illusion of news but actually contained little important information.[3] Many Americans were shocked after the war to discover how seriously they had been misled by the nation's military leaders and, indirectly at least, by the press. Surprisingly, there was little press protest of this censorship. Early public skepticism about the Gulf war had been largely muted by an intensive public relations campaign orchestrated by the Republican party and a group called the Citizens for a Free Kuwait, an organization created by the giant public

Surprisingly, there was little press protest of this censorship.

3. See, for example, Miller, "Operation Desert Sham," A17.

relations company Hill and Knowlton, which was working for the Kuwaiti government. The willingness by most members of the press to cooperate with the military rather than oppose the censorship stemmed less from patriotic zeal than from a fear that a failure to cooperate would leave them on the sidelines, unable to take part in the hoopla that characterized most media coverage of the war. A 1991 report by the Freedom Foundation, a distinctly pro-media organization, concluded that the press complained too little and too late about censorship.[4]

Lawsuits

At least two lawsuits resulted from the censorship. Some small media organizations such as The Nation, Harper's, Mother Jones, Pacific News Service, and a handful of writers including former New York Times writer Sydney Schanberg ("The Killing Fields") brought suit against the government, challenging the censorship on First Amendment grounds. These journalists and organizations had been largely excluded from the press pools. Interestingly, the television networks and larger newspapers, whose reporters were a part of the pools, refused to join the lawsuit. The fighting was over, the restrictions were ended; by the time the court heard the case, the issue was moot. The issue still could have been decided under an exception to the rule of mootness that permits a court to rule on a case if the subject matter "is capable of repetition yet evading review," that is, if the issue is likely to arise over and over again and continue to become moot each time before it can be resolved. The federal district court chose not to do this, however, saying that the issues were too abstract to be decided in the absence of an actual case.[5]

In April of 1993, a U.S. district court in the District of Columbia ruled that the government did not violate the First Amendment when it barred journalists from Dover Air Force Base during the conflict. Since 1972 the air base had been open to the press and public to witness the arrival of the bodies of U.S. military personnel who died overseas in the defense of their country. But the Bush administration did not want Americans to see video or still pictures of dead American servicemen and women coming home in body bags. The federal court supported the government. Citing several earlier rulings by the Supreme Court of the United States (see pages 306–308), the trial judge dismissed the complaint and ruled that the First Amendment does not "mandate a right of access to government information or sources of information within government's control."[6] The District of Columbia U.S. Circuit Court of Appeals affirmed the dismissal of the claim by the lower court.[7] The court ruled that the closure of the site did not violate the First Amendment because military bases have traditionally been closed to the public and the press. The court also stated that the burden placed on news gathering was modest at worst because the policy did not impede public and press acquisition of basic facts. These rulings were not unexpected, because for a variety of reasons, judges are quite unwilling to overturn Pentagon policies, policies that might affect the national security.

4. Dennis, et al., *The Media at War.*
5. *Nation Magazine* v. *U.S. Department of Defense,* 762 F. Supp. 1558 (1991).
6. *JB Pictures, Inc.* v. *Defense Department,* 21 M.L.R. 1564 (1993).
7. *JB Pictures, Inc.* v. *Defense Department,* 86 F. 3d 236 (1996).

Officials within the Defense Department and reporters worked in the wake of the war to establish new policies that might provide journalists significantly more access to information when the next war unfolded. Agreement was reached that press pools would no longer be used after the initial stages of any military operation. The Pentagon also agreed to limit the use of military escorts. But there remained a sharp disagreement over prepublication security review: the press seeking to return to the days of the Vietnam war when no such review occurred, the government unwilling to adopt a policy that it believes did not work in Southeast Asia.

Until NATO military forces began attacking the Serbs in Yugoslavia in 1999, reporters voiced fewer complaints about military censorship in the mid-to-late 1990s. Cooperation between the press and the government was reported to be good in 1994 when the United States sent troops to Saudi Arabia again and to Haiti. Of course, neither of these incursions carried with it the serious implications of the earlier Persian Gulf war. The Haitian press pool—which was disbanded after the invasion was called off—suffered through some logistical problems. Reporters complained that transportation and communication problems hampered their ability to transmit reports about the final preparations for combat. But, according to journalism professor Jacqueline Sharkey at the University of Arizona, many reporters agreed with military personnel who said several problems were caused because news organizations sent unprepared personnel to work in the pool. In an article in the December 1994 American Journalism Review, Sharkey quotes Scripps-Howard reporter Andrew Schneider as saying that the Pentagon's new game plan was to be "as open as possible."[8] Other than asking that the press not publish important information prior to the start of the invasion, "there were no restrictions on what we could report or how we could report it," Schneider said.

But the NATO bombing of Yugoslavia in 1999, in which the United States military played the leading role, once again brought charges of overt military censorship, especially in the early weeks of the campaign. From the time the bombings started until nearly mid-April, the U.S. government and NATO officials confined their remarks about the operation to broad generalities. Much of the material released focused on the problems related to the flood of refugees from Kosovo and ignored details of the bombing of Belgrade and other areas. At the same time the Clinton administration made certain that high-level government officials, like the secretaries of state and defense, were readily available, especially to the television networks, to defend U.S. policy. Independent observers in the United States and in Europe said the U.S. government was putting out propaganda at only a slightly slower rate than the state media in Yugoslavia. Implicit comparisons made by U.S. and NATO officials of Yugoslav President Slobodan Milosevic to Adolf Hitler and assertions that the refugee problem was the "worst humanitarian crisis in Europe since World War II" were just two examples of the kinds of exaggerations critics complained of. At the same time, in briefings by the Pentagon and by NATO, reporters were unable to find out how many attack missions had been made against Yugoslav forces, how many of the missions had been completed, how many bombs had been dropped and missiles had been fired, and precisely what they had hit. Reporters complained that the NATO briefings about the war were generally "baloney laden." Finally, in May of 1999, officials at The New York Times, the Washington Post, the Wall Street Journal, Associated Press,

---

8. Sharkey, "The Shallow End."

CNN, and other news media wrote a letter of protest to the secretary of defense. "Though the ongoing military campaign in the Balkans is one of the largest and most important U.S. military operations conducted in recent years," the letter said, "the Department of Defense has supplied far less information to the media and public than during the Persian Gulf War or the more recent Desert Fox operation." The letter broke up part of the information logjam.

But censorship remained a serious problem. Since World War II journalists who talk with servicemen and servicewomen have been able to report their names and their hometowns. Pilots and flight crews at the giant NATO air base at Aviano, Italy, were told by military public information officers that they could not reveal this information to journalists. When the Associated Press sought permission to send a correspondent to Albania to report on the dispatch of the U.S. Apache helicopters from Germany, the news agency was told that the reporter would have to stay in Albania for 14 days and would be bound to follow a three-page list of reporting restrictions. The Army finally relented after the AP complained.

The number of civilian casualties wrought by the massive bombing effort was the most sensitive issue during the brief military action. Even President Clinton publicly admitted that casualties were to be expected when aircraft bombed from 15,000 feet over civilian areas. The U.S. government was quick to admit to such casualties, but didn't like the idea of the matter becoming fodder for the nightly news. U.S. officials were highly critical of Serbian television reports that graphically displayed the death and destruction in civilian areas, calling the reports phony. The criticism did not deter Serbian television from putting such stories on the satellite for consumption by the U.S. press. Finally NATO bombed the Serb television stations off the air. Although shutting down the TV stations halted the diet of lies and propaganda being fed to the Serb viewers, one observer noted that the bombing also curbed the transmission to the West of disturbing pictures of collateral damage (civilian casualties) that were beginning to erode public support for NATO's escalating air strikes.[9]

American reporters were permitted to visit Belgrade and many did. Once there, of course, they were censored and shown only what the Yugoslav government wanted them to see. Kathleen Hall Jamieson, the dean of the School of Communications at the University of Pennsylvania, noted after studying much of the war reporting that both sides had an almost unlimited ability to create their own reality about the conflict. "We've got to be very careful about asking, what do we really know?" she said. "What is our first-hand experience of it? The answer at this point is, we can't know."[10]

SUMMARY

Censorship of war news was common in the United States until the fighting began in Vietnam in the 1960s. Reporters were required to follow general security guidelines in their coverage of the war in Southeast Asia, but nevertheless went nearly everywhere, talked with nearly everyone, and presented the American people with a frank account of both the good and bad in that

9. Slogan, "The Fog of War."
10. Bruni, "Dueling Perspectives."

conflict. Many in the American military thought that that frankness was wrong, and since Vietnam the Pentagon has exercised a heavy hand in controlling press coverage of U.S. military operations. After the press was excluded for 72 hours during the invasion of Grenada, a military and civilian panel recommended the formation of a small press pool that would accompany U.S. forces during the first three days of fighting in future military operations. This pool concept worked well at first, but was a failure when the United States invaded Panama.

The censorship of the press during the war in the Persian Gulf was the most extensive of any war. The censorship was prompted by senior military officials who still distrusted the press as a result of Vietnam, by the anti-democratic government of Saudi Arabia, and by the administration's fear of losing public support for the war. Reporters were kept on a very short leash: Those leaving the rear area had to travel in groups or pools, accompanied by a military escort. Reporters could only go where they were invited, and all stories were extensively reviewed before they were permitted to be published or broadcast. At the same time, the government tried to fill the vacuum created by this censorship with frequent news briefings that were usually incomplete and often dishonest. Two lawsuits brought against the government because of the censorship came to naught when the courts refused to consider the larger matter of prior restraint. Since the war the government and the press have tried, with only limited success, to establish new guidelines to govern the military and reporters in future conflicts. Press pool operations did work more smoothly when the United States sent troops to Haiti in 1994, but censorship problems arose again with the beginning of the 1999 war in the Balkans.

THE FIRST AMENDMENT IN THE SCHOOLS

Censorship of school newspapers and magazines is a serious First Amendment issue in America today. Not only does such censorship deprive students and others of information they should rightfully see, but censorship in the schools has the appearance of being the correct thing to do. School, after all, is where students are taught the difference between right and wrong, where students learn about the freedoms Americans enjoy under their constitution. The lesson many students may be learning is that if censorship is practiced by their school administrators, then it must be right. Teachers report that high school journalism students, accustomed to censorship on occasion, have come to accept it as the norm.[11] Nonjournalism students, the readers of the newspapers, often willingly accept the censorship, believing there must be a good reason for it. "The values [students] learn [in high school] are the values they take into their lives,"[12] noted Mark Goodman, the executive director of the Student Press Law Center in Washington, D.C.

---

11. Patten, "High School Confidential," 8.
12. Riskin, "Speech, Press Censorship."

CENSORSHIP OF THE HIGH SCHOOL PRESS

For centuries, students were presumed to have few constitutional rights of any kind. They were regarded as junior or second-class people and were told it was better to be seen and not heard. Parents were given wide latitude in controlling the behavior of their offspring, and when these young people moved into schools or other public institutions, the government had the right to exercise a kind of parental control over them: in loco parentis, in the place of a parent. During the social upheaval of the 1960s and 1970s, students began to assert their constitutional rights, and in several important decisions the federal courts acknowledged these claims. In 1969, in the case of *Tinker* v. *Des Moines,* for example, the Supreme Court ruled that students in the public schools do not shed at the schoolhouse gate their constitutional rights to freedom of speech or expression.

During the social upheaval of the 1960s and 1970s, students began to assert their constitutional rights, and in several important decisions the federal courts acknowledged these claims.

On December 16, 1966, Christopher Eckhardt, 16, and Mary Beth Tinker, 13, went to school wearing homemade black armbands, complete with peace signs, to protest the war in Vietnam. Mary Beth's brother John, 15, wore a similar armband the following day. All three were suspended from school after they refused requests by school officials to remove the armbands. School administrators said they feared that wearing the armbands might provoke violence among the students, most of whom supported the war in Vietnam. The students appealed to the courts to overturn their suspensions. Three years later Justice Abe Fortas, writing for the Supreme Court, said that students have a First Amendment right to express their opinions on even controversial subjects like the war in Vietnam if they do so "without materially and substantially interfering with the requirements of appropriate discipline in the operation of the school and without colliding with the rights of others."[13]

Unfortunately the legal legacy of the *Tinker* ruling failed to live up to Justice Fortas' bold language in the case. Lower federal and state courts consistently distinguished the Supreme Court ruling when faced with school censorship disputes.[14] Sensitive to the problems faced by school administrators and loathe to substitute their own judgment for rulings made by school superintendents and principals, judges slowly undermined the spirit if not the substance of the 1969 Supreme Court ruling.

By 1988, when the U.S. Supreme Court decided the case of *Hazelwood School District* v. *Kuhlmeier,* it became apparent that the promise of *Tinker* would not be fulfilled. Today, then, the place to begin to seek an understanding of students' First Amendment rights begins with *Hazelwood.*

The Hazelwood *Case*

In 1983 the principal at East Hazelwood High School near St. Louis censored the school newspaper by completely removing two pages from the publication. The pages contained articles about teenage pregnancy and the impact of parents' divorce on children. The articles

---

13. *Tinker* v. *Des Moines School District,* 393 U.S. 503 (1969).
14. See, for example, *Trachtman* v. *Anker,* 563 F. 2d 512 (1977) and *Frasca* v. *Andrews,* 463 F. Supp. 1043 (1978).

on pregnancy included personal interviews with three Hazelwood students (whose names were not used) about how they were affected by their unwanted pregnancies. There was also information about birth control in the story. The story on divorce quoted students—again not identified—about the problems they had suffered when their mothers and fathers had split up. The censorship of the articles was defended on the grounds of privacy and editorial balance. School officials said they were concerned that the identity of the three girls who agreed to anonymously discuss their pregnancies might nevertheless become known. School officials said they acted to protect the privacy of the students and the parents in the story on divorce as well. In addition, the principal said the latter story was unbalanced, giving the views of only the students. The federal district court upheld the censorship of the school newspaper, but this decision was overturned by a U.S. court of appeals.[15] In January of 1988 the Supreme Court reversed the appellate court ruling and ruled that the censorship was permissible under the First Amendment.

At the outset it is important to note that this ruling involved the censorship of a high school newspaper that was published as a part of the school curriculum. The court strongly suggested that the full force of the ruling would not necessarily apply to a high school paper published as an extracurricular activity where any student might contribute stories. Justice Byron White, author of the court's opinion, noted specifically in a footnote that the court did not at that time have to decide whether its ruling might also be applied to school-sponsored college and university newspapers.

The Court of Appeals had ruled the censorship of the newspaper unconstitutional because the articles could not have reasonably been forecast to "materially disrupt classwork, give rise to substantial disorder or invade the rights of others."[16] This is the standard from *Tinker*. But the Supreme Court rejected this standard by distinguishing the *Hazelwood* case from the earlier ruling. The *Tinker* ruling, Justice White said in the 5–3 decision, deals with the right of educators to silence a student's personal expression that happens to occur on school property. *Hazelwood* concerns the authority of educators over school-sponsored publications. "Educators are entitled to exercise greater control over this second form of student expression to assure that participants learn whatever lessons the activity is designed to teach, that readers or listeners are not exposed to material that may be inappropriate for their level of maturity, and that the views of individual speakers are not erroneously attributed to the school," he wrote. Educators do not offend the First Amendment by exercising editorial control over the style and content of student speech in school-sponsored publications so long as their actions are reasonably related to "legitimate pedagogical concerns." This means school officials could censor out material they found "ungrammatical, poorly written, inadequately researched, biased or prejudiced, vulgar or profane, or unsuitable for immature audiences." Justice White stressed at one point in the ruling that the education of the nation's youth is primarily the responsibility of parents, teachers, and state and local school officials, not federal judges. Only when the decision to censor has "no valid educational purpose" is the First Amendment directly and sharply involved.

Educators do not offend the First Amendment by exercising editorial control over the style and content of student speech in school-sponsored publications so long as their actions are reasonably related to "legitimate pedagogical concerns."

15. *Kuhlmeier* v. *Hazelwood School District*, 795 F. 2d 1368 (1986).
16. *Kuhlmeier* v. *Hazelwood School District*, 795 F. 2d 1368 (1986).

Justice William Brennan wrote a strong dissent for three members of the court. He complained of the crabbed view of the First Amendment rights of students outlined by Justice White in the court's opinion.

> Instead of teaching children to respect the diversity of ideas that is fundamental to the American system. . . . and that our Constitution is a living reality, not parchment under glass, the Court today teaches youth to discount important principles of our government as mere platitudes. The young men and women of Hazelwood East expected a civics lesson, but not the one the Court teaches them today.[17]

In the years since the *Hazelwood* ruling, censorship of the student press has escalated rapidly. In 1988 the Student Press Law Center reported that it received 550 calls from student journalists seeking legal help regarding censorship problems. In 1998 the Center reported that it received nearly 1,600 such calls. Since the killings in Columbine in April of 1999 problems have gotten even worse as school administrators crack down on the purveyors of any published

In 1988 the Supreme Court ruled that school administrators had broad powers to censor high school newspapers. Pictured above is Tammy Hawkins, one of the editors of the Hazelwood East High School newspaper, Spectrum, holding a copy of the newspaper that generated the high court ruling. AP/World Wide Photos.

17. *Hazelwood School District* v. *Kuhlmeier,* 108 S. Ct. 562 (1988).

prose that even hints at school violence. The focus of most censorship cases today is not stories about drugs or sex but stories that if published might, in the eyes of administrators, tarnish the image of the school. Typical of this kind of story is what happened at Naperville Central High School, located in an affluent suburb west of Chicago. Student journalists learned that school district administrators spent taxpayers' money to attend conferences in New York, New Orleans, San Francisco, and Phoenix. The four administrators spent a total of $5,600 in school funds to go to these meetings at a time when the district faced a serious budget crisis. When the Naperville school paper tried to publish an article on the travel expenses, the school principal ordered the student journalists to cut the names of the administrators from the article. "My concern was that there may have been an appearance that these administrators did something wrong and that would affect their ability to lead," said school principal Tom Paulsen. Some of the evidence uncovered by the students—including the administrators' expense vouchers—suggested at least the appearance of impropriety. The school official who visited San Francisco, for example, was reimbursed for five nights' lodging in a hotel, even though the conference lasted only two days.[18]

Other examples of censorship:

- Administrators in the Snohomish, Wash., school district blocked attempts by students to publish material about a high school vice principal who was suspended and later resigned in the face of charges of sexual harassment. The school paper was censored despite the fact that local newspapers had previously aired the facts of the story.
- Nine students at a suburban Miami high school were arrested at school for distributing a satirical pamphlet on campus. Authorities said the pamphlet, entitled "First Amendment," contained racist, obscene, and violent material. Criminal charges were never filed despite the arrests but the students faced suspensions and expulsion in the spring of 1998.
- The principal at a New Jersey high school cut a story about the school's sex education program that included instructions on how to use a condom.
- School officials at an Oregon high school refused to allow the school newspaper to publish stories on any of the school's sports losses.
- A Fort Wayne, Ind., principal censored an article that outlined financial improprieties by a school coach, even though the principal admitted it was accurate.
- A school administrator in Anchorage, Alaska, barred the publication of pictures taken of a fight in the school cafeteria.

The *Hazelwood* ruling has acted as a kind of imprimatur for high school officials to wield the censor's blue pencil with a heavy hand. But all the news is not bad. In 1994 The Freedom Forum in Arlington, Va., published the first comprehensive study of high school journalism in 20 years. "Death by Cheeseburger: High School Journalism in the 1990s and Beyond" provides readers with a lengthy summary of how high school administrators, teachers, and students are

---

18. "Students Censored."

responding to the *Hazelwood* ruling.[19] The authors point out that in addition to the problems now faced by student journalists in the wake of this court decision, positive developments have occurred as well. High school journalism remains vigorous in many schools, with newspapers filled with stories about problems associated with teenage pregnancy, crime, AIDs, gang violence, teen suicide, and other important issues. The legislatures in Colorado, Arkansas, Iowa, California, Massachusetts, and Kansas have passed statutes granting student journalists in those states a fuller measure of freedom of expression than granted by the Supreme Court in *Hazelwood.* Some community newspapers are now actively supporting the fight for freedom of expression in the schools. For example, when school officials forbade a student newspaper at a Dallas high school to publish a picture of a student smoking off campus to illustrate an article on health and school regulations, the Dallas Morning News said it would run the photo and an article about censoring the school newspaper unless the school superintendent relented. The student newspaper ran the photo as planned.

Censorship Guidelines

While the decision in *Hazelwood* surely gave school administrators a strong hand in censoring high school newspapers, all the questions regarding the scope of such censorship have not been answered. But some general guidelines have emerged.

The question, How can a high school newspaper be censored? cannot be answered until two other questions are. First, is the newspaper published at a public or private high school? Constitutional protections have substantially less meaning at private schools. The First Amendment is not considered an impediment to official censorship at such educational institutions. A newspaper at a private school can be censored in just about any way imaginable.

The next question to ask when focusing on public schools is, What kind of newspaper is it? Three kinds of publications are possible:

- A school-sponsored newspaper, generally defined as a paper that uses the school's name and resources, has a faculty adviser, and serves as a tool to teach knowledge or skills. Typically this kind of newspaper is produced as part of a journalism class.
- An unsupervised or student controlled newspaper produced on the school's campus as an extracurricular activity.
- A student newspaper produced and distributed off campus.

The *Hazelwood* ruling spoke only to the first kind of newspaper. This type of paper can be most heavily censored. Most authorities agree that school officials have less power to censor the second kind of publication, and no power to censor the third kind of newspaper, unless students attempt to distribute it on campus. School administrators can ban the on-campus distribution of material produced elsewhere, and this authority provides them with a kind of informal censorship power if students seek to circulate the material on school property.

Determining whether a newspaper has been distributed on campus or off campus is not a difficult task. But what about a Web site that is generated by a student on a home computer,

---

19. Bonner and Hines, *Death by Cheeseburger.*

but accessible through computers located both on and off campus? What rights do school officials have to censor this medium? This question was raised in a Missouri case when school officials suspended a student who, using his home computer, posted material on a Web site that was critical of both the school and school administrators, and contained crude and vulgar language. The student, Brandon Beussink, was told to clean up or abandon the Web site and was suspended from school for 10 days. The 10-day suspension resulted in Beussink failing all his classes during that semester. In December of 1998 a U.S. district court issued a preliminary injunction barring the school from enforcing the suspension, saying that the student's First Amendment challenge was very likely to succeed after a trial. The judge acknowledged that schools have narrowly limited rights to censor or punish student speech, but that the school exceeded these limits in this case.[20]

ACCEPTABLE CRITERIA APPLIED TO CENSOR HIGH SCHOOL NEWSPAPERS PRODUCED AS PART OF JOURNALISM CLASS

1. Stories or photos that materially and substantially interfere with the requirements of appropriate school discipline
2. Material that interferes with the rights of students
3. Material that fails to meet standards of academic propriety
4. Material that generates health and welfare concerns
5. Matters that are obscene, indecent, or vulgar

What kinds of content can be censored? Five general categories of material emerge from studying the case law.

1. Publications or stories that materially and substantially interfere with the requirements of appropriate discipline. This is the old *Tinker* standard; its viability remains solid.
2. Material that interferes with the rights of students. This too was a part of the *Tinker* standard. The school can protect students from damage to their reputation or invasion of their privacy. The school can also protect itself from liability in such instances.
3. School-sponsored newspapers can be censored for reasons of academic propriety, what the court in *Hazelwood* called "legitimate pedagogical concerns." This rationale is potentially boundless and includes everything from censoring stories that are ungrammatical or poorly written, to blue-penciling stories about topics that school administrators believe are inappropriate for students of high school age, to cutting stories that might interfere with the school's basic educational mission. This

---

20. *Beussink v. Woodland R-IV School District,* E.D.Mo., No. 1–98 CV00093 RWS, 12/28/98.

criterion supports censorship by administrators who fear damage to the school's image, since such damage might make it harder for the school to operate successfully. For example, administrators at a high school in Port Townsend, Wash., forbade the publication of an article in the school newspaper regarding allegations by several students—some of whom agreed to have their names used—that they had been sexually harassed by a school staff member. The publication of the story could disrupt the classroom, administrators said. Arguably, however, it would be much more difficult for school officials to censor extracurricular publications for these reasons.

4. Material that generates health and welfare concerns. School officials may censor stories and especially advertising that deals with tobacco and alcohol products, sexual behavior, and so on. This category is another seemingly open-ended one that can probably be applied to school-sponsored and nonsponsored publications with equal vigor.

5. Matters that are obscene, vulgar, or indecent. Obscenity is a narrowly, if not precisely, defined category of speech (see *Miller* v. *California* in Chapter 13). It is doubtful a high school publication would attempt to print such matter. Vulgarity and indecency, however, are open-ended kinds of concepts. The Supreme Court dealt with this issue in a 1986 ruling, *Fraser* v. *Bethel School District*,[21] a case involving a student speech. The ruling applies equally to newspapers, however.

A student named Matthew Fraser spoke before a student assembly on behalf of his friend who was running for a student government post. Fraser's speech, which he cleared beforehand with three teachers, contained the following remarks about his friend: "He is a man who is firm, he's firm in his pants, firm in his shirt, his character is firm—but most of all his belief in you, the students of Bethel, is firm." The speech contained another, similar double entendre. Fraser was suspended from school for two days by school officials who claimed the speech was obscene and vulgar.

Chief Justice Warren Burger wrote the high court's opinion that upheld Fraser's suspension. "The undoubted freedom to advocate unpopular and controversial views in schools must be balanced against the society's countervailing interest in teaching students the boundaries of socially appropriate behavior," the chief justice wrote. The schools could reasonably conclude, he said, that the essential lessons of civil, mature conduct cannot be conveyed in a school that tolerates "lewd or offensive speech." Burger added that the "pervasive sexual innuendo" in Fraser's speech was plainly offensive to both teachers and students.[22] Dissenter John Paul Stevens questioned whether "a group of judges who are at least two generations and three thousand miles away from the scene of the crime" were as well-qualified as Fraser to determine whether the speech would offend his contemporaries, who went on to elect the candidate for whom he spoke.

Although censorship of any kind is a problem, what deeply troubles most observers is the elasticity of many of the concepts used to justify the censorship of school newspapers,

"The undoubted freedom to advocate unpopular and controversial views in schools must be balanced against the society's countervailing interest in teaching students the boundaries of socially appropriate behavior."

21. 106 S. Ct. 3159 (1986).
22. *Fraser* v. *Bethel School District*, 106 S. Ct. 3159 (1986).

concepts like academic propriety, health and welfare, vulgarity. An additional problem is that the advisor to the newspaper, the adult supervisor, is an employee of the censoring agency, the school district. This person, who is in the best position to fight for the rights of the student journalists, may literally be putting a teaching career on the line if petty school administrators choose to use the annual teacher evaluation to punish an outspoken advisor.

CENSORSHIP OF COLLEGE NEWSPAPERS

It is more difficult to outline the power of school authorities to censor college newspapers; there are fewer court decisions. The court ruling that gave college and university journalists First Amendment protection actually preceded the *Tinker* decision by two years. In 1967 a U.S. district court in Alabama ruled that the administration at Troy State College could not punish student Gary Dickey because he refused to print an article approved by the administration in place of an editorial that it had banned. The editorial was critical of the state legislature and governor. Dickey instead left a blank space in the newspaper under the headline he had chosen and wrote "Censored" across the blank space. The court ruled that the "state cannot force a college student to forfeit his constitutionally protected right of freedom of expression as a condition to his attending a state-supported institution . . . where the exercise of that right does not materially and substantially interfere with . . . the operation of the school."[23] Since 1967 both the spirit and intent of this ruling have remained largely intact.[24]

Although the Supreme Court sidestepped the question of whether the *Hazelwood* ruling applied to college and university publications, a 1999 decision by the 6th U.S. Circuit Court of Appeals suggests that it does. In 1997 a U.S. district court ruled that the administrators at Kentucky State University, a public school in Frankfort, had the right to confiscate and withhold distribution of the entire 2,000 copies of the school's yearbook.[25] Administrators at the school cited as reasons for the confiscation the yearbook's overall lack of quality, the fact that the color of the cover did not match the school's colors, the yearbook's title ("Destination Unknown"), a lack of captions under photographs, and the inclusion of too many photographs depicting current events and celebrities. The students appealed the ruling, but the appellate court affirmed the lower-court decision despite the fact that the yearbook was not produced as a part of any class, a seemingly critical element in the *Hazelwood* ruling. The court ruled in a 2–1 decision that the students had failed to prove that the university intended at any time to relinquish control of the yearbook to the students, and thus the school was entitled to regulate the yearbook in a reasonable manner. It was reasonable, the court said, for the school to confiscate the book if administrators believed it failed to accomplish its intended purpose. Judge Alan Norris wrote:

> It is no doubt reasonable that KSU [Kentucky State University] should seek to maintain its image to potential students, alumni, and the general public. In light

---

23. *Dickey* v. *Alabama State Board of Education,* 273 F. Supp. 613 (1967).
24. See, for example, *Thonen* v. *Jenkins,* 491 F. 2d 722 (1973) and *Lentz* v. *Clemson University,* 24 M.L.R. 1765 (1995).
25. *Kincaid* v. *Gibson,* Civ. No. 95-98, E.D. Ky., 11/14/97.

IN the SPIRIT of THINGS!

A page from the edition of the Kentucky State University yearbook that was confiscated by school officials because they said they did not approve of its content.
Courtesy, Student Press Law Center/Photo by David Hathcox.

of the undisputedly [sic] poor quality of the yearbook, it is also reasonable that KSU might cut its losses by refusing to distribute a university publication that might tarnish, rather than enhance, that image.[26]

The court dismissed arguments that the action violated the students' First Amendment rights, supporting the trial court's notion that the students failed to demonstrate any injury because of the actions of the school. The students asked for an en banc rehearing of the case. Failing that, an appeal to the Supreme Court is contemplated, according to officials at the Student Press Law Center.

In a 1994 speech to college newspaper advisers, Mark Goodman listed some of the most important threats to the freedom of the campus press. College journalists are not immune from harassment by police and prosecutors (see Chapter 10), the executive director of the Student Press Law Center said.[27] Student journalists have difficulty gaining access to reports on faculty performance, student government meetings, and school disciplinary hearings. Gaining information on the latter kind of proceeding is a special problem since university administrators routinely push serious crimes like hazing, gay bashing, embezzlement, and sexual assault from the legal system into university disciplinary hearings, Goodman said. Advertising for

26. *Kincaid* v. *Gibson,* 191 F 3d 719 (1999).
27. Garneau, "Top 10 Threats," 31.

alcohol has been attacked, as well as advertising for other controversial products and ideas. Letters to the editors and commentaries written by columnists, especially conservative columnists, are frequently the target of protests. Although the federal courts have spoken sharply and clearly on the constitutionality of censoring newspapers by reducing their funding (see pages 94–95), this issue remains a critical one for college journalists. Traditionally censorship takes the form of sanctions against a journalist or publication, but Goodman notes that in the 1990s the theft of campus newspapers by those who disagree with material published in the newspaper is a growing problem. Thirty to 40 such thefts occur each year, and police often decline to even pursue the thieves because the campus newspapers are free, Goodman reported. The entire press run of The Daily Californian, the free student newspaper at the University of California at Berkeley, was stolen in November 1996. The 23,000 copies were apparently taken to protest an editorial printed in that edition that supported a state referendum to end affirmative action programs.

Attempts by the college press to report crimes that occur on campus are often blocked by college and university officials. Many post-secondary educational institutions are scrambling to keep their classrooms filled with new students. News reports about rapes, assaults, burglaries, robberies, and other crimes are not considered good publicity for the schools. A lot of administrators like to pretend their campuses are immune from the problems that take place in the real world. But crime is a fact of life on campus. Researchers at Cornell University and Southern Illinois University reported in 1997 that nearly one million college students may be carrying weapons. Three students at the University of Cincinnati were charged with starting a dormitory fire that forced the evacuation of 700 students and resulted in $200,000 in damage to the building. Twenty-four robberies occurred in a one-month period at the University of Pennsylvania. In addition, a research associate was stabbed to death and a student was shot and wounded as he fled a holdup.[28]

Administrators often cite a 25-year-old-federal law when they try to keep reporters away from campus police reports. The Family Educational Rights and Privacy Act (see page 355 for an outline of this law) was adopted to provide students with greater access to their own school records while ensuring the confidentiality of educational records (transcripts, results on tests, etc.). Some campus administrators have argued that crime reports that name students as victims, suspects, or even witnesses are educational records and hence inaccessible under this law. If the press cannot see the police reports, the stories can't be written. In the early 1990s the U.S. Department of Education endorsed this novel interpretation of the law and warned colleges and universities that the disclosure of the names or identities of students noted in the police reports could result in a loss of federal funding.

The Student Press Law Center won a federal court order blocking the Department of Education from enforcing its threatened action.[29] Congress has also stepped in, with both the House and Senate approving legislation altering the federal law to exclude all law enforcement records. In addition the Congress considered an even broader measure to ensure access

28. Paulk, "Campus Crime."
29. *Student Press Law Center* v. *Alexander,* 778 F. Supp. 1227 (1991); see also *Bauer* v. *Kincaid,* 759 F. Supp. 575 (1991).

to crime reports as a part of the Reauthorization of the Higher Education Act. The Accuracy in Campus Crime Reporting Act was drafted by the Society of Professional Journalists, a victims' rights group, and a coalition of organizations representing both student and professional journalists.[30] It had not been adopted as of the spring of 2000.

In 1997 the Ohio Supreme Court ruled that records of student disciplinary hearings at Miami University were not educational records as defined by the Family Educational Rights and Privacy Act. The school's newspaper sought to see the records under the state's open records law when university administrators blocked its access to the material. In its opinion the court noted, "Unfortunately, at present, crimes and other student misconduct are escalating at campuses across the nation. For potential students, and their parents, it is imperative that they are made aware of all campus crime statistics and other types of student misconduct in order to make an intelligent decision of which university to attend."[31]

Differences Between College and High School Newspapers

College and university student newspapers have some advantages over their high school counterparts in fending off attempts at censorship. First, most four-year college and university newspapers are not produced as a part of the curriculum at the school, as is typical of most high school newspapers. Typically, the newspaper is produced in a school building but generates most of its revenue from its own advertising sales. Student fees often provide a small but important part of the newspaper's income. A board of student publications, usually made up of students and faculty, nominally oversees the publication, selecting the editor and appointing an advisor to guide the newspaper.

A second advantage the college newspaper journalist has is the age of the audience. The high court in the *Fraser* case noted with dismay that the young man's speech was accessible to impressionable 13- and 14-year-olds. The college audience is adult in all but name.

Finally, courts have actually encouraged public college and university administrators to keep their hands off the operation of the school papers. There are numerous rulings in both state and federal courts that if a college or university does not censor or control the content of the school newspaper, it cannot be held liable for what the students publish.[32] The basis for this well-settled holding is that the constitutional guarantee of freedom of expression protects the press from government censorship, and this protection applies with no less force on college campuses than it does in the community at large. University newspapers are not immune from censorship, however. At many schools content control by the administration is a fact of life. This is especially true at private colleges, particularly those operated by a religious organization. Censorship also takes place at some public universities, especially smaller colleges.

Three reasons more than any others seem to be used to justify censorship of college newspapers. The first is disruption of the school, and this includes material that may interfere

---

30. Paulk, "Campus Crime."
31. *Ohio ex rel The Miami Student* v. *Miami University,* 79 Ohio St. 3d 168 (1997).
32. *Lentz* v. *Clemson University,* 24 M.L.R. 1765 (1995). See also *Scovil* v. *Bd. of Educ.,* 425 F. 2d 10 (1970) and *Quarterman* v. *Byrd,* 453 F. 2d 54 (1971).

with the purpose of the university or may interfere with the message the university is attempting to communicate to both its students and to the larger community. For example, the school will argue that it welcomes all students to campus. Articles that are racially insensitive interfere with this message.

Universities have argued as well that students need to be protected from offensive speech and contend that racist material is so harmful to minorities that it should not be protected by the First Amendment. Finally, colleges and universities have attempted to justify censorship on the grounds that it is in the school's interest to ensure that certain beliefs or ideas are not attributed to the school. The question of whether college publications are official university publications or student publications often makes it difficult to determine who is speaking in the campus newspaper.

Reducing Publication Funding

College newspapers also face threats of reduced financial support as a means of punishing them for past improprieties or to ensure future good behavior. It is not terribly hard for a school to drop its financial support for a campus newspaper. But it is harder now than it was prior to an important court ruling in 1983, the case of *Stanley* v. *McGrath.*[33]

At the end of the 1978–79 school year, the University of Minnesota Daily published its "Finals Edition," which offended thousands of persons both on and off the Twin Cities campus. "The newspaper," wrote University of Minnesota journalism professor Don Gillmor, "through gabble and toilet talk, was designed to irritate Third World students, Blacks, Jews, feminists, gays, lesbians, and Christians."[34] Through what it called an exclusive interview with Jesus Christ, the newspaper "revealed" to readers that Christ was a druggie, a bootlegger, a lecher, and a homosexual, for example.

The newspaper, the university administration, and the board of regents were inundated with complaints from all segments of the state's population. Hundreds of students were upset enough to begin a drive to change the student-fee support system for the newspaper. The Daily is typical of many university newspapers in that a small portion of student activity fees—in this case $2 per student per semester—was automatically given to the newspaper. It was suggested that students should be given the right to choose not to support the newspaper. The regents liked this idea as well, and despite the advice of two review committees, which recommended just the opposite, voted in 1980 for a refundable fee system that would permit students to refuse to financially support the newspaper. A court case resulted, and in 1983 the U.S. Court of Appeals for the 8th Circuit ruled that the regents' action violated the First Amendment. If the fee system had been changed, the court said, simply to respond to student complaints of being coerced into supporting views in the newspaper that they opposed, there would be no problem. But the Daily carried a wide variety of views, something for virtually everyone on campus. More importantly, it was clear under the circumstances that the fee system was

33. 719 F. 2d 279 (1983).
34. Gillmor, "The Fragile First," 277.

changed because the regents were unhappy with the 1979 Finals Edition. "Several Regents tes-tified that one of the reasons that they voted in favor of the resolution was that students should not be forced to support a paper which was sacrilegious and vulgar," the court noted. The heavy political pressure on the regents and their two resolutions deploring the content in the Finals Edition added weight to the conclusion that they were attempting to punish the news-paper. Finally, the University of Minnesota has several state campuses, but the fee-support sys-tem was changed only on the Twin Cities campus, home of the offending newspaper. "Our study of the record . . . leaves us with the definite and firm conviction that this change in fund-ing would not have occurred absent the public hue and cry that the *Daily*'s offensive contents provoked. Reducing the revenues available to the newspaper is therefore forbidden by the First Amendment," the court concluded.[35]

"Reducing the revenues available to the newspaper is therefore forbidden by the First Amendment."

Reducing the financial support for a student newspaper is clearly something a school administrator or school board can do—but only if it is done for the proper reasons. Any hint that censorship is behind the reduction could result in such an action running afoul of the First Amendment.

BOOK BANNING

In 1995 author David Guterson's novel "Snow Falling on Cedars" was named book of the year by the American Booksellers Association and won the prestigious PEN/Faulkner Award. The book, a story about a Japanese-American man charged with murdering a fellow salmon fish-erman in Washington state after World War II, was on The New York Times best-seller list for more than a year and has sold in excess of three million copies. But the administrators at the high school in Boerne, Texas, a small community about 30 miles northwest of San Antonio, ruled in September of 1999 that the book was unfit for senior English students to read. The book, they said, contained too much profanity, graphic violence, racial bigotry, and sex. Eng-lish teacher Frances Riley, who assigned the book with the approval of the administration, said she assigned the book to teach students about morals, values, and issues. Administrators revoked the authorization after receiving a few complaints, and Riley faced disciplinary action. Most students supported using the book and said that many of their fellow students who protested against using the book were not offended by the content of the novel but were distressed because the book was 460 pages long*. At the same time parents of elementary stu-dents at schools in many states were protesting classroom readings of the wildly popular Harry Potter books (for example, "Harry Potter and the Sorcerer's Stone"), because, the par-ents claimed, the books were anti-Christian. The books, written by Scottish author J.K. Rowl-ing, contain tales of witchcraft, evil spells, and magic. According to a report in The New York Times, there was a whispering campaign suggesting that the success of the books—five mil-lion hardcover and two million paperback books sold in the United States by November of 1999—was evidence of the strength of Satan.[36]

35. *Stanley* v. *McGrath,* 719 F. 2d 279 (1983).
36. MacCormack, "No Snow," and Wilgoren, "Don't Give Us Little Wizards."

*In May of 2000 the book was barred from high school reading lists in the South Kitsap, Wa. School district, a community adjacent to the area in which the story in the novel takes place and where Guterson taught for several years.

Book banning is certainly not a new phenomenon in the United States. Periodically the issue rises to the fore, and often intense pressure is put on the nation's librarians to purge the bookshelves of what the protesters call smut, racist, or anti-Semitic matter; satanic or anti-Christian tracts; or attacks on American values. Book censors have also complained about books that depict unorthodox family arrangements; speculations about Christ; sexual explicitness (even in a biological context); unflattering portraits of American authority; criticism of American authority and business and corporate practices; and radical political philosophy. (See the following box for a list of books commonly attacked by parents and school officials.)

LIST OF COMMONLY BANNED BOOKS

Several books by Judy Blume, a best-selling children's author

"Daddy's Roommate" by Michael Wilhoite

"Heather Has Two Mommies" by Leslea Newman

"Scary Stories to Tell in the Dark" by Alvin Schwartz

"The Bridge to Terabithia" by Katherine Paterson

"The Chocolate War" by Robert Cormier

"The Diary of Anne Frank"

"Manchild in the Promised Land" by Claude Brown

"The Martian Chronicles" by Ray Bradbury

"Catch-22" by Joseph Heller

"Where the Sidewalk Ends" by Shel Silverstein

"One Flew Over the Cuckoo's Nest" by Ken Kesey

The "Goosebumps" series by R.L. Stine

"One Day in the Life of Ivan Denisovitch" by Aleksander Solzhenitsyn

The American Heritage Dictionary

The Dictionary of American Slang

"Understanding AIDS and Your Immune System"

"Our Bodies, Ourselves" by the Boston Women's Health Book Collective

"Clan of the Cave Bear" by Jean Auel

"Of Mice and Men" by John Steinbeck

"Show Me," a sex education book

"I Know Why the Caged Bird Sings" by Maya Angelou

"Oliver Twist" by Charles Dickens

"A Farewell to Arms" by Ernest Hemingway

"1984" by George Orwell

"Brave New World" by Aldous Huxley

"The Catcher in the Rye" by J.D. Salinger

"The Grapes of Wrath" by John Steinbeck

"The Adventures of Huckleberry Finn" by Mark Twain

"The Merchant of Venice" by William Shakespeare

"Annie on My Mind" by Nancy Garden

The most recent episode of book banning activity reached a peak level in the mid-1990s. Attacks on the libraries have slowly declined since then, according to a study by the American

Library Assocation.[37] Attempts to ban books from school and public libraries occur all over the nation, although efforts appear to be the strongest in the South, Southwest, and along the West Coast. While locally mounted, the attacks are usually orchestrated by one of a number of national groups with names like National Citizens for Excellence in Education, Association of Christian Educators, the Eagle Forum, or Concerned Women for America. In recent years much of the censorship attack has shifted to public school curriculum materials. Textbooks—especially those that discuss evolution—have been the target of protests in many school districts. In Oak Harbor, Wash., members of a local chapter of Citizens for Excellence in Education attempted to force the school board to remove a fourth-grade reader in the "Impressions" series. Complaints about the reader, which contains myriad well-known stories and essays, included assertions that the stories taught the occult and witchcraft, encouraged children to steal and disobey their parents, and taught New Age religion. For example, members of the pressure group argued that a condensed version of "The Wizard of Oz" contained in the book "teaches children that human traits like courage and compassion are gained through one's own efforts and not bestowed as gifts from God."

In this case the school board voted unanimously to retain the book, but in many other instances local pressure succeeded in forcing the opposite decision. Unfortunately, most school board members are woefully unprepared to deal with an organized campaign against parts of the school curriculum or books contained in the library. And the courts have given little guidance in this matter. The Supreme Court has looked at this issue but once, and its somewhat ambiguous ruling left many questions unanswered.

Members of the Board of Education of the Island Trees School District in eastern New York removed nine books from the high school library. Included among the banished books were "The Fixer" by Bernard Malamud, "Slaughterhouse Five" by Kurt Vonnegut, "The Naked Ape" by Desmond Morris, "Soul on Ice" by Eldridge Cleaver, and the "Best Short Stories by Negro Writers." Student council president Steven Pico and four other students challenged this action in the U.S. district court. They argued that their First Amendment rights to read these books had been violated. But U.S. District Judge George Pratt rejected these arguments and ruled that a school board has the right to remove books that are irrelevant, vulgar, immoral, and in bad taste. The First Amendment was not violated by such action, Pratt ruled, citing a seven-year-old U.S. Court of Appeals decision, *President's Council District 25* v. *Community School Board.*[38] The judge's ruling came on the board of education's motion for summary judgment. No trial was ever held to establish the facts, including the school board's motives for removing these volumes.[39]

The U.S. Court of Appeals for the 2nd Circuit reversed Judge Pratt's order and ordered the district court to hold a trial. The appellate court stood by its earlier decision that permitted school authorities to remove vulgar or immoral books from the school library. But the court ruled that Steven Pico and the other students should have been given a chance at trial to persuade the court that the school board's ostensible justification for removing the books (that

37. Sterngold, "For Artistic Freedom."
38. 457 F. 2d 566 (1972).
39. *Pico* v. *Island Trees,* 474 F. Supp. 387 (1979).

they were in bad taste, vulgar, etc.) was merely a pretext for the suppression of freedom of speech. The board could not ban the books if their decision to remove them was based on their political or moral disagreement with the content of the works.[40]

In March 1982 the Supreme Court heard arguments in the case and three months later affirmed the court of appeals decision and returned the case to district court for trial. However, the high court was fractured into several groups, and seven different opinions were written.

The court's opinion was written by Justice William Brennan. A school board cannot, under the First Amendment, remove books from a school library simply because it disapproves of the political ideas or philosophies expressed in the books, wrote Justice Brennan. Books may be removed if they are persuasively vulgar or if they are educationally unsuitable. But the First Amendment guarantees to students a right to receive ideas, and the board of education cannot interfere with that right simply because it disagrees with those ideas. Brennan mustered the support of justices Thurgood Marshall and John Stevens behind his opinion.

A school board cannot, under the First Amendment, remove books from a school library simply because it disapproves of the political ideas or philosophies expressed in the books.

Justice Harry Blackmun concurred with all of Brennan's opinion except his reference to a "right to receive ideas," a controversial notion Brennan promulgated. Blackmun said he based his opinion on a principle narrower and far more basic than the right to receive ideas. The state may not suppress exposure to ideas for the sole purpose of suppressing exposure to those ideas, he wrote. The fifth vote in the 5–4 decision came from Justice Byron White, who seemed dismayed at Brennan's exploration of constitutional issues. A trial was needed, he said, to find out what motivated the removal of the books. When the facts are established, he wrote, the court can develop constitutional law on the matter.

Chief Justice Warren Burger and Justices Lewis Powell, William Rehnquist, and Sandra O'Connor all dissented. All the dissenting opinions reflected the position that it was the responsibility of the school board, not of a federal court, to run the school. "The plurality [Brennan, Marshall, Blackmun, and Stevens] concludes that the Constitution requires school boards to justify to its teenage pupils the decision to remove a particular book from a school library,"[41] Burger wrote. Other dissenters echoed Burger's complaint.

The ruling was particularly unsatisfactory because the court failed to provide any clear guidance on an issue that is plaguing scores of school libraries across the nation. The splits within the court left even a careful reader of the decision with little certainty about how the court would act in a subsequent case. Four justices said school boards cannot remove books from a library for political or moral reasons; four justices said school boards can remove books for any reason; and Justice White refused to say where he stands on the issue. "We should not decide constitutional questions until it is necessary to do so," he wrote. Even the language in the court's opinion lacks clarity. Brennan said that a book can be removed from the shelves if it is "persuasively vulgar" or "educationally unsuitable." What do these terms mean?

While attempts to ban books increase each year, few of these disputes have found their way into the courts. And when they have, the high court's decision in Pico has proved to be a

---

40. *Pico* v. *Island Trees,* 638 F. 2d 404 (1980).
41. *Island Trees* v. *Pico,* 457 U.S. 853 (1982).

flawed precedent. The 5th U.S. Circuit Court of Appeals, faced with what appeared to be a blatant attempt to remove a book on the basis of ideology from all the public schools in St. Tammany Parish, La., refused to grant a summary judgment to parents opposed to this censorship.[42] The book, "Voodoo and Hoodoo," by Jim Haskins, is a serious, scholarly work that outlines the foundations of African tribal religion and discusses how it evolved after it was transplanted to the United States by slaves brought to the Western Hemisphere. The second half of the work includes a description of various spells, tricks, and hexes. Both a school-level committee and a parishwide appeals committee said the book should be available to students in the eighth grade and above who have written permission from their parents. The school board, however, voted 12–2 to ban the book, ignoring the committee recommendations. One member said the book promoted practices that were not conducive to sound moral values. A U.S. district court overturned the school board decision, ruling that the action was taken only to deny students access to ideas that board members believed were objectionable. But the court of appeals overturned this ruling and sent the case back to the district court for a trial to determine the specific reasons for the removal of the book.

A federal district court in Kansas also ruled that it was necessary to hold a trial to determine specifically why the school board of United School District No. 233 near Kansas City removed the book "Annie on My Mind," by Nancy Garden, from school libraries.[43] The book, which describes a fictional relationship between two girls, won many awards, including the American Library Association designation as Best of the Best Books for Young Adults. The book contains no vulgarity, offensive language, or explicit sexual conduct, but was deemed by some members of the board of education to be a "glorification of the gay lifestyle." At the trial, school board members said the book was educationally unsuitable, parroting the rationale outlined by Justice Brennan in *Pico*. The court, however, called this testimony incredible and said what board members really meant was that they disagreed with the ideas expressed in the book. The court ordered the book back on library shelves.[44] In this case censors failed to ban a book with which they disagreed. But the litigation process was long and costly, and school board members failed only because a trial judge refused to accept their sworn assertions that the work in question was "educationally unsuitable."

No Supreme Court decision since 1982 has helped to clarify the meaning of the ruling in *Pico*. But school administrators have taken the strong mandate given to them in *Hazelwood School District* v. *Kuhlmeier*[45] to censor student publications and used it to justify the removal of books and other curricular material about which parents and other groups have complained. Courts have ruled such actions are permissible since they relate to the legitimate pedagogical concerns noted by the Supreme Court in *Hazelwood*.[46]

42. *Campbell* v. *St. Tammany Parish School Board*, 64 F. 3d 184 (1995).
43. *Case* v. *United School District No. 233*, 895 F. Supp. 1463 (1995).
44. *Case* v. *United School District No. 233*, 908 F. Supp. 864 (1995).
45. 108 S. Ct. 562 (1988).
46. Kaplan, "Removal of Books," 259.

SUMMARY

In the 1960s courts ruled that both high school and college students enjoyed the rights of freedom of expression guaranteed by the First Amendment. But despite a seemingly broad First Amendment ruling by the Supreme Court in the case of *Tinker* v. *Des Moines,* lower courts refused to apply the high court's mandate and the censorship of high school publications and presentations continued. In 1988 even the Supreme Court turned its back on *Tinker* and gave high school authorities broad rights of censorship over newspapers produced as a part of the journalism curriculum. Today school authorities may censor publications or presentations for legitimate academic reasons. They may also censor stories that materially and substantially interfere with the requirements of discipline in the school, that interfere with the rights of students, that generate health and welfare concerns, and that are obscene or vulgar. Censorship in the high school press is common at many schools; at other institutions, however, journalism seems to be robust. The college press suffers less censorship, but recently attempts have been made to censor college and university publications that present material deemed by authorities to be "politically incorrect," that present the college or administrators in a bad light, or that report on crime on the campus.

Book banning, a traditional problem in the United States, has been more intensive in the past decade because the courts have failed to articulate specific standards to guide school administrators and, at the same time, protect the rights of students.

TIME, PLACE, AND MANNER RESTRICTIONS

Most attempts by the government to use prior censorship are based on the content of the material it seeks to censor. National security interests may be at stake, or a school official might fear that a news story in a student newspaper deals with a subject too mature for high school students. But the government can also base its attempts at prior censorship on other factors—specifically, the time, the place, or the manner of the communication. There would certainly be few content-based objections to an individual presenting a speech on how to grow mushrooms. But the government (as well as citizens) would surely object if the speaker wanted to give the speech while standing in the middle of Main Street, or on a sidewalk at 2 a.m. in a residential neighborhood. These are called **time, place, and manner restrictions.**

But the government can also base its attempts at prior censorship on other factors—specifically, the time, the place, or the manner of the communication.

Such rules generate no serious First Amendment problems so long as they meet a set of criteria the courts have developed during the past 50 years. Let's look at the criteria first, and then see how they have been applied.

1. **The rule must be content neutral, both on its face and in the manner in which it is applied.** A rule that is content neutral is applied the same way to all communications, regardless of what is said or printed. Oftentimes a community will pass regulations limiting the distribution of certain kinds of material but not other kinds of material. Brentwood, Tenn., adopted an ordinance prohibiting the

distribution of commercial handbills in public places. But the law did not prohibit the distribution of newspapers, or political or religious material in these same places. The Tennessee Supreme Court ruled that this law was not content neutral.[47] And the U.S. Court of Appeals struck down a Gladstone, Mo., ordinance that prohibited landowners from placing political signs on their property more than 30 days prior to an election. The court said the ordinance was not content neutral, that it singled out political speech for special regulation.[48] Sometimes a law will appear to be content neutral but is not because of the way it is applied. The most common problem in such a law is that it gives a government official too much discretion in deciding when the law should be applied and when it shouldn't. A Clark County (Las Vegas), Nev., ordinance banned the distribution of advertising leaflets along Las Vegas Boulevard, commonly called the Las Vegas Strip. Officials said the canvassers who passed out the leaflets advertising erotic dance entertainment services interfered with the flow of pedestrian traffic, among other objections. The 9th U.S. Circuit Court of Appeals ruled that the ordinance was content based because it applied only to persons distributing commercial handbills. If the flow of pedestrian traffic along the Strip was a problem, the court asked, where was the evidence that only distributors of commercial handbills caused the problem? Didn't persons handing out noncommercial materials likewise interfere with pedestrians?[49]

In 1992 the Supreme Court struck down a county ordinance in Georgia that forced persons or groups seeking to have a rally or march to pay up to $1,000 to help defray county expenses in providing extra police protection and other services.[50] The fee was variable and was supposed to reflect the county's costs, but whether it included all costs or just some, or whether the fee was required at all, was left to the discretion of the county administrator. "The decision [of] how much to charge for police protection or administration time—or even whether to charge at all—is left to the whim of the administrator," wrote Justice Harry Blackmun. "There are no articulated standards either in the ordinance or in the county's established practice," he added in the 5–4 ruling.[51]

2. **The law must not constitute a complete ban on a kind of communication.** There must be some alternative means of accomplishing this communication. In the 1980s several states sought to ban exit polling outside voting booths. The polling was conducted by the news media for several reasons, including an attempt to find out what kind of people (age, political affiliation, occupation, etc.) voted for which candidates. Many of these statutes were struck down at least in part, the courts

---

47. *H & L Messengers v. Brentwood,* 577 S.W. 2d 444 (1979).
48. *Whitton v. Gladstone,* 354 F. 3d. 1400 (1995).
49. *S.O.C. v. Clark County, Nevada* 26 M.L.R. 2198 (1998).
50. *Forsyth County v. The Nationalist Movement,* 112 S. Ct. 2395 (1992).
51. *Forsyth County v. The Nationalist Movement,* 112 S. Ct. 2395 (1992).

GUIDELINES FOR TIME, PLACE, AND
MANNER RESTRICTIONS

1. Rules must be content neutral.
2. Rules must not constitute a complete ban on communication.
3. Rules must be justified by a substantial state interest.
4. Rules must be narrowly tailored.

---

ruled, because the press could not ask these questions at any other place or in any other manner and expect to get the same data. There is no assurance, for example, that persons responding to such questions in a telephone survey had voted for anyone.[52] The ban on exit polling, then, constituted a complete ban on the kind of questions reporters sought to ask.

3. **The state must articulate a substantial interest to justify this restraint on speech.** A ban against using loudspeakers to communicate a political message after 10 p.m. could surely be justified on the grounds that most people are trying to sleep at that time. A ban against passing out literature and soliciting money in the passageways between an airport terminal and the boarding ramps could also be justified by the state, which wants to keep these busy areas clear for passengers hurrying to board airplanes.[53] But attempts by the government to ban distribution of handbills on city streets because many people throw them away and cause a litter problem are typically rejected.[54] The state interest in keeping the streets clean can be accomplished by an anti-litter law. Some communities have attempted to raise aesthetic reasons to justify limiting or banning newspaper boxes. Most courts have refused to permit these concerns alone to justify limits on First Amendment freedoms, especially when so many other common objects on the streets (telephone poles, trash cans, fire hydrants, street signs) are also eyesores.[55] But some courts have accepted this justification. The 3rd U.S. Circuit Court of Appeals permitted the city of Coral Gables, Fla., to require that newspaper boxes be of a certain size, shape, and color.[56] And the 1st U.S. Circuit Court of Appeals in late 1996 approved an ordinance adopted by the Beacon Hill Architectural Commission to ban all newspaper boxes from the public streets of this historic section of Boston. The commission was trying to architecturally restore the district as a reminder of what old Boston looked like in the early days of the commonwealth, a period when there

---

52. See, for example, *Daily Herald* v. *Munro,* 838 F. 2d 380 (1988).
53. See, for example, *International Society for Krishna Consciousness* v. *Wolke,* 453 F. Supp. 869 (1978).
54. *Schneider* v. *New Jersey,* 308 U.S. 147 (1939) and *Miller* v. *Laramie,* 880 P. 2d 594 (1994).
55. See *Providence Journal* v. *Newport,* 665 F. Supp. 107 (1987), and *Multimedia Publishing Co. of South Carolina, Inc.* v. *Greenville-Spartanburg Airport District,* 991 F. 2d 154 (1993).
56. *Gold Coast Publications, Inc.* v. *Corrigan,* 42 F. 3d 1336 (1995).

were no newspaper boxes. The court said that the rule was content neutral, said in this case that aesthetic concerns represented a substantial government interest, and pointed out that there were ample places to buy newspapers within the district.[57]

In addition to asserting a substantial interest, the state is required to bring evidence to court to prove its case. Southwest Texas State University in San Marcos attempted to restrict the distribution of a small community newspaper on its campus. It told the 5th U.S. Circuit Court of Appeals that it sought such restrictions in order to preserve the academic environment and the security of the campus, protect privacy on campus, control traffic, preserve the appearance of the campus, prevent fraud and deception, and eliminate unnecessary expenses. These were all laudable goals, but the court said the university presented no evidence to support the notion that restricting the sale of these newspapers to a few vending machines or direct delivery to subscribers on campus would accomplish these goals. "[T]he burden is on the defendants [university] to show affirmatively that their restriction is narrowly tailored to protect the identified interests. Defendants failed to carry this burden," the court ruled.[58]

4. **The law must be narrowly tailored so that it furthers the state interest that justifies it, but does not restrain more expression than is actually required to further this interest.** "A regulation is narrowly tailored when it does not burden substantially more speech than is necessary to further the government's legitimate interests."[59] Officials in the city of Sylvania, Ga., believed they had a litter problem. The Penny-Saver, a weekly free newspaper, was thrown on the lawn or driveway of each residence in the city. Oftentimes residents just left the paper where it fell. These unclaimed papers were unsightly and sometimes wound up on the street or in the gutter. The city adopted an ordinance that made it illegal to distribute free, printed material in yards, on driveways, or on porches. The publisher of the Penny-Saver sued, claiming the new law was a violation of the First Amendment. The Georgia Supreme Court agreed, rejecting the city's argument that this was a proper time, place, and manner rule. The ordinance was certainly content neutral, but was not narrowly tailored. The law blocked the distribution of the Penny-Saver but also barred political candidates from leaving literature on doorsteps, stopped many religious solicitors who hand out material, and blocked scores of others from passing out pamphlets door-to-door. In addition, the court ruled, the problem could be solved in other ways that do not offend the First Amendment. The city could require either the Penny-Saver publisher or the city residents to retrieve the unclaimed papers or could punish the publisher for papers that end up in the ditch or on the street.[60]

---

57. *Globe Newspaper Company* v. *Beacon Hill Architectural Commission,* 100 F. 3d 175 (1996).
58. *Hays County Guardian* v. *Supple,* 969 F. 2d 111 (1992).
59. *Ward* v. *Rock Against Racism,* 491 U.S. 781 (1989).
60. *Statesboro Publishing Company* v. *City of Sylvania,* 516 S.E. 2d 296 (1999); see also *Houston Chronicle* v. *Houston,* 630 S.W. 2d 444 (1982) and *Denver Publishing Co.* v. *Aurora,* 896 P. 2d 306 (1995).

The City of Los Angeles adopted an ordinance banning the sale of goods or the solicitation of donations along the Venice Beach Boardwalk. The only exceptions were the sale of newspapers or other periodicals and solicitation or selling by nonprofit groups. City officials said the ordinance was needed to protect local merchants from unfair competition and to ensure the free flow of traffic on the boardwalk. The 9th U.S. Circuit Court of Appeals ruled that the ordinance was not narrowly tailored. If the city was truly concerned about unfair competition and traffic flow, there was no justification for allowing some vendors—those who sold newspapers or solicited for nonprofit groups—to use the boardwalk while barring all others. "There is no evidence," the court ruled, "that those without nonprofit status are any more cumbersome upon fair competition or free traffic flow than those with nonprofit status."[61]

A law or rule can be declared invalid for failing to pass any of the four tests listed above. The manner in which the rules are applied by the court (How much justification must the state have? for example) is usually dependent on the kind of place to which the rule applies. The place is called a "forum" in the law, and what is called forum analysis has become quite popular with contemporary judges.

FORUM ANALYSIS

Courts have identified four kinds of forums:

Traditional Public Forum: Traditional public forums are public places that have by long tradition been devoted to assembly and speeches, places like street corners, public parks, the steps in front of a student union building, or a plaza in front of city hall. The highest level of First Amendment protection is given to expression occurring in traditional public forums.

Designated Public Forum: Designated public forums are places created by the government to be used for expressive activities, among other things. A city-owned auditorium, a fairgrounds, a community meeting hall, and even a student newspaper intended to be open for use by all students are examples of designated public forums. First Amendment protections surely apply in such places, but the government has greater power to use time, place, and manner rules to regulate speech and press in these areas than in traditional public forums.

Public Property That Is Not a Public Forum: Some kinds of public property not considered to be public forums are obvious—prisons and military bases, for example. But other kinds of public property are also regarded as off-limits for expressive activity. Concourses leading to boarding areas in airports are not considered public forums, although the public areas in the airport terminal (where the restaurants, shops, and other facilities are located) are likely to be counted as designated public forums.[62] Courts in New York have ruled that subway stations are not public forums;[63] a court in South Dakota said that an interstate highway

61. *Perry* v. *Los Angeles Police Department,* 121 F. 3d 1365 (1997).
62. *International Society for Krishna Consciousness* v. *Lee,* 112 S. Ct. 2701 (1992) and *Lee* v. *International Society for Krishna Consciousness,* 112 S. Ct. 2709 (1992).
63. *Rogers* v. *New York City Transit Authority,* 89 N.Y. 2d 692 (1997).

rest stop is not a public forum;[64] and a U.S. district court in Oklahoma ruled in 1997 that the Oklahoma University computer network used by faculty and students is not a public forum.[65] At least three U.S. Courts of Appeals have had to decide whether the advertising space on the sides and backs of public transit buses constitute public forums. And the answer seems to focus less on where the space is located than on the transit systems' policies regarding the use of the space for advertising. Ad spaces on buses in both Chicago and New York were ruled to be designated public forums because the transit authorities permitted advertising for a wide variety of commercial, noncommercial, and political advertising.[66] The 9th U.S. Circuit Court of Appeals in 1998 ruled that the buses in Phoenix were not public forums because the city only sold space to commercial advertisers. "The city has not designated the advertising space on the exterior of its buses as a place for general discourse," the court said.[67]

Private Property: Owners of private property, which includes everything from a backyard patio to a giant shopping mall, are free to regulate who uses their property for expressive activity. There are no First Amendment guarantees of freedom of expression on private property.

Let's examine briefly how the courts have treated First Amendment rights in a variety of public and private forums.

PUBLIC FORUMS

The public streets have historically been regarded as places where people can speak and distribute handbills, pamphlets, and other materials. But history isn't law, and before 1938 whether public streets were legally open to such activity was not a settled matter. But in the landmark case of *Lovell* v. *Griffin,*[68] the Supreme Court established that the First Amendment protects the distribution as well as the publication of ideas, opinions, and news.

The city of Griffin, Ga., had an ordinance that prohibited distribution of circulars, handbooks, advertising, and literature of any kind without first obtaining written permission from the city manager. Under the law, the city manager had considerable discretion as to whether to give permission. Alma Lovell was a member of the Jehovah's Witnesses religious sect, an intense and ruggedly evangelical order that suffered severe persecution in the first half of this century. But the Witnesses doggedly continued to spread their word, passing out millions of leaflets and pamphlets and attempting to proselytize anyone who would listen.

Alma Lovell didn't even attempt to get a license before she circulated pamphlets, and she was arrested, convicted, and fined $50 for violating the city ordinance. When she refused to pay the fine, she was sentenced to 50 days in jail. At the trial the Jehovah's Witnesses freely admitted the illegal distribution, but argued that the statute was invalid on its face because it violated the First Amendment guarantees of freedom of the press and freedom of religion.

---

64. *Jacobsen* v. *Howard,* 904 F. Supp. 565 (1995).
65. *Loving* v. *Boren,* DC WOkla. No. CIV. 96-657-A 1/28/97.
66. *Planned Parenthood Association/Chicago Area* v. *Chicago Transit Authority,* 767 F. 2d 122 (1985) and *New York Magazine* v. *Metropolitan Transit Authority,* 136 F. 3d 123 (1998).
67. *Children of the Rosary* v. *City of Phoenix,* 154 F. 3d 972 (1998).
68. 303 U.S. 444 (1938).

On appeal the Supreme Court agreed that the law did indeed violate freedom of the press. Chief Justice Charles Evans Hughes wrote, "We think that the ordinance is invalid on its face" because it strikes at the very foundation of freedom of the press by subjecting it to license and censorship. The city argued that the First Amendment applies only to newspapers and regularly published materials like magazines. The high court disagreed, ruling that the amendment applies to pamphlets and leaflets as well: "These indeed have been historic weapons in the defense of liberty, as the pamphlets of Thomas Paine and others in our own history abundantly attest. The press in its historic connotation comprehends every sort of publication which affords a vehicle of information and opinion."[69]

Lawyers for Griffin also argued that the First Amendment was not applicable because the licensing law said nothing about publishing, but only concerned distribution. Again the court disagreed, noting that liberty of circulation is as essential to freedom of expression as liberty of publication. Chief Justice Hughes wrote, "Without the circulation, the publication would be of little value."

"The press in its historic connotation comprehends every sort of publication which affords a vehicle of information and opinion."

Public Streets

Nineteen months after the Lovell decision the Supreme Court handed down a second distribution decision, a ruling involving laws in four different cities. The four cases were decided as one, *Schneider* v. *New Jersey*.[70] A Los Angeles ordinance prohibited the distribution of handbills on public streets on the grounds that distribution contributed to the litter problem. Ordinances in Milwaukee, Wis., and Worcester, Mass., were justified on the same basis—keeping the city streets clean.

An Irvington, N.J., law was far broader, prohibiting street distribution or house-to-house calls unless permission was first obtained from the local police chief. The police department asked distributors for considerable personal information and could reject applicants the law officers deemed not of good character. This action was ostensibly to protect the public against criminals.

The Supreme Court struck down all four city ordinances. Justice Owen Roberts wrote for the court that cities can certainly enact regulations in the interest of public safety, health, and welfare. Pedestrians, for example, could be prohibited from blocking a street or sidewalk in order to distribute pamphlets. And a city can certainly punish persons who litter the streets with paper. But a community cannot justify an ordinance that prohibits the distribution of handbills—conduct that is protected under the First Amendment—by asserting an interest in keeping the streets clean. The fourth ordinance, the one in Irvington, was declared unconstitutional because it was not content neutral. It gave police the discretion to determine who could express their ideas and who could not, Roberts said.[71]

The following year the Supreme Court voided another anti-solicitation law, one enacted in New Haven, Conn. Solicitation of money for religious causes was prohibited unless the

69. *Lovell* v. *Griffin*, 303 U.S. 444 (1938).
70. 308 U.S. 147 (1939).
71. *Schneider* v. *New Jersey*, 308 U.S. 147 (1939).

solicitors first gained the approval of local officials, whose job it was to determine what was and was not a "bona fide object of charity." Justice Roberts, writing for a unanimous court, ruled that a community could, in order to protect its citizens from fraudulent solicitations, require strangers in the community to establish identity and authority to act for the cause they purport to represent. A community could also adopt reasonable rules limiting the time such door-to-door solicitation might be made.

> But to condition the solicitation of aid for the perpetuation of religious views or systems upon a license, the grant of which rests in the exercise of a determination by state authority as to what is a religious cause, is to lay a forbidden burden upon the exercise of a liberty protected by the Constitution.[72]

Other Public Forums

Courts have ruled that a wide variety of public places are public forums for the purpose of communication. Government attempts to regulate speech and press activity in an airport, for example, have frequently been challenged on First Amendment grounds. (See, for example, *International Society for Krishna Consciousness* v. *Wolke*[73] and *International Society for Krishna Consciousness* v. *Lee*.[74]) Airports are created to facilitate air travel, and are often filled with hurried passengers who stream down concourses from one boarding area to another. Courts have generally ruled that the government has the right to limit the distribution of materials in the busy and crowded zones of an airport. Airport terminals, that area often containing shops, restaurants, rental car agencies, and other businesses, are another matter. Generally, First Amendment concerns are more pronounced in these areas and a greater amount of speech activity is permitted. In 1992, however, the Supreme Court issued a pair of rulings that suggested the high court was having difficulty deciding how much solicitation should be permitted in air terminals. In the first case, *International Society for Krishna Consciousness* v. *Lee*,[75] a majority of the court ruled that airport terminals were not traditional public forums and that the government could forbid individuals to use the terminals to solicit money for any cause. But in the companion ruling, the high court declared that a government ban on the distribution of literature in these same terminals was a violation of the First Amendment, even though the terminal was not regarded as a traditional public forum.[76] The first decision was explained in a lengthy opinion written by Chief Justice Rehnquist. The second ruling, however, was contained in a one-paragraph, unsigned opinion. Justices Kennedy and O'Connor shifted their votes in the two cases.

In 1981 the Supreme Court ruled that the state of Minnesota could regulate communication activities by a religious group, the Hare Krishnas, at the Minnesota State Fair. The crowds on the fairgrounds were too thick to permit the Krishnas to perform their ritualistic face-to-face

---

72. *Cantwell* v. *Connecticut,* 310 U.S. 296 (1940).
73. 453 F. Supp. 869 (1978).
74. 925 F. 2d 576 (1991).
75. 112 S. Ct. 2701 (1992).
76. *Lee* v. *International Society for Krishna Consciousness,* 112 S. Ct. 2709 (1992).

solicitations. But the high court added that the group members could mingle with the crowds, talk with people, and propagate their views. The court added that the religious group members should also have the opportunity to have a booth at the fair like scores of other solicitors.[77]

Attempts by communities to regulate the street-corner vending machines that dispense newspapers and other publications is a common issue to confront the courts. Such regulations are permissible so long as the rules meet the normal tests for time, place, and manner rules. In 1988 the Supreme Court voided a Lakewood, Ohio, ordinance because the city tied the placement of the machines to permit fees, insurance requirements, design standards, and any other "such terms and conditions" the mayor deems reasonable and necessary. The high court ruled that the ordinance was invalid because it gave the mayor unbridled authority to reject a permit request. "It is apparent that the face of the ordinance itself contains not explicit limits on the mayor's discretion," wrote Justice William Brennan.[78] A similar regulation, struck down in New York, required vending machine owners to obtain permission from the city attorney to place their boxes on the streets, but the city council failed to give the city attorney any criteria to apply in the placement of these machines.[79]

What kind of regulations are permissible? Generally, fees or license costs are permissible.[80] Some states require that the fees can be no higher than necessary to cover the actual administrative cost of providing the permit.[81] Regulations regarding the location of the stands are also permissible, so long as they are reasonable. Rules that prohibit the placing of stands too close to fire hydrants or crosswalks are clearly acceptable. And it is possible to ban newsstands completely from some parts of a community. But the government must justify such a total ban.[82]

Finally, rules on clustering or limits on the number of stands on a single corner are possible. California courts approved a Glendale ordinance that permits only eight newsstands in any one location and 16 on each side of a block. The ordinance also employed a preference system for newspapers wishing to place stands on the streets, giving priority to newspapers that are published most frequently and circulated most widely in Los Angeles County. The court said that space was limited and the city had an obligation to allocate it. The preference for one kind of newspaper over another was "simply a means of balancing the problem of public demand and supply."[83]

Several states and cities have attempted to regulate the placement of billboards, with mixed results. The problem in such regulation is coping with the rights of store owners to advertise their businesses. The dilemma is best illustrated by a 1981 U.S. Supreme Court ruling on a San Diego billboard ordinance. The ordinance prohibited all outdoor advertising except on-site commercial signs that promoted goods or services offered by businesses on the premises. That is, owners of hardware stores could erect on their property signs that advertised

77. *Heffron* v. *International Society,* 452 U.S. 640 (1981).
78. *Lakewood* v. *Plain Dealer Publishing Co.,* 486 U.S. 750 (1988).
79. *New York City* v. *American School Publications,* 509 N.E. 2d 311 (1987).
80. *Phoenix Newspapers, Inc.* v. *Tucson Airport Authority,* 22 M.L.R. 1504 (1993).
81. See *Jacobsen* v. *Crivaro,* 15 M.L.R. 1958 (1988).
82. *Chicago Newspaper Publishers Association* v. *Wheaton,* 697 F. Supp. 1464 (1988); and *Globe Newspaper Co.* v. *Beacon Hill Architectural Commission,* 847 F. Supp. 178 (1994).
83. *Socialist Labor Party* v. *Glendale,* 82 Cal. App. 3d 722 (1978).

materials sold in the hardware store. Acknowledging that the ban was prompted by substantial state interests in the aesthetic quality of the city and in traffic safety, the Supreme Court nevertheless struck down the city law. The flaw in the ordinance was the broad exemption granted for on-site commercial speech. "Insofar as the city tolerates billboards at all," Justice White wrote in the plurality court opinion, "it cannot choose to limit their content to commercial messages." The law is not content neutral; it reaches into the realm of protected speech, he wrote. To be constitutional, then, the ordinance must allow noncommercial (Save the Whales, Abortion Is a Crime, etc.) on-site billboards as well. A total ban on billboards, if properly justified, might also be acceptable.[84] But courts have permitted governments to regulate the content of billboards. The 4th U.S. Circuit Court of Appeals rejected First Amendment challenges to two ordinances adopted by Baltimore in the mid-1990s.[85] Outdoor advertisements for both alcoholic beverages and cigarettes were banned from certain parts of the city. The ordinances were based on the desire by city officials to keep such messages out of places where children were more likely to see them, such as close to schools. The Supreme Court refused to hear an appeal of both rulings.

"Insofar as the city tolerates billboards at all, it cannot choose to limit their content to commercial messages."

Are public television stations public forums? Does the public have a right to participate in determining what programming should be aired on a government-funded station or to appear on programs relating to public issues? In 1982 the 5th U.S. Circuit Court of Appeals ruled that the managers of public television stations enjoyed the same rights as managers of privately owned televisions to select programming to be broadcast.[86] While citizens may have a voice in setting broad policies regarding programming, they don't have the right to influence day-to-day programming choices. In 1998 the Supreme Court reinforced this earlier decision when it ruled that public television station managers can determine which political candidates will appear on political debates aired by the station. Ralph Forbes, a perennial independent candidate for Congress, was excluded from a debate sponsored by and aired on a public television station between the Democrat and Republican candidates for Arkansas' 3rd Congressional District seat. The Court of Appeals ruled that Forbes should have been included,[87] but the Supreme Court reversed. The court ruled that public broadcasting stations do have the discretion to exclude minor party candidates from political debates, so long as the exclusion is not based on the candidate's views. The candidate debate was not a public forum, like a park or a street corner, but a "nonpublic" forum subject to reasonable restrictions, the court said. Justice Anthony Kennedy, writing for the six-person majority, noted that Nebraska public television stations had canceled their candidate debates in 1996 as a result of the earlier court of appeals ruling. "A First Amendment jurisprudence yielding these results does not promote

84. *Metromedia v. San Diego,* 101 S. Ct. 2882 (1981); see also *Donnelly v. Campbell,* 639 F. 2d 6 (1980); *Metromedia v. Baltimore,* 583 F. Supp. 1183 (1982); and *Norton v. Arlington Heights,* 433 N.E. 2d 198 (1982).
85. *Anheuser-Busch, Inc. et al. v. Mayor and City Council of Baltimore City,* 63 F. 3d 1305 (1995); and *Penn Advertising of Baltimore Inc. v. Mayor and City Council of Baltimore City et al.,* 63 F. 3d 1318 (1995).
86. *Muir v. Alabama Educational Commission,* 656 F. 2d 1012 (1981); 688 F. 2d 1033 (1982); see also *Chandler v. Georgia Public Telecommunications Commission,* 917 F. 2d 486 (1990).
87. *Forbes v. Arkansas Educational Television Communications Network Foundation,* 22 F. 3d 1423 (1994); *Forbes v. The Arkansas Educational Television Commission,* 93 F. 3d 497 (1996).

speech but represses it," Kennedy said. Even the dissenters agreed that the lower court was mistaken in ruling that every candidate on the ballot had a presumptive right to appear on the televised debate. The dissenters, however, argued that any decision to include or exclude a particular candidate must be based on "pre-established, objective criteria."[88]

Finally, in 1997 a U.S. district court ruled that a public university's computer network was not a public forum. The University of Oklahoma, fearful of violating a state law that barred the distribution of obscene or indecent material over a computer-generated communication system, installed a two-tier access system to sites on the network. Anyone could gain access to a set of university-approved sites in the first tier. But users who sought access to a full-service server that carried a wider variety of sites had to click a button acknowledging that their use of the server was for legitimate research and teaching activities and that they were at least 18 years old. The limited access was challenged by a faculty member at the university, but the lawsuit failed when the professor was unable to introduce any evidence that his First Amendment rights had been violated. Nevertheless the court took the occasion to note that the university computer and Internet services did not constitute a public forum because there was no evidence that the facilities had ever been open to the general public or used for public communication. "The state, no less than a private owner of property, has the right to preserve the property under its control for the use to which it is lawfully dedicated. In this case the OU [Oklahoma University] computer and Internet services are lawfully dedicated to academic and research uses."[89] Although the issue was imperfectly argued at trial, the ruling is still the first judicial effort to define what kind of a forum is represented by a computer-generated communication system.

PRIVATE FORUMS

The cases just noted concern public forums. Courts have generally tolerated much more restriction on expression exercised in private forums—shopping centers and private residences, for example. Residential distribution and solicitation have consistently been a vexing problem as the rights of freedom of expression are measured against the rights of privacy and private property.

In 1943 the Supreme Court faced an unusual ordinance adopted by the city of Struthers, Ohio, which totally prohibited door-to-door distribution of handbills, circulars, and other advertising materials. The law also barred anyone from ringing doorbells to summon householders for the purpose of distributing literature or pamphlets.

Justice Hugo Black wrote the opinion for the majority in the divided court. He said the arrest of Thelma Martin, another Jehovah's Witness, for ringing doorbells in behalf of her religious cause was a violation of her First Amendment rights. Door-to-door distributors can be a nuisance and can even be a front for criminal activities, Justice Black acknowledged. Further, door-to-door distribution can surely be regulated, but it cannot be altogether banned. It is a valuable and useful means of the dissemination of ideas and is especially important to those

88. *Arkansas Educational Television Commission* v. *Forbes,* 118 S. Ct 1633 (1998).
89. *Loving* v. *Boren,* DC WOkla. No. CIV-96-657-A, 1/28/97.

groups that are too poorly financed to use other, expensive means of communication with the people. Black said a law that makes it an offense for a person to ring the doorbell of house-holders who have appropriately indicated that they are unwilling to be disturbed would be lawful and constitutional. However, the city of Struthers cannot by ordinance regulate this decision on behalf of all its citizens—especially when such a rule clearly interferes with the freedom of speech and of the press. "The right of freedom of speech and press has broad scope. The authors of the First Amendment knew that novel and unconventional ideas might disturb the complacent, but they chose to encourage a freedom which they believed essential if vigorous enlightenment was ever to triumph over slothful ignorance."[90] But the Appellate Division of the New York Supreme Court ruled in 1996 that if a property owner tells the distributor of a free newspaper that he or she does not want the newspaper delivered, the distributor does not have a First Amendment right to continue to deliver the newspaper.[91]

The problem of dealing with distribution of materials at privately owned shopping centers has also been a troubling one. In 1968, in *Amalgamated Food Employees Local 590* v. *Logan Valley Plaza*,[92] the Supreme Court ruled that the shopping center was the functional equivalent of a town's business district and permitted informational picketing by persons who had a grievance against one of the stores in the shopping center. Four years later in *Lloyd Corp.* v. *Tanner*,[93] the court ruled that a shopping center can prohibit the distribution of hand-bills on its property when the handbilling is unrelated to the shopping center operation. Protesters against nuclear power, for example, cannot use the shopping center as a forum. Persons protesting against the policies of one of the stores in the center, however, can use the center to distribute materials.

In 1976 the Supreme Court recognized the distinctions it had drawn between the rules in the *Logan Valley* case and the rules in the *Lloyd Corp.* case for what they were—restrictions based on content. The distribution of messages of one kind was permitted, while the distribution of messages about something else was banned. In *Hudgens* v. *NLRB*,[94] the high court ruled that if, in fact, the shopping center is the functional equivalent of a municipal street, then restrictions based on content cannot stand. But rather than open the shopping center to the distribution of all kinds of material, *Logan Valley* was overruled, and the court announced that "only when . . . property has taken all the attributes of a town" can property be treated as public. Distribution of materials at private shopping centers can be prohibited.

Just because the First Amendment does not include within its protection of freedom of expression the right to circulate material at a privately owned shopping center does not mean that such distribution might not be protected by legislation or by a state constitution. That is exactly what happened in California. In 1974 in the city of Campbell, Calif., a group of high school students took a card table, some leaflets, and unsigned petition forms to the popular Pruneyard Shopping Center. The students were angered by a recent anti-Israel U.N. resolution

---

90. *Martin* v. *City of Struthers,* 319 U.S. 141 (1943).
91. *Tillman* v. *Distribution Systems of America , Inc.,* 648 NYS 2d 630 (1996).
92. 391 U.S. 308 (1968).
93. 407 U.S. 551 (1972).
94. 424 U.S. 507 (1976).

and sought to hand out literature and collect signatures for a petition to send to the president and Congress. The shopping center did not allow anyone to hand out literature, speak, or gather petition signatures, and the students were quickly chased off the property by a security guard. They filed suit in court, and in 1979 the California Supreme Court ruled that the rights of freedom of speech and petitioning are protected under the California Constitution, even in private shopping centers, as long as they are "reasonably exercised."[95] The shopping center owners appealed the ruling to the U.S. Supreme Court, arguing that the high court's ruling in *Lloyd Corp.* v. *Tanner* prohibited the states from going further in the protection of personal liberties than the federal government. But six of the nine justices disagreed, ruling that a state is free to adopt in its own constitution individual liberties more expansive than those conferred by the federal constitution.[96]

A state is free to adopt in its own constitution individual liberties more expansive than those conferred by the federal constitution.

Courts in many states (Washington, Colorado, New Jersey, Oregon, New York, and others) have interpreted their state constitutions as providing broader free speech and press rights than those provided by the First Amendment to the U.S. Constitution. This trend becomes particularly noticeable when the federal courts narrow the meaning of the First Amendment.

SUMMARY

The prior restraint of expression is permissible under what are known as time, place, and manner regulations. That is, the government can impose reasonable regulations about when, where, and how individuals or groups may communicate with other persons. Time, place, and manner rules apply to both public forums (settings owned or controlled by a government, such as a public street or an airport) and private forums (privately owned settings, such as residences and shopping centers). In order to be constitutional, time, place, and manner restraints must meet certain criteria:

1. The regulation should be content neutral; that is, application of the rule should not depend on the content of the communication.
2. The regulation must serve a substantial governmental interest, and the government must justify the rule by explicitly demonstrating this interest.
3. There cannot be total prohibition of the communication. The speakers or publishers must have reasonable alternative means of presenting their ideas or information to the public.
4. The rules cannot be broader than they need to be to serve the governmental interest. For example, the government cannot stop the distribution of literature on all public streets if it only seeks to stop the problem of congestion on public streets that carry heavy traffic.

95. *Robins* v. *Pruneyard Shopping Center,* 592 P. 2d 341 (1979).
96. *Pruneyard Shopping Center* v. *Robins,* 447 U.S. 74 (1980).

OTHER PRIOR RESTRAINTS

Major issues regarding prior restraint have been outlined in the previous pages. Yet each year other instances of prior restraint are challenged in the courts and frequently the Supreme Court is called on to resolve the issue. Here is a brief outline of some of these cases.

SON OF SAM LAWS

Americans have always been interested in crime and criminals. But in the past two decades our desire to know more about this sordid side of contemporary life has spawned a seemingly endless host of books and television programs about killers, rapists, robbers, hijackers, and their victims. Indeed, it is often jokingly said of those accused of high profile crimes that when they are captured they are more eager to contact an agent than a defense attorney. Efforts have been made by government to stop felons from receiving money that might be earned by selling stories about their crimes. Many civil libertarians say this is a prior censorship. The laws in question, which have been adopted in one form or another by 42 states and the federal government, are colloquially called "Son of Sam" laws after a serial killer in New York who was dubbed with that name by the press. Before the Son of Sam (David Berkowitz) was caught, reports circulated that the press was offering to pay for the rights to his story. The New York legislature responded to those reports by passing a law that permits the state to seize and hold for five years all the money earned by an individual from the sale of his or her story of crime. The money is supposed to be used to compensate the victims of the crimes caused by the felon. The criminal/author collects what is left in the fund after five years.

Two separate challenges to the New York law were mounted in the late 1980s and early 1990s. Simon & Schuster contested the law when it was applied against the best-selling book "Wiseguys" (the basis for the film "GoodFellas"). Career mobster Henry Hill was paid for cooperating with the book's author, Nicholas Pileggi. Macmillan Publishing Co. also challenged the validity of the law when New York sought to seize the proceeds of Jean Harris' autobiography, "Stranger in Two Worlds," because some of the material in the work was based on her trial for the murder of her lover, diet doctor Herman Tarnower.

The statute was upheld in both federal and state courts. The 2nd U.S. Circuit Court of Appeals ruled in *Simon & Schuster* v. *Fischetti*[97] that the purpose of the law was not to suppress speech but to ensure that a criminal did not profit from the exploitation of his or her crime, and that the victims of the crime are compensated for their suffering. A compelling state interest is served, and the fact that this imposes an incidental burden on the press is not sufficient to rule the law a violation of freedom of expression.

But in late 1991 the U.S. Supreme Court disagreed and in an 8–0 decision ruled that the Son of Sam law was a content-based regulation that violated the First Amendment.[98] "The

---

97. 916 F. 2d 777 (1990).
98. *Simon & Schuster, Inc.* v. *New York Crime Victims Board*, 112 S. Ct. 501 (1991); see also *Bouchard* v. *Price*, 694 A. 2d 670 (1998) in which the Rhode Island Supreme Court struck down a similar law.

statute plainly imposes a financial disincentive only on a particular form of content," wrote Justice Sandra Day O'Connor. In order for such a law to pass constitutional muster, the state must show that it is necessary to serve a compelling state interest and that the law is narrowly constructed to achieve that end. The members of the high court agreed with the ruling of the lower court that the state has a compelling interest in ensuring that criminals do not profit from their crimes, but this law goes far beyond that goal; it is not narrowly drawn. The statute applies to works on any subject provided they express the author's thoughts or recollections about his or her crime, however tangentially or incidentally, Justice O'Connor noted. The statute could just as easily be applied to "The Autobiography of Malcolm X" or Thoreau's "Civil Disobedience" or the "Confessions of St. Augustine," she added. While Justice O'Connor specifically noted that this ruling was not necessarily aimed at similar laws in other states because they might be different, the decision has forced substantial changes in most of the existing laws. In Massachusetts, however, the Supreme Judicial Court of that commonwealth approved a probationary scheme that had clear earmarks of a Son of Sam law. Katherine Power, a 1970s radical who participated in a bank robbery in which a police officer was killed, surrendered to authorities in 1993 after spending 23 years as a fugitive. She pleaded guilty to her crimes and a trial court ordered the defendant to serve 20 years probation as part of her sentence. Attached to the probation sentence was a provision that Power could not in any way profit from the sale of her story to the news media during those 20 years. Power appealed the provision, citing the First Amendment and the Supreme Court ruling in *Simon & Schuster.* The Massachusetts high court rejected this appeal, arguing that a specific condition of probation (which frequently restricts a probationer's fundamental rights) is not the same as a Son of Sam law, which is a statute of general applicability.[99] So, are Son of Sam laws constitutional? They certainly can be, but most of the current laws are not narrowly tailored in such a way as to pass muster. Because the laws are content-based statutes, the state has to first demonstrate that a compelling state interest is at stake and then prove that the law does not bar more speech than is necessary to further that interest. The state has to convince the court that its law stops a criminal from profiting from his or her crime while the victim remains uncompensated. In addition the law must be aimed at only significant commercial exploitation, not at all expressive activity in which the author reflects his or her thoughts or recollections about the crime, however incidental they might be.

PRIOR RESTRAINT AND PROTESTS

Two 1994 decisions by the Supreme Court focus on the prior restraint of those seeking to demonstrate or protest. In June the Supreme Court unanimously ruled that cities may not bar residents from posting signs on their own property. Margaret Gilleo had challenged the Ladue, Mo., ordinance by posting an 8-by-11-inch sign in a window of her house protesting the Persian Gulf War. The lower courts ruled that the ban on residential signs was flawed because the city did not ban signs on commercial property; the law favored one kind of speech over

99. *Massachusetts* v. *Power,* 420 Mass. 410 (1995)

another. But the Supreme Court struck down the ordinance in a broader fashion, ruling that the posting of signs on residential property is "a venerable means of communication that is both unique and important. A special respect for individual liberty in the home has long been part of our culture and law," wrote Justice John Paul Stevens. "Most Americans would be understandably dismayed, given that tradition, to learn that it was illegal to display from their window an 8-by-11-inch sign expressing their political views," he added.[100]

In another ruling involving the right to protest, the high court upheld a Florida state court injunction that established a 36-foot buffer zone between an abortion clinic in Melbourne, Fla., and anti-abortion protesters.[101] The buffer zone, or ban on picketing, was designed to keep protesters away from the entrance to the clinic, the parking lot, and the public right-of-way. Chief Justice Rehnquist, who wrote the 6–3 ruling, said the ban "burdens no more speech than is necessary to accomplish the governmental interest at stake." The court did strike down, however, a 300-foot buffer zone within which protesters could not make uninvited approaches to patients and employees, as well as a buffer zone the same size around the houses of clinic doctors and staff members. The Chief Justice said a smaller zone or restriction on the size and duration of demonstrations would be constitutional.

Finally, in 1995 the Supreme Court struck down an Ohio law (and for all intents and purposes laws in almost every other state in the nation) that prohibited the distribution of anonymous campaign literature. Margaret McIntyre had circulated leaflets opposing an upcoming school levy, but failed to include her name and address on the campaign literature as required by law. She was fined $100. The state argued the statute was needed to identify those responsible for fraud, false advertising, and libel, but seven members of the high court said the law was an unconstitutional limitation on political expression. "Under our constitution, anonymous pamphleteering is not a pernicious, fraudulent practice, but an honorable tradition of advocacy and of dissent," wrote Justice John Paul Stevens for the majority. "Anonymity is a shield from the tyranny of the majority." Stevens said anonymity might in fact shield fraudulent conduct, but our society "accords greater weight to the value of free speech than to the dangers of its misuse."[102]

A wide variety of legal issues relate to prior restraint. In recent years the Supreme Court of the United States has voided a statute aimed at denying criminals the right to earn profits from books or films about their crimes and voided a city ordinance that barred residents from putting signs on their front lawns or in their windows. At the same time, the high court has permitted limited restrictions aimed at those seeking to protest abortion at a clinic in Florida.

SUMMARY

---

100. *City of Ladue* v. *Gilleo*, 114 S. Ct. 2046 (1994).
101. *Madsen* v. *Women's Health Center*, 114 S. Ct. 2516 (1994).
102. *McIntyre* v. *Ohio Elections Commission*, 115 S. Ct. 1511 (1995).

HATE SPEECH

Succeeding generations tend to create their own words and phrases to describe events or phenomena that have existed for many years but were frequently called something else. In the 1980s Americans began to hear about something called "hate speech": invective, written or spoken, attacking individuals or groups because of their race, ethnic background, religion, gender, or sexual preference. Of course such abusive language did not first manifest itself in the 1980s; intolerance is not unique to contemporary times. The term "hate speech" is the only thing that is new about this phenomenon.

Few openly acknowledge a value in such speech, but there is considerable debate over what to do about it. Many argue that the state should act on behalf of these minorities and punish the public utterance or publication of such abusive language, or permit these individuals or groups to pursue their own legal recourse through civil suit. Such rules would help deliver the 14th Amendment's guarantee of equal protection by offering members of historically disadvantaged groups a tool to protect themselves, it is argued. Law professor Richard Delgado has noted that while punishing racial or ethnic insults would not prevent all such expression, at least punishment would deter whomever could be deterred.[103] To permit such invective means that the state is in fact promoting such speech, according to many who support censorship of this language. Professor Mari Matsuda explains this argument:

> Further, the law's failure to provide recourse to persons who are demeaned by the hate messages is in effect second injury to that person. The second injury is the pain of knowing that the government provides no remedy, and offers no recognition of the dehumanizing experience that the victims of hate propaganda are subjected to. The government's denial of personhood by denying legal recourse may be even more painful than the initial act of hatred. One can dismiss the hate group as an organization of marginal people, but the state is the official embodiment of the society we live in.[104]

While others agree that hate speech is certainly abhorrent and perhaps even harmful, they contend that such speech has always been a dark thread in this nation's fabric. Abusive language or hate speech is founded in ill-conceived beliefs and prejudice. Abolishing the language reflected by these beliefs will not change the way people think; it will simply drive this racial or ethnic hatred underground, in the dark, where it is most comfortable, according to writers like Nat Hentoff.[105] More importantly, it is argued by those who oppose legal sanctions for hate speech, such rules are clear violations of the First Amendment. We may not like everything that people say or write or publish on the Internet, but the Constitution guarantees that they shall have the opportunity to say or write what they wish. But there is a line that has been drawn by the Supreme Court, a line that a speaker cannot cross. Those who print racial epithets in newspapers or broadcast them on the radio or paint them on a fence are generally

Few openly acknowledge a value in such speech, but there is considerable debate over what to do about it.

103. Delgado, "Words That Wound," 133.
104. Matsuda, "Racist Speech," 2320.
105. Hentoff, *Free Speech for Me.*

protected by the First Amendment. But the same words uttered in a face-to-face confrontation may not enjoy this same protection. The Supreme Court established this principle in 1942 in a ruling in the case of *Chaplinsky* v. *New Hampshire.*

FIGHTING WORDS DOCTRINE

Chaplinsky was a member of the Jehovah's Witnesses. Face-to-face proselytization or confrontation is a part of the religious practice of the members of this sect. Chaplinsky attracted a hostile crowd as he attempted to distribute religious pamphlets in Rochester, N.H. When a city marshal intervened, Chaplinsky called the officer a "God-damned racketeer" and a "damned fascist." The Jehovah's Witness was tried and convicted of violating a state law that forbids offensive or derisive speech or name-calling in public. The Supreme Court affirmed the conviction by a 9–0 vote. In his opinion for the court Justice Frank Murphy outlined what has become known as the *fighting words doctrine:*

> There are certain well-defined and narrowly limited classes of speech, the prevention and punishment of which have never been thought to raise any constitutional problems. These include . . . fighting words—those which by their very utterance inflict injury or tend to incite an immediate breach of the peace. It has been well observed that such utterances are no essential part of any exposition of ideas, and are of such slight social value as a step to the truth that any benefit that may be derived from them is clearly outweighed by the social interest in order and morality.[106]

"There are certain well-defined and narrowly limited classes of speech, the prevention and punishment of which have never been thought to raise any constitutional problems."

Fighting words may be prohibited, then, so long as the statutes are carefully drawn and do not permit the application of the law to protected speech. Also, the fighting words must be used in a personal, face-to-face encounter—a true verbal assault. The Supreme Court emphasized this latter point in 1972 when it ruled that laws prohibiting fighting words be limited to words "that have a direct tendency to cause acts of violence by the person to whom, individually, the remark is addressed."[107] It is important to note that the high court has given the state permission to restrict so-called fighting words because their utterance could result in a breach of the peace, a fight, a riot; not because they insult or offend or harm the person at whom they are aimed.

The 1970s brought more litigation on this question as members of the racist and anti-Semitic National Socialist Party (Nazis) sought to confront the residents of a community in upstate Illinois. In 1976 Nazis said they planned a peaceful demonstration in Skokie, a community with a large Jewish population, to protest the racial integration of nearby Chicago schools. Village officials prohibited the protest, saying that the protesters had failed to obtain a $350,000 liability/property insurance policy required by Skokie Park District ordinance.

After the Nazis announced that they planned to protest against the insurance ordinance, the village obtained a temporary restraining order blocking the demonstration and then adopted three new ordinances regarding public marches and protests. In addition to the insurance requirements, the village ruled that a member of a political party cannot march in a

106. *Chaplinsky* v. *New Hampshire,* 315 U.S. 568 (1942).
107. *Gooding* v. *Wilson,* 405 U.S. 518 (1972).

military-style uniform and ruled that it is not permissible to disseminate material intended to incite racial hatred. State and federal courts in Illinois invalidated all the ordinances, ruling that they were discriminatory or abridged constitutionally protected rights of free speech.[108]

The Illinois Supreme Court, in refusing to enjoin the display of the swastika and other Nazi symbols, rejected the contention that such display constituted fighting words sufficient "to overcome the heavy presumption against the constitutional validity of a prior restraint." "Peaceful demonstrations cannot be totally precluded solely because that display [of the swastika] may provoke a violent reaction by those who view it. . . . A speaker who gives prior notice of his message has not compelled a confrontation with those who voluntarily listen."[109]

In 1992 the Supreme Court reaffirmed the right of the government to censor so-called fighting words, but ruled in *R.A.V. v. St. Paul* that the government could not be selective by banning only certain categories of fighting words. In 1990 a group of teenagers burned a crude wooden cross inside the fenced yard of a black family in St. Paul. The city had banned such hate crimes by an ordinance that forbade the display of a burning cross or a Nazi swastika or any writing or picture that "arouses the anger, alarm or resentment in others on the basis of race, color, creed, religion or gender." Minnesota courts had previously construed the phrase "arouses anger, alarm or resentment in others" to be conduct that amounts to fighting words. The U.S. Supreme Court struck down the statute, however, because it was a content-based regulation. Justice Antonin Scalia wrote that while it is clear that the law is aimed at stopping fighting words, which is permissible, it is also clear that the law only applies to fighting words that insult or provoke violence on the basis of race, color, creed, or gender. "Those who wish to use fighting words in connection with other ideas to express hostility, for example, on the basis of political affiliation, union membership, or homosexuality are not covered. The First Amendment does not permit St. Paul to impose special prohibitions on those speakers who express views on disfavored subjects," Scalia wrote. St. Paul, he said, has not singled out an especially offensive mode of expression, but rather has proscribed fighting words of any variety that communicate what it regards as an especially offensive message, a message of racial, religious, or gender intolerance. "Let there be no mistake about our belief that burning a cross in someone's front yard is reprehensible. But St. Paul has sufficient means at its disposal to prevent such behavior [i.e., laws that ban making terroristic threats, criminal damage to property, trespass] without adding the First Amendment to the fire," Scalia added.[110] In fact, Robert A. Viktora, R.A.V., was subsequently prosecuted and convicted of criminal trespass.

Perhaps the best example of rules against hate speech was the speech codes promulgated at more than 300 universities and colleges in the 1980s and early 1990s. The codes placed absolute limits on what students, faculty, and staff could say, write, broadcast, or publish. However, when the codes were challenged in court, more often than not they were ruled to be unconstitutional violations of the First Amendment.[111]

---

108. *Collin v. Smith,* 578 F. 2d 1197 (1978); *Village of Skokie v. National Socialist Party,* 373 N.E. 2d (1978).
109. *Village of Skokie v. National Socialist Party,* 373 N.E. 2d 21 (1978).
110. *R.A.V. v. St. Paul,* 112 S. Ct. 2538 (1992).
111. See, for example, *John Doe v. University of Michigan,* 721 F. Supp. 852 (1989) and *UWM Post v. Board of Regents of the University of Wisconsin,* 774 F. Supp. 1163 (1991).

The courts tended to apply the principles from the *Chaplinsky* and *Gooding* decisions (see page 117) that limit the prosecution of such hate speech to face-to-face encounters that could result in physical injury or incite violent acts. One by one universities and colleges abandoned these codes because they were ineffective in situations other than those face-to-face instances of fighting words and were too costly to defend in court. The problems of so-called hate speech have not disappeared from the college campuses; schools today, however, spend more time trying to educate young people on the impropriety of such speech than punishing student and faculty offenders.

SUMMARY

Hate speech is not a new problem in America, but for the first time in many years the courts have been called in to determine just how far the state may go in limiting what people say and write about other people when their language is abusive or includes racial, ethnic, or religious invective. In the early 1940s the Supreme Court ruled that so-called fighting words could be prohibited, but these words have come to mean face-to-face invective or insults that are likely to result in a violent response on the part of the victim. The high court voided a St. Paul, Minn., ordinance that punished such abusive speech because, the court said, the law did not ban all fighting words, merely some kinds of fighting words (i.e., racial or religious invective) that the community believed were improper. The decision in this case has sharply limited attempts by state universities and colleges to use speech codes to discourage hate speech or other politically incorrect comments or publications.

THE FIRST AMENDMENT AND THE INFORMATION SUPERHIGHWAY

One of the most perplexing First Amendment issues facing this nation today relates to the regulation of messages that travel over the so-called information superhighway. Communication via computer networks, once only a dream of computer engineers, has become a reality for tens of millions of Americans. While communicating via cyberspace is not yet a serious rival to communication through the traditional mass media and point-to-point message systems (i.e., the telephone), use of computer networks for an increasingly wide range of message transmissions is becoming more common each day, especially in American business. Not surprisingly, legal problems have arisen because of messages transmitted via the information superhighway. In the next 14 chapters of this text, you will find references to problems of libel, invasion of privacy, access to information, obscenity, and other issues that relate directly to communication via computer networks. In these cases the courts have attempted to apply traditional legal principles, principles that apply to newspapers or broadcasting stations or whatever, to solve the problems that have arisen in cyberspace. Sometimes this solution has proved satisfactory; sometimes it has not.

How the government regulates a message communicated by any medium is generally determined by the content of that particular message. A plea to burn down city hall and kill the mayor is sedition; a call to vote the mayor out of office is not. Calling Mary Smith a thief is libelous; calling Mary Smith a good student is not. The law is applied, then, based on what the message says. But in some instances the regulation of a message is based on more than the content of the message; it is also influenced by the kind of medium through which the message is transmitted.

At least four categories of traditional communications media are in common use today, and each is regulated somewhat differently by the law. The printed press—newspapers, magazines, books, and pamphlets—enjoys the greatest freedom of all mass media from government regulation. The over-the-air broadcast media—television and radio—enjoy the least amount of freedom from government censorship. Cable television is somewhere between these two, enjoying more freedom than broadcasting but less than the printed press. Few limits are placed on the messages transmitted via the telephone, and those that are must be very narrowly drawn.[112] There are some ifs, ands, or buts in this simple outline, but it is an accurate summary of the hierarchy of mass media when measured by First Amendment freedom. It should be noted, however, that many experts predict growing convergence in the mass media that will blur the lines among these four distinct media. The 1996 Telecommunications Act, for example, gave telephone companies the power to transmit television signals via phone lines to compete with cable television. At the same time cable companies were given the right to provide telephone service by buying phone systems or using the wires currently devoted to cable to carry telephone calls.[113]

Courts have distinguished among these four media by applying four basic criteria:

- **The capacity of the medium to carry messages.** Are there an unlimited number of channels, or is capacity limited in some way?
- **The traditional relationship between the government and the medium.** Has the medium traditionally been free, or has regulation been imposed from the inception of the medium?
- **The pervasiveness or invasiveness of the medium.** What role does the receiver play in receiving the message? Does the receiver have to actively seek the message, or can he or she be a largely passive recipient?
- **The accessibility of the medium.** How easy is it for children to gain access to the messages communicated by the medium?

Why is the printed press allotted the most protection by the First Amendment? Using these criteria it is obvious. There are no physical limits on the number of newspapers and magazines or handbills that can be published. (Economic limits is another matter, but one not considered by the courts in this context.) Since the founding of the Republic in 1789, the printed press has traditionally been free. The receiver must generally take an active role in purchasing a book or a magazine or newspaper. Young people must have the economic wherewithal to buy a newspaper or magazine, and then have the literacy skills to read it.

112. *Sable Communications* v. *FCC,* 492 U.S. 115 (1989).
113. See Lively, "Information Superhighway"; see also "Message Is the Medium."

It is just as obvious, applying these criteria, why broadcast media have fared the poorest in First Amendment protection. There is an actual physical limit on the number of radio and television channels that exist. All but a very few are in use. Since not everyone who wants such a channel can have one, it is up to the government to select who gets these scarce broadcast frequencies and to make certain those who use the frequencies serve the interests of all listeners and viewers. Because of this, and other reasons, broadcasting has been regulated since nearly its inception. It has no tradition of freedom. All the receiver must do to listen to the radio or watch television is to flick a switch. Even children who don't know how to read can do this; radio and television are easily accessible to kids.

Cable television and telephones fit somewhere in between. There is potentially an unlimited capacity for messages to be transmitted by each medium. Both have been historically regulated, but not to the extent that broadcasting has been regulated. Although a receiver can watch a cable television channel as easily as he or she can watch an over-the-air channel, the receiver must take a far more active role in subscribing to a cable system. While this may seem like a trivial distinction, the courts have made much of it. Judges have presumed that the persons who subscribe to cable television should know what they will receive. Federal law mandates that cable television companies provide safeguards (called cable locks) for parents who want to shield their children from violent or erotic programming*. Such screening technology is only now coming into use for over-the air television. The use of a telephone also requires a more active role by the receiver than simply switching on a radio or television set.

The application of these criteria over the past 60 years by judges in a wide variety of cases has resulted in the establishment of a hierarchy of mass media in relation to the First Amendment—the hierarchy just outlined. Where do computer-mediated communication systems fit into this hierarchy? In June of 1997 the Supreme Court ruled in a 7–2 decision that communication via the Internet deserves the highest level of First Amendment protection, protection comparable to that given to newspapers, magazines, and books.[114] (The dissenters on the court agreed with this portion of the ruling.) The high court made this decision as it ruled that the central provisions of the 1996 Communications Decency Act that restricted the transmission of indecent material over the Internet violated the U.S. Constitution. Recognizing that each medium of communication may present its own constitutional problems, Justice John Paul Stevens wrote that the members of the high court could find no basis in past decisions for "qualifying the level of First Amendment scrutiny that should be applied to this medium [the Internet]."

The court rejected the notion prevalent among those in Congress who voted for the Communications Decency Act that communication via the Internet should be treated in the same manner as communication via over-the-air radio and television. The court said that the scarcity of frequencies that had long justified the regulation of broadcasting did not apply in the case of the Internet, which, it said, can hardly be considered a "scarce" expressive commodity. "The Government estimates that as many as 40 million people use the Internet today, and that figure is expected to grow to 200 million by 1999," Justice Stevens wrote. "This dynamic, multifaceted category of communication includes not only traditional print and

114. *Reno* v. *American Civil Liberties Union,* 117 S. Ct. 2329 (1997).

*But in a May, 2000, ruling, *U.S. v Playboy Entertainment Group,* the Supreme Court suggested that cable television enjoys the full protection of the First Amendment. See page 629.

news services, but also audio, video, and still images, as well as interactive, real time dialogue. Through the use of chat rooms, any person with a phone line can become a town crier with a voice that resonates farther than it could from any soapbox," Stevens added.

Neither before nor after the enactment of the Communications Decency Act have the "vast democratic fora of the Internet been subject to the type of government supervision and regulation that has attended the broadcast industry," Justice Stevens wrote. There is no tradition of censorship in cyberspace. The court added that computer-mediated communication is not invasive as are radio and television. Communications over the Internet do not "invade" an individual's home or appear on one's computer screen "unbidden." Almost all sexually explicit images are preceded by warnings as to content, and odds are slim that a user would come across a sexually explicit site by accident.

Finally, the Supreme Court rejected the government's assertion that the shielding of children from indecent communication was critical if the Internet was to grow as an important communications medium, that adults would not embrace the Internet because of the risk of exposing their children to offensive and harmful content. "We find this argument singularly unpersuasive," wrote Justice Stevens. The dramatic expansion of this new marketplace of ideas contradicts the factual basis of this contention, he said. "As a matter of constitutional tradition, in the absence of evidence to the contrary, we presume that governmental regulation of the content of speech is more likely to interfere with the free exchange of ideas than to encourage it," Stevens wrote. "The interest in encouraging freedom of expression in a democratic society outweighs any theoretical but unproven benefit of censorship," he added.

The importance of this ruling cannot be overestimated. Not only did the court strike down a restrictive federal law that was certain to retard the growth of computer-mediated communication, it ruled that any other governmental agency that seeks to regulate communication via the information superhighway must treat this medium in the same manner it would treat a newspaper or a book. The impact of the high court ruling is just now being felt. For example, in September of 1999 the Ford Motor Company tried but failed to block the publication on the Internet of information taken from confidential Ford documents. Newspapers and magazines had won cases in the past when corporations tried to block them from publishing confidential information. In this case the U.S. district court in Detroit ruled that an Internet site enjoys the same free-press rights as these traditional publications.[115] Judge Nancy G. Edmunds wrote: "In the realm of law, we are only beginning to grapple with the impact of the communications revolution, and this case represents just one part of the skirmish—a clash between our commitment to the freedom of speech and the press, and our dedication to the protection of commercial innovation and intellectual property. In this case, the battle is won by the First Amendment." A companion lawsuit brought by Ford against the site owner for trademark and copyright violations is still pending. The confidential documents related to fuel efficiency and emission technology for sport utility vehicles.

But the battle over controlling the content of the Internet is really just starting. The Supreme Court's ruling on the Communications Decency Act was not the end of the matter, or even the beginning of the end. The ruling by the court in *Reno* was, as Winston Churchill

115. *Ford Motor Co.* v. *Lane,* 97 F Supp 2d 745 (1999). See also Bradsher, "Ford Loses Bid."

said after the British held off the Germans in the Battle of Britain, only the end of the beginning. States continue to try to regulate Internet content and are continually rebuffed by the federal courts, who block their efforts with the First Amendment.[116] And the Congress has not given up. In October of 1998 it passed the Child Online Protection Act, which was an attempt to impose restrictions on using the Internet to sell or transfer materials that are harmful to minors. And efforts by public libraries to use software programs that filter out objectionable sites also became an issue when citizens in some communities challenged these policies in court. These topics and others are fully explored in Chapter 13 in the section entitled "Erotic Materials in Cyberspace" (pp. 487–493). Finally, in January of 1999 a federal jury in Oregon ordered that $107 million in damages be paid by a group of militant abortion opponents who created a Web site that plaintiffs said targeted doctors and others who supported a woman's right to abortion. The plaintiffs called the content of the Web site domestic terrorism and deadly threats, but the anti-abortionists argued that nothing in their materials specifically advocated violence against abortion providers. Many observers said that this case, or one like it, would one day wind up in the Supreme Court as a major test of the line between free speech on the Internet and unlawful intimidation.

BIBLIOGRAPHY

Avery, Kay Beth, and Robert J. Simpson. "The Constitution and Student Publications: A Comprehensive Approach." *Journal of Law and Education* 16 (1987):1.

Barron, Jerome, and C. Thomas Dienes. *Handbook of Free Speech and Free Press.* Boston: Little, Brown, 1979.

Bonner, Alice, and Judith Hines. *Death by Cheeseburger: High School Journalism in the 1990s and Beyond.* Arlington, Va.: The Freedom Forum, 1994.

Boot, William. "Covering the Gulf War: The Press Stands Alone." *Columbia Journalism Review,* March/April 1991.

Bradsher, Keith. "Ford Loses Bid to Keep Documents Off Internet." *The New York Times,* 8 September 1999, A12.

Bruni, Frank. "Dueling Perspectives: Two Views of Reality Vying on the Airwaves." *The New York Times,* 18 April 1999, A11.

Buckley, T.D., Jr. "Student Publications, the First Amendment, and State Speech." *Cleveland State Law Review* 34 (1986):267.

Committee to Protect Journalists Update, no. 38, May 1990.

Cranberg, Gilbert, "The Gulf of Credibility." *Columbia Journalism Review,* March/April 1988, 19.

Delgado, Richard. "Words That Wound: A Tort Action for Racial Insults, Epithets, and Name Calling." *Harvard Civil Rights–Civil Liberties Law Review* 17 (1982):133.

Dennis, Everette, et al. *The Media at War: The Press and the Persian Conflict.* New York: Gannett Foundation Media Center, 1991.

---

116. See, for example, *American Civil Liberties Union* v. *Johnson,* 10th Cir., No. 982199, 11/2/99.

Denniston, Lyle. "Son of Sam Law vs. First Amendment." *Washington Journalism Review,* May 1991, 56.

DePalma, Anthony. "Battling Bias, Campuses Face Free Speech Fight." *The New York Times,* 20 February 1990, B10.

Dunn, Donald J. "Pico and Beyond: School Library Censorship Controversies." *Law Library Journal* 77 (1984–85):435.

"Editorials Support Censorship Decision." *Editor and Publisher,* 23 January 1988, 11.

Fialka, John J. *Hotel Warriors.* Washington, D.C.: Woodrow Wilson Press Center, 1992.

Fitzgerald, Mark. "Editorials support censorship decision." *Editor & Publisher,* 23 January 1988, 11.

Garneau, George. "Top 10 Threats to Campus Press." *Editor and Publisher,* 17 December 1994, 31.

Gillmor, Donald M. "The Fragile First." *Hamline Law Review* 8 (1985):277.

Hamilton, Patricia Anne. "Freedom of Expression in Public Schools: Regulation of Student Newspapers and Other Publications." *Cumberland Law Review* 18 (1987):181.

Hanson, Christopher. "Ecological Crisis Still Foe in Gulf." *Seattle Post-Intelligencer,* 6 April 1991, 1.

Harmon, Amy. "The Self-Appointed Cops of the Information Age." *The New York Times,* 7 December 1997, section 4, 1.

Hentoff, Nat. *Free Speech for Me—But Not for Thee: How the American Left and Right Relentlessly Censor Each Other.* New York: HarperCollins, 1992.

Jacobs, Matthew J. "Assessing the Constitutionality of Press Restrictions in the Persian Gulf War." *Stanford Law Review* 44 (1992):674.

Kaplan, Julie B. "The First Amendment Standard for Removal of Books from Public School Curricula." *Dickinson Law Review* 95 (1991):259.

Knightly, Phillip. *The First Casualty.* New York: Harcourt, Brace, Jovanovich, 1975.

———. "Here is the Patriotically Censored News." *Index on Censorship,* April/May 1991.

Lamb, David. "Pentagon Hardball." *Washington Journalism Review,* April 1991, 33.

Lewis, Peter. "Judges Turn Back Law to Regulate Internet Indecency." *The New York Times,* 13 June 1996, A1.

Lively, Donald. "The Information Superhighway: A First Amendment Roadmap." *Boston College Law Review* 35 (1994):1066.

MacArthur, John R. *Second Front: Censorship and Propaganda in the Gulf War.* New York: Hill and Wang, 1992.

MacCormack, Zeke, "No Snow: Texas School Bans Book." *Seattle Post-Intelligencer,* 10 September 1999, A1.

Matsuda, Mari. "Public Response to Racist Speech: Considering the Victim's Story." *Michigan Law Review* 87 (1989):2320.

"The Message Is the Medium: The First Amendment on the Information Superhighway." *Harvard Law Review* 107 (1994):1062.

McFadden, Robert F. "Internet Laws Overturned in New York and Georgia." *The New York Times,* 14 June 1997, A9.

Miller, Mark Crispin. "Operation Desert Sham." *The New York Times,* 24 June 1992, A17.

Patten, Jim. "High School Confidential." *Columbia Journalism Review,* September/ October 1990, 8.

Paulk, Crystal. "Campus Crime Real Despite What You Read." *Quill,* September 1997, 48.

Riskin, Cynthia. "Communications Students Support Some Speech, Press Censorship." *The Washington Newspaper,* January/February 1994.

Schanberg, Sydney H. "Censoring for Political Security." *Washington Journalism Review,* March 1991, 23.

Schmeisser, Peter. "The Pool and the Pentagon," *Index on Censorship,* April/May 1991, 32.

———. "Shooting Pool." *New Republic,* 18 March 1991, 21.

"School Censorship on Rise, Civil Liberties Group Says." *Seattle Post-Intelligencer,* 29 August 1991.

Sharkey, Jacqueline. "The Shallow End of the Pool." *American Journalism Review,* December 1994, 43.

Sloyan, Patrick J. "The Fog of War." *American Journalism Review,* June 1999, 32.

Sterngold, James. "For Artistic Freedom. It's Not the Worst of Times." *The New York Times,* 20 September 1998, Section 2, pg. 1.

"Students Censored, But Issue Lives On." *The New York Times,* 7 September 1997, A9.

Tenhoff, Greg C. "Censoring the Public University Student Press." *Southern California Law Review* 64 (1991):511.

Utter, Robert. "State Constitutional Law, the United States Supreme Court, and Democratic Accountability: Is There a Crocodile in the Bathtub?" *Washington Law Review* 64 (1989):27.

Wilgoren, Jodi. "Don't Give Us Little Wizards, The Anti-Potter Parents Cry." *The New York Times,* 1 November 1999, A1.

Libel
Establishing a Case

The law of libel is centuries old. Its roots in this country spring directly from the British common law. Throughout most of this nation's history the states were left to fashion their own libel laws. But since the mid-1960s the U.S. Supreme Court has "federalized" basic elements of defamation law, obligating the states to keep their rules and regulations within boundaries defined by the First Amendment. This development has transformed what was a fairly simple aspect of American law into a legal thicket akin to a blackberry patch. In this first of three chapters about defamation, I characterize some basic dimensions of this common tort action and outline requirements that have been placed on the plaintiff to establish a cause of action for libel.

THE LIBEL LANDSCAPE

Defamation, or libel, is undoubtedly the most common legal problem faced by persons who work in the mass media. In simple terms **libel** is the publication or broadcast of a statement that injures someone's reputation, that lowers that person's esteem in the community. While reporters, news writers, and editors at newspapers, broadcasting stations, and magazines are at the greatest risk from libel, advertising copywriters, public relations specialists, in-house magazine editors, and scores of others in the communications business can easily fall prey to the many snares that are a part of modern defamation law. A large number of libel cases involve defendants who don't even work in the mass media, people who perhaps wrote a letter to the editor, or gave an interview, or spoke at a public meeting.[1]

Libel suits have been a serious problem for the mass media since the dawn of printing, but during the past 20 years they emerged as perhaps the most serious legal problem faced by the press in the United States. The news media was inundated by a large number of high-profile, high-cost legal actions in the 1980s and early 1990s. Although this tide seems to be ebbing, according to reports from the Libel Defense Resource Center, significant problems continue to exist. A substantial number of libel suits are still filed and plaintiffs often seek astronomically high damage awards. The lawsuits can go on for years, diverting reporters and editors from other more important tasks. Legal costs have escalated as well, with skilled defense lawyers often billing clients hundreds of dollars an hour for their services. For example, book publisher Simon & Schuster and author James B. Stewart were embroiled in a libel suit since 1992 over the publication of the book "Den of Thieves," an account of powerful Wall Street figures (some of whom ended up in prison) who participated in the corporate takeover madness of the late 1980s. The suit was brought by a lawyer, Michael Armstrong, who is briefly mentioned in the book. Armstrong claims that the author accuses him of preparing a false affidavit for a witness to sign. By late 1999 both sides had spent more than $1million on legal costs. As a result the entire book industry became extremely wary about publishing critical investigative books because the potential costs of dealing with libel suits could destroy a book's profitability. Author Stewart told New York Times reporter Doreen Carvajal that from the beginning of the suit he felt as though someone was trying to punish or harass him. "It is unpleasant, time consuming and distracting. Its existence has clouded my credit rating and made it difficult for me to get a mortgage. I am sure it has intimidated other journalists and publishers," he said.[2] Efforts by some of the best minds in the field during the past 15 years have failed to generate a solution to this libel mess that is acceptable to the press, the public, and the legal community.

---

1. See, for example, *600 West 115th Street Corp.* v. *von Gutfeld,* 80 N.Y. 2d 130 (1992) and *Underwager* v. *Salter,* 22 F. 3d 730 (1994).
2. Carvajal, "Libel Wrangle over Miliken Book." The Appellate Division of the New York Supreme Court granted Simon & Schuster's motion for a summary judgment on September 27, 1999, and dismissed the lawsuit. See *Armstrong* v. *Simon & Schuster,* 27 M.L.R. 2289 (1999).

WINNING AND LOSING LIBEL SUITS

Libel suits can deprive the mass media of two essential commodities: time and money. These lawsuits can go on for years, in and out of court.* And because of the complex nature of the law, reporters and editors are frequently involved for long periods of time, talking with their own attorneys, talking with the plaintiff's attorneys, gathering records, and testifying in court. The periodic loss of key staff members can damage even a large newspaper or broadcasting station. But money is the bigger problem.

The size of damage judgments sought by plaintiffs frequently bears little resemblance to the actual harm, if any, that was suffered. In 1994 Philip Morris Co. sought $10 *billion* in damages when it filed a libel action against ABC, claiming the network defamed the company when it reported that cigarette makers add nicotine to the cigarettes they manufacture. The suit was settled out of court a year later when ABC agreed to apologize to Philip Morris twice during prime-time broadcasts and to pay up to $3 million for the tobacco company's legal fees. The Church of Scientology sued Time Warner for $416 million for publishing an article in 1991 that described the church as a global racket.[3] The Nation of Islam sought $4.4 *billion* in damages from the New York Post for a column that quoted the widow of Malcolm X discussing whether Louis Farrakhan was connected to her husband's death. Plaintiffs rarely get what they ask for, but the size of libel judgments rose steadily beginning in the 1980s.

Multimillion dollar jury awards are common. In 1996 a Florida jury awarded Bank-Atlantic Financial Corp. and its chief executive officer $10 million in a lawsuit brought against ABC for a "20/20" story critical of the bank's security transactions. In 1997 a Texas jury awarded a bond brokerage firm, MMAR Group, $222.7 million in a libel action against Dow Jones & Company for an article that appeared in the Wall Street Journal. The *average* jury award against a mass media defendant exceeded $1 million in the 1990s. In 1996 the average libel and right of privacy award was $3 million, according to a study by the Libel Defense Resource Center. Most of these huge jury awards are subsequently reduced by the judge or an appellate court. The trial judge in the MMAR Group–Dow Jones case first reduced the damage award to $22.7 million, for example, and later vacated the entire judgment, ruling that the verdict for the plaintiff had been tainted by deception by the plaintiff. The case was to be retried. But even a relatively low award can cause problems for some defendants. Barricade Books, a small but successful publishing house in New York, faced potential bankruptcy after it was ordered to pay $3 million in damages to a millionaire Las Vegas casino owner, Steve Wynn, who sued the company for stating in a catalog description of a book it published that a confidential Scotland Yard report alleged that Wynn was a front man for an organized crime family. Wynn denied the charges. The plaintiff got a restraining order from a Nevada court that

3. *Church of Scientology International* v. *Time Warner Inc.,* 903 F. Supp. 637 (1995). The case brought by the church was ultimately dismissed in July 1996. Time Warner settled a parallel libel suit brought by church member Michael Bayback in November 1996. This suit was based on the same 1991 article.

*In April of 1996 the Knight-Ridder Co. settled a lawsuit with a former Philadelphia prosecutor, Richard Sprague. The case, which went through two trials and numerous appeals, began in 1973, 23 years earlier.

barred Barricade publisher Lyle Stuart from distributing any books in his warehouse until the damage judgment was paid. Stuart said he did not have enough money to appeal the ruling and that the court ban on distribution of his books threatened the extinction of the company.[4]

Some observers suggest that things are likely to get somewhat better in the future. They predict fewer jury verdicts against the press and lower damage awards. This trend in libel law seems to reflect what is happening in personal injury lawsuits. Juries are becoming tougher on all personal injury plaintiffs, according to a study by Jury Verdict Research.[5] Several theories have been advanced to explain this shift in jury behavior. Some legal scholars have suggested that people are beginning to believe that the huge damage awards granted in civil suits are harmful to the nation. Other scholars believe that there is a greater public realization that large damage awards ultimately cost all Americans money because insurance companies will raise their rates to make up for the larger amounts of money they must pay out.

A mass media libel defendant typically will lose the case at trial, but will win on a reversal of the decision by an appellate court. Only 30 percent of the libel judgments won against the mass media between 1983 and 1993, for example, were upheld on appeal. Why does the press tend to lose in trial court? Several reasons have been suggested. The law is very complicated, and few trial judges see a libel case. Improper instructions to the jury or improper rulings from the bench are common. The press, the "dreaded media," as one commentator described the mass communications industry, has been losing favor with the public for nearly 25 years. Public opinion polls frequently reveal that less than 20 percent of Americans who are asked say they have substantial trust in journalists. The press has always been better at bringing problems to the attention of the public than supplying solutions to these problems. There is a tendency among many people to want to shoot the messenger. The pressure for television news programs to sustain ratings and newspapers and magazines to hold readers has pushed some in journalism to provide news coverage that emulates the bottom-feeding tabloid press. All these reasons and many others have resulted in the press losing favor with the American people, the people who sit on juries. In a libel suit these Americans have an opportunity not only to judge the behavior of the press, but to punish what they regard as inappropriate behavior.

Jurors frequently don't understand the law, and sometimes they personally don't approve of the First Amendment protections enjoyed by the press in a libel suit. A Gallup survey in the late 1980s revealed that the public strongly supported libel suits against the press, and two-thirds of those questioned said that a newspaper should be held liable for publishing a story that contained erroneous information, even if the reporters and editors had checked out the story and believed it was correct. Modern libel law dictates just the opposite outcome.

Ultimately winning a libel suit on appeal is generally good news for the press. But such a victory is not without cost. Defense expenses are extraordinarily high today. A simple case that doesn't even go to trial can cost a newspaper $25,000 in defense costs. With a tenacious plaintiff and an unsympathetic judge, pretrial costs can easily hit $50,000. Throw in a trial and one or two appeals, and costs can quickly approach $1 million. The Libel Defense Resource Center recently reported that the *average* cost of defending a libel suit (and remember, most

4. Carvajal, "Defamation Suit."
5. Perez-Peña, "U.S. Juries Grow Tougher."

don't go to trial) is $100,000. That amount may not be a major financial headache for CBS or Time Warner, but it can devastate a small publication or broadcasting station. Even a major medium, however, can be seriously affected in other ways by defense costs. In 1982 the president of Mobil Oil, William Tavoulareas, sued the Washington Post for libel. The trial lasted 19 days. The jury misunderstood the judge's instructions and awarded Tavoulareas and his son $1.8 million in damages. The trial judge set aside the jury verdict, but a three-judge panel of the U.S. Court of Appeals for the District of Columbia Circuit reinstated the judgment. The full court reheard the appeal and reversed, affirming the trial judge's decision to set aside the jury's ruling.[6] The Post won, but it had cost the newspaper $1.3 million to defend the lawsuit. Editor Ben Bradlee later commented that this experience clearly had an impact on how he looked at future news stories. If a reporter comes into the office with a terrific story, but says that it will cost the newspaper $1.3 million to run it, it had better be a really terrific story, Bradlee said, because the newspaper simply cannot afford the cost of defending itself for anything less.

THE LAWSUIT AS A WEAPON

Throughout its history, libel law has been premised on the idea that when a reputation has been damaged by something that was said or published, the injured party deserves the opportunity to go to court to repair this damage. A ruling by a court that the libelous comments were untrue helps restore the reputation; money damages provide solace to the injured person or business. Libel suits are often filed today with other purposes in mind: to punish an individual or business that has been critical of the plaintiff, and to warn others not to publish or broadcast similar criticisms. The Liberty Lobby, a conservative political group in Washington, D.C., constantly tried to harass and punish its critics by suing them for libel. The Church of Scientology is an extremely active litigant, using libel suits (and other legal claims such as copyright infringement) in an effort to block or soften criticism of its activities.

Most often the press is the target of such harassment lawsuits, but private citizens have not escaped this trend. An entire new genre of libel suits called SLAPP suits (Strategic Lawsuits Against Public Participation) has developed, according to University of Denver law professor George Pring and sociologist Penelope Canan, experts in the field. The lawsuits are not aimed at the restoration of reputation but at punishing and harassing anyone who is critical of the plaintiff or the plaintiff's operations. For example, Victor Monia and several citizens' groups were sued for more than $40 million in a libel action brought by a land developer after they successfully led a fight to impose a one-year moratorium on real estate development in Saratoga, Calif. A school bus company sued parents who complained to the state that the school buses were unsafe. A coal company sued a blueberry farmer for telling the Environmental Protection Agency about the company's pollution of a river. And the Police Benevolent Association of Nassau County, N.Y., filed 50 lawsuits against citizens who complained of police misconduct.

---

6. *Tavoulareas* v. *The Washington Post Co.,* 817 F. 2d 726 (1987). See also Brill, "1982: Behind the Verdict," 31.

The plaintiffs rarely win these lawsuits; of the cases that go to trial, defendants win more than 90 percent of the time. But the plaintiffs don't expect to win. The suits are aimed solely at stopping public criticism about what the plaintiffs have done or plan to do. The lawsuits, one authority has said, are brought to obtain an economic advantage over the defendant, not to vindicate a legally recognized right of the plaintiff.[7] The legislatures in at least nine states* have passed statutes that bar or severely limit these SLAPP suits either by immunizing from such lawsuits citizens who make good faith complaints to government or by providing for an early dismissal of such legal complaints. In California persons who make comments in a public forum in connection with an issue of public interest are provided through a broad anti-SLAPP law with the right to seek a motion to dismiss the lawsuit in furtherance of either the right to petition the government or the right of free speech. The term "person" has been applied to mass media defendants in that state, and recently a federal court dismissed a libel suit brought by the maker of a weight-loss product against a television station that asserted the anti-SLAPP statute in its defense. The court said that the TV broadcast constituted a public forum, that the safety of products intended for human consumption is a matter of public concern, and that the lawsuit was filed primarily to chill the exercise of free speech.[8]

But SLAPP suits are not the only problem. Some aggrieved parties who don't think they can win a libel suit against the press use other kinds of lawsuits to try to harass or frighten their critics. Dale Cohen, an attorney who represents the Chicago Tribune, said that the trend today is for lawyers to attack the conduct of the journalists rather than the content of the news stories.[9] Suits are brought for trespass, invasion of privacy, misrepresentation, and breach of contract. "There are a lot of benefits for plaintiff's lawyers who want to do that," Cohen said. "They can avoid many of the constraints of the First Amendment, like the burden of having to prove actual malice." At times journalists do stray beyond the tenets of responsible news gathering. Examples of such instances are documented at various places elsewhere in this book. But too often these "trash lawsuits," as Cohen calls them, are simply a legal ploy to try to frighten away a news medium from publishing or broadcasting a story.

In late 1995 CBS News became entangled in a dispute with Brown and Williamson, the nation's third largest tobacco company. CBS had tangled with this company before. In 1983 a federal court awarded the cigarette maker a $3 million judgment in a libel suit brought against a CBS-owned television station in Chicago.[10] This time a producer at "60 Minutes" was preparing a story that included an interview with a former Brown and Williamson executive who contended, among other things, that the tobacco company knowingly used a cancer-causing flavoring in its pipe tobacco. The executive, Jeffrey Wigand, was fired from his $300,000-a-year job as vice president of scientific research in March of 1993. Brown and

---

7. Pring, "SLAPP," 8, and Pring and Canan, "Strategic Lawsuits," 506; see also Dill, "Libel Law Doesn't Work."

8. *Metabolife International Inc.* v. *Wornick*, 27 M.L.R. 2597 (1999). See also *Lafayette Morehouse Inc.* v. *Chronicle Publishing Co.*, 37 Cal. App. 4th 1023 (1995).

9. Shepard, "Fighting Back."

10. *Brown and Williamson* v. *Jacobson*, 713 F. 2d 262 (1983).

*California, Delaware, Georgia, Massachusetts, Minnesota, Nevada, New York, Rhode Island, and Washington.

Williamson provided Wigand with a substantial severance package after he signed a nondisclosure agreement, a promise that he would not discuss company business with outsiders.

Wigand was paid $12,000 by CBS to help them develop a story on the tobacco industry, and the network also agreed to indemnify or financially protect Wigand should he be sued for libel by Brown and Williamson. As the story featuring the interview with Wigand reached its final editing stages, CBS attorneys advised network management to kill the story, fearing legal action by Brown and Williamson should the interview be broadcast. The lawyers were not worried about a libel suit but said they were concerned that Brown and Williamson might try to sue the network for inducing Wigand to break the confidentiality agreement he signed with the tobacco company. Judgments against the network in the billion dollar range were considered possible, especially since the suit, if brought, would go to trial in the tobacco-friendly state of Kentucky.

CBS decided not to broadcast the story as scheduled ("60 Minutes" later broadcast a modified version of the story as Wigand began to testify before legal authorities in Mississippi, something that reduced the likelihood of a successful breach of contract suit against CBS). The network's travails in this case are complicated by myriad extraneous issues. It was not a simple case.[11] First Amendment attorneys remain at odds over the possibility that Brown and Williamson might succeed in a breach of contract suit. CBS attorneys were obviously convinced the network would be in serious jeopardy. The point to remember, however, is this: A powerful interest like a tobacco company can use the law to block the dissemination of an important and possibly truthful news story. Many persons regard this proposition as distinctly unhealthy for the nation.

RESOLVING THE PROBLEM

Going to court in a libel action is rarely a happy experience for any of the participants. Plaintiffs are rarely gratified. Lawyers' fees can take as much as 50 percent of their winnings. The typical case takes four years to litigate, four years during which their lives are disrupted. Two-thirds of the plaintiffs questioned by researchers in the massive Iowa Libel Research Project said they were dissatisfied with their litigation experience.[12]

Going to court in a libel action is rarely a happy experience for any of the participants.

The press isn't happy either. Defense costs and damage awards cut into revenues. Reporters and editors are immobilized for long periods of time. Publicity about the lawsuit only reinforces the negative attitudes many persons have about the news media, further damaging the press's most valuable asset, its credibility. Even the public suffers in the end. Tax dollars subsidize the cost of litigation. Lawsuits often result in a more conservative press that may, to avoid the threat of lawsuits, deny readers and viewers important information.

Does every dispute between a mass medium and an injured party have to result in a lawsuit? Are there other means to solve these problems? Three-fourths of all plaintiffs interviewed in the Iowa Libel Research Project revealed that they would never have filed a lawsuit if the news medium would have published or broadcast a correction, retraction, or apology. Many journalists

11. See Grossman, "CBS, 60 Minutes" and Shepard, "Fighting Back." This incident was the basis for the 1999 film "The Insider."
12. Bezanson, Cranberg, and Soloski, *Libel Law and the Press.*

are reluctant to do this. Editors and reporters often reject the notion that the story is erroneous. In addition, some in journalism believe that publications and broadcasting stations that publish frequent corrections or retractions risk losing credibility with their readers or viewers.

Other schemes have been proposed as well. In the Iowa Dispute Resolution Program mediators are asked to determine the truth or falsity of the libelous allegations and then publicize the findings. No money damages are involved. A similar project was underway in Florida. But the researchers at the University of Iowa reported in late 1991 that mediation schemes lose their effectiveness unless they are initiated very early in the dispute.

A group of lawyers, journalists, and others working under the auspices of the Annenberg Washington Program in Communication Policy Studies proposed a Libel Reform Act in 1988. Under this plan, the plaintiff would first have to seek a retraction or apology. If a retraction or apology was published, the matter would end. Failure to seek a retraction within 30 days barred the plaintiff from suing later. If a retraction or reply was published, the matter would end. If no retraction was published, then either party could seek a ruling from a court on the matter of the truth or falsity of the defamatory material. The court would rule that one side was right, the other wrong. But a winning plaintiff would not get money damages; only reimbursement for his or her legal expenses. Plaintiffs' lawyers did not like this scheme because it eliminated damage awards. The press did not like it because it perceived the plan to force the publication or broadcast of retractions. Project director Rodney A. Smolla, a professor of law at William and Mary College, acknowledged the failure of the plan to gain acceptance, calling it "a dog that won't hunt."[13]

In 1994 the House of Delegates of the American Bar Association approved a Uniform Correction or Clarification of Defamation Act proposed by the National Conference of Commissioners on Uniform State Law, a private organization of judges, lawyers, and law professors. Under the proposed act, the publication or broadcast of a correction of a damaging mistake would shield a newspaper or broadcasting station from both punitive damages and damages for harm to reputation. If a suit was filed after the correction was made, the defendant would still enjoy the full protection of the First Amendment libel defenses. Damage awards would be confined to actual monetary losses the defamed person suffered as a result of the libel. About 30 states already have such retraction or correction statutes (see pages 230–231). But they tend to vary in many ways. Adoption of a uniform statute like the one proposed would simplify matters for both plaintiffs and media defendants. A state legislature must decide to adopt the Uniform Act before it will become law in that state, and in August of 1995 North Dakota became the first state to legally embrace this new libel reform. The press has been more positive in its response to this proposal than any of the earlier suggestions.

The press has also tried to fight back by countersuing plaintiffs for filing frivolous lawsuits or for abuse of process or malicious prosecution.[14] These countersuits have not been notably successful. In the end, probably the best way to solve the problem of libel is to know the law well enough to avoid a lawsuit. Explaining that law is the purpose of the rest of this chapter.

---

13. See Dill, "Libel Law Doesn't Work."
14. See, for example, *Ward* v. *Roy H. Park Broadcasting Co.,* 400 S.E. 2d 758 (1991) and *Mitchell* v. *The Herald Co.,* 137 A. 2d 213 (1988).

Libel is the most common legal problem faced by persons who work in the mass media. In the 1980s the press was hit by a large increase in the number of libel suits, but that trend may be abating. Many libel suits are filed to harass or silence the press by plaintiffs who do not expect to win the case. This strategy works because of libel judgments that now average more than $1 million and defense costs that are prohibitive for many small publications. Many attempts have been made to try to resolve this problem. Researchers have demonstrated that most libel plaintiffs are unhappy about their experiences in litigation and would not sue if the mass medium simply corrected or retracted the libelous statement. The press, however, seems reluctant to follow this strategy. More ambitious schemes to resolve the libel problem have generally met with opposition or indifference from the press and from organizations of trial lawyers.

SUMMARY

LAW OF DEFAMATION

The law of defamation is ancient; its roots can be traced back several centuries. Initially, the law was an attempt by government to establish a forum for persons involved in a dispute brought about by an insult or by what we today call a defamatory remark. One man called another a robber and a villain. The injured party sought to avenge his damaged reputation. A fight or duel of some kind was the only means of gaining vengeance before the development of libel law. It was obvious that fights and duels were not satisfactory ways to settle such disputes, so government offered to help solve these problems. Slowly the law of defamation evolved. Today the process of going to court to avenge one's honor is highly institutionalized.

In other parts of the world, different schemes are used to accomplish similar ends. In continental Europe libel suits are uncommon. When a newspaper defames a person, that person has the right—under law—to strike back, using the columns of the same newspaper to tell his or her side of the story. This right is called the right of reply, and it exists in the United States in a far less advanced form, as is noted near the end of Chapter 6. Many people favor this notion of letting the parties fight it out in print or by broadcast. They say it is far better to set out after the truth in this fashion than to rattle the chains on the courthouse door every time an insult is flung in the public press.

Parts of the law of libel do not concern those who work in mass communications. For example, elements of libel deal with allegations contained in private communications, a letter from one person to another, a job recommendation from a former employer to a prospective employer. The material in this chapter focuses on public communications—material that is published or broadcast via the mass media, using that term in its broadest sense to include advertising, company magazines, trade association newsletters, press releases, and so on. Similarly, because newspapers, broadcasting stations, magazines, and the like tend to focus on material considered to be of public concern, courts often treat them differently from nonmedia defendants.[15] Unless otherwise stated, it can be presumed the discussion in this text focuses on the rights and responsibilities of media defendants.

15. See, for example, *Philadelphia Newspapers, Inc.* v. *Hepps,* 475 U.S. 767 (1986).

Additionally, it must be remembered that libel law is essentially state law. It is possible to describe the dimensions of the law in broad terms that transcend state boundaries, and that is what this text attempts to do. But important variations exist in the law from state to state, as will be demonstrated in the next chapter in the discussion of fault requirements. It is important for students to focus on the specific elements of the law in their states after gaining an understanding of the general boundaries of the law.

Another problem in the law has to do with whether a communication is a libel (written defamation) or a **slander** (an oral defamation). The law in many states distinguishes between the two. The problem was simple 100 years ago. Because of the state of technology, a public communication, one meant for a wide audience, was a printed communication—a newspaper, magazine, or handbill. Therefore a law that dealt with libel more harshly than with slander made sense; libel caused more severe damage. A libel lasted longer than a slander since a libel was printed, more people saw it, and it was generally considered to be planned defamation, not words accidentally spoken in the heat of argument. Film, radio, and television have made these distinctions meaningless. If a performer defames someone on "The Tonight Show," the defamation still has immense impact and is heard by millions despite the fact that the defamation is not printed. Although the law varies slightly from state to state, today published defamation, whether it is in a newspaper, on the Internet, on radio or television, in the movies, or whatever, is regarded as libel. And libel rules apply. Most authorities also agree that online defamation should be governed by the rules of libel, not the rules of slander.

The purpose of this chapter is to give persons in mass communications guidance and rules to apply in the process of gathering, writing, publishing, and broadcasting news, information, or advertising. People who want to learn to litigate a lawsuit should go to law school. My goal is to keep media practitioners out of libel suits or at least to keep them from losing libel suits.

ELEMENTS OF LIBEL

There are many definitions of defamation, and they are all about the same. In their book "Libel," Phelps and Hamilton include this definition:

> Defamation is a communication which exposes a person to hatred, ridicule, or
> contempt, lowers him in the esteem of his fellows, causes him to be shunned, or
> injures him in his business or calling.[16]

The "Restatement of Torts," a compilation by the American Law Institute of what it thinks the common law says, defines libel this way:

> a communication which has the tendency to so harm the reputation of another as
> to lower him in the estimation of the community or to deter third persons from
> associating with him.[17]

---

16. Phelps and Hamilton, *Libel.*
17. American Law Institute, *Restatement of Torts.*

Here is another definition: Defamation is any communication that holds a person up to contempt, hatred, ridicule, or scorn.

Each of the preceding definitions reveals common and important elements of defamation:

1. **Defamation is a communication that damages the reputation of a person, but not necessarily the individual's character.** Your character is what you are; your reputation is what people think you are. Reputation is what the law protects.

2. **To be actionable defamation, the words must actually damage a reputation. There must be proof offered that the individual's reputation was harmed.** A U.S. district court in Oklahoma recently granted a summary judgment to the defendant in a libel suit because the plaintiff, a man who was wrongly named as a seller of T-shirts and other memorabilia "celebrating" the death and destruction caused by the bombing of the federal building in Oklahoma City, failed to provide sufficient evidence that his reputation had been harmed.[18] Without proof of this harm, a party who claims injury will not be able to recover damages for the injury. But the awarding of damages by juries is hardly a science, and often a plaintiff is compensated for suffering emotional harm or loss of self-esteem. Such awards should be possible only if the suffering or loss of esteem is a direct result from the actual harm to reputation. Courts have ruled in some instances that a particular plaintiff is "libel proof." This ruling means that the plaintiff's reputation was seriously tarnished even before the libel was published; the defamatory words were incapable of causing additional harm to the plaintiff's reputation.

   A Texas physician named Tommy Swate sued a reporter and a small Texas newspaper, alleging that an article published in the newspaper questioned his competence as a doctor. In their defense the defendants presented 24 previously published newspaper articles and three disciplinary orders from boards of medical examiners related to Swate's medical practice. Included were references to prior litigation involving the doctor and various instances of misconduct. He had been accused of failing to complete abortions on patients and to repair lacerations that occurred during abortion procedures. He had been placed on probation for five years, but continued to practice medicine anyway. The court said the plaintiff was libel proof. "Let it suffice to say," Judge Lopez wrote, "that Swate has been the target of extensive negative media attention for at least ten years, so much that it is imossible to believe Swate's reputation could have been further damaged."[19] Someone who is libel proof simply cannot prove injury to his or her reputation.

3. **At least a significant minority of the community must believe that the plaintiff's reputation has been damaged, but the minority must not be an unrepresentative minority.** A Delaware superior court ruled that it was not defamatory for a television newscaster to refer to a convict as "an alleged FBI informant." The plaintiff complained that the statement hurt his reputation among

Defamation is any communication that holds a person up to contempt, hatred, ridicule, or scorn.

18. *Zeran v. Diamond Broadcasting Inc.,* 26 M.L.R. 1855 (1998).
19. *Swate v. Schiffers,* 975 S.W. 2d 70 (1998).

his fellow prisoners at the state penitentiary. Conceding that the "informant" label might harm his prison reputation, the court ruled that "it is not one's reputation in a limited community in which attitudes and social values may depart substantially from those prevailing generally which an action for defamation is designed to protect." The public in general would not think any less of the plaintiff for being an informant for the FBI.[20] To summarize this point: The defamation must lower a person's reputation in the eyes of a significant number of people, and unless unusual circumstances exist, these people must fairly reflect representative views.

Persons can be injured through a libel in numerous ways. The statement may simply hurt their reputation, or it may be that lowering their reputation deprives them of their right to enjoy social contacts, which is a fancy way of saying that their friends don't like them anymore or their friends want to avoid them. A man's or woman's ability to work or hold a job or make a living may be injured. A person need only be injured in *one* of these three ways to have a cause of action for libel. If plaintiffs can show actual harm in any one of these areas, chances are good they will recover some damages. That is one of the reasons libel law exists—to compensate the plaintiff for injury. There are other reasons. A libel suit can help vindicate the plaintiff, help restore the damaged reputation. A victorious plaintiff can point a finger at the newspaper or television station and say, "See, they were wrong, they lied, they made an error." A damage judgment is also considered punishment for the defendant. Editors and broadcasters who have to pay a large damage award may be more cautious in the future. It can stand also as an example to other journalists to avoid such behavior.

Any living person can bring a civil action for libel. A dead person can't sue; that's obvious. The common law bars suits by the relatives of someone who has died in behalf of the deceased. Note, however, that if a living person is defamed, brings suit, and then dies before the matter is settled by the court, it is possible in some states that have what are called **survival statutes** for relatives to continue to pursue the lawsuit.[21] A business corporation can sue for libel, as can a nonprofit corporation, if it can show that it has lost public support and contributions because of the defamation. There is a division in judicial opinion about whether unincorporated associations like labor unions and political action groups can sue for libel. Some court rulings say no; others say yes. Find out what the law is in your state. Cities, counties, agencies of government, and governments in general cannot bring a civil libel suit. This question was decided years ago and is settled law.[22]

One important key to understanding any lawsuit is to understand the concept of the burden of proof. Which party must prove what? While this sounds like a trivial matter to many laymen, it is a very significant element in a lawsuit. Remember, under our adversarial legal system, the court does nothing but evaluate and analyze the material that is brought before it by the adversaries. Judges and juries don't go out and look for evidence themselves. So the matter of who must bring the evidence before the court is a critical one. If a plaintiff, for

---

20. *Saunders* v. *WHYY-TV,* 382 A. 2d 257 (1978).
21. See *MacDonald* v. *Time,* 554 F. Supp. 1053 (1983) and *Canino* v. *New York News,* 475 A. 2d 528 (1984).
22. *City of Chicago* v. *Tribune Publishing Co.,* 139 N.E. 2d 86 (1923).

example, is required to prove a specific element in a case and fails to bring sufficient evidence before the court to convince the judge or jury, the plaintiff loses the case. Theoretically, the defendant can just sit on his or her hands and do nothing until the plaintiff has brought forth the needed material to prove the point. But this is not likely to happen; the defendant is more likely to fight the plaintiff every step of the way, arguing that the evidence is not acceptable or is insufficient to prove the point.

In a libel case the plaintiff bears the initial burden of proof. He or she must establish five separate elements of the case in order to have any chance of winning (see following boxed text).

TO WIN A LIBEL SUIT A PLAINTIFF MUST PROVE:

1. The libel was published.
2. Words were of and concerning plaintiff.
3. Material is defamatory.
4. Material is false.
5. Defendant was at fault.

Each of the five elements in this box is outlined in detail shortly. Items four and five are probably only required if the plaintiff is suing a mass media defendant. These elements are fairly recent additions to the law of libel, and the courts have not yet fully resolved the question of how far they should be extended.[23] Since this book is about mass media law, it is written with the assumption that plaintiffs will generally have to prove the falsity of the matter. The fifth element, proof of fault, is also presumed to be a requirement to be met by the plaintiff for purposes of this discussion. Fault will be discussed in Chapter 5.

PUBLICATION

Before the law recognizes a statement or comment as a civil libel (**criminal libel** is different; see pages 232–234), the statement must be published. In the eyes of the law, **publication** occurs when one person, in addition to the writer and the person who is defamed, sees or hears the material.* Think of the situation as a kind of triangle. The writer or broadcaster (ultimately

---

23. See *Columbia Sussex* v. *Hay,* 627 S.W. 2d 270 (1981); *Mutafis* v. *Erie Insurance Exchange,* 775 F. 2d 593 (1985); and *Philadelphia Newspapers* v. *Hepps,* 475 U.S. 767 (1986).

*This statement may confuse some people who see it as a contradiction of an earlier statement that to be defamatory something must lower an individual's reputation in the eyes of a significant minority of the community. It is not a contradiction. Publication is what is being discussed here: How many people must see something before the law considers it to have been published. The earlier remark refers to damage to an individual: How many people must think less of a person upon hearing or reading the statement. It is necessary for the plaintiff to convince the court that a significant number of people in the community would think less of him or her because of the libelous remark, but it is not necessary that the plaintiff show that these people have actually seen the libelous remark.

the defendant) is at the first point: the subject of the defamatory statement (ultimately the plaintiff) is at the second point; and a third person is at the third point. All three are necessary for a libel suit. In defamation by the mass media, publication is virtually presumed. In fact, some cases are on record in which courts ruled that if a statement was published in a newspaper or broadcast over television, it is presumed that a third party saw it or heard it.[24]

Technically, every republication of a libel is a new libel. Judge Leon Yankwich ("It's Libel or Contempt If You Print It") wrote more than four decades ago:

> In brief, the person who repeats a libel assumes responsibility for the statement and vouches for its truth as though it had been of his own making or on his own information, no matter how emphatically the qualifying words show that the statement is made on the basis of a source other than the writer himself.[25]

Imagine this hypothetical situation. Television station WWTV reports that government inspectors have closed down the Warm Loaf Bread Co. because they found unhealthy conditions at the bakery. This is a libelous allegation. The editor of the company newsletter at competing Tres French Baking Company decides Tres French employees should hear this, so she publishes this item in the newsletter: "Government inspectors are closing down the Warm Loaf Bread Company because of unhealthy conditions at the bakery, according to WWTV." This is a republication of the libel, and the newsletter can also be sued by Warm Bread for defamation.

Some people mistakenly believe that attributing a libel to a third party will shield them from a lawsuit, but this is one of the great myths of American journalism. For example, most good reporters know that it is libelous to label someone a murderer. But a remarkably high percentage of professionals erroneously believe you can label someone a murderer, so long as you attribute the statement to a third party. "Jones killed his wife" is obviously defamatory. So is "Jones killed his wife, according to neighbor Ned Block." The newspaper or broadcasting station has simply republished Block's original libel of Jones. (The relationship between quoting an official as the source of a libelous assertion and fault, another element of the case that must be proved by the plaintiff, is discussed on pages 186–189.) Because of the republication rule, nearly everyone in the chain of production of a news story is technically liable in a lawsuit.

Some people mistakenly believe that attributing a libel to a third party will shield them from a lawsuit, but this is one of the great myths of American journalism.

A long-standing exception to the republication rule is the notion that news vendors, bookstores, libraries, and others who actually distribute the finished printed product cannot be held responsible for republishing the defamation unless the defendant can show that these people or institutions knew the printed matter contained a defamation, or should have had reason to know. This concept is called **scienter,** or guilty knowledge, and is fundamental in many areas of the law. For example, a federal court in eastern Washington state ruled in late 1991 that local television stations that are network affiliates are not responsible for the libelous content of programming that they transmit for the network. The court ruled that the stations are mere conduits for the network programs and have no prior knowledge of the content of these programs before they are actually broadcast.[26]

24. *Hornby* v. *Hunter,* 385 S.W. 2d 473 (1964).
25. Yankwich, *It's Libel or Contempt If You Print It.*
26. *Auvil* v. *CBS "60 Minutes,"* 800 F. Supp. 928 (1991).

Libel on the Internet

The great bulk of the law of libel that is outlined in this chapter and the next two applies to defamation that is transmitted via the Internet. Courts regard communication on the World Wide Web the same way they regard material published in newspapers, magazines, or books. Two issues have arisen, however, that have forced the courts and the Congress to consider the relationship between libel and the Internet. The first has to do with the status of online service providers (OSPs) in the transmission of a libel; the second has to do with jurisdiction, a subject that will be discussed in Chapter 6.

There are many contexts in which a libel might be published on the Internet. A defamatory message might be sent to every person who logs on to an OSP's computers. Libelous material might be contained in a database that is viewed or downloaded by a user. Defamation might be posted on a bulletin board generally accessible to some or all of the OSP's customers. A libelous remark might be made during an online real-time discussion among users connected to an OSP. Or, defamation might be contained in a message sent to an e-mail addressee.

If the OSP is the author or the originator of the libelous message, it will be regarded as a publisher in a libel suit. That is, the OSP will be treated in the same manner as a newspaper that publishes a libelous statement. The OSP is liable for the defamatory publication and can be sued. But if, as is more common, the OSP simply transmits a libel originated by someone using the system for e-mail or to post a message on a bulletin board or for some other purpose, the system operator will be regarded as a distributor, not a publisher. Included in the Communications Decency Act adopted by the Congress in 1996 is the provision that "No provider . . . of an interactive computer service shall be treated as the publisher or speaker of any information provided by another information content provider."[27] This protection may not be applicable if the OSP is aware of the libelous material it is transmitting and fails to remove it.

Prior to the 1996 congressional action courts had come to varying conclusions regarding the status of the OSP in a libel suit. A federal court in New York ruled in 1991 that an OSP should be considered a distributor, not a publisher. A New York state court reached the opposite conclusion four years later.[28] But since 1996 courts have accepted the congressional mandate, sometimes grudgingly, that relieves the OSPs of liablility. For example, a U.S. district court in Virginia ruled that America Online was not liable in a negligence action brought against the OSP by a man who claimed he was harmed when someone posted a notice on a bulletin board advertising T-shirts and other items glorifying the Oklahoma City bombing. Affixed to the ad were the plaintiff's name and telephone number. The court said the imposition of common law liability in the case would directly contradict the congressional mandate.[29] A Palm Beach trial court reached a similar conclusion in a case brought by a mother who claimed that a subscriber to America Online used the interactive service to solicit sales of videotapes and photographs of sexual acts committed by the subscriber with a child. None of the material was transmitted online; the subscriber simply asked people to call him on the telephone if they were interested in

---

27. 47 U.S.C. § 230 (C) (1).
28. See *Cubby, Inc.* v. *CompuServe, Inc.,* 776 F. Supp. 135 (1991) and *Stratton Oakmont, Inc.* v. *Prodigy Services,* 23 M.L.R. 1794 (1995).
29. *Zeran* v. *America Online Inc.,* 958 F. Supp. 1124 (1997); off'd. 129 F. 3d 327 (1997).

such items. The court said the provisions in the Communications Decency Act prohibited it from finding the OSP liable; the federal statute pre-empted state law on the matter. The 4th U.S. Circuit Court of Appeals affirmed this ruling in 1997.[30] In April of 1998 a federal judge in Washington, D.C., dismissed a libel action against America Online by a high-ranking aide to President Clinton. Sidney Blumenthal claimed he had been libeled by comments included in the online "Drudge Report," a political gossip Web site generated by Matthew Drudge and transmitted by America Online. U.S. District Judge Paul Friedman said he was reluctant to dismiss the suit, but that the clear intent of Congress—to protect Internet service providers from liability for materials disseminated by them but created by others—left him no choice.[31] The $30 million suit against Drudge, however, was allowed to proceed.

A court in New York recently ruled that OSPs are not liable for defamation that they simply transmit, regardless of what the Congress wrote in the Communications Decency Act. The high court in that state ruled that the role of Prodigy (an OSP) in transmitting e-mail "is akin to that of a telephone company, which one neither wants nor expects to superintend the content of its subscribers' conversations." The defendant is not a publisher under New York common law because it played only a passive role in the transmission of the libelous e-mail message, the court ruled.[32]

While the U.S. law protecting online service providers appears to be effective in protecting the OSPs from libel suits initiated in the United States, it is unlikely it will protect the OSPs from lawsuits filed in other countries. British law, for example, does not protect online service providers who simply act as distributors of a defamatory message that has been posted on the Web by a third party. An OSP in Great Britain, Demon Internet, agreed to pay $25,000 in damages plus several hundred thousand dollars in court costs to British physicist Laurence Godfrey in March of 2000 for transmitting alleged defamatory comments that had been part of a discussion in a news group carried by Demon's new servers. If Demon had been a U.S. OSP and the suit brought in a U.S. court, Godfrey would have had no chance of winning. But British libel law is more heavily weighted toward plaintiffs than the law in the United States, and the British government has not given OSPs immunity from libel actions when they merely act as distributors of the material.[33] Authorities disagree on whether a U.S. OSP could be successfully sued in a British court if it distributed defamatory matter about a British subject to Internet users in Great Britain. Courts will have to sort this out. The basic points to remember are these: At this time only U.S. law provides protection for OSPs regarding the content they simply distribute as opposed to originate. And the Internet, as a global medium, reaches nations with laws fundamentally different from those in the United States.

IDENTIFICATION

The second element in a libel suit is **identification:** the injured party must show the court that the allegedly defamatory statement is "of and concerning him, her, or it." Failing to do this, the plaintiff will lose the suit. Author William Peter Blatty sued The New York Times for libel

30. *Doe* v. *America Online, Inc.,* 25 M.L.R. 2112 (1997).
31. *Blumenthal* v. *Drudge,* 992 F. Supp. 44 (1998). See also Stout, "America Online."
32. *Lunney* v. *Prodigy Services Co.,* 28 M.L.R. 1090 (1999).
33. Kaplan, "Suit Against," and Lyall, "British Internet Provider."

when the newspaper did not list one of the writer's novels on its best-selling book list. Blatty, who wrote "The Exorcist" among other thrillers, argued that his book had sold more than enough copies to be included on the list, and that the newspaper, by keeping him off the list, was publishing a false and defamatory statement about him. But the California Supreme Court dismissed the case, noting that because Blatty was not on the list, he could not establish that anything The New York Times implied was "of and concerning him."[34] This was surely an unusual suit, but it makes the point: The plaintiff must be identified. And it is important to note that not all readers or viewers need to know to whom the libel refers. Some authorities say it is sufficient if only a single person can identify the subject of the report.[*] A person can be identified in a number of ways. He or she may be explicitly named. The individual can be described, for example, as the host of the quiz show "Jeopardy" or the city's superintendent of public works. A picture or a drawing, even without a caption, can be sufficient if the likeness is recognizable. Even descriptive circumstances can sometimes point the finger at someone. In 1991 a young woman, after attending a party, was abducted as she was standing outside a house near the University of Pennsylvania campus. She was raped by her abductor. A local television station reported the attack, including comments by a police officer that cast some doubts on the victim's story. She claimed these comments defamed her. The station did not use the victim's name, but described her as a female Bryn Mawr student (Bryn Mawr is a small college near the University of Pennsylvania that enrolls less than 1,500 undergraduates) who had been raped on a certain day, that she lived in a dorm at Bryn Mawr, that she drove a Nissan, and that she had attended a party at the University of Pennsylvania shortly before her abduction. The station claimed that broadcasting these facts did not constitute identification. But a U.S. district court disagreed, noting the small school environment at Bryn Mawr. "In this type of environment, it would not be surprising if some people could identify the plaintiff from the information supplied in the broadcast."[35] In fact, the plaintiff presented affidavits from students attesting to the fact that the story of her rape had spread rapidly across campus after the broadcast. The Illinois Supreme Court recently held the publishers of Seventeen magazine liable for publishing a short story labeled fiction that described as a slut a girl identified only as Bryson. The author of the story, Lucy Logsdon, a native of southern Illinois, wrote a first-person narrative that recounts a conflict she said she had with a high school classmate. The classmate in the short story bore a slight physical resemblance to the plaintiff, Kimberly Bryson, who had attended high school with Logsdon. The court said that third persons familiar with both the plaintiff and the defendant would understand that the story was referring to the plaintiff despite the fiction label.[36]

---

34. *Blatty* v. *The New York Times,* 728 P. 2d 1177 (1986).
35. *Weinstein* v. *Bullock,* 827 F. Supp. 1193 (1994).
36. *Bryson* v. *News America Publications Inc.,* 672 N.E. 2d 1207 (1996).

[*]This situation should not be confused with damage to the plaintiff. Only one person has to see a story for it to have been published. Some authorities (e.g., Phelps and Hamilton) also say that only one person has to identify the plaintiff. However, when a judge and jury consider whether the material is defamatory and damaging to the plaintiff, they must decide whether the statement can lower the plaintiff's reputation in the eyes of a significant minority of the community.

It is possible for the plaintiff to put two or more stories together to establish identification. Police arrested eight people in Brookline, Mass., in connection with drug smuggling. One of the persons arrested was identified as a former employee of Haim's Deli in Brookline. Police said gang members at times met at the deli. An area radio station mistakenly reported that "The owner of a Brookline deli and seven other people are arrested in connection with an international cocaine ring." Haim Eyal, the owner of Haim's Deli, sued for libel. The radio station attempted to defeat the suit by arguing that its report did not include the name of the delicatessen and that there were scores of delis in Brookline. Therefore, it had not identified Mr. Eyal. But the Massachusetts Supreme Judicial Court ruled that because nearly all other news stories about the incident had mentioned Haim's Deli, listeners to the erroneous radio report would know which deli was involved and would think Haim Eyal was arrested as a gang member.[37]

If a libelous statement does not make an explicit identification, then the plaintiff must somehow prove that the defamatory words refer to him or her. There have been a handful of cases recently in which plaintiffs have sued for libel, arguing that they have been fictionally portrayed in a novel. This is not as difficult to prove as it sounds, as some publishers have recently discovered. The U.S. Court of Appeals for the 2nd Circuit ruled in 1980 that an identification might be established if "a reasonable reader rationally suspects that the protagonist is in fact the plaintiff, notwithstanding the author's and publisher's assurances that the work is fiction." To do this, the court said, the plaintiff must show that the fictional work "designates the plaintiff in such a way as to let those who knew her understand that she was the person meant. It is not necessary that all the world should understand the libel; it is sufficient if those who knew the plaintiff can make out that she is the person meant."[38] What courts tend to do in such cases is first look at the similarities between the character and the plaintiff, and then look at the dissimilarities. In the early 1980s Lisa Springer sued Viking Press, alleging that she had been depicted as a character in Robert Tine's novel "State of Grace." The heroine of the fictional work was Lisa Blake, the mistress of a ruthless Italian industrialist, a woman who had an unusual sexual appetite. Springer had had a personal relationship with the author just before the book was published, and both she and the fictional Lisa Blake had similar physical characteristics, attended college, and even lived on the same street in New York. But the court found that the dissimilarities between the two were more striking, noting that Springer lived a fairly modest, quiet life, while the fictional Blake inhabited a far more luxurious world. "The dissimilarities both in manner of living and in outlook are so profound that it is virtually impossible to see how one who had read the book and who knew Lisa Springer could attribute to Springer the lifestyle of Blake."[39]

One of the most common problems in libel is careless identification that results in a case of mistaken identity. Years ago the Washington Post ran a story about a District of Columbia attorney named Harry Kennedy who was brought back from Detroit to face charges of forging a client's name. The attorney charged was Harry P.L. Kennedy, a man who used his middle

---

37. *Eyal* v. *Helen Broadcasting Corp.,* 583 N.E. 2d 228 (1991).
38. *Geisler* v. *Petrocelli,* 616 F. 2d 636 (1980).
39. *Springer* v. *Viking Press,* 457 N.Y.S. 2d 246 (1982).

initials when he gave his name. The Post left out the middle initials. Harry F. Kennedy, another District of Columbia attorney who did not use his middle initial in business, sued the newspaper and won a substantial judgment.[40] That was sloppy journalism.

Journalists face somewhat of a conundrum today regarding identification. Traditionally, reporters have been taught to include full identification when writing or talking about someone: John Smith, 36, of 1234 Boone Street, a carpenter. This information will separate this John Smith from any other person with the same name. But the issue of privacy is of great concern today, and many persons don't want their ages or addresses in the newspaper or broadcast on television. Some news organizations now permit less than complete identification in sensitive situations. A reporter needs to get complete identification for someone in the news; newspaper or broadcast station policy will dictate how much of it is used.

A reporter needs to get complete identification for someone in the news; newspaper or broadcast station policy will dictate how much of it is used.

GROUP IDENTIFICATION

A troublesome question regarding identification is group identification. Can a member of a group sue when the group as a whole is libeled? Remember, the plaintiff must show the court that the injurious remarks are "of and concerning him or her." If the group is very small, the plaintiff usually has little difficulty convincing a court that identification has occurred. If the editor of a company's employee newsletter asserts that the three-person employee benefit board is incompetent, each member could claim identification. On the other hand, if the group is very big it is improbable that a suit will stand. A group of commercial net fishermen in Florida was blocked in their attempt to sue four North Florida television stations that broadcast an advertisement depicting the purported negative environmental consequences of commercial net fishing as practiced along the Florida coast. The ad was sponsored by a group called Save Our Sea Life and was prepared as part of a campaign to amend the state constitution to limit net fishing. The Florida Circuit Court dismissed the action, noting that there were hundreds of commercial net fishermen in the state, a number far too large for the purpose of identification.[41]

But what about the groups in between very small and very big? The "Restatement of Torts" says this:

> One who publishes defamatory matter concerning a group or class of persons is subject to liability to an individual member of it, but only if (A)the group or class is so small that the matter can reasonably be understood to refer to the individual, or (B)the circumstances of publication reasonably give rise to the conclusion that there is particular reference to him.[42]

There is really no magic number; it is not possible to say, for example, that a group with more than 40 is safe, or that groups with less than 25 pose problems. Courts will look at the circumstances as well as the number in the group. A police undercover agent reported to the

40. *Washington Post* v. *Kennedy*, 3 F. 2d 207 (1924).
41. *Thomas* v. *Jacksonville Television, Inc.,* 24 M.L.R. 1894 (1996); see also *Adams* v. *WFTV Inc.,* 691 So. 2d 557 (1997).
42. American Law Institute, *Restatement of Torts.*

owner of a paper mill in Maine that employee Harry Hudson had been drinking on the job. The agent was assigned to the mill to look for illegal drug use. A dozen workers at the mill were ultimately fired, 11 for illegal drug use, and Hudson for drinking on the job. A local television station subsequently reported that 12 workers had been terminated at the mill for involvement with illegal drugs. No names were given, but the mill was identified. Hudson sued and argued that it was common knowledge in the small community who the 12 workers were—and as such he had been erroneously identified as an illegal drug user. The station sought to have the suit dismissed, but the Maine Supreme Court refused, ruling that it was a jury question whether or not the broadcast had identified Hudson.[43] Courts have ruled that groups of 29 teachers,[44] 30 firefighters,[45] and 21 police officers[46] were all too large to permit identification.

Despite these victories by the press, caution is urged on reporters who describe even a very large group in a defamatory manner. Caution is especially appropriate if only a small number of the defamed group live in the community. If the charge is made that all astrologers are frauds and there is only one astrologer in the community, the remark can be dangerous. The plaintiff could convince a sympathetic jury that he or she has been severely harmed by the remark. Saying "all" members of a group are corrupt is worse than saying "most" members are corrupt. Saying "most" is worse than saying "some," and saying "some" is worse than saying "one or two."

DEFAMATION

The third element in the plaintiff's case is the words themselves. There are two kinds of defamatory words. The first kind consists of words that are libelous on their face, words that obviously can damage the reputation of any person. Words like *thief, cheat,* and *traitor* are libelous per se—there is no question that they are defamatory.

The second kind of words are innocent on their face and become defamatory only if the reader or viewer knows other facts. To say that Duane Arnold married Jennifer Carter appears safe enough. But if the reader knows that Arnold is already married to another woman, the statement accuses Arnold of bigamy. And that is a libelous accusation.

The distinction between these two kinds of words was once more important than it is now. At one time plaintiffs had to prove they were specifically harmed by the words in the second category, usually called "libelous per quod." Damage was presumed from the words in the first category, usually called "libelous per se." All plaintiffs today must prove they were damaged by the publication of the libel. Still, in many jurisdictions, courts have erected significant barriers that make it more difficult for persons who sue for libel per quod to win their case than persons who sue for words that are clearly defamatory on their face.

The law does not contain a list of words that are defamatory. In each case a court must examine the particular words or phrase or paragraph and decide whether these words lower

43. *Hudson* v. *Guy Gannett Broadcasting,* 521 A. 2d 714 (1987).
44. *O'Brien* v. *Williamson Daily News,* 735 F. Supp. 218 (1990).
45. *Olive* v. *New York Post,* 16 M.L.R. 2397 (1989).
46. *Arcand* v. *Evening Call,* 567 F. 2d 1163 (1987).

the individual's reputation among a significant number of so-called right-thinking people in the community. Sometimes a precedent or many precedents will exist. Numerous cases, for example, establish that stating a woman is unchaste is libelous. But sometimes precedents aren't always that useful. Times change; the meanings of words change. At one time calling someone a socialist was defamatory because socialists were hated and feared by many. Today the use of such a word would likely be harmless. Author Oscar Hijuelos used these phrases in his novel "The Mambo Kings Play Songs of Love": "Gloria huddled at a table drinking daiquiris." She touched the "skin and gnarly hair" of the Mambo King before saying to him, "Come on, ya big lug, why don't you kiss me?" Eighty years ago such a description of a woman's behavior might in fact harm her reputation. But in 1991, a U.S. district court ruled that "reporting that a person has requested a kiss or [was] sipping a daiquiri, true or not, simply does not subject [a person] to the scorn of the average reader."[47]

At a libel trial a judge and jury are supposed to consider the words in light of their ordinary meaning unless the evidence is persuasive that the defendant meant something else when the statement was published. As a general rule, the judge will decide as a matter of law whether particular words are capable of conveying a defamatory meaning. Sometimes even negative descriptions of a person won't qualify as libel. Comedienne Martha Raye sued late-night television host David Letterman for a parody of her ads for denture cleaner. The ads always began, "Here is Martha Raye, actress, denture wearer." Letterman told his audience that he had seen "the most terrifying commercial on television last night, featuring Martha Raye, condom user." The court said that the words were not defamatory. "No one could reasonably understand this passage as expressing that the plaintiff actually uses condoms, that she is promiscuous, that she actually had made a condom commercial, or any other statement of fact," the California Superior Court judge ruled, dismissing the case.[48] Former NBC late-night host Johnny Carson was sued by Mr. Blackwell for making a joke about the fashion guru's annual list of worst dressed celebrities. Carson commented in his monologue that Blackwell said of Mother Teresa, "Miss Nerdy Nun is a fashion no-no." Blackwell never made the statement, and charged that it made him look bad to have such a remark attributed to him. The judge, however, got the joke and ruled the statement could not reasonably have been understood in a defamatory sense. It was a joke, and anyone who heard it would realize it was a joke.[49]

If the judge rules that the words *are capable* of a defamatory meaning, the fact finder— the jury, if there is one, or the judge—then must determine whether the words *in fact convey* a defamatory meaning. For example, a U.S. court of appeals ruled that it was up to a jury to decide whether the allegation that a scientist charged as much as $5,000 per day to testify as an expert in court cases carried with it the implication that the scientist was selling his testimony to the highest bidder, a clearly defamatory assertion.[50]

---

47. Cohen, "Use of Real Name."
48. *Raye* v. *Letterman,* 14 M.L.R. 2047 (1987).
49. *Blackwell* v. *Carson,* 22 M.L.R. 1665 (1994). See also *Buttons* v. *National Broadcasting Co., Inc.,*858 F. Supp. 1025 (1994).
50. *McBride* v. *Merrell Dow,* 717 F. 2d 1460 (1984).

Innuendo as opposed to a flat assertion can be defamatory. Read the following actual news item from the Boston Record:

> The Veterans Hospital here suspected that 39-year-old George M. Perry of North Truro, whose death is being probed by federal and state authorities, was suffering from chronic arsenic poisoning.
>
> State police said the body of Perry, and of his brother, Arthur, who is buried near him, would probably be exhumed from St. Peter's Cemetery in Provincetown.
>
> George Perry died in the VA hospital last June 9, forty-eight hours after his tenth admission there. . . . His brother, who lived in Connecticut and spent two days here during George's funeral, died approximately a month later. About two months later, in September, George's mother-in-law, seventy-four-year-old Mrs. Mary F. Mott, who had come to live with her daughter, died too. Her remains were cremated.

While the story lacked a good deal in journalistic clarity, it didn't take Perry Mason or Matlock to understand what the reporter was trying to suggest. Mrs. Perry murdered her husband, her brother-in-law, and her mother. The insinuations are that Arthur died after visiting the plaintiff's home and that the mother had "died too." Isn't it too bad that her remains were cremated? This story cost the Hearst Corporation, publishers of the Boston Record, $25,000.[51]

A libel suit cannot be based on an isolated phrase wrenched out of context. The article as a whole must be considered. A story about baseball's legendary base stealer, Maury Wills, might contain the sentence "Wills might be the best thief of all time," referring to his base-stealing ability. Wills cannot sue on the basis of that single sentence. The story itself makes it clear the kind of thievery the writer is discussing. Nevertheless, a libelous remark in a headline—even though it is cleared up in the story that follows—can be the basis for a libel suit.

One week after O.J. Simpson was acquitted of the criminal charge of murdering his wife and her companion the National Examiner carried a headline on its cover, "COPS THINK KATO DID IT—He fears they will want him for perjury, pals say." The story appeared on page 17 and carried the headline, "KATO KAELIN . . . COPS THINK HE DID IT." The story said the police were trying to prove that Kaelin lied under oath, that he committed perjury. The headlines suggest, Kaelin argued, that he was a suspect in the murders. Attorneys for the National Examiner said no, that was not what was intended. The word "it" meant perjury. Judges on the Ninth U.S. Court of Appeals ruled that under California law the meaning of the publication must be measured by the effect it would have on the mind of the average reader, and in this case it was highly likely that an average, reasonable reader might conclude that the word "it" referred to murder.[52] Kaelin and the Examiner settled this suit in October of 1999.

In a recent case in Indiana the state supreme court was confronted with a situation in which a restaurant owner argued that a newspaper headline defamed his establishment. The court adopted the rule that if a headline fairly indicates the substance of an otherwise accurate

---

51. *Perry v. Hearst Corp.,* 334 F. 2d 800 (1964).
52. *Kaelin v. Globe Communications Corp.,* 162 F. 3d 1036 (1998).

article, the headline is not defamatory. In this case a county health inspector reported that there was evidence of roaches and rodents in the restaurant. The headline in the Ft. Wayne Journal Gazette stated: "Health board shuts doors of Bandido's. Inspectors find rats, roaches at local eatery." The state high court ruled that the headline was not an accurate indication of the article, because it contained the word "rats," and the story only referred to "rodents." Every rat is a rodent, the court ruled, but not every rodent is a rat.[53]

Sometimes a court will even allow reader habits to be taken into account. A story of about 50 paragraphs published in the Seattle Post-Intelligencer was a generally accurate account of the redemption of a home mortgage by a local attorney. But the headline and the first few paragraphs strongly hinted that the attorney had done something wrong. The jury agreed with the plaintiff that it was unlikely that most readers would follow the lengthy story as it was jumped onto the inside pages of the newspaper and would absorb only the defamatory connotations in the first few paragraphs. The lawyer won a $100,000 judgment.[54]

Factual assertions can obviously be defamatory. What about an opinion? A pure opinion, one that does not imply a defamatory fact, is not defamatory. The Supreme Court has defined an opinion as a statement that cannot be proven to be true or false. "I think Mayor Frank Jones is a lousy leader for our city" is a pure opinion. There is no way to prove that true or false. But the statement, "I think Mayor Frank Jones lied to the people when he said he would clean up crime in the city" is not a pure opinion. Whether or not Jones is a liar can be tested by evidence. We will talk much more about this in Chapter 6.

If there is not a catalog of defamatory words, there are at least categories of words to which writers and editors need to pay special attention. Imputations of criminal behavior are responsible for a great many libel suits. Saying someone has done something illegal—from jaywalking to murder—is libelous. The use of the word "alleged" in these cases is often of little help. The meaning of the word "alleged" is "to be declared or asserted to be as described." An alleged murderer is someone who has been declared or asserted to be a murderer. But by whom? If the state has charged Jones with murder, the state has alleged that he is a murderer. If that is the case, a reporter should say so: "Jones, who has been charged with murder" rather than simply, "the alleged murderer Jones." But if Jones is merely being questioned in connection with the murder, he is not an alleged murderer, he is an alleged suspect. To call him an alleged murderer is inaccurate and libelous. The best guide for the reporter is this: Report what you know to be true. If Jones is being questioned as a suspect, say that. If police consider him a suspect, say that. Take the word "alleged" and put it in circular file next to the desk.

Sexual references and implications are also responsible for a great many libel suits. A statement that a woman is unchaste or is sleeping with a man to whom she is not married is defamatory. An allegation that a woman has been raped is equally libelous. The law traditionally has been less protective of men in this regard, but times may be changing. A young male model sued the publishers of gay and lesbian publications for including his photo in advertising

53. *Journal-Gazette Company* v. *Bandido's Inc.,* 27 M.L.R. 2089 (1999).
54. *McNair* v. *Hearst Corp.,* 494 F. 2d 1309 (1974).

for "Lust," a collection of photographs of naked, sexually aroused men engaged in explicit sex acts. The defendant was alone in the photo and was clothed from the waist down, but he argued that the use of the photo in advertising for such a publication suggests that he is sexually promiscuous. The defendants tried to argue that even if the use of the photo did imply sexual promiscuity, this was not a defamatory statement when made about a man rather than a woman. The Appellate Division of the New York Supreme Court disagreed. "[T]he notion that while the imputation of sexual immorality to a woman is defamatory per se, but is not so with respect to a man, has no place in modern jurisprudence. Such a distinction, having its basis in gender-based classification—would violate constitutional precepts," the court said.[55] Comments about other kinds of sexual behavior are also sensitive. But times change, and words that were once considered defamatory may no longer sustain a libel suit. During the First World War it was libelous to call someone a slacker for it meant he had refused to join the military service. Today the word means only that someone is not doing his or her share of the work and is not defamatory. So it is with sexual terms. Twenty years ago it was settled law that to call someone a homosexual was libelous. It may still be in many jurisdictions, but courts in at least a few states have ruled that the description is no longer defamatory.[56]

Material about the personal habits of an individual need to be carefully screened. To raise questions about an individual's honesty, integrity, or financial responsibility can be dangerous. Comments about consumption of alcohol or drugs can also cause problems. Libel law has traditionally protected persons from false assertions that they have a contagious disease. Such an allegation can cause friends and acquaintances to shun the supposed victim because they don't want to be infected by the disease themselves. This is not a common libel problem today. But suggesting that someone suffers from a medical condition that implies, for example, sexual promiscuity or unsavory behavior on the part of the victim is a problem. The Nebraska Supreme Court in 1990 sustained a jury award of $23,350 to a Springfield, Neb., man who was falsely accused of having AIDS. This was a slander suit, and resulted when a prominent woman in a small town began spreading rumors about the plaintiff.[57] Finally, comments about an individual's personal religious faith ("She doesn't live up to the teachings of her church"), patriotism, or political activities have also generated libel actions.

A person can be libeled by ridicule. Not all humorous stories about someone are necessarily defamatory; only those in which the subject of the story is made to appear "uncommonly foolish" tend to be dangerous. Newspapers are commonly victimized by false obituaries. At times the "deceased" has brought a libel suit in response to such a publication, but the courts have consistently ruled that to say someone has died is not defamatory; it does not lower that person's reputation. But once a New England newspaper ridiculed a man by saying he was so thrifty that he built his own casket and dug his own grave. This story made the man appear to be foolish or unnatural.[58]

---

55. *Rejent* v. *Liberation Publications, Inc.,* 197 A.D. 2d 240 (1994).
56. See, for example, *Donovan* v. *Fiumara,* 114 N.C. App. 524 (1994) and *Miles* v. *National Enquirer,* 38 F. Supp. 2d 1226 (1999), a Colorado ruling.
57. Robbins, "A Rumor of AIDS."
58. *Powers* v. *Durgin-Snow Publishing Co.,* 144 A. 2d 294 (1958).

Business Reputation

Libel law probably goes furthest in protecting persons in their business and occupations. Any comment that injures people's ability to conduct a business, harms them in their job, or makes it more difficult for them to pursue their occupation is generally defamatory. And businesspeople are generally more likely to sue. They tend to be more acquainted with law and more comfortable with a legal suit. And while fear of dragging one's personal life through a courtroom to sue for something published about a home life or sexual practice often deters a would-be plaintiff, the same cannot be said for suits based on comments about a business practice.

There are some interesting quirks in libel law as it relates to comments about the way an individual does business. To report that a businessperson or professional person has made an error is not always defamatory. Business and professional people are not expected to be perfect. Everyone makes a mistake now and then. A story, for example, that suggests a physician has misdiagnosed a case or that a real estate developer has botched a deal may not be considered defamatory under what is called the **single mistake rule.** The community would not think less of a doctor or businessperson who made a single error, the reasoning goes. Hence, the statement is not defamatory. Stories that suggest a pattern of incompetence, that go beyond asserting a single error, are defamatory, however.[59] The single mistake rule should not be used as an excuse for sloppy reporting, but it can come in handy if an error is inadvertently made.

Corporations that believe their credit has been damaged or their reputation has been harmed can do exactly what an individual plaintiff can do and sue for this injury. The list of kinds of defamatory accusations is long. Assertions that a company is involved in illegal business or that it fails to pay its bills on time or that it deliberately manufactures unsafe products or that it is trying to break a union are all libelous. The law, however, does not hold a public business responsible for the bad behavior of its customers. The owner of a Biloxi lounge sued for a story that said a man had been killed in a fight in the bar. Actually the fight took place outside, about one-half block down the street. The Mississippi Supreme Court refused to hold the newspaper responsible, ruling that there was nothing in the story that harmed the lounge or its owner.[60] A suggestion that the proprietor of a public business encourages rowdy behavior, or tolerates fighting, or permits drug deals to be made is a different matter. In these cases the story does reflect on the behavior of the owner and would be libelous.

Criticism of a Product

Criticism of a product falls into a different legal category called "disparagement of property." Such criticism is often called **trade libel,** but it is not really libel at all. What is the difference between libeling a business and disparaging a product? Persons who seek to sue for defamation of a business must demonstrate that the libel somehow suggests that the men and women who run the business are incompetent or too greedy or cheaters. An allegation, for example, that Acme automobiles won't operate during a rainstorm is an attack on the product itself but not

Criticism of a product falls into a different legal category called "disparagement of property."

---

59. *Bowes* v. *Magna Concepts, Inc.,* 561 N.Y.S. 2d 16 (1990); see also *Sermidi* v. *Battistotti,* 27 M.L.R. 2523 (1999).
60. *Chatham* v. *Gulf Publishing,* 502 So. 2d 647 (1987).

necessarily on the Acme car company. However, allegations that Acme automobiles won't run in a rainstorm because they are assembled improperly, or because the company has tried to cut costs by using parts that are not waterproof, is a defamation of the company as well as the product.

It is very difficult for a plaintiff to win a trade libel suit. First, the plaintiff must show that the statements about the product are false. This is often hard if the writer has been careful. Note the product evaluations in the magazine Consumer Reports. Consumers Union, which publishes the magazine, never reports that a particular model of car, a Ford Escort for example, handles poorly or starts hard. It reports that the particular car it tested handled poorly and started hard. Ford could not prove that statement was false, even if it could show that every other Escort manufactured handled well and started quickly.

Next, the plaintiff must show specific monetary loss because of the false comments about the product. The courts insist on precise dollars-and-cents losses from canceled orders, for example, or a dip in sales. Finally, the plaintiff has to show that the false comments about the product were motivated either by ill will and bad feelings, or actual malice. All three elements—falsity, monetary loss, and some kind of malicious conduct—must be proved, and this is a substantial burden for the plaintiff to bear. Simply proving the statement is false raises a considerable challenge.

For example, in 1989, the television program "60 Minutes" suggested that apples grown in Washington state were unsafe because they had been treated with a chemical called Alar, which some scientists contend causes an increased risk of cancer, especially to children. Farmers in the state sued CBS and others for $100 million, alleging among other things product disparagement, or trade libel. But the case came to an abrupt ending four years later when a U.S. district court granted the network's motion for a summary judgment, ruling that the plaintiffs in the case could not possibly prove that the statements were false.

The apple growers contended that three statements made in the broadcast were false.

1. Daminozide (the active ingredient in Alar) is the most potent cancer-causing agent in our food supply.
2. Daminozide poses an imminent hazard and unacceptable cancer risk.
3. Daminozide is most harmful to children.

Judge Nielsen said that there was substantial debate within the scientific community about the potential harm caused by daminozide. CBS presented evidence that the Environmental Protection Agency considers daminozide to be among the most carcinogenic synthetic pesticides, and that ingesting a carcinogen at any time could create the hazard of suffering a cancer in the future. He said that researchers have sharp differences of opinion regarding the potential harm that daminozide might cause to children. If science is seemingly in disagreement about the danger posed by this chemical, Judge Nielsen said, how did the plaintiffs think they were going to prove that these allegations were false?[61] The 9th U.S. Circuit Court of Appeals upheld this decision in 1995.[62]

61. *Auvil v. CBS "60 Minutes,"* 836 F. Supp. 740 (1993).
62. *Auvil v. CBS "60 Minutes,"* 67 F. 3rd 816 (1995).

Banks, Insurance Companies, and Vegetables

Many states have adopted statutes aimed at protecting the reputations of specific kinds of businesses. Banks and insurance companies in many jurisdictions are shielded by special statutes designed to protect them from attacks on their fiscal integrity. If successful, such an attack could turn customers against these businesses and destroy them quite easily. In recent years 13 states* have adopted statutes that outlaw publication of intentional lies about the fruits and vegetables grown in the state. These so-called veggie hate laws are aimed at preventing the kind of damage suffered by Washington apple growers because of the Alar controversy noted earlier. These laws generally give farmers and growers a cause of action to sue anyone who makes a statement about the health risks of a particular food product that is not based on "verifiable fact or scientific or other reliable evidence." Some of these laws also shift the burden of proving truth or falsity from the plaintiff to the defendant. Although such laws as these seem odd, they nevertheless exist and could result in legal woes for the careless journalist.

Talk show producer and host Oprah Winfrey was sued in 1998 by Texas cattle ranchers under that state's False Disparagement of Perishable Food Products Act. A guest on Winfrey's talk show had alleged that thousands of head of U.S. cattle were infected with bovine spongiform encephalopathy, the so-called mad cow disease, prompting the talk show host to declare that she was giving up eating hamburgers. Cattle prices dropped precipitously after the broadcast, and the ranchers sought millions of dollars in damages. Experts who viewed the case as the first important test of the constitutionality of the veggie hate laws were disappointed when U.S. District Judge Mary Lou Robinson ruled that the case could not proceed under the Texas law because the plaintiffs had not proved that cattle are "perishable food" as defined by the statute, or that "knowingly false" statements had been made, a requirement under the Texas law.[63] The lawsuit reverted to a run-of-the-mill product disparagement case, which Winfrey won.[64]

FALSITY

Libel plaintiffs who sue the mass media must generally prove that the defamatory statements are false. This comment must be qualified because it is not completely accurate, and to make this qualification you must be introduced to one of the anomalies of libel law, something that will be discussed at far greater length on page 207.

The world of libel plaintiffs is divided into two groups, public persons and private persons. A public person is a government official, an elected officer, someone who is leading a public crusade, a prominent entertainer, a visible religious or business leader. A private person is someone who is not a public person. As you will soon see, the law makes it far more difficult for a public person, as opposed to a private person, to win a libel suit.

63. *Texas Beef Group* v. *Winfrey,* 11 F. Supp 2d 858 (1998).
64. Verhovek, "Turf Was Cattlemen's." The 5th U.S. Court of Appeals upheld this verdict in February of 2000.

*As of late 1999, Alabama, Arizona, Colorado, Florida, Georgia, Idaho, Louisiana, Mississippi, North Dakota, Ohio, Oklahoma, South Dakota, and Texas have adopted these produce-protection measures.

In every instance a public-person plaintiff must prove that the libelous remarks are not truthful. But the Supreme Court has ruled that a private-person plaintiff must prove the falsity of the libelous statements only when the subject of the statement is a matter of public concern.[65] What is a matter of public concern? The Supreme Court has not given a definition but, in another case, noted that whether a statement dealt with a matter of public concern must be determined on the basis of the statement's "content, form and context."[66] Not a very clear definition.

The legal definition of a "matter of public concern" will undoubtedly be litigated heavily in the years to come, and someday a good set of criteria will be developed. It is my belief that this definition will be a broad definition, perhaps as broad as this: Something that is published in a newspaper or magazine of general circulation or aired on radio or television must be a matter of public concern. Please note, this definition is only an educated guess at this point.

Most plaintiffs, then, must prove that the defamatory material is false. In those few instances when a private person sues for a story that is not a matter of public concern, the defendant must prove that the material is truthful. How does one prove falsity or truth?

The first rule of proving truth or falsity is that the evidence presented in court must go to the heart of the libelous charge.

The first rule of proving truth or falsity is that the evidence presented in court must go to the heart of the libelous charge.

The proof must be direct and explicit. If there is conflicting evidence, the fact finder—the judge or the jury—will decide who is telling the truth. Every word of a defamatory charge need not be truthful, only the part that carries the gist or the sting.

What the court is looking for is substantial truth. For example, a Maryland television station reported that an AIDS counseling and testing business was under investigation by state authorities, that it failed to have a proper license, and that many health professionals were strongly opposed to businesses and clinics that issued the kind of AIDS-free ID cards provided by the business in this case. The cards were meaningless, the doctors said, because the cardholder could be exposed to the HIV virus the moment he or she left the clinic with the AIDS-free ID card.

The business had heavily promoted its service and sued for libel, alleging that the television story contained some errors. And it did. The TV report said the AIDS center sold the ID cards. It didn't. The cards were free, after the client paid $50 for the AIDS test. The report also said the company was closing one of its offices. It was not. In fact, it was opening a new office. And so on. But the 4th U.S. Circuit Court of Appeals ruled that the story was substantially true, that the minor inaccuracies were immaterial to the thrust of the story, that the business was under state investigation and failed to have a proper license.[67]

The Georgia Supreme Court ruled in 1999 that a statement published in a newspaper that said the plaintiff was serving jail time for rape and aggravated child molestation was substantially true, even though the plaintiff had been charged only with child molestation, not aggravated child molestation.[68] Similarly, a federal court in Pennsylvania ruled that a

65. *Philadelphia Newspapers, Inc.* v. *Hepps,* 475 U.S. 767 (1986).
66. *Dun & Bradstreet* v. *Greenmoss,* 472 U.S. 749 (1985).
67. *AIDS Counseling and Testing Centers* v. *Group W Television,* 903 F. 2d 1000 (1990).
68. *Weaver* v. *Jensen,* 27 M.L.R. 2146 (1999).

newspaper report that the plaintiff was convicted of embezzlement when the actual charges were tax evasion and mail fraud was substantially true and not actionable.[69] After James Mortensen pleaded guilty in federal court in 1997 to unlawfully selling archeological artifacts, newspapers in Nevada called him a looter, a robber, and a grave robber. Mortensen admitted illegally removing valuable artifacts from Indian burial sites, but he said the terms used by the newspapers made him appear to be a common thief and were not a truthful report of his crime. The Nevada Supreme Court agreed with the newspapers and said while the terms used were colloquial, they were nevertheless a truthful characterization of Mortensen's conduct.[70]

The context of any remark is important in determining truth or falsity. Poet Harold Norse objected to a statement made by author Ted Morgan in Morgan's biography of beat-generation author William Burroughs. Morgan said he was trying to describe Norse when the poet lived in Tangier in the 1960s: "Harold thought of himself as 'dark horse Norse,' ignored and unpublished." The plaintiff argued that the comment made it appear that he had not published any poetry by 1963, which was untrue. The 9th U.S. Circuit Court of Appeals disagreed with Norse, saying that when the statement is judged in the context in which it is presented, it is clearly not intended to be an account of Norse's publishing history, but rather a description of his state of mind at that time. He viewed himself, the court said, as "unfairly neglected and ignored, a poet who believed that he was not as successful as he deserved to be in his publishing efforts at that stage of his career.[71]

But don't be misled. It is not the size of the error that counts. The court will ask whether the inaccurate statement is defamatory. And a detail can be just as libelous as a major assertion. Take the case of Anthony S. Jones, for example. Jones was hired as a firefighter in 1984 under a federal court order that required the employment of more minorities in the Des Moines (Iowa) Fire Department. Eighteen months later he was fired. Authorities said he had failed to pass a written emergency medical technician examination, a requirement to hold the job. Fire Chief Robert Armstrong told reporters that Jones had a reading problem. He had been tutored in reading at taxpayers' expense, Armstrong said, but the test revealed he still read at the third-grade level. Jones sued when the story was broadcast. The television station and other defendants asked the trial court to dismiss the case because the story was substantially true. The trial court denied the motion, and the Iowa Supreme Court sustained the denial. The state high court said there were two errors in the story. Jones personally had paid for a substantial part of the tutoring. Also, Jones was tested as reading at a level comparable with the lower one-third of community college students, not the third-grade level. These were details, but they were an important part of the substance of the story. The story was not substantially true, the court ruled, and sent the case back for trial.[72]

Reporters must remember that a jury in a libel suit will determine the truth or falsity of a story based on what the story said, not what the reporter meant. ABC was sued by the maker

---

69. *Reilly v. North Hills News Record,* 27 M.L.R. 1569 (1998).
70. *Mortensen v. Gannett Co.,* 26 M.L.R. 1415 (1997).
71. *Norse v. Henry Holt and Co.,* 991 F. 2d 563 (1993).
72. *Jones v. Palmer Communications, Inc.,* 440 N.W. 2d 884 (1989).

of a garbage recycling machine. Lundell Manufacturing sold the $3 million machine to a county in Georgia. After using the machine for a year or so, some people in the county said that the new machine had not solved the garbage problem. An ABC "World News Tonight" story included these comments:

> In this south Georgia county of tobacco farms and pecan groves taxpayers are
> angry that they are stuck with a three million dollar debt for this garbage recy-
> cling machine that they never approved and does not work.

Network attorneys argued that the reporter meant that the machine does not work in the larger sense, that it doesn't solve the county's garbage problem. But a jury agreed with the plaintiff instead and said that they interpreted the comment to mean that the garbage recycling machine did not work, that it was defective. In 1996 the 8th U.S. Circuit Court of Appeals upheld the more than $1 million jury award and ruled that a jury could conclude that the network's statement about the machine was false.[73]

How does the court evaluate the truth of the charge? The jury does this with guidance from the judge. The jurors are presented with both the libelous untruthful statement about the plaintiff and the truth about the plaintiff. The untruthful statement will leave a certain impression about the plaintiff in the jurors' minds. Does learning the truthful statement change that impression? For example, a television station refers to Hal Jones as a wife beater. Jurors gain an impression of Jones based on that statement. In truth, Jones struck his wife only once, during an argument, after she threw a coffee pot at him. Does the truth leave a different impression of Jones in the jurors' minds? One court said, "a workable test of truth is whether the libel as published would have a different effect on the mind of the reader from that which the pleaded truth would have produced."[74]

The case of *Haynes* v. *Alfred A. Knopf, Inc.* provides a good example of this test. Author Nicholas Lemann wrote a best-selling book called "The Promised Land: The Great Black Migration and How It Changed America." In this work he recounted the migration of more than 5 million African-Americans from impoverished rural areas in the South to the North between 1940 and 1970. In some parts of the book he focused on the experiences of individuals to tell his story. What happened to Ruby Lee Daniels when she moved north from Mississippi was an important segment in the book. Seven years after she arrived in Chicago, Ruby Lee met Luther Haynes. Haynes had a good job at the time and he and Ruby lived together and had children. But then, according to Lemann, Luther began to drink too much and problems began. The author recounted a whole series of incidents that reflected very badly on Haynes and certainly hurt his reputation. Included were allegations that Haynes was fired from a job for drinking, that he was arrested for assaulting a police officer, that he refused to support his family, and that he walked out on Ruby and the children. In a libel suit that followed, Haynes did not dispute the accuracy of most of these statements, but said that three of them were false. The court ruled that even if three of the many statements were false, most of

---

73. *Lundell Manufacturing Co.* v. *ABC Inc.,* 98 F. 3d 351 (1996).
74. *Fleckstein* v. *Friedman,* 195 N.E. 537 (1934).

the material written about Haynes was true. The reputation was damaged by the truthful statements. The harm caused by the three false statements really didn't hurt Haynes that much more. "Falsehoods that do not harm the plaintiff's reputation more than a full recital of the true facts about him would do are thus not actionable," the court said.[75]

While it seems contrary to logic, the fact that every statement in a news story is true does not mean the total story could not be viewed as false if it leaves the wrong impression in the readers' minds. A South Carolina woman named Nora Richardson was driving a car that struck and seriously injured the police chief of Eastover, S.C. She pleaded guilty to charges of driving too fast for the road conditions. One year later the police chief, Nathaniel Williams, died. The newspaper wrote that Williams' death came "after being on medical leave for more than a year following a traffic accident in which a passing motorist hit him." The paper said he never fully recovered from his injuries and went on to detail the circumstances of the accident. Two days later the newspaper reported that Richardson would not face additional charges despite Williams' death. "It would be illegal to charge her for a second time for the same crime, Christy Cox [spokeswoman for the Highway Patrol] said."

Every statement in both stories was accurate, but the totality of the reports left readers with the impression that Williams died from injuries suffered in the accident; that Richardson had killed him. The newspaper failed to report that Williams had died from rectal cancer, something that had nothing to do with the traffic accident. The South Carolina Court of Appeals said that the "truth of each sentence of the articles, viewed separately, is irrelevant." The truth must be as broad as the sting or gist of the libel. The appellate court reversed a summary judgment granted to the newspaper and ordered the trial court to send the case to a jury.[76]

One more point should be stressed about truth and falsity. Correctly quoting someone or accurately reporting what someone else has told you does not necessarily constitute publishing a truthful statement. Imagine that John Smith tells a reporter that the police chief changes arrest records of certain prisoners to simplify their getting bail and winning acquittal. This charge, attributed to John Smith, is contained in the reporter's story, which is subsequently published. The police chief sues for libel. It is not sufficient for the reporter to prove merely that the statement in the story was an accurate copy of what Smith said. Even if the reporter's story contained an exact duplicate of Smith's charge, truth can be sustained only by proving the substance of the charge, that the police chief has altered arrest records. It is the truth of the libelous charge that is at issue, not merely of the accuracy of the quote in the story. Accuracy, then, is not always the same thing as truth.

The initial burden in the libel suit rests with the plaintiff, who must prove five important elements: that the defamation was published, that it was of and concerning the plaintiff, that the words were defamatory, that the allegations were false, and that the defendant was at fault in causing this legal harm. The first four elements have been discussed in this chapter. Proving fault, the most complicated of the five elements, is the subject of Chapter 5.

"Falsehoods that do not harm the plaintiff's reputation more than a full recital of the true facts about him would do are thus not actionable."

---

75. *Haynes* v. *Alfred A. Knopf, Inc.,* 8 F. 3d 1222 (1993); see also *Schmalenberg* v. *Tacoma News Inc.,* 943 P. 2d 350 (1997).
76. *Richardson* v. *State-Record Co.,* 499 S.E. 2d 822 (1998).

A plaintiff in a libel suit must first prove that the defamatory material was published; that is, that one additional person besides the plaintiff and the defendant has seen the material. The plaintiff must next show that the libel is of and concerning him or her. An individual can be identified for purposes of a libel suit by a name, nickname, photograph, or even through a report of circumstances. Statements made about a very large group of people cannot be used as the basis for a libel suit for a single member of that group. However, if the group is smaller, individual members of the group may be able to sue for comments made about the entire group. The plaintiff must also prove that the words in the offensive statement are defamatory; that they lower his or her reputation. The most common kinds of defamatory statements contain allegations about criminal acts or sexual impropriety, include comments about personal habits or characteristics, or reflect on the plaintiff's patriotism, political beliefs, or competence and qualifications in a business or occupation. Corporations or other businesses can be defamed, and the manufacturer of a product can sue, with great difficulty, for product disparagement. In lawsuits against the mass media the plaintiff normally must prove that the damaging statements are false. The evidence presented in court must go to the heart of the libelous charge; the gist or sting of the libel must be false. Minor errors, unless they relate directly to the gist of the libel, will not usually result in a finding of falsity. The test of falsity is whether the proven truth leaves a different impression of the plaintiff in the minds of the jury than the impression created by the defamatory falsehood.

SUMMARY

BIBLIOGRAPHY

"Amazing and All True! Lawyers Reveal Secrets for Protecting Tabloids." *The New York Times,* 1 January 1991.

American Law Institute. *Restatement of Torts,* 2d ed. Philadelphia: American Law Institute, 1975.

Ashley, Paul. *Say It Safely,* 5th ed. Seattle: University of Washington Press, 1976.

Bezanson, Randall P. "The Libel Tort Today." *Washington and Lee Law Review* 45 (1988):535.

———, Gilbert Cranberg, and John Soloski. *Libel Law and the Press.* New York: The Free Press, 1987.

Brill, Steven. "1982: Behind the Verdict in the Washington Post Libel Trial." *The American Lawyer,* May 1994, 31.

Carvajal, Doreen. "Defamation Suit Leaves Small Publisher Near Extinction." *The New York Times,* 8 October 1997, C1.

———. "Libel Wrangle Over Miliken Book Drags On." *The New York Times,* 28 June 1999, C1.

Cohen, Roger. "Suit Over Novel's Use of Real Name Is Dismissed." *The New York Times,* 19 July 1991.

Dienes, C. Thomas. "Libel Reform: An Appraisal." *Journal of Law Reform* 23 (1989):1.

Dill, Barbara. "Libel Law Doesn't Work, But Can It Be Fixed?" in *At What Price? Libel Law and Freedom of the Press,* essays by Martin London and Barbara Dill. New York: Twentieth Century Fund Press, 1993.

Goodchild, Seth. "Media Counteractions: Restoring the Balance to Modern Libel Law." *Georgetown Law Journal* 75 (1986):315.

Grossman, Lawrence K. "CBS, 60 Minutes, and the Unseen Interview." *Columbia Journalism Review,* January/February 1996, 39.

Jones, Alex S. "Iowa Experiment Offers Arbitration for Settling Libel Disputes Out of Court." *The New York Times,* 4 May 1987, 17.

———. "Libel Awards: Million-Dollar Barrier is Breached." *The New York Times,* 13 April 1988, 36.

Kaplan, Carl S. "Suit Against Cornell Dropped in International Libel Case." *The New York Times Cyber Law Journal,* 7 November 1998.

Libel Law: A Report of the Libel Reform Project. Washington, D.C.: The Annenberg Washington Program, 1988.

Lyall, Sarah. "British Internet Provider to Pay Physicist Who Says E-Bulletin Board Libeled Him." *The New York Times,* 1 April 2000, A5.

Perez-Peña, Richard. "U.S. Juries Grow Tougher on Plaintiffs in Lawsuits." *The New York Times,* 17 June 1994, A1.

Phelps, Robert, and Douglas Hamilton. *Libel.* New York: Macmillan, 1966.

Pring, George. "SLAPPS: Strategic Lawsuits Against Public Participation." *Pace Environmental Law Review,* fall 1989, 8.

———, and Penelope Canan. "Strategic Lawsuits Against Public Participation." *Social Problems* 35 (1988):506.

Prosser, William L. *Handbook of the Law of Torts.* St. Paul: West Publishing, 1963.

Robbins, William. "A Rumor of AIDS, a Slander Suit." *The New York Times,* 23 July 1990.

Shepard, Alicia C. "Fighting Back." *American Journalism Review,* January/February 1996, 34.

Smolla, Rodney A. "Dun & Bradstreet, Hepps, and Liberty Lobby: A New Analytic Primer on the Future Course of Defamation." *Georgetown Law Journal* 75 (1987):1519.

———, and Michael J. Garetner. "The Annenberg Libel Reform Proposal: The Case for Enactment." *William and Mary Law Review* 31 (1989):25.

Stout, David. "America Online Libel Suit Dismissed." *The New York Times,* 23 April 1998, A15.

Verhovek, Sam Howe. "A Gain for Winfrey in Suit by Beef Producers in Texas." *The New York Times,* 18 February 1998, A10.

———. "Turf Was Cattlemen's, But Jury Was Winfrey's." *The New York Times,* 27 February 1998, A10.

Yankwich, Leon R. *It's Libel or Contempt If You Print It.* Los Angeles: Parker & Sons Publications, 1950.

Libel
Proof of Fault

In 1964, for the first time, the Supreme Court of the United States ruled that a libel plaintiff was required to show that a defendant had been at fault when the defamatory material was published. Until that time, civil libel law had been governed by what is known as the doctrine of strict liability. Under this doctrine a libel defendant was responsible for harming a plaintiff regardless of how cautious and careful he or she had been in preparing and publishing or broadcasting the story. This ruling changed the face of libel law. What had been a relatively simple tort became a complex legal morass when it was infused with First Amendment considerations. In this chapter we outline the two basic considerations relevant to fault:

    Who is the plaintiff?

    How was the story or material processed or prepared?

NEW YORK TIMES v. SULLIVAN

A difficult and often violent struggle for civil rights was taking place in much of the Deep South in the early 1960s. Blacks, often accompanied by white civil rights workers, used various acts of nonviolent civil disobedience to challenge a wide range of voting, accommodation, and education laws that had left them as second-class citizens. Network television news was still in its early adolescence in this era; NBC and CBS carried only fifteen minutes of news each night. The story of the civil rights movement was carried throughout the nation via a handful of prestigious and frequently liberal newspapers, especially The New York Times. Segregationist leaders in the South hated these newspapers, which each day carried stories and pictures of another peaceful civil rights protest that had been met with violence or some other illegal act by city, county, or state officials or by angry southern citizens.

On March 29, 1960, The Times carried a full-page editorial-advertisement entitled "Heed Their Rising Voices." The ad was placed by an ad hoc coalition of civil rights leaders called the "Committee to Defend Martin Luther King and the Struggle for Freedom in the South." The text of the ad leveled charges against public officials in the South who, the committee contended, had used violence and illegal tactics to try to quell the peaceful civil rights struggle. The basic thrust of the charges contained in the advertisement was true; but the ad was filled with small, factual errors. Several public officials in Alabama brought suit against the newspaper. The first case to go to trial was one brought by Montgomery, Ala., police commissioner L.B. Sullivan, who sought $500,000 in damages for false and defamatory statements about the conduct of the Montgomery police department. Sullivan was never named in the ad but contended that comments about the behavior of the police reflected on him. A trial court ruled on behalf of Sullivan, and his $500,000 damage award was upheld by the Alabama Supreme Court. This despite the fact that only 35 copies of the offending issue of The New York Times were circulated in Montgomery County.

The U.S. Supreme Court unanimously reversed the decision, ruling that Sullivan could not recover damages in this case unless he proved that The New York Times published the false and defamatory advertisement knowing it was false, or that the paper exhibited reckless disregard for the truth when it printed the material.[1] That is, the Montgomery police commissioner had to show that the newspaper had actually lied when it printed the ad (knowledge of falsity), or that the persons who published the ad (both the members of the committee and the members of the newspaper's staff) had been extraordinarily careless by not examining the charges made in the statement much more carefully (reckless disregard for the truth). Justice William Brennan labeled these two elements "actual malice"; proof of knowledge of falsity or proof of reckless disregard for the truth was proof of actual malice. The language in the court's opinion extended the ruling in this case to all persons whom the court called public officials. All public officials who sought to win a libel suit based on defamatory allegations about how they did their jobs or whether they were fit to hold those jobs henceforth would have to prove actual malice. Before examining the various elements in this new libel standard, let's look briefly at the rationale Brennan and his colleagues used to support this fundamental change in the law.

---

1. *New York Times Co. v. Sullivan,* 376 U.S. 254 (1964).

The following are excerpts from the advertisement, "Heed Their Rising Voices," that was published in The New York Times on March 29, 1960, by the Committee to Defend Martin Luther King and the Struggle for Freedom in the South. The sections of the ad published below provoked a libel suit by L.B. Sullivan, police commissioner of Montgomery, Ala. against The New York Times, which resulted in the Supreme Court's application of the First Amendment as a shield against libel actions brought by public officials against the mass media.

"HEED THEIR RISING VOICES"

"As the whole world knows by now, thousands of Southern Negro students are engaged in widespread non-violent demonstrations in positive affirmation of the right to live in human dignity as guaranteed by the U.S. Constitution and the Bill of Rights. In their efforts to uphold these guarantees, they are being met by an unprecedented wave of terror by those who would deny and negate that document which the whole world looks upon as setting the pattern for modern freedom. . . .

"In Montgomery, Alabama, after students sang 'My Country, Tis of Thee' on the State Capitol steps, their leaders were expelled from school, and truckloads of police armed with shotguns and tear-gas ringed the Alabama State College Campus. When the entire student body protested to state authorities by refusing to re-register, their dining hall was padlocked in an attempt to starve them into submission. . . .

"Small wonder that the Southern violators of the Constitution fear this new, non-violent brand of freedom fighter . . . even as they fear the upswelling right-to-vote movement. Small wonder that they are determined to destroy the one man who, more than any other, symbolizes the new spirit now sweeping the South—the Rev. Dr. Martin Luther King, Jr., world-famous leader of the Montgomery Bus Protest. . . .

"Again and again the Southern violators have answered Dr. King's peaceful protests with intimidation and violence. They have bombed his home almost killing his wife and child. They have assaulted his person. They have arrested him seven times—for 'speeding,' 'loitering,' and similar 'offenses.' And now they have charged him with 'perjury'—a felony under which they could imprison him for ten years. . . .

"We urge you to join hands with our fellow Americans in the South by supporting, with your dollars, this Combined Appeal for all three needs—the defense of Martin Luther King—the support of the embattled students—and the struggle for the right-to-vote."

THE RATIONALE FOR THE RULING

▪ **Stripped of its cover, this case was clearly one of seditious libel.** A government official was criticized for the way he handled his public office. The newspaper was punished for publishing this criticism. The issues that generated the court ruling and the penalty for the newspaper were really not much different than what occurred in prosecutions under the Alien and Sedition Acts of 1798 and the

Espionage and Sedition Acts of 1917 and 1918. Rulings by the Supreme Court had sharply limited the government's power to use seditious libel to punish those who criticize it (see pages 52–56). What Sullivan and his co-plaintiffs were attempting to do was to resurrect sedition law via a civil libel action.

■ **The nation has a profound and long-standing national commitment to the principle that debate on public issues should be uninhibited, robust, and wide open.** Debate on public issues is a fundamental part of the democratic process. All citizens are encouraged to take part in this debate. In the heat of any discussion it is inevitable that erroneous statements will be made by the participants. Many people will be fearful of taking part in the debate if they think they might be sued for libel if they make a misstatement that harms someone's reputation. Whatever is added to the field of libel, wrote Justice Brennan, is taken away from the field of free debate. Freedom of expression, Brennan noted, needs breathing space to survive.[2]

Freedom of expression, Brennan noted, needs breathing space to survive.

■ **When a public official like Sullivan takes a government post, he or she must expect that their work will be closely scrutinized and even criticized by the people they serve.** Officers of government have ample means to rebut this criticism. They usually have easy access to the press to deny allegations made against them, to give their side of the story, and to even verbally attack their critics. This kind of speech is also a part of the important debate within a democracy. Police commissioner Sullivan could have easily talked to reporters in Montgomery if he sought to establish the truth. Instead he chose to punish The New York Times.

The actual malice rule imposed on the law of libel by the Supreme Court was already a part of the law in a handful of states prior to the 1964 ruling in *New York Times* v. *Sullivan.* In the wake of the Sullivan decision, all state and federal courts had to follow this rule. By the end of the decade, the Supreme Court had extended the actual malice rule to persons called public figures. Persons outside of government frequently try to lead public debate on important issues. These people should not be any more immune to criticism and complaints than government officials, the court rationalized.[3] Public figures would also have to prove actual malice in order to sustain a successful libel suit. Finally, in 1974, the high court added the final element to the libel fault rule when it declared that even private persons, persons who are not part of government or who have not tried to influence public opinion, must prove that the mass medium was at fault when the libel was published or broadcast.[4] The state courts were given some freedom in this ruling to determine just what kind of fault the private party suing a mass medium must prove. Under the First Amendment the private-person plaintiff at least must prove that the broadcasting station or magazine failed to exercise reasonable care in preparing and transmitting the story, or was negligent, the high court said. But a state could ask that these plaintiffs prove even more to sustain their libel suits, the court added. The issue of the level of fault that the plaintiff must prove will be discussed in the second half of this chapter (see pages 185–198).

2. *New York Times Co.* v. *Sullivan,* 376 U.S. 254 (1964).
3. *Curtis Publishing Co.* v. *Butts, A.P.* v. *Walker,* 388 U.S. 130 (1967).
4. *Gertz* v. *Robert Welch, Inc.,* 418 U.S. 323 (1974).

Several words have been used in the past few pages that beg for fuller explanation. Who is a public official? Who is a public figure? How do you define negligence? How do you define actual malice? The next section of this chapter attempts to add flesh to these bones, to make these legal concepts come a bit more alive. Before moving to that, let's briefly summarize the fault rules to this point.

1. Private persons who sue the media for defamation must at least prove that the material was published through negligence. Negligence is defined in the law as the failure to exercise reasonable care.
2. Individuals who have been deemed to be public persons for purposes of a libel suit against a mass medium have to prove that the defendant exhibited actual malice when the material was published. Actual malice is defined in the law as publishing with the knowledge that the libelous assertion is false, or with reckless disregard for whether it is true or false.

PUBLIC PERSONS VERSUS PRIVATE PERSONS

All libel plaintiffs who sue the mass media must prove that the defendant in the case was at fault, that the publication or broadcast of the libelous material was not simply the result of an innocent error. Public officials and public figures have to prove a higher level of fault than do private individuals. But who are public officials and public figures in the eyes of the law? Before exploring this issue a brief caution is warranted. One of the problems in the law of libel is that courts have taken perfectly good words that most of us use daily and have attached a slightly different meaning to these words. Students need to exercise caution because of this. Most of us could probably agree on a general definition of a public figure, for example. But in libel law these words mean something different. What we need to remember is the legal definition of these words, not the common, ordinary, everyday definition.

WHO IS A PUBLIC OFFICIAL?

Two questions must be asked to determine whether a libel plaintiff should be considered a public official:

1. Who is this plaintiff; that is, what kind of government job does this person have?
2. What was the allegedly libelous story about?

Let us consider these questions separately.

Job Description

A person who is *elected* to any government position, even the most lowly job, clearly qualifies to be regarded as a public official for purposes of a libel suit. Conversely, not every person who works for the government will be regarded as a public official. In attempting to draw some kind of a line regarding who is and who is not a public official the Supreme Court has said, "It is clear that the 'public official' designation applies at the very least to those among the hierarchy of government employees who have or appear to have to the public a substantial responsibility for or control over the conduct of governmental affairs." Justice Brennan added that when a position in government has such apparent importance that the public has an independent interest in the qualifications and performance of the person who holds it, beyond the general public interest in the qualifications and performance of all government employees, the person in that position qualifies as a public official.[5] Taxpayers are concerned that everyone who works for the government does his or her job efficiently and correctly. The people are concerned about the conduct of all public employees. But some people have jobs with responsibilities that go beyond the responsibilities given to the average government worker. We have a special interest in their qualifications and how well they do their jobs. These people qualify to be public officials.

The Supreme Court added that the person must hold a position that invites public scrutiny of the person holding it, entirely apart from the scrutiny and discussion occasioned by the particular charges in the controversy. In the late 1980s in Minneapolis, Minn., one of two Beluga whales kept by the city zoological park was injured and the wound refused to heal. News coverage of these problems continued for nearly three years until the whale and its female partner were sent to Sea World in San Diego. When zoo officials shortly thereafter announced they were contemplating buying two new whales, animal rights groups threatened to sue. The dispute prompted a study of what had caused the previous problem with the Beluga whale. A committee concluded that the curator of marine mammals at the zoo, Austin McDevitt, had been negligent because he maintained a level of chlorine in the whale tanks that was too high and that that was why the wound would not heal. McDevitt disputed the finding and when the report was made public, he sued for libel. The defendants in the lawsuit claimed McDevitt was a public official. Was he? McDevitt clearly worked for the government as curator of marine mammals at the zoo. But did he have substantial responsibility for the conduct of government affairs? Should the people in Minneapolis have an interest in the way he conducted his office beyond their general interest in how all government employees do their jobs? The defendants pointed to the controversy over the care of the whales, but the court rejected that argument. The critical aspect in determining who is and who is not a public official is the public interest in the person's job before the controversy began, not the public interest once a controversy has arisen. In this case the court ruled that the record did not manifest an independent interest in McDevitt's performance over and above an interest in how all government employees do their jobs.[6] In 1998 the 4th U.S. Circuit Court of Appeals ruled that Rex Baumback, timber management officer and contracting officer for timber sales in the Eldorado National Forest, was a public official. ABC News called the plaintiff "a bureaucrat who got away with a $25 million mistake" after he was accused of making serious errors in awarding 16 contracts for the sale of timber on federal lands. The Forest Service ultimately had to cancel the contracts and was being sued by timber companies. The appellate court said

The critical aspect in determining who is and who is not a public official is the public interest in the person's job before the controversy began.

5. *Rosenblatt v. Baer,* 383 U.S. 75 (1966).
6. *McDevitt v. Tilson,* 453 N.W. 2d 53 (1990).

that Baumback's role in management of the sale of U.S. resources clearly marked him as one who had substantial responsibility for the administration of government matters.[7]

Some state courts have developed criteria that are a little different from those used by the U.S. Supreme Court. The Tennessee Supreme Court ruled that a junior state social worker was a public official because her job carried with it "duties and responsibilities affecting the lives, liberty, money or property of a citizen that may enhance or disrupt his enjoyment of life."[8] The Washington Supreme Court in 1979 said that the administrator of a small county motor pool, who worked without direct supervision, had two assistants, and could independently spend up to $500 of county money on open charge accounts at several local parts dealers, was a public official. "The public quite naturally has a legitimate and continuing interest in how local tax revenues are spent by those county employees vested with the power to utilize the public purse," wrote Chief Justice Robert Utter for the court.[9] The defamation in this case was an allegation that the plaintiff had used small amounts of county funds to repair private vehicles. Similarly, police officers, who are relatively low-level government employees, have usually been held to be public officials because they hold the power of life and death over the citizens in a community.[10] The Washington Supreme Court ruled that a research analyst for the state Senate Energy and Utilities Committee was a public official. She was a top expert in nuclear waste management and was the major source of information to senators on all matters concerning radioactive waste.[11]

What about a consulting firm that advises a government on a controversial but important government policy question? The Iroquois Research Institute was hired by Fairfax County, Va., to evaluate the historical and archeological value of an island in the Potomac River on which the county hoped to construct water-intake facilities. Lowes Island was the subject of a great zoning controversy in the community, and when Iroquois reported that the work could be done without harming the island, the research institute became the focus of sharp criticism. The Loudoun (Va.) Times Mirror published a story that challenged the competence of Iroquois researchers, and a libel suit followed. The U.S. Court of Appeals for the 4th Circuit ruled that the consulting firm could not be considered a public official in terms of the libel suit.[12] The court said that the institute made no recommendations to the county, participated in no policy determinations, and exercised no discretion. In short, it had no control over the conduct of governmental affairs. "Its position was not of such apparent importance that the public has an independent interest in its qualifications," the court ruled. The court conceded that in some instances a consultant employed by the government entity can be classified a public official, but not this time.[13]

7. *Baumback* v. *American Broadcasting Cos.,* 26 M.L.R. 2138 (1998).
8. *Press* v. *Verran,* 589 S.W. 2d 435 (1978).
9. *Clawson* v. *Longview Publishing Co.,* 589 P. 2d 1223 (1979).
10. See, for example, *Soke* v. *The Plain Dealer,* 69 Ohio St. 3d 395 (1994) and *Clark* v. *Clark,* 21 M.L.R. 1650 (1993).
11. *Price* v. *Washington State Senate,* 12 M.L.R. 2035 (1986).
12. *Artic* v. *Loudoun Times Mirror,* 624 F. 2d 518 (1980). But see also *Adey* v. *Action for Animals, Inc.,* 361 F. Supp. 457 (1973), where another federal court came to a contrary conclusion.
13. *Artic* v. *Loudoun Times Mirror,* 624 F. 2d 518 (1980).

The context in which the defamation occurs is often important. A planner with a state geological survey office might not normally hold a position that invites public scrutiny. But if this person is appointed by the governor to conduct a study of the feasibility of constructing a hazardous waste dump site near the state capital, this special assignment brings with it closer public scrutiny. In such a case a person who was not a public official might suddenly become one in terms of libel law.

The Nature of the Story

If the plaintiff's position with the government fails to meet the criteria just outlined, that is, if the individual is not elected to office or fails to hold a job with substantial responsibilities, he or she will not be regarded as a public official for purposes of the libel action and will normally only bear the burden of proving that the defendant was negligent in publishing the defamation. But even if the plaintiff is an elected official or holds a responsible job in government, the actual malice requirement is only applied if the libelous remarks concern:

1. the way the plaintiff conducts himself or herself in office; the way the plaintiff does his or her official job; or
2. the plaintiff's general fitness to hold that job.

The first criterion relates to the plaintiff's official duties and focuses on matters directly related to public responsibilities. It must be remembered that public officials have private lives and not everything a government employee does in public necessarily relates to his or her official conduct. Dr. Lazelle Michaelis was the coroner of Otter Tail County, Minn., a position of substantial responsibility. She was also a private physician employed by a medical association. Because of her expertise in pathology she occasionally, as a favor, performed autopsies for the coroner in neighboring Becker County. A controversy developed when Michaelis concluded that the death of a young woman in Becker County was a suicide. Claiming her reputation was damaged by the publicity, she sued CBS broadcasting station WCCO for libel. The station argued that because Michaelis was the coroner in Otter Tail County she was a public official, obligated to prove actual malice. The court disagreed, saying that when Michaelis performed the autopsy in Becker County she was acting as a private doctor; she was paid by the medical association for which she worked. Her position in Otter Tail County had no relevance in this case.[14]

The second criterion is much broader and can relate to a public official's private life, personal habits, or traits that may make someone unfit to hold a responsible job. For example, the fact that the fire chief's personal financial affairs are in considerable disarray probably doesn't have much to do with how well she performs her job as fire chief. But a city treasurer who has problems with personal finances could be a different story. This might suggest the treasurer is not fit to manage the city's financial affairs. The decision whether a particular allegation reflects on a public official's fitness to hold the job will necessarily be a subjective one. And it is complicated by the fact that courts, in making this determination, seem to use an

---

14. *Michaelis* v. *CBS, Inc.,* 119 F. 3d 697 (1997).

elastic standard that relates to the importance of the plaintiff's job. It seems that almost anything about the personal life of the president of the United States is considered a measure of his or her fitness to hold that office. But the courts are unwilling to say the same thing about lower government officials. And the lower you go on the totem pole of public office holders, the more the courts seem willing to rule that stories about private life have little to do with being a public official for purposes of a libel suit. It is incumbent on any journalist preparing a story on a public official's private life to demonstrate within the story just how these revelations affect the government officer's official responsibilities. This, in itself, could thwart a lawsuit.

ALL-PURPOSE PUBLIC FIGURES

Persons deemed to be public figures must also prove actual malice when suing for libel. The Supreme Court has said that there are two kinds of public figures: all-purpose public figures and limited-purpose public figures. It was Justice Lewis Powell who established these twin categories in his opinion in *Gertz* v. *Welch*.[15] He identified all-purpose public figures as those persons who "occupy positions of such pervasive power and influence that they are deemed public figures for all purposes."

Only a handful of libel plaintiffs have been deemed to be all-purpose public figures. Entertainers Johnny Carson[16] and Wayne Newton[17] were both declared all-purpose public figures. So was conservative writer and editor William Buckley.[18] A few plaintiffs, puffed up with self-importance, have happily admitted that they were all-purpose public figures.[19] Federal courts refused to classify the former president of Mobil Oil, William Tavoulareas, as an all-purpose public figure, saying that such a person must be a well-known celebrity, that his or her name must be a household word. There is a lack of case law on this particular legal point, so we can only speculate on whether people like Ted Turner or Tom Hanks or Madonna might fit into this category. Professors Jerome Barron and Thomas Dienes suggest in their "Handbook of Free Speech and Free Press," "It is almost as if the courts are saying that a plaintiff will have to be totally exposed to constant media attention in order to be classified as a total [all-purpose] public figure."[20] Barron and Dienes suggest the keys might be instant national recognition and constant media exposure.

On a national level this definition of a general or all-purpose public figure may be accurate, but there is another way of looking at the problem: the general notoriety of a person within the area in which the libel is circulated. It is quite probable that there are persons in small communities who, in the right circumstances, might have the status of all-purpose public figures. Consider the woman who lives in a community of 6,500 persons. She was formerly the mayor, has served on the school board in the past, and has been a perennial choice for president of the Parent-Teacher Association. She is the president of the largest real estate company

15. 418 U.S. 323 (1974).
16. *Carson* v. *Allied News,* 529 F. 2d 206 (1976).
17. *Newton* v. *NBC,* 677 F. Supp. 1066 (1985).
18. *Buckley* v. *Litell,* 539 F. 2d 882 (1976).
19. *Masson* v. *New Yorker Magazine, Inc.,* 881 F. 2d 1452 (1989).
20. Barron and Dienes, *Free Speech and Free Press.*

in town, is a director on the board of the local bank, and owns the local pharmacy and dry cleaners. She is active in numerous service clubs, is a leader in various civic projects, and is instantly recognizable on the street by the town's residents. Her family founded the town 150 years earlier. If she is libeled in a community newspaper whose circulation remains almost exclusively in the community, it could be argued persuasively that this woman is an all-purpose public figure in the community. (See *Steere* v. *Cupp*,[21] in which the Kansas Supreme Court ruled such an individual was a total or all-purpose public figure.) In 1982, the Montana Supreme Court ruled that investment and commodity advisor Larry Williams was an all-purpose public figure for his libel suit based on a state Democratic party press release that erroneously charged that he had been under federal indictment for political dirty tricks. The court listed the following activities by Williams, which convinced the court that he was an all-purpose public figure for the purposes of a libel suit based on the circulation of defamatory allegations in Montana: he published an investment advisory service; he wrote three books on stocks; he was the subject of an article in Forbes magazine and another article in the Wall Street Journal; he frequently gave speeches and ran unsuccessfully for the U.S. Senate; he was chairman of the Republican party in Montana; and he was an active member of the National Taxpayers Union.[22]

But what if the defamatory material circulates outside the local community, as well, to persons who may not be familiar with the plaintiff? This question arose in 1985 in a libel suit by businessman George Martin against the Chariho Times in Rhode Island. Martin was clearly well known in the village of Shannock, where he owned and had developed a considerable amount of property over a period of 15 years. The Times was widely read by the 300 residents of the village, and a trial court ruled that Martin was a local all-purpose public figure. On appeal Martin argued that the newspaper had 3,000 subscribers, a far larger readership than just among the village residents by whom he was so well known. The Rhode Island Supreme Court, noting that Martin's fame had spread beyond the Shannock village limits, added that "very few individuals will be known to all subscribers or purchasers of any publication."[23] Wally Butts and Major General Edwin Walker were not known to all subscribers of the Saturday Evening Post, yet were declared to be public figures by the Supreme Court,[24] the Rhode Island justice noted, recalling that famous 1967 decision (see pages 191–193). "It is sufficient to attain a public figure status that the plaintiff should have been known to a substantial portion of the publication's readership," the court ruled.[25] And Martin met this test.

LIMITED-PURPOSE PUBLIC FIGURES

The second category of public figure outlined by Justice Powell in the *Gertz* decision is called the limited-purpose public figure. "More commonly," he said, "those classed as public figures have thrust themselves to the forefront of particular public controversies in order to influence

"More commonly, those classed as public figures have thrust themselves to the forefront of particular public controversies in order to influence the resolution of the issues involved."

21. 602 P. 2d 1267 (1979).
22. *Williams* v. *Pasma*, 565 P. 2d 212 (1982).
23. *Martin* v. *Wilson Publishing*, 497 A. 2d 322 (1985).
24. *Curtis Publishing Co.* v. *Butts, AP* v. *Walker*, 388 U.S. 130 (1967).
25. *Martin* v. *Wilson Publishing*, 497 A. 2d 322 (1985).

the resolution of the issues involved."[26] This kind of libel plaintiff is regarded as a public person for a discrete part of his or her life, usually because of steps the person has taken to influence public opinion on a public issue. In a series of four rulings in the mid-1970s the Supreme Court developed three criteria to determine whether someone is a limited-purpose public figure:

- **There must be a public controversy in existence before the publication or broadcast of the libelous matter.**
- **The plaintiff must have in some way participated voluntarily in attempting to resolve this controversy.**
- **The plaintiff's participation must be such that he or she is actively seeking to influence public opinion regarding the controversial issues.**

While there have only been a handful of cases that focused on whether a plaintiff was or was not an all-purpose public figure, there have been scores of rulings regarding limited-purpose public figures. The three criteria highlighted here stem from four decisions handed down by the Supreme Court of the United States. State courts and lower federal tribunals have often offered their own somewhat different guidelines. Most observers who have studied the troublesome question of who is and who is not a limited-purpose public figure regard the criteria generated by the high court to be a conservative definition; state and lower federal courts frequently regard as limited-purpose public figures plaintiffs who would not be regarded as such under the standards set by the Supreme Court. We spend the next few pages focusing on the four Supreme Court cases that generated the three-part test. We then look briefly at the ways in which the lower court rulings most commonly disagree with this test.

In *Gertz* v. *Welch* plaintiff Elmer Gertz was a well-known and widely respected Chicago attorney who had gained prominence in civil rights disputes in that city. He had written several books and articles, and on many occasions had served on commissions and committees in Chicago and Cook County. When a young man was slain by a Chicago police officer, Gertz agreed to represent the family in a civil action against the officer. The policeman had been tried and convicted of murder in the shooting, but Gertz played no role in that criminal action. His only role in the entire matter was as an attorney representing the family in the action for civil damages. He became the subject of a vicious attack by American Opinion, a magazine published by the John Birch Society, which accused him of being a communist fronter, a Leninist, and the architect of a frame-up against the police officer. It also charged that Gertz had a long police record.

In the libel suit that followed, the Supreme Court ruled that despite his prominence in the civil rights area, Elmer Gertz was not a public figure for the purposes of this lawsuit. The words of Justice Powell stand as an important guideline:

> It is preferable to reduce the public figure question to a more meaningful context
> by looking to the nature and extent of an individual's participation in the partic-
> ular controversy giving rise to the defamation.[27]

26. *Gertz* v. *Robert Welch, Inc.,* 418 U.S. 323 (1974).
27. *Gertz* v. *Robert Welch, Inc.,* 418 U.S. 323 (1974).

The key phrase is "extent of an individual's participation in the particular controversy giving rise the defamation." To be a limited-purpose public figure, the plaintiff must be shown to have played a prominent role in the particular controversy giving rise to the defamation, the controversy prompting publication of the defamatory statement or comment. Gertz would have been considered a limited-purpose public figure if the dispute in the case had involved civil rights in Chicago. But the particular controversy that gave rise to the article in American Opinion was the murder of the young man and the subsequent trial of the police officer. Gertz was not an important participant in that issue. He was simply acting as an attorney—which is his profession—in representing the family of the youth in a civil action. He was acting as a private individual.*

Two years later the court ruled that a socially prominent Palm Beach woman was not a public figure with regard to the divorce action in which she was involved. The case, *Time, Inc.* v. *Firestone,*[28] resulted from a short notice published in Time magazine that Russell Firestone was granted a divorce from his wife on grounds of extreme cruelty and adultery. Firestone was in fact granted a divorce from his wife, but on grounds that neither member of the couple was "domesticated." Mary Alice Firestone sued Time for libel, claiming she had been called an adulteress. Time argued that her prominence in the Palm Beach community made her a public figure. On the record she clearly appeared to be a public figure, a leading member of the "Four Hundred of Palm Beach Society," an "active member of the sporting set," a person whose activities attracted considerable public attention. She even maintained a clipping service to keep track of her publicity. The divorce case became a cause célèbre in the community, prompting 43 articles in a Miami newspaper and 45 stories in the Palm Beach newspapers. She held several press conferences during the course of the 17-month legal dispute. Nevertheless, the Supreme Court refused to acknowledge that Mary Alice Firestone was a public figure in the context of the divorce case, the subject of the Time article that was defamatory. Justice William Rehnquist wrote:

> Respondent did not assume any role of especial prominence in the affairs of society, other than perhaps Palm Beach society, and she did not thrust herself to the forefront of any particular public controversy in order to influence the resolution of the issues involved in it.[29]

Time argued that because the trial was well-publicized, it must be considered a public controversy and Mary Alice Firestone a public person. "But in doing so," Justice Rehnquist wrote, "petitioner seeks to equate 'public controversy' with all controversies of interest to the public." The justice said that a divorce proceeding is not the kind of public controversy referred to in *Gertz*. While there was public interest in the proceedings, the case was not an important public question.

---

28. 424 U.S. 448 (1976).
29. *Time, Inc.* v. *Firestone*, 424 U.S. 448 (1976).

*This libel case, which began in 1969, finally ended in the summer of 1982 when a $400,000 judgment against American Opinion was upheld by the 7th U.S. Circuit Court of Appeals.

Rehnquist also pointed out that Mrs. Firestone was not a voluntary participant in the divorce proceeding. She was forced to go into public court to dissolve her marriage. The subtle difference, then, that Rehnquist points to is the difference between voluntarily becoming involved in a public controversy and voluntarily becoming involved in something that results in a controversy. Firestone did the latter—she voluntarily went to court to get a divorce, and the divorce trial resulted in the controversy. Justice Powell did note in *Gertz* that "it may be possible for someone to become a public figure through no purposeful action of his own, but the instances of truly involuntary public figures are exceedingly rare."[30]

The meaning of *Gertz* and *Firestone* was re-emphasized in 1979 in two rulings by the Supreme Court that clearly indicated that the high court intended the limited-purpose public-figure category to be narrow. In both cases, *Hutchinson* v. *Proxmire*[31] and *Wolston* v. *Reader's Digest*,[32] the Supreme Court reversed rulings by lower federal courts, rulings that had declared that the plaintiffs were in fact limited-purpose public figures.

The plaintiff in the *Hutchinson* case was the research director at a public mental hospital in Michigan. He was also the recipient of about $500,000 in federal grants to support his research on animal aggression. Believing that such research was unimportant, Senator William Proxmire bestowed his monthly Golden Fleece Award on several federal agencies that had funded Hutchinson's research for nearly seven years. In the process the Wisconsin lawmaker accused Hutchinson of putting the "bite" on the American taxpayer and making "a monkey" out of the American people. Hutchinson sued.

Chief Justice Burger refused to consider the plaintiff a public figure. He said there was no controversy about the research until Proxmire's defamatory comments about Dr. Hutchinson. The scientist did not thrust himself or his views into a public dispute or issue. In fact, Burger said, the defendants "have not identified such a particular controversy; at most they point to concern about general public expenditures." Hutchinson, the chief justice noted, at no time assumed any role of public prominence in the broad question of concern about expenditures. The researcher, then, had no part in the controversy that gave rise to the defamation, according to Burger. Simply taking public money to do research is not enough to make a person like Hutchinson into a public figure, the court ruled. "If it were, everyone who received or benefited from the myriad public grants for research could be classified as a public figure."[33]

Finally, the chief justice drew on a basic rationale for the distinction between private and public persons and said that "we cannot agree that Hutchinson had such access to the media that he should be classified as a public figure." His access, Burger noted, was limited to responding to Proxmire's announcement of the Golden Fleece Award. The decision of the court was 8–1 in favor of Hutchinson's status as a private figure. The single dissenting vote by Justice Brennan was based solely on how the court had responded to another question, not to the public-figure issue.

30. *Time, Inc.* v. *Firestone,* 424 U.S. 448 (1976).
31. 443 U.S. 111 (1979).
32. 443 U.S. 157 (1979).
33. *Hutchinson* v. *Proxmire,* 443 U.S. 111 (1979).

The facts in the *Wolston* case are somewhat more complicated. Ilya Wolston was identified in a 1974 book, "KGB: The Secret Works of Soviet Secret Agents," as a Soviet agent. His description as such stemmed from events that had taken place nearly 20 years earlier when a federal grand jury in New York state was investigating the activities of Soviet agents in the United States. Wolston's aunt and uncle, Myra and Jack Soble, were well-publicized American Communists who were arrested in January 1957 and charged with spying. Wolston himself was interviewed by the Federal Bureau of Investigation and testified several times before a New York grand jury. In July 1958 he failed to respond to a grand jury subpoena. His failure to appear was reported in the press. He said he had not testified because he was in a state of mental depression. Later he changed his mind and offered to give testimony. He subsequently pleaded guilty to a charge of contempt and was sentenced to three years' probation. During the six weeks between the time he refused to testify and his sentencing, 15 news stories were published about Ilya Wolston in New York and Washington newspapers. He was never indicted for espionage.

Wolston's libel suit was based on his misidentification in the "KGB" book published by Reader's Digest. The publication argued that because of his contempt conviction in 1958, Wolston was a limited-purpose public figure for purposes of a discussion of Soviet agents and espionage. Eight members of the Supreme Court disagreed. Justice William Rehnquist, writing for the majority, stated that Wolston did not "inject" himself into any controversy, that he was dragged into the controversy when the government pursued him during the investigation of Soviet agents. "The mere fact that petitioner voluntarily chose not to appear before the grand jury, knowing that his action might be attended by publicity, is not decisive on the status of public figure," Rehnquist said.[34] The justice noted that Wolston played a minor role in whatever controversy there might have been over Soviet espionage, that he had never talked about this matter with the press. "We decline to hold that his mere citation for contempt rendered him a public figure for purposes of comment on the investigation of Soviet espionage."

Rehnquist stressed that Wolston had made no effort to influence the public on the resolution of any issue. The plaintiff did not in any way seek to arouse public sentiment in his favor or against the investigation. Quoting his own opinion in the *Firestone* case, Rehnquist wrote:

> While participants in some litigation may be legitimate "public figures," either generally or for the limited purpose of that litigation, the majority will more likely resemble respondent [Mary Firestone or Ilya Wolston], drawn into a public forum largely against their will in order to attempt to obtain the only redress available to them or to defend themselves against actions brought by the state or by others.[35]

"The mere fact that petitioner voluntarily chose not to appear before the grand jury, knowing that his action might be attended by publicity, is not decisive on the status of public figure."

34. *Wolston* v. *Reader's Digest,* 443 U.S. 157 (1979).
35. *Wolston* v. *Reader's Digest,* 443 U.S. 157 (1979).

The question now is, What can we learn from the language in these Supreme Court rulings? Three basic points seem to emerge:

1. Limited-purpose public figures normally must voluntarily step into the public spotlight. The court said it would be exceedingly rare for someone to be an involuntary public figure. Such instances as rising to deny charges made against you and going to court to end a marriage or to defend yourself from government charges do not represent voluntary behavior. They represent a response to the behavior of someone or something else.

2. A limited-purpose public figure is someone who plays a role in the resolution of an important public or social issue. A messy divorce, an investigation of aggression in animals, a charge of contempt for failure to testify before a grand jury are not the kinds of "affairs of society" that the court considers to be important. One gets the impression that the justices are looking to the discussion of social issues (abortion, discrimination), economic issues (taxpayers' revolt, city budget), educational problems (busing, minimum competency requirements), governmental rulings (censorship, arms control), and the like to find the kinds of persons they would consider limited-purpose public figures. A public controversy might be defined as a controversy in which the resolution of the issues will affect the general public or at least a wider group of persons than those individuals directly involved in the controversy.

3. There must have been some attempt by the plaintiff to influence public opinion in the resolution of these issues. This speaks to the basic point made by Justice Powell in the *Gertz* case—the nature and extent of the individual's participation in the particular controversy giving rise to the defamation. In *Hutchinson* the issue was wasteful expenditures, but Dr. Hutchinson had said little, if anything, about that before being libeled by Senator Proxmire. Similarly, Ilya Wolston had said nothing about the issue of Soviet agents in this country—which is what the defendant contended was the issue in *Wolston v. Reader's Digest.*

Inherent in an attempt to influence the outcome of a public issue is the ability of the plaintiff to get access to the mass media. The plaintiff generally must have some means of speaking out on the issue or of responding to criticism. Also, the media cannot create the controversy by defaming the plaintiff and then argue that the role of the plaintiff is important to the resolution of the issue. These are the key points, then, in determining whether an individual is a limited-purpose public figure:

1. **There must be an important public controversy.**
2. **The plaintiff must inject himself or herself voluntarily into the controversy.**
3. **The plaintiff must attempt to influence public opinion about the resolution of the issue and have some access to the press to accomplish this feat.**

LOWER-COURT RULINGS

The four Supreme Court rulings discussed here provide important guideposts that can assist anyone seeking to determine whether a particular plaintiff is a limited-purpose public figure. But the set of cases is not a talisman that answers all questions in all circumstances. For one thing the four cases did not reveal who was a public figure, only who was *not* a public figure. For the past three decades the lower courts have been somewhat at sea, struggling with lawsuits involving different kinds of circumstances and different kinds of plaintiffs. It is not surprising, then, that in 1993 legal scholars Harry Stonecipher and Don Sneed concluded, after examining numerous lower court rulings in which the limited-purpose public figure question was an issue, that state courts and lower federal courts are coming to some of their own conclusions regarding this question.[36] The tests emerging from the lower courts surely reflect the language of the high court rulings, but often four or five rather than three criteria are applied. In Washington state,[37] for example, the test requires the judge to answer five questions:

- Did the plaintiff have access to the media?
- What was the nature of the plaintiff's role in the controversy?
- Were the defamatory comments germane to the controversy?
- Did the controversy exist before the defamation was published?
- Was the plaintiff still a public figure at the time of defamation?

In Wisconsin, courts have used this test:

- Was there a public controversy?
- What was the scope of the controversy?
- What was the plaintiff's role in the controversy?
- Was the defamatory statement germane or related to the plaintiff's participation in the controversy?

When looking at lower-court rulings on who is and who is not a public figure, students of libel law will not always find the clear, consistent path forged by the U.S. Supreme Court in the four previously discussed cases. While many judges have attempted to conform to the basic criteria, it is not unusual to find divergence as well. For example, lower courts seem willing to listen to the argument that by knowingly taking certain actions an individual may draw legitimate

---

36. Stonecipher and Sneed, "Survey," 328.
37. *Clardy v. The Cowles Pub. Co.,* 912 P. 2d 1078 (1996).

public attention to himself or herself, even though he or she did not intend to come under the glare of public scrutiny. A criminal rarely seeks to attract attention; yet some courts have said that by committing a criminal act an individual can legitimately expect to draw the kind of public attention that fosters a definition of a public figure. But there is disagreement among the courts as well. In March of 1998 a U.S. district court in Connecticut ruled that the wife of a physician who had continuing legal problems was a public figure. The doctor, on probation for five years because of charges of incompetence, was arrested and charged with 20 counts of fraud. "Despite the fact that plaintiff has not sought a public role, she has been thrust into the role of a public figure by virtue of her marriage to Dr. Zupnik—who clearly is a public figure."[38] Three months later the Appellate Division of the New York Supreme Court ruled that the ex-husband of prominent television celebrity Joan Lunden was not a public figure simply because he was married for many years to the co-host of ABC's "Good Morning America." The Globe tabloid had suggested that prior to the divorce, while the couple was separated, Lunden's husband had an affair with a prostitute. "Plaintiff is not famous in his own right and his marriage to Ms. Lunden certainly did not bestow upon him the sort of fame that is necessary to be considered a general public figure."[39] The two cases present almost identical circumstances, yet the courts reached contrary decisions. What follows is a sampling of lower-court rulings that demonstrate both the consistencies and inconsistencies in the law.

The Nature of the Controversy

The kind of controversy that generated the libel is an obviously important factor in determining whether a plaintiff is a limited-purpose public figure. In 1994 in a decision that echoed earlier Supreme Court rulings, the 4th U.S. Circuit Court of Appeals declared that "a public controversy is a dispute that in fact has received public attention because its ramifications will be felt by persons who are not direct participants."[40] This is the same standard applied by the Georgia Supreme Court when it ruled that a group of plastic surgeons who were involved in a fight with other physicians over what kinds of medical specialists were qualified to perform plastic surgery were not public figures. This was a dispute that affected only members of the medical community, not the general public.[41] An interesting ruling from Colorado demonstrates the difference between varieties of controversies. Linda Lewis was arrested and convicted for shoplifting at a J.C. Penney store in Aurora, Colo. Linda and her husband then filed suit against the store, claiming that Mrs. Lewis, an African-American, had been beaten when she was detained by store security personnel. Despite the publicity about the $15 million lawsuit, at this point Mrs. Lewis was still just a private citizen attempting to use the court system to correct what she believed was a legal wrong. Then local and national civil rights organizations became involved in the dispute. Public meetings were held at which the Lewis' charges against J.C. Penney were aired. The possibility of a boycott of the Penney stores was raised. Mrs. Lewis appeared and spoke at these meetings. Videotape of her arrest in the store was shown at the meetings.

The kind of controversy that generated the libel is an obviously important factor in determining whether a plaintiff is a limited-purpose public figure.

38. *Zupnik* v. *Associated Press Inc.*, 26 M.L.R. 2084 (1998).
39. *Krauss* v. *Globe International Inc.*, 674 NYS 2d 662 (1998).
40. *Foretich* v. *Capital Cities/ABC, Inc.*, 37 F. 3d 1541 (1994).
41. *Georgia Society of Plastic Surgeons* v. *Anderson*, 363 S.E. 2d 710 (1987).

Chapter 5

A television station aired a report based on erroneous information that Mrs. Lewis had a prior criminal record. She sued for libel. The TV station contended that she was a public figure; Mrs. Lewis said she was a private citizen forced to go to court to protect her rights. The Colorado Court of Appeals agreed that the plaintiff was indeed a private citizen when she filed the lawsuit against the J.C. Penney Co. But when Mrs. Lewis began participating in the public protests about the department store, when she spoke at public meetings to rally support for this cause, when she aired the videotape of her arrest, she became a leading player in a public controversy. Because of the actions she took after she filed the lawsuit, she became a public figure and would have to prove actual malice.[42]

In several instances courts have ruled that the mass media cannot generate a controversy and then label those persons ensnared in that controversy as limited-purpose public figures. Courts call these attempts "bootstrapping." In 1989 The Globe tabloid newspaper claimed that an agent of the Central Intelligence Agency had named Khalid Khawar as the real assassin of Sen. Robert Kennedy; Sirhan Sirhan was innocent. The killing had been arranged by the Shah of Iran's secret police and the Mafia, the newspaper reported. The newspaper carried a photo of Khawar standing with a group of people who were talking with Kennedy shortly before he was killed. At the time of the killing Khawar was a free lance photographer. The camera that hung around the plaintiff's neck in the photo was really a gun, The Globe reported. The newspaper got its story from a book that made the same allegations. The book was highly controversial and focused considerable attention on Khawar, who sued the author and the publisher, as well as The Globe. Book author Robert Morrow defaulted (did not defend himself) and the publisher settled the suit and retracted the allegations. The Globe fought the lawsuit and argued that Khawar was a public figure because of all the publicity that was focused upon him when the book was published. The California Supreme Court disagreed, saying that Khawar had done nothing to bring about the publicity; it was generated by the press during the controversy.[43] This is a classic case of bootstrapping, which is not permitted. A jury found the allegations false and defamatory.

Voluntary Actions

Voluntary actions taken by the plaintiff are often critical in defining a limited-purpose public figure. The Washington Court of Appeals ruled that two women who often brought pro se lawsuits (they represented themselves, had no attorney) against a variety of government agencies were limited-purpose public figures. As plaintiffs in a variety of lawsuits, the pair sought to resolve a number of controversial issues, the court said.[44] And the 10th U.S. Circuit Court of Appeals ruled that a man involved in a widely publicized custody battle was a public figure because he actively sought to resolve this issue by appearing on nationally televised talk shows to discuss a father's custody rights.[45] However, the U.S. Court of Appeals for the 4th Circuit ruled in 1994 that Vincent and Doris Foretich, who had been publicly accused by their

42. *Lewis* v. *McGraw-Hill Broadcasting Co., Inc.*, 832 P. 2d 1118 (1992).
43. *Khawar* v. *Globe International Inc.*, 965 P.2d 696 (1998).
44. *Camer* v. *Seattle Post-Intelligencer*, 723 P. 2d 1195 (1986).
45. *Anderson* v. *Rocky Mountain News*, 15 M.L.R. 2058 (1988).

daughter-in-law of sexually abusing their granddaughter, were not limited-purpose public figures simply because they denied these charges at press conferences and at public rallies. The court said so long as the reply was responsive to the accusation, was not substantially stronger than the charge, and was disseminated to approximately the same audience that heard the original allegation, the plaintiffs remained private persons. "We see no good reason why someone dragged into a controversy should be able to speak publicly only at the expense of foregoing a private person's protection for defamation," the court said.[46]

In 1999 a Georgia court ruled that Richard Jewell was a limited-purpose public figure for purposes of his libel suit against Cox Enterprises Inc., publisher of the Atlanta Constitution and the Atlanta Journal. Jewell, a former deputy sheriff, is the man who discovered a bomb in a knapsack in a park during the 1996 Summer Olympic Games in Atlanta and then herded spectators out of the area before the device exploded. One person was killed, 11 others were injured. Jewell was regarded as a hero at first, and then law enforcement officers focused their attention on him as a suspect in the bombing. After the incident Jewell gave about a dozen interviews to local and national media about his role in clearing people out of the area after he discovered the bomb and about park security in general. He sued the Atlanta newspapers for comments published while he was regarded as a prime suspect in the bombing. He was later cleared. The court ruled that Jewell was a public person because he voluntarily stepped into the controversy by giving the interviews to the press. He was not at the time defending himself from accusations. "It is beyond argument," the court ruled, "that plaintiff did not reject any role in the debate, was a prominent figure in the coverage of the controversy, and, whatever his reticence regarding his media appearances, encountered them voluntarily."[47]

But courts in some states have ruled that an individual need not voluntarily inject himself or herself into a controversy to qualify as a limited-purpose public figure. In Wisconsin, for example, a state court ruled that a man who was falsely accused of a crime was a public figure for purposes of a libel suit because of his past behavior and the nature of the controversy. A teenager told police the plaintiff, Todd Erdmann, had come to his house looking for his sister. The boy told police that when he couldn't find the girl, Erdmann shot him. The plaintiff, who had earlier been warned about stalking the woman, was arrested five hours later. Police described the suspect as a survivalist who had access to several weapons. The following day the teenage boy admitted that he had made up the story, that he had in fact shot himself. Erdmann sued a local television station for libel for statements broadcast while he was a suspect. In the lawsuit the TV station contended that the plaintiff was a public figure. The Wisconsin Court of Appeals agreed. The court ruled that it was unfortunate that Erdmann had been thrust into the controversy primarily because of the boy's false report to the police and because of conclusions by the police that Erdmann was violent and dangerous and had access to automatic weapons. "Although the police formulated these conclusions without any conduct or action by Erdmann, it is clear that it may be possible for someone to become a public figure through no purposeful action of his own," the court ruled.[48]

---

46. *Foretich v. Capital Cities/ABC, Inc., 37 F. 3d 1541 (1994).*
47. *Jewell v. Cox Enterprises Inc., 27 M.L.R. 2370 (1999).*
48. *Erdmann v. SF Broadcasting of Green Bay Inc., 599 NW 2d 1 (1999).*

A Minnesota court reached a similar conclusion in 1993 when it ruled that the owner of many rental units around the University of Minnesota was a limited-purpose public figure when he brought a lawsuit against the Minnesota student daily newspaper after it published an article that identified him as a slumlord.[49] The controversy over the problems in rental housing was a real one, but Sherwood Nelson, the landlord, surely did not voluntarily inject himself into the dispute or try to lead public opinion on the matter. Nevertheless, the court said Nelson had gained sufficient notoriety to become a public figure because of his consistent presence in court and before other government forums to defend himself against charges of housing code violations and unlawful detainer. In one year alone he was charged with 16 housing code violations, involved in 11 unlawful detainer cases, and participated in 23 conciliation cases, all involving his rental properties.

Contradictory decisions like these are often confusing, even to lawyers who specialize in libel law. They are evidence of two things. First, that the law of libel is still evolving, as it has during the past several centuries. And second, as noted in Chapter 4, libel is still basically state law. While the constitutionalization of the tort has added some consistency to the development of the libel law, state judges still have considerable room to shape their own law.

BUSINESSES AS PUBLIC FIGURES

Businesses and corporations can sue for libel; they can also be classified as public figures for purposes of a libel suit. Surely if a business attempts to lead public opinion during a controversy over an important public issue, it could be categorized as a limited-purpose public figure. For example, General Motors could be classified as a limited-purpose public figure if it was libeled as it attempted to lead public opinion against government-imposed automobile emission standards. But businesses have been regarded as public figures based on other criteria as well, criteria hammered out over the past two decades. Some of the standards used to determine whether a business is a public figure include:

Businesses and corporations can sue for libel; they can also be classified as public figures for purposes of a libel suit.

- **Whether a business has used a highly unusual advertising or promotional campaign to draw attention to itself.**
- **Whether a business is regulated by the government.**
- **Whether the libelous comment about the business focuses on a matter of great public concern.**

Not all courts agree that these criteria are applicable. Here are some cases that offer guidelines in the application of these standards.

A company called Steaks Unlimited was deemed a public figure because it used a highly unusual method to advertise its low-priced, inspected, ungraded, frozen, tenderized, boxed beef. The advertising campaign featured unusually heavy radio and newspaper advertising, large signs erected at the sales location, and distribution of handbills to persons walking near

---

49. *Nelson v. University of Minnesota,* 22 M.L.R. 1089 (1993).

the store. The sale attracted wide public attention, beyond the attention from consumers who sought to buy the meat.[50] And a U.S. district court ruled in 1981 that the Bose Corporation was a limited-purpose public figure when it sued Consumer Reports because the audio equipment manufacturer had advertised its new 901 speakers in a highly unconventional manner that precipitated a public discussion on the merits of the product. The company intentionally emphasized the unconventional design of the product in its advertising and publicity.[51]

But normal advertising will not generally establish the level of notoriety required to turn a business into a public figure. A spirited, but typical, comparative advertising campaign between U.S. Healthcare, Inc., and Blue Cross in Pennsylvania did not propel either company into the public-figure status, according to the 3rd U.S. Circuit Court of Appeals.[52] Similarly, extensive advertising and promotion by entrepreneur Thomas Jadwin of a double tax-exempt, no-load bond mutual fund he had developed did not make him a limited-purpose public figure. Soliciting media attention for such an offering is normal, the Minnesota Supreme Court ruled.[53]

A nursing home in Rhode Island was declared to be a public figure by the state's high court because it was regulated by the government and because there was considerable public concern about the conditions at such facilities.[54] And the Ohio Court of Appeals ruled in 1997 that despite the novelty of interactive computer systems, advertising on the Internet is not unusual enough to turn a software company into a public figure in a libel suit.[55] In 1984 a U.S. district court in Kansas ruled that the Beech Aircraft Company was a limited-purpose public figure for the purposes of a libel suit against the Aviation Consumer Magazine, which had published a story about Beech aircraft involved in accidents. The court said that "the defamatory statements relate to part of Beech's business that is federally regulated and arose in the context of a federal investigation." By entering into a regulated activity like the manufacture of aircraft, the company, in essence, invited public scrutiny, the court said.[56] And in 1988 the U.S. Court of Appeals for the 11th Circuit ruled that two businessmen who owned jai alai frontons in Florida were public figures in their libel suit brought against ABC. The court ruled the pair had put themselves in the public eye by becoming involved in a heavily regulated industry.[57] In 1995 the New Jersey Supreme Court said it would not consider an ordinary business to be a public figure unless the business was concerned with matters of public health and safety or was subject to substantial government regulation. The court added, however, that it would also regard as a public figure a business accused of consumer fraud when the allegations, if true, would constitute a violation of New Jersey's Consumer Fraud Act. In this case a lawn mower repair business was accused of cheating its customers. The supreme court

---

50. *Steaks Unlimited* v. *Deaner,* 623 F. 2d 624 (1980).
51. *Bose Corp.* v. *Consumers Union of the United States, Inc.,* 508 F. Supp. 1249 (1981), rev'd 629 F. 2d 189 (1982), aff'd. 446 U.S. 485 (1984).
52. *U.S. Healthcare, Inc.* v. *Blue Cross of Greater Philadelphia,* 898 F. 2d 914 (1990).
53. *Jadwin* v. *Minneapolis Star,* 367 N.W. 2d 476 (1985).
54. *Harris Nursing Home Inc.* v. *Narragansett Television Inc.,* 24 M.L.R. 1671 (1995).
55. *Worldnet Software Co.* v. *Gannett Satellite Information Network, Inc.,* 25 M.L.R. 2331 (1997).
56. *Beech Aircraft* v. *National Aviation Underwriters,* 11 M.L.R. 1401 (1984).
57. *Silvester* v. *ABC,* 839 F. 2d 1491 (1988).

affirmed a lower-court ruling that the plaintiff business would have to prove actual malice to win its libel suit.[58] Other courts have rejected the government-regulation criteria, however. The Supreme Court of Oregon did not even consider the rationale that a regulated business is a public figure when it ruled that the Bank of Oregon was not a public figure for purposes of a lawsuit against the Willamette Week newspaper. "There simply is no public controversy into which plaintiffs arguably thrust themselves. Merely opening one's doors to the public, offering stock for public sale, advertising, etc., even if considered a thrusting of one's self into matters of public interest, is not sufficient to establish a public figure," the court ruled.[59]

Two court rulings in the 1990s, including one by the 5th U.S. Circuit Court of Appeals, have provided additional criteria that might be applied when determining whether a business is a public figure for purposes of a libel suit. In *Snead* v. *Redland Aggregates, Ltd.,* the Court of Appeals ruled that the notoriety of a business to the average person in the relevant geographical area (the area in which the libel is circulated), the public prominence of the business because it manufactures widely known consumer goods, and the frequency and intensity of media scrutiny of the business are all factors that need to be considered when a court makes a determination about the public figure status of a business.[60] Also to be considered, the court said, is whether the libelous speech involves a matter of public or private concern. In this case the court ruled that a British firm that quarried sand, gravel, and crushed stone was not a public figure. And a U.S. district court in Pennsylvania ruled that a business's relative access to the media and the manner in which the risk of defamation came upon the business (i.e., the context of the dispute that generated the libel) must be considered when deciding whether a business was a public figure or not.[61] While the criteria in both these decisions lack precision, these rulings indicate that some courts seem willing to consider the public figure status of businesses in a broader light.

As noted by the 5th U.S. Circuit Court of Appeals in the *Snead* decision, generalizations that have some value when determining the public or private status of an individual don't work well when applied to a business.[62] Most courts seem more comfortable approaching the problem on a case-by-case basis. The lack of clear standards is an important reason journalists should be cautious when communicating about businesses, even those that have a high visibility in the community.

THE PUBLIC FIGURE OVER TIME

If someone is a public person (public official or public figure) today, will he or she still be regarded as a public figure 20 years from now? Yes, but only in regard to the issues or matters that generated the public-person status today. If Foster Pierson is a public figure today because he is at the forefront of a fight against a gun control initiative on the ballot in Indiana,

---

58. *Turf Lawnmower Repair, Inc.* v. *Bergen Record,* 655 A. 2d 417 (1995).
59. *Bank of Oregon* v. *Independent News,* 963 P. 2d 35 (1985).
60. 998 F. 2d 1325 (1993).
61. *Rust Evader Corp.* v. *Plain Dealer Publishing Co.,* 21 M.L.R. 2189 (1993).
62. *Snead* v. *Redland Aggregates Ltd.,* 998 F. 2d 1325 (1993).

he will still be regarded as a public figure in any story published or broadcast 20 years from now regarding this initiative battle. Similarly, a woman who retires to private life after being mayor of Houston will still be regarded as a public person if she sues for libel for a story published 25 years from now that focuses on her conduct while she was mayor.

The 6th U.S. Circuit Court of Appeals ruled that a woman named Victoria Price Street was still a limited-purpose public figure in 1981 with regard to the incident that made her a public figure some 50 years earlier. Ms. Street charged that she had been raped by a group of young African-American men while she rode on a freight train in Alabama. The trial in 1931 of the so-called Scottsboro Boys created a national sensation. In the late 1970s NBC presented a dramatization of the incident and legal struggle endured by the defendants. Viewers of the program were left with the distinct impression that Ms. Street had lied when she charged rape. The network was surprised when Victoria Price Street sued for libel; they thought she was dead. The network argued that she was a public figure for purposes of the lawsuit; she conceded that she was a public figure when the original trial took place, but said she stayed out of the public spotlight for the past five decades. The court of appeals disagreed with the plaintiff, ruling that "once a person becomes a public figure in connection with a particular controversy, that person remains a public figure thereafter for purposes of later commentary or treatment of that controversy."[63] The Supreme Court of the United States agreed to hear Ms. Street's appeal, but the plaintiff and NBC agreed on an out-of-court settlement before the case was heard by the high court.

Subsequent court decisions have consistently reinforced this ruling.[64] A U.S. district court ruled that a U.S. Secret Service agent who was assigned to protect President Gerald Ford must still be regarded as a public person for purposes of a libel suit based on a story about an assassination attempt on Ford in 1975.[65] Two attempts were made on Ford's life in September of 1975. Agent Larry Buendorf deflected the arm of assailant Lynette "Squeaky" Fromme on Sept. 5, 1975, and saved the life of President Ford while he was visiting Sacramento, Calif. Two weeks later a private citizen, Oliver Sipple, pushed away the arm of assailant Sara Jane Moore as she attempted to shoot the president when he was in San Francisco. This second incident became a major issue in the Bay area when newspaper columnist Herb Caen speculated in print that the White House had not thanked Sipple for his heroic act because he was a homosexual. Sipple was gay, but sued the newspaper for invasion of privacy.[66] (See page 278 for more on this case.) Researchers at National Public Radio got the two incidents mixed up and commentator Daniel Schorr, in a report on how the press tramples on the privacy of public people, said it was revealed after he saved the president's life that agent Buendorf was a homosexual. The court ruled that Buendorf would have to prove actual malice to win his libel suit, something he was unable to do.[67] Most recently the Arkansas Supreme Court ruled that

---

63. *Street* v. *NBC*, 645 F. 2d 1227 (1981), cert. dismissed 454 U.S. 1095 (1981).

64. See *Newsom* v. *Henry*, 443 So. 2d 817 (1984) and *Contemporary Mission* v. *New York Times*, 665 F. Supp. 248 (1987), 842 F. 2d 612 (1988).

65. *Buendorf* v. *National Public Radio, Inc.*, 822 F. Supp. 6 (1993).

66. *Sipple* v. *Chronicle Publishing Co.*, 154 Cal. App. 3d 1040 (1984).

67. *Buendorf* v. *National Public Radio*, 822 F. Supp. 6 (1993).

J. Michael Fitzhugh, a former federal prosecutor, was not a public person for purposes of a libel action he brought against the Arkansas Democrat-Gazette. The newspaper published a story that federal prosecutor Robert Fiske Jr. was about to initiate the first prosecution in the Whitewater investigation. Two men, Charles Matthews and Eugene Fitzhugh, were the defendants in the case. The newspaper ran what it thought were pictures of the pair. The Matthews photo was correct, but the Democrat-Gazette ran J. Michael Fitzhugh's photo instead of a picture of Eugene Fitzhugh. The newspaper argued that because the plaintiff had been a federal prosecutor for eight years—clearly a public official during those years—he surely should be considered a public person for the purposes of this lawsuit. The court disagreed, ruling that while J. Michael Fitzhugh was and still is a public person for any story relating to his work as a federal prosecutor, he was not a public person for stories about matters outside that realm, including the Whitewater investigation. The simple error cost the newspaper $50,000 in damages.[68]

PRIVATE PERSONS

In a libel action, if the plaintiff does not meet the definition of a public official, an all-purpose public figure, or a limited-purpose public figure, the court will regard the individual as a private person. This designation means the plaintiff will not be required to prove that the defendant lied or exhibited reckless disregard for the truth in publishing the libel. The plaintiff in most jurisdictions will only have to demonstrate that the defendant failed to exercise reasonable care in preparing and publishing the defamatory material. There are, however, a few exceptions to this rule. A few states, including California,[69] Colorado,[70] Indiana,[71] Alaska,[72] and New York,[73] have decided that plaintiffs who are considered private persons must prove a higher degree of fault than simple negligence when they sue a mass medium for libel based on a story about a matter of public interest. In some states these plaintiffs must prove gross negligence or gross irresponsibility; in others these private-person plaintiffs must prove actual malice. Gross negligence is a higher degree of fault than simple negligence, but a lesser degree of fault than actual malice. To find out the rule in your state, locate the most recent state supreme court ruling on libel. Within the text of this decision there is very likely to be a reference to the level of fault required by private-person plaintiffs.

Under the fault requirement all persons who sue a mass medium for libel must prove that the defendant was somehow at fault in publishing the defamatory material, that the publication (or broadcast) did not result from an innocent error. Private persons generally need prove only

SUMMARY

68. *Little Rock Newspapers* v. *Fitzhugh,* 954 S.W. 2d 187 (1997).
69. *Rollenhagen* v. *City of Orange,* 172 Cal. Rptr. 49 (1981).
70. *Walker* v. *Colorado Springs Sun, Inc.,* 538 P. 2d 450 (1975).
71. *AAFCO Heating and Air Conditioning Co.* v. *Northwest Publications, Inc.,* 321 N.E. 2d 580 (1974).
72. *Gay* v. *Williams,* 486 F. Supp. 12 (1979).
73. *Chapadeau* v. *Utica Observer-Dispatch, Inc.,* 341 N.E. 2d 569 (1975).

negligence. What the courts call a "public person" must normally prove that the defendant acted with actual malice in publishing the libel; that is, the defendant knew the material was false but still published it or exhibited reckless disregard for the truth. What the courts define as "private persons" must prove at least that the defendant acted negligently, that is, in such a way as to create an unreasonable risk of harm. The courts have ruled that there are three kinds of "public persons":

I. *Public officials:* Persons who work for a government in a position of authority, who have substantial control over the conduct of governmental affairs, and whose position in government invites independent public scrutiny beyond the general public interest in the qualifications and performance of all government employees. Libelous comments must focus on the plaintiff's official conduct (the manner in which the plaintiff conducts his or her job) or on the plaintiff's general fitness to hold public office.

II. *All-purpose public figures:* Persons who occupy persuasive power and influence in the nation or in a community, persons who are usually exposed to constant media attention.

III. *Limited-purpose public figures:* Persons who voluntarily inject themselves into an important public controversy in order to influence public opinion regarding the resolution of that controversy. The key elements are:

    a. Public controversy, the resolution of which must affect more persons than simply the participants. The outcome must have an impact on people in a community.

    b. Plaintiffs who voluntarily thrust themselves into this controversy. An individual who has been drawn involuntarily into a controversy created by someone else (such as the press) is not a limited-purpose public figure.

    c. Plaintiffs who attempt to influence the outcome of the controversy, to shape public opinion on the subject. This implies that a plaintiff has some access to the mass media to participate in the public discussion surrounding the controversy.

Using a variety of criteria, courts have ruled that businesses can be deemed public figures in a libel suit. Persons who become public persons remain public persons throughout their lives with regard to stories published or broadcast that relate to incidents or events that occurred while they were public persons.

THE MEANING OF FAULT

Negligence = Failure to Exercise Reasonable Care

Actual Malice = Knowledge of Falsity or Reckless Disregard for the Truth

---

NEGLIGENCE

"Negligence" is a term that has been commonly used in tort law for centuries, but has only been applied to libel law since 1974. In simple terms, **negligence** implies the failure to exercise ordinary care. In deciding whether to adopt the negligence or the stricter actual malice fault requirements, state courts are providing their own definitions of the standard. Washington state adopted a "reasonable care" standard. Defendants are considered negligent if they do not exercise reasonable care in determining whether a statement is false or will create a false impression.[74] The Tennessee Supreme Court has adopted a "reasonably prudent person test": What would a reasonably prudent person have done or not have done in the same circumstance? Would a reasonably prudent reporter have checked the truth of a story more fully? Would such a reporter have waited a day or so to get more information? Would a reasonably prudent reporter have worked harder in trying to reach the plaintiff before publishing the charges?[75] In Arizona negligence has been defined as conduct that creates unreasonable risk of harm. "It is the failure to use that amount of care which a reasonably prudent person would use under like circumstances," the Arizona Supreme Court ruled.[76]

Some of the more common reasons a defendant might be found negligent include:

- **Reliance on an untrustworthy source**
- **Not reading or misreading pertinent documents**
- **Failure to check with an obvious source, perhaps the subject of the story**
- **Carelessness in editing and news handling**

The question the court will always ask is, **Did the reporter make a good faith effort to determine the truth or falsity of the matter?** Here are some cases that illuminate these criteria.

Did the reporter make a good faith effort to determine the truth or falsity of the matter?

In Massachusetts a reporter relied on a source whom police described as not having been reliable as an informant. Even the reporter testified that he found some of this source's information to be off the mark on critical points. The Massachusetts Supreme Judicial Court ruled that a jury might find negligence in such a case.[77] But in several cases courts have ruled that a reporter's reliance on a source who had been trustworthy in the past was not negligent behavior. This was the finding, for example, in a Florida case when a reporter based his story on inaccurate information provided by an "official" source who had always been reliable in the past.[78] And the courts have consistently ruled that a newspaper or broadcast station is not negligent when it relies on reports received from the Associated Press, Reuters, or other news services.[79]

Reportorial techniques are often scrutinized when a plaintiff asserts that a news medium has been negligent. But courts do not expect superhuman efforts from journalists, only general competence. The San Antonio Express-News was sued for libel when it inadvertently ran

---

74. *Taskett* v. *King Broadcasting Co.,* 546 P. 2d 81 (1976).
75. *Memphis Publishing Co.* v. *Nichols,* 569 S.W. 2d 412 (1978).
76. *Peagler* v. *Phoenix Newspapers,* 547 P. 2d 1074 (1976).
77. *Jones* v. *Taibbi,* 512 N.E. 2d 260 (1987).
78. *Karp* v. *Miami Herald,* 359 So. 2d 580 (1978).
79. *Appleby* v. *Daily Hampshire,* 395 Mass 2 (1985); and *McKinney* v. *Avery Journal, Inc.,* 393 S.E. 2d 295 (1990); *Cole* v. *Star Tribune,* 26 M.L.R. 2415 (1998).

the wrong picture with a story it published on a woman convicted of prostitution, selling a child into prostitution, and drug-related offenses. The plaintiff who had the same name as the woman described in the Express-News story had also been convicted of selling a child into prostitution, but was clearly not the woman described in the newspaper. Was there negligence in this case? The reporter had seven years of experience covering the courthouse and had spent six months researching the series of articles on the Texas Department of Correction's parole system. She had submitted a request to the county sheriff's office for a mug shot of the woman who was the subject of the story. The request included the woman's name, date of birth, and Department of Corrections identification number. The sheriff's office gave her the wrong photo. The plaintiff insisted that the reporter failed to verify that she had the correct photo, that the reporter should have checked with the woman's mother to make certain the correct photo was being used. The court disagreed. "The issue was not what Fox [the reporter] could have done to avoid the mistake. It is whether she acted reasonably; that is, as a reasonable reporter under similar circumstances would have acted." The court said there was no negligence in this case.[80]

The South Carolina Supreme Court ruled that the failure of a reporter to examine a public judicial record when writing about a criminal case could be negligence. The plaintiff in the case had been arrested with four other men and charged with pirating stereo audiotapes. Two months later four of the men arrested pleaded guilty to the charges, but the charges were dismissed against the plaintiff. The newspaper published a story saying that the plaintiff had also pleaded guilty to the charges. The reporter had gotten his information about the case in a telephone conversation with the prosecuting attorney. The attorney testified that he had given the reporter the correct information. Six days elapsed between the dismissal of charges and the erroneous story. The South Carolina high court concluded that the correct information was available to the reporter in the court records and that he could have looked at this material before publishing the story. He instead chose to rely on a telephone conversation and in doing so got the story fouled up. The jury could readily conclude that the reporter was negligent, the court ruled.[81] In a similar case in Washington state, the supreme court ruled that there was no evidence of negligence when a reporter relied on erroneous information from a city attorney in attempting to explain a court order. The plaintiff was convicted in municipal court of assault. A superior court later dismissed the charges. Legally, this meant that the municipal court conviction was voided as well. The news story related that the superior court had dismissed the charges, but also reported that the plaintiff had been convicted in municipal court. Nowhere in the superior court dismissal order—which was read to the reporter over the telephone—did it state that the municipal court conviction was reversed as well. The reporter checked with a city attorney on this point, and he confirmed her impression that the dismissal did not negate the previous conviction. There is no evidence of negligence in this case, the state's high court ruled. The reporter exercised reasonable care by checking with the city attorney, whom she might reasonably presume to understand the meaning of the dismissal order.[82]

80. *Garza* v. *The Hearst Corporation,* 23 M.L.R. 1733 (1995).
81. *Jones* v. *Sun Publishing,* 292 S.E. 2d 23 (1982).
82. *Lamon* v. *Butler,* 722 P. 2d 1373 (1986).

Finally, the Virginia Supreme Court ruled that when a newspaper published a very negative story about a local teacher, based largely on complaints from parents who called the newspaper, it exhibited negligence. Parents were quoted in the article as saying the teacher was erratic, disorganized, forgetful, unfair, and demeaning to students. The reporter who wrote the story talked to a couple of students, the principal, and two of the teacher's colleagues, but got very little information. As such, the story was very one-sided. The court said that the reporter could have contacted many more students to try to verify the accusations since there was no deadline pressure. It was obvious, the court ruled, that the parents who contacted the reporter bore the teacher ill will. This should have pushed the reporter to do a more thorough job.[83]

The editorial process itself may be examined when a plaintiff seeks to prove negligence. And carelessness in the way that editors handle news copy can result in a finding of fault. In 1985 the editors at USA Today planned to run a special feature commemorating the 10th anniversary of the capture of Saigon by the North Vietnamese, the end of the Vietnam War. In typical USA Today fashion, the editors wanted a short story from each state. An editor in Virginia called the paper's stringer in Vermont and asked him for a contribution. The stringer, Ron Wyman, talked with an acquaintance, Jeffrey Kassel, a clinical psychologist at a Veterans Administration hospital, and asked if he had any ideas for a short story. The thrust of Kassel's remarks was the notion that many American soldiers who fought in Vietnam felt as if they were victims, forced to fight in a war they didn't want. As Wyman was leaving, Kassel noted that he had recently seen an article in another newspaper that said that former Vietnamese soldiers were amused by the idea that their painful experiences in the war might leave them with "post-traumatic stress disorder," the scourge of many U.S. veterans. Wyman put his notes together and read them over the telephone to his editor in Virginia. She in turn routed the notes to another editor who wrote the final story, which quoted Kassel as saying, "We've become a nation of handwringers. . . . It's amusing that vets feel they are the victims when the Vietnamese had the napalm and bombs dropped on them."[84] This, of course, was not what Kassel had said. USA Today had attributed to the psychologist the observations in the newspaper article he noted to reporter Wyman. Testimony at the trial revealed that no one ever called Kassel before publication to check the quote, no editor checked with Wyman after the story was written, and the individual who wrote that short story never even checked with the editor who had transcribed Wyman's notes over the telephone. The 1st U.S. Circuit Court of Appeals ruled that a jury might certainly construe this behavior as negligent.[85]

The definition of the term "negligence" will undoubtedly vary from state to state and possibly from judge to judge within a state. It is going to be some time before any kind of broad, consistently applied guidelines emerge. The U.S. Supreme Court will be of little help in this case, as it appears to be the intention of the court to leave the matter to the states.

83. *Richmond Newspapers v. Lipscomb,* 362 S.E. 2d 32 (1987).
84. *Kassel v. Gannett Co., Inc.,* 875 F. 2d 935 (1989).
85. *Kassel v. Gannett Co., Inc.,* 875 F. 2d 935 (1989).

ACTUAL MALICE

Defining actual malice is somewhat easier than defining who is and who is not a public figure or public official. In *New York Times Co.* v. *Sullivan,*[86] Justice Brennan defined **actual malice** as "knowledge of falsity or reckless disregard of whether the material was false or not." The two parts of this definition should be considered separately.

Knowledge of Falsity

"Knowledge of falsity" is a fancy way of saying "lie." If the defendant lied and the plaintiff can prove it, actual malice has then been shown. In 1969 Barry Goldwater was able to convince a federal court that Ralph Ginzburg published known falsehoods about him during the 1964 presidential campaign in a "psychobiography" carried in Ginzburg's Fact magazine. Ginzburg sent questionnaires to hundreds of psychiatrists, asking them to analyze Goldwater's mental condition. Ginzburg published only those responses that agreed with the magazine's predisposition that Goldwater was mentally ill and changed the responses on other questionnaires to reflect this point of view. Proof of this conduct, plus other evidence, led the court to conclude that Ginzburg had published the defamatory material with knowledge of its falsity.[87]

"Knowledge of falsity" is a fancy way of saying "lie."

What if a reporter fabricates a quotation, and this quotation turns out to be defamatory to the person to whom it is attributed? Is this knowledge of falsity or actual malice? This was the question faced by the Supreme Court of the United States in 1991 when it heard an appeal by psychoanalyst Jeffrey Masson of an adverse lower-court ruling in his lawsuit against the New Yorker magazine and writer Janet Malcolm. For many years Masson was projects director of the prestigious Sigmund Freud Archives. As time went on, he became disillusioned with some of Freud's ideas and began to advance his own theories. His superiors disapproved of this and fired the noted psychoanalyst. Writer Malcolm talked with Masson for more than 40 hours about Freud, his own ideas about psychoanalysis, and his relationship with others who worked at the archives. The New Yorker published a long article that resulted from the interviews, and the piece was expanded and ultimately published as a book. Malcolm's article presented an unflattering picture of Jeffrey Masson. Some of the most damning prose came from long quotations that the writer attributed to the psychoanalyst. Malcolm had taken these quotes from 18 hours of taped interviews, as well as notes she had kept during the interviews. But Masson contended that he had never said many of the things attributed to him, that Janet Malcolm had fabricated these quotes. And these quotes made him look egotistical, irresponsible, sexually promiscuous, and dishonest. Malcolm said she had made only minor changes in the quotations.

In the lawsuit that followed, Masson stipulated he was a public figure. But he argued that when Malcolm changed or fabricated his remarks for the article, she was guilty of actual

---

86. 376 U.S. 254 (1964).
87. *Goldwater* v. *Ginzburg,* 414 F. 2d 324 (1969).

malice. The trial court granted the defendant's motion for a summary judgment, and the case went into appeal. The key question was whether evidence of changing the words in a direct quote is, in and of itself, proof of knowledge of falsity.

In a 7–2 ruling, the high court reversed the lower-court ruling. It said that readers presume that the words contained within quote marks are a verbatim reproduction of what the speaker said. But, Justice Kennedy wrote, to demand that the press meet such a high standard is unrealistic. "If every alteration [of a quote] constituted the falsity required to prove actual malice, the practice of journalism, which the First Amendment is designed to protect, would require a radical change, one inconsistent with our precedents and First Amendment principles," he added. "We conclude that a deliberate alteration of the words uttered by a plaintiff does not equate with knowledge of falsity . . . unless the alteration results in a *material change* [author's emphasis] in the meaning conveyed by the statement."[88]

The case was sent back to lower court for a jury trial on critical fact issues in the case. The appeal to the Supreme Court, after all, was based on the unproven premise that Malcolm had in fact altered the quotes. The Supreme Court insisted the jury answer three questions affirmatively:

1. Were the statements attributed to Masson false (i.e., the meaning of the quotes had been materially changed)?
2. Did these false statements defame Masson?
3. Did Malcolm act with actual malice; did she know the quotes were false but publish them anyway, or exhibit reckless disregard for the truth?

In 1993 a jury in San Francisco found that five quotations attributed to Masson were false, that two were libelous, and that there was sufficient evidence of actual malice to sustain a conviction for libel. But the jury members could not agree on a damage award to the plaintiff.[89] A new trial on both damages and liability was scheduled. In late 1994 another San Francisco jury ruled that two quotes were false, and one of those defamed Masson, but that Janet Malcolm had not acted with actual malice in publishing these quotes. In other words, the jury believed the reporter when she said she believed that what she wrote was what Jeffrey Masson had told her. Trial observers attributed the reversal in the verdict to two factors. The defense spent much more time in the second trial on the actual malice standard, trying to educate jurors in how irresponsible or careless a journalist must be for a libel claim to prevail. Also, most observers said that Janet Malcolm was far more persuasive in her testimony in the second trial, that jurors seemed more inclined to believe her.[90] Masson appealed the adverse verdict on the grounds that the trial judge erred in instructing the jury on actual malice. In June of 1996 the U.S. Court of Appeals affirmed the lower court verdict and barred Masson from trying to bring another libel action against The New Yorker based on the same libel claims.[91]

88. *Masson* v. *The New Yorker, Inc.,* 111 S. Ct. 2419 (1991).
89. Gross, "Impasse Over Damages," A1.
90. Margolick, "Psychoanalyst Loses Libel Suit," A1.
91. *Masson* v. *The New Yorker, Inc.,* 85 F. 3d 1394 (1996).

Reckless Disregard for the Truth

Reckless disregard for the truth is a bit more difficult to define. In 1964 the Supreme Court said that reckless disregard could be shown by proving that the defendant had "a high degree of awareness of [the] probable falsity" of the defamatory material when it was published.[92] Four years later the Supreme Court said that in order to show reckless disregard for the truth, the plaintiff must bring forth "sufficient evidence to permit the conclusion that the defendant in fact entertained serious doubts as to the truth of his publication."[93] Proof that the defendant failed to investigate a charge that later turns out to be false is not in and of itself sufficient evidence to prove actual malice.

These definitions of reckless disregard are certainly useful in a theoretical sense. It is surely possible to envision a reporter or editor entertaining serious doubts about the truth of an allegation and publishing it anyway. However, neither of these definitions is terribly helpful in a practical sense. As Judge Kozinski of the 9th U.S. Circuit Court of Appeals wrote in his decision in a case involving the National Enquirer and Clint Eastwood, "As we have yet to see a defendant who admits to entertaining serious subjective doubt about the authenticity of an article it published, we must be guided by circumstantial evidence."[94] There is language in a 1967 Supreme Court ruling that has been extremely helpful to both jurists and journalists in charting a course by using such evidence. The ruling involved two cases, *Curtis Publishing Co. v. Butts* and *AP v. Walker.*[95] Justice John Harlan outlined a test in his opinion to evaluate the conduct of both defendants in these libel cases. It is important to note that Justice Harlan never called the criteria he outlined a test for reckless disregard for the truth. He said he was attempting to establish a test to see whether the defendants in the two cases had seriously departed from the standards of responsible reporting. A few courts have rejected the Harlan criteria as a test for actual malice.[96] But even some members of the Supreme Court have referred to this test as a measure of reckless disregard. And it has become the most commonly used test in the lower courts.

The two cases that generated these criteria came before the Supreme Court at about the same time and were joined and decided as one case. In the first case, Wally Butts, the athletic director at the University of Georgia, brought suit against the Saturday Evening Post for an article it published alleging that Butts and University of Alabama football coach Paul "Bear" Bryant had conspired prior to the annual Georgia-Alabama football game to "fix" the contest. The Post obtained its information from a man who said that while making a telephone call, he had been accidentally plugged into a phone conversation between Butts and Bryant. George Burnett, who had a criminal record, told the Post editors that he had taken careful notes. The story was based on these notes.

Proof that the defendant failed to investigate a charge that later turns out to be false is not in and of itself sufficient evidence to prove actual malice.

92. *Garrison v. Louisiana,* 379 U.S. 64 (1964).
93. *St. Amant v. Thompson,* 390 U.S. 727 (1968).
94. *Eastwood v. National Enquirer Inc.,* 123 F. 3d 1249 (1997).
95. 388 U.S. 130 (1967).
96. See, for example, *Clyburn v. News World Communications,* 903 F. 2d 29 (1990).

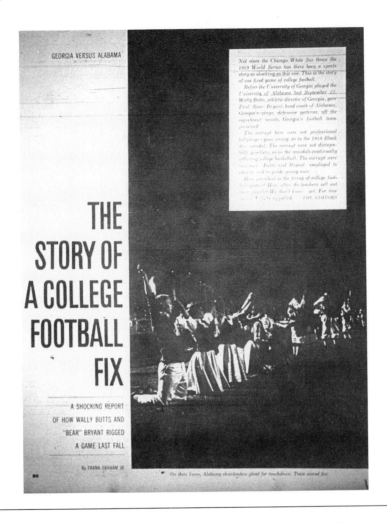

In the other case, Major General (retired) Edwin Walker, a political conservative and segregationist from Texas, brought suit against The Associated Press (AP) and a score of publications and broadcasting stations for publishing the charge that he led a mob of white citizens against federal marshals who were attempting to preserve order at the University of Mississippi during the crisis over the enrollment of James Meredith. Walker was on campus during the disturbances, but did not lead a mob. The AP report was filed by a young AP correspondent on the scene.

The court ruled that in the *Butts* case the Post had exhibited highly unreasonable conduct in publishing the story but that in the *Walker* case no such evidence was present. Again, it is important to note that although Justice John Marshall Harlan did not call the conduct reckless disregard at the time, most authorities accept these cases as good indicators of what the court means by reckless disregard. Look at the details of each case.

The Saturday Evening Post alleged that Wally Butts and Paul "Bear" Bryant conspired to fix the Georgia-Alabama football game during the 1962 college football season. Publication of this article ultimately resulted in the famous Curtis Publishing Co. v. Butts *ruling in 1967. Used with permission from the Saturday Evening Post © 1963*

In the *Butts* case, the story was not what would be called a hot news item. It was published months after the game occurred. The magazine had ample time to check the report. The source of the story was not a trained reporter, but a layperson who happened to be on probation on a bad-check charge. The Post made no attempt to investigate the story further, to screen the game films to see if either team had made changes in accord with what Bryant and Butts supposedly discussed. Many persons were supposedly with Burnett when he magically overheard this conversation and none were questioned by the Post. The magazine did little, then, to check the story, despite evidence presented at the trial that one or two of the editors acknowledged that Burnett's story needed careful examination.

In the *Walker* case, different circumstances were present. For the AP editor back in the office who was responsible for getting the story on the wires, it was hot news, a story that should be sent out immediately. It was prepared in the "heat of battle" by a young, but trained, reporter who in the past had given every indication of being trustworthy. All but one of the dispatches from the correspondent said the same thing: Walker led the mob. So there was internal consistency. Finally, when General Walker's previous actions and statements are considered, the story that he led a mob at Ole Miss was not terribly out of line with his prior behavior. There was nothing to cause AP to suspect that the story was wrong as, for example, would be a report that the Archbishop of New York led a mob down Fifth Avenue. A red light should signal those instances that suggest further checking because the story doesn't sound very likely.[97]

When all this is sorted out, three key factors emerge:

1. Was the publication of the story urgent? Was it a hot news item? Or was there sufficient time to check the facts in the story fully?

2. How reliable was the source of the story? Should the reporter have trusted the news source? Was the source a trained journalist? Should the editor have trusted the reporter?

3. Was the story probable? Or was the story so unlikely that it cried out for further examination?

It is very difficult for a plaintiff to prove actual malice. Proving that a defendant did in fact entertain serious doubts about the truth or falsity of the matter that was subsequently published or broadcast is an imposing task. But the Supreme Court has placed additional burdens on the plaintiff as well.

■ **The plaintiff must prove actual malice with "clear and convincing" evidence.**[98] Normally in a civil lawsuit the plaintiff must prove his or her allegations with a "preponderance of the evidence," which means that the plaintiff has more evidence than the defendant. "Clear and convincing" means that there can be little or no dispute about the evidence.

---

97. *Curtis Publishing Co.* v. *Butts, AP* v. *Walker,* 388 U.S. 130 (1967).
98. *Gertz* v. *Robert Welch, Inc.,* 418 U.S. 323 (1974).

■ **The Supreme Court has instructed appellate courts to re-examine the
evidence in the case to determine that the record "establishes actual malice
with convincing clarity."**[99] Typically an appellate court is bound to accept the
evidentiary findings of the trial court (see pages 15–17). But in a libel case the
appellate court is mandated to take a close look and make certain the evidence
supports the finding of malice. Allotting the appellate court such evidentiary power
not only gives the defendant a second chance to win the case on the basis of the
facts, but it also forces trial court judges to take extra pains when examining the
facts, knowing that their work will likely be closely scrutinized in the future. The
following overview of court rulings on actual malice will help illuminate both the
criteria for such a finding and these two defense advantages.

A financial advisor by the name of Brian Freeman sued for libel, saying he was mis-
quoted in a book by reporter Moira Johnson called "Takeover: The New Wall Street Warriors—
The Men, The Money, The Impact." Freeman is a lawyer and was representing a machinists'
union during the closed-door negotiations about the future of Trans World Airlines. Two finan-
ciers, Carl Ichan and Frank Lorenzo, were fighting over control of the airline. Johnson wrote:
"Brian Freeman, the lawyer to represent the machinists, compounded the threats of a strike,
warning that being sold into bondage to Lorenzo would provoke nighttime trashing of airplanes
and other sabotage." Reporter Johnson did not attend the meeting, but two people who did
talked with her about what Freeman had said during the negotiations. The first person Johnson
talked to said the quoted statement accurately reflected what Freeman had said. The other person, who testified in the lawsuit for Freeman, said he didn't exactly remember what Freeman
said, but that Freeman was cautious as a lawyer. "It was no big deal," the witness said. Freeman
contended that the two witnesses to the conversation obviously disagreed, and that Johnson
should have done more checking on the quote because of this disagreement. Failure to do so
amounted to actual malice. The New York Court of Appeals disagreed, noting that nothing the
second witness said actually contradicted what the first witness told Johnson. "Given these different possible interpretations, no rational fact finder could, in this case, find actual malice by
clear and convincing evidence."[100]

Disputes over the validity of evidence, often scientific evidence, frequently figure in
libel disputes. That a reporter accepts one set of findings rather than another is not regarded as
evidence of actual malice. Documentary filmmaker Michael Moore produced a segment of his
"TV Nation" program on a company that disposed of New York City sewer sludge by shipping
it to Texas and spreading it over a large plot of land. The company, Merco Joint Venture, said
the application of the sludge increases vegetation on arid grassland, adds nutrients to the soil,
and conditions the soil to make better use of limited water. Moore's "Sludge Train" broadcast
made light of this process and questioned the safety of such an application of waste matter.
Merco sued for libel, claiming that there was scientific evidence that the matter was safe. The
Fifth U.S. Circuit Court of Appeals ruled that there was no consensus from experts on whether

---

99. *Bose Corporation v. Consumers Union of the United States, Inc.,* 446 U.S. 485 (1984).
100. *Freeman v. Johnson,* 614 N.Y.S. 2d 377 (1994).

land application of the sludge was safe. And even if there were, it would not be proof that the defendants knew the broadcast was false or should have known it was false. "Because an 'expert' endorses a certain practice does not mean that all reasonable debate on the merits or safety of that practice is foreclosed," the court said as it reversed the $5 million judgment against the defendants.[101]

The U.S. Supreme Court spoke to the question of actual malice again in 1984 when it ruled that a sound engineer employed by Consumer Reports had not acted with actual malice when he knowingly changed the wording of the results of a test panel that had evaluated an audio speaker system, even though his testimony that he didn't think he had changed the meaning of the statement was unbelievable.[102] In its review of the Bose 901 speakers, Consumer Reports magazine said the sound from the speakers "tended to wander about the room." This statement was written by engineer Arnold Seligson, who supervised the test. But the listener panel had actually said that the sound tended to move along the wall, in front of and between the two speakers. At the trial Seligson testified that he believed the two statements meant the same thing. The district court found this testimony incredible and said that Seligson obviously knew he had changed the meaning of the statement.[103] This was evidence of actual malice. The Supreme Court disagreed, saying Seligson's testimony, in and of itself, was not evidence of actual malice. "He had made a mistake," Justice John Paul Stevens wrote, "and when confronted with it he refused to admit it and steadfastly attempted to maintain that no mistake had been made—that the inaccurate was accurate. The attempt failed, but the fact that he made the attempt does not establish that he realized the inaccuracy at the time of publication."[104]

The lower courts have been somewhat more consistent in applying the criteria developed by the Supreme Court regarding actual malice than they have in applying criteria used to determine who is and who is not a public figure. Many courts have used elements of the three-part Harlan test to measure actual malice. For example, Was the journalist on a deadline? A reporter for the St. Louis Globe-Democrat, preparing a story on deadline, told a rewrite person on the city desk that a city alderwoman admitted at a public meeting to having had two abortions. The copydesk botched the story and attributed the statement to another alderwoman, an outspoken foe of abortion. The Missouri Supreme Court said the journalists' behavior was negligent but not reckless disregard for the truth. The deadline pressure made rechecking the information impossible.[105]

The law does not require the complete verification of a story, especially a breaking story. (Most editors, however, will demand the most thorough verification possible.) The District of Columbia U.S. Circuit Court of Appeals ruled that evidence that a book publisher failed to completely verify defamatory allegations written by an author whose credibility had been frequently questioned was not sufficient to demonstrate that the publisher had in fact entertained serious doubts about the truth of these allegations. The book in question is "Profits of War" by

The law does not require the complete verification of a story, especially a breaking story.

101. *Peter Scalamandre & Sons, Inc.* v. *Kaufman,* 113 F. 3d 556 (1997).
102. *Bose Corporation* v. *Consumers Union of the United States, Inc.,* 446 U.S. 485 (1984).
103. *Bose Corporation* v. *Consumers Union of the United States, Inc.,* 508 F. Supp. 1249 (1981).
104. *Bose Corporation* v. *Consumers Union of the United States, Inc.,* 446 U.S. 485 (1984).
105. *Glover* v. *Herald Co.,* 549 S.W. 2d 858 (1977).

Ari Ben-Menashe, a man, the publisher acknowledged, whose credibility was often suspect. But Ben-Menashe was relied on as a credible source by many writers and television producers. The book contained allegations that Robert C. McFarlane, a former national security adviser, was really an Israeli agent who facilitated spying by the Israelis on the United States. Many of Ben-Menashe's allegations about McFarlane were proved to be false four months after the book was published when a congressional task force released a report on many topics related to relations between the United States and Middle Eastern nations. At the time the book was published, however, much of the evidence contained in the task force report had not yet been made public.

McFarlane argued that because Ben-Menashe's credibility was dubious at best, the book publisher had a duty to verify every one of his defamatory assertions. The court disagreed with that argument. "When the source of potentially libelous material is questionable . . . the investigatory efforts of the publisher are important only to the extent that they serve as evidence that it did not publish the material in reckless disregard for the truth," the judges said. The publisher does not have to corroborate every allegation, the court said. In this case the publisher did attempt to verify all the defamatory statements but was unable to find evidence to substantiate many of the charges. At the same time no contradictory evidence was uncovered either. "To hold that a publisher who relies upon a questionable source must not only investigate the allegations but actually corroborate them . . . would be to turn the inquiry away from the publisher's state of mind and to inquire instead whether the publisher satisfied an objective standard of care," the court ruled. The plaintiff had failed to demonstrate actual malice.[106]

The 11th U.S. Circuit Court of Appeals handed down a similar ruling in 1999 in a libel suit brought by a financial corporation against ABC television for a "20/20" broadcast. The plaintiff claimed that the network had portrayed BFC Financial Corporation as knowingly misleading investors about the benefits and risks of limited real estate partnerships. ABC countered with the argument that it interviewed many sources and not one of them regarded what BRC had done as being fair to investors. The plaintiff argued that the network reporters had not interviewed the real estate expert it had recommended and this was proof of actual malice. The court disagreed. "ABC was not required to continue its investigation until it found somebody who would stand up for Levan [the plaintiff]," the court said. The law only required that the network reporters not proceed to broadcast while entertaining serious doubts as to the truth of the allegations.[107]

The 9th U.S. Circuit Court of Appeals ruled in 1998 that a plaintiff, in this case a state court judge, must show that the defendant, ABC, had "obvious reasons to doubt the veracity of its reporting, but deliberately avoided learning the truth" in order to demonstrate actual malice. The judge was one of three judges profiled on the program "Prime Time Live" during a critical examination of the disciplinary processes for judges accused of misconduct. Among other allegations made by the network, ABC said that Judge Bruce Dodds used a crystal ball

---

106. *McFarlane* v. *Sheridan Square Press Inc.,* 91 F. 3d 1501 (1996).
107. *Levan* v. *Capital Cities/ABC Inc.,* 27 M.L.R. 2555 (1999).

he kept in his office to support judicial decisions and pressure litigants into settlements. The network said it had several sources for its story about the crystal ball and that ABC personnel had seen the device. Dodds admitted having it, but said common sense should have dictated to the program producers that he used the crystal ball simply to infuse some levity into his jurisprudence. He claimed that the ABC investigation was shoddy and incomplete. The court said common sense had little to do with it. "People, even judges, do peculiar things and engage in bizarre conduct. That, in fact, was precisely ABC's point about Judge Dodds."[108]

Lower courts have ruled that publication or broadcast of allegations against a person who has denied these allegations is not by itself a display of reckless disregard for the truth.[109] And the Illinois Supreme Court has ruled that refusal to retract a story does not constitute actual malice, either.[110]

Perhaps the one area in which a few lower courts have strayed slightly from the rulings by the U.S. Supreme Court is that of ill will. Before the decision in *New York Times Co. v. Sullivan*,[111] the term "malice" meant ill will. If a broadcasting station reported a story simply to hurt someone because the reporter or editor didn't like this person, this action was considered evidence of malice. But since the *Sullivan* decision, the U.S. Supreme Court has ruled several times that the actual malice standard is not satisfied merely through a showing of ill will or malice in the ordinary sense of the term.[112] Most lower courts have followed that rule.

But at least two state supreme courts have ruled that evidence of ill will can be used as evidence of actual malice, so long as other evidence exists as well. The Kentucky Supreme Court ruled in 1990 that evidence that a reporter had an apparent grudge against a local prosecutor was one factor the jury could consider in finding that the newspaper acted with reckless disregard for the truth.[113] Three years earlier the Washington Supreme Court upheld a finding of actual malice against a television station in part because a reporter had reportedly yelled, "You will regret doing this. I will get you" at the assistant to the subject of his defamatory news story. There was also considerable other evidence of reportorial malpractice in this case, however.[114]

Ill will alone will not support a finding of actual malice. But it is obvious that some courts will look at ill will as part of the evidence, and it could be the part that pushes the court to a finding of reckless disregard for the truth. Reporters obviously have feelings about the subjects of their stories. They should keep these feelings to themselves. News coverage should be motivated by a search for truthful information, not revenge or anger.

Ill will alone will not support a finding of actual malice.

108. *Dodds* v. *American Broadcasting Co.,* 145 F. 3d 1053 (1998).
109. *Roberts* v. *Dover,* 525 F. Supp. 987 (1981).
110. *Costello* v. *Capital Cities Communications, Inc.,* 15 M.L.R. 2407 (1986).
111. 376 U.S. 254 (1964).
112. See *Harte-Hanks Communications Inc.* v. *Connaughton,* 109 S. Ct. 2678 (1989) and *Beckley Newspapers* v. *Hanks,* 389 U.S. 81 (1967).
113. *Ball* v. *E.W. Scripps Co.,* 801 S.W. 2d 684 (1990).
114. *Herron* v. *King Broadcasting Co.,* 746 P. 2d 295 (1987).

In a lawsuit against a mass medium, a private person must prove that the defendant was at least negligent in publishing the defamatory matter. Negligence has been defined as the failure to exercise reasonable care or as acting in such a way as to create a substantial risk of harm. In some states, in certain cases private persons will be required to prove more than simple negligence. They may be required to prove gross negligence, which is a standard that implies a greater degree of carelessness on the part of the defendant. An individual who has been declared to be a public person for the purposes of a libel suit must prove actual malice. Actual malice is defined as knowledge of falsity or reckless disregard of the truth. Transmitting a story with the knowledge of its falsity means that the publishers of the story knew it was not true but still communicated it to the public. To prove reckless disregard for the truth, the plaintiff must show that the publisher of the defamation had a "high degree of awareness of the probable falsity of the material" when it was published or that the publisher in fact "entertained serious doubts about the truth of the material" before it was published. The courts have established a set of three criteria to help determine whether material was published with reckless disregard for the truth. The jurists tend to look at these factors:

SUMMARY

1. Whether there was time to investigate the story or whether the material had to be published quickly
2. Whether the source of the information appeared to be reliable and trustworthy
3. Whether the story itself sounded probable or farfetched

If the item was hot news, if the source was a trained journalist, and if the information in the story sounded probable, there can be no finding of reckless disregard. However, if there was plenty of time to investigate, if the source of the material was questionable, or if the information in the story sounded completely improbable, courts are more likely to permit a finding of reckless disregard for the truth.

BIBLIOGRAPHY

"Amazing and All True! Lawyers Reveal Secrets for Protecting Tabloids." *The New York Times,* 1 January 1991.

American Law Institute. *Restatement of the Law of Torts,* 2d ed. Philadelphia: American Law Institute, 1975.

Ashley, Paul. *Say It Safely,* 5th ed. Seattle: University of Washington Press, 1976.

Barron, Jerome, and C. Thomas Dienes. *Handbook of Free Speech and Free Press.* Boston: Little, Brown, 1979.

Gross, Jane. "Impasse Over Damages in *New Yorker* Libel Case." *The New York Times,* 4 June 1993, A1.

Languardt, Arlen W. "Media Defendants, Public Concerns, and Public Plaintiffs: Toward Fashioning Order from Confusion in Defamation Law." *University of Pittsburgh Law Review* 49 (1987):91.

Lee, Douglas E. "Public Interest, Public Figures, and the Corporate Defamation Plaintiff: Jadwin v. Minneapolis Star and Tribune." *Northwestern University Law Review* 81 (1987):318.

Lewis, Anthony. *Make No Law.* New York: Random House, 1991.

Margolick, David. "Psychoanalyst Loses Libel Suit Against a *New Yorker* Reporter." *The New York Times,* 3 November 1994, A1.

O'Connor, Clint. "Setting the Paper of Record Straight." *Washington Journalism Review,* September 1987, 10.

Prosser, William L. *Handbook of the Law of Torts.* St Paul: West Publishing, 1963.

Smolla, Rodney. *Suing the Press.* New York: Oxford University Press, 1986.

Smolla, Rodney A. "Dun & Bradstreet, Hepps, and Liberty Lobby: A New Analytic Primer on the Future Course of Defamation." *Georgetown Law Journal* 75 (1987):1519.

Stonecipher, Harry, and Don Sneed. "A Survey of the Professional Person as Libel Plaintiff." *Arkansas Law Review* 46 (1993):303.

Libel
Defenses and Damages

C ommon-law libel defenses are hundreds of years old. Before the mid-1960s when the Supreme Court began to add substantial new burdens upon libel plaintiffs, defenses were the primary means of warding off a defamation lawsuit. Most plaintiffs in the 1990s lose because they can't meet the required burden of proof; but common-law defenses remain a viable and important part of the law. A libel defense can not only protect a defendant from a successful suit, it can stop a plaintiff's case quickly, saving the publication or broadcasting outlet both time and money. Citing an appropriate defense, a defendant can ask a judge to dismiss a case even before a hearing is held. Such a dismissal is called a summary judgment. The judge may issue such a ruling if he or she does not think the plaintiff can prove what is required, as outlined in Chapters 4 and 5, or believes the defendant had a legal right (a defense) to publish or broadcast the defamatory material. Libel defenses are the primary subject of this chapter. Following this material is a brief outline of both civil libel damages and criminal libel.

SUMMARY JUDGMENT/STATUTE OF LIMITATIONS

The **summary judgment** is undoubtedly one of the best friends the mass media libel defendant has. Between 1986 and 1996, motions for summary judgment made by mass media defendants were granted 82 percent of the time, according to a study by the Libel Defense Resource Center. If the defendant's request for such a judgment is granted by the court, the case ends without a trial. Trials cost a lot of money and the press has not established a good track record for winning cases sent to a jury. Here is a brief outline of what happens in the summary judgment procedure:

After the plaintiffs have made their initial written allegations to the court, but before the trial begins, the defendants can argue that the lawsuit should be dismissed either because the plaintiff has failed to prove what is necessary to sustain the libel suit (publication, identification, defamation, falsity, and the requisite level of fault), or because there is a legal defense that blocks a successful lawsuit. As it considers this motion by the defense, the court is obligated to look at the plaintiff's allegation in the most favorable possible way. And if there is any dispute regarding facts (which would be cleared up at a subsequent trial), it must be for now resolved in favor of the plaintiff. If, having considered these factors, the court determines that a reasonable juror, acting reasonably, could not find for the plaintiff, then the motion for summary judgment will be granted.[1] (Please note that the plaintiff can also ask for a summary judgment, arguing there is no possible way a juror could find for the defendant.)

Here's a hypothetical example of how the summary judgment works. Imagine that Beth Smith, who publishes the newsletter for the Wyoming Cattle Breeders' Association, libels rancher Tom Brand in an article on meat inspection by the Department of Agriculture. Brand is the leader of a group of activist ranchers who have been protesting government inspection policies with rallies, appearances on local television shows, and marches. Smith's newsletter states that almost 50 percent of Brand's cattle have been rejected by inspectors as being unsafe to eat. Brand sues for libel. In his complaint Brand states that the allegations are false, that only 15 percent of his cattle were rejected. Smith and the breeders' association ask the court for a summary judgment. They claim that Brand is a public figure and will have to prove actual malice, for which no evidence exists. For the purpose of reviewing this motion, the court will assume that the allegation that 50 percent of Brand's cattle have been rejected is false. If the court finds for the defendant and grants the summary judgment, the case is finished, unless Brand appeals this decision. If the court rejects the motion, Smith can appeal as well. If this appeal is rejected, the case will go to trial. At that point the assumption that Smith's allegation that 50 percent of Brand's cattle were rejected is no longer valid. Brand will have to offer evidence that the statement is false and will, in all likelihood in this case, have to prove it was published with actual malice.

The Supreme Court has given both trial and appellate courts wide latitude in granting summary judgments in libel cases, especially in suits brought by public persons. In 1986 the justices said that federal courts must grant a summary judgment in favor of the media defendants in cases involving actual malice unless the plaintiffs can demonstrate that they will be

The Supreme Court has given both trial and appellate courts wide latitude in granting summary judgments in libel cases.

---

1. See, for example, *Nader* v. *DeToledano,* 408 A. 2d 31 (1979).

able to offer a jury clear and convincing evidence of actual malice.[2] Some trial judges had been hesitant about granting summary judgments because they believed that proof of actual malice calls the defendant's state of mind into question, which is a matter better considered at trial. But judges who force a trial even in the face of a weak libel claim are playing into the hands of those litigants who like to use the law to harass the press. Federal Judge Stanley Sarokin explained the importance of a summary judgment to the press in an 1985 ruling:

> Possibly the giants of the industry have both the finances and the stamina to run the risk in such situations [the threat of a libel suit]. But the independent will of smaller magazines, newspapers, television and radio stations undoubtedly bends with the spectre of a libel action looming. Even if convinced of their ultimate success on the merits, the costs of vindication may soon be too great for such media defendants to print or publish that which may entail any risk of a court action. If that is the result, it is a sorry state of affairs for the media, and, more important, for the country. Therefore, probably more than any other type of case, summary judgments in libel actions should be readily available and granted where appropriate.[3]

STATUTE OF LIMITATIONS

For nearly all crimes and most civil actions, there is a **statute of limitations.** Courts do not like stale legal claims. They have plenty of fresh ones to keep them busy. Prosecution for most crimes except homicide and kidnapping must be started within a specified period of time. For example, in many states if prosecution is not started within seven years after an armed robbery is committed, the robber cannot be brought to trial. He or she is home free. (However, the robber can still be prosecuted for failing to pay income tax on money taken from a bank, but that is another story.)

The duration of the statute of limitations for libel actions differs from state to state, varying from one to three years (figure 6.1). In most states the duration is one or two years. What this means is that a libel suit must be started within one or two years following publication of the offending material. The date of publication on a newspaper determines when the duration of the statute begins. In television and radio the statute of limitations begins on the day the program is telecast or broadcast. Magazines pose a somewhat different problem. The publication date on the magazine rarely coincides with the date the publication is actually distributed. Magazines dated November are usually distributed in October, sometimes even in late September. Courts have ruled that the statute of limitations begins on the date that a magazine is distributed to a substantial portion of the public. For example, Business Week magazine was sued for libel for an article published in its issue dated Sept. 12, 1994. The lawsuit was filed on Sept. 11, 1997, the day before the three-year statute of limitations expired. Attorneys for the magazine demonstrated to the court that the Sept. 12, 1994, edition of Business

2. *Anderson v. Liberty Lobby,* 477 U.S. 242 (1986).
3. *Schiavone Construction v. Time,* 619 F. Supp. 684 (1985).

MAP SHOWING DURATION OF STATUTE OF LIMITATIONS IN LIBEL ACTIONS

FIGURE 6.1

Plaintiffs must file libel suits before the statute of limitations expires. This chart indicates the duration of this filing period in the 50 states.

Week was on the newsstands and on its way to subscribers on Sept. 6, 1994. The U.S. District Court in New Mexico ruled that under the single publication rule, the statute of limitations begins on the earliest date that the publication is available to a substantial portion of the public rather than the cover date on the magazine.[4] Case dismissed.

The libel republication rule can be a factor in considering the statute of limitations. In some states buying a back issue of a publication is considered new publication, and the statute of limitations starts over. More and more jurisdictions have rejected this rule and substituted the single publication rule. This rule states that the entire edition of a newspaper or magazine is a single publication and that isolated sales in the months or years to come do not constitute republication. Therefore the statute of limitations starts on the day the edition hit the newsstands and ends one or two or three years later. The statute cannot be reactivated by a later sale. More than one-half the states have this progressive rule. Find out if your state does.

Posting the contents of a magazine online has generated a new problem with regard to publication date. A businessman in New York, which has a one-year statute of limitations, brought a libel action against Business Week magazine exactly one year after the magazine appeared on newsstands. The magazine, however, was posted on America Online a day before

4. *Printon Inc.* v. *McGraw-Hill Inc.,* 35 F. Supp. 2d 1325 (1998). See also *MacDonald* v. *Time,* 554 F. Supp. 1053 (1983); *Wildmon* v. *Hustler,* 508 F. Supp. 87 (1980); *Bradford* v. *American Media Operations, Inc.,* 882 F. Supp. 1508 (1995); and *Williamson* v. *New Times Inc.,* 980 S.W. 2d 706 (1998).

it appeared on the street. The magazine's attorneys argued that uploading the magazine onto the Internet and making it available to America Online's five million subscribers constitutes publication of the magazine. The plaintiff's attorney disputed this argument, claiming the day the magazine appeared on the newsstands was the day the statute of limitations started running. The issue had not been settled when this book was published.[5]

Jurisdiction

Is it possible for a plaintiff who has not filed a libel suit within the statute of limitations in his or her home state to file an action in another state that has a longer statute of limitations? The answer is yes, so long as the libel has been circulated in this other state. The Supreme Court clarified this question in two 1984 rulings, *Keeton* v. *Hustler*[6] and *Calder* v. *Jones*.[7] Kathy Keeton, a resident of New York, sued Hustler magazine, an Ohio corporation, for libel in the state of New Hampshire. Hustler challenged the action, arguing that the suit should be brought in New York or Ohio but not New Hampshire, which had a six-year statute of limitations. (The statute of limitations is now three years in New Hampshire.) Only about 15,000 copies of the 1-million-plus circulation of the magazine were sold in New Hampshire, the defendant argued. A court of appeals ruled that the plaintiff had too tenuous a contact with New Hampshire to permit the assertion of personal jurisdiction in that state, but the Supreme Court unanimously reversed the ruling. Hustler's regular circulation of magazines in New Hampshire is sufficient to support an assertion of jurisdiction in a libel action, Justice William Rehnquist wrote. "False statements of fact harm both the subject of the falsehood and the readers of the statement: New Hampshire may rightly employ its libel laws to discourage the deception of its citizens," the justice continued. The state may extend its concern to the injury that in-state libel causes to a nonresident as well, he added.[8]

The same day, the high court ruled that California courts could assume jurisdiction in a case brought by a California resident against the authors of a story that was written and published in a newspaper in Florida but circulated in California. Shirley Jones sued two journalists for an article they wrote and edited in Florida and that was then published in the National Enquirer. At that time the Enquirer had a national circulation of about 5 million and distributed about 600,000 copies each week in California. A trial court ruled that Jones could certainly sue the publishers of the Enquirer in California, but not the reporters. Requiring journalists to appear in remote jurisdictions to answer for the contents of articles on which they worked could have a chilling impact on the First Amendment rights of reporters and editors, the court said. But again a unanimous Supreme Court disagreed, with Justice Rehnquist noting that the article was about a California resident who works in California. Material for the article was drawn from California sources and the brunt of the harm to both the career and the personal reputation of the plaintiff will be suffered in California, he added. "An individual injured in

---

5. Pogrebin, "Publication Date Open."
6. 465 U.S. 770 (1984).
7. 465 U.S. 783 (1984).
8. *Keeton* v. *Hustler,* 465 U.S. 770 (1984).

California need not go to Florida to seek redress from persons who, though remaining in Florida, knowingly cause the injury in California," Rehnquist wrote. The justice said that the potential chill on protected First Amendment activity stemming from libel actions is already taken into account in the constitutional limitations on the substantive law governing such suits. "To reinforce those concerns at the jurisdictional level would be a form of double counting," he said.[9]

Jurisdiction and the Internet

These two Supreme Court rulings stand for the proposition that publishers may be sued in any jurisdiction in which they distribute even a relatively small portion of their publication—even if the plaintiff does not reside in that jurisdiction. How does this principle apply to communication on the Internet? Any message contained on any Web site is conceivably accessible in any state in the nation. Can the Web site operator be sued in any jurisdiction? Or must there be evidence that the message was read or downloaded by residents of the jurisdiction? These are open questions, and it is likely to be some time before the issues are resolved. Courts have made a handful of rulings regarding jurisdiction. A U.S. district court in the District of Columbia recently rejected the notion that a plaintiff can choose virtually any state jurisdiction in bringing an action for defamation simply because the content of the Internet appears in all 50 states. A Seattle company had posted a message on a bulletin board maintained by America Online, which is located in Virginia. In the defamation suit that followed, the plaintiff brought suit in the District of Columbia, claiming that 200,000 America Online subscribers in the District of Columbia had access to the message. The court rejected the argument, noting that the original message was sent to Virginia, not to the District of Columbia; that the subject matter of the message had nothing to do with the District of Columbia; and that neither party in the case was located or incorporated in the District of Columbia. "There is no nationwide jurisdiction for defamation actions," the court said, "and the advent of the Internet and Internet service providers such as America Online does not change that."[10]

In May of 1999, however, a federal court in Virginia rendered a somewhat different ruling when it decided that Texas residents could be sued in Virginia after posting allegedly defamatory statements on a Virginia-based America Online Usenet server. The message must have been stored, at least temporarily, in the server in Virginia, the court said, which gives Virginia courts jurisdiction.[11] These two cases are just a sample of the kind of litigation that is taking place. The best advice for Web users is to be careful about the content of any message sent via an interactive computer system, thus avoiding a potential libel action in any state.

---

9. *Calder* v. *Jones,* 465 U.S. 783 (1984).

10. *Mallinckrodt Medical Inc.* v. *Sonus Pharmaceuticals Inc.,* DCDC Civil Action No. 97-1732 (PLF), 1/5/98. See also *Advanced Software Inc.* v. *Datapharm Inc.,* C.D. Cal CV 98-5943 DDP, 11/3/98.

11. *Bochan* v. *La. Fontaine,* 27 M.L.R. 2057 (1999). See also *Telco Communications Inc.* v. *Apple A Day Inc.,* DC E. Va. Civil No. 97-542-A, 9/24/97; *Nicosia* v. *DeRooy,* N.D. Cal., No. C98-3029 MMC, 7/7/99; and *Remick* v. *Manfreddy,* E.D. Pa. 99-CV-0025, 4/22/99.

A libel suit must be started before the statute of limitations expires. Each state determines how long this period will be. In all states it is one, two, or three years. A libel suit started after the expiration of the statute of limitations will be dismissed.

SUMMARY

TRUTH

The First Amendment provides defendants in libel suits considerable protection. The defendant in a lawsuit filed against a newspaper or other mass medium is in fact well defended by the constitutional requirements placed on the plaintiff. But there were defenses for libel even before the ruling in *New York Times* v. *Sullivan.*[12] These emerged through the common law and via statutes in many states. Truth, privileged communication, fair comment, consent, and right of reply all work to protect the libel defendant—no matter who he or she might be. The applicability of each of these defenses in a particular case is determined by the facts in the case—what the story is about, how the information was gained, and the manner in which it was published.

Traditionally, truth has been regarded as an important libel defense that completely protected defendants in lawsuits for defamation. To use this defense, the defendant was required to prove the truth of the libelous allegations he or she published. Truth is still a defense in a libel action, but it has lost much of its importance in light of recent rulings that require most libel plaintiffs to carry the burden of proving a defamatory allegation to be false when the story focuses on a matter of public concern. In those few instances when a private-person plaintiff sues for a libelous statement that does not focus on something of public concern and therefore does not have to show the falsity of the matter as a part of proving negligence, the libel defendant can escape liability in the case by showing that the defamatory matter is true. But the defendant carries the burden of proof; truth becomes a defense. The same rules apply to proving truth that apply to proving falsity, only they are reversed. The defendant must show that the allegations are substantially true. Extraneous errors will not destroy the defense. See pages 153–158 to refresh your memory on these matters.

PRIVILEGED COMMUNICATIONS

Traditionally in the United States, we value robust debate as a means of discovering those elusive truths that we continually pursue. The law takes pains to protect this debate, making sure that speakers are not unduly punished for speaking their minds. Article 1, Section 6, of the federal Constitution provides that members of the Congress are immune from suits based on their remarks on the floor of either house. This is called a privilege. The statement in question is referred to as a privileged communication.

12. 376 U.S. 254 (1964).

ABSOLUTE PRIVILEGE

Today, privilege attaches to a wide variety of communications and speakers. Anyone speaking in a legislative forum—members of congress, senators, state representatives, city council members, and so forth—enjoys this privilege. Even the statements of witnesses at legislative hearings are privileged. But the comments must be made in the legislative forum. The Supreme Court ruled in 1979 that while a speech by a senator on the floor of the Senate would be wholly immune from a libel action, newsletters and press releases about the speech issued by the senator's office would not be protected by the privilege. Only speech that is "essential to the deliberations of the Senate" is protected, and neither newsletters to constituents nor press releases are parts of the deliberative process.[13]

Today, privilege attaches to a wide variety of communications and speakers.

Similarly, the privilege attaches to communications made in judicial forums—courtrooms, grand jury rooms, and so forth. Judges, lawyers, witnesses, defendants, plaintiffs, and all other persons are protected so long as the remark is uttered during the official portions of the hearing or the trial. Finally, persons who work in the administrative and executive branches of government enjoy privilege as well. Presidents, mayors, governors, department heads—official communications or official statements by these kinds of persons are privileged. In 1959 in *Barr* v. *Mateo,* the Supreme Court suggested that the privilege applies to any publication by government officials that is in line with the discharge of their official duties. This case involved a press release from a department head explaining why two federal employees had been fired. "A publicly expressed statement of the position of the agency head," the court ruled, "announcing personnel action which he planned to take in reference to the charges so widely disseminated to the public was an appropriate exercise of the discretion which an officer of that rank must possess if the public service is to function effectively."[14]

More recently, the court of appeals in New York state ruled that a press release issued by an assistant attorney general concerning the investigation of possible fraudulent activities by fund-raisers was protected from a lawsuit by privilege. The court said that since the attorney general as an executive official enjoys absolute privilege while exercising the functions of his office, the same privilege applies to his subordinates, who exercise delegated powers.[15] The difference in the treatment of the assistant attorney general by the New York court and Senator Proxmire by the U.S. Supreme Court over essentially the same item—a press release—stems from the different roots of the privilege. Congressional privilege stems directly from the U.S. Constitution and is limited by the constitutional language. The privilege applied to the state attorney general stems from the common law. Also, the functions of the two offices are different. Senators are supposed to deliberate and make legislative policy. Reporting to the public on the results of an official investigation is one of the governmental functions of an attorney general.

The privilege just discussed is an **absolute privilege.** The speaker cannot be sued for defamation on the basis of such a remark. A similar kind of privilege applies also to certain kinds of private communications. Discussions between an employer and an employee are privileged; the report of a credit rating is privileged; a personnel recommendation by an

---

13. *Hutchinson* v. *Proxmire,* 443 U.S. 111 (1979).
14. *Barr* v. *Mateo,* 353 U.S. 171 (1959).
15. *Gautsche* v. *New York,* 415 N.Y.S. 2d 280 (1979).

employer about an employee is privileged. These kinds of private communications remain privileged so long as they are not disseminated beyond the sphere of those who need to know.

QUALIFIED PRIVILEGE

What is called **qualified privilege** goes far beyond the absolute immunity granted to speakers at public and official meetings and the conditional immunity granted to certain types of private communications. Under the qualified privilege, an individual may report what happens at an official governmental proceeding or transmit the substance of an official government report or statement and remain immune from libel even if the publication of the material defames someone. This is how the privilege is outlined in the "Restatement of Torts":

> The publication of defamatory matter concerning another in a report of any official proceeding or any meeting open to the public which deals with matters of public concern is conditionally privileged if the report is accurate and complete, or a fair abridgment of what has occurred.[16]

Actually, this definition of the privilege in the "Restatement" is a bit conservative, as courts continually extend the protection of qualified privilege to reports of more diverse kinds of government activity. This qualified privilege is sometimes called the privilege of the reporter, as opposed to the absolute immunity noted previously, which is often referred to as the privilege of the participant. The use of the term "reporter" signifies someone who reports on what has happened, as opposed to the journalistic meaning of the term, a newspaper or television reporter.

CRITERIA FOR APPLICATION OF QUALIFIED PRIVILEGE

▪ Report of a privileged proceeding or document
▪ A fair and accurate summary published or broadcast as a report

---

At the start it is important to note that qualified privilege is a conditional privilege; that is, the privilege only works as a libel defense if certain conditions are met. First, the privilege only applies to reports of certain kinds of meetings, hearings, proceedings, reports, and statements. Second, the law requires that these reports be a fair and accurate or truthful summary of what took place at the meeting or what was said in the report. In the past there was a third condition—that the report containing the defamatory charges was published or broadcast in order to inform the people, not simply to hurt the plaintiff. It is generally considered today that this third condition no longer applies; the defendant's motivation for publishing or broadcasting the material is irrelevant.[17]

The defendant bears the burden of proving that the privilege applies to the libelous material. The court will determine whether the particular occasion (meeting, proceeding,

---

16. American Law Institute, *Restatement of Torts.*
17. See *Schiavone Construction* v. *Time,* 569 F. Supp. 614 (1983).

report) is privileged. The jury will determine whether the defendant's report of the occasion is a fair and accurate report.

Before going into the details relating to the application of this defense, let's look at a brief hypothetical example. During a meeting of the Mayberry City Council, Councilman Floyd Lawson, while discussing an increase in the garbage rates for city residents, says this: "Allied Garbage Co., which supposedly gives us a good rate to pick up the trash, is run by a bunch of crooks who are intent on cheating this city and all its citizens. I mean, I read it in the newspaper. These guys are a part of organized crime." Because of the protection of the absolute privilege, the owners of Allied Garbage cannot sue Lawson. When the reporter who attended the meeting includes this comment in her story, the newspaper also is shielded from a lawsuit so long as the story is a fair and accurate summary of what Lawson said: "Councilman Floyd Lawson charged last night during a city council meeting that the owners of Allied Garbage Co. are a part of organized crime and are cheating the city."

Let's first examine the kinds of occasions that courts have found to be covered by the privilege.

Legislative Proceedings

The privilege applies to what occurs during meetings of legislative bodies, from the U.S. Congress down to the lowly village council meeting. But courts have ruled that only what is said during the official portion of the meeting is included within the protective ambit of the defense. A Pennsylvania superior court recently ruled that the privilege did not apply to a newspaper report of comments made by citizens while a township board of supervisors meeting was in recess.[18] The privilege also applies to the reports of committee meetings of such organizations as well as to stories about petitions, complaints, and other communications received by these bodies. The only requirement that must be met with regard to this aspect of the privilege is that the official body, such as a city council, must officially receive the complaint or petition before the privilege applies. If the Citizens for Cleaner Streets bring to a city council meeting a petition charging the street superintendent with incompetence and various and sundry blunders in his or her job, publication of these charges is privileged as soon as the city council officially accepts the petition. Nothing has to be done with the document. It must merely be accepted. The privilege usually applies to stories about the news conferences of members of a legislative body following a session, to stories about what was said during a closed meeting by the body, and to stories about what was said during an informal gathering of legislators before or after the regular session, especially if what is said or what occurs during these kinds of events is of great public interest.

Judicial Proceedings

The privilege of the reporter also applies to actions that take place in judicial forums: testimony and depositions of witnesses, arguments of attorneys, pronouncements of judges, and so forth. Stories about trials, decisions, jury verdicts, court opinions, judicial orders and decrees,

18. *DeMary v. Latrobe Printing and Publishing Co.,* 28 M.L.R. 1337 (2000).

and grand jury indictments are all protected by the privilege. Probably the most difficult problem a reporter on the court beat has to face is what to do when a lawsuit is initially filed. Under our legal system a lawsuit is started when a person files a complaint with a court clerk and serves a summons on the defendant. The complaint is filled with charges, most of which are libelous. Can a reporter use that complaint as the basis for a story?

Traditionally states have followed one of two rules on this question. In some states a complaint that has been filed is not considered privileged until some kind of judicial action has been taken. The scheduling of an appearance by the litigants may be sufficient. This rule, which requires a judge to become involved in the matter before the complaint is privileged, is designed to protect an innocent party from being smeared in a news report written about a lawsuit that has been filed but then quickly withdrawn. Advocates of this system argue that it is much more difficult to withdraw such a lawsuit after a judge has gotten involved in the proceeding. Those who oppose this rule say the idea is a good one but it is out of date. Libel expert Bruce Sanford contends that "courts now recognize that the old rule can be easily circumvented by anyone determined to defame; judicial action may be obtained simply by filing a procedural motion."[19] Consequently, more and more states today follow the rule that the complaint becomes privileged as soon as it has been filed with the court and a docket number has been assigned or the defendant has been issued a summons. Two cautionary notes are important. A reporter should never take a lawyer's word that the lawsuit has been filed. The announcement may be a hoax to get publicity favorable to a client. A call to the courthouse is always in order. Also, ignore what the lawyer says about the case when he or she proclaims that the legal action has been filed. Normally, only comments or material contained in the formal judicial proceedings or court documents are protected by privilege. The Iowa Supreme Court recently ruled that comments made to a reporter by an attorney after the lawyer had filed the complaint initiating the lawsuit were not protected by privilege.[20]

Stories about those parts of the judicial process that are closed to the public are normally not protected by the privilege. For example, court sessions for juveniles and divorce proceedings are frequently closed to protect the privacy of the individuals involved. Some states regard these closures as important public policy and attempt to discourage publicity about such proceedings by denying the mass media the opportunity to apply the privilege if a lawsuit should result from press coverage. But this rule is changing. The 9th U.S. Circuit Court of Appeals has ruled that under California law, the press enjoyed the privilege to publish reports of proceedings in a family court that excluded the general public during its hearings.[21] And a broad reading of U.S. Supreme Court rulings in certain privacy lawsuits that were generated because of press reports of court hearings suggests that the First Amendment may place substantial limits on libel plaintiffs as well who are suing because of a report of a closed legal proceeding.[22] (See pages 277–282 for a discussion of these cases.)

19. Sanford, *Libel and Privacy.*
20. *Kennedy* v. *Zimmerman,* 28 M.L.R. 1188 (1999).
21. *Dorsey* v. *National Enquirer, Inc.,* 973 F. 2d 1431 (1992).
22. See *Cox Broadcasting Co.* v. *Cohn,* 420 U.S. 469 (1975) and *Florida Star* v. *B.J.F.,* 109 S. Ct. 2603 (1989).

Executive Actions

Reports of the statements and proceedings conducted by mayors, department heads, and other persons in the administrative and executive branches of government are generally privileged. The best guideline is that the privilege is confined to stories about actions or statements that are official in nature, the kinds of things that are substantially "acts of state." By law, administrators are required to prepare certain reports and to hold certain hearings, and the privilege certainly covers stories on these activities. Although not required by law, other actions are unmistakably part of the job. Reports on these activities are protected as well. For example, the district attorney of Delaware County in Oklahoma held a news conference to discuss a drug investigation previously conducted by his office. At the news conference he distributed the transcript of a conversation between two undercover narcotics agents who had worked on the investigation. A local newspaper published a verbatim report of the conversation and was sued by a man named Ace Wright, who said it defamed him. The Oklahoma Supreme Court ruled that the publication was privileged. "District attorneys in Oklahoma have historically used press conferences to distribute information about the activities of their office to the citizens they represent," the court said.[23] The news conference was an activity conducted as a part of the official duties of the district attorney's office. But the Massachusetts Supreme Judicial Court refused to extend the privilege to remarks made by a small-town police chief about an internal investigation into whether one of his officers was working part-time at a second job while he was supposed to be on duty. "The conditional privilege to publish defamatory material is designed to allow public officials to speak freely on matters of public importance in the exercise of their official duties," the court said.[24] But it was not an official duty of the chief to report to the press on an internal departmental investigation. An Ohio court ruled that reports of health inspections of restaurants are privileged.[25] The New York Supreme Court ruled that reports of investigations by an environmental agency are privileged also.[26] Even stories based on confidential government documents that focused on possible government misconduct were declared to be privileged under Massachusetts law.[27] Finally, a Nevada court ruled that defamatory remarks contained in an official press release issued by the Bureau of Land Management, a federal agency, were privileged.[28]

Reports of police activities also fall under the heading of executive actions. It is fairly well settled that a report that a person has been arrested and charged with a crime is privileged. Official statements made by police about an investigation are privileged in many instances. The U.S. Court of Appeals for the 2nd Circuit ruled that public statements made by the head of the New York City office of the Federal Bureau of Investigation about an FBI search of law offices in Brooklyn were privileged. The Cable News Network had quoted the

> *"The conditional privilege to publish defamatory material is designed to allow public officials to speak freely on matters of public importance in the exercise of their official duties."*

23. *Wright* v. *Grove Sun Newspaper Co., Inc.,* 873 P. 2d 983 (1994).
24. *Draghetti* v. *Chimielewski,* 416 Mass. 808 (1994).
25. *McCain* v. *KTVY, Inc.,* 738 P. 2d 960 (1987).
26. *Quarcini* v. *Niagara Falls Gazette,* 13 M.L.R. 2340 (1987).
27. *Ingerere* v. *ABC,* 11 M.L.R. 1227 (1984).
28. *Mortensen* v. *Gannett Co.,* 24 M.L.R. 1190 (1995).

FBI agent as describing the offices as the headquarters for a dangerous left-wing group that sought to topple the U.S. government.[29] The U.S. Court of Appeals for the 3rd Circuit ruled that information obtained legally by Time magazine from FBI investigatory documents is also protected by a qualified privilege.[30] Caution needs to be exercised here, however. The privilege surely does not apply to every statement made by every police officer on every topic. The Idaho Supreme Court refused to apply the privilege to statements that were made privately to a reporter by a police officer. The court said these statements went beyond the official police reports, which are clearly privileged documents.[31]

The privilege is not confined to those instances of reporting official government proceedings. The Washington Supreme Court ruled that the reporting of the charges on recall petitions is privileged.[32] A federal court in Idaho ruled that the privilege applied to a story about a meeting called by citizens to protest the actions of a judge. It clearly was not an official meeting but concerned important public business, the conduct of a public official. The court said, "There is a general doctrine that what is said at a public meeting, at which any person of the community or communities involved might have attended and heard and seen for himself, is conditionally privileged for publication."[33]

The "Restatement of Torts" says that reports of what occurs at meetings open to the public at which matters of public concern are discussed are privileged.[34] Paul Ashley, libel authority and author of "Say It Safely," wrote that the privilege probably applies to a public meeting even though admission is charged, so long as everyone is free to pay the price. "By supplying them with information about public events," Ashley writes, "the publisher is acting as the 'eyes and ears' of people who did not attend."[35] In such a circumstance, the report of a public meeting, the key element undoubtedly is the subject of debate. Was it of public concern? Was it of limited public concern? Was it a purely private matter?

NEUTRAL REPORTAGE

Qualified privilege has taken on a somewhat different form in a handful of jurisdictions in a defense that has been labeled **neutral reportage.** The few courts that have embraced this idea, such as the 2nd U.S. Circuit Court of Appeals[36] and the 8th U.S. Circuit Court of Appeals,[37] have done so rather warmly. But many other courts that have been confronted with the defense have rejected it,[38] arguing that the doctrine is incompatible with the Supreme Court's ruling in

29. *Foster* v. *Turner Broadcasting,* 844 F. 2d 955 (1988).
30. *Medico* v. *Time,* 634 F. 2d 134 (1981).
31. *Wiemer* v. *Rankin,* 790 P. 2d 347 (1990).
32. *Herron* v. *Tribune Publishing Co.,* 736 P. 2d 249 (1987).
33. *Borg* v. *Borg,* 231 F. 2d 788 (1956).
34. American Law Institute, *Restatement of Torts.*
35. Ashley, *Say It Safely.*
36. *Edwards* v. *National Audubon Society, Inc.,* 556 F. 2d 113 (1977), cert. den. 434 U.S. 1002 (1977).
37. *Price* v. *Viking Penguin, Inc.,* 881 F. 2d 1426 (1989).
38. See, for example, *Dickey* v. *Columbia Broadcasting System, Inc.,* 583 F. 2d 1221 (1978) and *Young* v. *The Morning Journal,* 76 Ohio St. 3d 627 (1996).

Gertz v. *Robert Welch, Inc.,* or that it is unnecessary because of the protection provided by the actual malice rule in *New York Times* v. *Sullivan.* As you read the following description of this defense, you must remember that neutral reportage is not regarded as a legitimate libel defense in most jurisdictions.

The neutral reportage privilege developed most directly from an interesting suit in New York state concerning the annual Audubon Society Christmas bird count. The New York Times printed charges made by an official of the Audubon Society that any scientist who argues that the continued use of the pesticide DDT has not taken a serious toll of bird life is "someone who is being paid to lie about it or is parroting something he knows little about." The implication was, of course, that certain scientists were being paid by the pesticide industry to lie about the impact of the chemicals on wildlife. The Times story included the names of several scientists given to the reporter by Robert Arbib, the official at the Audubon Society. Some of these scientists sued for libel, but the U.S. Court of Appeals for the 2nd Circuit ruled that the story published by The Times containing the libelous charges was privileged. The court ruled this way even though reporter John Devlin might have believed the charges made by Arbib were false when he published them. The court called the privilege "neutral reportage" and described it in the following manner:

> When a responsible prominent organization like the National Audubon Society makes serious charges against a public figure, the First Amendment protects the accurate and disinterested reporting of those charges, regardless of the reporter's private views regarding their validity. What is newsworthy about such accusations is that they were made. . . . The public interest in being fully informed about controversies that often rage around sensitive issues demands that the press be afforded the freedom to report such charges without assuming responsibility for them. We must provide immunity from defamation where the journalist believes, reasonably and in good faith, that his report accurately conveys the charges made.[39]

The status of the neutral reportage rule remains unresolved at best. Courts in only a handful of jurisdictions (Ohio, Florida, and the 2nd and 8th U.S. Circuit Courts of Appeals) have fully accepted the privilege. Courts in more jurisdictions have rejected it. Many people view it as a good idea whose time may never come. Based on the decision in the *Edwards* case and a few other rulings, application of this privilege seems to have four distinct requirements:

- **The charges must be newsworthy charges that create or are associated with a public controversy.**
- **The charges must be made by a responsible and prominent source.**
- **The charges must be reported accurately and neutrally.**
- **The charges must be about a public official or public figure.**[40]

39. *Edwards* v. *National Audubon Society, Inc.,* 556 F. 2d 113 (1977), cert. den. 434 U.S. 1002 (1977).
40. See *Khawar* v. *Globe International Inc.,* 46 Cal. App. 4th 22 (1996); aff.'d 79 Cal. Rptr. 2d 178 (1998).

ABUSE OF PRIVILEGE

Whether qualified privilege applies to a particular story is only part of the problem. The privilege can be destroyed if the story in question is not a fair and accurate or true report of what took place. *Fair* means balanced. If at a public meeting speakers both attack and defend John Smith, the story should reflect both the attack and the defense. A story that focuses just on the charges is not fair, and the privilege will have been abused. Similarly, if the story concerns a continuing kind of an affair—a legislative hearing, a trial, and so forth—in which testimony is given for several days, the press is obligated to publish stories about each day's events if the privilege is to be used. There has to be balance. If a story about a civil suit based on the charges listed in the complaint is prepared, it is important to get the defendant's response as well. Balance is the key.

An accurate or true report means just that; it should honestly reflect what took place or what was said. In 1988 Glamour magazine printed a story about a widely publicized child custody case. The writer used a variety of sources for the story, including some depositions filed during the custody battle. These are privileged documents. A deposition from a clinical psychologist who had talked with the father in this case, Eric Foretich, discussed the death of his infant sister. The psychologist said that Foretich "was making funeral arrangements, selecting burial plots, you know, seeing the dead infant, things of that sort. . . . He spoke about his dead infant sister and being given this child to hold as his mother is running screaming through the house." The story in Glamour, however, contained these phrases: "When he [Foretich] was in his teens, a sister died shortly after birth. Eric's mother handed him the dead infant, and he arranged for the funeral."

A U.S. district court in the District of Columbia said the magazine's statement was not a fair and accurate summary of the material in the deposition. The description of Eric's mother in the deposition suggests a woman who was distraught, distressed by grief. The description of her in the magazine shows a cold, uncaring woman.[41]

Small errors in a story will not usually destroy the privilege, but an Ohio newspaper was judged to have abused its privilege when it botched its reporting of an attorney's name. The publication, using official court records, reported that "Amherst attorney James Young is facing a contempt of court citation." James C. Young was the attorney cited for contempt. James H. Young, another Amherst attorney, sued for libel. The Ohio Supreme Court ruled that the simple error rendered the story not substantially accurate.[42] More typical is a case in which a Florida television station broadcast a report based on privileged police records that a school bus driver had been convicted of attempted murder and had served four years in jail. The television report was wrong; the police records clearly stated that the bus driver had actually only served two years in jail. Nevertheless the court ruled that this was a substantially accurate story and the privilege protected the erroneous report.[43] Attorney F. Lee Bailey wrote in a

The privilege can be destroyed if the story in question is not a fair and accurate or true report of what took place.

41. *Foretich v. Advance Magazine Publishers, Inc.,* 18 M.L.R. 2280 (1991).
42. *Young v. The Morning Journal,* 76 Ohio St. 3d 627 (1996).
43. *Woodward v. Sunbeam Television Corp.,* 616 So. 2d 501 (1993).

book that Lawrence D. Murray, a former San Francisco assistant district attorney, was arrested for driving while under the influence of alcohol and for assault and battery of police officers. In fact Murray was arrested for being intoxicated in a public place and resisting arrest. "The slight inaccuracy in the details will not prevent a judgment for the defendant," a federal judge ruled, "if the inaccuracy does not change the complexion of the affair so as to affect the reader of the article differently than the actual truth would." The error in Bailey's book was a small one.[44]

The story should also be in the form of a report. If defendants fail to make it clear that they are reporting something that was said at a public meeting or repeating something that is contained in the public record, the privilege may be lost. The law says the reader should be aware that the story is a report of what happened at a public meeting or at an official hearing or is taken from the official record. These facts should be noted in the lead and in the headline if possible, as noted in the following boxed example. The U.S. Court of Appeals for the District

---

AT CITY COUNCIL SESSION: MAYOR BLASTS CONTRACTOR WITH CHARGES OF FRAUD

Mayor John Smith during a city council meeting today charged the Acme Construction Company with fraudulent dealings.

---

of Columbia Circuit ruled that qualified privilege did not apply to a magazine summary of statements contained in an official report from the National Transportation Safety Board. The report is an official record; it is clearly covered by the reporter's privilege. But the summary in the magazine gave readers no clue that the statements constituted a summary of an official document. "The challenged [defamatory] assertion is simply offered as historical fact without any particular indication of its source," the court said. The reader was left with the impression that the author of the article reached the conclusion contained in the defamatory allegations based on his own research.[45]

The privilege protects only that part of a story based on an official proceeding or a public record or report. Anything added to the story from outside these sources will not be protected by the qualified privilege.

One last point needs to be made. Traditionally, under the common law, if even a fair and true report was published not to inform the public but because the publisher wanted to hurt the target of the defamation, the privilege could be lost. Courts called this intent to harm the plaintiff common-law malice because the publisher had a malicious intent. In most states today, even if the plaintiff is able to prove common-law malice, the privilege will still protect the publisher. But this protection is not the law everywhere. The Minnesota Court of Appeals decided in June of 1999 that proof of common-law malice can defeat the privilege in that state.[46] Be forewarned.

---

44. *Murray* v. *Bailey,* 11 M.L.R. 1369 (1985).
45. *Dameron* v. *Washingtonian,* 779 F. 2d 736 (1985).
46. *Moreno* v. *Crookston Times Printing Co.,* 594 NW 2d 555 (1999).

SUMMARY

The publication of defamatory material in a report of a public meeting, legislative proceeding, or legal proceeding or in a story that reflects the content of an official government report is conditionally privileged. The privilege extends to the meetings of all public bodies, to all aspects of the legal process, to reports and statements issued by members of the executive branch of government, and even to nonofficial meetings of the public in which matters of public concern are discussed. Such reports cannot be the basis for a successful libel suit as long as the report presents a fair (balanced) and accurate (truthful) account of what took place at the meeting or what is contained in the record.

PROTECTION OF OPINION

The law has traditionally shielded statements of opinion from suits for defamation. Opinion is a basic part of mass media in the 21st century, with art, music, film, and television reviews, political commentary, news analysis, and editorials. Opinion-filled exchanges, often heated and exaggerated, are part of the basic political and social discourse in the United States. For several centuries a common-law defense, called fair comment and criticism, was the shield used to protect opinion statements from libel suits. In the past 30 years, however, two other defenses have been added, and there is some question whether the common-law protection afforded to opinion statements by the fair comment defense is needed or viable. In the following pages we examine all three of these potential defenses.

RHETORICAL HYPERBOLE

In the late 1960s, a real estate developer had engaged in negotiations with a local city council for a zoning variance on some land he owned. At the same time the developer was also negotiating with the same city council on another parcel of land that the city wanted him to buy. The local newspaper published articles on the bargaining and said that some people had characterized the developer's negotiating positions as "blackmail." The libel suit that followed ultimately found its way to the U.S. Supreme Court. The high court rejected the plaintiff's notion that readers would believe the developer had committed the actual crime of blackmail. The court said the stories gave readers all the background needed to understand the negotiations. "Even the most careless reader must have perceived that the word was no more than rhetorical hyperbole, a vigorous epithet used by those who considered the [developer's] negotiating position extremely unreasonable."[47]

Four years later the high court rendered a similar ruling in a case involving a dispute among postal workers. The National Association of Letter Carriers was trying to organize workers at a post office in Virginia. The monthly union newsletter included the names of those who had not yet joined the union under the heading, "List of Scabs." To emphasize their point,

47. *Greenbelt Publishing Assn., Inc. v. Bresler,* 398 U.S. 6 (1970).

the editors of the newsletter published a definition of a scab written years ago by American author Jack London. London said, among other things, that a scab carries a tumor of rotten principles where others have a heart, and is a traitor to his god, his country, his family, and his class. A postal worker sued, claiming he was not a traitor. The high court cited the earlier decision in *Greenbelt* and said it was impossible to believe that any readers would have understood the newsletter to be charging the plaintiff with the criminal offense of treason. It was rhetorical hyperbole—lusty, imaginative expression.[48]

The New York Court of Appeals ruled in 1992 that comments made during a heated public hearing on a proposal to create a sidewalk cafe outside the ground floor of a multistory apartment unit were rhetorical hyperbole, not capable of a defamatory meaning. The defendant in the case, a tenant who had lived in the building for 30 years and had been a former president of the tenants' board of managers, complained that the existing indoor restaurant already caused severe problems for the tenants in the building. He said that the cafe had "denigrated" the building, that the plaintiff's lease on the space was "as fraudulent as you get and it smells of bribery and corruption," and that the permit to build the sidewalk eatery was "fraudulent." The court ruled that, "Given the loose nature of the language, the general tenor of the remarks made at the public hearing, and the skepticism a reasonable listener brings to such proceedings, we [do not] believe . . . that a reasonable listener would conclude factual assertions were being made about the plaintiff."[49]

Opinion statements, then, may be defended as being unbelievable rhetoric. Here are some examples of the kinds of statements lower courts have ruled are rhetorical hyperbole:

> A television station compared a local politician to Manuel Noriega, and said he had stolen democracy from the people.[50]
>
> A school board member referred to a former president of a local Parent-Teachers Association as a "new nightrider of the K[u] K[lux] K[lan]."[51]
>
> A TV commentator said a chiropractor was a part of an "international network of medical quackery," and said his patients were victims of "cancer con artists" and "unscrupulous charlatans."[52]
>
> A statement was made in an editorial that a mayor's zoning proposal was "extortion" and blackmail."[53]
>
> A teacher was described as a "babbler."[54]

Rhetorical hyperbole is protected, then, because the language is so expansive that the reader or listener knows it is only an opinion, that it is not an assertion of fact.

Opinion statements, then, may be defended as being unbelievable rhetoric.

---

48. *Old Dominion Branch No. 496, National Association of Letter Carriers* v. *Austin,* 94 S. Ct. 2770 (1974).
49. *600 West 115th Street Corp.* v. *Von Gutfeld,* 80 N.Y. 2d 130 (1992).
50. *Maholick* v. *WNEP TV,* 20 M.L.R. 1022 (1992).
51. *Hunter* v. *New York City,* 22 M.L.R. 1189 (1993).
52. *Kirk* v. *CBS,* 14 M.L.R. 1263 (1987).
53. *Fasi* v. *Gannett Co.,* 114 F. 3d 1194 (1997).
54. *Moyer* v. *Amador Valley Joint Union High School District,* 225 Cal. App. 3d 720 (1990).

THE FIRST AMENDMENT

The Supreme Court ruled in 1991 that a statement of "pure opinion" on a matter of public concern is protected by the First Amendment.[55] A libel action based on such a statement cannot succeed. Courts across America have adopted this principle as a fundamental aspect of libel law. There has been substantially less agreement, however, on how to identify a statement of "pure opinion." Chief Justice Rehnquist, the author of the 1991 ruling, said a statement of pure opinion is a statement that is incapable of being proved true or false. Pure opinion, Rehnquist said, does not assert or even imply a provably false fact.

The Supreme Court decision flowed from a case in which an Ohio sports columnist wrote that a high school wrestling coach and a school superintendent "lied" during a hearing in which they argued for the reinstatement of the wrestling team, which had been disqualified from participating in the state wrestling tournament. It's hard to know what writer Ted Diadiun really meant when he wrote his column, but after a libel suit was filed against the newspaper, the sportswriter argued that he was simply stating his opinion that the coach and the school superintendent had not been honest when they testified at the hearing.

The case meandered through state and federal courts for nearly 15 years before the Supreme Court ultimately ruled in 1991 that Diadiun's statement was an assertion of a fact, not simply an opinion. Rehnquist said the columnist would not have helped his case had he written "In my opinion, Milkovich [the coach] lied" or "I think Milkovich lied." He is still asserting a fact. He is telling readers, the chief justice said, that "I know something that leads me to believe that this man lied under oath." And this is the assertion of a fact, nothing more, nothing less. The newspaper ultimately paid $116,000 in damages to the plaintiffs. More important, perhaps, the publication spent close to a half million dollars defending itself.

It is unusual for lower courts to reject outright a principle of law enunciated by the Supreme Court, but that is what has happened in this case. The majority of lower courts in the United States that since 1991 have decided cases involving statements of opinion have indicated a dissatisfaction with the *Milkovich* standard. The consensus seems to be that defining an opinion statement using the single criterion of proving a statement true or false is far too conservative, that it would deny First Amendment protection to statements that an author intended to be opinion and that a reader or viewer would assume was opinion.

Many courts have gravitated to a different test for determining whether a remark is intended an assertion of fact or a statement of opinion. This test includes the criterion outlined by the high court—can the statement be proved true or false—but requires the court to look at other dimensions of the published comment as well.

The Ollman Test

In 1984 the U.S. Court of Appeals for the District of Columbia Circuit outlined a four-part test to determine whether a statement should be regarded as the assertion of a fact or as simply the

---

55. *Milkovich* v. *Lorain Journal Co.,* 110 S. Ct. 2695 (1991).

speaker's or writer's opinion. The test, which emerged from the case of *Ollman* v. *Evans*,[56] is known as the *Ollman* test for obvious reasons. Here are the four elements:

- **Can the statement be proved true or false?** This is the basic test from *Milkovich*.
- **What is the common or ordinary meaning of the words?** Some words that appear to be factual assertions are more often used as statements of opinion. If you call someone a turkey, you don't really mean to suggest that the person has feathers and says gobble-gobble. Calling someone a moron doesn't normally mean that his or her IQ score is way below average.
- **What is the journalistic context of the remark?** Newspaper readers expect to find factual assertions in news stories on the front page. They don't expect to find facts in editorial columns, they expect to find opinions. Dan Rather gives us the news; Rush Limbaugh gives us his opinions, no matter how he happens to word these statements.
- **What is the social context of the remark?** Certain kinds of speech are common to certain kinds of political or social settings. The audience attending a lecture by an eminent scientist on the need to vaccinate young children is expecting to hear facts. In a debate between two candidates for the legislature, the audience is prepared to hear opinion. Labor disputes, political meetings, protest rallies, and other such settings usually generate high-spirited and free-wheeling commentary. People don't usually expect to hear factual assertions.

OLLMAN TEST

1. Can the statement be proved true or false?
2. What is the common or ordinary meaning of the words?
3. What is the journalistic context of the remark?
4. What is the social context of the remark?

The first important court to reject the single-criterion *Milkovich* test was the New York Court of Appeals, the high court in that state. The case, *Immuno, A.G.* v. *Moor-Jankowski*,[57] involved a letter to the editor of a scholarly scientific journal. Jan Moor-Jankowski was a professor of medical research at New York University and the editor of the Journal of Medical Primatology. He published a letter in the Journal from Dr. Shirley McGreal that was highly critical of a plan by Immuno, A.G., an Austrian medical company, to establish a facility in Sierra Leone that would use chimpanzees for hepatitis research. McGreal said the company's motivation to construct the facility in Africa was to avoid legal restrictions on the importation

---

56. 750 F. 2d 970 (1984).
57. 77 N.Y. 2d 235 (1991).

of chimps, an endangered species, into the United States. She also alleged that the plan could seriously deplete the chimpanzee population, and that Immuno's stated intention of returning the animals to the wild after they had been used for research could result in spreading hepatitis throughout the chimpanzee population. The letter was published in the letters-to-the-editor section of the journal. Moor-Jankowski included an editor's note that the author of the letter was an animal rights advocate (she was the head of the International Primate Protection League) and that Immuno, A.G. considered the charges reckless and inaccurate.

In 1990 the New York high court had ruled that the letter was opinion and protected. Immuno, A.G. appealed to the U.S. Supreme Court, which granted certiorari and ordered the New York Court of Appeals to reconsider its decision in light of the *Milkovich* ruling.

The court did, and once again ruled the letter to be an opinion. Judge Judith Kaye identified possible assertions of fact in the letter, determined that under *Milkovich* they were likely verifiable, but concluded that Immuno, A.G. had not satisfied the burden of proving the falsity of any of these assertions. But the New York court went further, almost thumbing its nose at the U.S. Supreme Court's *Milkovich* ruling, which it called "hypertechnical." Judge Kaye said the Supreme Court ruling required "fine parsing" of the publication at issue, and isolated the challenged speech and "extracted its express or implied factual statements" without regard to context. The First Amendment may not require a broad protection for opinion statements, Judge Kaye wrote, but the New York State Constitution does.[58] She wrote that the context of this defamation, the fact that it was a letter to the editor where readers have a common expectation of opinion statements, was material in this case. The letters page carried the warning that the views expressed in the letters were the views of the letter writers. Judge Kaye also noted that the readers of the Journal were highly specialized, aware of the debate going on over such research projects. This context meant that the statements at issue were protected as a matter of law under the state constitution.

Whereas the New York Court of Appeals finally rested its ruling on its own state constitution, other courts have based their application of the *Ollman* test squarely on the First Amendment, rejecting in a direct way the Chief Justice's opinion in *Milkovich* v. *Lorain Journal Co.* A U.S. district court in California ruled in 1998 that a statement published about Johnnie Cochran, one of O.J. Simpson's lead defense attorneys, in a column in the New York Post was an opinion, protected by the First Amendment. Cochran had signed on to represent Abner Louima, a Haitian immigrant who said he was beaten by New York police. The newspaper columnist, Andrea Peyser, wrote that Louima was a very sympathetic plaintiff in the lawsuit against the city, but that he would weaken his otherwise strong case by permitting a "legal scoundrel" to join his team. Peyser added that Cochran "will say or do just about anything to win, typically at the expense of the truth." The court said its decision that the statement was opinion protected by the First Amendment was based on the general tenor of the entire work, the specific content and context of the statements, and because the statement was not sufficiently factual that it could be proved true or false.[59]

---

58. *Immuno, A.G.* v. *Moor-Jankowski*, 77 N.Y. 2d 235 (1991).
59. *Cochran* v. *NYP Holdings Inc.*, 27 M.L.R. 1108 (1998). See also *Phantom Touring, Inc.* v. *Affiliated Publications*, 953 F. 2d 724 (1992).

Another important example of the application of the broader *Ollman* standard was the 1994 ruling by the District of Columbia Circuit of the U.S. Court of Appeals in *Moldea* v. *New York Times Co.*[60] (This was the same court that fashioned the *Ollman* test nearly 10 years earlier.) The lawsuit was based on a review of Dan Moldea's book, "Interference: How Organized Crime Influences Professional Football" by The New York Times sportswriter Gerald Eskenazi. In his review Eskenazi said the book was marred by "too much sloppy journalism." In February a three-judge panel split 2–1 and ruled that Eskenazi's statement could be the basis for a libel suit because it "reasonably can be understood to rest on provable, albeit unstated, defamatory facts."[61] The sentence, Judge Harry Edwards said, was a conclusion that "implies certain facts—that Moldea plays fast and loose with his sources." This ruling rejected the *Ollman* criteria and reflected the narrower *Milkovich* test.

In a rare occurrence, however, Judge Edwards and his colleague Judge Patricia Wald changed their minds and on May 3 reversed their earlier ruling. Edwards noted an aphorism, previously expressed by Supreme Court Justice Felix Frankfurter, that "Wisdom too often never comes, and so one ought not to reject it merely because it comes late." Then he and his two colleagues applied the elements of the broader *Ollman* test to Eskenazi's review. "*Moldea I* is shortsighted," he wrote, "in failing to take account of the fact that the challenged statements were evaluations of a literary work which appeared in a forum in which readers expect to find such evaluations." Edwards said that "when a reviewer offers commentary that is tied to the work being reviewed, and that is a supportable interpretation of the author's work, that interpretation does not present a verifiable issue of fact that can be actionable in defamation." Edwards wrote that the court was not backing away from its earlier determination that statements of opinion can be actionable if they imply a provably false fact. But courts must consider elements beyond the defamatory statement itself. "We now recognize . . . that *Milkovich* did not disavow the importance of context, but simply discounted it in the circumstances of that case." The ruling in *Ollman* established, Edwards noted, that readers will approach different genres of writing differently. "While *Milkovich* could be interpreted as we read it in our initial decision, we are unwilling to assume that the Court meant to sweep away so much settled law without a clearer indication that this was indeed its intent."[62] The proper standard to apply in cases involving critical reviews, Edwards said, would make commentary actionable only when the *interpretations are unsupportable by reference to the written work* (author emphasis).

"Wisdom too often never comes, and so one ought not to reject it merely because it comes late."

Other decisions have echoed the ruling in *Moldea II* in their own ways.[63] But simply because a defendant says a statement is an opinion when the libel suit is filed does not mean that the courts will always agree. Milwaukee Journal columnist Gregory Stanford, in a piece on a fellow journalist's career, recounted her journalistic sparring with a community activist

60. 22 F. 3d 310 (1994).
61. 15 F. 2d 1137 (1994).
62. *Moldea* v. *New York Times Co.*, 22 F. 3d 310 (1994).
63. See *Dworkin* v. *L.F.P., Inc.*, 839 P. 2d 903 (1992); *Maynard* v. *The Daily Gazette Co.*, 447 S.E. 2d 293 (1994); *Keohane* v. *Stewart*, 882 P. 2d 1285 (1994); *Stolz* v. *KSFM 102 FM*, 30 Cal. App. 4th 195 (1995); *Vail* v. *The Plain Dealer Publishing Co.*, 72 Ohio St. 3d 279 (1995); *Portington* v. *Bugliosi*, 56 F. 3d 1147 (1995); and *Biospherics, Inc.* v. *Forbes, Inc.*, 26 M.L.R. 2164 (1998).

named James Milsap. Milsap, who ran a job training program from a facility called Inner City Hall, was fired from this post when financial irregularities turned up. Stanford, in commenting on what had happened, wrote this in his column: "And nobody knew where the money was coming from for the Hall or his Cadillac. (No mystery, if my case was typical. He simply reneged on paying people.)" Milsap claimed that the last sentence was defamatory, but the U.S. District Court ruled that it was a statement of opinion and granted the defendant a summary judgment. The 7th U.S. Circuit Court of Appeals reversed and ruled that a jury might find that the statement suggested undisclosed defamatory facts. The clear implication was that Milsap had not paid Stanford money he was owed. Milsap said that was not true. Because a genuine issue of material facts exists, it is inappropriate to resolve the case through a summary judgment, the court said.[64]

The implication of a defamatory fact was also at issue in a Rhode Island case. A man picketing and protesting the dismissal of an employee at a YMCA branch collapsed. The president of the branch was a physician who was conducting a board meeting while protesters marched outside. When he was informed that a picketer had collapsed, he offered his assistance. He was told his help was not needed because an aid unit was expected momentarily. When the protester died the story received widespread publicity. The press reports included criticism of the doctor for not aiding the stricken man. All the stories left out the fact that the physician had offered to help the victim. The doctor sued and argued that the stories made him appear to be indifferent, uncaring, and even callous. The defendants argued that the defamatory criticisms were opinions. A jury agreed with the plaintiff, noting that by leaving out the essential fact that the doctor had offered to help the stories implied something that was not truthful.[65] The absence of this information turned protected opinion statements into defamatory factual allegations.

FAIR COMMENT AND CRITICISM

Fair comment is a common-law defense that protects the publication of statements of opinion. It has worked satisfactorily for several centuries. But like many other elements in the law of libel, fair comment has been seriously affected by the application of First Amendment protections to libel law. With the emergence of the First Amendment privilege for statements of opinion that has been outlined in the previous section, most lawyers say it makes more sense to rely on the power of the Constitution to protect their clients as opposed to using a workable, but less powerful, common-law defense. Hence, the status of the fair comment defense is in a kind of legal limbo right now. The hundreds of fair comment precedents remain on the books as good law, but no one seems to cite them anymore.

The use of a fair comment defense requires the court to apply a three-part test:

64. *Milsap* v. *Journal/Sentinel Inc.,* 100 F. 3d 1265 (1996). When this case was remanded for trial, the U.S. District Court granted the defendant's motion to dismiss because Milsap had failed to properly ask for a retraction. The 4th U.S. Circuit Court of Appeals affirmed this dismissal. *Milsap* v. *Stanford,* 139 F. 3d 902 (1998).
65. *Healy* v. *New England Newspapers,* 520 A. 2d 147 (1987).

1. **Is the comment an opinion statement?** Courts have traditionally used a single-criterion test to answer this question: Can the statement be proved true or false?

2. **Does the defamatory comment focus on a subject of legitimate public interest?** The courts have defined legitimate public interest very broadly to include everything from cultural artifacts to religion to medicine to advertising. If the defamatory comment is aimed at an individual it must focus on that person's public life, not his or her private life. What Madonna does on stage is one thing; what she does in her bedroom is something else.

3. **Is there a factual basis for the comment?** The third requirement of the three-part test is critical, for it is grounded in the legal rationale for the defense: the notion that both our democratic system of government and our culture are enhanced by the free exchange of ideas and opinions. Almost 200 years ago, Great Britain's Lord Ellenborough wrote that "Liberty of criticism must be allowed, or we should have neither purity of taste nor of morals. Fair discussion is essentially necessary to the truth of history and the advancement of science."[66] Those who read the opinions of others certainly have the right to express opinions of their own on the same topic. But it is impossible for a person to challenge another individual's opinion without knowing the basis for that opinion. The facts supporting the opinion must accompany the opinion.

Under fair comment the facts may be outlined in the article or broadcast that contains the opinion. For example:

> In 1995 Mayor Robert Allen bought six road graders for the city, none of which were needed or used. Two years later he spent $3 million of the people's money to build an auditorium which stands vacant 350 nights a year. Last year he sent four of his staff to Europe to study how mass transit is operated there, and three of the cities his staff visited have no mass transit system. Mayor Allen has been squandering taxpayers' money for too long; he is wasteful and pays little heed to need for fiscal caution.

The opinion—that Allen has been squandering taxpayers' money—was supported by the factual statements in the first part of the story.

But if the facts regarding a situation are already widely known, it is not necessary for the commentator to spell them out afresh for readers or viewers. For example, the comment that "No U.S. president has lowered the moral threshold in the White House more than Bill Clinton" need not be accompanied by a litany of the Clinton-Lewinsky affair. On the other hand there is a well-regarded school of thought in libel law that suggests it is a good idea in any commentary or analysis to present the facts that support the opinion. This inclusion can enhance even the First Amendment defense for opinion statements. A presentation of the facts gives the defamatory remarks important context. It can help explain what is meant. And it is more equitable to readers and listeners, and to the individual who is the focus of the criticism. In any lawsuit, judges and jurors are always impressed by fairness.

It is a good idea in any commentary or analysis to present the facts that support the opinion.

66. *Tabart v. Tipper,* 1 Camp. 350 (1808).

The defendant who is sued for defamatory opinion, then, may attempt to defeat the lawsuit using any or all of the three strategies just outlined. The defendant can argue that the defamatory statements are so broad, so exaggerated, that no one would regard them as factual assertions; that they are rhetorical hyperbole. The defendant may also argue that the statement is a pure opinion and protected by the Constitution. Finally, the defendant can argue that the common-law defense of fair comment provides a shield against a lawsuit.

TIPS ON AVOIDING A LIBEL SUIT BASED ON STATEMENTS OF OPINION

Journalists can take steps to avoid such a lawsuit in the first place. Mass media attorney David Utevsky suggests the following:

- When stating an opinion, try to make certain it is understood as such. But remember the words "in my opinion" don't change a statement of fact into protected opinion.
- Don't rely on journalistic context to protect you. Just because the libel appears in a review or a column or a commentary does not mean a court will regard it as opinion.
- Clearly state and summarize the facts on which your opinion is based. Ask yourself whether you believe a court could find that these facts support your opinion about the matter.
- Make certain the facts are true. If there is a dispute about the fact, refer to both sides of the dispute when stating your opinion.

SUMMARY

Statements of opinion are often immune to a successful libel action. The courts have said that rhetorical hyperbole—broad, exaggerated comments about someone or something—are obviously not assertions of fact and cannot stand as the basis for a successful libel suit. The Constitution also protects statements of opinion, but only pure opinion, according to the Supreme Court. Opinion statements that imply the assertion of falsehoods are not protected. The Supreme Court has ruled that the test to determine whether a statement is opinion or not is whether the statement may be proved false. Other courts have applied somewhat broader tests for opinion that focus on the ordinary meaning of the words and the journalistic and social context of the statement in addition to whether the statement can be proved to be false. Finally, opinion is protected by the common-law defense of fair comment. A plaintiff cannot recover damages for an opinion statement about a subject of legitimate public interest that is based on true facts that are clearly stated or well known.

DEFENSES AND DAMAGES

The privilege of the reporter and the defenses for opinion are not the only means at hand to thwart a libel suit. At least two other common-law defenses exist: **consent** and **right of reply.** Like fair comment, these defenses are old. Both have been used on occasion in the past with substantial success. Yet they are not universally accepted, and only rarely have they been applied in a libel suit in the last 30 years. Let's briefly examine each.

CONSENT

Many legal authorities agree that an individual cannot sue for libel if he or she consented to the publication of the defamatory material.[67] Imagine that Mary Jones, a reporter for the River City Sentinel, hears rumors that John Smith is a leader of organized crime. Jones visits Smith and tells him that she has heard these rumors. Then Jones asks Smith if he cares if the rumors are published in the newspaper. Smith says it is OK with him, and Jones writes and publishes the story. In this instance Smith consented to publication of the defamation. Now this event is not too likely to happen, is it? Cases of this kind of express consent are extremely rare. Courts insist that the plaintiff either knew or had a good reason to know the full extent of the defamatory statement in advance of its publication before consent can be said to exist.

But there is another kind of consent that some courts have recognized. It is called indirect or implied consent. A plaintiff can give this kind of consent in at least a couple ways. One court has ruled that when an individual comments on a defamatory charge and this response is published with the charge, the injured party has given indirect consent to publish the libel.[68] The logic to this argument is simple: If the response is printed, the charge must be printed as well or the story won't make any sense. Courts have also ruled that if the defendant has told others of the defamatory charges against him or her, this amounts to implied consent to publication elsewhere.[69] Implied consent is constructed on sound legal theory, but only a handful of courts have accepted this theory. Nevertheless, getting a comment from an individual you are about to libel is a very good idea. Giving the subject of the story a chance to reply might reveal mistakes in the story, mistakes that can be corrected before publication or broadcast. It is the fair and equitable thing to do as well. Judges and jurors appreciate fairness. The goal, after all, is to publish the truth. There is no reason to believe that the subject of the story might not have information that would help the reporter attain that goal.

Implied consent is constructed on sound legal theory, but only a handful of courts have accepted this theory.

RIGHT OF REPLY

Right of reply is another secondary defense. Like consent, it has not been commonly applied in recent years. Right of reply is sometimes called "the self-defense." If an individual has been defamed, he or she may answer the defamation with a libelous communication and not be

---

67. Phelps and Hamilton, *Libel,* and Sanford, *Libel and Privacy.*
68. *Pulverman* v. *A.S. Abell Co.,* 228 F. 2d 797 (1956).
69. *Pressley* v. *Continental Can Co.,* 250 S.E. 2d 676 (1978).

subject to a successful libel suit. It might be termed "giving as good as you got." The only limitation here is that the reply must approximate the original defamation in magnitude. Self-defense has this same limitation. The response cannot greatly exceed the provocation. The court will not accept a claim of self-defense if you shoot and kill someone because he or she threw a spitwad at you.

In a famous lawsuit two American journalists assailed one another in print. Newsman Quentin Reynolds suggested that columnist Westbrook Pegler had once called a third journalist, Heywood Broun, a liar. This bothered Broun, Reynolds wrote, to the extent that he could not sleep. Broun became ill and finally died. Pegler was incensed by this comment, claiming it charged him with moral homicide. So he attacked Reynolds, calling him sloppy, a sycophant, a coward, a slob, and a four-flusher. Pegler accused Reynolds of public nudism, of being a war profiteer, and of being an absentee war correspondent. Pegler also attacked the deceased Broun, calling him a liar and someone who made his living by controversy.

In the libel suit that followed, Pegler raised the defense of right of reply. The court agreed that Pegler's comments about Broun bore a resemblance to a reply but determined that the columnist had gone too far in his attack on Quentin Reynolds. This portion of the article had no conceivable relationship to a reply. Reynolds was awarded $175,000 from Pegler, the New York Journal-American, and the Hearst Corporation.[70]

The case just described is not a typical lawsuit. Journalists still fight with one another, but they rarely settle the matter in court. As such, what good is the right of reply defense for those who work in the mass media? Some authorities have argued that the mass media has the right to publish a reply to a defamatory attack and remain immune from a libel suit.[71] In several cases it was held that where the plaintiff's charge was made in a newspaper, the newspaper was privileged to carry the defendant's reply.[72] Otherwise the right of reply is of no avail to the defendant; no one would be able to see or read the reply if the defendant were denied use of the press. Similarly, it was held that the reply can even be carried in a newspaper or a medium different from the medium used for the attack.

In "Cases and Materials on Torts," law professors Charles Gregory and Harry Kalven wrote:

> The boundaries of this privilege are not clearly established and it gives rise to questions amusingly reminiscent of those raised in connection with self-defense: How vigorous must the plaintiff's original aggression have been? Must the original attack itself have been defamatory? What if it [the original attack] is true or privileged? How much verbal force can the defendant use in reply? Can he defend third parties?[73]

Questions like these continue to reduce the true effectiveness of the defense of right of reply.

---

70. *Reynolds* v. *Pegler,* 223 F. 2d 449 (1955).
71. See Phelps and Hamilton, *Libel.*
72. See *Fowler* v. *New York Herald,* 172 N.Y.S. 423 (1918).
73. Gregory and Kalven, *Cases and Materials on Torts.*

DAMAGES

If the court gets to the point in a libel suit of assessing damages, it is obvious that the plaintiff has met all requirements, including proving fault, and that none of the defenses just outlined have worked. How damages are assessed is not an essential piece of information for a journalist to carry; yet some feeling for the subject is useful. Libel law operates with four kinds of damages today. In each instance, before any damages can be awarded, the plaintiff must prove one thing or another to the court.

Actual Damages

The most common libel damages are called **actual damages,** or damages for actual injury. Plaintiffs have to convince the jury that because of the injury to their reputation, they have suffered actual harm. What kind of harm? Not physical harm, obviously. The best definition of actual damages (as they are now defined) comes from the *Gertz* case.[74] Justice Powell wrote that actual injury is not limited to out-of-pocket loss or money loss, which is how many authorities defined actual damages prior to this decision. Powell said, "Indeed, the more customary types of actual harm inflicted by defamatory falsehood include impairment of reputation and standing in the community, personal humiliation, and mental anguish and suffering." This statement is a very broad definition of actual damage. How can someone prove that he or she has suffered mental anguish? What is evidence of personal humiliation? These are very hard questions to answer. Libel damages have never been precise, and this formulation does not promise additional precision. The plaintiff has to bring evidence of some kind of injury. The jury will be the key factor in making the determination of how much harm and how much damage.

The most common libel damages are called actual damages, or damages for actual injury.

In 1985 the Supreme Court made a ruling in *Dun & Bradstreet* v. *Greenmoss Builders*[75] that somewhat modified the high court's 1974 *Gertz* v. *Welch* ruling on damages. In the *Dun & Bradstreet* ruling, the court relieved a heavy burden of proof from private persons who were suing for libel on the basis of statements that do *not* focus on an issue of public concern. These changes are reflected in the summaries below.

Special Damages

Special damages are specific items of pecuniary loss caused by published defamatory statements. Special damages must be established in precise terms, much more precise terms than those for the actual damages just outlined. If a plaintiff can prove that he or she lost $23,567.19 because of the libel, that amount is then what the plaintiff can ask for and what will likely be awarded if he or she can convince the jury of the validity of the case. Special damages represent a specific monetary, and only monetary, loss as the result of the libel. Most plaintiffs do not seek special damages. However, in some cases special damages are all that can be sought. In trade libel, for example, the only award a plaintiff can get is special damages.

74. *Gertz* v. *Robert Welch, Inc.,* 4118 U.S. 323 (1974).
75. 472 U.S. 479 (1985).

Presumed Damages

Presumed damages are damages that a plaintiff can get without proof of injury or harm. A public-person plaintiff or a private-person plaintiff suing for a libelous statement that focuses on a matter of public concern can only be awarded presumed damages (sometimes called general or compensatory) damages on a showing of actual malice, knowledge of falsity, or reckless disregard of the truth. However, a private person suing on the basis of a libelous statement that focuses on a private matter and not a public concern need only show negligence to collect presumed damages.

Punitive Damages

Lawyers used to call **punitive damages,** or exemplary damages, the "smart money." Punitive damage awards are usually very large. The other kinds of damages just discussed are designed to compensate the plaintiff for injury. Punitive damages are designed to punish defendants for their misconduct and to warn other persons not to act in a similar manner.

A public-person plaintiff or a private-person plaintiff suing for a libelous statement that focuses on a matter of public concern can only win punitive damages on a showing of actual malice, knowledge of falsity, or reckless disregard for the truth. A private person suing for libel based on remarks made about a private matter, and not a public concern, can win punitive damages on a showing of negligence.

Punitive damages are the most onerous aspect of any libel suit, and many persons think they are grossly unfair. Punitive damages have been barred in Louisiana, Massachusetts, Nebraska, New Hampshire, Oregon, and Washington, and have been limited in Colorado, Florida, Georgia, Kansas, Montana, Mississippi, North Dakota, and Virginia.[76] Legislatures in other states, such as Alabama, Illinois, and Indiana, have considered placing some kind of limits on punitive damages. Some have argued that high punitive damage awards violate the Eighth Amendment to the U.S. Constitution, which forbids the levying of excessive fines. But the Supreme Court has consistently rejected this argument. The common-law method for assessing punitive damages is not itself so inherently unfair as to be per se unconstitutional, said Justice Harry Blackmun in 1991.[77] "We need not and indeed cannot draw a mathematical bright line between the constitutionally acceptable and constitutionally unacceptable that would fit every case," he added. "We can say, however, that general concerns of reasonableness and adequate guidance from the court when the case is tried to a jury properly enter into the constitutional calculus."

In 1996 the high court did overturn as "grossly excessive" an award of $2 million to an Alabama man who sued BMW for selling him, as a new car, a BMW that had been repainted to correct minor paint damage incurred in shipping. Justice John Paul Stevens declined to provide lower courts with a specific formula to determine the fairness of punitive damage awards. He instead offered three guideposts that lower courts could use: the degree of reprehensibility of the defendant's conduct, the ratio between the punitive and actual damages, and a comparison

76. Dill, "Libel Law Doesn't Work."
77. *Pacific Mutual Life Insurance Co. v. Haslip,* 111 S. Ct. 1032 (1991).

between the punitive damage awards and any civil or criminal fines available in the state for similar conduct. Most observers suggested that the ruling left more questions unanswered than it resolved, especially as it related to mass media law.[78]

RETRACTION STATUTES

The phrase "I demand a retraction" is common in the folklore of libel. What is a **retraction**? A retraction is both an apology and an effort to set the record straight. Let us say you blow one as an editor. You report that Jane Adams was arrested for shoplifting, and you are wrong. In your retraction you first tell readers or viewers that Jane Adams was not arrested for shoplifting, that you made a mistake. Then you might also apologize for the embarrassment caused Ms. Adams. You might even say some nice things about her. At common law a prompt and honest retraction is usually relevant to the question of whether the plaintiff's reputation was actually harmed. After all, you are attempting to reconstruct that part of her reputation that you tore down just the day before. She might have difficulty proving actual harm.

The phrase "I demand a retraction" is common in the folklore of libel.

RETRACTION STATUTE FROM STATE OF OREGON

A typical retraction statute looks much like this one from the state of Oregon. Publishers and broadcasters who meet the letter of such laws can substantially reduce the amount of damages a plaintiff can win in a libel suit.

30.165 Publication of correction or retraction upon demand.

1. The demand for correction or retraction shall be in writing, signed by the defamed person or the attorney of the person and be delivered to the publisher of the defamatory statement, either personally or by registered mail at the publisher's place of business or residence within 20 days after the defamed person receives actual knowledge of the defamatory statement. The demand shall specify which statements are false and defamatory and request that they be corrected or retracted. The demand may also refer to the sources from which the true facts may be ascertained with accuracy.

2. The publisher of the defamatory statement shall have not more than two weeks after receipt of the demand for correction or retraction in which to investigate the demand; and, after making such investigation, the publisher shall publish the correction or retraction in:

   (a) The first issue thereafter published, in the case of newspapers, magazines or other printed periodicals.

   (b) The first broadcast or telecast thereafter made, in the case of radio or television stations.

---

78. Greenhouse, "Justices Reject Punitive Award," A1.

> (c) The first public exhibition thereafter made, in the case of
>   motion picture theatres.
> 3. The correction or retraction shall consist of a statement by the
>   publisher substantially to the effect that the defamatory statements
>   previously made are not factually supported and that the publisher
>   regrets the original publication thereof.
> 4. The correction or retraction shall be published in substantially as
>   conspicuous a manner as the defamatory statement. [1955 c.365 §3]

Thirty-three states have some kind of retraction law, according to libel authority Bruce Sanford.[79] Some of these laws are very comprehensive, others provide extremely limited protection. The Washington state law, for example, only relates to the liability of editors and others who process the news, and most persons who work in the media in Washington don't even regard the law as a retraction statute.[80] Under a typical retraction statute, a plaintiff must give the publisher an opportunity to retract the libel before a suit may be started. If the publisher promptly honors the request for a retraction and retracts the libelous material in a place in the newspaper as prominent as the place in which the libel originally appeared, the retraction will reduce, and in some instances cancel, any damage judgment the plaintiff might later seek in a lawsuit. Failure to ask for a retraction or failure to ask for a retraction in the way prescribed by the statute can result in a dismissal of the libel complaint.[81]

In at least two states, retraction statutes adopted by the legislature have been ruled unconstitutional. In both Arizona[82] and Montana,[83] the state high courts have ruled that the state constitution gives citizens the right to sue for injury to person, property, or character. The retraction statute diminishes that right and is hence unconstitutional, the courts ruled.

Retraction laws make good sense. It is the truth we seek, after all; a successful libel suit results in compensating the plaintiff monetarily but it is not very effective in correcting the errors in people's minds resulting from publication of the defamation. Widespread adoption of the Uniform Correction or Clarification of Defamation Act (see page 134) in the states will increase the importance and frequency of timely retractions.

SUMMARY

Secondary defenses, consent and right of reply, exist and may in rare instances aid a libel defendant. To collect damages in a libel suit, plaintiffs must demonstrate to the court that there was actual harm to their reputations. These are called *actual damages.* If plaintiffs can demonstrate

79. Sanford, *Libel and Privacy.*
80. Washington Rev. Code Ann. § 9: 58. 040 (1977).
81. *Milsap* v. *Stanford,* 139 F. 3d 902 (1998).
82. *Boswell* v. *Phoenix Newspapers,* 730 P. 2d 186 (1986).
83. *Madison* v. *Yunker,* 589 P. 2d 126 (1978).

specific items of monetary loss, *special damages* may be awarded. Plaintiffs may also seek to win *punitive damages*. In many states, a timely retraction of the libel can reduce damages significantly and even lessen the likelihood of a libel suit. These rules are governed by state laws called *retraction statutes.*

CRIMINAL LIBEL

Criminal libel has been a part of the law of defamation for as long as the law has existed. It is a close cousin to seditious libel and civil libel. Chapters 4, 5, and the first part of this chapter have dealt with civil libel, one person suing another for defamation. Criminal libel is founded on the theory that sometimes it is appropriate for the state to act on behalf of the party injured by the libel and bring criminal charges against the defendant. Criminal libel has been justified traditionally with the argument that if the state fails to act, the injured party or parties may take violent action against the libeler to compensate for the damage they have suffered. The state has a substantial interest in preventing this violence from occurring. This, of course, is 17th-century thinking. Because of that, fewer than half the states have criminal libel statutes today, and these laws are rarely invoked in those states that still have them; they are relics of the past. But they are not forgotten and in some jurisdictions, especially in the southern United States, prosecutions for criminal libel do occur. For example, in the summer of 1988, the editor of a small weekly newspaper in Kingstree, S.C., was indicted for criminal libel after he wrote that two local politicians were involved in "corrupt dealings." Jim Fitts, editor of the weekly The Voice, faced a possible fine of $5,000 and a year in jail. The state criminal libel law had only been used three times in the past 40 years. As will be noted shortly, the difficulty in prosecuting such a case made it unlikely that Fitts would ever be convicted. And as a matter of fact, charges were eventually dropped against Fitts.[84]

The authorities in most states are unwilling to take on someone else's trouble and sue for criminal libel so long as a civil remedy is readily available. A prosecutor has very little to gain from such an action. In fact, he or she would probably be roundly criticized for instituting criminal libel charges. In an age when people are mugged, robbed, raped, and murdered with alarming frequency, damage to an individual's reputation—or even to the reputation of a large number of persons—somehow does not seem too serious. Forty years ago in New York, a judge stated this proposition very well:

> The theory, in simplest terms, is that when an individual is libeled, he has an adequate remedy in a civil suit for damages. The public suffers no injury. Vindication for the individual and adequate compensation for the injury done him may be obtained as well in the civil courts. Thus the rule has always been that the remedy

84. Smothers, "Editor Faces Criminal Libel Charges," p.18; see also *Fitts* v. *Kolb,* 779 F. Supp. 1502 (1991).

> of criminal prosecution should only be sought where the wrong is of so flagrant
> a character as to make a criminal prosecution necessary on public grounds.[85]

Criminal libel differs from civil libel in several important respects. First of all, it is possible to criminally libel the dead. The state can use a criminal libel statute to prosecute an individual for damaging the reputation of someone who is deceased. In some states criminal libel is tied to causing or potentially causing a breach of the peace. This charge used to be quite common. If a publication, speech, or handbill so provoked the readers or listeners that violence became possible or did in fact occur, criminal libel charges might result. In 1966 the U.S. Supreme Court undermined most of the "breach of the peace" statutes as well as the actions of those states that brought criminal libel actions under the common law. The case was *Ashton* v. *Kentucky*[86] and involved a mining dispute in Hazard, Ky. An agitator was arrested for circulating a pamphlet that contained articles attacking the chief of police, the sheriff, and a newspaper editor, among others. At the criminal libel trial, the judge defined the offense as "any writing calculated to create a disturbance of the peace, corrupt public morals or lead to any act, which when done, is indictable."

The Supreme Court reversed the conviction. Writing for a unanimous court, Justice William O. Douglas said the crime, as defined by the trial court, was too general and indefinite. It left the standard of responsibility—whether something is illegal or not—wide open to the discretion of the judge. Also, Douglas noted, the crime is determined not by the character of the person's words, not by what that person says or writes, but rather by the boiling point of those who listen to or read those words. The law makes someone a criminal simply because his or her neighbors have no self-control and cannot refrain from violence. This decision was an important factor, but only one factor, in the passing of "breach of the peace" as an aspect of criminal libel. It is extremely rare for such a case to occur today.

The Supreme Court has heard one criminal libel case since *The New York Times* v. *Sullivan*[87] ruling. The court ruled in *Garrison* v. *Louisiana*[88] that when the defamation of a public official is the basis for a criminal libel suit, the state has to prove actual malice on the part of the defendant; that is, knowledge of falsity, reckless disregard for the truth, or falsity of the matter. Justice Brennan wrote that the reasons that persuaded the court to rule that the First Amendment protected criticism of public officials in a civil libel suit apply with equal force in a criminal libel suit. "The constitutional guarantees of freedom of expression compel application of the same standard to the criminal remedy," he added. However, the question of what the court would do with a group libel suit of the kind it faced in 1952 is still not answered.

Criminal libel is not a real problem for journalists and broadcasters. Of the few criminal libel cases on record since World War II, cases in which the media were the defendants can be counted on one hand. Normally the action is brought against the writer of the article or the speaker of the words, not against the medium publishing the comments.

Criminal libel is not a real problem for journalists and broadcasters.

85. *People* v. *Quill,* 177 N.Y. 2d 380 (1958).
86. 384 U.S. 195 (1966).
87. 376 U.S. 254 (1964).
88. 379 U.S. 64 (1964).

INTENTIONAL INFLICTION OF EMOTIONAL DISTRESS

While persons working in mass communications continue to struggle with the libel imbroglio, a new threat to the right to publish has emerged in the past two decades—a tort called the intentional infliction of emotional distress. Lawsuits alleging this tort injury first appeared in the late 19th century, according to Susan Kirkpatrick in an article in the Northwestern University Law Review.[89] But it wasn't recognized by the "Restatement of Torts," the synthesis of tort law published by the American Law Institute, until 1948. In 1965 the "Restatement" provided for the first time a definition of the tort, which has four parts.

- **The defendant's conduct was intentional or reckless.**
- **The defendant's conduct was extreme and outrageous.**
- **The defendant's conduct caused the plaintiff emotional distress.**
- **The emotional distress was severe.**[90]

In practice, Kirkpatrick said, courts really focus on a single criterion—whether the defendant acted outrageously. Or as one court put it, the defendant's conduct went beyond all possible bounds of decency and was regarded as atrocious and utterly intolerable in a civilized community. An Illinois appellate court ruled in late 1998 that ethnic slurs, like "stupid Polack," the portrayal of a buffoonish Polish Pope, and Polish jokes on three separate NBC programs were not sufficiently outrageous to maintain an action for intentional infliction of emotional distress.[91]

An unusual case from Florida demonstrates the kind of communication that might support such a finding. A six-year-old boy was abducted in June of 1985. Two years later police found a child's clothing and parts of a skeleton, but it took authorities another year to make the connection between the grisly remains and the missing child. In August of 1988 a television reporter and camera operator went to the chief of police and asked to see the child's skull. The officer was videotaped as he lifted the skull out of the box containing the remains, and the video was shown on the evening news. Family members unexpectedly saw the video and were shocked. They sued for invasion of privacy and outrage, the Florida version of the emotional distress tort. The Florida Court of Appeals ruled against the invasion of privacy claim, but said that the video had clearly exceeded the bounds of decency. "Indeed," the court said, "if the facts as alleged herein do not constitute the tort of outrage, then there is no such tort."[92]

A lawsuit for intentional infliction of emotional distress can be premised on a wide range of conduct, much of which has nothing to do with publishing or broadcasting. Many journalists fear such a lawsuit because they are not aware of the enormous burdens placed on the plaintiff in such a lawsuit. Not many plaintiffs file such actions against the press; it is too difficult to win such a case.[93] In recent years courts have been more hospitable to emotional distress claims based on how the reporter got the information rather than whether the

89. Kirkpatrick, "Intentional Infliction of Emotional Distress," 993.
90. American Law Institute, *Restatement of Torts.*
91. *Polish-American Guardian Society* v. *General Electric Co., 27* M.L.R. 1443 (1998).
92. *Armstrong* v. *H & C Communications, Inc.,* 575 So. 2d 280 (1991).
93. Mead, "Suing Media for Emotional Distress," 24.

information was published or broadcast. In 1995 a judge in California refused to dismiss an emotional distress claim against television journalists who, knowing no parent was present, told three young children that their neighbor had killed herself and her three children, and then videotaped the youngsters' reactions for later broadcast. (The video was never shown on television.) The court said a jury could surely find the TV reporter's behavior so outrageous that it went "beyond all possible bounds of decency."[94]

In the early 1980s some public-person plaintiffs sought to use the emotional distress tort to circumvent the libel requirement that they had to offer clear and convincing proof of actual malice. The Supreme Court recognized the ploy and in 1988 blocked this strategy.

The case began in November of 1983 when Hustler magazine published a parody of a Campari liquor ad. The real Campari ads were interviews with celebrities who talked about their first taste of the liquor, but with a clear suggestion of sexual connotation. The Hustler parody was a fictitious interview with the Reverend Jerry Falwell, who described his first sexual experience as an incestuous encounter with his mother. Falwell was also characterized by the parody as a drunkard. There was a small disclaimer at the bottom of the parody, and it was listed in the table of contents as fiction.

Falwell sued the magazine for libel, invasion of privacy, and intentional infliction of emotional distress. The trial judge dismissed the invasion of privacy claim, but sent the other two to the jury. Jurors rejected the libel claim on the grounds that the parody was so far-fetched, no person could possibly believe that it described actual facts about Falwell. The jury did award the Baptist preacher $200,000 in damages for emotional distress.

Hustler appealed the ruling, but a unanimous three-judge panel of the U.S. Court of Appeals for the 4th Circuit upheld the damage award, noting that all the proof that was needed in such a case was that the item was sufficiently outrageous as to cause emotional harm, and that it was published intentionally.[95] While most journalists did not condone the Hustler style of parody, they nevertheless viewed the decision as a serious threat to freedom of expression. The sturdy First Amendment barrier built up to protect the mass media from libel suits brought by persons in the public eye was neatly circumvented by Falwell in this case. Because of his presence as a spokesman for the conservative religious right in this nation, Falwell would likely be considered a public figure in a libel action and be forced to prove actual malice before he could collect damages. In this suit he did not even have to show negligence. Nor did the broad First Amendment protection granted statements of opinion apply outside the law of libel. In the future persons suing for satire or parody could avoid having to surmount the constitutional barriers in libel law by instead filing an action for intentional infliction of emotional distress.

Hustler appealed to the Supreme Court and in 1988, in a unanimous ruling, the high court reversed the appellate court ruling. Chief Justice Rehnquist, noting that most persons would see the Hustler parody as gross and repugnant, nevertheless rejected Falwell's argument that because he was seeking damages for severe emotional distress rather than reputational harm, a standard different than that applied in libel should apply. "Were we to hold otherwise,"

94. *KVOR-TV Inc.* v. *Superior Court of Sacramento County,* 37 Cal. Rept. 2d 431 (1995).
95. *Falwell* v. *Flynt,* 797 F. 2d 1270 (1986).

the chief justice wrote, "there can be little doubt that political cartoonists and satirists would be subjected to damages awarded without any showing that their work falsely defamed its subject." Rehnquist added:

> The appeal of the political cartoon or caricature is often based on exploration of unfortunate physical traits or politically embarrassing events—an exploration often calculated to injure the feelings of the subject of the portrayal. The art of the cartoonist is often not reasoned or evenhanded, but slashing and one-sided.[96]

Falwell contended it was making a mockery of serious political cartoons to compare them to the Hustler parody, which was truly outrageous. The law should protect even public figures from such outrageous caricatures. Rehnquist disagreed, noting the outrageousness standard of liability would not work.

> "Outrageousness" in the area of political and social discourse has an inherent subjectiveness about it which would allow a jury to impose liability on the basis of jurors' tastes and views or perhaps on the basis of their dislike of a particular expression.[97]

The court ruled that in order for a public figure or public official to win an emotional distress claim, it would be necessary to prove three things:

1. That the parody or satire amounted to statement of fact, not an opinion.
2. That it was a false statement of fact.
3. That the person who drew the cartoon or wrote the article knew it was false, or exhibited reckless disregard for the truth or falsity of the material. In other words, proof of actual malice is necessary.

SUMMARY

Persons who work in mass communications need to be aware of two additional legal problems closely related to civil libel: criminal libel and the intentional infliction of emotional distress. Most states have criminal libel statutes, but it is rare that public prosecutors will bring an action under these old-fashioned laws. In a criminal libel action involving a public person, the state must carry the same fault burden as a civil-libel plaintiff would carry—proof of actual malice. The intentional infliction of emotional distress is a new tort and punishes a wide range of conduct, including the publication or broadcast of material that is outrageous and causes severe emotional distress. Courts have made it extremely difficult for plaintiffs to win such suits by placing a substantial burden of proof on the injured party. The Supreme Court added to this burden in 1988 when it ruled that public-person plaintiffs would have to show actual malice as well to win their lawsuits.

96. *Hustler Magazine* v. *Falwell*, 108 S. Ct. 876 (1988).
97. *Hustler Magazine* v. *Falwell*, 108 S. Ct. 876 (1988).

BIBLIOGRAPHY ⟶

American Law Institute. *Restatement of Torts.* 2d ed. Philadelphia: American Law Institute, 1975.

Ashley, Paul. *Say It Safely.* 5th ed. Seattle: University of Washington Press, 1976.

Dill, Barbara. "Libel Law Doesn't Work, But Can It Be Fixed?" In *At What Price? Libel Law and Freedom of the Press,* by Martin London and Barbara Dill. New York: The Twentieth Century Fund Press, 1993.

Gleason, Timothy W. "The Fact/Opinion Distinction in Libel." *Hastings Journal of Communications and Entertainment Law* 10 (1988):763.

Greenhouse, Linda. "For First Time Justices Reject Punitive Award." *The New York Times,* 21 May 1996, A1.

Gregory, Charles O., and Harry Kalven. *Cases and Materials on Torts.* 2d ed. Boston: Little, Brown, 1969.

Kirkpatrick, Susan. "Falwell v. Flint: Intentional Infliction of Emotional Distress as a Threat to Free Speech." *Northwestern University Law Review* 81 (1987):993.

Mather, Michael. "Experience with *Gertz* 'Actual Injury' in Defamation Cases." *Baylor Law Review* 38 (1986):917.

McGraw, David. "The Right to Republish Libel: Neutral Reportage and the Reasonable Reader." *Akron Law Review* 25 (1991):335.

Mead, Terrance C. "Suing Media for Emotional Distress: A Multi-Method Analysis of Tort Law Evolution." *Washburn Law Journal* 23 (1983):24.

Phelps, Robert, and Douglas Hamilton. *Libel.* New York: Macmillan, 1966.

Pogrebin, Robin. "Publication Date Open to Dispute in Internet Age." *The New York Times,* 3 November 1997, C1.

Pring, George. "SLAPPS: Strategic Lawsuits Against Public Participation." *Pace Environmental Law Review,* fall 1989, 8.

Prosser, William L. *Handbook of the Law of Torts.* St. Paul: West Publishing, 1963.

Sanford, Bruce W. *Libel and Privacy.* 2d ed. Englewood Cliffs, N.J.: Prentice-Hall Law & Business, 1993.

Smolla, Rodney A. "Dun & Bradstreet, Hepps, and Liberty Lobby: A New Analytic Primer on the Future Course of Defamation." *Georgetown Law Journal* 75 (1987):1519.

Smothers, Ronald. "Editor Faces Criminal Libel Charges." *The New York Times,* 28 June 1988, 18.

Thomas, Jeffrey. "Statements of Fact, Statements of Opinion, and the First Amendment." *California Law Review* 74 (1986):1001.

Invasion of Privacy
Appropriation and Intrusion

I nvasion of privacy is a multifaceted tort that is designed to redress a variety of grievances. These
include commercial exploitation of an individual's name or likeness, the intrusion on what might be
called our private domains, the revelation of intimate information about someone, and the libellike publication of embarrassing false reports about a person. As our population increases and government, business, and the mass media intrude further into private life, the value of the right to privacy seems to grow.
And while strong legal defenses have been erected to defend legitimate incursions by the mass media into
the private parts of a person's life, journalists and others face the prospect of losing public and legal support in the future for some reportorial practices considered common today. In this chapter we introduce
the subject of the right to privacy and explore two of the four tort areas, appropriation and intrusion.

THE GROWTH OF PRIVACY LAW

The right to privacy is one of the newest legal concepts you will encounter in this book. Privacy was not articulated as an important value in the largely rural America of the 18th and 19th centuries. It wasn't until the end of the 19th century that the need for a right to privacy became a public issue. Of course the nation had changed dramatically. America was rapidly becoming an urban nation. The streets of many cities were clogged with poor immigrants or first-generation Americans. Big city daily newspapers used a variety of sensational schemes to attract these potential readers. Editors often played out the lives of the "rich and famous" on the pages of their newspapers, permitting their readers to vicariously enjoy wealth, status, and celebrity.

It was this kind of journalism that apparently pushed two Boston lawyers, Samuel D. Warren and Louis D. Brandeis, to use the pages of the Harvard Law Review to propose a legally recognized right to privacy. Warren, the scion of a prominent Boston family, urged his friend (and future Supreme Court justice) Brandeis to help him write the piece, "The Right to Privacy."[1] The article appeared in 1890 and can be legitimately regarded as the fountain from which the modern law of privacy has flowed.

The pair argued, "Instantaneous photographs and newspaper enterprise have invaded the sacred precincts of private and domestic life; and numerous mechanical devices threaten to make good the prediction that 'what is whispered in the closet shall be proclaimed from the house-tops.' " Warren and Brandeis said they were offended by the gossip in the press, which they said had overstepped in every direction the obvious bounds of propriety and decency:

> To satisfy a prurient taste the details of sexual relations are spread broadcast in the columns of the daily papers. To occupy the indolent, column upon column is filled with idle gossip, which can only be procured by intrusion upon the domestic circle. . . .
>
> The common law has always recognized a man's house as his castle, impregnable, often, even to its own officers engaged in the execution of its commands. Shall the courts thus close the front entrance to constituted authority, and open wide the back door to idle or prurient curiosity?[2]

To stop this illicit behavior, the two young lawyers proposed that the courts recognize the legal right of privacy; that is, citizens should be able to go to court to stop such unwarranted intrusions and also secure money damages for the hardship they suffered from such prying and from publication of private material about them.

It was 13 years from the time the Warren and Brandeis article was first published until the first state recognized the law of privacy. The state of New York adopted a law that prohibited the commercial exploitation of an individual and called it a right to privacy. Interestingly, the right this new statute sought to safeguard was not even mentioned in the famous Harvard Law Review article.

1. Warren and Brandeis, "The Right to Privacy," 220.
2. Warren and Brandeis, "The Right to Privacy," 220.

The law of privacy grew slowly and sporadically over the next 90 years. All but four states today recognize some kind of legal right to privacy. Minnesota and North Dakota have thus far refused to recognize the tort, and there have been no reported privacy cases in either Vermont or Wyoming.[3] Other states have rejected one or more of the four torts that constitute the modern right to privacy.[*]

The law of privacy grew slowly and sporadically over the next 90 years.

Privacy law is far more idiosyncratic from state to state than is libel law. In other words, it is somewhat easier to make generalizations about libel law that reflect the law in every state or in most states than it is to make these generalizations about the law of privacy. Part of the problem is that some states have protected the right to privacy through statutes, and these often are very particular. The New York statute, for example, is quite explicit about how the right to privacy is protected in that state, and some aspects of the law common in most states are not a part of the New York law.

Today the law of privacy encompasses protection for at least four separate legal wrongs. Three of these have absolutely nothing to do with the law as outlined in 1890 by Warren and Brandeis. Let's briefly summarize these four areas of the law before we outline each in detail.

FOUR AREAS OF PRIVACY LAW

1. Appropriation of name or likeness for trade purposes
2. Intrusion upon an individual's solitude
3. Publication of private information about an individual
4. Publishing material that puts an individual in a false light

---

The first kind of invasion of privacy is called **appropriation** and is defined as taking a person's name, picture, photograph, or likeness and using it for commercial gain without permission. Appropriation is technically the only right of privacy guaranteed in some of the states that have privacy statutes. The laws are limited to outlawing this one kind of behavior. But as a matter of fact, judicial construction of these laws has allowed them to encompass some of the other aspects of invasion of privacy as well.

Intrusion is the second type of invasion of privacy, an area of the law growing rapidly today, and is what most people think of when invasion of privacy is mentioned. Intrusion upon the solitude and into the private life of a person is prohibited.

The third arm of the law prohibits **publication of private information**—truthful private information—about a person. What is truthful private information? Gossip, substance of private conversations, and details of a private tragedy or illness have all been used as the basis of a suit.

---

3. Sanford, *Libel and Privacy.*

[*]For example, Alaska, Arizona, Delaware, Hawaii, Iowa, Mississippi, Missouri, Montana, Nebraska, New Hampshire, New York, North Carolina, Ohio, Rhode Island, Tennessee, Texas, Utah, and Wisconsin in addition to Minnesota, North Dakota, Vermont, Washington, and Wyoming have not yet recognized or have refused to recognize the somewhat controversial false light tort. See Sanford, *Libel and Privacy.*

Finally, the publication of material that places a person in a **false light** is the fourth category of the law of privacy. This category is an outgrowth of the first area of the law, appropriation, and doesn't at first glance seem like an invasion of privacy at all, but it is.

Some caveats or warnings are appropriate before each of these aspects of the law is detailed. First, only people enjoy protection for their right to privacy. Corporations, labor unions, associations, and so forth can protect their reputations through libel law, but they do not have a right to privacy. (Other laws protect businesses against unfair commercial exploitation.)

Because of the relative youth of the right to privacy and the ragged way in which the law of privacy has grown, variations in the protection of the right to privacy from state to state are even more common than are state-by-state differences in libel law. What is perfectly legal in one state might result in a successful tort action in a neighboring jurisdiction.

The right to privacy is most easily understood if each of the four areas of the law is considered as a discrete unit. Don't try to apply the defenses that may be applicable in appropriation to publication of private information. They don't work.

Next, there is much about the law of privacy that defies logic. Why is putting someone in a false light considered an invasion of privacy, for example? Challenging the logic of the law serves little purpose and usually makes learning the law more difficult.

The law of privacy is young—just over 100 years old if you start with the Warren and Brandeis proposal. There are a lot of legal questions that haven't been answered, or at least answered satisfactorily. Bad court decisions are abundant. Trial judges rarely see invasion-of-privacy cases; most lawyers are equally distant from the law. If you mix those two elements together, it is not uncommon for courts to render wrong-headed decisions. A trial court in Louisiana once ruled that a house had a right to privacy, for example.

Finally, it is worthwhile to raise the issues of ethics and morality. The following pages provide for journalists, photographers, and advertising and public relations practitioners a kind of road map of how to stay within the law. But these aren't necessarily the roads that should be followed at all times. Today, more than ever, many readers and viewers are asking the mass media to exercise restraint in certain areas, restraint that often falls well within the boundaries of what is legal. Journalists would do well to ponder these requests. Publish and be damned is still an appropriate response in some situations. But more often a thoughtful journalist will take a different tack.

PRIVACY AND THE INTERNET

The intersection of the right of privacy with the information superhighway has generated tremendous public and governmental interest. The Congress and state legislatures across the nation considered scores of bills aimed at reducing public concern about the ability of Internet users to protect their private lives as they surfed the World Wide Web. A 1997 study conducted by the Boston Consulting Group revealed that 70 percent of nearly 10,000 Net users questioned were more concerned about privacy on the Internet than they were about the privacy of information they transmit by telephone or mail. Public fears focus on two primary topics: the ease with which third parties can collect private information about persons who use the Internet and how simple it is for people who have this data to publish it to others via the information superhighway. The collection problem fits most comfortably within the discussion of intrusion and will be outlined there. The publication problem is closely akin to the private facts tort and will be discussed in that context.

APPROPRIATION

It is illegal to appropriate an individual's name or likeness for commercial or trade purposes without consent.

Appropriation is the oldest of the four privacy torts. Until recently it was the most comprehensible. Appropriation protects an individual's name or likeness from commercial exploitation. In June of 1999, for example, celebrity Paula Abdul sued the maker of the Hollywood 48-Hour Miracle Diet for suggesting in advertising that Abdul used the product.[4] The plaintiff in an appropriation suit will argue that she or he has been humiliated and embarrassed by having her or his photograph or name or image publicly associated with a commercial endeavor. As such, this tort protects the individual's right to privacy. In 1953 Judge Jerome Frank of the U.S. Court of Appeals "discovered" another right that naturally falls under the appropriation tort: the right of publicity.[5] The case involved a fight between two bubble gum companies over the right to include trading cards containing the photographs of professional athletes in the packages that contained their gum. One company had the athletes' permission, the other did not. But it was difficult for these professional athletes, who spent most of the time in the public spotlight, to argue that they suffered embarrassment or humiliation because of this additional publicity. What they were complaining about was that they had been commercially exploited; that someone was using their identities to reap a commercial benefit and the athletes were not getting their share. Judge Frank agreed, saying that individuals had the right to control the commercial exploitation of their likenesses.

In most respects the two rights encompassed by appropriation, the right of privacy and the **right of publicity,** are identical. But they differ in at least three important ways. First, the right to privacy protects only the exploitation of the individual's name and likeness. The right to publicity will protect the individual's identity as well. What is an identity? Identity includes name and likeness, but it is broader and can include, among other things, an image created by someone through playing a character.

In most respects the two rights encompassed by appropriation, the right of privacy and the right of publicity, are identical.

For example, George "Spanky" McFarland sued the owner of a New Jersey restaurant called Spanky McFarland's for infringement on his right of publicity. McFarland played the character called Spanky in the "Our Gang" comedies in the 1920s, '30s, and '40s. The movie series was later shown on television as the "Little Rascals." Hal Roach Studios owned the rights to the comedy series until 1938. Today the rights to the movies are jointly controlled by Turner Entertainment Company and King World Productions. Until his death in 1992, McFarland was receiving income from the licensing of products based on the series. (McFarland died after this suit began. Under the New Jersey survival statute, the court permitted the actor's estate to maintain the lawsuit.)

4. "Abdul Serves Lawsuit."
5. *Haelan Laboratories, Inc.* v. *Topps Chewing Gum,* 202 F. 2d 866 (1953).

The restaurant opened in 1989. It featured more than 1,000 photos and other Our Gang memorabilia, and patrons could buy such items as Spanky's Steak Sandwich, Rascal's Choice, Buckweet's [*sic*] Basket, and Alfalfa's Sprout Burger, all named after characters in the films. A U.S. district court dismissed McFarland's claim, stating that whatever rights the plaintiff may have had to exploit the name Spanky were passed on to Hal Roach Studios in 1936 when McFarland relinquished all rights to the name except the right to continue to use the nickname Spanky. The restaurant might have appropriated someone's right to the name Spanky, but it was not McFarland's right, the court said.

The 3rd U.S. Circuit Court of Appeals disagreed. "The district court held, in effect, that an actor who portrays a character in such a manner that the character becomes inextricably intertwined with the individual, to such an extent that the individual comes to utilize the character's name as his own, has no proprietary interest in the exploitation of the name or image. We disagree," the appellate court said. "Where an actor's screen persona becomes so associated with him that it becomes inseparable from the actor's own public image, the actor obtains an interest in the image which gives him standing to prevent mere interlopers from using it without authority," the court added. "We hold," Judge Hutchinson wrote, "that there exists at least a triable issue of fact as to whether McFarland had become so inextricably identified with Spanky McFarland that McFarland's own identity would be invoked by the name Spanky."[6]

The 9th U.S. Circuit Court of Appeals reached the same conclusion three years later when it reversed a summary judgment granted to Host International, which had installed animatronic robots that resembled "Cheers" patrons Norm Peterson and Cliff Clavin in airport bars modeled on the set of the long-running television comedy. Host named the figures Bob and Hank. The company said that since Paramount owned the copyright to the characters as well as the set design, actors George Wendt (Norm) and John Ratzenberger (Cliff) could not claim that their identities had been appropriated. The appellate court sent the case back for trial, stating that an actor or actress does not lose the right to control the commercial exploitation of his or her likeness merely by portraying a fictional character owned by someone else.[7]

The marketing of celebrity and sports figure images grew to enormous proportions in the United States in the 1990s. More and more right to publicity challenges were mounted by individuals and organizations. In the late 1990s former major league all-star pitcher Don Newcombe sued the Adolph Coors Company for using what he claimed was his image in an advertisement for Killian's Irish Red ale; actor Dustin Hoffman sued Los Angeles magazine for including a computer-altered image of him in a fashion spread in the periodical; and ETW Corporation, which holds the marketing rights to golfer Tiger Woods, sued well-known sports artist Rick Rush, who produced a limited number of serigraphs called "The Masters of Augusta" that featured a painting of the 1997 Masters Tournament winner.[8]

In addition to protecting an individual's identity as well as a name or likeness, the right to publicity differs from the right to privacy in two other important ways:

6. *McFarland* v. *Miller,* 14 F. 3d 912 (1994).

7. *Wendt* v. *Host International,* 125 F. 3d 800 (1997).

8. *Newcombe* v. *Adolph Coors Co.,* 157 F. 3d 686 (1998); Kuczynski, "Dustin Hoffman"; and Chambers, "Lawsuit Pits."

- The right to privacy dies with the individual because it is a personal right; the right to publicity, a property right, can be passed on to the heirs of the deceased (see pages 259–260).
- It is generally accepted that only the famous, persons who have a property value in their name, can assert a right to publicity.

EARLY CASES

Two of the earliest privacy cases on record are good examples of how the appropriation tort is supposed to protect an individual from commercial exploitation. In 1902 young Abigail Roberson of Albany, N.Y., awoke one morning to find her picture all over town on posters advertising Franklin Mills Flour. Twenty-five thousand copies of the advertisement had been placed in stores, warehouses, saloons, and other public places. Abigail said she felt embarrassed and humiliated, that she suffered greatly from this commercial exploitation, and she therefore sued for invasion of privacy. But she lost her case, and the state's high court ruled:

> an examination of the authorities leads us to the conclusion that the so-called "right of privacy" has not yet found an abiding place in our jurisprudence, and, as we view it, the doctrine cannot now be incorporated without doing violence to settled principles of law by which the profession and the public have long been guided.[9]

Following this decision a great controversy arose in New York, led by the press, much of which expressed outrage at the way the court had treated Abigail. The controversy settled on the state legislature which, during the following year, 1903, adopted the nation's first privacy law. The statute was very narrow; that is, it prohibited a very specific kind of conduct. Use of an individual's name or likeness without the individual's consent for advertising or trade purposes was made a minor crime. In addition to the criminal penalty, the statute allowed the injured party to seek both an injunction to stop the use of the name or picture and money damages.

Two years later Georgia became the first state to recognize the right of privacy through the common law. Paolo Pavesich, an Atlanta artist, discovered that a life insurance company had used his photograph in newspaper advertisements. Pavesich's photograph was used in a before-and-after advertisement to illustrate a contented, successful man who had bought sufficient life insurance. A testimonial statement was also ascribed to the artist. He sued for $25,000 and won his case before the Georgia Supreme Court, which ruled:

> the form and features of the plaintiff are his own. The defendant insurance company and its agents had no more authority to display them in public for the purpose of advertising the business . . . than they would have had to compel the plaintiff to place himself upon exhibition for this purpose.[10]

---

9. *Roberson* v. *Rochester Folding Box Co.,* 171 N.Y. 538 (1902).
10. *Pavesich* v. *New England Mutual Life Insurance Co.,* 122 Ga. 190 (1905).

USE OF NAME OR LIKENESS

Everybody knows what a name is, and it is therefore unnecessary to dwell on that term. It should be noted, however, that stage names, pen names, pseudonyms, and so forth count the same as real names in the eyes of the law. If the name of rock star Elton John is used in an advertisement for dental floss without his permission, the suit cannot be defended on the basis that because Elton John's real name is Reginald Kenneth Dwight, his "name" was not appropriated illegally. It should also be noted that the law of privacy protects only people's names. Company names, trade names, and corporate names are not protected. Only people enjoy the right of privacy. Businesses, corporations, schools, and other "things" are not protected under the law. However, the use of a trade name like Kodak or Crest can create other serious legal problems (see Chapter 14).

What is a likeness? Obviously a photograph, a painting, and a sketch—anything that suggests to readers and viewers that the plaintiff is pictured—is a likeness. Federal courts in New York state ruled that a sketch of a black man sitting in the corner of a boxing ring was, for purposes of an invasion-of-privacy suit, the "likeness" of former heavyweight champion Muhammad Ali. The boxer looked a little like Ali, and the sketch was accompanied by a verse that referred to the boxer as "the Greatest."[11]

Whether a likeness or representation of a plaintiff has been appropriated is often a jury question. Susan Cohen sued a cosmetics maker in 1984 after the firm published an ad containing what Cohen said was a photo of herself and her daughter bathing in a stream while nude. But only the backs and the sides of the bathers can be seen, and the company argued no appropriation had taken place because the plaintiffs were not identifiable. Cohen's husband said he recognized his wife and daughter, as did friends of the family. A lower court dismissed the suit, ruling that the plaintiff's identities cannot be determined from the picture. But the appellate division of the New York Supreme Court overturned the dismissal. The requirement that a portrait or picture of a plaintiff be appropriated "does not require that there be an identifiable facial representation as a prerequisite to relief," the court said. A jury should decide whether the advertisement contains a recognizable likeness.[12] In January of 1997 a U.S. district court ruled that a baby, photographed as she was carried by a firefighter away from the bombed Alfred P. Murrah Federal Building in Oklahoma City on April 19, 1995, was not identifiable. The judge rejected the plea from the child's mother to bar the use of the photograph for commercial purposes without her consent. The photographer had sold the rights to use the picture to several publications as well as to a T-shirt manufacturer and a commemorative statuette maker.[13]

Look-Alikes and Soundalikes

Does using a look-alike in an advertisement constitute appropriating someone's likeness? Beginning in the 1980s, performers who look like or sound like someone more famous have been in demand for public appearances and to work in advertising. Barbara Reynolds, a woman

Does using a look-alike in an advertisement constitute appropriating someone's likeness?

11. *Ali* v. *Playgirl,* 447 F. Supp. 723 (1978).
12. *Cohen* v. *Herbal Concepts,* 473 N.Y.S. 2d 426 (1989).
13. Queary, "Mother Denied Say," A8.

who bears a striking resemblance to the late Jackie Kennedy Onassis, was featured in a Christian Dior ad, along with three real celebrities. Reynolds was made up and dressed to look like Onassis, who sued, arguing that her likeness had been appropriated for the advertisement. The New York Supreme Court agreed, noting that the law prohibits the use of a representation "which conveys the essence and likeness of an individual." Reynolds, as Reynolds, could pose for ads or make public appearances, but she could not attempt to convey the appearance of someone else, someone much better known.[14] Phil Boroff, who might easily be mistaken for Woody Allen, appeared in several ads for firms like National Video and Men's World. In April 1986 he appeared in a Men's World ad in Newsday holding a clarinet, very reminiscent of the character played by Allen in the film "Annie Hall." Beneath the photo, in small, lightfaced type, were these words: "This is a Ron Smith celebrity look-alike." Allen sued. A U.S. district court ruled that despite the disclaimer and despite the fact that it was Phil Boroff, not Woody Allen, in the photo, "the use of Boroff's photograph in their [Men's World] advertisement creates a likelihood of consumer confusion over plaintiff's endorsement or involvement."[15] A bigger, bolder disclaimer might have solved the legal problem, the judge ruled.

Contemporary advertising strategies include the notion of attempting to build an emotional bond between the product and the consumer, to suggest a sharing of values. Advertisers have found that the use within television and radio ads of songs that were popular at the time members of the target audience came of age will invoke favorable memories among the viewers and the listeners; a great summer trip, a special prom, a wedding day. But many performers are reluctant to re-perform the song in a commercial. So the advertiser sometimes does the next best thing and hires another artist to imitate the singer's original performance. The ad may or may not include a disclaimer, "celebrity voice impersonator."

Singer Bette Midler was the first to go to court because of such an impersonation. She sued the Ford Motor Company and its ad agency, Young & Rubicam, for using a "soundalike" to imitate a song—"Do You Want to Dance?"—that she made popular in the 1970s. (The Beach Boys originally made the song popular in the 1960s.) The agency first asked Midler to do the commercial, but she refused. The agency then hired a performer who had worked as a backup singer for Midler for 10 years to imitate Midler's performance.

The U.S. Court of Appeals for the 9th Circuit ruled in favor of Midler and sustained a jury verdict of $400,000 against Young & Rubicam. "The singer manifests herself in the song. To impersonate her voice is to pirate her identity," the court ruled. Not every voice imitation to advertise goods is necessarily actionable, the court noted; however, "we hold that when a distinctive voice of a professional singer is widely known and is deliberately imitated in order to sell a product, the sellers have appropriated what is not theirs and committed a tort in California."[16]

In the wake of the Midler ruling, other performers sought to block similar voice impersonations in commercials. Singer Tom Waits successfully sued Frito-Lay for using an impersonator to imitate him on a commercial jingle for Salso Rio Dorito corn chips. The jingle was a copy of Waits' hit song "Step Right Up." A jury awarded the singer $2.5 million. Performers

14. *Onassis v. Christian Dior,* 472 N.Y.S. 2d 254 (1984).
15. *Allen v. Men's World Outlet,* 679 F. Supp. 360 (1988).
16. *Midler v. Ford Motor Co.,* 849 F. 2d 460 (1988).

247

Chris Isaak, Mitch Ryder, and Carlos Santana also sought to stop similar voice impersonations. A variety of legal strategies were used by the plaintiffs in these cases. Midler won her case using a California statute that specifically prohibits the misappropriation of an individual's "voice" or "likeness" for advertising or selling without the individual's consent. Waits used the federal Lanham Act (see pages 554–557), a statute that prohibits unfair competition. To win, Waits had to prove that he had a distinctive voice that was recognizable by the public and that the advertiser attempted to pass off the commercial as being performed by the singer. Jurors had to find that they recognized Waits' voice in the commercial, not merely that they thought it was Waits' voice because he had popularized the song used in the jingle.

The power of the right of publicity to protect identity as well as name and likeness was demonstrated in 1992 when a federal court ruled in favor of game show hostess Vanna White in her "look-alike" suit against Korean electronics manufacturer Samsung. White, of course, is the very recognizable young woman whose claim to fame is turning letters on the game board of America's most popular syndicated television quiz show, "Wheel of Fortune." Samsung Electronics America and its advertising agency developed a campaign in the early 1990s that tried to suggest that while lots of things in our society might change or become dated, Samsung products would remain state-of-the-art despite the passage of time. The ads featured two illustrations purporting to display items from the 21st century. One would contain a picture of a Samsung product like a VCR, the other a humorous message. In one ad, for example, there was a picture of a raw beefsteak with the caption, "Revealed to be health food, 2010 A.D."

White sued Samsung for publishing an ad that included a photo-parody of the celebrated letter turner. Near the center of the color photo was a robot, reminiscent of C3PO of "Star Wars" fame, decked out in a blond wig, evening dress, and jewelry, standing next to a video board with large letters on it. Beneath the illustration was the caption, "Longest running game show, 2012 A.D." The joke in the parody ad was that Samsung products would still be around after Vanna White had been replaced by a robot on "Wheel of Fortune." A lower court dismissed the lawsuit, but the 9th U.S. Circuit Court of Appeals reinstated the action, ruling that the use of the image of the formally dressed robot in the advertisement surely could effectively "eviscerate" White's right to publicity. "The identities of the most popular celebrities are not only the most attractive for advertisers, but the easiest to evoke without resorting to obvious means such as a name or likeness or voice," the court ruled.[17] Performers need to be protected from such exploitation.

Four years later in 1996 the 10th U.S. Circuit Court of Appeals was also faced with a lawsuit based on what was arguably a commercial parody. A company called Cardtoons has published since 1992 a series of baseball cards that feature caricatures of well-known major league baseball players. The back of the cards contain humorous commentary. The card depicting Barry Bonds of the San Francisco Giants, for example, carries a recognizable likeness of Bonds on the front, with the name Treasury Bonds of the Gents. The commentary on the back of the card describes Treasury Bonds and focuses on his high salary and his interest in money. Ricky Henderson of the Oakland Athletics is referred to as Egotisticky Henderson of the Pathetics.

---

17. *White* v. *Samsung Electronics America, Inc.,* 971 F. 2d 1395 (1992); rehearing den. 989 F. 2d 1512 (1992).

The Major League Baseball Players Association sued to block distribution of the cards. The suit alleged, among other things, that the cards violated the ballplayers' right to publicity. Their likenesses were used for commercial purposes without their consent. The lower court ruled in favor of Cardtoons and the Court of Appeals affirmed. The court ruled that the cards were parodies, social commentary on popular American celebrities, and protected by the First Amendment. "While not core political speech . . . this type of commentary on an important social institution constitutes protected expression," Judge Tacha wrote.[18] The players association argued that this case was identical to *White* v. *Samsung* and that the same outcome was warranted. Judge Tacha disagreed, noting that the White case involved an advertisement for a product and this case did not. But that didn't matter, the judge wrote, because he and his colleagues disagreed with the result of the earlier case. The court stressed the importance of parody and said that the Major League Baseball Players Association would never consent to a parody of its members. "Because celebrities are an important part of our public vocabulary, a parody of a celebrity does not merely lampoon the celebrity, but exposes weakness of the idea or value that the celebrity symbolizes in society," Judge Tacha added.

The court ruled that the cards were parodies, social commentary on popular American celebrities, and protected by the First Amendment.

With two circuit courts at odds on this matter, it is quite possible the Supreme Court will eventually have to resolve the issue. The White case is certainly at the outer limits of protection for the images of the famous and near famous. The Cardtoons decision reflects a more realistic picture of the status of the law.

Is an advertiser who seeks to create the illusion of a celebrity with a look-alike or a voice impersonator protected from an appropriation suit if the ad contains a disclaimer? Yes, if the disclaimer is prominent in the ad. Small type at the bottom of a full-page ad will not do the trick, nor will an audio disclaimer camouflaged by music or noise in a radio spot. And, of course, a disclaimer would not have helped in Vanna White's case. It was obviously not the game show hostess in the advertisement; it was a robot!

ADVERTISING AND TRADE PURPOSES

What are advertising and trade purposes? While minor differences exist among the states—especially among the states with statutes—a general guideline can be set down: advertising or trade purposes are commercial uses; that is, someone makes money from the use. Here are examples of the kinds of actions that could be regarded as a commercial use:

1. **Use of a person's name or photograph in an *advertisement* on television, on radio, in newspapers, in magazines, on posters, on billboards, and so forth.**
2. **Display of a person's photograph in the window of a photographer's shop to show potential customers the quality of work done by the studio.**
3. **A testimonial falsely suggesting that an individual eats the cereal or drives the automobile in question.**

18. *Cardtoons* v. *Major League Baseball Players Association*, 95 F. 3d 959 (1996).

4. **The use of someone's likeness or identity in a commercial entertainment vehicle like a feature film, a television situation comedy, or a novel.**[19]

5. **Use of an individual's name or likeness in a banner ad or some other commercial message on a Web site.**

In 1992 the former wife of National Football League Hall of Fame running back John Riggins decided to sell the house the two had lived in, a home she had won as a part of the divorce settlement. As a real estate agent she created a brochure that used John Riggins' name in several spots to advertise the house. The Virginia Supreme Court ruled that this was a commercial purpose and sustained the award of more than $50,000 to the former NFL star.[20]

In Utah a broadcaster announced the name of a person on the "Dialing for Dollars" television feature. The individual sued, arguing that the program was simply an advertising device used by the station to attract viewers and that since no consent had been given for the use of the name over the air, the use was an invasion of privacy. The Utah Supreme Court agreed with the plaintiff, declaring that the name had been used to promote a commodity—the television station.[21]

NEWS AND INFORMATION EXCEPTION

What about this argument? A newspaper runs a photograph of John Smith on the front page after his car rolled over several times during a high-speed police pursuit. Smith sues for invasion of privacy, arguing that his picture on the front page of the newspaper attracted readers to the paper, resulted in the sale of newspapers, and therefore was used for commercial or trade purposes. Despite the arguments of many persons—even today—courts have consistently rejected this claim.

This plea was first made in 1907 by a New Yorker who objected to having his picture appear on the front page of the New York World. The state supreme court rejected the argument, noting that surely the intent of the state legislature was not to prohibit a newspaper or magazine from publishing people's names or pictures in a single issue without their consent.[22] Two years later another New York court reiterated this stand, ruling that advertising and trade purposes referred to commercial use, not to the dissemination of information.[23] The U.S. Supreme Court has ruled that the fact that newspapers and books and magazines are sold for profit does not deny them the protection of liberty of expression.[24]

---

19. But not always. A New York court, faced with a privacy suit by a Michael Costanza against Jerry Seinfeld and the producers of the "Seinfeld" television show for using his name (Costanza) and likeness (short, fat, and bald) in the TV program, dismissed the action, claiming that a fictional television program falls outside a trade or advertising use as defined by the New York statute. See *Constanza* v. *Seinfeld*, 693 NYS 2d 897 (1999).
20. *Town & Country Properties, Inc.* v. *Riggins*, 457 S.E. 2d 356 (1995).
21. *Jeppson* v. *United Television*, 580 P. 2d 1087 (1978).
22. *Moser* v. *Press Publishing Co.*, 109 N.Y.S. 963 (1908).
23. *Jeffries* v. *New York Evening Journal*, 124 N.Y.S. 780 (1910).
24. *Time, Inc.* v. *Hill*, 385 U.S. 374 (1967). See *Small* v. *WTMJ Television Station*, 542 N.W. 2d 239 (1995) for a recent statement of this rule.

Anyone who has worked in journalism for very long knows that material created for promotional or public relations purposes is often published or broadcast under the guise of news or information. Women's magazines often publish makeover sections in which ordinary women are given cosmetics, clothing, new hairstyles, and advice from professionals to try to improve their appearance. Seventeen magazine published articles on makeovers for many years. Each article accompanying the before-and-after photos discussed the makeover and listed the brand names of the products used, generally products from regular advertisers. One young woman featured in the section inadvertently failed to sign a release and, when the magazine was published, sued the publication for using her name or likeness for purposes of trade. She lost. A court ruled that the article about grooming, makeup, and clothing was newsworthy to the teenage audience at which it was aimed. Mention of the brand names of products was incidental to the article and pictures.[25]

A professional model argued that the use of a picture of her modeling a jacket in the "Best Bets" column of the New York magazine was an illegal appropriation of her likeness for advertising purposes. The column features short articles and photos about new and unusual products and services, and the photo of the model carried this caption:

> Yes Giorgio—from Giorgio Armani. Based on his now classic turn on the
> bomber jacket, this cotton-twill version with "fun fur" collar features the same
> cut at a far lower price—about $225. It'll be available in the stores next week.
> Henry Post Bomber Jacket/Barney's, Bergdorf Goodman, Bloomingdale's.

The plaintiff said this was an advertisement and that in order to get a product featured in the "Best Bets" column, a merchant had to advertise elsewhere in the magazine. The New York Court of Appeals disagreed that use of the photo was an appropriation, ruling that the "newsworthiness exception applies not only to reports of political happenings and social trends, but also to news stories and articles of consumer interest, including developments in the fashion world." The plaintiff argued that she certainly was not newsworthy. The court said that was immaterial—the jacket she modeled was newsworthy.[26]

But what might be regarded as a newsworthy fashion feature by one judge might be considered a commercial appropriation by another. Actor Dustin Hoffman was awarded $3 million in damages in early 1999 after Los Angeles magazine used his photo in a fashion feature called Grand Illusions. Using computer imaging technology, the magazine mixed still photos of actresses and actors (both living and dead) with photos of models wearing the latest spring fashions by many designers who were major advertisers in the magazine. Hoffman's picture came from a publicity still for the movie "Tootsie," in which the actor is made up like a woman. Hoffman's face and head were attached to the body of a female model over this caption: "Dustin Hoffman isn't a drag in a butter-colored silk gown by Richard Tyler and Ralph Lauren heels." The court ruled that the use of the photo was for the purpose of selling or advertising goods.[27] It was not newsworthy. Elvis Presley's estate was also suing the magazine for use of the dead singer's photo in the same fashion feature.

25. *Lopez* v. *Triangle Communications,* 421 N.Y.S. 2d 57 (1979).
26. *Stephano* v. *News Group W Publications,* 485 N.Y.S. 2d 220 (1984).
27. *Hoffman* v. *Capital Cities/ABC Inc.,* 33 F. Supp. 2d 867 (1999).

OTHER EXCEPTIONS

The right to publish or broadcast an individual's name or likeness for news and information purposes is a broad exception to the appropriation rule. Other courts have found other exceptions as well, but this is where the law of privacy gets a little dicey. Not all courts view the same actions as exceptions to the appropriation rule. The doctrine of incidental use, for example, is recognized in many jurisdictions and permits a fleeting or brief use of an individual's name or likeness in some kinds of commercial creations. A U.S. district court in California said that the use of a retired actress's name and likeness in advertising for videos of two feature films in which she had appeared 30 years earlier was incidental to the release of the videos themselves. The use of her image and name in the video was protected by a release she had signed when she made the original movies.[28] A brief filmed scene of a pedestrian walking on the street that ends up in a feature motion picture may not support an action for appropriation either. A U.S. district court in New York rejected Pamela Preston's claim that her likeness had been appropriated when she appeared for a total of nine seconds walking on a New York street in a scene that ran behind the opening credits of the film "Sea of Love." "The doctrine of incidental use was developed to address concerns that penalizing every unauthorized use, no matter how insignificant or fleeting, of a person's name or likeness would impose undue burdens on expressive activity," the court ruled.[29] In 1994 a federal court in New York ruled that it was an incidental use when publisher Random House used, without permission, the names and photographs of five other authors in advertising for its book on the Kennedy assassination, "Case Closed" by Gerald Posner. In his book Posner argued that the conspiracy theories proposed by the five pictured authors were bogus. The headline "Guilty of Misleading the American Public" was above the pictures. The court acknowledged that this case was somewhat unusual, in that earlier applications of the incidental use doctrine in this regard had generally related to the media's reuse of previously published material for the purposes of self-promotion. (This is called the *Booth* rule; see the following section.) "Nonetheless," Judge Martin said, "it is clear that what drives the exception is a First Amendment interest in protecting the ability of the media to publicize its own communications."[30]

The doctrine of incidental use, for example, is recognized in many jurisdictions and permits a fleeting or brief use of an individual's name or likeness in some kinds of commercial creations.

Booth *Rule*

The *Booth* rule is closely related to the incidental use doctrine; in fact, some courts refer to it as part of that doctrine. The rule has developed slowly over the past 38 years and today provides fairly broad protection to the mass media in most states if an individual's name or likeness is used in advertising for a particular medium. In other words, the use of a person's name or likeness in an advertisement *for* a magazine or a newspaper or a television program is usually not regarded as an appropriation if the photograph or name has been or will be a part of the medium's news or information content.

28. *Page* v. *Something Weird Video,* 25 M.L.R. 1489 (1996).
29. *Preston* v. *Martin Bregman Productions, Inc.,* 765 F. Supp. 116 (1991). See also *University of Notre Dame* v. *20th Century Fox,* 22 App. Div. 2d 452, 15 N.Y.S. 2d 907 (1962).
30. *Groden* v. *Random House Inc.,* 22 M.L.R. 2257 (1994), aff'd. 61 F. 3d 1045 (1995).

The controversy that sparked this rule involved actress Shirley Booth. She was photographed in Jamaica, and the picture was published in a feature story in Holiday magazine. Holiday then used the same picture to advertise the magazine itself. The full-page advertisement told readers that the picture was typical of the material appearing in Holiday magazine and urged people to advertise in the periodical or subscribe to Holiday. Ms. Booth did not object to her photograph in the feature story, only to its use in the subsequent advertisement. The courts, however, refused to call the use an invasion of privacy. The New York Supreme Court ruled that the strength of a free press depends on economic support from advertisers and subscribers, and hence a publication or broadcasting station must promote itself. Since the picture in this case was first used in an information story, its subsequent use in a promotion for the magazine was really only incidental to its original use and was merely to show the quality and content of the magazine. The picture was not used to sell spaghetti or used cars. Hence the use did not constitute an invasion of privacy.[31]

Originally it was believed that the *Booth* rule protected only the *republication* or *rebroadcast* of material previously used in the medium. And some courts still follow this rule. But other courts have enunciated a broader protection. For example, a U.S. district court ruled that it is permissible for a newspaper or magazine to use previously published material in a television advertisement for the publication.[32] That is, a name or likeness that appeared in a newspaper story can be *republished* in a television advertisement for that newspaper. In New Jersey a woman was photographed as a part of a television news story on the dangers of smoking in the presence of infants. Her photo was used in station promotions for the news story, but her comments and picture were cut from the story when it was broadcast. The court ruled that this use still was an incidental and protected use.[33] The California Court of Appeals in 1995 ruled that when the San Jose Mercury News reprinted news stories and photos that it had originally used to report the San Francisco 49ers' 1989 Super Bowl victory over Cincinnati, it was not actionable. The newspaper created a poster from the clippings, which it sold. The court rejected Joe Montana's lawsuit, saying the publication of the material on a poster that promoted the newspaper's coverage of the game was simply an adjunct of the original protected publication.[34] In 1995 the New York Supreme Court ruled that the use of radio personality Howard Stern's photo without his permission in advertisements for an online service was not an invasion of privacy under this incidental republication rule. After Stern announced he was a candidate for the job of governor of New York, the Delphi online service set up a bulletin board for debates on his political candidacy. It used an outlandish photo of Stern (which he had earlier posed for) showing him with bare buttocks. The picture appeared in ads in New York Magazine and the New York Post with the caption, "Should this man be the next governor of New York?" Readers were invited to debate the issue on the bulletin board. Stern argued that Delphi wasn't a news or information medium like a newspaper or magazine and shouldn't be allowed to raise the incidental republication exception. The court

31. *Booth* v. *Curtis Publishing Co.*, 11 N.Y.S. 2d 907 (1962).
32. *Friedan* v. *Friedan*, 414 F. Supp. 77 (1976).
33. *Linder* v. *Capital Cities ABC Inc.*, 27 M.L.R. 2375 (1999).
34. *Montana* v. *San Jose Mercury News, Inc.*, 34 Cal. App. 4th 6790 (1995).

disagreed, stating that the online service is analogous to news vendors, bookstores, letters to the editor, and other news disseminators.[35] No one yet knows just how far the courts will go in extending the *Booth* rule. The tendency, however, seems to be to expand the protection, rather than restrict it.

Clearly the use of a name or photo to promote a medium cannot be an explicit or even implied endorsement of the medium. Cher won a lawsuit against Forum magazine after it used her photo to promote an edition of the publication. The advertisements clearly implied that the actress-singer endorsed Forum, which was not true. That issue of the magazine did contain an interview with Cher, but the court ruled that the advertisements went far beyond establishing the news content and quality of the publication for potential readers.[36] On the other hand, The Village Voice regularly uses a cover from a recent edition as an advertisement for new subscribers. The reproduced cover is always embellished by the addition of a cartoon balloon emanating from the mouth of the personality featured on the cover. The balloon usually contains the words "We'll be right over," or "What's your address?" Ramon Velez, an activist in New York, sued The Village Voice, arguing that the use of his photo in this way implied an endorsement. The appellate division of the Supreme Court disagreed, noting that no reasonable reader would believe that the plaintiff had endorsed The Village Voice.[37] The fact that the entire cover, and not just Velez's photo, had been used probably helped the defendant in this case.

Finally, the use of an individual's name or likeness in a political advertisement is not regarded as an appropriation. A campaign advertisement that says "Vote for Jones, not Smith," would not give Smith a legal right to sue for appropriation. The use of an individual's name or likeness in an issue-oriented advertisement such as "Save the Whales" or "Stop Racism" likewise would not sustain an appropriation lawsuit. What about the use of a name or likeness in an advertisement or promotion for a nonprofit organization like the YMCA or the Red Cross? Many such groups put out brochures or pamphlets to stimulate donations to further their community work. Would the unauthorized use of the picture of a child swimming in the pool at the YMCA sustain a lawsuit? That is unlikely, but the 6th U.S. Circuit Court of Appeals did uphold a small damage award to a child whose picture was used without permission in a direct mail solicitation by a Kentucky religious order. The Little Sisters of the Assumption Order included the photo with a letter that was sent to 125,000 homes asking for donations for the poor. The appellate court affirmed the lower court award of $100 in damages for appropriation.[38] And the New York Supreme Court came to a similar conclusion in 1995 when it found that the use of an individual's photo on a solicitation by a nonprofit corporation, the Community Service Society of New York, is an advertisement under the terms of the New York privacy statute. The defendant had used the plaintiff's picture in its newsletter aimed at soliciting funds for needy New Yorkers.[39] These two cases stand alone at present, but suggest that

---

35. *Stern* v. *Delphi Internet Services Corp.*, 626 N.Y.S. 2d 694 (1995).
36. *Cher* v. *Forum International*, 692 F. 2d 634 (1982).
37. *Velez* v. *V V Publishing Corp.*, 524 N.Y.S. 2d 186 (1988).
38. *Bowling* v. *The Missionary Servants of the Most Holy Trinity*, 972 F. 2d 346 (1992).
39. *Vinales* v. *Community Service Society of New York, Inc.*, 23 M.L.R. 1638 (1995).

caution should be exercised by any organization, commercial or otherwise, that seeks to use the names and faces of real people in fund-raising efforts. The simplest solution to the problem is to get consent from these persons.

CONSENT AS A DEFENSE

The law prohibits only the unauthorized use of a name or likeness for commercial or trade purposes. States with privacy statutes require that written authorization or consent be given before the use. The rule in the states that follow the common law is less specific with regard to the need for written consent. But in any legal action the defendant is going to have to prove that he or she had consent to use the name or photograph. Written consent is generally uncontestable. Attempts to convince a court that oral consent was given can be met by the plaintiff's denial, and then the fact finder will have to decide who is telling the truth. Also, oral consent can be withdrawn up to the moment of publication or broadcast.[40]

The law prohibits only the unauthorized use of a name or likeness for commercial or trade purposes.

The consent issue is most easily resolved if the subject has signed a model release similar to the one printed on page 256. But such legal documents are not always required to establish consent. Two rulings make this point. Sam and Joseph Schifano sued the Greene County Greyhound Park, a dog racing track, for including their photo in an advertising brochure for the facility. The plaintiffs, who visited the park often, were photographed while they sat with several other persons in what is called The Winner's Circle, a section of the park that can be reserved by interested groups of spectators. There was no written consent for the use of their picture, but there was ample evidence that park officials had told the plaintiffs why they were taking the photos and gave them a chance to leave if they did not want to be in the picture. "Plaintiffs, neither by objecting nor moving, when those options were made available by park employees, consented to having their photograph taken at the Park," the Alabama Supreme Court ruled in 1993.[41]

A year later the 9th U.S. Circuit Court of Appeals handed down a similar ruling in a lawsuit involving a popular television situation comedy called "Evening Shade." Country music songwriter and performer Wood Newton sued the producers of the program because the lead character in the show, played by Burt Reynolds, was also named Wood Newton. The creator of the program, Linda Bloodworth-Thomason, grew up in the same town as the real Wood Newton, and there are some similarities between the real and fictional characters. Newton never signed a release for the use of his name, but when the program was first telecast he sent a letter to the producers that said, "I want you to know that I'm flattered that you are using my name, everyone who I've talked to thinks it's exciting and so do I." The lawsuit was filed many months later, after the producers of the program had rejected music that Newton had written and submitted for use on the program. "Although Newton never uttered the words 'I consent,' it is obvious that he did consent," the court ruled.[42]

40. *Durgom v. CBS,* 214 N.Y.S. 2d 752 (1961).
41. *Schifano v. Greene County Greyhound Park, Inc.,* 624 So. 178 (1993).
42. *Newton v. Thomason,* 22 F. 3d 1455 (1994).

> ## MODEL RELEASE OR CONSENT FORM
> ## USED BY A PHOTOGRAPHER
>
> For and in consideration of my engagement as a model/subject by (insert photographer's name), hereafter referred to as the photographer, on terms or fee hereinafter stated, I hereby give the photographer, his/her legal representatives, and assigns, those for whom the photographer is acting, and those acting with his/her permission, or his/her employees, the right and permission to copyright and/or use, reuse, and/or publish, and republish photographic pictures or portraits of me, or in which I may be distorted in character, or form, in conjunction with my own or a fictitious name, on reproductions thereof in color, or black and white made through any media by the photographer at his/her studio or elsewhere, for any purpose whatsoever; including the use of any printed matter in conjunction therewith.
>
> I hereby waive any right to inspect or approve the finished photograph or advertising copy of printed matter that may be used in conjunction therewith or to the eventual use that it might be applied.
>
> I hereby release, discharge and agree to save harmless the photographer, his/her representatives, assigns, employees or any person or persons, corporation or corporations, acting under his/her permission or authority, or any person, persons, corporation or corporations, for whom he/she might be acting, including any firm publishing and/or distributing the finished product, in whole or in part, from and against any liability as a result of any distortion, blurring, or alteration, optical illusion, or use in composite form, either intentionally or otherwise, that may occur or be produced in the taking, or processing or reproduction of the finished product, its publication or distribution of the same, even should the same subject me to ridicule, scandal, reproach, scorn, or indignity.

When Consent Won't Work

There are times when even written consent does not work as a defense, and the media must be aware of such situations:

1. **Consent given today may not be valid in the distant future, especially if it is gratuitous oral consent.** In Louisiana a man named Cole McAndrews gave permission to the owner of a health spa to use his before-and-after pictures in advertisements for the gym. But the owner, Alvin Roy, waited 10 years to use the photographs, and in the interim McAndrews' life had changed considerably. He sued Roy, who argued that it was McAndrews' responsibility to revoke the consent if he no longer wanted the pictures used. But a Louisiana court of appeals agreed instead with the plaintiff. Judge Robert D. Jones wrote:

   > We are of the opinion that it would be placing an unreasonable burden on the
   > plaintiff to hold he was under duty to revoke a gratuitous authorization given

many years before. As the defendant was the only person to profit from the use of the pictures then, under all the circumstances, it seems reasonable that he should have sought renewal of the permission to use the old pictures.[43]

Reauthorization is needed when a name or photograph is used many years after consent was first given. A professional actor in New York gave the manufacturer of artificial Christmas trees permission to use his picture in a commercial for one year. When the commercial was used after one year, he sued for appropriation, and the New York high court sustained his privacy suit against the challenge by the defendant that only an action for breach of contract should be permitted.[44]

2. **Some persons cannot give consent.** A teenage girl is perfect to appear in an Acme Shampoo advertising campaign. She agrees to pose and signs a release authorizing use of her picture in the advertisements. The pictures are great, the advertisements are great, everything is great—until notice arrives that the model is suing for invasion of privacy! But she signed the permission form. Right. But she is only 16 years old, and under the law minors cannot give consent. Parental consent is required in such instances. What if the girl said she was 18 years old? The court will determine how believable such a statement was and will frequently ask whether the defendant sought any proof of this claim. If parents or guardians do give consent for the use of a minor's name or picture, under the common law in many states it is possible for the minors to revoke that consent when they reach the legal age.

Other people are unable to give consent as well. CBS was sued on behalf of David Delan by his guardian for including the young man in its film "Any Place But Here," a documentary about mental illness. Delan had been hospitalized for more than five years as a psychotic at the Creedmor State Hospital in New York. He was legally incompetent to sign a consent form, and the network failed to gain a signed release from a physician. A psychologist gave CBS permission to film David, but the New York state law specifically requires the signature of a medical doctor on the release agreement before patients in the state's mental hospitals can be photographed or interviewed.[45] CBS ultimately prevailed in the case when the appellate division of the New York Supreme Court ruled that the broadcast was not made for advertising or trade purposes, and therefore consent from David Delan was not required.[46] But the point made by the trial court is well taken. Persons who are unable to give consent because, for one reason or another, they are wards of the state, are risky subjects for publications or broadcasts that are made for advertising or trade purposes. It is important to know that the person from whom consent is obtained is legally able to give consent.

It is important to know that the person from whom consent is obtained is legally able to give consent.

43. *McAndrews v. Roy,* 131 So. 2d 256 (1961).
44. *Welch v. Mr. Christmas Tree,* 57 N.Y. 2d 143 (1982).
45. *Delan v. CBS,* 445 N.Y.S. 2d 898 (1981).
46. *Delan v. CBS,* 458 N.Y.S. 2d 698 (1983).

3. **Consent to use a photograph of a person in an advertisement or on a poster cannot be used as a defense if the photograph is materially altered or changed.**

Several years ago a well-known and well-paid New York fashion model posed for pictures to be used in an advertising campaign for a bookstore. After the photography session, model Mary Jane Russell signed this standard release form:

> The undersigned hereby irrevocably consents to the unrestricted use by Richard Avedon [the photographer], advertisers, customers, successors, and assigns, of my name, portrait, or picture for advertising purposes or purposes of trade, and I waive the right to inspect or approve such completed portraits, pictures, or advertising matter used in connection therewith.

It sounds as though she signed her life away, and with regard to the pictures Avedon took, she did. However, the bookstore sold one of the photographs to a maker of bedsheets. The bedding manufacturer had a reputation for running sleazy advertising campaigns and consequently had trouble getting first-class models to pose for advertising pictures. The manufacturer substantially retouched the Avedon photographs, changing the context. Mary Jane Russell sued for invasion of privacy, but the manufacturer answered by telling the court that the model had given irrevocable consent for anyone to use those pictures, that she had waived her right to inspect the completed pictures and the advertising, and so forth.

The court agreed that Russell had given up her right of privacy with regard to the pictures Avedon took. But the picture used by the sheet maker in its advertising was not the same picture taken by Avedon. It had been altered. And Russell won her case. Justice Matthew Levy of the New York Supreme Court wrote:

> If the picture were altered sufficiently in situation, emphasis, background, or context, I should think that it would no longer be the same portrait, but a different one. And as to the changed picture, I would hold that the original written consent would not apply and that liability would arrive when the content of the picture has been so changed that it is substantially unlike the original.[47]

What is substantial alteration? It probably means something other than minor retouching, but how much retouching is permissible before a privacy suit can accrue is difficult to say. This is one of the few cases on this legal point. Persons who want to retouch a photograph should be careful, even when they have written consent. They might change the picture sufficiently so that the consent would not apply.

The reference to altering the context of a picture arose in New York when a model sued and won after her seminude photograph was used to advertise an allegedly obscene movie. She had signed a release permitting the use of her photograph for "any purpose whatsoever," but the New York Supreme Court ruled that "any purpose whatsoever" does not include a "degrading use."[48]

---

47. *Russell v. Marboro Books,* 183 N.Y.S. 2d 8 (1959).
48. *Dittner v. Troma,* 6 M.L.R. 1991 (1980).

LIFE AFTER DEATH

The right to privacy is a personal right and dies with the individual. The right to publicity may live on after death. The operative word in the previous sentence is "may," since there is considerable dispute among courts in the United States about this proposition. The legislatures in at least nine states have passed statutes guaranteeing that the right to commercially exploit the name or likeness of a dead public figure may be passed on to heirs and protected for as long as 50 years.* At the same time, the state of New York doesn't recognize a descendant's right to control publicity at all.

The law in most states is governed by court decisions rather than statute, and these rulings tend to lack consistency. Initially, some states rejected the notion that the right to publicity could be protected after death, that it was something that could be passed on to an heir.[49] But such decisions seem to be out of step with the way the law is developing in most states. A few state courts have ruled that the right to publicity may be passed on to an heir, but only if the deceased had attempted to exploit this right during his or her lifetime. This was the direction the law was taking in California before the state adopted a statute to govern this issue.[50] Most commonly, however, state courts are ruling that the right of publicity is descendible— may be passed on to an heir—under any circumstance.[51]

The use of dead celebrities to sell products is a growing phenomenon. Viewers of the Super Bowl telecast in 1997 saw Fred Astaire, who died in 1987, dancing with a Dirt Devil vacuum cleaner. James Dean sells Levi's jeans and Converse shoes; Charlie Chaplin sells IBM personal computers. There are at least two major American companies—the Curtis Management Group and the Roger Richman Agency—that do nothing but license the likenesses of dead celebrities. Advertisers who seek to associate their products with images of dead celebrities must be wary of the law in this area, which is generally unsettled in most states. It is usually worth the money and the effort to pay for the licensing rights rather than risk a lawsuit, which can be costly even if it is successfully defended.

New challenges in this area of privacy law will emerge in the coming years. Computer technology called reanimation, the kind of technology that brought dinosaurs to life in the film "Jurassic Park," is now capable of bringing dead celebrities to life again on video. Simpler film splicing technology has already been used to create commercials like the one for Diet Coke in which singer Elton John performed for an audience that included Humphrey Bogart, James Cagney, and Louis Armstrong. But in this case these were real images of these dead performers technically joined with contemporary footage of John. The advertiser must get permission for such a use because both the right to publicity and copyright are involved. Under reanimation, a brand new image of Bogart or Cagney could be digitally created. And

---

49. See, for example, *Reeves* v. *United Artists,* 572 F. Supp. 1231 (1983).
50. See, for example, *Lugosi* v. *Universal,* 160 Cal. App. 3d 323 (1979) and *Acme* v. *Kuperstock,* 711 F. 2d 1538 (1983).
51. See *The Martin Luther King Center* v. *American Heritage Products,* 296 S.E. 2d 697 (1982).

*California, Florida, Indiana, Kentucky, Nebraska, Oklahoma, Tennessee, Utah, and Virginia all have statutes that speak to this matter in some way.

legal experts are not certain whether, under existing law, permission to use this image is necessary. Right to publicity claims should still be applicable if the reanimated image appears in an advertisement. But in many states, right to publicity laws do not prevent the use of the image of a dead celebrity in something other than an advertisement.

SUMMARY

Appropriation of a person's name or likeness for commercial or trade purposes without permission is an invasion of privacy and may be a violation of a person's right to publicity. Use of an individual's photograph, a sketch of the person, a nickname, or a stage name are all considered use of a name or likeness. However, the publication of news and information in magazines, books, newspapers, and news broadcasts is not considered a trade purpose, even though the mass medium may make a profit from such publication. Consequently, persons who are named or pictured in news stories or other such material cannot sue for appropriation. Also, a news medium may republish or rebroadcast news items or photographs already carried as news stories in advertising for the mass medium to establish the quality or kind of material carried by the medium.

Anyone who seeks to use the name or likeness of an individual for commercial or trade purposes should gain written consent from that person. Even written consent may be invalid as a defense in an invasion-of-privacy suit if the consent was given many years before publication, if the person from whom the consent was gained cannot legally give consent, or if the photograph or other material that is used is substantially altered.

Courts have also recognized what is known as the right to publicity. Right-to-publicity actions are most often instituted by well-known persons who believe the unauthorized use of their name or likeness has deprived them of an opportunity to reap financial gain by selling this right to the user. In some states the right to publicity can be passed on to heirs like any other piece of property, which means that a performer's estate can control the use of his or her name and likeness after the performer's death.

INTRUSION

It is illegal to intrude, physically or otherwise, upon the seclusion or solitude of an individual.

Intrusion is what many people think of when they hear the phrase "invasion of privacy." Wiretapping, cameras with telephoto lenses, hidden microphones—all of these are associated with intrusion. Intrusion is different from the other three privacy tort categories in an important way: Intrusion involves the collection of data about someone; the other three involve the publication of information about an individual. In an intrusion case, if the information has been gathered illegally, an intrusion has taken place. It really doesn't matter what the defendant does—if anything—with the data. The legal wrong takes place when the material is gathered.

Under appropriation, publication of private facts, and false light privacy, it is the publication of the data that creates the legal wrong. How the information has been gathered is generally immaterial to those causes of action.

The key to understanding intrusion is to understand the phrase "reasonable expectation of privacy." If the plaintiff enjoys a reasonable expectation of privacy when the intruder snaps the picture or overhears the conversation or whatever, courts will generally regard the defendant's actions as an intrusion. But if there is no reasonable expectation of privacy for the plaintiff when the data is taken, then there is no intrusion. The intrusion tort, then, focuses on how information is gathered.

Most states and the federal government have a variety of laws that regulate the way information can be gathered, laws that limit the recording of a conversation with a hidden microphone, prohibit wiretapping and eavesdropping, and regulate many other behaviors. (See pages 317–320 for more information on these kinds of laws.) These laws provide penalties for illegal information gathering that go beyond a civil lawsuit for invasion of privacy.

INTRUSION AND THE INTERNET

The explosive use of interactive computer systems has greatly outpaced the ability of society to police the Internet to protect against the illegal collection of data about Web users. Studies reveal that Internet users are concerned. A 1999 Harris poll for Business Week found that fear of losing privacy was the primary reason people cited for not going online. Of those who do go online, only three of 10 said they gave valid information when asked to register at a Web site.[52]

But giving information away is not the most serious problem. Adults are generally aware of what may be in store for them if they pass on sensitive information to others, whether it is over the Internet, in a printed survey they receive in the mail, or to a telephone solicitor. A legal doctrine followed in many states, called the assumption of risk analysis, clearly stipulates that an individual loses a privacy interest in personal information that is made accessible to another person or otherwise placed in the flow of commerce. In these states the courts have said there is no reasonable expectation of privacy in bank records, numbers dialed on a telephone, or even the contents of curbside trash.[53] Internet users who are asked for information at least have the choice of providing the requested data or walking away from the Web site. Any information given to an online service provider ceases to be private unless there is an agreement between the OSP and the user ensuring the privacy of this data. At least this was a ruling by a U.S. district court in Virginia in 1999.[54]

But voluntarily giving information to an OSP or site operator is not the greatest fear of most Web users. More serious is the problem of users giving up private information without even knowing they are doing so. So-called online profiling, the practice of aggregating information about users gathered primarily by tracking their movements on the Web, is an important issue that has yet to be fully resolved. When Intel introduced its Pentium III processor in

52. Fixmer, "New Way to Travel."
53. Stuckey, *Internet and Online Law.*
54. *U.S. v. Hambrick,* W. D. Va. No. 98-0042-C, 7/7/99.

early 1999 it was revealed that a chip in the processor contained a unique serial number (a different number for each processor), and this chip would permit the tracking of the users' movements on the Web. The inclusion of this tracking device did not violate any U.S. laws, and Intel said the device would enhance security on the Internet by permitting e-commerce sellers to verify with whom they are communicating or doing business. But after an outcry from privacy advocates and others, the processor manufacturer agreed to eliminate the identifying number for consumers who sought such a deletion. In November of 1999 RealNetworks, a Seattle company that leads the market for software used to play online music and video, admitted it was secretly monitoring users' listening habits. The company was tapping into users' hard drives each time they accessed the company's software programs. The day after this monitoring was revealed, RealNetworks' executives apologized and said they had released a patch on their Web site that would in the future prevent the program from relaying personal information about users to third parties. In the wake of these revelations at least two class-action lawsuits were filed against the company, claiming that the secret acquisition of the personal data violated various state consumer protection laws.

The language of the Internet is filled with exotic words like "cookies" and "mouse droppings" and "sniffers," slang terms that identify programming devices that, in a clandestine way, capture data about the Net user while he or she surfs the Web. A cookie, for example, is a tiny file that can collect data about a Web user. When the user connects his or her computer to a Web-site server through the Internet, the Web-site server sends a small data file (cookie); the user's computer saves it on the hard drive. As the user and the Web site communicate, some data are stored in the cookie. When the user disconnects, the cookie remains in the user's computer. Other data about the user's Internet use may be automatically stored in the cookie later. The next time the user connects to that Web site, the site reads the cookie for information on the user.[55] Cookies are designed to help the Web-site operators provide better service to those who use their sites by making the sites more easily accessible. But cookies can and do gather considerable personal information about the Web user, and most Web-site operators don't disclose their use of this data-gathering device. In 1998, the Federal Trade Commission surveyed 1,400 Web sites and found that 92 percent still collected personal data from users but only 14 percent disclosed their information-gathering practices. A year later another survey revealed that gains in the protection of privacy had been made. Researchers found that 93 percent of the commercial Web-site operators collect some kind of personal information from site users, but almost 66 percent warned users that this data was being gathered.

Kids are especially vulnerable to the collection of data by Web-site operators. Of 186 World Wide Web sites geared toward children checked by the Federal Trade Commission in 1997, 86 percent collected personally identifiable data from the children without seeking parental approval. Colgate-Palmolive invites kids to submit their names, age, and e-mail address to the Colgate Tooth Fairy, according to The Seattle Times reporter O. Casey Corr. Kids are not told to check with their parents first, and few of the children understand the implications of legal statements carried by the site operator, which, if clicked on by the child, discloses that the information collected can be used for any purpose, including marketing.

55. Lewis, "Web Cookies: Trail of Crumbs."

Clandestine data gathering can go way beyond dropping cookies on hard drives. Many regular computer users were surprised when reading Special Prosecutor Kenneth Starr's report on the President Clinton–Monica Lewinsky scandal to find footnotes that revealed that information had been gathered from computer files and e-mail. In some instances the government investigators had actually retrieved files that the computer owner had deleted or erased. "Recovering files that were deleted from a computer directory is a trivial process," Joel R. Reidenberg, a professor of law at Fordham University, told New York Times reporter Peter Lewis.[56] Deleting a file only hides the file so it no longer shows up on the computer directory of files. "When a user deletes a file, the computer stops listing it in the file directory and marks the disk space as available for reuse," Lewis wrote. But as long as the hard drive has open space, the computer has no need to write over the space occupied by the deleted file. The file remains on the hard disk and is easily retrievable. Today, as hard-drive capacity commonly grows larger, the likelihood that the deleted file space will be overwritten becomes more remote. There is software that will actually erase the file, but even that solution is not 100 percent foolproof. Lewis reports that in 1997 a woman in Nevada bought a used computer at an auction and found that it contained the names, addresses, social security numbers, and prescription information for 2,000 people, including people being treated for AIDS and mental illness. The pharmacy that first owned the machine had failed to properly delete these files.

E-mail is another problem. The e-mail message passes through several exchange points on its way to the recipient, and it is possible to copy, reroute, or tamper with the message at any one of these points, Lewis noted. While federal law makes reading another person's e-mail off-limits in many cases, the law does not, for example, forbid an employer from exploring an employee's messages. In May of 1997 the American Management Association released the results of its survey of more than 900 mid-sized to large companies. More than a third of these employers admitted they recorded employee telephone calls or voice mail, checked employee computer files and e-mail, or videotaped employees as they worked. Another 37 percent said they monitor the telephone numbers their employees call.[57] Computer programs called packet filters make it possible for unauthorized snoops to conduct surveillance of e-mail. These programs permit data thieves to target all communications to a single address, invisibly making copies of targeted messages to be read later.[58]

Other privacy concerns voiced by legal experts focus on the growing amount of government data that is now online and accessible by anyone with a home computer and a modem. This information was formerly open to inspection, but those who wanted to see it had to request it in writing—giving their names and addresses—or go to the government agency and ask for it in person. Now it is obtainable electronically from the home or office. Some law enforcement officers express worries that criminals will use the data, such as driver's license records, to find people they seek to harm. In at least one instance in California, a killer used data obtained online to locate the victim he later killed. The California law has since been changed, making such data less accessible.

56. Lewis, "What's on Your Hard Drive."
57. "AMA Survey Charts Extent of Workplace Monitoring," 2 E.P.L.R. 560 (1997).
58. Markoff, "New Frontier of Eavesdropping."

Legislative Action

American business believes that intrusive information-gathering on the Internet is a problem that business can take care of through self-regulation. President Clinton and many members of Congress agree. The only government agency that argued that new laws were needed was the Federal Trade Commission. But the FTC is fighting an uphill battle. Both White House officials and Congressional leaders called a proposal by the agency in May, 2000, to increase protection of privacy on the Internet "premature," and refused to support it.[59]

There are laws that affect communication on the Internet. Nearly 15 years ago the Congress amended an existing statute that regulated wiretapping so it applied to many more kinds of electronic communication, including communication via the Internet. The Electronic Communications Privacy Act, or ECPA, has many provisions.[60] The law makes it illegal, for example, to intentionally intercept a cellular telephone conversation or disclose or air the communication with knowledge or reason to believe that the call was intercepted illegally. The law forbids the manufacturers and importers of radio scanners from making or selling scanners that can intercept communications on frequencies used for cellular telephones. Scanners that are sold should not be easily modified to enable them to intercept such communications, but most authorities agree that it is fairly easy for someone with a rudimentary training in radio electronics to make such modifications. The 1986 law also prohibits the intentional interception of online communication and outlaws such practices as keystroke monitoring, tapping a data line, and rerouting electronic communication to provide contemporaneous acquisition. It is also illegal under the ECPA to use or disclose the contents of any electronic communication if the user or discloser knew or had reason to know that the information was obtained through an illegal interception. This means it is illegal to use any device to read other users' private messages and to divulge the contents of another person's electronic mail. The online system provider cannot read the contents of users' e-mail, but the law does not apply to employers. The statute also prohibits "hacking," or gaining unauthorized access to other users' files or documents.

In 1994 Congress adopted the Drivers' License Protection Act, which barred state departments of motor vehicles from disclosing personal information about individuals that is contained in driver's license records, information including photos, names, addresses, telephone numbers, and the like. This data is used by many nongovernment entities, like the press, and many state governments do a lucrative business in selling this information to all sorts of businesses that market goods and services to drivers and automobile owners. Several states challenged the law, claiming that it violated the 10th Amendment to the U.S. Constitution because it forced state officials to perform a federal task—the protection of personal privacy. State officials said this federal mandate exceeded Congress' authority under the commerce clause and encroached on state authority. U.S. Courts of Appeals in four circuits ruled on the new law. Two said it was constitutional,[61] two said it was not.[62] In January of 2000 the Supreme Court ruled

59. Labaton, "White House and Agency."
60. See Stuckey, *Internet and Online Law.*
61. *Travis* v. *Reno,* 163 F. 3d 1000 (1998) and *Department of Public Safety* v. *United States,* 161 F. 3d 1266 (1998).
62. *Condon* v. *Reno,* 155 F. 3d 453 (1998) and *Reno* v. *Pryor,* 171 F. 3d. 1281 (1999).

unanimously that the law did not violate the 10th Amendment. The court said the statute regulated states as owners of databases containing information that is an article of interstate commerce; it did not compel states to enact any laws or commandeer their officials to assist in administering federal programs.[63]

In late 1998 Congress adopted the Children's Online Privacy Protection Act, which authorizes the Federal Trade Commission to regulate Internet sites that collect personal information from children under the age of 13. A year later the FTC issued final rules that implement the federal law, rules that went into effect in April of 2000. Site operators who collect personal information from children, including name, address, social security number, e-mail address, and telephone number, by any means (home page posting, pen pal service, electronic mail service, contest, message board, or chat room) are required to:

- provide notice of what information is being collected;
- obtain verifiable parental consent for the collection, use, or disclosure of the information;
- provide at a parent's request a description of the type of personal information collected and give the parents an opportunity to refuse the further use of the information and to obtain that information already collected about the child; and
- maintain reasonable procedures to protect the confidentiality and security of the information collected from children.

Participation in games or contests cannot be conditioned on the child disclosing more personal information than is necessary to participate in the activity. There are some exceptions to the parental consent requirement, such as instances in which the online contact information collected from a child is used to respond directly on a one-time basis. The new rules also include instructions on how Web site operators may obtain acceptable (under law) verifiable parental consent. These rules provide a kind of sliding scale for the site operators, requiring a more reliable consent before sensitive information can be gathered, and less rigorous consent rules for less sensitive information. For example, if the child wants to participate in a chat room or if the site operator wants to be able to make the information it gathers available to third parties, consent must be obtained via postal mail, fax, credit card, or tamper-resistant digital signatures. But if the information is being gathered only for use internally by the Web site, operators will be able to accept e-mail consent as long as they take steps to confirm the parent's identity through a follow-up e-mail or a telephone call. The FTC said the sliding scale rules, which took effect in April 2000, will expire in two years in favor of a more secure electronic form of consent.[64]

The collection of data via the Internet about people who use the system could in many instances qualify as an illegal intrusion. The problem, however, is that the user usually doesn't know the data has been collected. Also, because of the international nature of the Internet, while such data collection may be illegal in the United States, it might not be in another part of

---

63. *Reno* v. *Condon,* 28 M.L.R. 1281 (2000).
64. Clausing, "New Privacy Rules."

the world. Where did the intrusion take place? when the information was snatched from the user's computer, which is located in Detroit? or when it was downloaded by the site operator, who lives in Brussels, Belgium?

What happens to the data that is gathered by cookies and intercepted e-mail and other means? It is often sold or released to the public for other purposes. These problems will be explored when publication of private facts is discussed in Chapter 8.

INTRUSION AND THE PRESS

An illegal intrusion can occur in myriad ways. Eavesdropping to overhear a conversation could be an intrusion. Gathering personal information from an individual's private records could also be an intrusion. The use of a telephoto lens on a camera to photograph a subject might violate the law as well. The court will ask in every case in which an intrusion is alleged whether the subject of the intrusion "enjoyed a reasonable amount of privacy" when the information was collected. This is the key to determining whether an invasion of privacy took place. A reporter who sits at a table in a restaurant and eavesdrops on the conversation at the next table is not committing an intrusion. If other diners can hear the conversation, the speakers did not enjoy a reasonable expectation of privacy.[65] If, however, the reporter hides in a closet in the subject's office and listens to a conversation, this would be an intrusion. Two people talking in a private office have a reasonable expectation of privacy. A U.S. district court in Ohio ruled in 1997 that the user of an online service who participated in a chat room conversation and sent e-mail messages to other chat room participants could not have a reasonable expectation of privacy with regard to the content of these messages.[66]

An intrusion suit cannot be based on the recording of activities that occur in public. If what is done is visible or what is said is audible by any person who happens to be in the vicinity, there cannot be a legitimate expectation of privacy. But this legal maxim does not stop plaintiffs from suing in such circumstances.

NO PRIVACY IN PUBLIC

A pharmacist in Seattle, Wash., sued KING-TV for invasion of privacy after the television station photographed the interior of his pharmacy through the front window. The druggist had been charged with cheating the state out of Medicaid funds. He refused to talk with reporters after the charges were made, so the KING-TV camera operator placed the camera against the outside of the store's front window and photographed the druggist as he talked on the telephone. The filming was done from the exterior of the building, from a place open to the public. The court ruled that an intrusion must be something that the general public would not be free to view. In this case any passerby could have seen what was recorded on film by the KING-TV camera operator. There was no unwarranted intrusion.[67]

---

65. See *Simtel Communications* v. *National Broadcasting Company Inc.,* 84 Cal. Rptr. 2d 329 (1999).
66. *U.S.* v. *Charbonneau,* DC, S. Ohio, CR-2-97-83, 9/30/97.
67. *Marks* v. *KING Broadcasting,* 618 P. 2d 572 (1980).

American Airlines flight attendant Beverly Deteresa sued the American Broadcasting Company for secretly recording a conversation she had with ABC producer Anthony Radziwill. The plaintiff worked the flight that O.J. Simpson took to Chicago the night that Nicole Brown Simpson and Ronald Goldman were killed. Radziwill asked Deteresa to appear on television as the two talked at her front door. She declined, but Radziwill secretly taped the conversation and instructed a camera crew across the street to videotape the discussion between the producer and the flight attendant. A brief segment was later shown on ABC news. The 9th U.S. Circuit Court of Appeals affirmed a lower-court decision granting a summary judgment to the television network. The court ruled that there was no reasonable expectation of privacy when the plaintiff was talking with a journalist in plain sight of anyone who passed by on the public street.[68]

It is just as unreasonable for individuals to expect privacy in other settings where people gather. A woman sitting in a restaurant complained of intrusion after a television news crew videotaped patrons sitting in the room. The Iowa Supreme Court ruled that someone sitting in a restaurant could not have a legitimate expectation of privacy. If the patron was in a private dining room in the restaurant such an expectation may exist, but what happens in a public dining room happens in public.[69] But the courts have recognized gradations in an expectation of privacy as well. ABC sent a reporter to work as a telephone psychic at a telemarketing company. While there the reporter secretly photographed and tape-recorded conversations with several co-workers. The network was sued for intrusion, among other things. ABC argued that there was no legitimate expectation of privacy in the office setting because workers shared small, three-walled cubicles. Conversations could be heard by other employees. The California Supreme Court disagreed with the network, ruling that

> in an office or other workplace to which the general public does not have unfettered access employees may enjoy a limited, but legitimate expectation that their conversations and other interactions will not be secretly videotaped by undercover television reporters, even though their conversations may not have been completely private.[70]

One of the most controversial privacy cases of the last ten years occurred in California. A car containing four members of the Shulman family accidentally left Interstate 10, tumbled down an embankment, and came to rest upside down in a drainage ditch. Rescue apparatus arrived at the scene, including a Mercy Air helicopter with a medic and a flight nurse. Also on board was a camera operator who worked for a television production company. The photographer was accumulating footage for a television program called "On Scene: Emergency Response." Nurse Laura Carnahan was wearing a microphone that supplied the audio stream for the video. As rescue workers cut Ruth Shulman out of the car, she was comforted by Carnahan. The conversation was recorded as the photographer videotaped the rescue. Shulman was placed in the rescue helicopter, and during the flight to the hospital more video and audio material was gathered. Shulman, who ended up a paraplegic because of her injuries, sued for invasion of privacy, both intrusion and publication of private facts. The California courts dismissed the private

68. *Deteresa* v. *American Broadcasting Co. Inc.,* 121 F. 3d 460 (1997).
69. *Stressman* v. *American Blackhawk Broadcasting Co.,* 416 N.W. 2d 685 (1987).
70. *Sanders* v. *American Broadcasting Companies,* 978 P. 2d 67 (1999).

facts claim, noting that there was tremendous public interest in what happened in this case. (See pages 276–294 for an explanation of this aspect of the right of privacy.) But the California Supreme Court said a jury could certainly find a valid intrusion claim with regard to the video and audio recordings of Mrs. Shulman while she was in the rescue helicopter on the way to the hospital, and the audio recording of conversations between the flight nurse and the victim as firefighters removed Mrs. Shulman from the wrecked car.[71]

The question that can be asked in the wake of the death of Princess Diana is, Could she have sued for intrusion the pesky paparazzi who followed her everywhere? The answer is no, at least not in most of the United States. As long as what took place occurred in public places, she had no legitimate expectation of privacy. (This does not mean, however, that another kind of lawsuit might not stand in court if the photographers jeopardized the safety of the princess.) Even what happens on the deck of a private yacht in the middle of the ocean is visible to any other boater who happens to pass by. There can be no reasonable expectation of privacy in such a situation. Is there anything that a celebrity like Diana could do to chase away determined photographers? In 1973 Jacqueline Kennedy Onassis obtained an injunction from a federal court barring a particular photographer, Ron Galella, from coming within 24 feet of her and within 30 feet of her children, Caroline and John Jr. Galella had pestered the Kennedy children and their mother for years. In one instance his action caused a horse John Jr. was riding to bolt. Galella was also barred under the injunction from blocking any movements of the children or doing anything that might put them in danger or harass, alarm, or frighten them and from entering the children's play area at their school. In 1982 a U.S. district court found Galella in contempt for violating parts of the order on 12 separate occasions.[72] A similar order was recently granted to a family in Pennsylvania that was the subject of intense scrutiny by a pair of reporters from the television infotainment program, "Inside Story"[73] (see pp. 314–315). Such a carefully tailored court order can offer some protection to the celebrity who is hounded by photographers and reporters. In 1998 a California Superior Court found two free-lance photographers guilty of false imprisonment for hounding Arnold Schwarzenegger and his wife, Maria Shriver, and blocking their car as they drove their son to school. Shriver was five months pregnant when the incident occurred, and Schwarzenegger had only been out of the hospital for one week following open-heart surgery. The paparazzi were each fined $500 and sentenced to jail.[74] In the wake of these high-profile paparazzi incidents the California state legislature adopted what was popularly dubbed the anti-paparazzi law, which became effective January 1, 1999. The law creates tort liability for "physical" and "constructive" invasions of privacy through photographing, videotaping, or recording a person engaging in a "personal or familial activity."[75] While many of the activities prohibited by the new law were already prohibited by other California laws (trespass, for example), the penalties for these

---

71. *Shulman* v. *Group W. Productions Inc.,* 955 P. 2d 469 (1998).
72. *Gallela* v. *Onassis,* 487 F. 2d 986 (1973), 533 F. Supp. 1076 (1982).
73. *Wolfson* v. *Lewis,* 924 F. Supp. 1413 (1996).
74. Weinraub, "2 Paparazzi Convicted."
75. California Civil Code, Section 1708.8.

actions were substantially stiffened. Critics of the law said it could hinder legitimate news gathering activities as well as block intrusions by the paparazzi. In the end, the law of privacy offers little protection to the rich and famous who travel each day on the public highways and become the focus of photographers and reporters who feed the seemingly insatiable American appetite for information about and photographs of celebrities.

THE USE OF HIDDEN RECORDING DEVICES

The miniaturization of video and audio equipment has made it possible for anyone, including reporters, to secretly record conversations, confrontations, meetings, and other happenings. Please note that such secret video and audio recording is outlawed in some states. (See page 317 for a discussion of this problem.) But if it is not prohibited by the state, can it nevertheless constitute an intrusion, an invasion of privacy? It is not easy to answer this question definitively.

In 1971 a U.S. court of appeals in California ruled that such surreptitious recording could constitute an illegal intrusion. The case was an odd one. Two reporters for Life magazine agreed to cooperate with Los Angeles police who sought to arrest a man who was practicing medicine without a license. Posing as man and wife, the pair went to the "doctor's" home where he conducted his practice. While A.A. Dietemann examined the woman, the man secretly photographed the procedure. At the same time the conversation was secretly recorded. Police arrested Dietemann several weeks later, and following his apprehension the magazine published a story with a transcript of the recorded conversation and some of the photos taken in his home. The appellate court sustained his suit for intrusion, ruling that a homeowner should not "be required to take the risk that what is heard or seen [in his or her home] will be transmitted by photography or recording . . . to the public at large."[76] Other courts have not followed this precedent, although none of the subsequent cases involved recording or photography in a private home.

For example, in 1975 Arlyn Cassidy and several other Chicago police officers were acting as undercover agents, investigating massage parlors in the city. The owner of one massage parlor where police previously had made arrests believed he was being harassed by the officers and invited a television news camera crew to come in and secretly film an encounter between an undercover agent and a model at the parlor. The camera was set up behind a two-way mirror and was filming when officer Cassidy came in, paid $30 for deluxe lingerie modeling, and subsequently arrested the girl for solicitation. Three other agents came into the room at about the same time the television news crew burst through another door, filming as they left the building. The officers sued the station for intrusion, using the *Dietemann* case as precedent.

But an Illinois appellate court ruled in favor of the journalists, distinguishing the *Dietemann* case in some important ways. First, Cassidy and the other plaintiffs were public officers acting in the line of duty as the filming took place. Second, the film crew was not in a private home but in a public business. And third, the crew was on hand at the invitation of the operator

76. *Dietemann v. Time, Inc.,* 499 F. 2d 245 (1971).

269

of the premises. "In our opinion," the court ruled, "no right of privacy against intrusion can be said to exist with reference to the gathering and dissemination of news concerning discharge of public duties."[77]

A Kentucky circuit court ruled that it was not an intrusion when a young woman, at the instigation of a newspaper, secretly recorded a conversation she had with an attorney in the attorney's office. After the newspaper published a transcript of the conversation, during which attorney John T. McCall proposed an unethical fee arrangement with the woman, the lawyer sued for intrusion. Again, the court distinguished *Dietemann,* noting that the woman was in McCall's office at his invitation. "A lawyer, an officer of the court, discussing a public court with a potential client, is not in seclusion within the meaning of the law," the court ruled.[78] A Kentucky appellate court subsequently upheld this ruling.[79]

Finally, a U.S. district court in Illinois in 1994 rejected an intrusion claim made against ABC News after it had secretly photographed and recorded eye examinations at an ophthalmic clinic. The owners of the clinic sued. The court ruled that the plaintiffs in the case had alleged no damage from the recording, other than that it had been broadcast. The court also rejected the claim that the recording violated the doctor-patient privilege. That privilege, the court said, belongs to the patient, not the doctor. If the doctor had filmed the examination, it would have been a violation of this privilege and likely an intrusion. But when the patients authorized the recording (they were working for the network), no legal wrong occurred.

The 5th U.S. Circuit Court of Appeals upheld this ruling in early 1995. The appellate court specifically rejected the plaintiff's arguments that the 1971 *Dietemann* ruling should control in this situation. The court said Dietemann was operating out of his home, not a public place of business like the ophthalmic clinic. And Dietemann did no advertising whereas the eye clinic actively solicited the public to visit the facility.[80] Cases like those cited here have chipped away at the substance of the *Dietemann* ruling.

The use of hidden cameras or concealed microphones generates controversy among journalists as well as among the public. In some states (see pages 317–319), laws regulate the use of these reporting tactics. But whether such reporting techniques are illegal or not, they are regarded by many people as sneaky, intrusive, and unethical. A journalist who uses such means without careful consideration of the alternatives risks undermining the public trust in his or her work and in the craft in general. In 1992 the Society of Professional Journalists and the Poynter Institute for Media Studies drafted guidelines for the use of hidden cameras. These guidelines, outlined in the *American Journalism Review,*[81] state that hidden cameras should be used only

- when the information is of profound importance;
- when all other alternatives for obtaining the same information have been exhausted;

"A lawyer, an officer of the court, discussing a public court with a potential client, is not in seclusion within the meaning of the law."

77. *Cassidy* v. *ABC,* 377 N.E. 2d 126 (1978).
78. *McCall* v. *Courier-Journal,* 4 M.L.R. 2337 (1979).
79. *McCall* v. *Courier-Journal,* 6 M.L.R. 1112 (1980).
80. *Desnick* v. *Capital Cities/ABC, Inc.,* 851 F. Supp. 303 (1994), aff'd. *Desnick* v. *American Broadcasting Companies, Inc.,* 44 F. 3d 1345 (1995).
81. Lissit, "Gotcha," 17.

■ when the individuals involved and their news organizations apply—through outstanding quality of work as well as the commitment of time and funding—the excellence needed to pursue the story fully;

■ when the harm prevented by the information revealed through deception outweighs any harm caused by the act of deception;

■ when the journalists involved have conducted a meaningful, collaborative, and deliberative decision to justify deception.

The guidelines say that winning a prize, beating the competition, getting a story cheaply, doing it because others have done it, or doing it because the subjects of the story are unethical are not sufficient reasons to justify the use of hidden cameras.

INTRUSION AND THE PUBLICATION OF INFORMATION OBTAINED ILLEGALLY

It is unlikely that a plaintiff can successfully sue a newspaper or broadcasting station for intrusion if the news medium publishes or broadcasts information obtained from an illegal intrusion by a third party not connected with the mass medium. At least three appellate court rulings suggest that the press is not liable in such instances. In the 1960s the late newspaper columnist Drew Pearson obtained documents from private files of the Liberty Lobby, a right-wing political group in Washington, and from the files of former Connecticut senator Thomas Dodd. Employees of both Dodd and Liberty Lobby took the files from the private offices, made copies of them (which were given to Pearson), and then returned the purloined files. In both cases the court ruled that the publishers could not be held responsible for the actions of the intruders.[82]

Judge J. Skelly Wright wrote in the *Dodd* case:

> If we were to hold appellants liable for invasion of privacy on these facts, we would establish the proposition that one who receives information from an intruder, knowing it has been obtained by improper intrusion, is guilty of a tort. In an untried and developing area of tort law, we are not prepared to go so far.[83]

This principle was supported in 1978 by a Maryland circuit court when several former and current members of the University of Maryland basketball team sued the Washington Evening Star for publishing an article that revealed portions of their academic records. Somebody gave the newspaper the information. There was no evidence presented that the reporters had either personally inspected the records or asked someone else to do it. Consequently, no suit could be maintained by the athletes on the intrusion theory.[84]

But these three decisions don't really answer all the important questions. First, the plaintiffs brought their actions under the intrusion tort. Other older and more exotic tort laws exist that might be used as the basis for a successful lawsuit. (Something called conversion

---

82. *Liberty Lobby* v. *Pearson,* 390 F. 2d 489 (1968) and *Pearson* v. *Dodd,* 410 F. 2d 701 (1969).
83. *Pearson* v. *Dodd,* 410 F. 2d 701 (1969).
84. *Bilney* v. *Evening Star,* 406 A 2d (1979).

and trover is one of these laws.) Next, the cases noted here surely do not insulate the journalists from legal action if they make the actual intrusion or steal documents or files. And, if the journalists are given actual documents as opposed to photocopies of documents, it is conceivable that they might be charged with possession of stolen property. Finally, as noted previously, the Electronic Communications Privacy Act makes it illegal to knowingly use the contents of any electronic communication if the user knew or should have known that the information was gained through an illegal interception. This statute has not been applied to news reporters—yet. Investigative reporters and other journalists who depend on information gained in illegal ways operate in a murky legal environment. The ethical environment is an even more dismal swamp. Perhaps the most important thing for the journalist to remember is that the public good that might accrue from publishing or broadcasting important stories founded on illegally obtained information will rarely protect the reporter from the legal consequences of breaking the law to get this information (see pages 310–320).

SUMMARY

Intruding on an individual's solitude, or intrusion, is an invasion of privacy. The legal wrong occurs as soon as the information about the individual is illegally collected. Subsequent publication of the material is not required. To establish an intrusion the plaintiff must demonstrate that he or she enjoyed a reasonable expectation of privacy when the information was collected by the defendant. One of the most serious legal problems associated with the Internet is the unauthorized collection of data about Net users. Such intrusions are usually hard to detect, and the Congress has made only limited headway in generating laws or other means to protect Internet users from this kind of invasion of privacy. The general rule is that there can be no privacy in a public place. What happens on the streets, in public places, in open view, are not situations in which a person enjoys a reasonable expectation of privacy. Contrary rulings exist on whether the use of hidden cameras and microphones constitutes an intrusion. Some plaintiffs try to sue for other kinds of legal wrongs instead of invasion of privacy in these cases. The publication or broadcast of information obtained through an intrusion by a third party, not associated with the publisher or broadcaster, is generally not regarded as a violation of the law.

BIBLIOGRAPHY

"Abdul Serves Lawsuit to Diet Promoter." *The Seattle Post-Intelligence,* 16 June 1999, A3.

Bernstein, Nina. "Proposals to Protect Privacy Seem to Face Stalemate on Contradictory Goals." *The New York Times,* 20 October 1997, A12.

Blanck, Katherine. "Restricting the Use of Sound-Alikes in Commercial Speech by Amending the Right of Publicity Statute in California." *San Diego Law Review* 26 (1989):911.

Bloom, Seth. "Preventing the Misappropriation of Identity: Beyond the 'Right of Publicity.'" *Hastings Comm/Ent. Law Journal* 13 (1991):489.

Brooks, Brian. *Journalism in the Information Age.* Boston: Allyn and Bacon, 1997.

Chambers, Marcia. "Lawsuit Pits Artists' Rights vs. Athletes'." *The New York Times,* 16 February 1999, C19.

———. "New Privacy Rules for Children's Web Sites." *The New York Times,* 21 October 1999, D11.

Corr, O. Casey. "Cybersnoops on the Loose." *The Seattle Times,* 10 August 1997, B5.

Davis, Melissa. "Voicing Concerns: An Overview of the Current Law Protecting Singers' Voices." *Syracuse Law Review* 40 (1989):1255.

Fixmer, Rob. "New Way to Travel the Web while Leaving Fewer Footprints." *The New York Times,* 16 August 1999, C5.

Kuczynski, Alex. "Dustin Hoffman Wins Suit on Photo Alteration." *The New York Times,* 23 January 1999, A30.

Labaton, Stephen. "White House and Agency Split on Internet Privacy." *The New York Times,* 23 May 2000, C–1.

Levine, Marla E. "The Right of Publicity as a Means of Protecting Performers' Style." *Loyola of Los Angeles Law Review* 14 (1980):129.

Lewis, Peter. "Web Cookies: Trail of Crumbs." *The Seattle Times,* 9 August 1998, C1.

———. "What's on Your Hard Drive." *The New York Times,* 8 October 1998, D1.

Lissit, Robert. "Gotcha." *American Journalism Review,* March 1995, 17.

Lohr, Steve. "Industry Group to Offer Standards for Privacy on Internet." *The New York Times,* 26 May 1997, C3.

Markoff, John. "At the New Frontier of Eavesdropping." *The New York Times,* 19 January 1997, B5.

Pember, Don R. "The Burgeoning Scope of Access Privacy and the Portent for a Free Press." *Iowa Law Review* 64 (1979):1155.

Pember, Don R. *Privacy and the Press.* Seattle: University of Washington Press, 1972.

Pember, Don R., and Dwight L. Teeter. "Privacy and the Press Since *Time* v. *Hill.*" *Washington Law Review* 50 (1974):57.

Prosser, William L. "Privacy." *California Law Review* 48 (1960):383.

Queary, Paul. "Mother Denied Say over Baby's Photo." *The Seattle Times,* 19 January 1997, A8.

Rubiner, Michael. "Style Is One Thing, Defining It Is Another." *The New York Times,* 5 July 1992.

Sanford, Bruce W. *Libel and Privacy,* 2d ed. Englewood Cliffs, N.J.: Prentice-Hall Law & Business, 1993.

Sims, Andrew B. "Right of Publicity: Survivability Reconsidered." *Fordham Law Review* 49 (1981):453.

Stuckey, Kent. *Internet and Online Law.* New York: Law Journal Seminars-Press, 1996.

Warren, Samuel D., and Louis D. Brandeis. "The Right to Privacy." *Harvard Law Review* 4 (1890):220.

Weber, Bruce. "High-Tech Film Casting: Death Is No Drawback." *The New York Times,* 11 March 1994, B15.

Weinraub, Bernard. "2 Paparazzi Convicted of Stalking Celebrities." *The New York Times,* 4 February 1998, A36.

Zimmerman, Kevin. "Singers May Say 'No,' But the Sound Remains the Same." *Variety,* 10 January 1990, 1.

Invasion of Privacy
Publication of Private Information and False Light

Giving publicity to private facts about someone's life is what provoked legal scholars Samuel D. Warren and Louis D. Brandeis to propose in 1890 that the law should protect an individual's right to privacy. Some label this gossipmongering, others describe it as legitimate journalism. Whatever it is called, it has become the stock-in-trade of a growing number of American periodicals and television programs. And the law, as you will see in the next section of this text, has been largely ineffective in stopping it. We also explore in this chapter the strangest of the privacy torts, false light invasion of privacy.

PUBLICITY ABOUT PRIVATE FACTS

It is illegal to publicize private information about a person if the matter that is publicized

   a. would be highly offensive to a reasonable person, and
   b. is not of legitimate public concern or interest.

"Keyhole journalism" is what critics in the late 19th century called it. The snooping, prying, gossipy, scandal-driven reporting that many of us today have come to take for granted in both the print and electronic media was just emerging at the end of the last century. A lot of people believed it was offensive and should be stopped. Attorneys Samuel Warren and Louis Brandeis even proposed a legal solution, a right of privacy, enforceable in a court of law.[1] But American courts have been less than enthusiastic in their support for such ideas. Of all the four tort actions encompassed by the right to privacy, this one, giving publicity to private facts, has gained the least acceptance from the judiciary. The courts in at least 11 states have not yet recognized or have refused to recognize this tort.[*] The North Carolina Supreme Court, in refusing to recognize the tort action, called it "constitutionally suspect."[2] What makes this tort "constitutionally suspect" in the eyes of many judges and legal scholars is that it punishes the press, or whomever, for publishing truthful information that has been legally obtained. Making the press liable in such instances seems to run against basic American First Amendment tenets and a substantial body of case law. So although the courts in about 80 percent of U.S. jurisdictions are willing to hear arguments in such a case, plaintiffs rarely win these arguments. More than one legal scholar has argued that few would suffer if this entire tort area of privacy simply disappeared. University of Chicago law professor Harry Kalven wrote more than 30 years ago that the size and strength of the defenses in a private facts lawsuit raise the question of whether it is a viable tort remedy. "The mountain, I suggest, has brought forth a pretty small mouse," he said.[3]

But the courts and legal scholars may be out of step with public opinion on this question. Many persons outside journalism and the law exhibit strong feelings that the press goes too far in prying into the lives of both those in public life and others who happen to become newsworthy momentarily because of a tragedy or some other event. For example, the vast majority of persons who responded to a 1990 survey conducted by researchers at Middle Tennessee State University said they believed the press deserves less than full protection from lawsuits when journalists delve into the past lives of public figures or report about the sexual activities of persons in the public eye. This area may be one of those in which journalists need to ask some tough questions of themselves before pushing the law to its outer limits. What is legal may not always be what is right, either on an ethical/moral scale or in the eyes of readers and viewers. There are times when it is absolutely essential for the journalist to have the protection to publish

But the courts and legal scholars may be out of step with public opinion on this question.

1. Warren and Brandeis, "The Right to Privacy," 220.
2. *Hall* v. *Post,* 15 M.L.R. 2329 (1988).
3. Kalven, "Privacy in Tort Law," 326.

[*]Alaska, Hawaii, Illinois, Indiana, Minnesota, Nebraska, Virginia, Montana, North Carolina, North Dakota, and Utah.

what many would regard as offensive and embarrassing private information. But the routine publication of this kind of information may someday seriously dilute this valuable protection.

It is easiest to understand this aspect of the law by taking the tort apart and looking at each element separately (see boxed text). The plaintiff in a private-facts case carries the burden of proving each element. Failure to convince the court of any one of these three parts of the law means the lawsuit is doomed.

PUBLICITY TO PRIVATE FACTS

1. There must be publicity to private facts about an individual.
2. The revelation of this material must be offensive to a reasonable person.
3. The material is not of legitimate public concern.

PUBLICITY

The words "publicity" and "publication" mean different things in privacy law than they do in libel law. In defamation, "publication" means to communicate the material to a single third party. The word "publicity" in privacy law implies far more. It means that the material is communicated to the public at large or to a great number of people, making it certain that the facts will shortly become public knowledge. This kind of publicity can usually be presumed when a story is published in a newspaper or broadcast over radio and television.

PRIVATE FACTS

Before an invasion of privacy suit can be successful, the plaintiff must demonstrate that the material publicized was indeed private. What happens in public is considered public information. A fan at a Pittsburgh Steelers football game urged a news photographer to take his picture. The photographer did, but when the photograph was published in Sports Illustrated, the fan sued for invasion of privacy, arguing that the photograph revealed that his trousers were unzipped, which was quite embarrassing. The District Court for Eastern Pennsylvania ruled against the plaintiff, primarily because the picture was taken in a public place with the plaintiff's knowledge and encouragement. It was not private information.[4] A Massachusetts court of appeals ruled that no privacy exists when a person is standing in a line at a government building. The plaintiff in the case was photographed while standing in a line of persons waiting to collect unemployment benefits at the state employment security office. "The appearance of a person in a public place necessarily involves doffing the cloak of privacy which the law protects," the court ruled.[5]

---

4. *Neff* v. *Time,* 406 F. Supp. 858 (1976).
5. *Cefalu* v. *Globe Newspaper,* 391 N.E. 2d 935 (1979). See also *Arrington* v. *New York Times,* 55 N.Y.S. 2d 433 (1982).

A U.S. district court in Ohio ruled that a video showing a man arrested by Cleveland police being taken from his home in handcuffs publicized a public event, not a private one, since the activity took place outside the house.[6] Another U.S. district court ruled that the publication in Penthouse magazine of pictures of celebrities Tommy Lee and Pamela Anderson Lee, showing them on their honeymoon in various states of undress, "sexually touching," would not support a private facts case since the photos had been previously published in other magazines. The scenes were no longer private when Penthouse published the pictures.[7]

If a large segment of the public is already aware of supposedly intimate or personal information, it is not private. Oliver Sipple, who deflected a gun held by a woman who tried to assassinate President Gerald Ford, sued the San Francisco Chronicle after a columnist noted that Sipple was a homosexual and that that may be the reason Ford had never thanked his benefactor for his heroic act. But Sipple's suit failed, in part at least, because his sexual orientation was hardly a secret in San Francisco. A California court of appeals noted that Sipple routinely frequented gay bars, marched in parades with other homosexuals, and openly worked for the election of homosexual political candidates, and that many gay publications had reported stories about his activities in the homosexual community. That he was a homosexual was not a private fact, the court ruled.[8]

A court in Massachusetts ruled that because the plaintiff in a privacy action had told three other persons about some embarrassing personal information, the information was not a private fact for purpose of an invasion of privacy lawsuit.[9]

Information that is contained in public records—documents that are open to public inspection—is not private. Even though this information may not have been previously publicized, its republication in a newspaper or magazine will not sustain a publication of private facts suit.[10] But one has to be careful, especially when dealing with health records. What seems to be a public record may not be. New York City was sued by an individual who complained to the City Commission on Human Rights that he had been discriminated against by his employer because he was infected with the AIDS virus. The commission arranged an agreement between the employer and the man, and then distributed a press release outlining the settlement. The plaintiff was not identified, but he alleged that there were sufficient details in the release that made him readily identifiable to persons who knew him or worked with him. The city maintained that when the man filed a complaint, he put his name on a public record. But Human Rights Commission staffers failed to realize that part of the arranged settlement included an agreement that the complainant would not be identified. The city code regarding such a conciliation agreement specifically states that the information shall be made public, *unless the complainant and the commission determine that disclosure is not required.* The 2nd U.S. Circuit Court of Appeals ruled that the plaintiff's medical status did not automatically become a public record when he filed his complaint.[11]

6. *Reeves* v. *Fox Television Network,* 25 M.L.R. 2104 (1997).
7. *Lee* v. *Penthouse International Ltd.,* 25 M.L.R. 1651 (1997).
8. *Sipple* v. *Chronicle Publishing Co.,* 154 Cal. App. 3d 1040 (1984).
9. *Peckham* v. *Levy,* 26 M.L.R. 1222 (1997).
10. *Langford* v. *Vanderbilt University,* 199 Tenn. 389 (1956).
11. *Doe* v. *New York,* 15 F. 3d 275 (1994).

Naming Rape Victims

There is, perhaps, no more difficult problem in privacy law today than whether the name of a rape victim can or should be published. The victim's name is frequently part of a public police file, the public information or indictment filed against the defendant, or a court record and hence, under the law, not really private information. A determined reporter can generally discover the name of a victim that is not included in the public record. Younger people tend to think that this has become an issue in the 1980s and 1990s because the popularity of tabloid journalism has pushed the press to abandon long-standing policies that protected the privacy of rape victims. Nothing could be further from the truth. Forty-five years ago most publications and broadcasting stations routinely identified rape victims. And few editors had any second thoughts about it. It was only recently, at least partially the result of the growth of the women's movement, that such routine identification was challenged. Today no more than 5 or 10 percent of all newspapers and even fewer broadcasting stations routinely identify the victims of sexual assault.[12]

Those who oppose the identification of rape victims in the press raise three arguments:

- Someone who is sexually assaulted is victimized three times: the first during the assault, the second during interrogation by often unsympathetic police and during public trial testimony and cross-examination, and the third by knowing that friends, neighbors, co-workers and others are aware of the rape because of the publicity.
- Society often judges the rape victim to be as guilty as the rapist. This attitude can stigmatize the victim for many years.
- Because of the two factors outlined above, victims who realize that their identities will be revealed frequently fail to report the crime, especially if the rape has been committed by an acquaintance. The rapist is not punished and is likely to attack another victim.

Few persons will deny the validity of these arguments. A handful of journalists believe that it is important for society to know the names of all crime victims, that names add credibility to news stories, and they publish these names regardless of the consequences. Other journalists, however, while accepting the logic of the arguments against publication, still assert that the identity should be made public. Some argue that to treat victims of rape differently from victims of a burglary or other crimes in which the victim's name is routinely reported insinuates that being raped is such a disgrace that the victim's name must be concealed, which reinforces the myth that rape victims are "damaged goods." "Now is the time for us to understand that keeping the hunted under wraps merely establishes her as an outcast and implies that her chances for normal social relations are doomed forevermore," said Karen DeCrow, former president of the National Organization for Women. "Pull off the veil of shame. Print the name," she added. Geneva Overholser, former editor of the Des Moines Register, argues that by not printing the name, the press is reinforcing the idea that rape is a different kind of attack,

---

12. Marcus and McMahon, "Limiting Disclosure," 1019.

not a crime of brutal violence. She said that this "sour blight of prejudice is best subjected to strong sunlight."[13] Some newspapers are trying to reach a compromise on this matter by not printing the victim's name unless she or he consents to the use. Victims who fear the publicity are protected; using the names of those who don't mind undermines the myth noted by Karen DeCrow.

Most social and political issues in the United States end up in court, and this one is no different. Judges have been asked to decide whether the press has a legal right to publish the name of a victim of a sexual assault or whether this is an invasion of privacy. Four states, Florida, Georgia, South Carolina, and Wisconsin, adopted statutes early in the century that prohibited the press from identifying the victim of a rape. Among other provisions, these laws gave victims a right to sue for invasion of privacy if their name was revealed. The statutes in both Wisconsin[14] and South Carolina[15] were tested and courts ruled that the laws did not infringe on freedom of the press. The Supreme Court of the United States first became involved in the issue in the mid-1970s. A reporter for an Atlanta, Ga., television station, in violation of station policy, broadcast the name of a young woman who had been raped and murdered. He had obtained the name from public court documents. The parents sued, using the Georgia rape victim identification law as the basis for the legal action. Georgia courts supported the privacy claim, but in 1975, in the case of *Cox Broadcasting Co. v. Cohn,* the U.S. Supreme Court overturned the decision. The high court ruled that the press cannot be held liable for invasion of privacy for reporting information that was already part of a public record. Justice Byron White noted that most persons depend on the mass media for information about the operation of government. The press gathers this information at public meetings and from the public record. Judicial proceedings are an important part of our governmental system and are something in which the public has always expressed a great interest. By making judicial records and proceedings public, the state of Georgia must have concluded that the public interest was being served:

> We are reluctant to embark on a course that would make public records generally available to the media but forbid their publication if offensive to the sensibilities of the supposed reasonable man. Such a rule would make it very difficult for the press to inform their readers about the public business and yet stay within the law. The rule would invite timidity and self-censorship and very likely lead to the suppression of many items that would otherwise be put into print and that should be made available to the public.[16]

Quoting the "Restatement of Torts," which attempts to summarize the law of torts, the court said, "There is no liability when the defendant merely gives further publicity to information about the plaintiff which is already public. Thus there is no liability for giving publicity to facts about the plaintiff's life which are matters of public record."

Judges have been asked to decide whether the press has a legal right to publish the name of a victim of a sexual assault or whether this is an invasion of privacy.

13. Marcus and McMahon, "Limiting Disclosure," 1019.
14. *State* v. *Evjue,* 253 Wis. 146 (1948).
15. *Nappier* v. *Jefferson Standard Life Insurance Co.,* 322 F. 2d 502 (1963).
16. *Cox Broadcasting Co.* v. *Cohn,* 420 U.S. 469 (1975).

But the 1975 ruling did not completely resolve the issue. The high court was confronted with a somewhat different case 14 years later. The Florida Star, a weekly newspaper in Jacksonville, mistakenly published the name of the victim of a sexual assault. Such publication was against the newspaper's own policy and in violation of a state policy that deemed that such records were not to be made public. Law enforcement officers inadvertently gave the record to a new reporter, and it was included in the weekly outline of police activity published by the newspaper. The privacy suit was based on a Florida law that made it illegal to "print, publish, or broadcast . . . in any instrument of mass communication" the name of the victim of a rape. Justice Thurgood Marshall, writing for the six-person majority, said the newspaper could not be held liable in this case. It had published accurate information that it had lawfully obtained, information contained in public records. The plaintiff argued that the police reports that were mistakenly given to the reporter were not public records. Marshall said that this fact was immaterial. "The fact that state officials are not required to disclose such reports does not make it unlawful for a newspaper to receive them when furnished by the government," Marshall wrote. But the jurist stressed that the court's ruling was not without limits.

> Our holding today is limited. We do not hold that truthful publication is automatically constitutionally protected, or that there is no zone of personal privacy within which the state may protect the individual from intrusion by the press, or even that a State may never punish publication of the name of a victim of a sexual offense. . . . We hold only that where a newspaper publishes truthful information which it has lawfully obtained, punishment may be imposed, if at all, only when narrowly tailored to a state interest of the highest order.[17]

The issue in Florida continued to play itself out two years later when the national tabloid newspaper The Globe and other print and broadcast media revealed the name of the young woman who claimed she was raped by William Kennedy Smith at the Kennedy estate in Palm Beach. Smith was acquitted of the charges, but Florida prosecuted The Globe under the statute just cited. In August of 1993, a Florida district court of appeals ruled that the state statute was unconstitutional. In an attempt to respond to Justice Marshall's instruction in the earlier Florida Star decision, the state of Florida argued that the statute was justified because the state had a high interest in protecting the identity of rape victims. State attorneys cited many of the same arguments previously noted on page 279 to support their contention that the victim's name should not be revealed. The court of appeals was apparently unimpressed. "The fact that forty-six states are able to conduct sexual assault investigations and trials without punishing the press criminally for disclosure of the victim's identity is, in itself, a circumstance which leads this court to conclude that the state's expressed concerns about a victim's safety and privacy are somewhat exaggerated and overblown," the court said.[18]

The debate on this issue goes on. And courts continue to be asked to rule in cases with circumstances different from those decided earlier. For example, the Georgia Supreme Court overturned a $100,000 damage award against a newspaper that had published the name of a woman

---

17. *Florida Star* v. *B.J.F.,* 109 S. Ct. 2603 (1989).
18. *Florida* v. *Globe Communications Corp.,* 622 So. 2d 1066 (1993), aff'd. by Florida Supreme Court, 648 So. 2d 110 (1994).

who had shot and killed an intruder in her home.[19] When Nancy Tatum shot and killed Shedrick Hill Jr., he had exposed himself and was approaching her with a knife in his hand. Police ruled that Tatum acted in self-defense and gave her name to the press only after a reporter promised not to use it. Officials said they were treating the case as a sexual assault and, as noted previously, Georgia has a statute aimed at protecting the identity of a victim of sexual assault.

The newspaper used the victim's name, but did not report that a rape or an assault with intent to commit rape had occurred. In one story the paper recounted that the assailant had his pants unzipped when he was shot; a second story recalled that there was an attempted rape in the same neighborhood several years earlier. The Georgia Court of Appeals affirmed a jury verdict in favor of the plaintiff, rejecting the argument that the U.S. Supreme Court decision in *Florida Star* v. *B.J.F.*[20] was controlling. In that case, the Georgia appellate court said, the state was attempting to sanction the press for identifying a rape victim. This case was a common-law privacy action brought by the injured party.[21] The Georgia Supreme Court rejected that rationale and ruled that the Florida Star ruling did control the outcome. The court said the newspaper merely published information about a matter of public importance, information it had obtained legally. The court acknowledged that the state did have an interest in protecting the identity of rape victims. But, the court added, "When she shot Hill, Tatum became the object of legitimate public interest and the newspaper had the right under the Federal and State Constitutions to accurately report the facts regarding the incident, including her name."[22]

Finally, the Texas Supreme Court ruled in 1995 that a newspaper that had revealed extensive personal details about the victim of a rape, including her age, the fact that she owned a private business and the address of that business, the make and model of her car, and her home address (which was the site of the attack), was not guilty of an invasion of privacy. The reporter had obtained this information from the police, information that the plaintiff contended revealed her identity to those who knew her. The court did not dispute this contention, but ruled that it could not hold the newspaper to the task of deciding which identifying details are safe to publish and which are not. "To require the media to sort through an inventory of facts, to deliberate and catalogue each of them according to their individual and cumulative impact under all circumstances, would impose an impossible task, a task which could cause critical information of legitimate public interest to be withheld until it becomes untimely and worthless to an informed public."[23]

OFFENSIVE MATERIAL

If the determination has been made that private facts about a person's life have been published, a court must then ask two subsequent questions:

1. Would the publication of the material offend a reasonable person?
2. Was the published material of legitimate public concern?

19. *Macon Telegraph Publishing Co.* v. *Tatum,* 436 S.E. 2d 655 (1993).
20. 109 S. Ct. 2603 (1989).
21. *Macon Telegraph Publishing Co.* v. *Tatum,* 430 S.E. 2d 18 (1993).
22. *Macon Telegraph Publishing Co.* v. *Tatum,* 436 S.E. 2d 655 (1993).
23. *Star-Telegram Inc.* v. *Doe,* 23 M.L.R. 2492 (1995).

Frequently, courts are faced with the real dilemma that while revelation of the material was extremely offensive and embarrassing, its publication was of great importance for the public. Except in extremely unusual circumstances, the press will win such decisions. The judiciary places great weight on the role of the press as an agent to inform and enlighten the public on matters of interest and importance. Judges have ruled time and again that it is the responsibility of the press to bring such "newsworthy" information to the people. And courts have been hesitant to define narrow limits on what the public needs to know or on the kinds of information in which the people have a genuine interest. And remember, the publication of the material must be offensive to a reasonable person. The feelings of a hypersensitive person or someone who is especially sensitive do not count. Peggy Jo Fry sued the Ionia (Mich.) Sentinel-Standard for invasion of privacy when it reported that her husband and another woman had died in a fire that destroyed a cottage near Lake Michigan. The story mentioned that Ted Fry had been seen with Rita Hill at a tavern prior to the fire and related details about Fry's wife and children. The court ruled that these details were simply not highly offensive to a reasonable person.[24] Another Michigan woman sued Knight-Ridder Newspapers after the Miami Herald published a story about the murder of her daughter. The plaintiff in the case was mentioned incidentally in the story. It was noted that four of her six children were deaf and that she was a hardworking woman who had great faith in her daughter's ability to succeed in life. The court said such information is not offensive.[25]

The judiciary places great weight on the role of the press as an agent to inform and enlighten the public on matters of interest and importance.

It has been previously noted that the law strongly favors the defendant in this tort area. Judges will often bend over backward to support the right of the press to publish truthful private information. But once in a while a reporter or editor or broadcaster will do something that the court thinks is so stupid or so outrageous that the judge is compelled to throw up his or her hands in despair and find for the plaintiff. The following three cases do not accurately represent the true nature of the private facts tort, but demonstrate how insensitive journalistic conduct sometimes pushes a court to rule in behalf of the plaintiff, in spite of the law.

Many years ago a woman with a rather unusual disorder—she ate constantly, but still lost weight—was admitted to a hospital. Journalists were tipped off and descended on her room, pushed past the closed door, and took pictures against the patient's will. Time magazine ran a story about the patient, Dorothy Barber, and in it referred to her, in inimitable Time style, as "the starving glutton." Mrs. Barber sued and won her case. The judge said the hospital is one place people should be able to go for privacy.[26] More than the patient's expectation of privacy in a hospital room influenced the ruling, because there are several decisions in which persons in hospitals have been considered to be the subject of legitimate concern and did not therefore enjoy the right to privacy. The story about the unusual disorder was surely offensive, almost mocking. The disorder was not contagious, and the implications for the general public were minimal. The Time story seemed to focus on Mrs. Barber almost as if she were a freak, and in doing so the revelation of this information was highly offensive to any reasonable person.

24. *Fry v. Ionia Sentinel-Standard,* 300 N.W. 2d 687 (1980).
25. *Andren v. Knight-Ridder Newspapers,* 10 M.L.R. 2109 (1984).
26. *Barber v. Time,* 159 S.W. 2d 291 (1942).

A Georgia housewife took her two sons to the county fair and finally succumbed to their pressure to be taken through the fun house. As she left the building, an air jet blew Mrs. Flora Bell Graham's dress up over her head, and she was exposed from the waist down except for her underclothing. As fate would have it, a local photographer was nearby and captured the moment on film. The picture was featured in the Sunday edition of the local newspaper as a publicity piece for the fair. Mrs. Graham sued. By logical legal analysis one could suggest that she should not have won. Many people saw her. It was a public occurrence. She could not be readily identified in the picture because her dress was over her head. However, persons who knew the children, who were also in the picture, could make the connection between mother and children. Mrs. Graham did win.[27] She had suffered an immense amount of embarrassment from the most intimate kind of revelation, and the public value of the photograph was extremely low.

Finally, the South Carolina Supreme Court affirmed a jury verdict against a newspaper that, in publishing a story about teenage pregnancies, had identified a young man—a minor—as the father of an illegitimate child. The teenage mother of the baby had given the reporter the father's name. The reporter talked to the young man, who understood that the newspaper was doing a survey on teenage pregnancy. He said he was never told that his name might be used in the story. The newspaper argued that the information—including the boy's name—was of great public interest. The state supreme court said that was a jury question, and a jury ruled it was not of great public interest.[28]

LEGITIMATE PUBLIC CONCERN

While the cases just cited do not stand alone, they are unusual. Far more often courts rule that public concern over the issues involved outweighs any embarrassment to plaintiffs. Several factors have been cited in weighing the public concern or interest in a particular matter.

In determining whether something is of public concern, courts have focused on such factors as what the story is about, whom the story is about, when the incidents described in the story took place, and sometimes where they took place. Factual stories, reports, or broadcasts that have great public interest have generally been protected in invasion-of-privacy suits. The courts have been quite liberal in defining public interest, not as something people should read about but as something they do read about, something in which people are interested.

A 12-year-old girl who gave birth to a baby,[29] the suffocation of two children in an old refrigerator,[30] the sterilization of an 18-year-old girl,[31] the death of a young man from a drug overdose,[32] the activities of a bodysurfer,[33] the photograph of a dead murder victim,[34] and

27. *Daily Times-Democrat* v. *Graham*, 162 So. 2d 474 (1962).
28. *Hawkins* v. *Multimedia*, 344 S.E. 2d 145 (1986).
29. *Meetze* v. *AP*, 95 S.E. 2d 606 (1956).
30. *Costlow* v. *Cuismano*, 311 N.Y.S. 2d 92 (1970).
31. *Howard* v. *Des Moines Register*, 283 N.W. 2d 789 (1979).
32. *Beresky* v. *Teschner*, 381 N.E. 2d 979 (1978).
33. *Virgil* v. *Time, Inc.*, 527 F. 2d 1122 (1975).
34. *Barger* v. *Courier-Journal and Louisville Times*, 20 M.L.R. 1189 (1992).

other subjects have all been ruled to be of legitimate concern and interest to the public. Even the seemingly frivolous subject of romance was declared to be newsworthy by a New York court that found no liability in the broadcast of a television film of a man and a woman walking hand in hand along Madison Avenue. The couple objected to being photographed; he was married to another woman, she was engaged to be married to another man. The court said that the film, used to show people behaving in a romantic fashion in order to explore the prevailing attitudes on this topic, is newsworthy.[35]

The courts have been most generous to the press in their understanding of American reading and viewing habits. In a 1975 ruling in California, the U.S. Court of Appeals for the 9th Circuit noted that "in determining what is a matter of legitimate public interest, account must be taken of the customs and conventions of the community; and in the last analysis what is proper becomes a matter of community mores."[36] Thirty-five years earlier, another federal judge noted that the public enjoyed reading about the problems, misfortunes, and troubles of their neighbors and other members of the community. The case involved an article in The New Yorker about the failure of a child prodigy to fulfill the promise many had predicted for him (see boxed excerpt). "When such are the mores of the community, it would be unwise for a court to bar their expression in the newspapers, books, and magazines of the day," Judge Charles Clark wrote.[37]

The following are excerpts from an article written by Jared L. Manley about William James Sidis. The piece was published in The New Yorker on August 14, 1937, and provoked one of the nation's most celebrated invasion-of-privacy lawsuits (Sidis v. F-R Publishing Co.).

"Where Are They Now?"
"April Fool!"

"One snowy January evening in 1910 about a hundred professors and advanced students of mathematics from Harvard University gathered in a lecture hall in Cambridge, Massachusetts, to listen to a speaker by the name of William James Sidis. He had never addressed an audience before, and he was abashed and a little awkward at the start. His listeners had to attend closely, for he spoke in a small voice that did not carry well, and he punctuated his talk with nervous, shrill laughter. . . . The speaker wore black velvet knickers. He was eleven years old. . . . When it was all over, the distinguished Professor Daniel F. Comstock of Massachusetts Institute of Technology was moved to predict to reporters, who had listened in profound bewilderment, that young Sidis would grow up to be a great mathematician, a famous leader in the world of science."

---

35. *DeGregario* v. *CBS*, 43 N.Y.S. 2d 922 (1984).
36. *Virgil* v. *Time, Inc.*, 527 F. 2d 1122 (1975).
37. *Sidis* v. *F-R Publishing Co.*, 113 F. 2d 806 (1940).

(The next section of the article explains how Sidis, as a small child, had become a kind of guinea pig for his psychologist father who used experimental techniques to educate his son when he was little more than a baby. Manley goes on to describe Sidis's education, his extreme efforts to hide from the spotlight of publicity, his series of mundane jobs, and his rejection of a career in science or mathematics.)

"William James Sidis lives today, at the age of thirty-nine, in a hall bedroom of Boston's shabby south end. . . . He seems to get a great and ironic enjoyment out of leading a life of wandering irresponsibility after a childhood of scrupulous regimentation. . . . Sidis is employed now, as usual, as a clerk in a business house. He said that he never stays in one office long because his employers or fellow-workers soon find out that he is the famous boy wonder, and he can't tolerate a position after that. 'The very sight of a mathematical formula makes me physically ill,' he said."

(Manley relates that Sidis has become a passionate collector of streetcar transfers, that he enjoys the study of certain aspects of the history of Native Americans, and that he is writing a treatise on floods.)

"His visitor [Manley] was emboldened, at last, to bring up the prediction, made by Professor Comstock . . . back in 1910, that the little boy who lectured that year on the fourth dimension to a gathering of learned men would grow up to be a great mathematician, a famous leader in the world of science. 'It's strange,' said William James Sidis, with a grin, 'but you know, I was born on April Fool's Day.'"

Even the way a story is presented is normally not a factor: sensationalism and sensational treatment generally do not remove the protection of newsworthiness. Concerning the story of the suffocation of the two young children, the parents found the sensational treatment of the story as objectionable as the story itself. However, the court ruled that the manner in which the article was written was not relevant to whether the article was protected by the constitutional guarantees of free speech and free press—which, by the way, it was.[38] In another case a Boston newspaper published a horrible picture of an automobile accident in which the bloodied and battered body of one of the victims was clearly visible and identifiable, and the court rejected the plaintiff's claim. The Massachusetts Supreme Court noted, "Many things which are distressing or may be lacking in propriety or good taste are not actionable."[39] And in 1994 the 5th U.S. Circuit Court of Appeals ruled that sensational television stories about the discovery of child pornography, including homemade sex films, among the belongings of a Roman Catholic priest did not turn newsworthy reports into invasion of privacy. The judge agreed the information was embarrassing and the news stories demonstrated a distinct lack of sensitivity on the part of the broadcasters, but ruled that the material was clearly of public interest. "We are not prepared to make editorial decisions for the media regarding information directly related to matters of public concern," the court declared.[40]

38. *Costlow* v. *Cuismano,* 311 N.Y.S. 2d 92 (1970).
39. *Kelley* v. *Post Publishing Co.,* 327 Mass. 275 (1951).
40. *Cinel* v. *Connick,* 15 F. 3d 1338 (1994).

Courts also take into account whom the story is about when deciding whether there is legitimate public concern regarding the information. It is no surprise that the famous and the infamous must endure far more publicity about their private lives than the average American. Such is the nature of celebrity in the early 21st century. Even people whose lives just happen to intersect with those who are well known sometimes lose their privacy as well. In September of 1988 Pamela J. Howell, a private person by all accounts, happened to be a patient at the Four Winds Hospital, a private psychiatric facility. Few of her friends or relatives knew she had been hospitalized. As she walked one day with several other patients outside a hospital building, a photographer from The New York Post, using a telephoto lens, snapped a picture of the group of women. The photographer was not interested in Mrs. Howell; what he wanted and got was a photo of Hedda Nussbaum, another patient at Four Winds who happened to be walking with Mrs. Howell and others. Hedda Nussbaum had been in the national news for many months as the adoptive mother of a 6-year-old girl who had died from child abuse. She was undergoing treatment at the psychiatric facility. Pamela Howell's name was not mentioned in the newspaper, but she was clearly recognizable in the photograph published in The Post. The New York Court of Appeals rejected her right to privacy suit, noting that "If plaintiff's picture accompanied a newspaper article on a matter of public interest, to succeed [in her lawsuit] she must demonstrate that the picture bore no real relationship to the article."[41] The plaintiff, who just happened to be in the wrong place at the wrong time, could not carry that burden of proof in this case.

Even the most widely known public person retains at least a small portion of his or her life that the courts seem willing to shield. How far can the press delve into the private affairs of a public person? While not officially enunciated, courts have nevertheless recognized that a kind of sliding scale is applicable. The more famous the person, the smaller the zone of privacy. Just as important in many instances, however, is the reason for the publication of private information. The press is not required to justify its publication of private information, but a court will frequently try to determine why the material was published. Did it help us understand something? Did it illuminate a problem? Did it give us important insights? Or was it merely an attempt to titillate readers or viewers, to satisfy a craving for the odd or unusual? A good example of this is a 25-year-old case from California.

How far can the press delve into the private affairs of a public person?

The story focused on Mike Virgil, widely regarded in southern California as one of the best bodysurfers along the Pacific Coast. Sports Illustrated decided to publish a story on bodysurfing, and writer Curry Kirkpatrick chose to emphasize the prowess of Virgil. Virgil was known for his almost total disregard for personal safety and talked freely with the writer about his private life as well as about his surfing. He told Kirkpatrick that he was reckless in private as well and described several incidents to demonstrate this attitude. These incidents include putting out a burning cigarette with his mouth, burning a hole in his wrist with a cigarette, diving headfirst down a flight of stairs, and eating live insects. After the interview, Virgil had second thoughts about the story and asked Sports Illustrated not to include the material about his private life. The magazine published the story as Kirkpatrick had written it, and Virgil sued. The U.S. Court of Appeals for the 9th Circuit ruled that the line between private and public

41. *Howell* v. *New York Post Co., Inc.,* 612 N.E. 2d 699 (1993).

information "is to be drawn when the publicity ceases to be the giving of information to which the public is entitled, and becomes a morbid and sensational prying into private lives *for its own sake* [emphasis added]." In applying this standard to the Virgil case, a U.S. district court ruled that "any reasonable person reading the article would conclude that the personal facts concerning the individual were revealed in a legitimate journalistic attempt to explain his extremely daring and dangerous style of bodysurfing."[42] Judge Thompson ruled that no one could reasonably conclude that these personal facts were included for any inherent morbid, sensational, or curiosity appeal they might have. If Sports Illustrated had published these personal details about Virgil without any other information, it might have been an invasion of privacy. But in the context of the story about his public life as a surfer, the publication was not an invasion of privacy.

This standard was applied by the Iowa Supreme Court when it ruled that a story about a girl who had been sterilized when she was 18 years old was not an invasion of privacy. The story focused on the activities at a county juvenile home that had come under investigation by the state. As an example of what occurred there, the Des Moines Register recounted the story of a girl who was sterilized against her will because a psychiatrist reported to officials that she was "impulsive" and "hair-triggered" and would probably have sexual problems in the future. The girl's name was used but was not prominent in the story. The court ruled that the paper had not pried into the girl's life simply to shock or outrage the community. The facts were presented to demonstrate to the community the kind of unethical, even illegal, activities taking place at the home. As such, the material was of legitimate public concern. But was it necessary to use the victim's name in this story? Was it not possible for the newspaper to present this story to readers without identifying an unfortunate victim of this county home? The Iowa high court ruled it was legitimate to conclude that the name was an essential ingredient in the story:

> In the sense of serving an appropriate news function, the disclosure [of the name] contributed constructively to the impact of the article. It offered a personalized frame of reference to which the reader could relate, fostering perception and understanding. Moreover, it lent specificity and credibility to the report. In this way the disclosure served as an effective means of accomplishing the intended news function. . . . Moreover, at a time when it was important to separate fact from rumor, the specificity of the report would strengthen the accuracy of the public perception of the merits of the controversy.[43]

The U.S. Court of Appeals for the 10th Circuit used this same argument to refute charges of invasion of privacy brought by a physician against the periodical Medical Economics. The story in the magazine was entitled "Who Let This Doctor in the O.R.? The Story of a Fatal Breakdown in Medical Policing," and described several patients of an anesthesiologist who suffered fatal or severely disabling injuries in the operating room. The article focused on the lack of self-policing by physicians and the lack of disciplinary action by hospitals. To document these allegations, the author of the story discussed the plaintiff anesthesiologist's

42. *Virgil v. Time, Inc.,* 527 F. 2d 1122 (1975).
43. *Howard v. Des Moines Register,* 283 N.W. 2d 789 (1979).

psychiatric and related personal problems. Her picture and name were included in the story. While the plaintiff conceded the story was newsworthy, she argued that the publication of her photograph, name, and private facts revealing her psychiatric and marital histories added nothing to the story and were an invasion of privacy. The court disagreed, stating that the inclusion of the name and photograph strengthened the impact and credibility of the article. "They obviate any impression that the problems raised in the article are remote or hypothetical, thus providing an aura of immediacy and even urgency that might not exist had plaintiff's name and photograph been suppressed," the court said. The plaintiff's psychiatric and marital problems were connected to the newsworthy topic by the rational inference that her personal problems were the underlying causes of the acts of alleged malpractice.[44]

What courts often look for in these kind of cases, then, is a nexus between the admittedly private and embarrassing information and the newsworthy subject of the story. How far the press can go in reporting the private life of public persons often depends not only on what was said—how private the information is—but also on why the material was used. When an individual's public life is explained, many parts of that person's private life are of legitimate public concern.

It is important at this point in our discussion of public persons and public figures to note that we are not using these terms as they are used in the law of libel. Recall, when discussing defamation, the label "public figure" had a distinct and quite narrow meaning. That is not the definition of public person used in privacy law. Also, libel law tends to reject the concept of the "involuntary public figure," a private individual who just happens to get caught in a big story. Since 1929 American courts have recognized that involuntary public figures do exist in privacy law. The Kentucky Supreme Court first noted such a person and gave this definition of the status:

> The right of privacy is the right to live one's life in seclusion, without being subjected to unwarranted and undesired publicity. In short, it is the right to be let alone. . . . There are times, however, when one, whether willing or not, becomes an actor in an occurrence of public or general interest. When this takes place he emerges from his seclusion, and it is not an invasion of his right of privacy to publish his photograph with an account of such occurrence.[45]

The court later noted that private citizens can become "innocent actors in great tragedies in which the public has a deep concern." The scope, therefore, of the rubric involuntary public figure is wide. In Kansas City a young man was arrested by police outside the local courthouse on suspicion of burglary. A local television news crew filmed the arrest, and it was broadcast on television that night. The young man, however, had been released by police, who admitted they had arrested the wrong man. An invasion-of-privacy suit followed, but the courts rejected it, stating that the plaintiff must show a serious, unreasonable, unwarranted, and offensive invasion of private affairs before recovery can be allowed:

44. *Gilbert* v. *Medical Economics,* 665 F. 2d 305 (1981).
45. *Jones* v. *Herald Post Co.,* 18 S.W. 2d 972 (1929).

In the case at bar, plaintiff was involved in a noteworthy event about which the public had a right to be informed and which the defendant [television station KCMO] had a right to publicize. This is true even though his involvement therein was purely involuntary and against his will.[46]

An Illinois appeals court ruled in 1978 that a story that reported the death of a boy from an apparent drug overdose and then went on to outline details of the youth's life was not an invasion of privacy. The subject was of legitimate concern; in addition, the youth became an involuntary public figure by his actions within the drug culture in the community. "It is not necessary for an individual to actively seek publicity in order to be found in the public eye," the court ruled.[47]

Some have speculated that because the Supreme Court has ruled in libel cases that a public figure must be a voluntary participant in a controversy or public event, a similar rule might be applied in the law of privacy. But there seems to be nothing on record to suggest that will happen. Indeed, two factors strongly mitigate against such a development. First, to abandon the involuntary public figure rule in privacy law would be to radically reshape a part of the law that is more than 70 years old. That seems unlikely. Second, remember we are dealing not with defamatory falsehoods in privacy law, but with truthful accounts of private affairs. American judges have been extremely reluctant to find liability where the charge is based on truthful or factual material. A narrowing of the definition of public figure to meet the criteria established in libel law would significantly enlarge the scope of liability. The records suggest most American jurists oppose such a move.

RECOUNTING THE PAST

A great number of privacy suits have resulted from both published and broadcast stories about people who were formerly in the public eye. In these cases the plaintiffs have consistently argued that the passing of time dims the public spotlight and that a person stripped of privacy because of great notoriety regains the protection of privacy after several years. Courts have not accepted this argument very often. The general rule is that once persons become public figures they remain public figures, at least with regard to the events or circumstances that originally pushed them into the public spotlight. Two kinds of stories fall into this category: (1) stories that merely recount a past event (14 years ago today, Walter Denton jumped off the Golden Gate Bridge and survived) and do not tell readers what the subject of the story does today and (2) stories that recount a past occurrence and attempt to focus as well on what the participant does today (14 years ago Walter Denton jumped off the Golden Gate Bridge and survived, and today he is principal of Madison High School).

Stories that fall in the first category are protected in almost every instance. In 1975 the Kansas Supreme Court, for example, ruled it was not an invasion of privacy when a newspaper republished in a "Looking Backward" column a story that a police officer had been suspended and then fired in 1964 after a complaint from a citizen. The court said that "official

---

46. *Williams v. KCMO Broadcasting Co.,* 472 S.W. 2d (1971).
47. *Beresky v. Teschner,* 381 N.E. 2d 979 (1978).

misconduct is newsworthy when it occurs, and remains so for so long as anyone thinks it worth retelling." The court added, "Once these facts entered the public domain, they remained there . . . plaintiff could not draw himself like a snail into his shell."[48] And the New Jersey Supreme Court ruled that the publication of a book about crimes that took place eight years earlier was not an invasion of privacy, despite the lapse of time. Joseph Kallinger and his son were apprehended by police in 1975 after their criminal rampage that included killing, robbing, and raping. In 1983 a professor of criminal justice at City University of New York published a book about Kallinger's life and crimes. One of Kallinger's victims sued, arguing that replaying this tragedy in public print was traumatic, disturbing, and would be highly offensive. The court agreed with that assessment but ruled that the case failed because the facts revealed were not private but public, and "even if they were private, they are of legitimate concern to the public."[49] The lapse of time did nothing to insulate the plaintiff from such publicity. The facts were taken from the public trial record in the case, and the court noted that the Supreme Court ruling in *Cox* v. *Cohn*[50] was not limited to contemporaneous events.

The second kind of story is more problematic. There have been too few cases to establish a clear guideline. Some courts have clearly gone on record permitting the "where-are-they-now" kind of story. But even these judges have suggested that stories designed to purposely embarrass or humiliate a person because of his or her past conduct might not be tolerated under all circumstances.[51] The North Carolina Court of Appeals refused to grant a summary judgment to a newspaper that had been sued for invasion of privacy for recounting a woman's search for a child she had given up for adoption 17 years earlier. The woman returned to Salisbury, N.C., looking for the girl she had left there in 1966. All of the adoption records were sealed under state law, but she found out the name and address of her daughter through a newspaper advertisement. A newspaper story later identified the girl and her adoptive parents, all of whom were extremely upset by the publicity. The court said that the question of whether the story was newsworthy and immune from a lawsuit depended on a standard of reasonableness in light of community mores. This is a jury question, the court ruled, not something that should be decided on a motion for summary judgment. The judges noted that whether the story of the adoption, which was likely a public issue in 1967, had become a private matter by 1984 was another question the jury should decide. In making this judgment, the court said, the jurors should consider whether state laws on the confidentiality of jury records reflect on the newsworthy nature of the story.[52] The North Carolina Supreme Court later dismissed the case, noting the state did not recognize the private-facts element of privacy law.[53]

There is a real risk in running a story about a local banker that includes the fact that he was arrested for car theft 20 years earlier. A judge may ask: Of what relevance is this information about past deeds? Surely if the man is running for public office, the public deserves to

"Once these facts entered the public domain, they remained there . . . plaintiff could not draw himself like a snail into his shell."

48. *Rawlins* v. *The Hutchinson Publishing Co.,* 453 P. 2d 288 (1975).
49. *Romaine* v. *Kallinger,* 537 A. 2d 284 (1988).
50. 420 U.S. 469 (1975).
51. See *Kent* v. *Pittsburgh Press,* 349 F. Supp. 622 (1972); *Sidis* v. *F-R Publishing Co.,* 113 F. 2d 806 (1940); and *Bernstein* v. *NBC,* 232 F. 2d 369 (1955).
52. *Hall* v. *Post,* 355 S.E. 2d 816 (1987).
53. *Hall* v. *Post,* 15 M.L.R. 2329 (1988).

have this information. No privacy suit would stand in such a case. Oftentimes such stories are published or broadcast for inspirational reasons—see how this person pulled him- or herself up by the bootstraps and succeeded despite the odds. In such cases the subjects of the stories will usually consent to the use of this information because they are proud of their accomplishments. But if, for example, the editor publishes this information to hurt a banker because an application for a loan was rejected, a court may very well rule that an invasion of privacy has taken place. This is another area in which the journalist has to exercise judgment and ask: Why am I publishing this potentially embarrassing information? If there is good cause, the journalist will find the courts will bar an action for invasion of privacy.

The publication of private facts generates many lawsuits, but few are successful. The key to avoiding successful litigation in this area is for the newsperson to stick to reporting the news. It is when the journalist makes a foray into non-newsworthy private lives of average persons in order to titillate or amuse readers or viewers that this area of invasion of privacy can prove extremely troublesome.

PRIVATE FACTS ON THE INTERNET

Chapter 7 described problems relating to the collection of personal information from Internet users. Once this data is gathered it is frequently offered to various individuals and agencies who can use it commercially or in other ways. While such exploitation rarely reaches the level of publication of private facts it nevertheless is dismaying to millions of people and the members of Congress. "Today, with commercial databases, networks, and CD-ROMs, you can match data sets with a few keystrokes in seconds and literally surf through people's lives," said Leslie L. Byrnes, the White House consumer affairs adviser, in 1997.[54] In 1996 members of Congress asked the Federal Trade Commission to evaluate the legality of several computerized databases. The legislators said they became concerned when it was discovered that the Lexis-Nexis P-Trak databases promised purchasers access to the names and addresses of 300 million people. Some of the P-Trak listings contained birthdates, telephone numbers, and prior addresses of the persons listed. The database also included the social security numbers of as many persons as possible until June of 1996 when the company was forced by government pressure to delete these numbers. (When the U.S. government first put its social security system online it too made every citizen's social security number easily accessible. It too stopped the practice under congressional pressure.) Armed with a social security number, an interested snooper can uncover an almost unlimited amount of personal information about someone. Other online databases promise buyers credit files, medical records, and even driver's license numbers.

In 1998 the Federal Trade Commission took action against GeoCities, a Web site with more than 2 million subscribers that offers users their own Web pages, e-mail addresses, and information on topics of interest to them. The commission and the company announced a

---

54. "White House Consumer Advisor Sees Role for Encryption in Privacy Protection," 2 E.L.P.R. 156 (1997).

settlement in August under which the Web site promised subscribers that it would not give out information collected during registration, including age, education, occupation, income, and personal interests, without permission. "GeoCities misled its customers, both children and adults, by not telling the truth about how it was using their personal information," said Jodie Bernstein, director of the Bureau of Consumer Protection at the FTC.[55] In May of 1999, in its second Internet-privacy enforcement action, the FTC forced a multi-billion-dollar investment company to agree to change the way its World Wide Web site treated information gathered from children and teenagers. The Liberty Financial Companies of Boston's Young Investor Web site had not kept its promise that all data collected from users would be kept totally anonymous. The site asked the young people about matters such as their weekly allowance, whether their parents were saving for their college education, and other financial matters. Actually, the company used the information to identify specific individuals, the FTC said. A company spokesman said the company had kept the information confidential, if not completely anonymous.

The freewheeling manner in which some American businesses have secretly gathered and circulated personal data about Web users has troubled not only U.S. citizens. European governments have also worried about some of these practices. In 1995 the European Union adopted the Data Protection Directive. This directive, which went into effect in the fall of 1998, requires member countries to adopt laws that protect the privacy of all personal information gathered by electronic commerce industries. The directive also prevents companies operating in the European Union from transmitting personal data electronically to third countries, including the United States, unless those countries provide "adequate protection" for the information.

The European Union sought similar legislation from the United States. But the president, Congress, and nearly all American businesses rejected the notion of legal restraints and instead sought to meet the European standards through self-regulation. Many American businesses, especially direct-marketing companies, make substantial amounts of money buying, selling, and developing business strategies based on huge data banks of personal information about consumers. These groups fought hard to block any legislation on this issue. Discussions went on for more than two years between the United States and the European Union. Although the directive went into effect in 1998, no interruptions of data flow occurred. Some data-reliant American businesses, like credit card companies such as American Express, reached individual agreements with European governments.[56] Then in early 2000, Undersecretary of Commerce David Aaron, who leads the U.S. negotiating team in the discussions with the European Union, indicated that the two sides had reached a tentative agreement on this matter. Although both sides called the agreement a breakthrough, critical details, including how it would apply in practice, remained unresolved. The outline of the pact seemed to represent a compromise, with Europeans agreeing that American businesses could police themselves and with the U.S. companies agreeing to post notices of how personal data would be

55. Brinkley, "Web Site Agrees."
56. Andrews, "European Law."

used and to gain consumer consent before transferring such data to others. U.S. companies also had to assent to four basic principles, including their agreement to subject themselves to a data protection commission in one of the EU nations; demonstrate that they are already covered by U.S. laws that regulate such matters as credit card applications; and sign up with a self-regulating privacy organization in the United States, such as the Better Business Bureau Online, or agree to refer privacy-related disputes with individuals to a panel of European data protection authorities for resolution.

SUMMARY

It is an invasion of privacy to publicize private information about another person's life if the publication of this information would be embarrassing to a reasonable person and the information is not of legitimate public interest or concern. To publicize means to communicate the information to a large number of people. There is no liability for giving further publicity to information that is already considered public. The press is free, for example, to report even embarrassing and sensitive matters contained in public records. The information that is publicized must be considered offensive to a reasonable person; the law does not protect hypersensitive individuals.

Courts use many strategies to determine whether information has legitimate public concern. Stories that are of great interest have legitimate public concern. Stories about both voluntary and involuntary public figures are normally considered of legitimate public concern. When private information is published or broadcast, it is important that a connection exists between the revelation of the embarrassing private information and the newsworthy aspects of the story. Embarrassing details about a person's private life cannot be publicized simply to amuse or titillate audiences. News stories that recount past events—including embarrassing details of an individual's life—are normally protected from successful privacy suits. However, courts will usually insist on a good reason for relating these embarrassing past events to an individual's current life or work. The nation is struggling to resolve issues relating to the use of personal data gathered via the Internet.

FALSE LIGHT PRIVACY

It is illegal to publicize material that places an individual in a false light if

　　a. **the false light in which the individual was placed would be offensive to a reasonable person, and**

　　b. **the publisher of the material was at fault when the publication was made.**

This fourth tort in the invasion of privacy quartet has engendered the most disputes within the law. What in the world does this have to do with invasion of privacy? Many state courts have refused to recognize this variety of invasion of privacy. For example, in 1998 the Minnesota Supreme Court for the first time recognized a cause of action for appropriation, private facts, and intrusion, but specifically rejected the false light tort. The court said that most false light claims are encompassed within defamation.[57] Yet false light lacks many of the procedural safeguards that accompany defamation, and this shortcoming increases the tension between state tort law and the First Amendment. The origins of the false light tort are murky. It is a hybrid of both the appropriation tort and the private facts tort, created more than 60 years ago by well-meaning judges who forced the development of the law in an attempt to resolve what appeared to be legitimate legal claims.

There are three important elements in the tort. The first is that the material must be substantially false. Minor errors, incorrect details, little mistakes really don't matter. The allegation made in the lawsuit is that the defendant published statement A, and that this statement made the plaintiff look bad and caused the plaintiff to experience humiliation and mental suffering. The plaintiff must prove that statement A, the remarks that caused the harm, is false. Proving that there are other errors in the story is insufficient to make the case.

FALSE LIGHT PRIVACY

1. Publication of material must put an individual in a false light.
2. The false light would be offensive to a reasonable person.
3. The publisher of the material was at fault.

The plaintiff next must prove that the false allegations would be considered offensive by a reasonable person. Finally, the plaintiff must prove that the defendant was at fault when he or she or it made the false allegation. Let's first look at some typical ways the plaintiff can establish the falsity of the matter, and then examine the second and third elements.

FICTIONALIZATION

Fictionalization is really the purposeful distortion of the truth, usually for dramatic purposes. Some of the earliest false light cases involved radio and television dramatizations of actual news events. Because they did not know exactly what happened, and because real life is generally boring, script writers often changed these events to increase the drama. False light suits were often a consequence of this creativity.[58] Today the creators of docudramas on television face real problems with potential false light privacy and libel lawsuits. Producers normally buy the rights to the story from the real people involved in the event to be dramatized. Once these people sign a contract, they forfeit their right to later sue if they are unhappy with the presentation. Those persons who refuse to sign are simply not included in the story. (And you always thought docudramas were accurate and truthful.) The passion for getting participants in real-life events to sign on to these television presentations means that television producers

---

57. *Lake* v. *Wal-Mart Stores Inc.,* 582 N.W. 2d 231 (1998).
58. See, for example, *Strickler* v. *NBC,* 167 F. Supp. 68 (1958).

often arrive on the scene of a tragedy at the same time the police and fire officials show up. In a different age of journalism, mainstream newspaper and magazine writers also were caught in false light lawsuits when they dramatized true stories by adding dialogue, or changing the scene slightly.[59] Today in print journalism it is the supermarket tabloid newspapers that are the target of such suits. A 96-year-old Arkansas resident sued the Sun for using her photo to illustrate a totally fabricated story about a 101-year-old female newspaper carrier who had to give up her route because she was pregnant. Plaintiff Nellie Mitchell's photo had been published 10 years earlier in another tabloid owned by the same company in a true story about the Mountain Home, Ark., woman. But the editors at the Sun needed a picture to illustrate their phony story and simply used Mitchell's, undoubtedly thinking she was dead. A U.S. district court jury awarded the elderly woman $1.5 million in damages.[60] The simple rule for writers who want to be dramatists is this: if you change the facts, change the names and don't use photos of real people.

The other side of this coin relates to using the name of a real person in what is clearly a piece of fiction. Simply using the name of an actual person in a novel or feature film or situation comedy is not actionable (page 144). A party in such a suit must prove that his or her identity was taken as well. What is the difference? Let's say that Joyce Carol Oates writes a novel about a popular actress who has AIDS. In the book, the actress's best friend is a short, chubby nurse named Julia Roberts. The writer has taken actress Julia Roberts' name, but not her identity. But if, in the novel, an actress who has AIDS is named Julia Roberts, if she is rather tall and thin, if she is a former model, if she had been married to a country/pop singer named Lyle Lovett, and so on, then the writer has taken the identity as well as the name. How many characteristics must be the same before plaintiffs can claim their identity was taken and they were placed in a false light? Courts decide this on a case-by-case basis.

Simply using the name of an actual person in a novel or feature film or situation comedy is not actionable.

For example, the author and publisher of a book entitled "Match Set" was sued by a woman who had the same name as the central character in the novel. Both women were named Melanie Geisler. The character in the novel was a female transsexual tennis player who was induced to participate in tennis fraud. The plaintiff in the case worked for a small publishing company for six months and was acquainted with the defendant author who also worked at the same company for a short time. The plaintiff and the fictional Melanie Geisler shared many physical characteristics. Geisler argued that the similarity of names and physical descriptions, coupled with the fact that she and the author were acquainted for a short time, led many persons to believe the book was about her. The U.S. Court of Appeals for the 2nd Circuit ruled that a reasonable person could come to such a conclusion, rejected the defendant's motion for dismissal, and sent the case back for trial.[61] Some authors can face a problem even if the plaintiff does not have the same name as a character in the novel. In a Florida case a novelist knowingly used a real person with whom she was acquainted as the basis for a character in a book;

---

59. See *Acquino* v. *Bulletin Co.*, 190 Pa. Super. 528 (1959).
60. *Peoples Bank & Trust Co. of Mountain Home* v. *Globe International, Inc.*, 786 F. Supp. 791 (1992). See also *Varnish* v. *Best Medium*, 405 F. 2d 608 (1968).
61. *Geisler* v. *Petrocelli*, 616 F. 2d 636 (1980).

but the name was changed in the book. She was sued for invasion of privacy and lost the case. The court ruled that because the character described in the novel was so unusual, many persons in the community recognized her even though the name had been changed.[62]

Novels and feature films often carry a disclaimer: "This is a work of fiction. All the characters and events portrayed are fictitious. Any resemblance to real people and events is purely coincidental." Will this ward off a false light suit? No. Although the statement has minimal value in showing the intent of the author or publisher or producer, the rule is simple: you cannot escape liability for committing a legal wrong by announcing that you are not liable. If you put a large sign on the top of your car that said, "Stay out of my way. I am a very bad driver and if I hit someone, it is not my fault," this would not relieve you from any liability if you caused an accident. Similarly, the disclaimer that a book is a work of fiction and the characters are fictitious will not prevent a successful privacy suit if the author has obviously appropriated someone's identity and put him or her in a false light.

OTHER FALSEHOODS

False light privacy suits based on fictionalization are not too common today. Today false light lawsuits more typically involve simple editing or writing errors, or errors in judgment. Misuse of photographs, both still and video, is a common problem. The Saturday Evening Post was plagued by such lawsuits in the 1940s and 1950s. For example, the magazine once published a picture of a little girl who was brushed by a speeding car in an intersection and lay crying in the street. The girl was the victim of a motorist who ignored a red traffic light, but in the magazine the editors implied that she had caused the accident herself by darting into the street between parked cars. The editors simply needed a picture to illustrate a story on pedestrian carelessness and plucked this one out of the files. The picture was totally unrelated to the story, except that both were about people being hit by cars. Eleanor Sue Leverton sued the Post and won. Judge Herbert F. Goodrich ruled that the picture was clearly newsworthy in connection with Eleanor's original accident.

Misuse of photographs, both still and video, is a common problem.

> But the sum total of all this is that this particular plaintiff, the legitimate subject for publicity for one particular accident, now becomes a pictorial, frightful example of pedestrian carelessness. This, we think, exceeds the bounds of privilege.[63]

WJLA-TV in the nation's capital was sued in a case that graphically demonstrates how a broadcasting station or publication can and cannot use unrelated pictures to illustrate a story. The station broadcast a story on a new medical treatment for genital herpes. The report appeared on both the 6 p.m. and 11 p.m. newscasts. Both reports carried the same opening videotape of scores of pedestrians walking on a busy city street. Then the camera zoomed in on one woman, Linda Duncan, as she stood on a corner. Duncan turned and looked at the camera. She was clearly recognizable. On the 6 p.m. news there was no narration during the opening

---

62. *Cason* v. *Baskin,* 159 Fla. 131 (1947).
63. *Leverton* v. *Curtis Publishing Co.,* 192 F. 2d 974 (1951).

footage. The camera focused on the plaintiff Duncan and then the tape cut to a picture of the reporter, who was standing on the street, and said, "For the twenty million Americans who have herpes, it's not a cure." The remainder of the story followed. But for the 11 p.m. news, the reporter's opening statement was read by the news anchor as viewers watched the opening videotape, including the close-up of Linda Duncan. A defense motion to dismiss the privacy and defamation actions was granted as it related to the 6 p.m. newscast. The court said there was not a sufficient connection between pictures of the plaintiff and the reporter's statement. But the court denied a summary judgment relating to the 11 p.m. broadcast. "The coalescing of the camera action, plaintiff's action (turning toward the camera), and the position of the passerby caused plaintiff to be the focal point on the screen. The juxtaposition of this film and commentary concerning twenty million Americans with herpes is sufficient to support an inference that indeed the plaintiff was a victim," the court ruled. A jury should decide whether the connection was strong enough.[64]

Sometimes an error simply occurs, and there is little anyone can do about it. A newspaper in Oklahoma published an article concerning the death of a former local schoolteacher who had been convicted of murder and who was reportedly mentally ill. But the photo used to accompany the story was that of Frenche Colbert, who lived in Phoenix, Ariz. Colbert's picture had been sent to the newspaper years earlier when he graduated from law school. Somehow, his photo got mixed up with that of the schoolteacher. There is no question that this publication put Colbert in a false light.[65] In such cases the fault requirement is a strong defense (see page 299).

A simple precaution will protect publishers and broadcasters against many false-light suits. Refrain from using unrelated photos to illustrate stories and articles. When you want to publish a story in the employee magazine about worker carelessness as a prime cause of industrial accidents, control the impulse to pull from the files a random picture of one of the employees working on the assembly line. That employee could contend that you are suggesting she is careless. Similarly, don't use old photos of kids hanging around the parking lot at a local park to illustrate your news story on neighborhood complaints about drug dealing in the park. Juxtaposing the wrong pictures with the wrong words could give viewers the impression that you are suggesting one of these kids is selling or using drugs.

HIGHLY OFFENSIVE MATERIAL

Before a plaintiff can win a false-light case, the court must be convinced that the material that is false is highly offensive to a reasonable person. Although the records contain a handful of cases where nonoffensive material was the basis for a successful false-light suit,[66] these cases are old and should not be regarded as authoritative today. Typical of modern decisions is the case of *Cibenko* v. *Worth Publishers*. The plaintiff is a New York–New Jersey Port Authority

---

64. *Duncan* v. *WJLA-TV,* 10 M.L.R. 1395 (1984).
65. *Colbert* v. *World Publishing,* 747 P. 2d 286 (1987).
66. See *Molony* v. *Boy Comics Publishers,* 65 N.Y.S. 173 (1948) and *Spahn* v. *Julian Messner, Inc.,* 18 N.Y. 2d 324 (1966).

police officer whose photograph appeared in a college sociology text. In a section of the book entitled "Selecting the Criminals," the picture depicts a white police officer (Cibenko) in a public place apparently prodding a sleeping African-American man with his nightstick. The caption for the picture states:

> The social status of the offender seems to be the most significant determinant of whether a person will be arrested and convicted for an offense and of the kind of penalty that will be applied. In this picture a police officer is preventing a black male from falling asleep in a public place. Would the officer be likely to do the same if the "offender" were a well-dressed, middle-aged white person?

Officer Cibenko claimed the photograph and caption made him appear to be a racist, and this portrayal was false. A U.S. district court in New Jersey disagreed and ruled that there was no offensive meaning attached to the photograph and caption, especially not a highly offensive meaning.[67] A U.S. district court in Maine dismissed a suit by a man who had fallen out of the hatch of a small airplane, but managed to cling to the door rails until the pilot made an emergency landing. An article in National Enquirer embellished the story somewhat, adding material on what the plaintiff had thought about as he clung to the airplane. The reporter had never communicated with the accident victim, and therefore could not have known what went through his mind. The court ruled that the description of physical sensations and predictable fears, though possibly exaggerated or maybe even fanciful, was not offensive to a reasonable person.[68]

THE FAULT REQUIREMENT

Since 1967, plaintiffs in false-light suits have been required to carry a fault requirement much like the one applied in libel cases. The case in which this fault requirement was applied to invasion of privacy was the first mass media invasion-of-privacy suit ever heard by the U.S. Supreme Court.[69] In the early 1950s the James Hill family was held captive in their home for nearly 24 hours by three escaped convicts. The fugitives were captured by police shortly after leaving the Hill home. The incident became a widely publicized story. A novel, "The Desperate Hours," was written about a similar incident, as were a play and a motion-picture script. Life magazine published a feature story about the drama, stating that the play was a reenactment of the ordeal suffered by the James Hill family (see figure 8.1). The actors were even taken to the home in which the Hills had lived (now vacant) and were photographed at the scene of the original captivity.

James Hill sued for invasion of privacy. He complained that the magazine had used his family's name for trade purposes and that the story put the family in a false light. "The Desperate Hours" did follow the basic outline of the Hill family ordeal, but it contained many differences. The fictional Hilliard family, for example, suffered far more physical and verbal indignities at the hands of the convicts than did the Hill family.

67. *Cibenko* v. *Worth Publishers,* 510 F. Supp. 761 (1981).
68. *Dempsey* v. *National Enquirer Inc.,* 687 F. Supp. 692 (1988).
69. *Time, Inc.* v. *Hill,* 385 U.S. 374 (1967).

THEATER

BANK ROBBERS HOLD FAMILY IN WHITEMARSH PRISONERS;

ACTUAL EVENT, as reported in newspaper, took place in isolated house about 10 miles from Philadelphia. There three convicts from

Lewisburg penitentiary held family of James Hill as prisoners while they hid from manhunt. All three convicts were later captured.

TRUE CRIME INSPIRES TENSE PLAY

The ordeal of a family trapped by convicts gives Broadway a new thriller, 'The Desperate Hours'

FIGURE 8.1

Life magazine published this article about the James Hill family, which led the family to sue for invasion of privacy. LIFE Magazine © 1955 Time Inc. Reprinted with permission. Photo © Cornell Capa/Magnum Photos.

The family won money damages in the New York state courts,[70] but the Supreme Court of the United States vacated the lower-court rulings and sent the case back for yet another trial. The Hill family gave up at this point, and no subsequent trial was held.

Justice William Brennan, in a 5–4 ruling, declared that the family's name and photographs had not been used for trade purposes. Brennan reminded all concerned that informative material published in newspapers and magazines is not published for purposes of trade (see pages 250–252), even though these publications generally are considered profit-making businesses.

Turning to the false-light action, Brennan applied the same First Amendment standards he had developed in *The New York Times* v. *Sullivan* libel suit to this category of invasion-of-privacy litigation (see pages 162–165). "We hold that the constitutional protections for speech and press preclude the application of the New York [privacy] statute to redress false reports of matters of public interest in the absence of proof that the defendant published the report with knowledge of its falsity or in reckless disregard of the truth."[71]

In the last 27 years, however, the Supreme Court has substantially modified the fault requirement in libel. Since 1974 and the case of *Gertz* v. *Welch,*[72] the Supreme Court has insisted that public persons must prove actual malice to win a libel suit but that states may permit private persons to win a libel judgment with proof of simple negligence, not actual malice. Six months after its ruling in *Gertz,* the Supreme Court issued a ruling in a false-light

70. *Hill* v. *Hayes,* 207 N.Y.S. 2d 901 (1960), 18 App. Div. 2d 485 (1963).
71. *Time, Inc.* v. *Hill,* 385 U.S. 374 (1967).
72. 418 U.S. 323 (1974).

invasion-of-privacy case, *Cantrell* v. *Forest City Publishing Co.*[73] In this case the high court ruled that there was evidence to show that the defendant had acted with reckless disregard for the truth. But because the plaintiff had managed to bear the higher burden of proof in the case and was able to prove actual malice, the Supreme Court didn't decide whether the *Gertz* ruling had changed the law of privacy as well as the law of libel. "This case presents no occasion to consider whether a state may constitutionally apply a more relaxed standard of liability for a publisher or broadcaster of false statements injurious to a private individual under a false-light theory of invasion of privacy or whether the constitutional standard announced in *Time, Inc.* v. *Hill* applies to all false-light cases," wrote Justice Stewart for the court.

Whether the *Gertz* variable-fault standard is applicable to false-light cases remains an open question. Most authorities tend to think that the rule of *Time, Inc.* v. *Hill*—that all plaintiffs are required to show actual malice, knowledge of falsity, or reckless disregard of the truth—will stand as the law in most jurisdictions. Several factors prompt this conclusion. The Supreme Court could have changed the rules in the *Cantrell* case, but did not. The high court could have modified the *Time, Inc.* v. *Hill* rule in *Gertz,* but did not. Finally, a statement that is not defamatory is likely to be far less damaging to a plaintiff. Less harm, higher fault requirement. Some courts have taken a different point of view and ruled that private-person false-light plaintiffs must prove only negligence.[74] But more courts have stayed the course, requiring all plaintiffs to show actual malice.[75]

Whether the Gertz variable-fault standard is applicable to false-light cases remains an open question.

Before the discussion of the right of privacy comes to an end, we need to recall a few points. First, remember that only people have the right of privacy. Corporations, businesses, and governments do not enjoy the legal right of privacy as such. Second, unlike libel, the law of privacy does provide that the plaintiff may seek an injunction to stop an invasion of privacy. Courts are very hesitant to enjoin tortious conduct, however, unless the plaintiff can show that the action will cause irreparable injury and that the tortious conduct will likely be continued. Such was the case in the *Galella* v. *Onassis*[76] suit. A plaintiff is far more likely to get an injunction in either an intrusion or an appropriation case than in a private-facts or false-light suit. Normally, courts refuse to grant injunctions because they believe an adequate legal remedy is available or because they believe that the injunction could constitute prior censorship in violation of the First Amendment. The plaintiff bears an immense burden in convincing a court that prior restraint is called for. While it is possible to get an injunction, it is difficult. Third, it is impossible to civilly libel a dead person, but a few state privacy statutes make it possible for an heir to maintain an action for invasion of privacy.

Although privacy law is not as well charted as libel law, and although there are fewer privacy cases, suits for invasion of privacy are a growing menace to journalists. If journalists stick to the job of responsibly reporting the news, they may rest assured that the chance for a successful privacy suit is slim.

73. 419 U.S. 245 (1974).
74. See *Wood* v. *Hustler,* 736 F. 2d 1084 (1984) and *Crump* v. *Beckley Newspapers,* 370 S.E. 2d 70 (1984).
75. See *Dodrill* v. *Arkansas Democrat Co.,* 5 M.L.R. 1090 (1979); *McCall* v. *Courier-Journal and Louisville Times Co.,* 4 M.L.R. 2337 (1979), aff'd 6 M.L.R. 1112 (1980); *Goodrich* v. *Waterbury Republican-American Inc.,* 448 A. 2d 1317 (1987); and *Colbert* v. *World Publishing Co.,* 747 P. 2d 286 (1987).
76. 487 F. 2d 986 (1973); 533 F. Supp. 1076 (1982).

It is an invasion of privacy to publish false information that places an individual into what is called a false light. However, this false information must be considered offensive to a reasonable person. Also, the plaintiff must prove that the information was published negligently, with knowledge of its falsity, or with reckless disregard for the truth.

One common source of false-light privacy suits is any drama that adds fictional material to an otherwise true story. The use of fictional rather than real names in such a drama will normally preclude a successful invasion-of-privacy suit. The coincidental use of a real name in a novel or stage play will not stand as a cause of action for invasion of privacy. Most false-light cases, however, result from the publication of false information about a person in a news or feature story. Pictures of persons who are not involved in the stories that the pictures are used to illustrate frequently provide false-light privacy suits.

SUMMARY

BIBLIOGRAPHY

Andrews, Edmund. "European Law Aims to Protect Privacy of Data." *The New York Times,* 26 October 1998, A1.

Brinkley, Joel. "Web Site Agrees to Safeguards in First On-Line Privacy Deal." *The New York Times,* 14 August 1998, A13.

Kalven, Harry, Jr. "Privacy in Tort Law—Were Warren and Brandeis Wrong?" *Law and Contemporary Problems* 31 (1966):326.

Marcus, Paul, and Tara L. McMahon. "Limiting Disclosure of Rape Victims' Identities." *Southern California Law Review* 64 (1991):1019.

"Naming Names." *Newsweek,* 29 April 1991, 26.

Nimmer, Melville. "The Right to Speak from *Times* to *Time:* First Amendment Theory Applied to Libel and Misapplied to Privacy." *California Law Review* 56 (1968):935.

Pember, Don R. "The Burgeoning Scope of Access Privacy and the Portent for a Free Press." *Iowa Law Review* 64 (1979):1155.

Pember, Don R. *Privacy and the Press.* Seattle: University of Washington Press, 1972.

Pember, Don R., and Dwight L. Teeter. "Privacy and the Press Since *Time* v. *Hill.*" *Washington Law Review* 50 (1974):57.

Pilgrim, Tim A. "Docudramas and False-Light Invasion of Privacy." *Communications and the Law,* June 1988, 3.

Prosser, William L. "Privacy." *California Law Review* 48 (1960):383.

Rubiner, Michael. "Style Is One Thing, Defining It Is Another." *The New York Times,* 5 July 1992.

Warren, Samuel D., and Louis D. Brandeis. "The Right to Privacy." *Harvard Law Review* 4 (1890):220.

Wyatt, Robert O. *Free Expression and the American Public.* Murfreesboro, Tenn.: Middle Tennessee State University, 1991.

Gathering Information
Records and Meetings

This chapter is about the role played by the law in the efforts of reporters and others to gather information. American government is divided into three parts: the executive branch, the judicial branch, and the legislative branch. This chapter focuses on the law as it relates to the executive branch and to news gathering in general. Access to judicial hearings and records is covered in Chapters 11 and 12. The legislative branch is usually regarded as a force unto itself in defining access to its meetings and records. It makes its own rules, and the law has little to do with it.

This chapter covers the use of the First Amendment, both as a shield to block government from prosecuting reporters because they have violated the law as they gathered information, and as a sword to force open closed meeting rooms, restricted disaster sites, file cabinets, and computer storage facilities. But the primary focus of the chapter is state and federal statutes that define the rights of all citizens, including reporters, to gain access to government-held information.

Chapter 9

Information is the lifeblood of American journalism and American politics. Because the government is the biggest and most important institution in our lives, information about the government and information gathered by the government is a central focus of the news media. For most of the history of this republic, government was not a major repository of information that most people wanted to see. But government has grown in size and scope in the past 70 years and today controls the access to more data than most of us can imagine. Vast social programs that began in the 1930s, increased law enforcement functions, myriad new environmental, consumer, health, welfare, and safety responsibilities, national security problems because of the Cold War and several hot wars, and scores of other new government obligations have generated mountains of records. Until the mid-20th century there were few significant rules that defined the rights of citizens, including journalists, to gain access to the information generated and kept by the government. Reporters developed sophisticated but informal schemes with news sources in government to get the material they needed. The average citizen was shut out.

Since the 1950s state and federal governments have passed laws defining public access to records and meetings. If there was a "Golden Age of Access" to information it was likely in the 1970s and early 1980s. Since then there has been a growing government resistance to public (especially press) access to such materials. While it is incorrect to argue that the public has taken an active role in supporting this government resistance, public support for the press, which is the most active agent seeking access to records and meetings, is not now strong, and seems to be diminishing each year. Seattle attorney Michael J. Killeen argues that there are several reasons for the lack of public support for access to information.[1] Most people don't understand the concept of open government, he says. Americans also say they are worried about protecting their personal privacy. Government agencies maintain records that include a substantial amount of private information about citizens. Attempts to gain access to any government records are often challenged by concerns over invasion of personal privacy. Finally, people say they are dissatisfied with news coverage of a wide range of issues. Many people are reluctant to back the press as journalists fight to keep tabs on government officials. Sensing this lack of public support, government agencies have become bolder in their attempts to curtail access to public records and public meetings.

Journalists and citizen activists are often forced to go to court to try to assert rights they believe have been abridged by government restrictions on access to information. But rights and liberties are grounded in the law. We don't enjoy rights in the United States just because they feel good, or because they are inherent to human nature. When someone goes to court and asks for something, the first thing the judge will say is "Show me the law." So if journalists hope to use the law for assistance, they must find support in one of those sources of the law discussed in Chapter 1.

But rights and liberties are grounded in the law.

1. Killeen, "Resistance to Public Access," 2.

NEWS GATHERING AND THE LAW

No legal right to gather news or attend meetings can be found in the common law. Despite the tradition of open government both in this country and in Great Britain, the common law provides only bare access to government documents and to meetings of public agencies. In Great Britain, where the common law developed, complete and total access to Parliament, for example, was not guaranteed until 1874, and even then the House of Commons could exclude the public by a majority vote. Initially the public was excluded because members of Parliament feared reprisal from the Crown for statements made during floor debate. Later this fear subsided, but secret meetings continued in order to prevent voters from finding out that many members of the legislative body were not faithful in keeping promises to constituents.

Secrecy in England had a direct impact on how colonial legislatures conducted their business. The Constitutional Convention of 1787 in Philadelphia was conducted in secret. The public and the press had almost immediate access to sessions in the U.S. House of Representatives, but it was not until 1794 that spectators and reporters were allowed into the Senate chamber. Although today access is guaranteed to nearly all sessions of Congress, much (maybe even most) congressional business is conducted by committees that frequently meet in secret.

Common-law precedents exist that open certain public records to inspection by members of the public, but distinct limitations have been placed on this common-law right. For example, under the common law a person seeking access to a record must have an "interest" in that record. And most often this interest must relate to some kind of litigation in which the person who seeks the record is a participant. Also, only those records "required to be kept" by state law are subject to even such limited disclosure under the common law. Many important records kept by the government are not "required to be kept" by law. Hence, the common law must be found wanting as an aid in the process of news gathering.

THE CONSTITUTION AND NEWS GATHERING

The U.S. Constitution is another source of the law in this nation. Does this document provide any assistance to the citizen who seeks to scrutinize government records or attend meetings of government bodies? Surprisingly, perhaps, the First Amendment plays a rather insignificant role in defining the rights of citizens and journalists in the news-gathering process. The amendment was drafted in an age when news gathering was not a primary function of the press. The congressional records of the drafting and adoption of the First Amendment fail to support the notion that the protection of the news-gathering process was to be included within the scope of freedom of the press. The adoption of antecedents to the First Amendment, such as the free speech provisions of the Virginia Declaration of Rights, and the letters and publications of men like Adams, Madison, and Jefferson, are also found wanting in support of this idea. On August 15, 1789, during the House debate on the adoption of the First Amendment, James Madison, its principal author in the Congress, stated that if freedom of expression means nothing more than that "the people have a right to express and communicate their sentiments and wishes, we have provided for it already" (in what was to become the First Amendment). "The right of freedom of speech is secured; the liberty of free press is expressly declared to be beyond the reach of this government; the people may therefore publicly address their representatives, may privately address them, or declare sentiments by petition to the whole body," Madison added. One is hard-pressed to find within this description of the First Amendment guarantee of freedom of expression expansive notions about the right to gather news and information. The First Amendment was seen as a means by which the public could confront its government, not necessarily report on its activities.[2]

But the U.S. Constitution is a living document, and as Justice Oliver Wendell Holmes reminds us, each age should be the mistress of its own law. Courts are surely not precluded today from finding a right to gather news within the ambit of the First Amendment, even if such a right did not exist in 1791. The argument could certainly be made that because the press of the late 18th century did not as such gather news (the newspapers of the day were more likely to be filled with essays than news stories), such a right could not have existed in 1791. So it does little harm to the intent of the drafters of the First Amendment to find such a right among the constitutional guarantees of the 21st century, when news gathering is the primary function of the press. This argument has been made but has not been well accepted by the courts.

The Supreme Court has had numerous occasions to explore the nexus between freedom of expression and news gathering. In a non-press-related case in 1964, the members of the high court ruled that the constitutional right to speak and publish does not carry with it the unrestrained right to gather information.[3] Eight years later Justice Byron White, speaking as well for three other members of the high court, said: "Nor is it suggested that news gathering does not qualify for First Amendment protection; without some protection for seeking out the news, freedom of the press could be eviscerated."[4] The statement was dictum in a case that involved the right of journalists to refuse to reveal the names of confidential news sources (see Chapter 10). But White said he couldn't find any connection at all between news gathering and a reporter's reluctance to reveal the name of a confidential news source, and one wonders whether he really meant what he said about news gathering and the First Amendment. In any case, such comments are as far as the Supreme Court has come in dealing with the matter in an abstract way.

The high court has been asked on three separate occasions whether the First Amendment guarantees a journalist the unobstructed right to gather news in a prison. In each case the court said no. In *Pell* v. *Procunier*,[5] reporters in California attempted to interview specific inmates at California prisons. In *Saxbe* v. *Washington Post*,[6] reporters from that newspaper sought to interview specific inmates at federal prisons at Lewisburg, Pa., and Danbury, Conn. In both instances the press was barred from conducting the interviews. The U.S. Bureau of Prisons rule, which is similar to the California regulation, states:

> Press representatives will not be permitted to interview individual inmates. This rule shall apply even where the inmate requests or seeks an interview.

2. See Rourke, *Secrecy and Publicity* and Padover, *The Complete Madison.*
3. *Zemel* v. *Rusk,* 381 U.S. 1 (1964).
4. *Branzburg* v. *Hayes,* 408 U.S. 655 (1972).
5. 417 U.S. 817 (1974).
6. 417 U.S. 843 (1974).

At issue was not access to the prison system. The press could tour and photograph prison facilities, conduct brief conversations with randomly encountered inmates, and correspond with inmates through the mails. Outgoing correspondence from inmates was neither censored nor inspected, and incoming mail was inspected only for contraband and statements that might incite illegal action. In addition, the federal rules had been interpreted to permit journalists to conduct lengthy interviews with randomly selected groups of inmates. In fact, a reporter in the Washington Post case did go to Lewisburg and interview a group of prisoners.

The argument of the press in both cases was that to ban interviews with specific inmates abridged the First Amendment protection afforded the news-gathering activity of a free press. The Supreme Court disagreed in a 5–4 decision in both cases. Justice Stewart's opinion was subscribed to by Chief Justice Burger, and Justices Blackmun, White, and Rehnquist. Justice Stewart wrote that the press already had substantial access to the prisons and that there was no evidence that prison officials were hiding things from reporters. Stewart rejected the notion that the First Amendment gave newspeople a special right of access to the prisons. "Newsmen have no constitutional right of access to prisons or their inmates beyond that afforded the general public," the justice wrote.[7] Since members of the general public have no right to interview specific prisoners, the denial of this right to the press does not infringe on the First Amendment.

The high court did not disagree with the findings of the district court in the *Saxbe* case that face-to-face interviews with specific inmates are essential to accurate and effective reporting about prisoners and prisons. What the court seemed to say was that while the First Amendment guarantees freedom of expression, it does not guarantee effective and accurate reporting. In fact, about five months after the *Saxbe* and *Pell* decisions, in a speech at the Yale Law School Sesquicentennial Convocation, Justice Stewart made this exact point:

> The press is free to do battle against secrecy and deception in government. But the press cannot expect from the Constitution any guarantee that it will succeed. There is no constitutional right to have access to particular governmental information, or to require openness from the bureaucracy. The public's interest in knowing about its government is protected by the guarantee of a free press, but the protection is indirect. The Constitution itself is neither a Freedom of Information Act nor an Official Secrets Act. The Constitution, in other words, establishes the contest, not its resolution.[8]

"There is no constitutional right to have access to particular governmental information, or to require openness from the bureaucracy."

In 1978 the high court split along similar lines on a case involving press access rights to a county jail.[9] An inmate at the Santa Rita County, Calif., jail committed suicide in 1975. Following the death and a report by a psychiatrist that jail conditions were bad, KQED television in San Francisco sought permission to inspect and take pictures in the jail. Sheriff Houchins announced that the media could certainly participate in one of the six tours of the jail facility that were given to the public each year. However, the tours did not visit the disciplinary cells nor the portion of the jail in which the suicide had taken place. No cameras or tape recorders were allowed, but photographs of some parts of the jail were supplied by the sheriff's office.

7. *Pell* v. *Procunier,* 417 U.S. 817 (1974).
8. Stewart, "Or of the Press," 631.
9. *Houchins* v. *KQED,* 438 U.S. 1 (1978).

Reporters at KQED took a jail tour, but were not happy at the limits placed on them. Sheriff Houchins contended that unregulated visits through the jail by the press would infringe on the inmates' right of privacy, could create jail celebrities out of inmates that would in turn cause problems for jailers, and would disrupt jail operations. Houchins noted that reporters did have access to inmates—they could visit individual prisoners, could visit with inmates awaiting trial, could talk by telephone with inmates, could write letters to prisoners, and so forth. But KQED argued that it had a constitutionally protected right to gather news and challenged the limits.

Chief Justice Warren Burger wrote the opinion for the court in the 4–3 decision in which neither Justice Blackmun nor Justice Marshall took part. "Neither the First Amendment nor the Fourteenth Amendment mandates a right of access to government information or sources of information within the government's control," Burger asserted. The chief justice seemed troubled by the argument of KQED that only through access to the jail could the press perform its public responsibility.

> Unarticulated but implicit in the assertion that the media access to jail is essential for an informed public debate on jail conditions is the assumption that the media personnel are the best qualified persons for the task of discovering malfeasance in public institutions. . . . The media are not a substitute for or an adjunct of government. . . . We must not confuse the role of the media with that of government.[10]

In 1980 in a case that many commentators hailed as the beginning of a general constitutionally guaranteed "right to know," the Supreme Court ruled that the First Amendment does establish for all citizens the right to attend criminal trials.[11] (See Chapter 12 for a full discussion of this case.) But while Chief Justice Burger's opinion was quite explicit regarding the First Amendment and attendance at criminal trials, it was obscure regarding the larger constitutional right to gather news in other contexts. And the high court has done little in the past two decades to clarify its position on this question. Although it has decided a number of right-of-access cases since *Richmond Newspapers,*[12] the Supreme Court has never explicitly recognized this right outside of judicial proceedings.

The lower federal courts and state courts tend to mirror the rulings by the Supreme Court that reject the notion of a First Amendment right of access to information and meetings. There are, however, significant exceptions:

- In 1950 a federal district judge in Rhode Island ruled that when public records are restricted from examination and publication, "the attempts to prohibit their publication is an abridgment of the freedom of the speech and the press."[13] The Pawtucket city council had given access permission to one newspaper but refused to grant similar access to another newspaper that editorially opposed the city

---

10. *Houchins* v. *KQED,* 438 U.S. 1 (1978).
11. *Richmond Newspapers* v. *Virginia,* 448 U.S. 555 (1980).
12. See, for example, *Press-Enterprise Co.* v. *Riverside Superior Court,* 464 U.S. 501 (1984).
13. *Providence Journal Co. et al.* v. *McCoy et al.,* 49 F. Supp. 186 (1950).

administration. A U.S. court of appeals upheld the lower-court rulings, but on the grounds that the denial of access to information to the opposition newspaper was a denial of equal protection of the laws as guaranteed by the 14th Amendment to the U.S. Constitution but was not necessarily a violation of the First Amendment.

- The 5th U.S. Circuit Court of Appeals ruled in 1977 that news gathering was protected by the First Amendment but still denied a reporter's request to film the execution of a condemned man.[14]

- When the White House staff tried to exclude camera crews with the Cable News Network from the pool of network television photographers who cover the president, a U.S. district court forbade the discriminatory action, noting that the First Amendment includes a "right of access to news and information concerning the operations and activities of government."[15]

- In 1985 a federal court in Utah ruled that the public and the press had a First Amendment right to attend a formal administrative fact-finding hearing by the Mine Safety and Health Administration to investigate the causes of a mine fire that killed 27 people. The 10th U.S. Circuit Court of Appeals later overturned this ruling, noting that the hearings had ended and the issue was moot.[16]

- Finally, a U.S. district court in Ohio ruled in 1988 that the press and the public have a qualified First Amendment right of access to the legislative process—in this case a city council meeting. The court said there was always a First Amendment presumption in favor of open government meetings, a presumption that can only be overcome by a formal showing of a need for privacy and confidentiality.[17]

Unfortunately decisions like these stand in stark contrast to a larger body of case law that denies this proposition. Most courts do not find that the First Amendment is an impediment to government actions that limit access to records, meetings, and even news gathering in general. A key point that must be remembered regarding these rulings: In virtually all the instances noted in which a court has ruled that the First Amendment does provide a means of gaining access to a meeting or a record, the court has emphasized that this right belongs to both the press and the public. Reporters are not given any special rights in this regard, only those rights that all citizens enjoy.

What we have just looked at is the use of the First Amendment as a kind of sword, a weapon or tool to gain access to information or records. In recent years journalists have been accused of invasion of privacy (see pages 260–272), trespass, disorderly conduct, and unlawful news gathering when they have attempted to get a news story. Has the First Amendment been an effective shield in warding off these prosecutions? The answer is no; the First Amendment has been of little use at all. Let's examine some of these issues.

---

14. *Garrett* v. *Estelle*, 556 F. 2d 1274 (1977).
15. *CNN* v. *ABC et al.*, 518 F. Supp. 1238 (1981).
16. *Society of Professional Journalists* v. *Secretary of Labor*, 11 M.L.R. 2474 (1985), rev'd. 832 F. 2d 1180 (1987).
17. *WJW* v. *Cleveland*, 686 F. Supp. 177 (1988).

The First Amendment Protection of News Gathering

At first glance the arguments sound compelling. An informed citizenry needs information to effectively undertake its responsibility to govern itself. The most important independent source of information is the American press: newspapers, magazines, television, radio, and the Internet. In order to provide citizens with needed information, journalists must go where news is happening. And sometimes the news is happening behind closed doors, on private property, or in restricted areas. To get the news, reporters may have to pretend they are someone else, lie about their backgrounds, use surreptitious techniques, and even deceive news sources. But news gathering serves a high public purpose. These transgressions by journalists—which might result in civil or even criminal liability if done by nonjournalists—must be forgiven. The journalist's illegal acts must be shielded by the First Amendment. Compelling arguments, indeed.

American courts, however, have been largely unswayed by these arguments. In 1998 a U.S. district court in Maryland refused to dismiss charges of transporting and receiving child pornography against a free-lance journalist who attempted to block the prosecution by arguing that he was gathering news, not child pornography. Laurence Matthews said that law enforcement officials were too zealous in their prosecution of Internet users and that the news stories resulting from his investigation would reveal this overly aggressive official action. His work was in the public interest, he said. But the court was not moved. "It is well settled that the First Amendment does not grant the press automatic relief from laws of general application," Judge Williams said. "If law enforcement officials are doing something improper in their investigations the court does not understand how the defendant would uncover malfeasance by receiving and disseminating the materials himself."[18]

The Matthews case, while stating the general rule of law, can surely be viewed as an aberration in some ways. Most reporters don't violate criminal statutes, as Matthews was charged with doing, to investigate how the police enforce those statutes. But reporters do break other laws. An overview of some of these kinds of situations will demonstrate that the courts are no more tolerant of these actions.

Trespass   Reporters don't have the right to **trespass** on private property if the owner or occupant of the property objects. It makes no difference that police or fire officials invite the reporters to cross the property line or enter the private premises. A state court in New York sustained a trespass action against a broadcasting film crew stemming from an incident at an exclusive New York City restaurant. The news crew had been sent to visit various restaurants cited by local authorities for health code violations. The crew entered the restaurant with its cameras rolling and floodlights on. Although the proprietor of the restaurant commanded the reporters to leave, the journalists stayed with the cameras and continued to film until they were physically escorted from the premises. In the meantime, customers ducked under tables, and some fled without paying their bills.

---

18. *U.S.* v. *Matthews,* 11 F. Supp. 2d 656 (1998). Matthews was sentenced to 18 months in prison in September 1998.

The broadcasting company, CBS, attempted to defend its action by using the First Amendment as a shield to protect itself from the trespass suit. The court disagreed. "Clearly, the First Amendment is not a shibboleth before which all other rights must succumb," the judge ruled:

> This court recognizes that the exercise of the right of free speech and free press demands and even mandates the observance of the co-equal duty not to abuse such right, but to utilize it with right reason and dignity. Vain lip service to "duties" in a vacuous reality wherein "rights" exist, sovereign and independent of any balancing moral or social factor, creates a semantical mockery of the very foundation of our laws and legal system.[19]

Since 1980 the courts have decided several cases in which reporters, broadcasters, or photographers have been charged with trespass or related illegal acts. The rulings have remained consistent and a few simple, basic rules have emerged. If the owner of the property or the resident of a dwelling refuses to permit journalists to enter the property or the dwelling, the journalists must stay off the property, whether or not news is happening there. Reporters in Oklahoma followed protesters into restricted areas during demonstrations at a nuclear facility. The protesters were arrested; so were the journalists. The Oklahoma Court of Appeals upheld the criminal trespass conviction of the journalists, ruling that the reporters were given reasonable access to the events at the facility and they did not need to trespass to get the story.[20] However, reporters who seek to gather news on private property that is generally open to the public are not normally regarded as committing a trespass, unless they refuse to leave when asked to do so. ABC photographers secretly filmed eye examinations given to patients in a private eye clinic. The owners of the clinic later sued for a variety of legal wrongs (see page 270 for a discussion of the invasion of privacy claim) including trespass. The 7th U.S. Circuit Court of Appeals rejected the trespass action, saying that there was no invasion in this case of any of the specific interests that the tort of trespass seeks to protect. The offices were open to anyone who sought the ophthalmologic services offered by the clinic. The activity in the office was not disrupted; there was no invasion of anyone's private space. The court compared the reporters to restaurant critics who secretly visit restaurants, or persons who pose as prospective homebuyers to gather evidence of the violation of laws barring discrimination in the sale or rental of housing.[21] On the other hand, if a reporter has consent from the property owner or occupant of the dwelling to proceed onto private property, then a subsequent trespass suit will not be sustained in court. After a woman permitted a CBS television crew to accompany a crisis intervention team that entered her home, she was later unable to maintain that this action had been a trespass.[22]

Government officials, however, cannot give reporters permission to enter private premises. If the occupant or owner protests, the journalists must leave. A Humane Society investigator obtained a search warrant to enter a home whose occupants had been the object of

Government officials, however, cannot give reporters permission to enter private premises.

19. *Le Mistral, Inc.* v. *CBS*, 402 N.Y.S. 2d 815 (1978).
20. *Stahl* v. *Oklahoma*, 665 P. 2d 839 (1983).
21. *Desnick* v. *American Broadcasting Companies, Inc.*, 44 F. 3d 1345 (1995).
22. *Baugh* v. *CBS, Inc.*, 828 F. Supp. 745 (1993).

numerous complaints of cruelty to animals. The investigator invited reporters and film crews from three television stations to accompany him in this foray. The journalists went inside the home, despite the protests of one of the occupants, filmed the interior of the home, and then broadcast the news story. In a lawsuit that followed, the television stations attempted to raise the defense of "implied consent through custom and usage," but the New York court disagreed vigorously. The so-called implied consent to enter a private home is a custom created by the press itself, the judge noted.[23] "This is a boot-strapping argument," he said, that does not eliminate the trespass in this case. Newspeople do not stand in any favored position with regard to trespass, the judge said. "If the news media were to succeed in compelling an uninvited and nonpermitted entry into one's private home whenever it chose to do so, this would be nothing less than a general warrant equivalent to the writs of assistance which were so odious to the American colonists," he added.

This reminder by the court is something many in the news business seem to have forgotten: The individuals who wrote the U.S. Constitution were as fearful of government intrusions into homes and churches as they were of censorship of the press. Some federal judges seem to be doing their best to remind journalists of this fact. Federal Judge Jack B. Weinstein lashed out at both government agents and producers for CBS in the wake of a particularly odious search of a home in Brooklyn. In March of 1992 federal agents, accompanied by a CBS news crew, searched the home of Babatunde Ayeni. The government agents were seeking evidence that Ayeni was involved in a credit card fraud scheme. The news crew, which manifested no CBS logos on their clothing or equipment, was seeking video footage for the TV show "Street Stories." Ayeni was not at home. Agents were met by his wife, Tawa, attired in a dressing gown, and his 4-year-old son. The search took two hours. Mrs. Ayeni objected to the videotaping, but later testified that she assumed the news crew was a government video crew. Agents wore microphones and made comments as they were videotaped holding up objects (personal letters and photos, etc.) they uncovered in the search. Nothing they found, however, was evidence of criminal wrongdoing. (Ayeni later did plead guilty to criminal conspiracy and was put on probation.) Before they left the home the agents were filmed explaining how credit card fraud schemes work, expressing disappointment that they did not uncover evidence, and assuring the camera crew (and the audience) that Ayeni was involved in these illegal schemes.

The incident has resulted in considerable litigation. When Ayeni was brought to trial for fraud, his attorneys subpoenaed to have the CBS tape for his defense. Ayeni's attorneys got the tape and later used it in a civil action against CBS for invasion of privacy and tortious news gathering.

CBS and its news personnel sought to have the privacy suit dismissed, claiming they were immune from suit, that they were acting with the permission of government agents and should therefore be shielded from a lawsuit. But the U.S. District Court disagreed. Judge Weinstein said that the federal agents went beyond the scope of the search warrant when they allowed the camera crew into the Ayeni home. The video pictures made by CBS constitute a seizure of property under the meaning of the 4th Amendment, he wrote. "CBS had no greater right than that of a thief to be in the home, to take pictures and to remove the photographic

23. *Anderson* v. *WROC-TV,* 441 N.Y.S. 2d 815 (1981).

record," he said.[24] "In this instance, the television crew took from the home, for the purpose of broadcasting them to the world at large, pictures of intimate secrets of the household, including sequences of a cowering mother and child resisting the videotaping," Weinstein added. After its motion to dismiss was denied, CBS quickly settled the lawsuit out of court.

Cooperation between the press and government agents, which for most reporters only 25 years ago was regarded as unthinkable, is becoming more and more common, especially as the so-called reality television shows try to satisfy their ever-increasing appetite to fill hours of programming. While it may not yet be the norm, reporters and photographers routinely accompany federal, state, and local police officers as they execute search warrants, arrest fugitives, and investigate crime. In 1999 the Supreme Court of the United States unanimously ruled that when law enforcement officers permit reporters to accompany them when they enter private homes to conduct searches or witness arrests, the officers violate "the right of residential privacy at the core of the Fourth Amendment." Two cases had found their way to the high court. The first, *Wilson* v. *Layne,* resulted when members of a joint federal and local law-enforcement task force invited a Washington Post reporter and photographer to accompany them when they arrested fugitives in Rockville, Md., just outside the nation's capital. The other case, *Hanlon* v. *Berger,* involved agents of the U.S. Fish and Wildlife Service who invited reporters and photographers from CNN to accompany them as they searched the property of a Montana rancher for evidence that the property owner was illegally poisoning wildlife. The issue the Supreme Court focused upon was whether the government agents who brought the journalists onto the private property could be held responsible for civil rights violations; in other words, could the property owners sue the government agents for violating their Fourth Amendment rights against an illegal search? The government agents attempted to justify the invitations by arguing that such close-up coverage of their action will assist the public in understanding law enforcement problems and help the police in getting more public cooperation. "Surely the possibility of good public relations for the police is simply not enough, standing alone to justify the ride-along intrusion into a private home," Chief Justice William Rehnquist wrote for the court. The chief justice quoted an almost 400-year-old British court ruling in supporting the high court's decision: "The house of everyone is to him as his castle and fortress, as well for his defence [*sic*] against injury and violence, for his repose." But because the law concerning media ride-alongs had not been developed when these arrests took place, the high court ruled that it would be unfair to subject the police officers in this case to money damages for their behavior. The officers could not have clearly foreseen that what they did would be a violation of the Constitution.[25]

The court chose not, at least for now, to rule on the matter of the liability of reporters and photographers who enter private premises with the permission of police. The *Berger* case was remanded to the 9th U.S. Circuit Court of Appeals for disposition in light of the high court ruling regarding the liability of the police.[26] In an earlier decision, the Court of Appeals had ruled that, because of the extremely close cooperation between the journalists and the

24. *Ayeni* v. *CBS, Inc.,* 848 F. Supp. 362 (1994).
25. *Wilson* v. *Layne,* 119 S. Ct. 1692 (1999).
26. *Hanlon* v. *Berger,* 119 S. Ct. 1706 (1999).

government agents who searched the Montana ranch, the television reporters and producers were actually "state actors" or "joint actors" with the wildlife agents and could be subject to the same kind of Fourth Amendment action brought against the federal officers.[27] After the Supreme Court decision, the appellate court ruled that the journalists did not enjoy the kind of qualified immunity that had shielded the government agents in the *Wilson* case, reinstated Berger's Fourth Amendment claim against the reporters, and also reversed a lower court's dismissal of claims for trespass and the intentional infliction of emotional distress against the media defendants.[28] The case was still being litigated in the late spring of 2000.

These rulings send a clear message that if a reporter wants to enter private property, he or she better have the permission of the occupant or the owner of the property. Government agents are unable to give the press this permission. The ruling does not spell the end of the dubious practice of media ride-alongs. The press can still accompany law enforcement officers as they enforce the law on public sidewalks, public streets, and other public places.

Harassment   In 1996 a federal judge in Pennsylvania took the extraordinary action of enjoining the news-gathering activities of two reporters who worked for the television info-tainment program "Inside Edition." Reporters Paul Lewis and Stephen Wilson were preparing a story on the high salaries paid to corporate executives at U.S. HealthCare while the company was imposing severe cost cutting on patients. The story focused on Leonard Abramson, chairman of the board, and Abramson's daughter and son-in-law, Nancy and Richard Wolfson, who also worked at U.S. HealthCare. The Wolfsons argued that the reporters used ambush interviews, shotgun microphones, and other electronic equipment to harass them and invade their privacy after they rejected requests for on-camera interviews. The reporters went so far, the couple said, as to follow their daughter to school and to follow the entire family when they took a vacation in Florida. The Wolfsons sued the reporters for tortious stalking, harassment, trespass, and invasion of privacy–intrusion upon seclusion, and asked the judge to stop the reporters from using the intrusive news-gathering techniques until a jury trial was held. The judge ruled that he thought the Wolfsons would prevail in their lawsuit against the reporters. He said that through their unreasonable surveilling, hounding, and following, the two news gatherers had effectively rendered the family captive in their own home. The judge barred Lewis and Wilson from any conduct, with or without the use of cameras, that invades the Wolfsons' privacy, actions including but not limited to harassing, hounding, following, intruding, frightening, terrorizing, or ambushing the family.[29]

Many in the press found the judge's actions frightening.[30] It is indeed rare for a court to enjoin—issue a prior restraint against—news-gathering activities. The court appeared highly sympathetic to the Wolfsons' concern about the safety of their children. But the court was also disturbed by the nontraditional reporting techniques of the two reporters. Neutral observers tend to view the ruling not as a blow to news gathering but as a sharp reaction to the overly aggressive behavior of the "Inside Edition" reporters.

---

27. *Berger* v. *Hanlon*, 129 F. 3d 505 (1997).
28. *Berger* v. *Hanlon*, 28 M.L.R. 1094 (1999).
29. *Wolfson* v. *Lewis*, 924 F. Supp. 1413 (1996).
30. Schulz, "Troubling Ruling," 5.

TIPS ON NEWS GATHERING AND TRESPASS

Kent Middleton makes the following observations in the Pepperdine Law Review:

- The person who is in possession of the property can give consent to a reporter to enter the property. It doesn't always have to be the owner; a tenant of a rental property, for example, can give consent.
- A property owner who gives consent to a public officer to enter the property is not automatically giving consent to reporters who accompany this official.
- Implied consent is an illusion more often than a reality. For example, the failure of a homeowner to object when reporters enter the home with police cannot be assumed to constitute consent, especially in tense or disorienting circumstances.
- Finally, a government official who legally enters property in an emergency lacks the authority to invite journalists or others to enter the property.

Fraud   Imagine this scenario. A newspaper editor hears well-founded rumors that a local retail business is cheating its customers. To check out this story, two newspaper reporters apply for jobs at the business to take a look at what goes on inside. The pair use false names, fake work histories, and tell the business owners they are looking for work. They do not reveal they are newspaper reporters and will be spying on the other workers at the business. Are the reporters' activities legal? In 1996 a jury in North Carolina ruled that such behavior constituted fraud and awarded a large grocery store chain over $5 million in damages, saying ABC television reporters committed trespass and other infractions as well as fraud when they hired on as employees for the food company.[31] ABC claimed in a broadcast of its "PrimeTime Live" television program that the food chain was selling unclean meat and produce. The trial judge reduced the damages to $315,000 several months later,[32] and in 1999 the Fourth U.S. Circuit Court of Appeals threw out most of the reduced damage award, ruling that the behavior of the ABC reporters did not meet the legal standard for fraud in North Carolina. The food chain's case lacked evidence that the company had been hurt when the ABC employees lied to get hired and secretly recorded activities in the store, the court said. The appellate court left a jury award of $2 intact: an award of $1 for trespass and $1 because the ABC reporters had breached their legal duty to be loyal employees of the company.[33]

The appellate court's reversal notwithstanding, it is possible that reporters who secretly infiltrate a private business looking for news could incur civil liability for fraud. The Minnesota Court of Appeals sustained just such a charge in 1998 when it ruled that a Minneapolis

31. Meier, "Jury Says ABC Owes"; *Food Lion* v. *Capital Cities/ABC, Inc.,* 951 F. Supp. 1224 (1996), 964 F. Supp. 956 (1997).
32. Mifflin, "Judge Slashes."
33. *Food Lion Inc.* v. *Capital Cities/ABC,* 194 F. 3d 505 (1999); see also Barringer, "Appeals Court Rejects Damages."

television station could be liable for both fraud and trespass after one of its reporters lied about her background and her intentions when she applied for a position as a volunteer at a care facility for mentally retarded persons. The reporter secretly videotaped activities at the facility and portions of the tape were later telecast.[34]

Misrepresentation   In the autumn of 1994 NBC approached Raymond Veilleux, owner of a trucking company in Maine, and sought permission to send a reporting team with a long-haul truck driver as he drove a California-to-Maine run. Veilleux and driver Peter Kennedy said they were suspicious of the offer because of the growing pressures for stricter regulation of truckers in the wake of a fatal accident in 1993. Four young people had been killed when the car in which they were riding was struck by a long-haul driver who had exceeded the number of hours he was legally allowed to drive. Veilleux and Kennedy conceded to work with the network only after NBC agreed to present a positive view of trucking. The network producers said that they would not ask Kennedy to violate any trucking regulations or deviate from his normal driving routine during the trip and that the report would not include any comments from an organization called Parents Against Tired Truckers, an advocacy group fighting for tougher trucking regulations. The 1995 "Dateline" segment did not portray the industry in a positive way. The opening line was, "American highways are a trucker's killing field." The report included interviews with members of Parents Against Tired Truckers, alleged that driver Kennedy repeatedly violated hours-of-service regulations, falsified his driver's log book, and lied to federal inspectors. NBC also revealed that Kennedy had previously tested positive for marijuana and amphetamine use in a random drug test. Kennedy was shown admitting to some of these allegations during the program. Veilleux and Kennedy sued. A U.S. district court rejected NBC's motion for a summary judgment and permitted a jury to hear allegations of misrepresentation, false light privacy, and negligent infliction of emotional distress.[35] In July of 1998 the jury awarded the plaintiffs $525,000 in damages. Twenty months later, the 1st U.S. Circuit Court of Appeals dismissed many of the charges against NBC on the grounds that most of the statements in the broadcast were not materially false and could not sustain a claim of intentional infliction of emotional distress or false light privacy. The court also said the claim of misrepresentation against the network for promises it made to portray the trucking company in a positive way could not be sustained because in the course of the investigation, NBC uncovered negative information about the trucking company that it was free to report. But the network remained liable for misrepresentation for failing to fulfill its promise not to involve the Parents Against Tired Truckers in the broadcast.[36]

Failure to Obey Lawful Orders   Police and fire officials at the scene of disasters, accidents, and fires frequently restrict the access of the press and public to the site. Reporters are bound to respect these rules or face charges of disorderly conduct or worse. The New Jersey Supreme Court upheld the disorderly person conviction of a press photographer who was charged with

---

34. *Special Force Ministries* v. *WCCO Television,* 584 N.W. 2d 789 (1998).

35. *Veilleax* v. *National Broadcasting Co.,* 8 F. Supp. 2d 23 (1998).

36. Schiesel, "Jury Finds NBC Negligent," *Veilleux* v. *National Broadcasting Co.,* 1st Cir., No. 98-2104, 3/6/00.

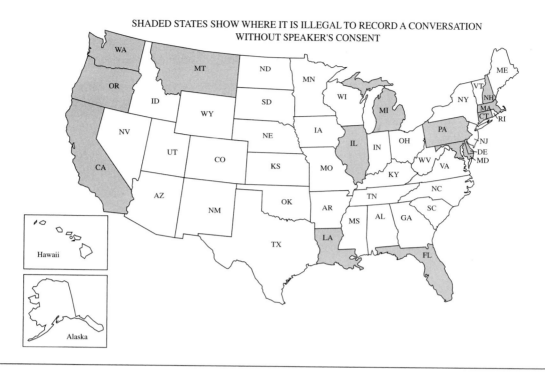

SHADED STATES SHOW WHERE IT IS ILLEGAL TO RECORD A CONVERSATION
WITHOUT SPEAKER'S CONSENT

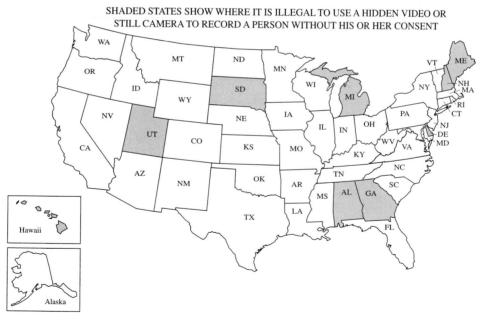

SHADED STATES SHOW WHERE IT IS ILLEGAL TO USE A HIDDEN VIDEO OR
STILL CAMERA TO RECORD A PERSON WITHOUT HIS OR HER CONSENT

impeding a police officer in the performance of his duty at the scene of a serious traffic accident. The photographer was standing near the wreckage when the state trooper, who feared a fire might begin and who also wanted to preserve the accident scene for investigation, ordered the area cleared of spectators. The news photographer moved back five feet, but when he refused to move any farther, he was arrested.

The journalist, Harvey J. Lashinsky, argued that the state's disorderly person statute was inapplicable to him because he was a member of the press. The state's high court disagreed, noting that "the constitutional prerogatives of the press must yield under appropriate circumstances to other important and legitimate interests." Acknowledging that the press does play a special role in society, the court nevertheless said that the photographer clearly impeded the officer by refusing his request to leave the area. While the officer was arguing with the journalist, he could have been giving assistance to the accident victims and beginning the investigation of the crash.[37]

When a commuter aircraft crashed near Billy Mitchell Field outside Milwaukee in September of 1985 police cordoned off the crash site so rescue workers and federal safety officials could do their work. WTMJ news photographer Peter Ah King and three other journalists who had run through a police roadblock to reach the crash site were told by authorities to leave the area. But Ah King jumped a fence and ran to the top of a small hill 30 yards away. When a police officer caught up with him he was told to leave, but he refused and continued to take video pictures of the crash site. He told authorities he would only leave if he was arrested, so police arrested him. Shortly thereafter the crash site was opened to the press. Ah King was convicted of disorderly conduct. He appealed his conviction to the Wisconsin Supreme Court, which affirmed the lower-court ruling. The court said that the refusal to obey a police command does not normally constitute disorderly conduct. But in this case the photographer's repeated refusal to obey the order to leave the area in a situation in which crowd control was a major concern, coupled with "his continued penetration into a nonpublic restricted area," must be regarded as disorderly conduct because the conduct had the tendency to disrupt good order. The court acknowledged that reporters have a right to gather the news by any means within the law, but they do not have a First Amendment right to access, solely because they are news gatherers, to the scene of an airplane crash from which the general public has been excluded.[38] (Note: At least one state, California, has a statute that gives the news media the right to enter disaster areas closed to the general public. But reporters must sign a waiver of liability of the government before access is allowed.)

Grand juries work behind closed doors, and courts are very sensitive when anyone attempts to elicit information from the jurors about what has taken place. Two reporters in Indiana were held in contempt of court when they attempted to induce former grand jury members to reveal secret testimony. But the Indiana Supreme Court dismissed the contempt charges in this case. The court bluntly affirmed that unlawful news-gathering activities are not protected by the First Amendment and that any attempt to induce grand jurors to reveal secret testimony can surely be punished by the courts. But in this case, the reporters attempted to

37. *State* v. *Lashinsky,* 404 A. 2d 1121 (1979).
38. *Oak Tree* v. *Ah King,* 436 N.W. 2d 285 (1989).

gain information from former grand jurors more than two years after the closure of the particular grand jury proceeding. The attempts to obtain information in this case could hardly impede the administration of justice, the state court declared.[39]

Note the point made in these cases that a journalist has an obligation to obey "lawful" orders by police and other officials. Photographer David Connell obeyed the orders of police officers, but he believed they were unlawful. A U.S. district court in New Hampshire agreed and ruled that Connell's civil rights had been violated when he was barred from taking pictures at an automobile accident. One person was killed, another seriously injured in the collision. Connell began taking pictures from a spot about 25 feet away from the accident. When the police asked him to move, he retreated to a spot about 30 yards away, and then 40 yards away. Police still weren't satisfied, so Connell went into a home and began taking pictures from a second-floor window. Others were viewing the wreck from a similar vantage point. Police and emergency medical technicians still weren't happy, and Connell was ordered to stop taking pictures or face arrest for disturbing the peace. He complied but brought the civil rights action against the town of Hudson. "It is hard to imagine how Connell could have interfered with police or emergency activities by taking pictures from the second floor of a house that others were using to view the accident," the court said. The real reason for the restriction on the photographer seemed to be that emergency personnel did not want Connell to take pictures of the dead and injured as they were removed from the automobiles. The court said this was an insufficient justification. The court awarded Connell only nominal damages, one dollar. But the ruling nevertheless makes the strong point that police and fire officials must respect the rights of journalists, who also have a job to do.[40]

Other Laws Many other laws may directly affect news gathering. And the First Amendment does not offer a shield to reporters who violate these, either. For example, in most states and the District of Columbia, a reporter can secretly record a conversation or interview with a news source. But in California, Connecticut, Delaware, Florida, Illinois, Louisiana, Maryland, Massachusetts, Michigan, Montana, New Hampshire, Oregon, Pennsylvania, and Washington, a reporter must ask for permission before a conversation may be recorded. These restrictions apply to journalists and nonjournalists alike, but the laws make allowances in some instances for recordings made during the coverage of news. For example, if a tape recorder is in plain sight during an interview or speech and the speaker does not object, consent to the recording is presumed. A U.S. district court in Washington state ruled that the audio portion of a videotape of a public demonstration was not covered by the state's statute, so long as the conversations recorded were held on a public street, within earshot of passersby, and the person making the tape was using a readily apparent recording device.[41] Nineteen states and the federal government have passed laws outlawing eavesdropping. In Alabama, Delaware, Georgia, Hawaii, Maine, Michigan, New Hampshire, South Dakota, and Utah, it is illegal to use a hidden video or still camera to record a person without his or her consent. Reporters should know the laws of their own states regarding such matters.

39. *Indiana* v. *Helzel,* 522 N.E. 2d 31 (1990).
40. *Connell* v. *Town of Hudson,* 733 F. Supp. 465 (1990).
41. *Fordyce* v. *Seattle,* 21 M.L.R. 2177 (1993).

The clear message the courts are sending to journalists, as exhibited by the rulings just outlined, is that reporters are not police or government agents. Reporters are not immune from the law simply because they are attempting to gather information about matters of substantial public interest. This message is not new law; for years reporters either respected these rules or were far more subtle when they disregarded them. The push—manifested largely by the info-tainment-oriented prime-time television shows—for more and more video footage of actual events has put great stress on the law and generated tension between news-gatherers, the courts, and the First Amendment. And many observers correctly note that it is usually a push for higher ratings, not service to the public interest, that motivates the sometimes outrageous behavior. Is it just coincidence, for example, that over the past few years ABC has broadcast "PrimeTime Live" programs using hidden cameras and microphones only during the month of November, the important rating sweeps month? If there is a common thread that runs through all the recent news-gathering rulings it is this: Journalists who think they are above the law are in legal peril.

SUMMARY

Gaining access to government-held information is an important problem for journalists and citizens alike. Since the early 1980s government has become more reticent about providing easy access by reporters to the vast amounts of information held by agencies within the government. Public opinion tends to support the government in this regard, and journalists have been forced to exercise legal means to accomplish some reporting tasks. But the law is not always helpful. The common law offers little assistance to persons attempting to inspect government records. The U.S. Constitution was drafted at a time when news gathering was not the central role of the press. There is little evidence to suggest that the right to gather news was intended to be guaranteed by the First Amendment. Federal courts have in recent years suggested that news and information gathering is entitled to some protection under the U.S. Constitution, but they have been stingy in granting such protection. The U.S. Supreme Court has limited the rights of reporters to gather information at prisons and jails to the same rights enjoyed by other citizens. The Supreme Court did rule that all citizens have the right to attend judicial proceedings, but the high court has not extended this First Amendment right beyond the criminal justice system. Lower courts have found broader, albeit qualified, constitutional rights of access. Courts have not permitted, however, the use of the First Amendment to immunize reporters from legal consequences that result when the law is broken while news is being gathered.

THE FREEDOM OF INFORMATION ACT

Neither the common law nor the Constitution has provided the clear and well-defined right of access to government information that most citizens believe is needed. Beginning in the early 1950s, there were concerted efforts by press and citizen lobbying groups to pass statutes that guarantee to public and press alike the right to inspect records and other information held by the government and to attend meetings held by public agencies. These laws now exist in

Between 1789 and 1966 access to the records of the federal government was largely an unsettled question.

almost every state. In addition, there are federal open-records and open-meetings laws. Let us look at the federal legislation first.

Between 1789 and 1966 access to the records of the federal government was largely an unsettled question. Various housekeeping laws, administrative procedure statutes, had been passed by Congress, but none were aimed at providing the kind of access to government records that both the press and a large segment of the population believed necessary for the efficient operation of our democracy. Before 1966 the laws Congress passed were really laws authorizing information to be withheld, rather than laws forcing government agencies to open their files. Also, reporters could do little when requests for information were denied. In 1966, after many years of hearings and testimony and work, Congress adopted the **Freedom of Information Act (FOIA),** which was ostensibly designed to open up records and files long closed to public inspection. The documentary evidence left by Congress relating to the passage of this measure leaves little doubt that the purpose of this bill was to establish a general philosophy of the fullest possible disclosure of government-held records. The Senate Report's Purpose of the Bill section quotes James Madison:

> Knowledge will forever govern ignorance, and a people who mean to be their own governors, must arm themselves with the power knowledge gives. A popular government without popular information or the means of acquiring it, is but a prologue to a farce or a tragedy or perhaps both.[42]

Both the public and the press have accepted this philosophy. Each year about 600,000 FOIA requests are made to the federal government.

The Freedom of Information Act has been an important tool for journalists seeking answers to important questions. In the past 35 years reporters have used the law to expose serious safety defects in the gas tank on the Ford Pinto, to find out why the Hubble Space Telescope mirror failed to work, and to alert citizens in several states about environmental crises at Department of Energy nuclear weapons plants. In 1995 the Dayton (Ohio) Daily News used the FOIA to uncover documents that showed that women in the military were routinely ignored or rebuffed when they brought charges of rape against enlisted men and officers. The Cleveland Plain Dealer used the act in 1996, following the crash of a ValuJet passenger jet in the Everglades, to reveal that the government had been previously aware of safety problems at the airline. In 1997 and 1998 reporters were using the FOIA to try to force the Department of Defense to be more forthcoming in revealing the cause of the illnesses that afflicted thousands of veterans of the Persian Gulf War. These are just a few examples of how the law has worked as it was intended to work. But using the law has not always been easy, for the government often has been genuinely hostile to Freedom of Information Act requests made by reporters. "From Lyndon Johnson's reluctant signing of the FOIA in 1966, every administration since has viewed it with some degree of distaste," said Professor Lotte Feinberg, an FOIA expert at John Jay College of Criminal Justice.

Some administrations have treated the law as an anathema and have done everything possible to subvert the fundamental purpose of the law. Presidents Ronald Reagan and George Bush were unusually skeptical of the idea that the public and the press should have a right of

---

42. U.S. Senate, *Clarifying and Protecting,* 2–3.

access to public documents. President Reagan told his attorney general to inform executive branch department heads to comply with the letter of the law, but not the spirit of the law. If there was any reason a document might be withheld from public scrutiny, withhold it, Attorney General William French Smith said. From 1980 until 1992 executive departments used a variety of ploys to block access to government-held information. Some department heads would purposely fail to hire enough people to meet FOIA requests, despite having the budget to fill these jobs. Steve Weinberg, executive director of Investigative Reporters and Editors, noted in an article in the Columbia Journalism Review some of the ways in which the bureaucrats in the executive branch interfered with the application of the Freedom of Information Act.[43] Agencies would levy very high fees for searching for documents and for copying documents, fees that smaller news organizations could not afford to pay. Agencies would respond to FOIA requests by claiming that documents were lost or that they had been moved to other departments. Government officials would fail to meet the legally mandated 10-day time limit for a response, and then claim that they lacked the needed staff to comply with the law. Finally, redacting, or editing out portions of documents for myriad legitimate or illegitimate reasons, was common. President Bill Clinton appeared, on the surface at least, to view the right of the public to have access to government-held information more favorably. Department heads were told to presume that the contents of federal records should be disclosed and to deny access only in those instances in which "it is reasonably foreseeable that the disclosure would be harmful." Many actions by Clinton seemed to demonstrate his resolve to reopen government to public scrutiny.

In the spring of 1995 President Clinton signed an executive order that substantially loosened secrecy rules in the executive branch of government, especially in regard to older records.[44] The order instructed federal agencies to open by April 2000 classified records that contain historical material and are more than 25 years old. The order does allow some agency heads, such as the director of the Central Intelligence Agency, to exempt some documents from disclosure, but all such exemptions must be reviewed by an Interagency Security Classification Appeals Panel. In addition, the new policy requires government agencies to err on the side of openness when weighing whether a new document should be classified. It also requires officials to justify their decisions to designate a document as secret.[45] By the late summer of 1999, 600 million pages of documents relating to everything from the war in Vietnam to UFOs had been declassified, but nearly 1 billion more pages still had not been reviewed.[46]

Policy is one thing; practice is something else. In the summer of 1996 Congressman David E. Skaggs, a member of the House intelligence committee, reported that the federal government spent $5.6 billion in 1995 keeping documents secret. This figure, roughly twice the combined annual budgets of both the Federal Bureau of Investigation and the Drug Enforcement Administration, does not include the funds spent by the Central Intelligence Agency to ensure the secrecy of documents it possesses. At the same time, the government spent less than one percent of this amount to declassify documents, Skaggs said. Military and

43. Weinberg, "Trashing the FOIA," 21.
44. Weiner, "U.S. Plans Secrecy Overhaul," A1.
45. Jehl, "Clinton Revamps Policy on Secrecy," A1.
46. Riechmann, "Congress Fears."

intelligence agencies said it costs too much to declassify documents. Freedom of information advocates have been disappointed in other ways in which the Clinton administration has carried out these new directives. The president has failed to insist that members of his administration carry out the policies he has publicly espoused.

Money is only part of the problem. The seemingly genetic bent of most bureaucrats to keep documents secret is another problem. When former Associated Press correspondent Terry Anderson asked the FBI for access to material in his personal files that related to Arab terrorists who had held him hostage in Lebanon for six years, the agency refused, claiming that releasing the records would violate the terrorists' right of privacy. Public ridicule forced Attorney General Janet Reno to reverse the FBI on this point, but she still denied Anderson's request, citing national security reasons. The projects editor of the Syracuse, N.Y., Post-Standard received a letter from the Department of Army Intelligence and Security Command in February of 1995, saying that a request he had made five years earlier for information about the crash of Pan Am Flight 103 would be answered within the required 10-day time limit.[47] Other horror stories abound. The fact of the matter is that no administration since the Freedom of Information Act was adopted 35 years ago has truly invested sufficient time and energy to make it work the way it was envisioned. Only the dogged efforts of private citizens, scholars, and journalists have occasionally broken down the walls between the bureaucracy and the citizenry it is supposed to serve.

FOIA AND ELECTRONIC COMMUNICATION

The Freedom of Information Act was born in an age when records were kept in folders that were stored in boxes or metal file cabinets. When the statute was adopted in 1966 the federal government owned only 3,000 computers. Today the federal government has millions of computers and spends billions of dollars each year on hardware, software, and other computer equipment. By the year 2000 the vast majority of government records were created, transported, and stored electronically. As computer technology replaced paper records, agencies within the federal government balked at allowing access to these electronic records. Most bureaucrats seemed to hold the opinion that the electronic records were a special class of data, outside the range of FOIA and off limits to the public.[48] Officials argued that if they had to perform even simple computer programming to retrieve the information sought by the requester, the information fell outside the broad mandate of disclosure of the Freedom of Information Act. This mindset was not confined to the lower echelons of the administration. High officials in both the Bush and the Clinton administrations fought efforts by the National Security Archives to force the government to save electronic messages (e-mail) sent by computer. Officials in the Bush administration sought to erase from computer files all records of communications among officials during the eight years of the Reagan presidency. The case was still in the courts when Clinton was inaugurated in 1993 and his administration continued to argue the position taken by the Bush administration that the government had a right to dispose of this information as it saw fit. The U.S. Court of Appeals for the District of Columbia Circuit rejected this argument

---

47. Wicklein, "FOIA Foiled," 36.
48. Morrissey, "FOIA Foiled?" 29.

in August of 1993, ruling that the government must preserve electronic messages and memos under the same standards that have always been applied to paper communications.[49]

In 1996, after a couple of previous tries, Congress finally adopted an amendment to the Freedom of Information Act that requires government agencies to apply the same standards of disclosure to electronic records that they have always applied to paper documents. This includes all e-mail correspondence as well as letters or notes. The bill was approved 402–0 in the House and passed on a voice vote in the Senate and President Clinton signed the measure. The Electronic Freedom of Information Act (EFOIA) also establishes priorities that the agencies must apply when faced with multiple requests for computer searches for records. Top priority goes to FOIA requests in which a delay would threaten the life or safety of an individual. Next in line comes the news media and others in the business of disseminating information to the public. The new law also requires agencies to publish an online index of the documents they have and to make a reasonable attempt to provide documents in the requested format, that is, on tapes, diskettes, paper, and so on. The law does not, however, define electronic information, instead leaving this important question to federal agencies and the courts.

This new law can resolve many of the issues regarding access to electronically stored material, at least at the federal level. But progress may be slow. In April 1998 the Office of Management and Budget reported that overall agency compliance with EFOIA amendments had been "overwhelmingly inadequate." It may take years for full compliance to occur. Reporters who cover any level of government face similar problems. The growing use of e-mail has made it possible for members of governmental boards or commissions to hold a "virtual" meeting via the computer. A freedom of information request from a reporter for the Spokane, Wash., Spokesman-Review recently revealed that two of three Spokane County Commissioners were engaged in substantial e-mail communication about important county issues. Since two of three members constitutes a quorum, these members could not have legally had these discussions in face-to-face meetings. But whether or not such e-mail discussions constitute a meeting has yet to be resolved. Some states, such as Arizona, are proposing penalties for those officials who try to use e-mail to avoid the requirements of open meetings laws.[50]

Freedom of information laws are only as helpful as the administration that must administer them. Multitudes of means exist for thwarting the law. Despite the problems, the federal FOIA continues to operate. Two thousand times a day people try to use the law to gain access to government-held information: sometimes a mere piece of paper, or an e-mail message, other times hundreds of pages of documents.[51]

AGENCY RECORDS

In the next few pages I sketch the broad outlines of the federal Freedom of Information Act, focus on the nine areas of exempted information, and suggest some ways in which a journalist or citizen can use the law. One can write an open-records law in two basic ways. The first way

49. Lewis, "Government Told to Save Messages," A1.
50. "Exchange of E-Mail Isn't Meeting," 1 E.P.L.R. 391 (1996). See also State ex rel Wilson-Simmons
     v. Lake City Sheriff's Dept., Ohio No. 97-797, 5/20/98, and Kelly, "Behind Closed E-Mail."
51. Feinsilber, "Agencies Try Hard to Answer," A10.

is to declare that the following kinds of records are to be accessible for public inspection and then list the kinds of records that are open. The second way is to proclaim that all government records are open for public inspection except the following kinds of records and then list the exceptions. Congress approved the second kind of law in 1966, and it went into effect in 1967. The law has been amended several times, with substantial changes being enacted in 1974, 1976, 1986, and 1996.

What Is an Agency?

The U.S. Freedom of Information Act gives any person access to all the records kept by all federal agencies, unless the information falls into one of nine categories of exempted material. An agency has been defined under the law as

> any executive department, military department, government corporation, govern- ment-controlled corporation or other establishment in the executive branch of government (including the executive office of the president), or any independent regulatory agency.

The law governs records held by agencies in the executive branch of government and all the independent regulatory agencies like the **Federal Trade Commission,** the Federal Aviation Agency, and the Securities and Exchange Commission. The law does not cover records held by Congress or the federal courts. Some agencies associated with the executive branch of govern- ment also fall outside the purview of the law. In 1985 the U.S. Court of Appeals for the District of Columbia Circuit ruled that the Council of Economic Advisors, which works closely with the president on economic matters, is not covered by the law because it exists solely to advise and assist the president and makes no policy on its own. The agency has no regulatory power; it can- not issue rules or regulations. Although the FOIA does govern some operations in the executive office of the president, the law does not reach "the president's immediate personal staff or units in the executive office whose *sole function* is to advise and assist the president," the court ruled.[52]

A U.S. district court ruled in 1995 that the National Security Council (NSC), which is also a part of the executive office of the president, is an agency under the FOIA because it oper- ates independently of the president in many instances.[53] The U.S. Court of Appeals reversed this decision a year later. The court said that three factors have to be considered when deter- mining whether a unit in the executive office of the president exercises enough substantial independent authority to be regarded as an agency. The court must look at how closely from an operational standpoint the group is to the president, at whether it has a self-contained structure, and at the nature of its delegated authority. The NSC certainly has a self-contained structure with its own staff and budget, the court acknowledged. But the "intimate organizational and operating relationship between the President and the NSC is . . . entitled to significantly greater weight in evaluating the NSC's arguable status as an agency than is the self-contained struc- ture of the entity,"[54] the court ruled. Also, in this case, the plaintiff failed to show that the NSC

---

52. *Rushforth* v. *Council of Economic Advisors,* 762 F. 2d 1038 (1985).
53. *Armstrong* v. *Executive Office of the President,* 877 F. Supp. 690 (1995).
54. "National Security Council Not Subject to FOIA," 1 E.P.L.R. 438 (1996).

exercised any meaningful nonadvisory authority. Because the NSC operates in close proximity to the president, and because it does not exercise substantial independent authority, the NSC is not an agency within the meaning of the law, the court concluded.

In 1990 the U.S. Court of Appeals ruled that the office of the Counsel to the President was also an agency functioning only to advise and assist the president, and it too was exempt from the provisions of the Freedom of Information Act.[55] But in another decision, the court did rule that the Defense Nuclear Facilities Safety Board is an agency within the meaning of the statute.[56] Congress created this board in 1988 to review and evaluate standards relating to the design, construction, and operation of defense nuclear facilities; investigate practices or events at such facilities that may adversely affect public health; and recommend measures to the secretary of energy to ensure adequate protection of public health and safety. The language in the FOIA defines agencies to include "other establishments in the executive branch of government." These exact words were used by the Congress when it created the board, the court said, making it hard to deny that this board was to be covered by provisions of the FOIA.[57]

What Is a Record?

Congress did not specify the physical characteristics of a record in the Freedom of Information Act. Certainly records are paper documents. But the term "record" also includes films, tapes, and even three-dimensional objects such as evidence in a criminal prosecution. Computer tapes and other electronic data also qualify as records, though few court decisions specifically assert that point.[58]

What Is an Agency Record?

"Agency" has been defined under the law; so has "record." What is an agency record? It is not, unfortunately, simply a combination of the definition of these two terms. In this case the whole, the term "agency record," involves a good deal more than the sum of its parts. Courts have established the following definition of an agency record:

If the agency has created the document and is in possession of that document, it is very likely an agency record.

If the agency has created the document but does not possess or control it, it is not an agency record.

If the agency merely possesses the document but has not created it, it might be an agency record, or it might not. If the agency came into possession of the document as a part of its official duties, it is probably an agency record. If it just happens to have the document, it is probably not an agency record.

---

55. *National Security Archives* v. *U.S. Archivist,* 909 F. 2d 541 (1990).
56. *Energy Research Foundation* v. *Defense Nuclear Facilities Safety Board,* 917 F. 2d 581 (1990).
57. *Energy Research Foundation* v. *Defense Nuclear Facilities Safety Board,* 917 F. 2d 581 (1990).
58. *Long* v. *IRS,* 596 F. 2d 362 (1979).

The great volume of case law supports this definition. The National Institute of Arthritis, Metabolism, and Digestive Diseases (NIAMDD) paid a consulting firm to conduct a study to determine the effectiveness of certain diabetes treatments. The researchers conducted the study and gave NIAMDD a report of the findings. But the consultants kept all the raw data, which was the object of the FOIA lawsuit. The Supreme Court said the materials sought were not agency records; they had not been created by NIAMDD; nor did the agency control this material.[59]

The same year the high court rejected the requests of the Reporters Committee to gain access to notes created by Henry Kissinger when he was secretary of state. Kissinger gave these notes to the Library of Congress when he left office. The high court refused to accede to the FOIA request, noting that the material had certainly been created by Kissinger, but that he was no longer in possession of the documents.[60]

The U.S. Court of Appeals refused to permit the inspection of telephone slips and desk calendars possessed by two different agencies because neither kind of document was related to agency business.[61] The same court also refused to provide access to a report prepared by members of Ronald Reagan's transition staff prior to his inauguration as president. The document was kept by the Department of Health and Human Services, an agency covered by FOIA. "In this case," the court said, "although copies of the report are physically located in HHS, the report was not generated by HHS, is not within the control of HHS, and indeed never entered the department's files or was ever used by the department for any purpose."[62]

In *Justice Department* v. *Tax Analysts*,[63] the Supreme Court ruled that the Justice Department was required to make available copies of district court decisions it receives in the course of litigating tax cases. The opinions were sought by a company called Tax Analysts, which publishes a weekly magazine called Tax Notes, a report on federal tax matters. Because the Justice Department is routinely sent these opinions, editors at Tax Analysts decided it would save the company a great deal of time to get copies of the opinions from the Department of Justice, rather than soliciting them from courts around the nation. But the Justice Department refused, arguing that these were not agency records. These decisions, the Justice Department lawyers argued, originated with the courts, agencies not covered by the Freedom of Information Act. But Justice Thurgood Marshall disagreed and wrote for the 8–1 majority that the relevant question is whether an agency covered by the Freedom of Information Act has "created or obtained the materials sought . . . not whether the organization from which the documents originated is itself covered by the FOIA." The Justice Department controls these records, even though it did not generate them. (This statement distinguishes the ruling from the case of *Wolfe* v. *Department of Health and Human Services,* in which the records were stored at the agency but were not under agency control.) If the Justice Department wanted to continue to refuse to provide these materials to the Tax Analysts, it would have to cite an appropriate exemption.

59. *Forsham* v. *Harris,* 445 U.S. 169 (1980).
60. *Kissinger* v. *Reporters Committee,* 445 U.S. 136 (1980).
61. *BNA* v. *Baxter; Environmental Defense Fund* v. *Office of Management and Budget,* 742 F. 2d 1848 (1984).
62. *Wolfe* v. *Department of Health and Human Services,* 539 F. Supp. 276 (1987); 711 F. 2d 1077 (1983).
63. 492 U.S. 136 (1989).

In 1999 a U.S. district court in Illinois added a somewhat dissenting note to the opinions just outlined when it ruled that a private contractor that had worked for the National Cancer Institute (NCI) had to hand over to the Chicago Tribune records relating to a study of breast cancer. The NCI hired EMMES Corporation to audit the results of the study. The contract clearly spelled out that EMMES would work independently and not as an agent of government. The NCI gathered the data, forwarded it to EMMES, which did a statistical analysis of the material and returned it to the NCI. The Tribune wanted the audit records, which the NCI did not have and which the agency claimed belonged to EMMES. The court said that an agency such as the NCI must obtain from contractors those documents that it has effectively loaned out for the purpose of having the contractor perform work. The work product of the contractor, that is, the records of the audit results, belongs to the government, not the contractor, the court added. Complicating the case was evidence that the NCI had taken overt steps to make certain that EMMES kept the audit results so the agency could avoid having to release this material under an FOIA request.[64]

FOIA EXEMPTIONS

A document or tape or file that has been determined to be an agency record accessible via the Freedom of Information Act may still be withheld from public inspection if it properly falls in one of the nine categories of exempted material. Please note, federal agencies *are not required* to withhold documents from disclosure simply because they are included in an exempted category.[65] The law simply says they may withhold such material. The nine exemptions outlined in the following pages are fairly specific, yet not specific enough to be free from substantial judicial interpretation. How a judge defines a word or phrase in these exemptions can result in a significant change in the meaning of the law, and lead to either expanded public access or, more likely in recent years, substantially reduced public access. We will examine each exemption separately, try to outline its meaning, and briefly explore case law that illuminates how the exemption is applied.

Federal agencies are not required to withhold documents from disclosure simply because they are included in an exempted category.

EXEMPTIONS TO DISCLOSURE UNDER THE FREEDOM OF INFORMATION ACT

1. National security matters
2. Housekeeping materials
3. Material exempted by statute
4. Trade secrets
5. Working papers/Lawyer-client privileged materials

---

64. *Chicago Tribune Co.* v. *U.S. Department of Health and Human Services,* 27 M.L.R. 1906 (1999).
65. See *Chrysler Corp.* v. *Brown,* 441 U.S. 281 (1979).

6. Personal privacy files
7. Law enforcement records
8. Financial institutions
9. Geological data

National Security

Exemption One: Matters specifically authorized under criteria established by an executive order to be kept secret in the interest of national defense or foreign policy and in fact properly classified pursuant to such an executive order. This exemption deals with a wide range of materials, but primarily with information related to national security and national defense, intelligence gathering, and foreign relations. The system has a three-tier classification. Material, the release of which could reasonably be expected to damage national security, is classified as "confidential," the lowest level of classification. The "secret" classification is used to shield material that if disclosed could be expected to cause serious damage to national security. "Top secret," the highest level of classification, is reserved for material that if revealed could be expected to cause exceptionally grave damage to national security.[66]

As originally adopted in 1966, this exemption excluded from disclosure any document or record that the president, through executive order, chose to classify in the name of national security. Courts, including the Supreme Court, ruled that there could be no challenge to the classification of the document or record, no judicial examination of whether the material was sensitive or even related to national security.[67] The exemption was abused by administrations, especially during the Nixon presidency, and was amended by the Congress in 1974. The change in the law has given the courts the power to inspect classified documents to determine whether they have been properly classified.

What is supposed to happen is this: The president (undoubtedly the staff) establishes criteria in an executive order for the classification of sensitive documents and records. Officials in federal agencies like the Defense Department or the State Department use these criteria to determine whether material in their possession should be classified as confidential, secret, top secret, or so on. If a document is classified, it is exempt from disclosure. There is a powerful tendency toward overclassification. This is the problem that Congress sought to correct. Now an individual seeking access to material can ask the court to determine whether the document was properly classified, that is, whether it properly falls within the criteria established by the executive order. A judge cannot question the criteria established by the president, but he or she can see if the criteria were properly applied.

But judges are seemingly loathe to do this. The law only states that a court *may* determine whether the material was properly classified, not that it *must* do so. Most courts refuse

---

66. Exec. Order No. 12958, 3 C.F.R. 333 (1996).
67. *Epstein* v. *Resor,* 296 F. Supp. 214 (1969), aff'd. 421 F. 2d 930 (1970), and *EPA* v. *Mink,* 401 U.S. 73 (1973).

to even examine the documents. Although occasionally a judge will take the initiative to apply the exemption as Congress intended,[68] more commonly judges refuse to evaluate the classification of the material, claiming they lack the expertise to make such a judgment.[69]

Exemption One is highly susceptible to administrative interpretation. Hence, its scope can expand or contract from administration to administration. President Jimmy Carter tended to support a wider access to government documents. He required all government agencies to consider the public interest that might be harmed as well as the government interest that might be served by making a document inaccessible through classification.

Presidents Reagan and Bush adopted a much more restrictive approach, classifying many more documents and keeping them classified for as long as possible. The Reagan administration even sought to reclassify material that had been previously declassified. In one case government agents raided the library at the Virginia Military Academy and removed documents that had been available to the public on open shelves for many years. President Clinton, as was previously noted, has taken an approach more like that of Carter and has sought to reduce the amount of classified material.

Under an executive order signed by President Clinton in 1995 someone seeking access to a classified document can forgo using the Freedom of Information Act and instead ask for a review of whether the document should be classified at all. This process takes longer and the requester loses the right to ask for an expedited review and fee waivers (see page 343). The requester also forfeits the right, for a time at least, to argue that the documents should be released under the Freedom of Information Act.

Housekeeping Practices

Exemption Two: Matters related solely to the internal personnel rules and practices of an agency. This exemption covers what are known as "housekeeping" materials: vacation schedules, coffee break rules, parking lot assignments, and so forth. Little harm would result if these materials were made public; the exemption is offered simply to relieve the agencies of the burden of having to maintain such material in public files.

The most controversial aspect of Exemption Two is whether it applies to agency staff manuals. For example, a citizen sought access to a Bureau of Alcohol, Tobacco, and Firearms staff manual entitled "Surveillance of Premises, Vehicles, and Persons." The bureau released all but 20 pages of the manual, which it said described internal personnel rules and practices of the agency. The U.S. Court of Appeals for the District of Columbia Circuit ruled in favor of the agency in the lawsuit that followed. The court noted that during the debate on the FOIA in Congress, members spoke without contradiction that Exemption Two was designed to shield material in law enforcement manuals on investigation procedures.[70] But in 1997 the 10th U.S. Circuit Court of Appeals ruled that maps depicting the location of the Mexican spotted owl that were

68. *Browde* v. *Navy,* 713 F. 2d 864 (1983).
69. *Knopf* v. *Colby,* 502 F. 2d 136 (1975).
70. *Crooker* v. *Bureau,* 670 F. 2d 1051 (1981); see also *Hardy* v. *Bureau of Alcohol, Tobacco, and Firearms,* 631 F. 2d 653 (1980).

used by the U.S. Forest Service to protect the owl habitat pursuant to the Endangered Species Act did not relate to the agency's personnel practices and were not exempt from disclosure.[71]

The exemption cannot be used to hide all agency procedures and policies, especially if they involve questionable agency practices. The Boston Globe sought information from the Federal Bureau of Investigation and the Drug Enforcement Administration regarding the amount of money these agencies paid to Charles Matta, a former confidential informant. During the 12 years Matta was a paid FBI/DEA informant he was continually in trouble with local law enforcement authorities. In 1990 he was convicted in state courts for gambling and alcohol- and drug-related offenses. The newspaper wanted to find out if the federal agencies had been inadvertently subsidizing Matta's local criminal activities. The federal law enforcement agencies rejected the Freedom of Information Act requests made by The Globe, citing various exemptions, including Exemption Two. Officials said that the amount of money paid to Matta related to internal agency practices. The U.S. District Court rejected government efforts to block the disclosure of these records. The court said two questions must be asked regarding the applicability of Exemption Two:

1. Is the matter about which information is sought predominantly internal, such that there can be no legitimate public interest in the information?

If there is public interest, then the court must determine

2. Would disclosure significantly risk circumventing any of the agencies' regulations or statutes?

This is not a balancing test, the court said. If there is no public interest in having this information released, then Exemption Two applies. Similarly, if release of this material might seriously compromise the operation of the agency, then the material must remain secret. In this case, the court said, "The public has a right to know whether in a combined effort to enforce criminal laws the agencies instead bankrolled Matta's ongoing criminal activities." In addition, the agencies failed to cite any regulations or statutes that might be circumvented by the release of this information. "Where the plaintiffs have demonstrated a strong public interest and where the identity of the informant has been publicly acknowledged, the total amount paid to the informant is not exempt [from disclosure]," the court concluded.[72]

Statutory Exemption

Exemption Three: Matters specifically exempted from disclosure by statute (other than section 552b of this title) provided that such statute (a) requires that the matters be withheld from the public in such a manner as to leave no discretion on the issue, or (b) establishes particular criteria for withholding or refers to particular types of matters to be withheld. This exemption is designed to protect from disclosure information required or permitted to be kept secret by scores of other federal laws. A wide range of records fall under this

---

71. *Audubon Society* v. *United States Forest Service,* 104 F. 3d 1201 (1997).
72. *Globe Newspaper Co.* v. *FBI,* 21 M.L.R. 1013 (1992).

exemption, including census bureau records, public utility information, trade secrets, patent applications, tax returns, bank records, veterans benefits, and documents held by both the Central Intelligence Agency and the National Security Agency.

Courts generally ask three questions when determining whether Exemption Three applies to a specific record or document:

1. Is there a specific statute that authorizes or requires the withholding of information?
2. Does the statute designate specific kinds of information or outline specific criteria for information that may be withheld?
3. Does the record or information that is sought fall within the categories of information that may be withheld?

If all three questions are answered yes, disclosure can be legally denied.

Via congressional action and numerous court rulings the Central Intelligence Agency has managed to use this exemption to almost completely shield its operations from public scrutiny. In 1984 Congress voted to exempt all CIA operational files from release under the Freedom of Information Act. In 1985 the Supreme Court ruled that records relating to CIA-funded research from 1952 to 1966 at 80 universities to study the effects of mind-altering substances on humans were off-limits to public inspection. A man named John Sims wanted to see the names of the schools and the individuals who had participated in the research projects. The agency argued that the names were exempt from disclosure because, under a 1947 law, the names of intelligence sources cannot be disclosed by the CIA. The Supreme Court agreed and ruled that the director of the spy agency had broad authority under the 1947 National Security Act to protect all sources of information, confidential or not.[73] In 1996 a U.S. district court ruled that the CIA didn't even have to respond to a formal FOIA request, since its response might reveal whether it even had a record sought by the requester. The court said the agency had to maintain its strict policy of not revealing sources.[74]

In recent years, federal agencies have cited nearly 100 different statutes to try to justify withholding documents. In some instances courts have rejected these attempts, but frequently the denial goes unchallenged, according to researchers at the Reporters Committee on Freedom of the Press. Courts have upheld denial of access to records based on laws governing the Census Bureau, Consumer Products Safety Commission, Internal Revenue Service, the Patent and Trademark Office, the Postal Service, National Security Agency, and a few others. It is expected that more and more government agencies will in the future seek specific congressional exemption from provisions of the FOIA.

The Central Intelligence Agency has managed to use this exemption to almost completely shield its operations from public scrutiny.

Trade Secrets

Exemption Four: Trade secrets and financial information obtained from any person and privileged or confidential. Two kinds of information are exempt from disclosure under this exemption—trade secrets and financial or commercial information. The trade secret exemption

73. *Sims* v. *CIA*, 471 U.S. 159 (1985).
74. *Earth Pledge Foundation* v. *Central Intelligence Agency*, DC SNY 96 Civ. 0257 (1996).

has not been heavily litigated. In 1983 the U.S. Court of Appeals for the District of Columbia Circuit fashioned a definition of a trade secret that considerably narrowed the exemption. In litigation initiated by Ralph Nader's Public Citizen Health Research Group, the court said a trade secret is "an unpatented, commercially valuable plan, appliance, formula, or process which is used for the making, preparing, compounding, treating, or processing of articles or materials which are trade commodities, and that can be said to be the end product of either innovation or substantial effort." The court rejected a broader definition of a trade secret proposed by the Food and Drug Administration: "any . . . compilation of information which is used in one's business and which gives him an opportunity to obtain an advantage over competitors who do not know or use it."[75]

The "financial information" exemption applies only to information supplied to the government by individuals or private business firms. It is this second section of the exemption that has undergone the most thorough judicial interpretation. When the Miami Herald sought records from the Small Business Administration regarding loans made to small contractors that had become delinquent, the agency said this was financial or commercial information which it did not have to disclose under Exemption Four. But courts had previously ruled that Exemption Four only applies if the disclosure of the information would either impair the government's ability to obtain similar information in the future, or would cause competitive harm to the individual or business which submitted the information. The SBA was unable to produce evidence that either of these conditions existed and the court ordered the material disclosed.[76] Federal courts have followed this doctrine consistently. In 1998 the Federal Aviation Administration attempted to use "financial information" arguments to support its decision not to reveal specific data to the Chicago Tribune when the newspaper sought documents relating to in-flight medical emergencies. There was nothing in the data originally given to the Tribune that identified the airlines that provided the data, including flight numbers, aircraft tail numbers, routes, remarks regarding individual medical emergencies, and portions of correspondence. Because the "events occurred while the aircraft were in revenue producing operations," the FAA said, the data were commercial or financial information. Noting at the outset that the fundamental premise of the FOIA is disclosure, not secrecy, the U.S. District Court said that only material that bears a direct relationship to the operations of a commercial venture is exempt from disclosure. The information must be commercial in nature. The flight information did not meet that standard.[77]

Working Papers/Discovery

Exemption Five: Interagency and intra-agency memorandums and letters which would not be available by law to a party other than an agency in litigation with the agency. This exemption shields two kinds of materials from disclosure. The first are best described as working papers; studies, reports, memoranda, and other sorts of documents that are prepared and circulated to assist government personnel to make a final report, an agency policy, or a

---

75. *Public Citizen Health Research Group* v. *Food and Drug Administration,* 704 F. 2d 1280 (1983).
76. *Miami Herald* v. *Small Business Administration,* 670 F. 2d 65 (1987).
77. *Chicago Tribune* v. *Federal Aviation Administration,* 27 M.L.R. 1059 (1998).

decision of some kind. This section of the law also exempts from disclosure communications between an agency and its attorney, material that is traditionally protected by the attorney-client privilege. (In any lawsuit, communications between an attorney and a client are private.)

The rationale for protecting working papers from public disclosure was well outlined in 1982 when the U.S. Court of Appeals refused to require the Air Force to give up materials that were used in preparing a final report on the use of herbicides in Vietnam. The court explained in *Russell* v. *Air Force:*[78]

> There are essentially three policy bases for this privilege. First, it protects creative debate and candid consideration of alternatives, within an agency, and thereby improves the quality of the agency policy decisions. Second, it protects the public from the confusion that would result from premature exposure to discussions occurring before the policies affecting it had actually been settled upon. And third, it protects the integrity of the decision-making process itself by confirming that "officials should be judged by what they decided, not for matters they considered before making up their minds."

The portions of the first draft of the report sought by the plaintiff in the case were considerations, not decisions, and part of the decision-making process designed to be protected by this exemption. Factual portions of predecisional documents are not normally exempt. For example, imagine there is a long policy memorandum containing advisory recommendations on a proposed jet fighter and the cost of the construction of the warplane. While the advisory recommendations are exempt, the factual cost data is not and must be segregated out of the memo and released on request.

Sometimes documents generated to help formulate a policy become the basis for that policy, and are noted or discussed in the final decision or policy statement. The Supreme Court ruled in 1975 that Exemption Five cannot be used to shield such documents. Once the decision has been made, the court said, public disclosure of these materials cannot damage the decision-making process.[79]

The courts have interpreted Exemption Five very broadly. For example, the U.S. Court of Appeals for the District of Columbia Circuit ruled that Exemption Five goes so far as to shield draft book manuscripts from disclosure. A historian working for the Office of Air Force History prepared a draft history of the role of the U.S. Air Force in South Vietnam in the early 1960s. Senior OAFH officers rejected the manuscript—the second time such a manuscript was turned down. A reporter sought a copy of the manuscript, believing it might contain information about unreported war crimes. The Air Force turned down the request, arguing that disclosure of the manuscript might reveal the deliberative editorial process used by the Air Force. The court agreed. "The simple comparison of the draft with the final manuscript would expose an editorial judgment made by Air Force personnel," the court ruled. This exposure of the editorial judgment would inhibit creative debate and candid considerations in the future, the court added.[80]

78. 682 F. 2d 1045 (1982).
79. *NLRB* v. *Sears, Roebuck and Company,* 421 U.S. 132 (1973).
80. *Dudman Communications Corp.* v. *Air Force,* 815 F. 2d 1565 (1987).

In 1991 the U.S. Court of Appeals ruled that when an agency invokes the "working papers" exemption to protect predecisional documents or other materials, it is not necessary for the agency to point to a particular decision or policy that was generated because of these materials. Access Reports sought from the Justice Department a copy of a single memo written by a department staff attorney that contained an analysis of amendments to the Freedom of Information Act that were being proposed by the department in 1981. A lower federal court rejected the government's argument that the memo was protected as a working paper because the Justice Department was unable to cite the decision that was influenced by the staff attorney's analysis. The Justice Department could not meet this requirement because the memo was prepared after the decision was made; it was an analysis of the decision.

The court of appeals applied a much looser requirement. It agreed that before Exemption Five could be applied, it must be shown that the document was part of the agency's deliberative process and was predecisional. But this language, the court said, cannot be taken to require that the document contribute to a single, discrete decision. "The key question in identifying deliberative material is whether the disclosure of the information would discourage candid discussion within the agency." In this case the memo writer testified at the trial that he thought he was creating an internal, working document. If he had been preparing something for public disclosure, he would have been more cautious in his analysis, he said. The court noted, "At the time of writing the author could not know whether the decision-making process would lead to a clear decision, establishing the privilege [Exemption Five], or a fizzle, defeating it. Hedging his bets he would be drawn into precisely the cautious or Aesopian language that the exemption seeks to render unnecessary."[81]

The second part of the exemption has been interpreted to shield from public disclosure material that would not be routinely or normally open to discovery in a civil proceeding. (The discovery process in litigation enables one party to gain access to evidence, testimony, and other material held by the other party, prior to the trial.) This includes communications between an agency and its attorneys, and material that might reveal case strategy in litigation. In 1984 the U.S. Supreme Court ruled that confidential statements obtained during an Air Force investigation of an air crash are protected from disclosure under Exemption Five. The public is entitled to all such memorandums or letters that a private party could discover in litigation with the agency, wrote Justice John Paul Stevens for a unanimous court. But the material in question would not normally or routinely be open to discovery in a civil proceeding. The high court ruled that Exemption Five incorporates the civil discovery privilege; Congress did not intend to create a situation in which litigants could use the FOIA to circumvent discovery privilege.[82] In 1988, however, the Supreme Court took another look at Exemption Five as it relates to discovery privileges and reached a different conclusion. Two federal inmates both sought copies of their presentence investigation reports. These reports are prepared by probation officers for use by district courts before sentencing. They are then forwarded to the Bureau of Prisons and finally to the Parole Commission. Some parts of these reports were clearly not to be disclosed because both a federal statute and federal court rules preclude the release of information that

81. *Access Reports* v. *Justice Department,* 926 F. 2d 1192 (1991).
82. *U.S.* v. *Weber Aircraft Corp.,* 465 U.S. 792 (1984).

relates to confidential sources, diagnostic opinions, and other information that may harm prisoners or third parties. (These rules apply through Exemption Three.) But the government sought to block the release of the remainder of the reports on the grounds that they are normally considered privileged communications in civil or criminal discovery proceedings. Chief Justice Rehnquist agreed that courts have been very reluctant to give third parties access to presentence reports. But he noted, "There is no indication, however, that similar restrictions on discovery of presentence investigation reports have been recognized by the courts when the individual requesting discovery is the subject of the report." Rehnquist and four other members of the court said they believed it was entirely reasonable to treat a claim of privilege under Exemption Five differently as to one class of those who make requests than as to another class. Here, there was good reason to differentiate between third-party requests and requests by the subject of the report. The inmates won their case.[83]

The long-term ramifications of the *Julian* decision might be far more important than the immediate impact, which is clearly narrow. This is the first time the Supreme Court ever differentiated between types of requesters in resolving an FOIA dispute. In other words, it is the first time the court said this exemption clearly precludes giving the information to some kinds of persons, but not to other kinds of persons. Whether or not this differentiation becomes an important element in litigating FOIA cases remains to be seen.

Exemption Five also incorporates the common-law concept called **executive privilege.** Beginning with President George Washington in 1794, American chief executives have asserted that the president enjoys a common-law privilege to keep secret all presidential papers, records, and other documents. Washington asserted the privilege when Congress called for all papers and records in the possession of the president that would facilitate its investigation of the negotiation of the Jay Treaty, a controversial agreement with Great Britain. Washington refused to comply with the congressional demand, citing executive privilege. Andrew Jackson refused to give Congress information relating to a boundary dispute in Maine. Millard Fillmore refused a request from the Senate that he provide that body with information regarding negotiations with the Sandwich (Hawaiian) Islands.

In 1974 in *U.S.* v. *Nixon*,[84] the Supreme Court sharply limited the boundaries of the traditional executive privilege. In this case copies of audiotape recordings of conversations that took place in the Oval Office were subpoenaed by the special prosecutor for use in the criminal trial of some of the Nixon aides. The former president argued that the tapes were protected by executive privilege. He said that revelation of the material on the tapes would damage the integrity of the decision-making process and that under our system of separation of powers, the courts were precluded from reviewing his claim of privilege. He also argued that even if his claim of absolute executive privilege should fail, the court should at least hold as a matter of constitutional law that his privilege superseded the subpoena.

However, in a unanimous opinion (8–0, since Justice Rehnquist did not participate in the decision), the Burger court rejected the notion of absolute privilege in this case. The court said that an absolute privilege can be asserted only when the material in question consists of

Exemption Five also incorporates the common-law concept called "executive privilege."

83. *Justice Department* v. *Julian,* 108 S. Ct. 1606 (1988).
84. 94 S. Ct. 3090 (1974).

military or diplomatic secrets. When other kinds of information are involved, privilege of the president must be balanced against other values—in this case, against the operation of the criminal justice system. The need for the privilege must be weighed against the need for the information.[85] No president in recent memory has asserted this privilege as many times as President Clinton. Citing the privilege the president rejected congressional attempts in 1996 to obtain documents related to White House travel office firings, a joint FBI–Drug Enforcement Agency memo to the president on drug enforcement, and foreign-policy documents on the administration's Haiti policy. In 1999 Clinton invoked the privilege again when Congress sought documents relating to his decision to offer clemency to jailed members of a Puerto Rican separatist group.[86] Clinton tried but failed to use executive privilege to protect his senior aides from questioning by prosecutors in the office of the independent counsel during the Monica Lewinsky investigation.

Personal Privacy

Exemption Six: Personnel and medical files and similar files the disclosure of which would constitute a clearly unwarranted invasion of privacy. This exemption shields "personnel and medical files and similar files." Personnel files and medical files are fairly easy to identify. The courts have had more of a problem determining the nature of a "similar file." At one time courts declared that similar files were files *like* personnel and medical files.[87] But the Supreme Court rejected that interpretation. The key consideration, the high court said, is not the kind of file that is at issue, but the kind of information in the file that is the object of the FOIA request. An individual's medical and personnel files contain highly personal information about an individual. A file is a "similar file" if it contains this same kind of personal information.[88] Not every file that contains personal information will be considered a similar file. "The test is not merely whether the information is in some sense personal," a U.S. court of appeals ruled, "but whether it is of the same magnitude—as highly personal in nature—as contained in personnel or medical records."[89]

In the late 1980s The New York Times sought access to the voice communications tape recorded aboard the space shuttle Challenger just before it exploded in January of 1987. The National Aeronautics and Space Administration argued that the tape was shielded from disclosure because it contained personal information similar to that contained in personnel and medical files. Both the U.S. District Court[90] and a panel of judges on the U.S. Court of Appeals[91] ruled that the tape contained nothing as personal as material in personnel or medical files. But the government petitioned for a rehearing of the case by the full membership of the appellate court, and in a 6–5 ruling the appellate court overturned the earlier decisions.

---

85. *U.S.* v. *Nixon,* 94 S. Ct. 3090 (1974).
86. Galvin, "Clinton Invokes Executive Privilege."
87. *Washington Post* v. *State Department,* 647 F. 2d 197 (1981).
88 *State Department* v. *Washington Post,* 456 F. 2d 595 (1982).
89. *Kurzon* v. *Health and Human Services,* 649 F. 2d 65 (1981).
90. *New York Times* v. *NASA,* 679 F. Supp. 33 (1987).
91. *New York Times* v. *NASA,* 852 F. 2d 602 (1988).

"While the taped words do not contain information about the personal lives of the astronauts, disclosure of the file would reveal the sound and inflection of the crew's voices during the last seconds of their lives," the court said. The information recorded through the capture of a person's voice is distinct and is in addition to the information contained in the words themselves, the six judges noted.[92]

A ruling that a file is a medical or personnel or similar file does not automatically bar the release of data in the file. Establishing that the information or material sought is the kind of information protected by Exemption Six is just the first step. The court must then determine that

1. the release of this information will constitute an invasion of personal privacy, *and*
2. this invasion of personal privacy is clearly unwarranted.

The Supreme Court made it clear in 1976 that exemption is not intended to preclude every incidental invasion of privacy, but rather "only such disclosures as constitute clearly unwarranted invasions of personal privacy."[93] The government normally carries the burden of proof that the release of the information will amount to an unwarranted invasion of privacy. But this burden is not a terribly heavy one. For example, a U.S. district court accepted government arguments that the release of the voice communications tape recorded aboard the space shuttle Challenger would be an unwarranted invasion of privacy.[94] The ruling was made despite the fact that a printed transcript of the tape had been previously released.

In 1991 the Supreme Court ruled that the revelation of personal information contained in U.S. State Department interviews with Haitian nationals who had been returned to their homeland after coming to the United States would constitute an invasion of privacy.[95] An attorney representing undocumented Haitian nationals sought copies of interviews that the U.S. government had conducted in an attempt to determine whether the Haitian government was harassing or harming the refugees who were forced to return to Haiti. The State Department provided almost 100 pages of documents describing the interviews and summarizing what had been discovered, but all identifying details, including names and addresses of the interview subjects, had been deleted. This is called a redacted document. The attorney went to court to get the full interviews. Lower federal courts ordered the government to produce the material it had deleted. But the U.S. Supreme Court sided with the State Department, ruling that release of the names, addresses, marital status, employment status, living conditions, and other material would be an invasion of privacy of the interview subjects. Justice John Paul Stevens said linking such data to the names of the former refugees would be a "significant" invasion of their personal privacy. The high court ruling was unanimous.

In 1994 the Supreme Court ruled that in some circumstances it is an unwarranted invasion of privacy to make public the home addresses of government employees. The issue arose as two labor unions sought the names and home addresses of employees of the Department of Defense and other federal agencies. The labor unions filed an unfair labor practices complaint

92. *New York Times* v. *NASA,* 970 F. 2d 1002 (1990).
93. *Department of the Air Force* v. *Rose,* 425 U.S. 352 (1976).
94. *New York Times* v. *National Aeronautics and Space Administration,* 782 F. Supp. 628 (1991).
95. *State Department* v. *Ray,* 112 S. Ct. 1287 (1991).

when the agencies refused to provide the sought-after data. Both the Federal Labor Relations Authority and a U.S. court of appeals ordered the agencies to provide the requested information.[96] But the U.S. Supreme Court overturned these rulings in a unanimous decision that said the names and addresses could be withheld from disclosure by virtue of Exemption Six.[97] Justice Clarence Thomas wrote that he couldn't imagine how this information would further citizens' rights to be informed about what their government was up to. In addition the privacy interests are substantial, he said. The union seeks the addresses of those employees who have chosen not to join the union. These employees may want to avoid an influx of union-related mail or telephone calls or visits. "Many people simply do not want to be disturbed at home by work-related matters," Thomas wrote. When the privacy interest outweighs the public interest in the information, the disclosure would constitute a clearly unwarranted invasion of privacy, the associate justice concluded.

Law Enforcement

Exemption Seven: Records or information compiled for law enforcement purposes, but only to the extent that the production of such law enforcement records or information (a) could reasonably be expected to interfere with enforcement proceedings, (b) would deprive a person of a right to a fair trial or an impartial adjudication, (c) could reasonably be expected to constitute an unwarranted invasion of personal privacy, (d) could reasonably be expected to disclose the identity of a confidential source, including a state, local or foreign agency or authority or any private institution which furnished information on a confidential basis, and, in the case of a record or information compiled by criminal law enforcement authority in the course of a criminal investigation or by an agency conducting a lawful national security intelligence investigation, information furnished by confidential source, (e) would disclose techniques and procedures for law enforcement investigations or prosecutions, or would disclose guidelines for law enforcement investigations or prosecutions if such disclosure could reasonably be expected to risk circumvention of the law, or (f) could reasonably be expected to endanger the life or physical safety of any individual.

Exemption Seven provides an agency a broad exception to the general rule of access. Like Exemption Six, Exemption Seven requires a two-tiered test in its application. The first tier or question (what lawyers and judges often call the threshold question) is:

Was the information or record sought compiled for law enforcement purposes?

If the government is unable to show that the records were compiled for law enforcement purposes, the exemption does not apply. But the courts are generally willing to grant the government a wide latitude in applying this test. For example, the Supreme Court ruled in 1982 that summaries of investigatory records qualified as law enforcement records. In 1969 presidential staff members requested that the FBI summarize and transmit to the president information in its files concerning particular individuals who had criticized the administration, a

96. *Department of Defense* v. *Federal Labor Relations Authority,* 975 F. 2d 1105 (1992).
97. *Department of Defense* v. *Federal Labor Relations Authority,* 114 S. Ct. 1006 (1994).

so-called enemies list. When Howard Abramson sought to see these summaries in 1976, he was told they were investigatory records shielded by Exemption Seven. Abramson argued that while the original records may have been compiled for law enforcement purposes, the summaries of these records sent to the president did not meet this criterion. The summaries were prepared, if for any reason, for political and not law enforcement purposes. But the high court disagreed in a 5–4 ruling. "We hold that information initially contained in a record made for law enforcement purposes continues to meet the threshold requirements of Exemption Seven where that recorded information is reproduced or summarized in a new document prepared for a non-law enforcement purpose," Justice Byron White wrote for the court.[98]

In another decision in 1989, the high court ruled that the reason the material is originally compiled is not relevant in determining whether Exemption Seven is applicable. The key question, the high court ruled, is whether the information is being used for law enforcement purposes when the response to the FOIA inquiry is sent to the person seeking the data.

The key question, the high court ruled, is whether the information is being used for law enforcement purposes when the response to the FOIA inquiry is sent to the person seeking the data.

Grumman Aircraft provided routine information for a government audit in 1978. The information compiled at this time by the Defense Contract Audit Agency was not compiled for law enforcement purposes. Seven years later a federal investigation into possible fraudulent practices by the company began and Grumman sought to gain copies of the information it had provided the auditors in 1978. The agency refused, citing Exemption Seven, and transferred the records to the FBI. Grumman then sought the records from the FBI. This agency said no, arguing that the records had been compiled for law enforcement purposes and their release could reasonably be expected to interfere with an ongoing proceeding. Grumman argued that the records were not originally compiled for law enforcement purposes, but the Supreme Court said this was immaterial. "The plain words [of the statute] contain no requirement that compilation be effected at a specific time. The objects sought merely must have been compiled [for law enforcement purposes] when the government invokes the exemption," Justice Harry Blackmun wrote for the court in the 6–3 ruling.[99]

Law enforcement agencies, however, are not given carte blanche discretion to designate any record they choose as one gathered for law enforcement purposes. Seth Rosenfeld sued the Department of Justice and the Federal Bureau of Investigation to gain access to records of FBI investigations of faculty, students, and journalists at the University of California in the early 1960s when the so-called Free Speech Movement challenged the university administration's regulations barring political activities on campus. The federal agencies argued that the material had been gathered for the purpose of examining whether the student movement had been captured from within by communists. The U.S. Court of Appeals for the 9th Circuit agreed that while some of the material sought by Rosenfeld had indeed been gathered for legitimate law enforcement purposes, other records were gathered long after the need for such an investigation ceased to exist. The law enforcement purpose argument was only a pretext, the court said, invoked to pursue routine monitoring of many individuals and to shield the harassment of the political opponents of the FBI.[100]

98. *FBI* v. *Abramson*, 456 U.S. 615 (1982).
99. *John Doe Agency* v. *John Doe Corporation*, 110 S. Ct. 471 (1989).
100. *Rosenfeld* v. *U.S. Dept. of Justice*, 57 F. 3d 803 (1995).

Information compiled for law enforcement purposes may still be accessible under the Freedom of Information Act. The court next must determine whether the release of the material would result in one of the six consequences outlined in *a* through *f* in the exemption; in other words, could the release of the information be expected to interfere with law enforcement proceedings or deprive a person of a right to a fair trial?

Congress amended Exemption Seven in 1986 and gave federal law enforcement agencies far broader authority to refuse FOIA requests. Courts have read the exemption in an expansive manner, giving the FBI, the Secret Service, the Drug Enforcement Administration, and other federal police agencies even more legal excuses to deny access to information they possess. For example, in 1989 the Supreme Court agreed that the release of computerized arrest records (often called "rap sheets") held by the FBI could reasonably be expected to constitute an unwarranted invasion of personal privacy. The rap sheets contain information indicating arrests, indictments, acquittals, convictions, and sentences on about 24 million people in the nation. Some of this material is highly sensitive, but much of it has been publicized previously when individuals were being processed by the criminal justice system. Additionally, all of this data is available from state and local law enforcement agencies across the nation. The FBI has simply put together all the bits and pieces of data about an individual held by various police agencies into a single, computerized file.

CBS reporter Robert Schnake sought such information from the FBI on Charles Medico. The agency denied the request, citing the personal privacy factor in Exemption Seven. A U.S. district court supported the agency, saying the material sought by Schnake would be personal to Medico. But the U.S. Court of Appeals for the District of Columbia Circuit reversed this decision, noting that the government cannot assert a privacy interest in records it holds when the records are already available from state and local authorities.[101] The Supreme Court reversed this ruling in an important 9–0 decision. The privacy interest in a rap sheet is substantial, wrote Justice John Paul Stevens for the court. "The substantial character of that interest is affected by the fact that in today's society the computer can accumulate and store information that would have otherwise surely been forgotten long before a person attains the age of 80, when the F.B.I.'s rap sheets are discarded," Stevens added. Stevens rejected the argument that because arrests and convictions are almost always public knowledge when they happen, an individual has only a minimal privacy interest in a federal compilation of such information. Federal computers, he said, make easily available information that would be difficult to obtain by other means. "Plainly there is a vast difference between the public records that might be found after a diligent search of courthouse files, county archives, and local police stations throughout the county and a computerized summary located in a single clearinghouse of information," Stevens noted.[102]

The protection of personal privacy exemption was also recently used by federal courts to block access to information in FBI files about possible disciplinary proceedings against an FBI agent for misconduct. The agent was accused of entrapping a suspect.[103] The protection

101. *Reporters Committee for Freedom of the Press* v. *Justice Department,* 816 F. 2d 730 (1987).
102. *Justice Department* v. *Reporters Committee,* 109 S. Ct. 1486 (1989).
103. *Dunkelberger* v. *Justice Department,* 906 F. 2d 779 (1990).

of both privacy and the identity of confidential sources were reasons given by the U.S. Postal Service when it refused to give television station KTVY nearly half of the 4,700-page record amassed by the agency when it investigated the shooting deaths of 14 postal service workers at the Edmond, Okla., post office in 1986. The 10th U.S. Circuit Court of Appeals supported the government's refusal to release the entire file.[104]

For a time in the early 1990s federal courts took the position that when a law enforcement agency invoked Exemption Seven *d* (the release of the information could reasonably be expected to disclose the identity of a confidential source), the court should presume that the agency had guaranteed confidentiality to the source.[105] In order to rebut the application of this exemption, the party seeking the data had to bring forth evidence to show that the agency had not promised confidentiality, usually an impossible task. In 1993 the Supreme Court seriously undercut this interpretation of the exemption when it ruled that a source should be presumed to be confidential only if the source furnished information with the understanding that the agency would not divulge the communication except to the extent the agency thought necessary for law enforcement purposes. Such a confidential relationship could not be presumed in every case, the court said. There must be either evidence of an explicit promise of confidentiality or evidence of the circumstances in the relationship between the investigator and the source that supports an inference of confidentiality. The court cited the relationship between an agent and a paid informer as an example of the latter.[106]

Records and documents held by federal law enforcement agencies enjoy additional shielding from public disclosure beyond the broad language of Exemption Seven. The 1986 amendment to the FOIA permits such agencies to refuse to confirm or deny the existence of

1. records concerning a criminal investigation, if disclosure could reasonably be expected to interfere with enforcement proceedings;
2. informant records requested by third parties, if the informant's status as an informant has not been officially confirmed; and
3. classified records of the FBI pertaining to foreign intelligence, counterintelligence, and international terrorism investigations.

The purpose of these additional limits on access to information is to try to stop the bad guys, crooks, spies, terrorists, and so on from using the Freedom of Information Act as a means of finding out how much the government knows about their activities. And if the limits are applied in this fashion, few will object. But remember, the government does not always work from such noble principles. Recall the case earlier where White House operatives wanted FBI files on persons who criticized the president. The broad law enforcement exemptions to the FOIA make it very difficult for the press or others to discover and publicize this kind of misuse of government power.

104. *KTVY-TV* v. *U.S. Postal Service,* 919 F. 2d 1465 (1990).
105. See, for example, *Schmerler* v. *FBI,* 900 F. 2d 333 (1990).
106. *Justice Department* v. *Landano,* 113 S. Ct. 2014 (1993).

Financial Records

Exemption Eight: Matters contained in or related to examination, operating, or condition reports prepared by, on behalf of, or for the use of any agency responsible for the regulation and supervision of financial institutions. This is a little-used exemption that is designed to prevent the disclosure of sensitive financial reports or audits that, if made public, might undermine the public confidence in banks, trust companies, investment banking firms, and other financial institutions.

Geological Data

Exemption Nine: Geological and geophysical information and data, including maps concerning wells. People who drill oil and gas wells provide considerable information about these wells to the government. This exemption prevents speculators and other drillers from gaining access to this valuable information.

HANDLING FOIA REQUESTS

Government departments must answer requests for records and documents within 20 days.[*] A journalist can, however, ask for an "expedited review" if there is an urgent need for the information. A requester is entitled to an expedited review if he or she is a person primarily engaged in disseminating information and there is an urgency to inform the public about an actual or alleged governmental activity. If an appeal is filed after a denial, the agency has only 20 days to rule on the appeal. Each agency must publish quarterly, or more frequently, an index of the documents and records it keeps.

Government departments must answer requests for records and documents within 20 days.

Agencies are required to report to Congress each year and must include in the report a list of the materials to which access was granted and to which access was denied and the costs incurred. If a citizen or a reporter has to go to court to get the agency to release materials and the agency loses the case, the agency may be assessed the cost of the complainant's legal fees and court costs. Finally, agency personnel are now personally responsible for granting or denying access, a requirement federal agencies object to strenuously. An employee of an agency who denies a request for information must be identified to the person who seeks the material, and if the access is denied in an arbitrary or capricious manner, the employee can be disciplined by the Civil Service Commission.

Agencies may charge fees to cover the actual cost of searching for and copying the records that are sought. These fees can be very high if a large amount of material is requested. The Reporters Committee for Freedom of the Press estimates that search charges range from $11 to $28 per hour, depending on the agency. Computer searches might cost considerably more, as high as $270 per hour. Photocopying costs range from 3 to 25 cents per page. In 1986 Congress passed legislation that set out specific fee provisions for four kinds of requesters:

[*]Requests had to be answered within 10 days until 1996. The Electronic Freedom of Information Act amendments to the law extended the response time to 20 days.

1. Commercial-use requesters must pay fees for document search, duplication, and review.
2. Noncommercial requesters from educational or scientific institutions pay no search fees and receive one hundred pages of free duplication.
3. Representatives of the news media pay no search fees and receive copies of one hundred pages free.
4. All other requesters receive two hours of search time and one hundred pages at no charge.

Anyone who seeks a fee waiver under the FOIA must show that the disclosure of the information is "in the public interest because it is likely to contribute significantly to public understanding of the operations or activities of the government and is not primarily in the commercial interest of the requester."

News media representatives are defined as persons actively working for an organization that publishes or broadcasts the news to the public. Free-lance writers working on magazine articles or books may qualify as a representative of the news media if they can demonstrate a solid basis for expecting publication of their work. This evidence could be a contract, a response to a query letter, or some other document or device that indicates probable publication. News has been defined as "information about current events or of current interest to the public."

The Freedom of Information Act is not difficult to use. There is a sample request letter on page 345. In addition, both the Student Press Law Center and the Reporters Committee for Freedom of the Press offer free automated open records request letters. The fill-in-the-blank format is easy to complete before printing it out on a computer. The online services of the Student Press Law Center can be accessed through http://www.splc.org. The online address for the Reporters Committee is http://www.rcfp.org. For only $3 (plus $1.50 for shipping and handling) it is possible to get a highly informative booklet, "How to Use the Federal FOI Act," 8th edition, published by the Reporters Committee for Freedom of the Press, 1101 Wilson Blvd., Suite 1910, Arlington, VA 22209. Longtime right-of-access proponent Sam Archibald offers these suggestions to journalists on making the law work:[107]

1. Find out which agencies have the material in which you are interested. The "United States Government Manual" lists all federal agencies, explains what they are supposed to do, and usually lists local addresses and telephone numbers.
2. Call or write the agency to get background information about the material and information in which you are interested.
3. When you have determined what records you seek, write an official request for the material. Address it to the head of the agency, describe as specifically as possible the material you seek, and state that the request is made under the Freedom of Information Act: 5 United States Code, Section 552.
4. If your request is rejected, file an appeal with the head of the agency. Send along the copy of the rejection letter and make a strong argument as to why you think the material is not exempt.

107. Archibald, "The Revised F.O.I. Law," 54.

SAMPLE FOI ACT REQUEST LETTER

Your address
Daytime phone number
Date

Freedom of Information Office
Agency
Address

FOIA Request

Dear FOI Officer:

Pursuant to the federal Freedom of Information Act, 5 U.S.C. § 552, I request access to and copies of *(here, clearly describe what you want. Include identifying material, such as names, places, and the period of time about which you are inquiring. If you think they will help to explain what you are looking for, attach news clips, reports, and other documents describing the subject of your research).* Please include any e-mail correspondence that relates to this matter.

(Optional:) I would like to receive the information in electronic *(or microfiche)* format.

I agree to pay reasonable duplication fees for the processing of this request in an amount not to exceed $ _____. However, please notify me prior to your incurring any expenses in excess of that amount.[1]

(Suggested request for fee benefit as a representative of the news media:) As a representative of the news media I am only required to pay for the direct cost of duplication after the first 100 pages. Through this request, I am gathering information on *(subject)* that is of current interest to the public because *(give reason)*. This information is being sought on behalf of (give the name of your news organization) for dissemination to the general public. *(If a free-lancer, provide information such as experience, publication contract, etc., that demonstrates that you expect publication.)*

(Optional fee-waiver request:) Please waive any applicable fees. Release of the information is in the public interest because it will contribute significantly to public understanding of government operations and activities.[2]

If my request is denied in whole or part, I ask that you justify all deletions by reference to specific exemptions of the act. I will also expect you to release all segregable portions of otherwise exempt material. I, of course, reserve the right to appeal your decision to withhold any information or to deny a waiver of fees.

Because I am making this request as a journalist *(or author or scholar)* and this information is of timely value, I would appreciate your communicating with me by telephone, rather than by mail, if you have questions regarding this request.[3] *(If you are a reporter or a person who is "primarily engaged in disseminating information," and your request concerns a matter of "compelling need," a request for expedited review may be honored. If so, include the next three paragraphs:)*

Please provide an expedited review of this request, which concerns a matter of urgency. As a journalist, I am primarily engaged in disseminating information.

The public has an urgent need for information about *(describe the government activity involved)* because *(establish the need for bringing information on this subject to the public's attention now.)*

I certify that my statements concerning the need for expedited review are true and correct to the best of my knowledge and belief. I look forward to your reply within 20 business days, as the statute requires.

Thank you for your assistance.

Very truly yours,

Your Signature

Footnotes

1. Most agencies will not consider your request properly filed unless you state something about the fees—either your willingness to pay or your request for a fee waiver. By setting an amount up front, the agency will begin to process your request, and you can retain some control over the ultimate amount you will have to pay.

2. You may wish to address each criterion for waiver, except that, as a representative of the news media, you need not show how you will use the information to contribute to public understanding or that its use is noncommercial. An author or scholar may show how the information will ultimately be available to the public. A library may identify researchers who will use it.

3. It is always a good idea to call the agency's FOI office several days after your request is mailed, to be sure of its arrival and to talk directly with the officer processing your request. Quite often you can resolve any minor problems concerning your request at that time and avoid delays.

Sample FOIA request letter, based on *How to Use the Federal FOI Act,* 8th ed., FOI Service Center Publication.

5. If the appeal is rejected—and you really want to get the material—go to court. This final point, more than any other, needs to be emphasized. As long as government agencies are confident that the press and public will not bother with lawsuits, the tendency to withhold information will be reinforced. But strong sanctions can be applied against government officials who are found to have deliberately withheld material illegally. Sanctions can only be applied, however, after judicial determination of the matter. The application of this kind of pressure on a regular basis by the press and the public can have a generally positive impact in the battle for open government.

TIPS ON HOW TO GET RECORDS

Many old journalistic hands argue that formal FOIA requests should be a last resort. Jack Briggs of the Tri-City (Wash.) Herald advises reporters to:

- Ask informally for documents—a formal FOIA request often takes much longer.
- Look to public court records for information that takes longer to get through an FOIA request.
- Cultivate trusted sources within federal agencies.
- Follow up FOIA requests with telephone calls.
- Don't kick and scream, unless kicking and screaming is justified. And don't forget to occasionally praise the FOIA officer who helps you.

Reporter Steve Weinberg, in an article in the Columbia Journalism Review, offers these additional tips for using the FOIA.[108] Be specific in your request. Know exactly what you want. To do this you must study the agency indexes closely. Try to direct FOIA requests to regional or local offices when possible. It is easier to communicate with a local office, and very often the people who operate these offices are not as "hardened" as their counterparts in Washington. Offer to pay reasonable fees in your request letter; if not, the agency will write you back in 20 days and ask if you are willing to pay the fees. This exchange will simply delay any action on your request.

FEDERAL OPEN-MEETINGS LAW

In 1976 Congress passed and the president signed into law the **Government in Sunshine Act, the federal open-meetings law.** The statute affects approximately 50 federal boards, commissions, and agencies "headed by a collegial body composed of two or more individual members, a majority of whom are appointed to such position by the president with the advice and consent

---

108. Weinberg, "Trashing the FOIA," 21.

of the Senate." These public bodies are required to conduct their business meetings in public. Notice of public meetings must be given one week in advance, and the agencies are required to keep careful records of what occurs at closed meetings. The law also prohibits informal communication between officials of an agency and representatives of companies and other interested persons with whom the agency does business unless this communication is recorded and made part of the public record.

Courts have strictly interpreted the requirement that the law only applies to bodies whose members are appointed by the president. In 1981 the U.S. Court of Appeals for the District of Columbia Circuit ruled that the Government in Sunshine Act did not govern meetings of the Chrysler Loan Guarantee Board, a body created by the Congress to oversee federal loan guarantees for the financially troubled automaker. Persons who served on the board were not actually named by the president, but served because they held other federal offices (i.e., secretary of the treasury, comptroller general, chairman of the Federal Reserve). "If Congress had wanted to subject the board to the provisions of the Sunshine Act, it could have so provided when the board was established," the court noted.[109] A board or agency must also have some independent authority to act or take action before the law applies. A U.S. court of appeals ruled that the law does not apply to the president's Council of Economic Advisors. The sole function of the CEA is to advise and assist the president, the court said. It has no regulatory power. It cannot fund projects, even though it may appraise them. It has no function, save advising and assisting the president. Hence, it is not subject to either the FOIA or the Government in Sunshine Act.[110] The same rationale—that the Government in Sunshine Act does not cover advisory bodies—was used to block access to meetings of a panel of experts convened in 1986 by the federal Energy Department to determine whether a nuclear reactor in Washington state could melt down, as did the Chernobyl reactor in the Soviet Union.[111] Even agencies or commissions that fall under the aegis of the law may meet behind closed doors. The 1976 law lists 10 conditions or exemptions under which closed meetings might be held. The first nine of these exemptions mirror the exemptions in the Freedom of Information Act. The 10th exemption focuses on situations in which the agency is participating in arbitration or is in the process of adjudicating or otherwise disposing of a case.

A court of appeals in Washington, D.C., ruled that agencies may not automatically hold budget deliberations behind closed doors. "The Sunshine Act contains no express exemption for budget deliberations as a whole. Specific items discussed at budget meetings might, however, be exempt and might justify closing portions of a commission meeting on an individual and particularized basis," Judge Skelly Wright ruled. In each case the agency must defend its closure of the meeting by demonstrating that the discussion would focus on material excluded

Courts have strictly interpreted the requirement that the law only applies to bodies whose members are appointed by the president.

---

109. *Symons* v. *Chrysler Corporation Loan Guarantee Board,* 670 F. 2d 238 (1981).
110. *Rushforth* v. *Council of Economic Advisors,* 762 F. 2d 1038 (1985).
111. *National Resources Defense Council, Inc.* v. *Secretary of Energy,* 637 F. Supp. 116 (1986). Note: The Federal Advisory Committee Act does contain open-meetings and open-records provisions, but only a limited number of groups must abide by these provisions. For example, a federal court ruled in June of 1993 that the National Health Care Task Force, headed by Hillary Clinton, was not an advisory committee within the meaning of the law and did not have to hold open meetings.

from public disclosure by one of the 10 exemptions.[112] The 10th exemption was used to block access to a meeting of the Nuclear Regulatory Commission. The NRC was discussing the reopening of the nuclear power plant at Three Mile Island in Pennsylvania. The federal district court ruled that this meeting would likely focus on the final adjudication of the federal action involving the nuclear reactor and hence could be closed to press and public.[113]

There has been relatively little litigation under the Government in Sunshine Act, and reporters who work in Washington, D.C., report that compliance with the law is not good. The same problems existed in the early years of operation of the Freedom of Information Act. Constant pressure and frequent litigation against agencies that refused to comply with the FOIA finally made the law more effective. The same pressure is needed to make the Government in Sunshine Act live up to its promise.

SUMMARY

Statutes provide public access to both federal records and meetings held by federal agencies. The federal records law, the Freedom of Information Act, makes public all records including electronic records and e-mail held by agencies within the executive branch of government and the independent regulatory commissions. Courts have given a broad meaning to the term "record" but have ruled that an agency must normally create and possess such a record before it becomes subject to the Freedom of Information Act. Nine categories of information are excluded from the provisions of the law. These include exemptions for national security, agency working papers, highly personal information, and law enforcement files. Agencies must publish indexes of the records they hold and must permit copying of these materials. It is important to follow specific procedures when making a Freedom of Information Act request to see certain records or documents.

The Government in Sunshine Act is the federal open-meetings law. This law reaches about 50 agencies in the executive branch and the regulatory commissions. Members of these organizations are not permitted to hold secret meetings unless they will discuss material that falls into one of 10 categories. These categories mirror the Freedom of Information Act exemptions but also include a provision that permits closed-door meetings to discuss attempts to arbitrate or adjudicate certain cases or problems. This act is a newer law and does not seem to work as well as does the Freedom of Information Act.

STATE LAWS ON MEETINGS AND RECORDS

It is not as easy to talk about access at the state level as it is at the federal level, for we are dealing with hundreds of different statutes. (Most states have multiple laws dealing with access to meetings, access to records, and other access situations.) We can at best make a few generalizations. Harold Cross made some of the most astute generalizations in 1953 in his pioneering

112. *Common Cause* v. *Nuclear Regulatory Commission*, 674 F. 2d 921 (1982).
113. *Philadelphia Newspapers* v. *Nuclear Regulatory Commission*, 9 M.L.R. 1843 (1983).

book "The People's Right to Know."[114] Cross was really the first scholar to present a comprehensive report on access problems. In his book he listed four issues, or questions, common to every case of access:

1. Is the particular record or proceeding public? Many records and meetings kept or conducted by public officers in public offices are not really public at all. Much of the work of the police, though they are public officers and work in public buildings, is not open to public scrutiny.

2. Is public material public in the sense that records are open to public inspection and sessions are open to public attendance? Hearings in juvenile courts are considered public hearings for purposes of the law, but they are often not open to the public.

3. Who can view the records and who can attend the meetings open to the public? Many records, for example, might be open to specific segments of the public, but not to all segments. Automobile accident reports by police departments are open to insurance company adjusters and lawyers, but such records are not usually open to the general public.

4. When records and meetings are open to the general public and the press, will the courts provide legal remedy for citizens and reporters if access is denied?

The last question is probably not as important today as it was when Cross wrote his book in 1953, for at that time access to many public records and meetings in the states was based on the common law. Today this fact is no longer true. Access to meetings and records is nearly always governed by statute, and these statutes usually, but not always, provide a remedy for citizens who are denied access. This provision is more widespread in open-meetings laws, which tend to be more efficient in providing access, than in open-records laws, which are still weak and vague in many jurisdictions.

STATE OPEN-MEETINGS LAWS

All 50 states have specific statutes that mandate open meetings, and these laws range from good to awful. The need for **open-meetings laws** is obvious. There never was a solid common-law right to attend the meetings of public bodies, and as noted earlier, the constitutional provisions regarding freedom of expression have proved inadequate with regard to access.

It is difficult to make generalizations about these 50 different state laws. The Reporters Committee on Freedom of the Press in 1997 published its third edition of "Tapping Officials' Secrets," a comprehensive examination of both the open-meetings laws and the open-records laws in all 50 states. A quick perusal of this volume demonstrates the variety in the laws among the states. One of the most important aspects of any open-meetings law is the strong sanctions that may be imposed on government officials who fail to follow the mandate of the law. Laws that provide for substantial personal fines against these individuals are generally more desirable than laws that impose only small fines or no personal penalties at all. Another important

114. Cross, *The People's Right to Know.*

part of an open-meetings law is the legislative declaration at the beginning of the law. A clear, strong statement in favor of open access to meetings of government bodies can persuade a judge who is trying to interpret the law to side with the advocates of access rather than with the government. For example, in the state of Washington the open-meetings law begins as follows:

> The legislature finds and declares that all . . . public agencies of this state and subdivisions thereof exist to aid in the conduct of the people's business. It is the intent of this chapter that their actions be taken openly and that their delibera-tions be conducted openly.

State open-meetings laws are normally written in one of two ways. Some laws declare that all meetings are open, except the following. Meetings that are closed are then listed. Other state laws simply list the agencies that must hold open meetings. The Congress of the United States is clearly excluded from the provisions of the federal open-meetings law. State legisla-tures are generally excluded from the provisions of their state open-meetings laws as well. But the issue is not quite as clear-cut as the situation at the federal level. Some state open-meetings laws do in fact cover some kinds of legislative proceedings. State open-meetings laws routinely do not include meetings of parole and pardon boards, of law enforcement agencies, of military agencies like the National Guard, of medical agencies like hospital boards, and so forth.

A good open-meetings law will specifically define a meeting by giving the number of members of the board or commission who must be present to constitute a public meeting (a quorum? at least two? etc.), by stating that all deliberative stages of the decision-making process are considered meetings and must be open to the public, and by stating that social gatherings and chance encounters are not considered meetings and are therefore excluded from the provisions of the law. Some laws are not this specific and merely refer to all meet-ings, all regular or special meetings, all formal meetings, or whatever.

The exclusion of chance meetings and social gatherings is often troublesome to the press, especially in small towns. It is not uncommon that all members of the school board or the city council happen to have dinner at the same restaurant just before a meeting. If the din-ner is obviously a ploy to avoid the law, a suit can be brought against the members. Often it is difficult to prove that the dinner is anything other than a chance encounter or a social gather-ing. But a good law specifies that all gatherings at which public business is discussed must be open, not just official decision-making sessions.

Most open-meetings laws provide for closed meetings, or **executive sessions,** in certain kinds of cases. Meetings at which personnel problems are discussed are an obvious example. A public airing of a teacher's personal problems could be an unwarranted invasion of privacy. The discussion of real estate transactions is another obvious example. When a school board considers buying a parcel of land for a new high school, premature public disclosure of this fact could cost the taxpayers money should the owner raise the price of the property or spec-ulators buy it and force the school district to pay far more than it is worth. Meetings involving public safety are sometimes best conducted in private rather than in public. Usually laws will permit an official body to meet with its attorney behind closed doors if potential or actual lit-igation is on the agenda. This exception is merely an extension of the traditional lawyer-client privilege. Labor negotiations may also be held in private in about half the states. All but 13 state open-meetings laws contain a provision that no final action can be taken at an executive session, that the board or commission must reconvene in public before a final determination can be made on any issue.

When a presiding officer of a governmental body announces at a meeting that the body is going into executive session, a reporter at the meeting should make certain of the following items:

1. The presiding officer has specified what topics will be discussed during the closed session, or why the executive session has been called.

2. A reporter who believes that a meeting is being closed improperly should formally object. He or she should ask members of the body specifically which provision in the law they are using to go into closed session. It is not inappropriate to ask for a vote of the body to make certain the required simple majority (or two-thirds majority in some states) approves of the closed session.

3. The reporter should also ask what time the closed session will end, so he or she can attend a reconvened public session.

Most open-meetings statutes require not only that meetings be open to the public, but also that the public be notified of both regular and special meetings far enough in advance that they can attend if they wish. Time requirements vary, but normally a special meeting cannot be held without an announcement a day or two in advance.

Virtually all laws provide some kind of injunctive or other civil remedy if the law is violated; almost half the statutes provide for criminal penalties if the statute is knowingly violated. In many states any action taken at a meeting that was not public, but should have been public, is null and void. The action must be taken again at a proper meeting. Most laws provide fines and short jail terms for public officers who knowingly violate the law, but prosecution is rare.

Although a few laws date from the 19th century, the open-meetings laws in most states are a relatively new phenomenon. Such laws, which owe their passage to strong, forceful pressure from the press, have developed largely since 1950. In 1959 only 20 states had such laws. Formation in the early 1970s of the public lobby Common Cause gave great impetus to the passage of open-meetings laws. In 1972 and 1973 alone, nine states passed such statutes.

What should a reporter do when asked to leave a meeting that he or she believes should be open to the press and public? First, find out who has denied you access to the meeting and ask for the legal basis of this denial. Never leave a meeting voluntarily; but if ordered to leave, do so and contact your editor immediately. Resistance is not advised, for criminal charges may be filed against you. While open-meetings laws provide a good means of access to proceedings, the reporter possesses what is probably a more powerful weapon—the power of publicity. Public officials don't like stories about secret meetings. If an agency abuses its right to meet in executive session, describe these meetings as they really are—secret sessions. A photo essay showing a meeting room door open, closing, and closed, accompanied by a caption citing appropriate parts of the open-meetings law, will often get a reporter back into a proceeding faster than a court action.

While open-meetings laws provide a good means of access to proceedings, the reporter possesses what is probably a more powerful weapon—the power of publicity.

OPEN-MEETINGS TIPS FOR REPORTERS

■ Ask for legal basis for closure.
■ Find out who is asking that meeting be closed and why.
■ Never leave a meeting voluntarily.
■ Call your editor immediately.
■ Use publicity as well as the law to gain access.

STATE OPEN-RECORDS LAWS

Every state in the union also has some kind of **open-records law.** The access laws either follow the federal formula—all records are open except the following—or list the kinds of records that the public does have a right to inspect. In a useful article in the George Washington Law Review, attorneys Burt Braverman and Wesley Heppler outlined the basic dimensions of state freedom of information.[115]

Most state laws permit inspection of records by any person, but a few limit access to public records to citizens of the state. The reason persons want to see a record is normally considered immaterial when determining whether they can gain access to the record. The freedom of information laws provide access to records held by public agencies in the state, and normally these statutes provide a broad definition of these agencies. Normally included are state offices, departments, divisions, bureaus, boards, and commissions. Records kept by local government agencies (cities, counties, villages) are also included, as are those kept by school districts, public utilities, and municipal corporations. In some states these laws also apply to records held by the governor.[116] These state laws do not normally govern records kept by courts or the legislature. Frequently these branches of government have established their own policies regarding access to records. Braverman and Heppler report that state laws follow either a liberal or conservative definition of a public record. *All records possessed by an agency* are deemed to be public records in those states with liberal definitions of a public record. But some state laws are more conservative and provide access only to those *records that are required to be kept by law.*

All state freedom of information laws provide exemptions to disclosure. Agencies *may* withhold material that falls under an exemption in some states; agencies *must* withhold this information in other states. Braverman and Heppler list the six most common substantive exemptions to the state open-records laws as follows:

1. Information classified as confidential by state or federal law
2. Law enforcement and investigatory information
3. Trade secrets and commercial information
4. Preliminary departmental memorandums (working papers)

115. Braverman and Heppler, "State Open-Records Laws," 721.
116. Bush, "Access to Governors' Records," 135.

5. Personal privacy information
6. Information relating to litigation against a public body

The attorneys report that although state laws vary widely, state courts have almost uniformly held that exemptions should be construed narrowly; that is, they should be read in such a way as to provide public access to the greatest amount of information. The federal Freedom of Information Act requires agencies to maintain an index of documents and records; not many state laws have the same requirement. But in every state, the right to inspect records includes the right to copy records. Procedures to gain access to state agency records follow the federal FOIA model. Two-thirds of the state statutes have provisions for judicial review of agency rulings in which the state bears the burden to show that the record should remain undisclosed.

Some states have attempted to keep the question of access to records out of court by developing commissions or committees to try to resolve access questions. Citizens of Connecticut, for example, can appeal the denial of an access request to an independent commission, which has 20 days to try to resolve the issue. A court appeal remains if either the agency or citizen seeks to overturn a commission ruling. In New York a Committee on Public Access to Records attempts to regulate and facilitate the access to public records. Florida added another new wrinkle to state access law when voters in 1992 approved an amendment to the state constitution authorizing public access to not only records and meetings in the executive branch of government, but to legislative and judicial records and meetings as well. The proposal was approved by 85 percent of the citizens who voted, by any definition a landslide and a strong indication of citizen interest in open government.

This brief summary of the state laws provides the barest of outlines and guidelines. Reporters, government information officers, and even just interested citizens should be well acquainted with state rules and regulations on public access to meetings and records. Such information is easily developed with a little research. Many state press associations or organizations of journalists publish handbooks or guides to the laws in their states. A simple phone call is often all that is needed to get one of these guides. Many of these same organizations periodically sponsor seminars on access, open to all for the price of the registration fee. Knowledge about state access laws is truly power. Without such knowledge reporters and citizens alike can be easily misled by misguided public officials. The challenges ahead will focus as well on the growing trend toward electronic storage and movement of government data. Some of these issues are just beginning to be discussed, let alone resolved. Electronic access task forces are meeting in many states to study problems relating to access, privacy, and other important issues. The press must play a central role in these discussions.

THE PRIVATIZATION OF PUBLIC GOVERNMENT

One of the real challenges facing the press in the 21st century results from the growing trend of private companies taking over what has been traditionally regarded as government business. For-profit and nonprofit organizations today are replacing the government in operating public schools, jails and prisons, state and local welfare agencies, and many other state services.

These private agencies are not generally regarded to have the same responsibilities as public agencies to maintain open records and hold meetings in public. State and federal open-meetings and open-records laws do not include private organizations under their access mandates. The privatization of government functions has started slowly, but because the federal government has recently assigned each state the lion's share of the nation's welfare programs, it is likely that privatization will expand rapidly. Corporations already see operation of state welfare programs as potential profit centers. In Texas, private companies now handle many of the state's social services responsibilities. Some prisons in Arizona are operated by for-profit companies. Agencies in Ohio use private search firms to help select appointed public officers, like chiefs of police. And some government agencies, frustrated with the time it takes to deal with record management and access problems, have turned over government records to private companies who sell access to these records for a profit. In DuPage County, Illinois, the administrators of the judicial system gave exclusive control of the court's records to a private firm who sold access to the records. Other counties considered using the same system before an editorial campaign by the state's newspapers stopped the practice from spreading.[117] In Indiana, Illinois, Michigan, Ohio, and Wisconsin, a company called CivicLink, owned by Ameritech, a telephone company, provides computer access to court proceedings, meetings, property and tax records, and other types of public information—for a price. Journalists seeking information about such "private" government systems are sure to face denials based on corporate privacy, confidentiality of private financial records, and other arguments that businesses have used for decades to shield their operations from public scrutiny. New laws will be needed to break down these walls.

SUMMARY

All states have laws that govern access to public meetings and public records. Good state open-meetings laws have strong legislative declarations in support of public meetings, specifically define a public meeting by listing the number of members who must gather to constitute a meeting, and declare void all actions taken during a meeting that was improperly closed to the public. Most laws provide for closed sessions to discuss such matters as personnel actions, real estate transactions, and litigation.

State open-records laws tend to mirror the federal law. Both state and local agencies are governed by the laws, which apply to most governmental bodies except the legislature and the courts. Most state laws govern all records kept by these agencies, but a few are applicable only to records that are required to be kept by law. Exemptions to state open-records laws include material specifically excluded by other statutes, law-enforcement investigatory information, working papers, and highly personal information. Most laws provide for access to the judicial system in case a request for data is rejected, but both New York and Connecticut have established commissions to act as arbiters in these matters, and Florida has adopted a constitutional amendment that governs access throughout state government.

117. Fought, "Privatization Threatens Access."

LAWS THAT RESTRICT ACCESS TO INFORMATION

Just as there are laws that provide for public access to government-held documents, there are laws that specifically preclude access to government-held information. There are provisions in scores of federal laws alone that limit the right of access. Tax statutes, espionage laws, legislation on atomic energy, and dozens of other kinds of laws are filled with limitations on the dissemination of information (e.g., personal information on taxes, national security questions, and matters relating to nuclear weapons). But in addition to these kinds of laws, the federal government has adopted in the past four decades at least three rather broad sets of regulations regarding information held by the government. All three were adopted in the name of protecting the right to privacy, a value that seems to have replaced national security as the most commonly asserted reason the government uses to keep things secret. While these regulations cannot be considered here in a comprehensive sense, persons who gather information for a living need to be aware of their implications.

All three were adopted in the name of protecting the right to privacy, a value that seems to have replaced national security as the most commonly asserted reason the government uses to keep things secret.

GENERAL EDUCATION PROVISIONS ACT

An amendment, the Family Educational Rights and Privacy Act, to the General Education Provisions Act (1974) is aimed at increasing both the parental access to, and the confidentiality of, educational records. On the one hand, the law forces all federally funded schools and educational agencies to permit parents to inspect and review their children's educational records. On the other hand, the statute prohibits the distribution of personally identifiable information, excluding what is called directory data, to unauthorized persons without consent of the parents. The result is that student records or files must be kept confidential. This goal is hardly a hardship on the press in most instances. However, because of the stiff penalty in the law—possible loss to the school of federal funds—educators have occasionally overreacted and declared data that are actually unprotected by the statute to be confidential. Some university officials, for example, have tried to use this provision to deny reporters access to campus police records in an effort to squelch stories about crime on campus (see page 92). In one absurd case, a reporter-photographer said that school officials chased him off school property when he attempted to photograph children playing outside at recess. The officials cited the 1974 law as a reason that picture taking was no longer permitted on school property. Of course, instances like that are rare, and the significance of the law is its indication of the extreme interest in privacy today rather than its threat to the legitimate news-gathering tasks of the press.

THE FEDERAL PRIVACY LAW

The **Privacy Act** of 1974 has two basic thrusts. First, it attempts to check the misuse of personal data obtained by the federal government, the quantity of which has, of course, reached staggering proportions. Second, the law is intended to provide access for individuals to records about themselves that are held by federal agencies. The first objective of the law could be the more troublesome to the press.

The act requires that each federal agency limit the collection of information to that which is relevant and necessary, to collect information directly from the subject concerned when possible, and to allow individuals to review and amend their personal records and information. Also, under the act agencies are forbidden from disclosing what is called "a personally identifiable record" without the written consent of the individual to whom the record pertains. Since this section of the law is seemingly contradictory to the spirit of the federal FOIA, Congress was forced to clarify the responsibilities of federal agencies with regard to the law. A provision was added to the Privacy Act that declares that records required to be disclosed under the FOIA are not subject to the provisions of the Privacy Act and consequently cannot be withheld from inspection. To the government official with control of information, however, neither the Privacy Act nor the FOIA is unambiguous.

The difficulty in resolving aspects of the Privacy Act and the Freedom of Information Act is graphically illustrated by a case decided by the U.S. Court of Appeals for the District of Columbia Circuit. Frank Greentree was indicted and convicted in federal court on drug charges. He filed a civil suit to block state prosecution based on the same events. Greentree sought information from both the Drug Enforcement Administration and the U.S. Bureau of Customs to assist him in his civil action. When the agencies refused to give him the material he sought, he filed both a Freedom of Information Act request and a Privacy Act request to get the information. The documents sought by Greentree were contained in something called the Investigations Record System, and this system of records has been declared to be exempt from the access provisions of the Privacy Act. Hence it was unavailable to Greentree through the federal privacy law. Because the information could not be released under the Privacy Act, the government argued that it was also unavailable under FOIA Exemption Three. Remember Exemption Three: it provides that the Freedom of Information Act does not apply to matters "specifically exempt from disclosure by statute." The material Greentree sought was exempt from disclosure under the federal privacy statute; therefore, the government argued, it was also exempt from disclosure under Exemption Three of the Freedom of Information Act. In two previous appellate court rulings, this government argument was sustained.[118] But in *Greentree,* the U.S. Court of Appeals for the District of Columbia Circuit denied the validity of this argument and ruled against the government. Judge Wald said that throughout its consideration of the Privacy Act, the Congress struggled to hold separate the Privacy Act and the FOIA. That effect was ultimately successful, he said. Judge Wald noted that section (b) (2) of the Privacy Act clearly states that "no agency shall disclose any record which is contained in a system of records . . . *unless disclosure of the record would be required under section 552 (The Freedom of Information Act) of this title* [author emphasis]." "We must conclude," Wald wrote, "that this section of the Privacy Act represents a congressional mandate that the Privacy Act not be used as a barrier to FOIA access." Congress could not have intended that a section of the Privacy Act could serve as a withholding statute under FOIA Exemption Three, the judge said. It is possible, he noted, that the government might still be able to block access to this information because of Exemption Seven (the law enforcement exemption of the FOIA), but the government would have to prove that the material sought by Greentree was exempt from disclosure.[119]

---

118. See *Terkel* v. *Kelly,* 599 F. 2d 214 (1979) and *Painter* v. *Federal Bureau of Investigation,* 615 F. 2d 689 (1980).

119. *Greentree* v. *Customs Service,* 674 F. 2d 74 (1982).

The Privacy Act imposes a cost on an agency if it releases a file that should remain private. To the bureaucrat, that presents a real dilemma, as was emphasized in the Harvard Civil Rights/Civil Liberties Law Review:

> If government officials refuse to disclose the material, they risk being sued by the party who requested the file under the Freedom of Information Act. Under the FOIA the court may award to a successful plaintiff his costs and attorney's fees. If, on the other hand, agencies release material, they risk being sued under the Privacy Act by the person who is the subject of the file. In that case, the plaintiff might win by showing that the file was exempt from disclosure under FOIA. A successful Privacy Act plaintiff can collect not only his costs and attorney's fees, but also actual damage sustained because of disclosure.[120]

Given this distinction between the statutes, it is easy to recognize that bureaucrats will choose to err on the side of caution—it is wiser to withhold the information and risk suit under the FOIA than possibly incur Privacy Act penalties.

Other conflicts exist in the administration of the two laws. Before passage of the Privacy Act, materials that were not required to be disclosed under the FOIA were nevertheless permitted to be disclosed at the discretion of a government agency. Now, information falling under an FOIA exemption, and thus not required to be disclosed, will routinely be withheld out of fear of violating the Privacy Act.

CRIMINAL HISTORY PRIVACY LAWS

In accordance with the broad scope of the Omnibus Crime Control and Safe Streets Act of 1968, the federal Law Enforcement Assistance Administration, an agency created by the Nixon administration to help local police forces fight crime, sought to develop a national computerized record-keeping system. The system that was established permits any police department in the nation to have access to the records of virtually all other police departments.

Congressional concern about the misuse of this record system led to limitations on access to the data. Police records have always contained a considerable amount of misinformation, information that is out of date, and information that is private. The centralized record-keeping system presents a problem referred to by some writers as the "dossier effect." The contrast between these computerized and centrally maintained records immediately accessible across the country and those police records of the past was sharp and immediately evident: fragmented, original-source records kept by a single police agency for a limited geographical area were not readily accessible because of their bulk and associated indexing problems. Hence, federal policy mandated that states, if they wish to participate in the national record-keeping system, adopt rules that, among other things, limit the dissemination of some criminal history nonconviction data.

The "Code of Federal Regulations" ("Criminal Justice Information Systems") defines nonconviction data as follows:

---

120. "Freedom of Information Act's Privacy Exemption," 596.

arrest information without disposition if an interval of one year has elapsed from the date of arrest and no active prosecution of the charge is pending, or information disclosing that the police have elected not to refer a matter to a prosecutor, or that a prosecutor has elected not to commence criminal proceedings, or that proceedings have been indefinitely postponed, as well as all acquittals and all dismissals.

As a result of the state laws, press access to criminal history records kept by the police has been virtually eliminated unless data sought pertain to an incident for which a person is currently being processed by the criminal justice system, are conviction records, or are original records of entry, such as arrest records, that are maintained chronologically and are accessible only on that basis. Reporters can also obtain information about arrests not resulting in conviction, however, if they are aware of the specific dates of the arrests. It is hard to determine whether these laws have substantially affected the press's ability to report on the criminal justice system. A good police reporter usually can gain access to information he or she wants to see. Nevertheless, potential problems are apparent. One commentator noted:

> On the one hand, the uncontrolled dissemination and publication of certain criminal history records can adversely affect the individual himself. On the other hand, the public and the press must have access to basic records of official action if they are to effectively scrutinize and evaluate the operations of the police, the prosecuting agencies, and the courts.[121]

The ability to achieve that scrutiny is important. For example, it is possible to envision a situation in which a prosecutor is accused of favoring friends or certain ethnic or racial groups when deciding whether to prosecute arrested persons. Without access to arrest records that can be compared with prosecution records, such a charge would be difficult to investigate. Persons within the criminal justice system could gain access to the needed records, but history indicates that these people must be prodded before they take action. And, of course, prodding is the function of the press.

STATE STATUTES THAT LIMIT ACCESS TO INFORMATION

All states have statutes that limit access to information that would otherwise be available under a freedom of information law. The state of Washington, for example, has more than 100 different laws that govern the access to particular information. Arizona has 39 laws that block access to specific records. Some of these state statutes are aimed at blocking access to trade secrets; others limit access to information submitted to the state in compliance with environmental laws. The working papers of assessors, poll lists from prior elections, and reports from oil and gas companies are also frequently exempted from disclosure by a specific statute. State privacy laws are the most common kind of statutory limitation on the access to information.

All states have statutes that limit access to information that would otherwise be available under a freedom of information law.

---

121. Higgins, "Press and Criminal Record Privacy," 509.

SUMMARY

All the states and the federal government have laws that specifically exclude certain kinds of information from the public scrutiny. Some of these exclusions were noted in the discussion of Exemption Three of the Freedom of Information Act. Today, the right to privacy has been erected as a substantial barrier to access to information held by government agencies. The federal government has adopted a law protecting the privacy of student records. The Congress passed a federal privacy law, which often conflicts with the provisions of the Freedom of Information Act. The federal government has also insisted that states pass statutes that control access to criminal history records. Much privacy legislation has been passed by the states themselves, and today the right to privacy is being used frequently to block access to public records.

BIBLIOGRAPHY ⟶

Adams, John B. *State Open-Meeting Laws: An Overview.* Columbia, Mo.: Freedom of Information Foundation, 1974.

Archibald, Sam. "The Revised F.O.I. Law and How to Use It." *Columbia Journalism Review,* July/August 1977, 54.

Barringer, Felicity. "Appeals Court Rejects Damages against ABC in Food Lion Case." *The New York Times,* 21 October 1999, A1.

Beesley, Susan L., and Theresa Glover. "Developments Under the Freedom of Information Act, 1986." *Duke Law Journal* 1987 (1987):521.

Braverman, Burt A., and Wesley Heppler. "A Practical Review of State Open-Records Laws." *George Washington Law Review* 49 (1981):721.

The Bush Administration and the News Media. Washington, D.C.: Reporters Committee for Freedom of the Press, 1992.

Bush, Ellen M. "Access to Governors' Records: State Statutes and the Use of Executive Privilege." *Journalism Quarterly* 71 (1994):135.

The Clinton Administration and the News Media. Washington, D.C.: Reporters Committee for Freedom of the Press, 1996.

Cross, Harold. *The People's Right to Know.* New York: Columbia University Press, 1953.

Denniston, Lyle. "Reagan Legacy: Law against Leaks." *Washington Journalism Review,* December 1988, 10.

Feinsilber, Mike. "Agencies Try Hard to Answer Blizzard of FOIA Requests." *The Seattle Times,* 19 June 1994, A10.

Fought, Barbara C. "Privatization Threatens Access." *Quill,* September 1997, 8.

"The Freedom of Information Act's Privacy Exemption and the Privacy Act of 1974." *Harvard Civil Rights/Civil Liberties Law Review* 11 (1976):596.

Galvin, Kevin. "Clinton Invokes Executive Privilege on Clemency Deal." *The Seattle Post-Intelligencer,* 17 September 1999, A3.

Genovese, Margaret. "Reagan Administration Information Policies." *presstime,* April 1985, 14.

Gersh, Deborah. "New FOIA Policy Directives Issued." *Editor & Publisher,* 9 October 1993, 18.

Greenhouse, Linda. "Police Violate Privacy in Home Raids with Journalists." *The New York Times,* 25 May 1999, A25.

Hayes, Michael J. "Whatever Happened to 'The Right to Know'? Access to Government-Controlled Information Since Richmond Newspapers." *Virginia Law Review* 73 (1987):111.

Higgins, Steven. "Press and Criminal Record Privacy." *St. Louis University Law Journal* 20 (1977):509.

How to Use the Federal FOI Act, 8th ed. Arlington, Va.: FOI Service Center, 1998.

Jehl, Douglas. "Clinton Revamps Policy on Secrecy of U.S. Documents." *The New York Times,* 18 April 1995, Al.

Kelly, Tina. "Behind Closed E-Mail." *The New York Times,* 1 April 1999, D1.

Killeen, Michael. "Resistance to Public Access Is Increasing." *Allied Daily Newspapers of Washington Briefing* 59 (February 1994):2.

Kirtley, Jane E., ed. *The First Amendment Handbook.* Washington, D.C.: The Reporters Committee for Freedom of the Press, 1986.

Lewis, Neil. "Government Told to Save Messages Sent by Computer." *The New York Times,* 14 August 1993, A1.

Malmgren, Lynn C. "First Amendment: Freedom of Press to Gather News." *Villanova Law Review* 20 (1974):189.

Marwick, Christine M., ed. *Litigation Under the Amended Freedom of Information Act,* 2d ed. Washington, D.C.: American Civil Liberties Union and Freedom of Information Clearing House, 1976.

Meier, Barry. "Jury Says ABC Owes Damages of $5.5 Million." *The New York Times,* 23 January 1997, A1.

Middleton, Kent. "Journalists, Trespass, and Officials: Closing the Door on *Florida Publishing Co.* v. *Fletcher.*" *Pepperdine Law Review* 16 (1989):259.

Mifflin, Laurie. "Judge Slashes $5.5 Million Award to Grocery Chain for ABC Report." *The New York Times,* 30 August 1997, A1.

Morrissey, David H. "FOIA Foiled?" *presstime,* March 1995, 29.

Padover, Saul, ed. *The Complete Madison.* New York: Harper & Row, 1953.

Pember, Don R. "The Burgeoning Scope of 'Access Privacy' and the Portent for a Free Press." *Iowa Law Review* 64 (1979):1155.

Riechmann, Deb. "Congress Fears Nuclear Secrets May Slip Out in Old Documents." *The Seattle Post-Intelligencer,* 25 August 1999, A5.

Ritter, Bob. *New Technology and the First Amendment.* Greencastle, Ind.: SPJ Reports, 1993.

Rourke, Francis. *Secrecy and Publicity.* Baltimore: Johns Hopkins University Press, 1961.

Schiesel, Seth. "Jury Finds NBC Negligent in 'Dateline' Report." *The New York Times,* 9 July 1998, A19.

Schulz, David A. "Troubling Ruling Restricts News Gathering." *Editor & Publisher,* 29 June 1996, 5.

Sherer, Michael D. "Free-Lance Photojournalists and the Law." *Communications and the Law* 10 (1988):39.

Stewart, Potter. "Or of the Press." *Hastings Law Journal* 26 (1975):631.

U.S. Senate. *Clarifying and Protecting Right of Public to Information.* 89th Cong., 1st sess., 1965, S. Rept. 813.

Weinberg, Steve. "Trashing the FOIA." *Columbia Journalism Review,* January/February 1985, 21.

Weiner, Tim. "Lawmaker Tells of High Cost of Data Secrecy." *The New York Times,* 28 June 1996, A9.

———. "U.S. Plans Secrecy Overhaul to Open Millions of Records." *The New York Times,* 18 March 1994, A1.

Wicklein, John. "FOIA Foiled." *American Journalism Review,* April 1996, 36.

Wright, Ann A. "The Definition of 'Agency' Under the Freedom of Information Act as Applied to Federal Consultants and Grantees." *Georgetown Law Journal* 69 (1981):1223.

Wright, William R., II. "Open-Meeting Laws: An Analysis and Proposal." *Mississippi Law Review* 45 (1974):1151.

Protection of News Sources/Contempt Power

The lifeblood of journalism is information; reporters have it, and others often want it. Most of what a journalist discovers appears in the columns of a newspaper or on the 6 o'clock news. Today it is not uncommon for government officials and attorneys representing both plaintiffs and defendants to seek that small amount of information that the reporter chooses to keep confidential. Judges, grand juries, and even legislative committees all have the power to issue subpoenas to try to force reporters to reveal this confidential information. In the first part of this chapter we explore exactly how much protection the law provides to reporters who refuse to cooperate when they are presented with subpoenas and how the actions of the journalist ultimately affect what we all read in our newspapers and magazines and see and hear on television and radio.

Anyone who refuses to submit to a court order can be punished with a citation for contempt of court, a swift judicial ruling in which the target can find himself or herself in jail in a matter of hours. Application of the contempt power is how judges and sometimes even legislators force compliance with their rulings and orders. The last portion of this chapter focuses on this power; where it comes from, how it can be applied, and how it is limited.

The jailing of a reporter who refuses to cooperate with government authorities who want him or her to divulge confidential information is not a common occurrence in the United States today. But it does happen. In 1993 Stuart (Fla.) News reporter Tim Roche served 18 days in jail because he refused to reveal the name of the person who gave him a copy of a sealed court order in a child custody case. In December of 1995 Houston Chronicle reporter Jennifer Lenhart was jailed for refusing to reveal the names of grand jury members who told her about secret deliberations in a police shooting case. In October of 1996 a judge in Florida sentenced Miami Herald reporter David Kidwell to 70 days in jail because he refused to answer questions about an interview he had with Joseph Zile, a man who is accused of killing his stepdaughter. Prosecutors said they wanted to confirm that Zile, who faces the death penalty if convicted, actually told Kidwell that he was furious with his stepdaughter on the night she was killed. The reporter spent two weeks in jail before a federal judge freed him and directed the state appeals court to reconsider the case in light of numerous federal court rulings that recognize a First Amendment privilege for reporters. The appellate court, however, ruled that Florida did not recognize such a privilege and upheld the contempt citation. One year later the Florida Supreme Court ruled that the state did recognize a qualified reporter's privilege and ordered the lower court to reconsider Kidwell's situation in light of this privilege.[1] And in June of 1999 a federal judge ordered two Atlanta Journal-Constitution reporters, Ron Martz and Kathy Scruggs, to be jailed for refusing to reveal who told them that security guard Richard A. Jewell was a leading suspect in the bombing at the 1996 Olympic Games in Atlanta. Cases like these are unusual enough that they are widely publicized in trade journals and professional journalism publications. But every journalist must face the fact that he or she could be put in exactly the same position as Tim Roche, Jennifer Lenhart, David Kidwell, Ron Martz, or Kathy Scruggs, because government officials remain persistent in their requests to journalists for a wide variety of information. A study by the Reporters Committee for Freedom of the Press revealed that in 1993 more than 3,500 **subpoenas** seeking notes, photographs, tapes, or testimony were served on 469 news organizations.[2] And the total number of subpoenas served on journalists that year might actually be twice that number because more than half of the 2,100 organizations surveyed did not respond. Why are journalists subject to all these court orders?

Most journalists are highly efficient information gatherers. Some information that journalists gather is not included in the newspaper stories or television reports they prepare. Sometimes the source of a story doesn't want to be named and asks the reporter to promise not to reveal his or her identity. But reporters are not only efficient gatherers, they are excellent record keepers as well. Unreported material is often retained in notebooks and computer memories, or on videotape and audiotape. For some persons this undisclosed information is important, even vital.

Law enforcement officials frequently want to know what a criminal suspect told a journalist during an interview—only parts of which have been published or broadcast. Libel plaintiffs often need to know the identity of the sources used by reporters in preparation of a story in

1. *Kidwell v. Florida*, 696 So. 2d 399 (1997); rev'd 26 M.L.R. 2466 (1998).
2. *Agents of Discovery.*

order to try to prove the story was untrue or fabricated or published with malice. Video recordings of a violent demonstration are often useful to police who seek to identify those who incited the violence or committed criminal acts. Hence, reporters are often asked to reveal information they have gathered but chosen not to publish or broadcast. Most of the time journalists comply with such requests. At times, however, they refuse. When this happens, the persons interested in getting this information often get a court order or subpoena to force the journalist to reveal the name of the news source or to disclose the confidential information. Or government agents may get a warrant to search a newsroom or a reporter's home to find the information they want.

In our society the press is supposed to represent a neutral entity as it gathers and publishes news and information. When the government or anyone else intrudes into the newsroom or the reporter's notebook, it compromises this neutrality. A news source who normally trusts journalists may choose not to cooperate with a reporter if government agents can learn the source's name by threatening the reporter with a court order. Television news crews will hardly be welcome at protest rallies if the demonstrators know that the government will use the film to identify and prosecute the protesters. The effectiveness of the reporter as an information gatherer may be seriously compromised if government agents or civil and criminal litigants can force journalists to reveal information they choose not to disclose. Society also may ultimately suffer because the flow of information to the public may be reduced.

This chapter is about the problems a reporter can face when government agents or other persons use the power of the judicial system to gain access to the news-gathering processes. We study the problems of source confidentiality and newsroom searches. We also look at recent judicial and legislative attempts to resolve these issues. Finally, we examine the powerful weapon the government may employ to get its way in these disputes: the contempt power.

In our society the press is supposed to represent a neutral entity as it gathers and publishes news and information.

NEWS AND NEWS SOURCES

If news and information are the lifeblood of the press, then news sources are one of the important wells from which that lifeblood springs. Many journalists, especially those who consider themselves investigative journalists, are often no better than the sources they can cultivate. News sources come in all shapes and sizes. Occasionally their willingness to cooperate with a reporter is dependent on assurances from the journalist that their identity will not be revealed. Why would a news source wish to remain anonymous? There are many reasons. Often the source of a story about criminal activities has participated in criminal activities and has no desire to publicize this fact. Frequently the source of a story about government mismanagement or dishonesty is an employee of that government agency, and revelation of his or her identity could result in loss of the job for informing the press of the errors made by the employee's superiors. Some persons simply do not want to get involved in all the hassle that frequently results when an explosive story is published; by remaining anonymous they can remain out of the limelight.

Journalists have always used confidential sources and obtained information that government officials sought to uncover. The earliest reported case of a journalist's refusal to disclose his sources of information took place in 1848 when a reporter for the New York Herald refused to reveal to the U.S. Senate the name of the person who had given him a secret copy of the treaty the United States was negotiating to end the Mexican-American War. He was held in contempt of the Senate and jailed. A U.S. court of appeals denied the journalist's petition for release.[3] But the issue of journalists protecting the identity of a confidential source surfaced infrequently in the next 120 years. In fact, from 1911 to 1968 only 17 cases involving a reporter's confidential sources were reported, according to an article in the California Law Review.[4]

In the past 30 years, requests to journalists to reveal confidential information or to share notes or video outtakes (television videotape that was not broadcast) with government officials have become far more common. In the late 1960s and 1970s, the press played a significant role in the confrontation between African-Americans and whites, between war protesters and police, between the dominant culture and the nascent counterculture. Oftentimes reporters who had information sought by the government were put on the spot. In 1999 Dan Rather and CBS News producers were told they would have to provide the videotape of an interview the CBS anchorman had with one of the men on trial in Texas for murdering a black man by dragging him behind a pickup truck. Portions of the interview were telecast on "60 Minutes II." Texas authorities wanted to see the entire interview.* The confidential relationship between a journalist and a news source often sparks the interest of authorities who are seeking to discover who leaked confidential information to the press. Leaks, apparently from the office of independent counsel Kenneth Starr, facilitated much of the early reporting about the Clinton-Lewinsky

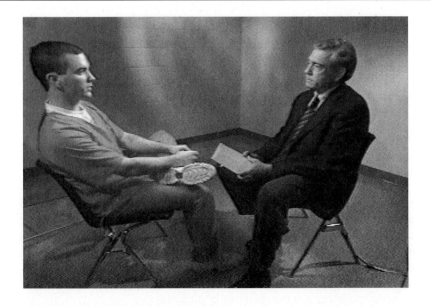

Law-enforcement officials frequently try to gain access to information generated by journalists, as Texas authorities did when CBS News reporter Dan Rather interviewed this murder suspect. Courtesy CBS News/60 Minutes II.

3. ex parte *Nugent,* 16 F. Cas. 471 (1848).
4. "The Newsman's Privilege," 1198.

*When Texas judicial authorities threatened to put a news producer in jail and the appellate courts rejected the television network's requests for help, CBS agreed to provide the material sought by the court.

affair. Stopping such "leaks" is given a high priority by others in government. Members of the U.S. Senate grilled reporters Nina Totenberg of National Public Radio and Timothy Phelps of Newsday in early 1992 to try to get them to reveal the names of confidential informants who leaked to them a statement made by law professor Anita Hill during the Senate confirmation hearings for Judge Clarence Thomas. Thomas was being considered for an appointment to the U.S. Supreme Court at the time, and Hill charged the jurist with sexual harassment. The pair of reporters were threatened with subpoenas and possible contempt charges for failing to cooperate. But leadership in the Senate finally abandoned the quest for the information, letting Totenberg and Phelps off the hook.

GROUNDS FOR SUCCESSFUL CHALLENGE OF SUBPOENA TO JOURNALIST

Shield law	18.4%
Information available elsewhere	27%
Lack of relevance	9.8%
Order too broad	9.8%
Constitutional privilege	8%
Information not needed	23.6%
Other	3.4%

Source: Reporters Committee for Freedom of the Press, 1995.

A 1995 study conducted by the Reporters Committee for Freedom of the Press looked at reporter source problems during 1993.[5] The data revealed that broadcasters received 70 percent of all subpoenas issued to the news media. Criminal litigation generated 44 percent of all subpoenas; civil cases spawned about one-quarter (see figure 10.1). The press complied with about 50 percent of the requests. The remaining subpoenas were either voluntarily withdrawn by the person seeking the information, or were challenged in court. About 350 court orders were challenged by the press in 1993, and the journalists succeeded in getting the subpoenas quashed, or set aside, in 80 percent of these cases. Finally, less than 40 percent of the subpoenas issued sought confidential information. Reporters and photographers are more commonly called on today to reveal what they saw as eyewitnesses or to share audiotaped or videotaped material that was gathered without any promise of confidentiality to anyone.

The journalist served with a subpoena has few options. The reporter or news organization can cooperate with those who seek the information and reveal what it is they want to know. This cooperation could damage the reporter/source relationship or threaten the image of independence fostered by most news media. The journalist can seek to have the subpoena withdrawn or attack the order in court and hope to have it quashed. Going to court can be

5. *Agents of Discovery,* 1995.

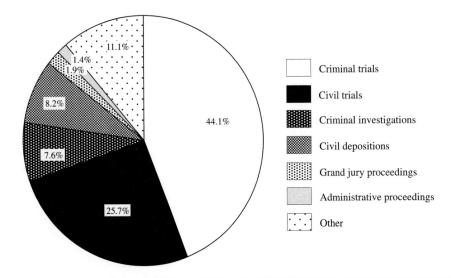

FIGURE 10.1

Kind of proceeding or process that generates subpoenas to reporters. Source: Reporters Committee on Freedom of the Press.

expensive and is time-consuming. The statistic cited earlier, that 80 percent of the subpoenas challenged by the press are quashed, is deceptive. The press usually only challenges a court order when it thinks it can win. Of the 3,519 subpoenas reported in 1993, only about 8 percent were actually quashed. Another 21 percent were ultimately withdrawn. If in the end the journalist refuses to cooperate, he or she will likely be held in contempt of court. A fine and a jail sentence usually follow. So the choice for the journalist is not an easy one.

But the choice for society is difficult as well. The interests that are involved in this dilemma are basic to our system of government and political values. On the one hand, it is clearly the obligation of every citizen to cooperate with the government and testify before the proper authorities. This concept was so well established by the early 18th century that it had become a maxim. John Henry Wigmore, in his classic treatise on evidence, cites the concept thus: "The public has a right to everyman's evidence."[6] The Sixth Amendment to the U.S. Constitution guarantees us the right to have witnesses and to compel them to testify in our behalf. And surely this right is a valuable one, both to society and to the individual seeking to prove his or her innocence of charges of wrongdoing. The Supreme Court has said on many occasions that it is a citizen's duty to testify. In 1919 the court wrote as follows on the duties and rights of witnesses:

> [I]t is clearly recognized that the giving of testimony and the attendance upon court or grand jury in order to testify are public duties which everyone within the jurisdiction of the government is bound to perform upon being properly summoned, . . . the personal sacrifice involved is a part of the necessary contribution to the public welfare.[7]

6. Wigmore, *Anglo-American System of Evidence.*
7. *Blair* v. *U.S., 250 U.S. 273 (1919).

On the other hand, society benefits from the free flow of information provided by the mass media. Many believe that when a reporter is forced to break a promise of confidentiality or is used as an arm of law enforcement investigators, it harms this free flow of information. People who know things, often important things, simply won't give this information to journalists for fear of being exposed if the reporter is squeezed for the information. The fragile reporter/source relationship may be damaged.

TIPS FOR REPORTERS ON
PROMISING CONFIDENTIALITY

Here are some suggestions that were given by newspaper attorney David Utevsky to reporters and writers at a seminar in Seattle.

- ∎ Do not routinely promise confidentiality as a standard interview technique.
- ∎ Avoid giving an absolute promise of confidentiality. Try to persuade the source to agree that you may reveal his or her name if you are subpoenaed.
- ∎ Do not rely exclusively on information from a confidential source. Get corroboration from a nonconfidential source or documents.
- ∎ Consider whether others (police, attorneys, etc.) will want to know the identity of the source before publishing or broadcasting the material. Will you be the only source of this information, or can they get it elsewhere?
- ∎ Consider whether you can use the information without disclosing that it was obtained from a confidential source.

The thrust of all these suggestions is for the reporter to try to avoid being served with a subpoena unless it is absolutely necessary.

A survey of reporters who had been nominated for the Pulitzer Prize revealed that these journalists used confidential or off-the-record information in the preparation of about one-third of their news stories.[8] Three-fourths of the respondents to this survey said their ability to report the news would be substantially affected if they were routinely forced to disclose confidential or background data they had gathered.

Society has responded to this real dilemma by giving journalists a qualified privilege that permits them in some circumstances to protect the names of confidential sources or to shield other information they have gathered and recorded. Such a privilege is not unique in our law. Doctors, lawyers, members of the clergy, even accountants in some instances, enjoy a privilege that requires them to protect the confidentiality of discussions they have with patients, clients, or parishioners.

The reporter's privilege is not a nice, neat, legal proposition. It more closely resembles a crazy quilt. The legal source of the privilege varies from jurisdiction to jurisdiction. In some places the U.S. or state constitution provides the privilege; in other places it is the common law.

---

8. Osborn, "The Reporter's Confidentiality Privilege," 57.

About half the states have a statutory privilege. While the source of the privilege varies, its scope often differs from place to place as well. In the following section, I draw a general outline of this reportorial privilege. Remember, however, journalists need to know the law in their particular state in order to protect their own interests, and the interests of their news medium.

Researchers in the 1970s who looked into the growing problems reporters were having with subpoenas discovered that too many journalists were promising to protect the identity of their news sources without thinking about whether it was truly necessary to do so to get the story.[9] This attitude caused a great many unnecessary problems for both the reporters and their news organizations. Today many newspapers, magazines, and broadcasting stations routinely instruct their reporters to promise confidentiality last, not first.

Today many newspapers, magazines, and broadcasting stations routinely instruct their reporters to promise confidentiality last, not first.

PROMISSORY ESTOPPEL

For years journalists have grounded their reluctance to reveal the name of a confidential source in an ethical or practical base. Reporters have argued that they are supposed to be neutral, uninvolved. To cooperate with the government or lawyers destroys this neutrality. Cooperation will also frighten away important sources. Today journalists can add a third basis for their refusal to reveal the name of a confidential source. They may be sued and be liable for civil damages if they break their promise of confidentiality.

This story begins in Minnesota about 20 years ago, in the last days of a political campaign. In 1982 Dan Cohen, who was closely associated with the Republican campaign for the governorship of Minnesota, approached reporters for both the Minneapolis Star and Tribune and the St. Paul Pioneer Press Dispatch and said he would give them previously unpublicized information about Marlene Johnson, the Democratic-Farmer-Labor candidate for lieutenant governor. All the reporters had to do was to promise never to reveal Cohen's name when asked where they got the information. The reporters agreed and Cohen supplied them with 12- and 13-year-old court records showing that Johnson had been arrested for unlawful assembly (she was at a protest rally) and that she had been convicted of petty theft for leaving a store without paying for $6 worth of sewing goods (the conviction was later vacated).

Editors at both newspapers decided to publish the information about the candidate, but because the election was just days away, they felt it was necessary to include Cohen's name as the source of the information to give readers the opportunity to evaluate the charges against Johnson. When Cohen's name was published, he lost his job. He angrily sued for breach of contract, claiming he and the reporters had entered into a contractual agreement when he provided the information for a promise of confidentiality. A Minnesota trial court agreed and awarded the public relations man $200,000 in compensatory damages and $500,000 in punitive damages. The Minnesota Court of Appeals affirmed the conviction but threw out the punitive damages, saying Cohen had failed to prove fraud in this case, the only claim that would permit a punitive damage award.[10] The Minnesota Supreme Court reversed the conviction.

---

9. Chamberlain, "Protection of Confidential News Sources," 18.
10. *Cohen v. Cowles Media Co.,* 445 N.W. 2d 248 (1989).

The state high court said the agreement between Cohen and the reporters was not an enforceable contract. The plaintiffs had raised an alternative theory of law at the oral argument, the doctrine of promissory estoppel. The high court said it was unnecessary to consider whether the agreement between Cohen and the reporters was governed by this doctrine, because enforcement of the doctrine would violate the First Amendment.[11]

Cohen appealed to the Supreme Court of the United States, which in June of 1991 reversed the Minnesota Supreme Court ruling and told the state court to reconsider whether the doctrine of promissory estoppel did in fact apply in this case. Enforcement of this doctrine, wrote Justice Byron White, would not violate the First Amendment. "Generally applicable laws [that is, laws that can be applied to all citizens equally] do not offend the First Amendment simply because their enforcement against the press has incidental effects on its ability to gather and report the news." Here, White added, "Minnesota law simply requires those making promises to keep them."[12]

Promissory estoppel is an old Anglo-American legal rule that was promulgated to prevent injustice when someone fails to keep a promise that he or she has made, a promise that by itself does not add up to an enforceable contract, but a promise someone else has relied on. It is typically codified in the common law in words like these: "A promise that the promisor reasonably expects to induce reliance and that does induce reliance is binding if injustice can be avoided only by enforcement of the promise." To prevail in an action for promissory estoppel the plaintiff is usually required to show

1. that the defendant made a clear and definite promise;
2. that the defendant intended to induce the plaintiff's reliance on the promise, and that plaintiff did rely on the promise to his or her detriment; and
3. that the promise made by the defendant must be enforced by the court to avoid an injustice to the plaintiff.

Assume that your uncle walks in while you are working in a fast-food restaurant and tells you that he will pay your college tuition and room and board for the coming year if you quit your job. He promises to give you $10,000 on demand. The day that you quit your job and rent a new apartment, your uncle dies. You visit your aunt and ask her for the money but she refuses to pay. You are in deep trouble without the money you have been promised. A suit under the doctrine of promissory estoppel would be appropriate and probably successful.

The four Supreme Court dissenters in the Minnesota case mentioned earlier argued that ruling against the newspapers amounted to punishing them for publishing legally obtained, truthful information. But Justice White and his supporters, Chief Justice Rehnquist and Justices Scalia, Kennedy, and Stevens, disagreed. There is no punishment here at all, Justice White said, noting that the punitive damage judgment had been reversed. "The payment of compensatory damages in this case is constitutionally indistinguishable from a generous

11. *Cohen v. Cowles Media Co.*, 457 N.W. 2d 199 (1990).
12. *Cohen v. Cowles Media Co.*, 111 S. Ct. 2513 (1991).

bonus paid to a confidential news source," he noted.[13] In January of 1992 the Minnesota Supreme Court awarded Cohen $200,000 in damages in his suit against the newspapers.[14]

The ink was barely dry on the Supreme Court's ruling in the *Cohen* case when the 8th U.S. Circuit Court of Appeals raised the specter of promissory estoppel again. The defendant in this case was the publisher of Glamour magazine, which had printed an article on therapist-patient sexual abuse. Among those interviewed was plaintiff Jill Ruzicka. Ms. Ruzicka had sued her former therapist and the state agency whose job it was to regulate such practitioners. She claimed the therapist had engaged in improper sexual conduct with her. The case was covered by the press before it was settled out of court. Ruzicka continued to be active in state commissions and public hearings regarding therapist sexual abuse, and her activities were reported in the Minnesota press. Glamour reporter Claudia Dreifus sought to interview Ruzicka about her case, but the Minneapolis attorney agreed to talk with the reporter only if she was not identified in the story. Dreifus consented to this condition. The reporter interviewed Ruzicka, wrote the story, and then read her draft of the story to Ruzicka, who approved the article. The story was set in a midwestern city and the plaintiff was not identified. But Glamour editors insisted on a substantial rewrite of the article, and the final version of the story contains material that Ruzicka says identifies her. She is called Jill Lundquist and described as a Minneapolis attorney. The story refers to her lawsuit against the offending therapist and State Board of Medical Examiners and indicates that she was a member of the state task force that helped write the law criminalizing sexual exploitation by a therapist. The key to identification, Ruzicka said, is that the list of participants on the state task force is public and she is the only woman in the group. The court of appeals threw out a breach-of-contract action instituted by the plaintiff, but remanded the case to the U.S. District Court to consider her claim brought under promissory estoppel.[15]

In 1992 the U.S. District Court dismissed the promissory estoppel action against Glamour on the grounds that the promise not to identify Ruzicka in the story was not sufficiently clear and definite to support a recovery under promissory estoppel. In the *Cohen* case, the court said, the defendants had made a clear and unambiguous promise to shield the identity of the source, and then made a conscious and calculated decision to violate that promise. In this case the defendants did in fact make an attempt to mask the plaintiff's identity, but in the plaintiff's opinion, failed to accomplish this goal. "Far from preventing an injustice," the court ruled, "enforcing such an ambiguous promise could create injustice by placing on editors and reporters the impossible burden of guessing at what steps such a promise requires."[16]

Again, however, the 8th U.S. Circuit Court of Appeals reversed and ordered the lower court to hold a trial in the case.[17] The appellate court said that the promise to shield Ruzicka's identity was definite enough under state law to support an action for promissory estoppel. The court said that because the magazine editors had added other identifying details to the article about the plaintiff after she had approved the original draft, a jury could find that the magazine had failed to keep its promise.

13. *Cohen* v. *Cowles Media Co.*, 111 S. Ct. 2513 (1991).
14. *Cohen* v. *Cowles Media Co.*, 479 N.W. 2d 387 (1992).
15. *Ruzicka* v. *Conde Nast Publications, Inc.*, 939 F. 2d 578 (1991).
16. *Ruzicka* v. *Conde Nast Publications, Inc.*, 794 F. Supp. 303 (1992).
17. *Ruzicka* v. *Conde Nast Publications, Inc.*, 999 F. 2d 1319 (1993).

Fears that the *Cohen* and *Ruzicka* cases would spark a firestorm of promissory estoppel lawsuits against the press appear to have been unwarranted. Only a couple of other lawsuits have been reported.[18] Most editors and broadcast news directors say the decisions simply reinforce existing policies at most news organizations that reporters must consult with their superiors before promising confidentiality to a source. A few journalists noted that these rulings might in some instances make it easier for a journalist who is willing to promise confidentiality to get a source to talk, since the source now has a means of recourse should the journalist fail to live up to the promise.

The best way for a reporter to beat a subpoena is not to get one in the first place. But that is not always possible. The next section of this chapter focuses on how a journalist can keep a promise of confidentiality and still stay out of jail when faced with a court order. The starting point for this discussion is the First Amendment.

TIPS FOR REPORTERS WHEN CONFRONTED WITH A SOURCE WHO DEMANDS CONFIDENTIALITY

1. Assume the interview is on the record unless the subject seeks anonymity.
2. There is no obligation to grant anonymity for information that has already been provided.
3. Before making any promise to a source, try to find something out about the information and where it comes from.
4. Try to talk with an editor or news director before making any promises to a source.
5. Keep any promise made to a source simple and easy to fulfill, and be certain both you and the source completely understand the conditions to which you have agreed.
6. Record any promise you make to a source.
7. Avoid adding material to a story that a source has already approved, or try to avoid promising the source that he or she has story approval.

CONSTITUTIONAL PROTECTION OF NEWS SOURCES

In 1972 the Supreme Court of the United States ruled, in a 5–4 decision, that there was no privilege under the First Amendment for journalists to refuse to reveal the names of confidential sources or other information when called to testify before a grand jury.[19] This ruling is the

---

18. See *Anderson* v. *Strong Memorial Hospital*, 573 N.Y.S. 2d 828 (1991) and *Morgan* v. *Calender*, 780 F. Supp. 307 (1992).
19. *Branzburg* v. *Hayes*, 408 U.S. 665 (1972).

last word the nation's high court has spoken on the subject. Yet today, a limited constitutional protection has been applied by U.S. appeals courts and U.S. district courts in many parts of the nation. The story of how judges in many of the lower and intermediate federal courts rewrote the *Branzburg* ruling is an example of the pragmatic genius of American law.

The Supreme Court consolidated three similar cases when it first faced the question of whether journalists could find a privilege in the First Amendment to permit them to refuse to testify when called before a grand jury. One case involved Paul Branzburg, a reporter for the Louisville Courier-Journal. Branzburg was called to testify in 1971 about drug use in Kentucky after he wrote two stories about drugs and drug dealers in the area. In the second case, Paul Pappas, a television reporter for a Massachusetts television station, was called before a grand jury to relate what he had seen and heard when he spent three hours at a Black Panther headquarters in July of 1970. Finally, The New York Times reporter Earl Caldwell was subpoenaed to appear before a grand jury investigating the activities of the Black Panthers in Oakland, Calif. Caldwell, an African-American, had gained the confidence of the leaders of the militant group and had consistently written illuminating stories about the Panthers that demonstrated an astute awareness of their activities. The decisions in the three cases are referred to collectively as the *Branzburg* ruling.

In two instances—*Branzburg* and *Pappas*—lower courts had rejected arguments that the First Amendment provided a privilege for the reporters, a privilege that would permit them to refuse to testify. In *Caldwell,* however, the U.S. Court of Appeals for the 9th Circuit ruled that forcing the journalist to even appear before a grand jury could damage the public's First Amendment right to be informed. The court therefore found that journalists enjoyed a qualified privilege that protected them when called to testify about confidential information. The government must show a compelling need for the witness's presence in order to overcome this privilege, the court ruled.

The Supreme Court fractured into three groups in deciding this case. Four justices, led by Byron White, who wrote the court's opinion, ruled that there was no First Amendment privilege for reporters called to testify before a grand jury. White said that although the court was sensitive to First Amendment considerations, the case did not present any such considerations. There were no prior restraints, no limitations on what the press might publish, and no order for the press to publish information it did not wish to. No penalty for publishing certain content was imposed. White wrote:

> The use of confidential sources by the press is not forbidden or restricted. . . .
>
> The sole issue before us is the obligation of reporters to respond to grand jury subpoenas as other citizens do and answer questions relevant to an investigation into the commission of crime. Citizens generally are not constitutionally immune from grand jury subpoenas; and neither the First Amendment nor other constitutional provisions protect the average citizen from the disclosing to a grand jury information that he has received in confidence.[20]

Reporters are no better than average citizens, White concluded.

20. *Branzburg v. Hayes,* 408 U.S. 665 (1972).

The four dissenters differed sharply with the other justices. Justice William O. Douglas took the view that the First Amendment protection provides the press with an absolute and unqualified privilege. In any circumstance, under any condition, the reporter should be able to shield the identity of a confidential source. Justices Potter Stewart, William Brennan, and Thurgood Marshall were unwilling to go as far as Justice Douglas and instead proposed that reporters should be protected by a privilege that is qualified, not absolute. These three dissenters argued that the reporter should be able to protect the identity of the confidential source unless the government can show the following:

1. That there is a probable cause to believe that the reporter has information that is clearly relevant to a specific violation of the law

2. That the information sought cannot be obtained by alternative means less destructive of First Amendment rights

3. That the state has a compelling and overriding interest in the information

When the government cannot fulfill all three requirements, Justice Stewart wrote for the dissenters, the journalist should not be forced to testify.

Justice Lewis Powell provided the fifth vote needed for the court to reject the notion of a constitutional privilege for reporters. But while Powell voted with those who could find no privilege in the First Amendment, his brief concurring opinion seemed to support the opposite proposition. "The Court does not hold that newsmen, subpoenaed to testify before a grand jury, are without constitutional rights with respect to the gathering of news or in safeguarding their sources," he wrote. No harassment of reporters will be allowed, and a balance must be struck between freedom of the press and the obligation of all citizens to give relevant testimony. "In short, the courts will be available to newsmen under circumstances where legitimate First Amendment interests require protection," Powell wrote. Two years later, in a footnote in another case, *Saxbe* v. *Washington Post,*[21] Powell emphasized that the high court's ruling in *Branzburg* was an extremely narrow one and that reporters were not without First Amendment rights to protect the identity of their sources.

LOWER-COURT RULINGS

Most lower federal courts have treated the high court's decision in *Branzburg* as the very narrow ruling that Justice Powell said it was in 1974. The *Branzburg* ruling focused on a reporter's responsibility to testify before a grand jury. And that is generally how the lower courts have applied the precedent, granting reporters a qualified right to refuse testimony in other kinds of circumstances. Note the language from the 3rd U.S. Circuit Court of Appeals in a 1979 ruling, which characterized *Branzburg* in this fashion:

> There (in Branzburg), the Supreme Court decided that a journalist does not have an absolute privilege under the First Amendment to refuse to appear and testify before a grand jury to answer questions relevant to an investigation of the commission of

Most lower federal courts have treated the high court's decision in Branzburg *as the very narrow ruling that Justice Powell said it was in 1974.*

---

21. 417 U.S. 843 (1974).

a crime. No Supreme Court case since that decision has extended the holding beyond that which was necessary to vindicate the public interest in law enforcement and ensuing effective grand jury proceedings.[22]

But not all the U.S. Courts of Appeals have looked at *Branzburg* in such an expansive manner. In 1998 a panel of judges in the 5th Circuit wrote:

> Although some courts have taken from Justice Powell's concurrence a mandate to construct a broad, qualified news reporters' privilege in criminal cases, we decline to do so. Justice Powell's separate writing only emphasizes that at a certain point, the First Amendment must protect the press from government intrusion.[23]

The court went on to require a television station to surrender the unaired portions of a video-tape interview with a man accused of arson.

Ten of 12 of the U.S. appeals courts have ruled that the First Amendment provides at least limited protection for reporters who are asked to testify or produce photos or other materials at hearings other than grand jury proceedings.* The 6th U.S. Circuit Court of Appeals (Kentucky, Michigan, Ohio, and Tennessee) rejected this notion in 1987. "Because we conclude that acceptance of the position . . . would be tantamount to our substituting, as a holding in *Branzburg,* the dissent written by Justice Stewart, we must reject that position. . . . That portion of Justice Powell's opinion certainly does not warrant rewriting the majority opinion to grant a First Amendment testimonial privilege to news reporters," the court ruled.[24] And the 7th U.S. Circuit Court of Appeals (Illinois, Indiana, and Wisconsin) has not directly faced the issue. Thirty-one of the United States have enacted a statutory protection called a shield law that offers reporters some protection against being forced to reveal the identities of confidential sources. (See page 388 for a list of those states.) Appellate courts in most of the remaining 19 states have recognized various kinds of constitutional or common-law testimonial privileges for reporters.

The constitutional privilege has considerable elasticity. Its successful application depends on several factors. What kind of proceeding is involved? The privilege is more readily granted to a journalist involved in a civil suit than to one called to testify before a grand jury. What kind of material is sought? A journalist is more likely to be protected by the privilege when the name of a confidential source is sought than when courts are seeking testimony about information that is not confidential or about events actually witnessed by the reporter. Finally, testimonial privilege derived by both federal and state courts through the constitution or the common law is qualified by the various tests that courts have developed, tests that usually mirror the one outlined by Justice Stewart in *Branzburg.* Is the information important? Is

---

22. *Riley* v. *Chester,* 612 F. 2d 708 (1979).
23. *U.S.* v. *Smith,* 135 F. 2d 363 (1998); see also *WTHR-TV* v. *Cline,* 693 N.E. 2d 1 (1998).
24. *Storer Communications* v. *Giovan,* 810 F. 2d 580 (1987).

*The 5th U.S. Circuit Court of Appeals is included among the ten because, despite the 1998 ruling in *U.S.* v. *Smith,* judges in the circuit have ruled that a privilege exists at least for civil suits. (See, for example, *Miller* v. *Transamerican Press, Inc.,* 621 F. 2nd 721 [1980]). The 1998 decision did not reject these earlier rulings, but argued that because a criminal case was at issue, a different standard should apply.

it clearly relevant to the proceedings? Is there somewhere else to get the information? In the next few pages, I sketch the rough outline of this reporter's privilege. It is important to remember, however, that without a binding Supreme Court ruling, the lower federal and state courts have been permitted to fashion their own rules; and there is distinct variance from state to state, federal circuit to federal circuit. Look to the court precedents in your region as the final authority in this matter.

Civil Cases

A reporter could be called to testify in three different kinds of court proceedings: a civil lawsuit, a criminal case, or a grand jury. Courts are most likely to recognize the right of a journalist to refuse to testify in a civil action, and least likely to recognize this right if the reporter is called before a grand jury. Recognition of the privilege in civil cases came only a year after the *Branzburg* ruling, when a U.S. district court in Washington, D.C., quashed a subpoena issued to reporters from a variety of newspaper and magazines who were thought to have materials obtained during their coverage of the Watergate break-in. The materials were sought by members of the Democratic National Committee who were suing to win damages from some of the Watergate burglars.[25] The court said that reporters had at least a qualified privilege under the First Amendment to refuse to answer such questions or provide such material. Four years later the 10th U.S. Circuit Court of Appeals ruled that filmmaker Arthur Hirsch could not be forced to reveal confidential information he had obtained in connection with a civil suit by the estate of Karen Silkwood against the Kerr-McGee Corporation.[26] Silkwood died mysteriously in an auto accident after she threatened to expose improper safety conditions at the nuclear facility at which she worked. Hirsch was preparing a documentary film on Karen Silkwood's life and death.

In a typical civil suit, the court will ask three questions when deciding whether to force the reporter to testify:

1. Has the person seeking the information from the reporter—normally the plaintiff—shown that this information is of *certain relevance* in the case? It must be related to the matter before the court.

2. Does this information go to the heart of the issue before the court? That is, is it critical to the outcome of the case?

3. Can the person who wants the information show the court that there is no other source for this information?

If all three questions are answered yes, the chances are good that the court will require the reporter to reveal the confidential information. But it is not easy for the plaintiff or the defendant to meet the requirements of this test. How rigorously the judge applies this test often depends on the reporter's relationship to the lawsuit. If the reporter is not a party to the lawsuit but merely has information that may be of value to one or both parties, a judge typically applies

---

25. *Democratic National Committee* v. *McCord,* 356 F. Supp. 1394 (1973).
26. *Silkwood* v. *Kerr-McGee,* 563 F. 2d 433 (1977).

the test very rigorously and normally the journalist will not be required to testify. But that is not always the case. In 1996 a federal judge in Connecticut ruled that a reporter had to testify in a securities case as to whether one of the defendants had actually made the statements that were attributed to him in a newspaper article written by the reporter.[27] The judge ruled that the testimony sought was directly relevant to the case and was unavailable from another source. The court also noted that it was not seeking information about a confidential source. If the reporter is a party in the lawsuit, either as a plaintiff or a defendant, courts are less willing to let the journalist off the hook. In these instances it is more likely, but still not common, for the court to require the reporter to cooperate.

There is but a single recorded case in which a reporter who was a plaintiff in the case was asked to testify and refused. Columnist Jack Anderson sued former President Richard Nixon and other former administration officials in 1978 for trying to deprive him of his civil rights. His lawsuit was founded on reports he said he received from confidential informants, but when asked by the defendants to reveal the names of these informants, Anderson refused. The court ruled that the columnist could not have things both ways. "He cannot ask for justice and deny it to those he accuses."[28] Anderson was forced to withdraw his lawsuit when he refused to testify.

Reporters far more commonly find themselves as defendants in lawsuits, typically a libel suit. Oftentimes the plaintiff seeks to know about sources the reporter used to prepare the libelous story, or where and how the reporter got information for the libelous story. Whether the court will force the reporter to testify in such instances usually depends on several factors, all of which are related to the three-part test outlined earlier. A plaintiff will often be required to show that the information held by the reporter goes to the very heart of the lawsuit. For example, the plaintiff may have to show that he or she cannot possibly prove negligence or actual malice (see pages 185–198 to refresh your memory on these matters) without information from the reporter.[29] Or, the court will require that the plaintiff show that the libel claim actually has merit, that it is not simply an attempt to harass the defendant.[30] Finally, the court will usually require the plaintiff to show that there is no other source for this information, that the plaintiff has exhausted all other potential means of gaining this information. In 1979 the U.S. Supreme Court ruled that it was not an infringement of the reporters' First Amendment rights for the defendant to ask reporters what they were thinking about as they prepared the libelous story.[31] Such questions may or may not involve confidential sources.

The reporter who refuses to obey a court order and give the plaintiff critical information in a libel suit surely faces a **contempt of court** charge and potentially a fine and a jail sentence. But that is not all. In a few cases when a reporter has refused to reveal his or her source for a libelous story, the court has ruled as a matter of law that no source for the story exists.[32]

---

27. *SEC* v. *Seahawk Deep Ocean Technology, Inc.,* 166 F.R.D. 268 (1996).
28. *Anderson* v. *Nixon et al.,* 444 F. Supp. 1195 (1978).
29. *Cervantes* v. *Time,* 446 F. 2d 986 (1972).
30. *Senear* v. *Daily Journal-American,* 641 P. 2d 1180 (1982).
31. *Herbert* v. *Lando,* 441 U.S. 153 (1979).
32. See *Downing* v. *Monitor Publishing,* 415 A. 2d 683 (1980) and *Sierra Life* v. *Magic Valley Newspapers,* 623 P. 2d 103 (1980).

This declaration effectively strips away the libel defense for a newspaper or broadcasting station. In effect, the judge is saying that the reporter made up the story. This is not a common occurrence, but certainly a frightening one.

Finally, the 9th U.S. Circuit Court of Appeals handed down an important ruling in mid-1993 when it extended the reporter's privilege in a civil suit to the authors of books as well. Typically the privilege has been granted to so-called working journalists, salaried employees of newspapers, magazines, and broadcasting stations. Free-lance writers like book authors were often denied the protection. The case involved a defamation action between Leonard Shoen, the founder of the U-Haul Corporation, and his sons, Mark and Edward. The libel case was an offshoot of a long-running and highly acrimonious fight among these family members over control of the company. Ronald Watkins, an author of books on topical and controversial subjects, was working on a manuscript about the family feud. He was subpoenaed to testify regarding his interviews with Leonard Shoen, but he refused, citing the First Amendment privilege among other reasons. The lower court rejected his argument and, when Watkins still refused to testify, held the author in contempt of court.

The Court of Appeals reversed the lower-court order. The court ruled that a book author clearly had a right to invoke the First Amendment privilege.[33] "The journalist's privilege is designed to protect investigative reporting regardless of the medium used to report the news to the public," Judge Norris wrote. And there was no question that when Watkins was gathering information as he interviewed Leonard Shoen, he intended to disseminate it to the public. The plaintiff raised the issue that Watkins had not given a promise of confidentiality when he interviewed the elder Shoen. Judge Norris said that fact was not controlling. The privilege could apply even in the absence of a promise of confidentiality. It is simply one factor to be considered when all the interests are balanced. In this case the plaintiffs failed to show that they exhausted other potential sources for the same information. Why didn't they talk directly with Leonard Shoen, the court asked. This factor alone meant that the plaintiffs had failed to demonstrate sufficient cause to overcome the First Amendment protection afforded Watkins, Judge Norris said.

Criminal Cases

Courts have granted the First Amendment privilege to reporters quite freely in civil actions in part, at least, because there is no competing constitutional right involved. In a criminal case, however, the privilege for the reporter must be balanced against the Sixth Amendment right of the defendant to compel testimony on his or her behalf. Consequently, it is somewhat less likely that a court will permit a reporter to refuse to answer questions about the identity of a confidential source or other confidential information. Courts most often apply slight variations of the Stewart test from the *Branzburg* case (see page 375) to determine whether the journalist will be compelled to testify.

In *U.S.* v. *Burke,* for example, the defendant was indicted for conspiracy in connection with a basketball point-shaving scheme at Boston College and attempted to impeach the

In a criminal case, the privilege for the reporter must be balanced against the Sixth Amendment right of the defendant to compel testimony on his or her behalf.

33. *Shoen* v. *Shoen,* 5 F. 3d 1289 (1993).

testimony of the prosecution's chief witness, a reputed underworld figure. The defendant asked the court to subpoena the unpublished notes and drafts of Sports Illustrated reporter Douglas Looney, who had interviewed the witness. The U.S. Court of Appeals for the 2nd Circuit quashed the subpoena, noting that a court may order reporters to reveal confidential sources only when the information is (1) highly material and relevant, (2) necessary or critical to the defense, and (3) unobtainable from other sources.[34]

This same test was recently applied in a New York case relating to the trial of mob boss John Gotti. Bruce Cutler had served as Gotti's attorney until he was disqualified by the court. Prior to Cutler's disqualification, the court had warned all lawyers in the case to refrain from making out-of-court statements about the highly publicized trial. During the course of the trial, and after his disqualification, Cutler made comments about the case that were published in newspapers and broadcast on television. Cutler was charged with criminal contempt of court for violating the court order. Before his jury trial Cutler subpoenaed several reporters, seeking their notes, video outtakes, and other materials. The journalists sought to quash the subpoena, but the 2nd U.S. Circuit Court of Appeals said that Cutler could have limited access to some of these materials because it constituted the only significant evidence he had to defend the charge of contempt that had been levied against him. In other words, the material he sought was relevant, unobtainable from other sources, and critical to his defense.[35]

In 1984 the Washington state Supreme Court ruled that an Everett (Wash.) Herald reporter did not have to reveal the names of several confidential sources he had used to prepare an article about alleged cult activities at an 80-acre farm near rural Snohomish, Wash. The owner of the farm, Theodore Rinaldo, had been convicted of statutory rape, assault, coercion, and intimidating a witness. A year after his conviction, several persons who had testified on Rinaldo's behalf at his trial stepped forward and admitted they had committed perjury. It was during his second trial for tampering with witnesses and other offenses that Rinaldo tried to force reporter Gary Larson to reveal the names of persons who gave the reporter information for six articles that had brought the activities at the farm to the attention of local authorities. Justice James Dolliver, speaking for the court, ruled that Rinaldo would have to show that the information was necessary or critical to his defense and that he had made a reasonable effort to get the material by other means. He could not make such a showing, and the subpoena was quashed.[36]

In 1980 the U.S. Court of Appeals for the 3rd Circuit ruled that Jan Schaffer, a reporter for the Philadelphia Inquirer, had to testify about a conversation she had had with a prosecuting attorney before a criminal trial. The defendants in a government prosecution moved for a dismissal of the charges on the grounds that massive pretrial publicity about the case would prevent their getting a fair trial. The defendants charged that the publicity was the result of misconduct by the prosecutor, who they said had improperly given reporters details of the sting operation. The prosecutor admitted talking with reporters about the case, but the defendants sought the reporter's testimony to confirm the prosecutor's statements. The court, applying the three-part

34. *U.S.* v. *Burke,* 700 F. 2d 70 (1983).
35. *U.S.* v. *Cutler,* 6 F. 3d 67 (1993).
36. *State* v. *Rinaldo,* 684 P. 2d 608 (1984).

test, ruled that Schaffer would have to testify. The reporter obviously had the information—the prosecutor admitted talking with her about the case. There was a compelling need for the information—it was central to the defendant's charges of misconduct by the prosecutor. And the defense had attempted to get the information elsewhere—from the prosecutor himself. The reporter was the only source left.[37]

Grand Jury Proceedings

While the qualified privilege for reporters to refuse to reveal the identities of confidential sources in civil and criminal actions has been recognized by most lower federal courts and state supreme courts that have considered the question, these same courts have routinely refused to extend the First Amendment privilege to grand jury proceedings. This refusal is true even though the grand jury's power to force disclosure is not constitutionally guaranteed, as is the criminal defendant's right to compel a witness to testify. The obvious explanation for this reluctance on the part of judges is that the single U.S. Supreme Court precedent on the question focused on grand jury testimony and in that case, *Branzburg* v. *Hayes*,[38] the high court ruled that no privilege existed.

Lower courts consistently reinforce this ruling. For example, in 1993 the 9th U.S. Circuit Court of Appeals rejected the notion that scholars enjoy a privilege under the First Amendment to resist a subpoena to appear before a grand jury. James R. Scarce was a Ph.D. student at Washington State University who was doing research on militant factions in the environmental movement and animal rights groups. About the time of an attack on animal research facilities at the university, Scarce communicated with Rodney Coronado, an individual who government investigators believed was involved in the vandalism. Scarce was subpoenaed to appear before a grand jury and answer questions about the vandalism and his conversations with Coronado. He appeared but refused to answer some questions, claiming that a scholar's privilege under the First Amendment supported his refusal. He argued that because scholars gather and disseminate information like journalists, they too should not be forced to reveal confidential information. The Court of Appeals rejected this argument, noting that not even journalists enjoy a First Amendment privilege to refuse to answer legitimate questions from a grand jury.[39]

This case is typical. There are, however, a few decisions that have recognized the journalist's privilege even in the face of a grand jury subpoena. In 1992 the 3rd U.S. Circuit Court of Appeals upheld a U.S. district court ruling that journalists as well as news-gathering agencies have a qualified privilege against disclosure, in grand jury proceedings, of the identity of news sources. Immediately prior to the end of a sensational criminal trial in Pittsburgh in 1990, the government learned that copies of Federal Bureau of Investigation reports produced for use by the defense counsel had been distributed to some members of the press. Distribution of such material had been earlier barred by the judge. The court issued an order demanding that the reporters produce any reports they may have been given. In addition, a grand jury

37. *U.S. v. Criden,* 633 F. 2d 346 (1980).
38. 408 U.S. 665 (1972).
39. *Scarce* v. *U.S.,* 5 F. 3d 397 (1993).

subpoena was issued ordering the reporters to produce the same documents. The U.S. District Court that heard the reporter's challenge to the subpoenas ruled that the government could only overcome that privilege enjoyed by the reporters if it could show they were the only source of this information and that this information was crucial to the government's claim. The appellate court sat en banc when it heard the appeal and split evenly in its decision. The tie vote sustained the trial court ruling.[40]

In July of 1991, the Massachusetts Supreme Judicial Court quashed a subpoena issued to WCVB-TV reporter David Ropeik. A grand jury was looking into the bizarre case of the deaths of Carol and Charles Stuart in the winter of 1989–90. The case received national publicity. Charles Stuart claimed that he and his wife had been attacked in the Mission Hill district of Boston by a gunman. Carol was killed, and her child, who was delivered by Cesarean section in an emergency room, died a few days later. Charles sustained a gunshot wound but survived. Days later he identified a suspect in a police lineup. But then the case started to unravel. Two months later Charles Stuart's brother Matthew told police that Charles had killed his wife. The next day Charles killed himself. A grand jury investigation began into the role played by Charles's brother and a third man in Carol's murder.

David Ropeik, in a television report, revealed that "according to a source close to the Stuart family," Matthew had brought the murder gun to Charles on the night of the killing. Ropeik was subpoenaed to appear before a grand jury and ordered to identify the family source. He appealed the court order. In mid-1991 the Massachusetts high court quashed the subpoena. The court said that common-law principles may justify the denial of enforcement of a grand jury summons issued for a news reporter if the public interest in the free flow of information outweighs the public interest in having everyone's evidence available. The grand jury had already talked with 80 people, family members and friends of the family, the court noted. It is fair to assume one of those persons is the unnamed source, but none admitted talking with any reporters. Assume Ropeik identified one of the 80 as his source, the court said. Since all had testified under oath that they did not have any information about the case, it is unlikely they would later change their story. Also, neither the reporter nor the source are eyewitnesses; their testimony in a trial would be of minimal value. Consequently, there is a very low likelihood of benefit to the commonwealth if Ropeik is forced to testify, the court ruled.[41]

But again, these rulings are really atypical; more often than not, reporters have found themselves forced to testify when subpoenaed to appear before a grand jury. If there is any good news in this state of affairs, it is that fewer and fewer such subpoenas are being issued today.

NONCONFIDENTIAL INFORMATION AND WAIVER OF THE PRIVILEGE

While U.S. courts have been willing to permit journalists to protect confidential sources and confidential information, most of the same courts have been far more reluctant to protect reporters when nonconfidential information is at issue. And most subpoenas issued today to journalists are to gain access to nonconfidential information.

40. in re *Grand Jury Subpoena,* 963 F. 2d 567 (1992).
41. in re *John Doe Grand Jury Investigation,* 410 Mass. 596 (1991).

In 1999 the 2nd U.S. Circuit Court of Appeals, vacating an earlier decision it had announced, ruled that the federal law does recognize a qualified privilege for journalists with regard to nonconfidential information. In order to get the unedited videotape possessed by NBC, the plaintiff, who filed a civil rights action against a Louisiana police officer, would have to show that the information contained on the tape was highly material and relevant, necessary, or critical to the maintenance of his civil rights claim and was not obtainable from other sources.[42] This is an unusual ruling, as most other courts have rejected this notion. More typical is a ruling by the 5th U.S. Circuit Court of Appeals a year earlier that said that reporters do not enjoy any privilege, qualified or otherwise, not to disclose nonconfidential information in a criminal case.[43] In this instance the Bureau of Alcohol, Tobacco, and Firearms sought a TV station's videotaped interview with a suspect in an arson fire. This ruling seems to be more in line with previous court rulings on this matter. A U.S. district court ruled in 1990 that a journalist who was said to have witnessed a beating of a criminal suspect by police had to testify on behalf of the injured party. "This court knows of no authority to support the proposition that such personal observations are privileged simply because the eyewitness is a journalist," the judge ruled.[44]

Photographers have been forced to surrender photos they have taken of building fires,[45] industrial accidents,[46] fatal auto accidents,[47] or even of an individual who has filed a personal injury lawsuit against an insurance company.[48] The press has generally been unable to convince judges that it has an important interest at stake when it refuses to cooperate with those who seek nonconfidential information. The arguments that have been made so well about the importance of protecting confidential sources aren't nearly as persuasive when nonconfidential material is at stake.

Reporters must worry about another aspect of the privilege, the problem that through some action they may actually waive their right to refuse to testify. A case in Washington, D.C., focuses on this dilemma. Six police officers brought a $9 million lawsuit against the city and top police officials. They were disciplined by the police department after a botched 1986 drug operation that failed to net the hundreds of arrests expected. In the wake of the failed raid, Washington Post reporter Linda Wheeler revealed in a newspaper story that the Post had obtained secret plans for the raid. The six officers who were disciplined argued that leaks from high-level police officials, not from them, caused the raid to fail. And they subpoenaed Wheeler to find out where she got the plans for the operation.

Reporters must worry about another aspect of the privilege, the problem that through some action they may actually waive their right to refuse to testify.

The reporter refused to identify her source and was found in contempt of court. The court said that any privilege a reporter might enjoy in such an instance was waived when, in 1986, she told her husband and another man, both officers in the U.S. Park Police, the name of her confidential source. "A reporter cannot choose in 1986 to disclose her source to others . . . and

42. *Gonzales* v. *National Broadcasting Co., Inc.,* 155 F. 3d 618 (1999).
43. *U.S.* v. *Smith,* 135 F. 3d 963 (1998).
44. *Dillon* v. *San Francisco,* 748 F. Supp. 722 (1990).
45. *Marketos* v. *American Employers Insurance Co.,* 460 N.W. 2d 272 (1990).
46. *Stickels* v. *General Rental Co., Inc.,* 750 F. Supp. 729 (1990).
47. *Idaho* v. *Salsbury,* 924 P. 2d 208 (1996).
48. *Weathers* v. *American Family Mutual Insurance Co.,* 17 M.L.R. 1534 (1990).

then choose in 1991—as a witness in a judicial proceeding—not to make this same disclosure," wrote Judge Richard A. Levie. The District of Columbia Court of Appeals upheld this ruling.[49]

Wheeler was excused from testifying in the summer of 1991 when a mistrial was declared in the lawsuit. But a retrial was scheduled. The reporter's husband, to whom she had revealed the identity of her source, was forced to testify before the hearing was adjourned. "This could become a very effective harassment technique," said Jane Kirtley, executive director of the Reporters Committee for Freedom of the Press. She suggested that a judge or attorney might say, "Well, journalists, I recognize you're covered by a shield law or a reporter's privilege, but I'm just going to bring in your spouse, your kid, your parents, your dog, anybody who's around, and see what they know."

There is really no bright line marking when and how a reporter may in fact waive the privilege. The law is too diffuse for such a generalization. But reporters who have promised confidentiality should keep the information completely confidential. In fact, if Wheeler did reveal the name of her source to her husband, and she still denies doing so, she broke a Washington Post rule that forbids a reporter from telling anyone outside the newspaper the name of a confidential source.

WHO IS A JOURNALIST?

An emerging problem relating to the constitutionally based journalist's privilege is, Who is a journalist? When the privilege was developed in the '70s and '80s the definition of a journalist was relatively clear: A journalist was someone who gathered news for a news medium. In the 21st century, with the growth of interactive computer communication and 900 number information services, virtually anyone can report the news, or what he or she might refer to as the news. Should anyone who uses the Internet or a 900 telephone number to spread information be regarded as a journalist for purposes of the law? This issue has not been resolved, but at least one court has attempted to solve the dilemma.

Mark Madden is an irrepressible professional-wrestling commentator who "broadcast" his commentary via 900 number telephone calls. His commentaries were usually sarcastic, sometimes fanciful, and always provocative. To listen to these messages callers paid $1.69 per minute. World Championship Wrestling owns the line and paid Madden $350 per week to operate it.[50] During a commentary Madden reported that the World Wrestling Federation, the arch rival of the WCW, was in serious financial difficulty. WCW and WWF are suing each other, claiming unfair competition. Madden was subpoenaed to testify about the sources for his report on WWF's financial difficulties. Madden raised the First Amendment privilege, claiming he was a journalist entitled to constitutional protection. A U.S. district court agreed in 1997,[51] but the U.S. Court of Appeals overturned the lower-court decision in July of 1998. The appellate judges said that Madden was an entertainer disseminating hype, not news.

---

49. *Wheeler* v. *Goulart,* 18 M.L.R. 2296 (1990); *Goulart* v. *Barry,* 18 M.L.R. 2056 (1991).
50. Glaberson, "Wrestling Insults."
51. *Titan Sports Inc.* v. *Turner Broadcasting Systems Inc.,* 967 F. Supp. 142 (1997).

In ruling that Madden was not a journalist, the three-judge panel from the 3rd U.S. Circuit Court of Appeals defined a journalist (for purposes of application of the privilege) in this fashion: a journalist is one

- who is engaged in investigative reporting;
- who is gathering news; and
- who possesses the intent at the beginning of the news-gathering process to disseminate this news to the public.[52]

Since this ruling two other cases have been reported. A U.S. district court in the District of Columbia has ruled that cyberjournalist/rumor-monger Matt Drudge was protected by the constitutional journalistic privilege in the libel suit brought against him by Sydney Blumenthal.[53] (See pages 373–383.) But a cyberscribe in Colorado who maintained a Web site offering information about the University of Colorado athletic programs does not have a constitutional right to be given the same privileges that school officials accord to other "accredited members of the news media." In other words, the U.S. District Court did not regard Theodore Smith as a journalist.[54] These cases are just the opening chapters of what is surely to be a long saga regarding who is and who is not a journalist.

TELEPHONE RECORDS

The names of confidential news sources, reporters' notes, news film, and photographs are not the only records that have been sought by government agents and attorneys through the use of a subpoena. In a 1994 libel action initiated by the Philip Morris Companies against ABC, the cigarette maker sought access to a reporter's credit card, airline and rental car bills, as well as private telephone records. The goal of this effort was to try to discover the identity of a former R.J. Reynolds Tobacco Co. executive who told the network reporter that tobacco companies regularly added nicotine to cigarettes. Telephone records present a special problem.

The telephone company maintains subscriber records for toll telephone calls for about six months. For long-distance calls billed to the subscriber's telephone number, these records indicate the telephone number called, as well as the date, time, and duration of the call. The records are no secret; a copy of the monthly toll-call record is provided to each subscriber with each month's bill.

In 1974 the American Telephone and Telegraph Company (AT&T) announced that in the future it would not release these records to the government without a subpoena and, as a general policy, would seek to notify subscribers immediately when their individual records had been subpoenaed by a government agency. However, when records were subpoenaed pursuant to a felony investigation, the telephone company said it would not notify the subscriber of the subpoena as long as the government certified that an official investigation was being conducted and that notification to the subscriber could impede the investigation.

52. In re *Madden,* 151 F. 3d 125 (1998).
53. *Blumenthal* v. *Drudge,* 186 F.R.D. 236 (1999).
54. *Smith* v. *Plati,* D. Colo., No. 99-K-491, 7/22/99.

The Reporters Committee for Freedom of the Press challenged the telephone company's policy of releasing *any* records to the government, arguing that the government could use such records to determine reporters' sources. Journalists raised both the Fourth Amendment and the First Amendment as bars to this cooperation between AT&T and the government.

A U.S. court of appeals seemed unpersuaded that this cooperation created a real problem and ruled against the Reporters Committee. The Fourth Amendment claim lacked merit, the court said, because the constitutional prohibition against illegal search and seizure "does not insulate all personal activity from official scrutiny." The First Amendment claim was similarly rejected. The court asserted that the First Amendment offers no additional protections against good faith criminal investigations beyond that afforded by the Fourth and Fifth amendments.

> The principle is clear. To the extent individuals desire to exercise their First Amendment rights in private, free from possible good faith law enforcement investigation, they must operate within the zone of privacy secured by the Fourth Amendment. When individuals expose their activities to third parties, they similarly expose these activities to possible government scrutiny.[55]

SUMMARY

In recent years more and more reporters have been called to testify in legal proceedings. Often they are asked to reveal confidential information to aid police in criminal investigations, to assist in the defense of a criminal defendant, or to help a libel plaintiff establish negligence or actual malice. Failure to comply with a court order can result in a citation for contempt of court. The Supreme Court of the United States ruled in 1972 that reporters were like all other citizens; they did not enjoy a First Amendment privilege that permitted them to refuse to testify before a grand jury. Despite this high court ruling, the lower federal courts and state courts have fashioned a constitutional, common-law privilege that often protects a journalist who has been subpoenaed to testify at a legal hearing. The privilege is qualified. In many instances a court will not require a journalist to testify unless the person seeking the information held by the journalist can demonstrate that the reporter has information that is relevant to the hearing, that there is a compelling need for the disclosure of this information, and that there are no alternative sources for this information.

Courts tend to apply this three-part test differently in different types of legal proceedings. Journalists are most likely to escape being forced to testify in a civil suit, especially if the reporter is not a party to the suit in some way. Reporters are more likely to be forced to testify in a criminal case, but there are numerous examples of reporters being granted a qualified privilege to escape such testimony as well. Reporters called to testify before a grand jury, however, usually are required to honor the subpoena. More and more courts are seeking journalists' testimony regarding nonconfidential information, and the law is of substantially less protective value in these cases. A U.S. court of appeals has ruled that the records of toll telephone calls made by journalists may also be subpoenaed to further legitimate law enforcement proceedings.

55. *Reporters Committee* v. *AT&T,* 593 F. 2d 1030 (1978).

LEGISLATIVE AND EXECUTIVE PROTECTION OF NEWS SOURCES

While the courts have erected limited barriers to protect journalists from subpoenas issued by government agencies, the state legislatures and the U.S. Department of Justice have attempted to protect reporters as well. Thirty-one states have passed statutes that shield reporters in one way or another from subpoenas that might force them to reveal confidential information. There is no federal shield law, but the Department of Justice has developed an extensive set of guidelines that sharply limit when and how federal agents may use subpoenas against journalists. First, let us look at the state statutes.

SHIELD LAWS

In 1896 Maryland granted journalists a limited privilege to refuse to testify in court proceedings. Thirty additional states have adopted similar statutes, called **shield laws.** The states that have such laws are Alabama, Alaska, Arizona, Arkansas, California, Colorado, Delaware, Florida, Georgia, Illinois, Indiana, Kentucky, Louisiana, Maryland, Michigan, Minnesota, Montana, Nebraska, Nevada, New Jersey, New Mexico, New York, North Carolina, North Dakota, Ohio, Oklahoma, Oregon, Pennsylvania, Rhode Island, South Carolina, and Tennessee.

In 1896 Maryland granted journalists a limited privilege to refuse to testify in court proceedings.

These laws, in more or less limited terms, outline the reporter's privilege that has been established by the state. The statutes generally establish who can use the privilege (i.e., who is a reporter?), the kinds of information the privilege protects (i.e., confidential and nonconfidential; sources only or sources and information), and any qualifications that might accrue (i.e., the privilege is waived through voluntary disclosure of other parts of the material; instances when disclosure is mandated).

For example, the Alabama shield law provides:

> No person engaged in, connected with, or employed on any newspaper (or radio broadcasting station or television station) while engaged in a news gathering capacity shall be compelled to disclose, in any legal proceeding or trial, before any court or before a grand jury of any court, or before the presiding officers of any tribunal or his agent or agents, or before any committee of the legislature, or elsewhere, the sources of any information procured or obtained by him and published in the newspaper (or broadcast by any broadcasting station or televised by any television station) on which he is engaged, connected with, or employed.[56]

Some have speculated that the mere existence of a shield law is valuable because it will deter the issuance of subpoenas to journalists. But the study by the Reporters Committee for Freedom of the Press doesn't support that notion. More than half the states have shield laws; more than half (59 percent) of the 3,519 subpoenas issued in 1993 were issued in those states. But shield laws do provide important protection for reporters in many instances. Shield laws were responsible for nearly 20 percent of subpoenas successfully challenged in 1993. In Illinois, for example, courts ruled that the state shield law prevented the editor of the Journal of the American Medical Association from being forced to reveal the name of a contributor who

---

56. Ala. Code, 12-21-142 (1986 & Supp. 1992).

SHADED STATES HAVE SHIELD LAWS

claimed he or she had euthanized a terminally ill patient. Under the statute, all other sources of information had to be exhausted and the disclosure of the information had to be essential to the public interest before the journalist could be required to reveal the information, the court ruled. The state's attorney failed to meet this burden.[57] In 1996 the New York shield law protected NBC when Graco Children's Products, a defendant in a wrongful death suit, sought access to portions of unused video interviews gathered by the network while it was preparing a report on the safety of a combination cradle and baby swing manufactured by the company. A lower court had ordered the network to comply with the subpoena and imposed a $5,000-a-day fine when it refused. The court said that in order to defeat the protection of the shield law the defendant would have to show that the material sought was highly relevant to the case, that it was critical for maintenance of the defense, and that it was not obtainable from other sources. Whereas NBC conceded the first point, the court ruled that Graco had failed to meet the requirements of the second and third prongs of the test. The U.S. Court of Appeals quashed the subpoena.[58] And in 1997 the Minnesota Court of Appeals ruled that before a reporter could be compelled to testify in a libel suit, the trial court must, because of the state's shield law, find that the information was unavailable from other sources, that it was clearly relevant to the case, and that the defamatory statements were false.[59]

Source: Reporters Committee for Freedom of the Press

57. in re *Grand Jury Investigation,* 15 M.L.R. 1469 (1988).
58. *Krase* v. *Graco Children Products Inc.,* 79 F. 3d 346 (1996).
59. *Bauer* v. *Gannett Co.,* 557 N.W. 2d 608 (1997).

Many other cases could be cited to show how shield laws have protected journalists. But these laws have problems as well. Not the least of these problems is that many judges don't like shield laws. They believe the laws unfairly impinge on judicial discretion, denying judges the authority to compel testimony when it is needed in a lawsuit. Hence, in many instances the laws are interpreted very narrowly. Judges follow the letter of the law, but not the spirit of the legislation. For example, the California Supreme Court ruled that while a reporter could not be held in contempt for refusing to produce unpublished photos he had taken of an automobile accident, he might still be subject to other sanctions, such as money damages, for failing to comply with the order. The state shield law only protects a reporter from a contempt citation.[60] The New York shield law failed to protect NBC when it was ordered to provide video outtakes of a protest demonstration staged in early 1998 by thousands of construction workers. The trial judge ruled that the government—which wanted to use the videotape to identify workers so they could be prosecuted—had demonstrated that the material was highly relevant and unavailable from other sources.[61] This showing defeated the protection of the shield law.

Shield laws suffer from other deficiencies as well. Here are some of the problems:

- Few of the laws give a protection that exceeds, or is even equal to, that given by the constitutional privilege.
- The laws in most of the states are significantly qualified. For example, the laws in Alaska, Louisiana, New Mexico, and North Dakota can be overcome by a mere judicial determination that justice or public policy requires the privilege to yield to some other interest.[62]
- In some states the reporter waives the privilege upon disclosure of any portion of the confidential matter.[63]
- In other states the shield law will not apply unless there was an understanding of confidentiality between the reporter and the source.[64]
- State shield laws often exclude free-lance writers, book authors, and cable television operators. Courts have not yet considered whether such laws apply to people who use a computer as a mass medium but it is unlikely that such laws would apply to Internet communicators.[65]
- Shield laws rarely cover what a reporter witnesses, only what a reporter has been told or given.[66]

The perfect shield law would likely be preferable to the First Amendment privilege; but the perfect shield law does not exist. Hence, even in those states that have a shield law, reporters frequently end up relying on the constitutional privilege.

---

60. *The New York Times* v. *Santa Barbara Superior Court*, 796 P. 2d 811 (1990).
61. in re *Grand Jury Subpoenas*, 27 M.L.R. 1723 (1998).
62. *Confidential Sources and Information.*
63. in re *Schuman*, 537 A. 2d 297 (1988).
64. *Outlet Communications, Inc.* v. *Rhode Island*, 588 A. 2d 1050 (1991).
65. Alexander and Cooper, "Words That Shield."
66. *Delaney* v. *Superior Court*, 249 Cal. Rept. 60 (1988); *Minnesota* v. *Knutson*, 523 N.W. 2d 909 (1994).

FEDERAL GUIDELINES

As a kind of corollary to a shield law, the Department of Justice has adopted rules that define when and how a federal prosecuting attorney can obtain a subpoena against a working reporter.[67] Here is a summary of the guidelines:

I. The Department of Justice must attempt to strike a balance between the public's interest in the free dissemination of ideas and information and the public interest in effective law enforcement when determining whether to seek a subpoena for a journalist's confidential information.

II. All reasonable attempts should be made to obtain the information from alternative sources before considering issuing a subpoena to a member of the news media.

III. Negotiations with the news media to gain the information sought shall be pursued in all cases in which a subpoena to a member of the news media is contemplated.

IV. If the negotiations fail (if the reporter won't provide the material voluntarily), the attorney general must approve the subpoena based on the following guidelines:

a. There must be sufficient evidence of a crime from a nonpress source. The department does not approve of using reporters as springboards for investigation.

b. The information the reporter has must be essential to a successful investigation—not peripheral or speculative.

c. The government must have unsuccessfully attempted to get the information from an alternative, nonpress source.

d. Great caution must be exercised with respect to subpoenas for unpublished information or where confidentiality is alleged.

e. Even subpoenas for published information must be treated with care, because reporters have encountered harassment on the grounds that information collected will be available to the government.

f. The subpoena must be directed to specific information.

TELEPHONE RECORDS

Rules 1 through 3 in the guidelines just listed apply as well when federal agents seek to subpoena the toll telephone records of members of the media. If the negotiations to get the records fail, the agents must seek permission from the attorney general to issue the subpoena. In such a case the following guidelines apply:

1. There should be reasonable grounds to believe that a crime has been committed, and that the information sought is essential to the successful investigation of that crime.

---

67. See 28 C.F.R. §50.10.

2. The subpoena should be directed at only relevant information regarding a limited subject matter and should cover a limited period of time.

3. The government should have pursued all reasonable alternative means before seeking the subpoena.

4. Reporters must be given timely notice that the government intends to issue a subpoena.

5. Information obtained through the subpoena must be closely guarded so that unauthorized persons cannot gain access to it.

These federal guidelines have worked well. In some federal cases judges have insisted that the government must demonstrate that it has followed these guidelines before it will force a reporter to testify.[68] Some state and local law enforcement agencies have adopted rules similar to these federal rules. The federal guidelines apply to criminal cases, civil matters, and subpoena of telephone records. It is true that these guidelines do not completely protect the working journalist, but the guidelines often work better than shield laws, and they go a considerable distance in reducing animosity that was mounting between the press, the police, and the courts.

NEWSROOM SEARCHES

Is a newsroom or a journalist's home protected by the First Amendment from a search by the police or federal agents? The Supreme Court of the United States refused to extend the First Amendment in such a manner in 1978.[69] Since then, however, the Congress and many state legislatures have provided qualified legislative protection for premises where news and scholarship are produced. The lawsuit that resulted in the Supreme Court ruling stemmed from the political turmoil of the early '70s, a period that generated many of the previously discussed cases regarding reporters' sources.

Is a newsroom or a journalist's home protected by the First Amendment from a search by the police or federal agents?

In April of 1971 police were asked to remove student demonstrators who were occupying the administrative offices of Stanford University Hospital. When police entered the west end of the building, demonstrators poured out of the east end, and during the ensuing melee outside the building, several police officers were hurt, two seriously. The battle between the police and the students was photographed by a student, and the following day pictures of the incident were published in the Stanford Daily student newspaper. In an effort to discover which students had attacked the injured police officers, law enforcement officials from Santa Clara County secured a warrant for a search of the Daily's newsroom, hoping to find more pictures taken by the student photographer. There was no allegation that any member of the Daily staff was involved in the attack or other unlawful acts. No evidence was discovered during the thorough search.

This type of search is known as an innocent third-party search, or simply a third-party search. Police search the premises or a room for evidence relating to a crime even though there is no reason to suspect that the owner of the premises or the occupant of the room is involved

---

68. See, for example, *U.S.* v. *Blanton,* 534 F. Supp. 295 (1982).
69. *Zurcher* v. *Stanford Daily,* 436 U.S. 547 (1978).

in the crime that is being investigated. Such searches are not uncommon, but in the lawsuit that followed, the student newspaper argued that this kind of search threatened the freedom of the press and should not be permitted unless police officials first obtain a subpoena—which is more difficult for police to get than a simple search warrant is. The subpoena process would also provide the press with notice prior to the search and allow editors and reporters to challenge the issuance of the subpoena.

The newspaper argued that the unannounced third-party search of a newsroom seriously threatened the ability of the press to gather, analyze, and disseminate news. The searches could be physically disruptive for a craft in which meeting deadlines is essential. Confidential sources—fearful that some evidence that would reveal their identity might surface in such a search—would refuse to cooperate with reporters. Reporters would be deterred from keeping notes and tapes if such material could be seized in a search. All of this, and more, could have a chilling effect on the press, lawyers for the newspaper argued.

The Supreme Court, in a 5–3 ruling, disagreed with the newspaper. Justice Byron White ruled that the problem was essentially a Fourth Amendment question (i.e., was the search permissible under the Fourth Amendment?), not a First Amendment question, and that under existing law a warrant may be issued to search any property if there is reason to believe that evidence of a crime will be found. "The Fourth Amendment has itself struck the balance between privacy and public need and there is no occasion or justification for a court to revise the Amendment and strike a new balance," White wrote. The associate justice conceded that "where the materials sought to be seized may be protected by the First Amendment, the requirements of the Fourth Amendment must be applied with 'scrupulous exactitude.'" He added, "Where presumptively protected materials are sought to be seized, the warrant requirement should be administered to leave as little as possible to the discretion of the officer in the field." But Justice White rejected the notion that such unannounced searches are a threat to the freedom of the press, arguing that the framers of the Constitution were certainly aware of the struggle between the press and the Crown in the 17th and 18th centuries, when the general search warrant was a serious problem for the press. Yet the framers did not forbid the use of search warrants where the press was involved, White asserted. They obviously believed the protections of the Fourth Amendment would sufficiently protect the press.[70]

Newsroom searches by the police, a rarity in the decades before the *Zurcher* case, suddenly became a common occurrence. Journalists sought legislative relief from this onslaught and Congress responded by adopting the Privacy Protection Act of 1980.[71] The law limits the way law officers and government agents can search for or seize materials that are in the hands of persons working for the mass media or persons who expect to publicly disseminate the material in some other manner (e.g., public speech). The statute designates two categories of material that are protected: work products and documentary materials. The law says a work product "encompasses the material whose very creation arises out of a purpose to convey information to the public." In layperson's language, work products are reporters' notes, undeveloped film, outtakes, and so forth. Documentary materials are described as "materials upon

---

70. *Zurcher* v. *Stanford Daily,* 436 U.S. 547 (1978).
71. See 42 U.S.C §§ 2000aa–2000aa-12.

which information is formally recorded," such as government reports, manuscripts, and the like. Congress based the statute on the commerce clause in the U.S. Constitution in order to extend the reach of the law to include state and local agencies, as well as federal law enforcement personnel. To obtain either work products or documentary materials, law enforcement agencies must obtain a subpoena; a search warrant will not do. There are, however, exceptions to the rule. A law enforcement agency may conduct a warranted search of a newsroom to find work products in either of the following two situations:

1. When there is a probable cause to believe that the person possessing such materials has committed or is committing a criminal offense to which the materials will relate.
2. Where there is reason to believe that the immediate seizure of such materials is necessary to prevent the death of or serious harm to a person.

A search warrant may be used instead of a subpoena to obtain documentary materials if either of the two conditions just listed is met or in either of these two situations:

1. There is reason to believe that the giving of notice pursuant to gaining a subpoena would result in the destruction, alteration, or concealment of such materials.
2. That such materials have not been provided in response to a court order directing compliance with a subpoena, all other legal remedies have been exhausted, and there is reason to believe that further delay in gaining the material would threaten the interests of justice.

In most instances, then, law enforcement personnel will be forced to seek a subpoena to gain access to information kept in a newsroom or a reporter's home. While the problem of newsroom searches has been alleviated, it has not been eliminated. In October of 1990, police with a search warrant raided the newsroom of the Macomb Daily, a suburban Detroit newspaper, and confiscated a reporter's notebook after riffling through files. In August of 1994 police searched the newsroom of television station WDAF in Kansas City, Mo., and seized a videotape the station had purchased from a tourist that showed a man dragging a woman across the street into an apartment building. The woman was later found murdered. The seizure was made despite the station's willingness to dub a copy of the tape for the police. A court later ruled that authorities had violated the federal Privacy Protection Act and awarded WDAF $1,000 in damages. In 1994 police in Spokane, Wash., searched the hotel rooms of a CBS news crew at 4:20 in the morning, seeking what they said was a videotape related to a civil lawsuit against the city. The city council later apologized to the network.[72]

HOW TO RESPOND TO A SUBPOENA

What should a reporter do if he or she is subpoenaed? First, try to avoid the problem altogether. Don't give a promise of confidentiality to a source without first carefully considering whether such a promise is actually needed to get the story. Discuss the matter with an editor

What should a reporter do if he or she is subpoenaed?

72. *Agents of Discovery.*

or the news director before agreeing to keep the name of a source confidential. Also, don't talk, even informally, with persons outside the newspaper about stories in which confidential information or sources are involved. Such discussions may be ruled to constitute a waiver of the privilege you seek to assert at a later date.

But if a subpoena should arrive, the first thing to remember is that the police are not coming to your door to arrest you. The subpoena is simply an order that you have been called to appear at some type of proceeding or supply certain documents. So don't panic. Tell your editor or news director immediately. Ask to talk with your news organization's legal counsel. Don't attempt to avoid being served with the subpoena. While a reporter is under no obligation to make the job easier for the person serving the subpoena, resistance to this service may result in the subpoena being abandoned and a search warrant issued in its place. Don't ever accept a subpoena for someone else.

If the subpoena requests only published material, or video that has previously been broadcast, the newspaper or broadcasting station may simply provide this material without dispute. It is unlikely that the news organization will so readily provide other kinds of materials, however. Journalists should be familiar with their news organization's policy on retaining notes, tapes, first drafts, and so on. If there is no policy, it is worthwhile to ask management to consider adopting one. Once the subpoena has been served, the material sought is considered official evidence, and if it is destroyed to avoid having to produce it, the reporter very likely will be held in contempt of court. So once you have been served, begin gathering the material together in case you have to surrender it at some later time.

If you believe that the material or names of sources should be withheld, and your news organization disagrees, it is in your interest to hire your own attorney to represent you. The company attorney is working for the company, not you. Finally, remember that the odds of being forced to give up the material or names are low. The law is, for the most part, on your side these days.

SUMMARY

State legislatures and the federal government have adopted statutes and rules that offer some protection to journalists who hold confidential information sought by government agents and other individuals. Thirty-one states have adopted so-called shield laws, which provide a qualified privilege for reporters to refuse to testify in legal proceedings. Although sometimes these statutes can be helpful, they are not without problems. There is a lack of consistency among the state shield laws. These laws have definitional problems that permit courts to construe them very narrowly if they choose to. The laws usually protect only what someone tells a reporter, not what a reporter personally sees or hears. Often courts see the statutes as legislative interference with judicial prerogatives and go out of their way to interpret the laws in the least useful manner.

The Department of Justice has adopted rules that govern when and how federal agents may subpoena journalists, records possessed by journalists, and journalists' telephone toll records. The rules require federal agents to strike a balance between the public's interest in the free flow of information and effective law enforcement. Federal prosecuting attorneys are instructed to attempt to obtain information from alternative sources or to negotiate with the journalist to get the material before seeking a subpoena. The attorney general must approve all subpoenas under guidelines outlined in these rules.

Congress passed the Privacy Protection Act of 1980 in response to a ruling by the U.S. Supreme Court that the First Amendment does not ban searches of newsrooms or reporters' homes. This act requires federal, state, and local police agencies who seek a journalist's work products or other documentary materials to get a subpoena for these materials rather than seize them under the authority of a search warrant. The statute does provide exceptions to these rules. For example, premises may be searched and materials seized under a search warrant if police believe the reporter has committed a crime, if there is reason to believe someone will be harmed if the materials are not seized, or if police fear the materials might be destroyed if a subpoena is sought.

THE CONTEMPT POWER

Those who work in the mass media and run afoul of judicial orders or the commands of legislative committees can quickly feel the sharp sting of a contempt citation. Reporters who refuse to respond to a subpoena, editors who criticize a judge, newspapers that refuse to pay a libel or invasion of privacy judgment, all of these and more can be held in contempt. American editors first encountered this kind of legal sanction in the 18th century when colonial legislatures used contempt to punish journalists who criticized their actions. The contempt power today remains a vestige of the rule of monarchs. It is a power once exercised only by kings and queens. Most judges and legislators today who can issue citations for contempt recognize that it is an authoritarian practice out of step with modern democratic concepts and contemporary due process of law. Yet judges especially argue they must retain this power to enforce their orders. A brief sketch of the history of contempt is followed by a discussion on the various kinds of contempt citations that can be issued. The limitations placed on the application of the contempt power concludes this section of the book.

HISTORY OF CONTEMPT

In 1631 in England, a British subject was convicted of a felony, a common enough event. This particular subject was angered at being found guilty, and after the sentence was read he threw a brickbat (a piece of broken brick) at the judge. The brickbat missed the judge, but the man was quickly seized, his right hand was cut off and nailed to the gallows, and he was immediately hanged in the presence of the court.[73]

While such judicial retribution is an uncommon exercise of the contempt power, it nevertheless is a representative example of the power of judges to control what goes on in their courtrooms. Even today, at the beginning of the 21st century, disobedience of or disrespect for the court is normally put down swiftly by exercise of the power of contempt. Any act that interferes

73. Goldfarb, *The Contempt Power.*

with the orderly processes of justice is usually promptly stopped and the offender is quickly punished. While other governmental bodies (legislative bodies, for example) can use the contempt power, its use by judges, which is the subject of this section, is far more common today.

In a nation like the United States with a long tradition of due process of law, the contempt power appears to be an anomaly, something out of character. One individual should not have the kind of unbridled power that a judge can wield via contempt. The contempt power can only be understood as an artifact of history. Hundreds of years ago in England, the monarch dispensed justice to the people. The king or queen was above the law, someone whose power was divinely inspired, and resistance to royal orders was a sin, punishable by damnation. When judges eventually began to administer the courts on behalf of the monarch, they retained much of this power since it was believed, though absent from the courtroom, the king or queen nevertheless was spiritually guiding the hand of justice.

As representative democracy developed in England and royal influence of the government diminished, judges retained the contempt power, and it became institutionalized in common-law courts in both Great Britain and the United States. Courts today rarely justify the exercise of the contempt power on the grounds that it protects the integrity of the judge. Instead, protection of the authority, order, and decorum of the court is the usual reason given for the use of the contempt power. Alternatively, the court will use contempt to protect the rights of the litigants using the court to settle a dispute.

KINDS OF CONTEMPT

Varieties of contempt are recognized through the common law, and efforts have been made to label these varieties. But these efforts have been unsatisfactory; there is frequently disagreement among courts about what kinds of behavior constitute what kinds of contempt. No attempt will be made to resolve these discrepancies in this book. It is sufficient to note that judges use the contempt power for two purposes:

A court can use the contempt power to protect the rights of a litigant in a legal dispute. A reporter who refuses to reveal the name of a source critical to the defense of a person charged with larceny could endanger the person's right to a fair trial. The contempt power can be used to force the reporter to testify. Similarly, a broadcasting station that refuses to pay the plaintiff a judgment after losing a libel case endangers the right of the injured party to repair his or her reputation. Again, the contempt power can be used to force the broadcaster to pay the judgment.

The contempt power can be used to vindicate the law, the authority of the court, or the power of the judge. A defendant who refuses to stop talking during a trial or an attorney who continually ignores judicial warnings against talking to reporters about the merits of the case can be punished with a contempt citation. So can a writer who carelessly and aggressively criticizes a court ruling in a newspaper editorial.

Judges who use the contempt power to protect the rights of litigants usually impose an indeterminate sentence against the target of the contempt. That is, a judge can jail a reporter until he or she is willing to reveal the name of the critical source. Or the court can fine the broadcaster a specific amount each day until the civil judgment is paid. The punishment is used to coerce the target of the citation to take some action.

Judges who use the contempt power to vindicate the law, the authority of the court, or the power of the judge will generally impose a determinate sentence. That is, a specific fine ($25,000) or jail sentence (30 days in jail). Here the sentence is strictly punishment; no coercion is implied.

The most onerous application of the contempt power occurs when it is summarily applied. When a judge uses summary contempt power, the jurist acts as a prosecutor ("I accuse you of . . ."), jury ("Guilty as charged") and judge (I sentence you to . . ."). This power is normally reserved for those occasions when the judge has actual firsthand knowledge of the contemptuous act; for example, if the defendant misbehaves in the courtroom or if the reporter refuses to answer questions relating to the identity of a source. When the summary power is applied, the accused has few of the rights normally associated with due process of law. There is no jury trial, no right to call witnesses. The accuser and the judge are one and the same.

Any contempt conviction can be appealed. As in any other case, the appeal is taken to the next higher court in the state or in the federal system. Normally the punishment is suspended pending the outcome of the appeal.

Contempt and the Press

The contempt power is broad and touches all manner of persons who run afoul of a judge. Journalists are among persons at jeopardy. What kinds of situations are most likely to result in contempt problems for the press? To list a few:

1. Failure to pay a judgment in a libel or invasion-of-privacy case.
2. Failure to obey a court order. The judge rules that no photos may be taken in the courtroom, or orders reporters not to publish stories about certain aspects of a case. If these orders are disobeyed, a contempt citation may result.
3. Refusal of a journalist to disclose the identity of a source or to testify in court or before a grand jury.
4. Critical commentary about the court. This might be an editorial critical of the court or a cartoon mocking the judge. Contempt citations have been issued to punish the press in such cases.
5. Tampering with a jury. A reporter tries to talk with jurors during a trial, asking questions about their views on the defendant's innocence or guilt.

These situations are some of the more common ways that members of the press might become involved in a contempt problem, although the list is by no means exhaustive.

LIMITATIONS ON CONTEMPT POWER

The early years of the 20th century must be regarded as a high-water mark for the contempt power, because since that time the opponents of this power have succeeded in placing rather severe limitations on its use. Make no mistake; it is not a sterile power. Judges can and still do use their contempt power. Great Falls (Mont.) Tribune reporter Melody Perkins found that out when she asked Judge John M. Marvel why the proceeding she had just been ushered out of was closed to the public. The judge declared that her question disrupted the courtroom, held her in contempt, and fined her $300. The Montana Supreme Court upheld the citation.[74] But today judges throughout the United States have far less freedom in how they use this power than they had in the first quarter of this century.

Legislative Limits

One important limitation on the power of the court to use contempt comes from legislatures. For example, for nearly 90 years, the Congress has passed laws that limit use of the summary power by federal judges to dispose of contempt citations. The 1914 Clayton Antitrust Act, for example, requires that judges provide a jury trial in a contempt case when the contemptuous action is also a crime under federal or state law. In 1932, as a part of the Norris-LaGuardia Act, the Congress mandated jury trials for all contempts arising out of labor disputes. The 1957 civil rights law provided for a jury trial for contempt when the sentence imposed exceeded 45 days in jail. The 1964 civil rights law contains the same provision.

Court-Imposed Limits

The bench itself imposes limitations on the use of the summary power. The Federal Rules of Criminal Procedure requires that in many instances notice be given the contemnor and a hearing be allowed. In addition, there is the right to counsel, the right to cross-examine witnesses, the right to offer testimony, and in many instances the right to a jury trial. If the contempt citation is based on criticism or disrespect of a judge, that judge is disqualified from the proceeding. Bail is also allowed. The courts and legislatures in many states also deem that a jury trial is a requirement in an indirect contempt.

In the instances just noted, the legislature or the bench itself grants the right to a jury trial. Is there a constitutional right to a jury trial in such cases? The U.S. Supreme Court has been grappling with this question since the 1960s.

In 1964 the high court ruled that there is no constitutional right to a jury trial in a contempt case in upholding the contempt conviction of the governor of Mississippi, Ross Barnett, who willfully disobeyed an order of the U.S. Court of Appeals for the 5th Circuit. As one might expect at that time and in that place, the substantive question involved was civil rights. However, a footnote to the court's opinion states, "Some members of the Court are of the view that, without regard to the seriousness of the offense, punishment by summary trial without a jury would be constitutionally limited to that penalty provided for petty offenses."[75]

Petty offenses generally carry a sentence of six months or less. What the court seemed to be hinting at is that a jury trial is constitutionally required if the penalty exceeds more than six months in jail. In 1966 in *Cheff* v. *Schnackenberg*,[76] the high court specifically said what it had implied in the *Barnett* case—that sentences exceeding six months cannot be imposed in

74. *Great Falls Tribune Co. v. Montana Eighth District Court*, 777 P. 2d 345 (1989).
75. *U.S. v. Barnett*, 376 U.S. 681 (1964).
76. 384 U.S. 373 (1966).

cases of criminal contempt without giving the accused a jury trial. Two years later, in *Bloom* v. *Illinois*,[77] the high court took the last step and ruled that criminal contempt is a crime in the ordinary sense and that since the U.S. Constitution guarantees the right to a jury trial in criminal cases, prosecutions by state courts for serious criminal contempts (those with more than a six-month penalty) must be heard by a jury.

In 1941 the U.S. Supreme Court placed a distinct limit on the power of federal judges to use their summary power in punishing contempts. An 1831 statute had limited the use of this power to contempts committed in the presence of the court or "so near thereto" as to obstruct the administration of justice. In 1918 the high court ruled that the words "so near thereto" had a causal meaning. Any act that was in close relationship to the administration of justice could be punished summarily.[78] Twenty-three years later the Supreme Court reversed itself on this matter in the case of *Nye* v. *U.S.*[79] Justice William O. Douglas cited research that had been done on the 1831 statute by legal scholars during the mid-1920s that showed Congress had intended the words to have a geographic, not a causal, meaning. Before the summary power can be used, Douglas wrote, the misbehavior must be in the courtroom or in the physical proximity of the courtroom. Most people today believe this interpretation permits a federal judge to exercise the summary power to punish acts that take place in the courtroom, in the hallway outside the court, and perhaps in the lobby of the courthouse, but not much farther. Conceivably, a noisy demonstration just outside the building might also be ruled to be "so near thereto" to affect the administration of justice.

Through various means, then, during this century the summary power of judges has been limited, and in turn the limitations have reduced the contempt power. Through statutes that explicitly limit the use of the summary power and through court rulings that limit the severity of punishment that may be applied in the absence of a jury, the absolute power of judges has been trimmed. Nevertheless, the summary power is still a threat. And even six months in jail is a long time!

First Amendment Limitations

The First Amendment was not raised as a barrier to contempt conviction until relatively modern times—in 1941 to be exact. In 1941, and again in 1946 and 1947, the U.S. Supreme Court ruled that freedom of the press to comment on the judiciary must be protected, except in those circumstances in which the commentary presents a serious threat to the proper functioning of the legal process. These three decisions—*Bridges* v. *California* and *Times Mirror Co.* v. *Superior Court*,[80] *Pennekamp* v. *Florida*,[81] and *Craig* v. *Harney*[82]—stand as the bedrock support for the argument that the First Amendment protects the press in writing about the judiciary.

---

77. 391 U.S. 194 (1968).
78. *Toledo Newspaper Co.* v. *U.S.*, 247 U.S. 402 (1918).
79. 313 U.S. 33 (1941).
80. 314 U.S. 252 (1941).
81. 328 U.S. 331 (1946).
82. 331 U.S. 367 (1947).

The first case, *Bridges* v. *California* and *Times Mirror Co.* v. *Superior Court*,[83] consisted of two appeals from decisions by California courts, and the cases were decided together by the Supreme Court. In the first case, labor leader Harry Bridges was held in contempt of court when he publicly threatened to take the dockworkers out on strike if the courts attempted to enforce a judicial ruling against Bridges and his union. In the second case, the Los Angeles Times was ruled in contempt for publishing a series of antilabor editorials. The trial court claimed that the editorials were aimed at influencing the disposition of cases concerning labor unionists that were before the court.

In a 5–4 decision, the high court repudiated the idea that the contempt power is valid because it is deeply rooted in English common law. Justice Hugo Black wrote that even if this were the case, the idea ignores the generally accepted historical belief that "one of the objects of the Revolution was to get rid of the English law on liberty of speech and press." Black said that before a judge can use the contempt power to close off discussion of a case, there must be a "clear and present danger" that the discussion will produce interference with the proper administration of justice. In applying Holmes's famous World War I clear-and-present-danger sedition test to contempt, Black meant that only those threats to justice that are imminent or immediate can be punished. The substantive evil must be extremely serious and the degree of imminence extremely high before utterances can be punished, he wrote.

The government argued in these cases that commentary on a case is clearly proper, but only *after* the case is completed so that the course of justice will not be influenced. Black rejected this notion, saying that it is while a trial is under way that the public interest about a case is highest. He wrote:

> We cannot start with the assumption that publications actually do threaten to change the nature of legal trials and that to preserve judicial impartiality it is necessary for judges to have a contempt power by which they can close all channels of public expression to matters touching on the pending cases.[84]

It should be noted parenthetically that in using the clear-and-present-danger test to block contempt convictions, Justice Black made better use of those four words than did the high court in its application of the test in sedition trials (see pages 52–54). The clear-and-present danger test indeed became an effective means of stopping contempt convictions against the press.

This concept was reinforced five years later when in the second case, *Pennekamp* v. *Florida*, the court reviewed an appeal from the Florida Supreme Court involving a contempt citation against the Miami Herald. The Herald had been highly critical of the trial courts in Dade County, Fla., for many months. In at least two editorials, it was argued that the courts worked harder to protect the criminals than they worked to protect the people. But the newspaper's evaluation of the courts' performance was founded on serious misstatement of facts. The court found both the editor, John D. Pennekamp, and the newspaper in contempt and levied fines against them both.

Black said that before a judge can use the contempt power to close off discussion of a case, there must be a "clear and present danger" that the discussion will produce interference with the proper administration of justice.

83. 314 U.S. 252 (1941).
84. *Bridges* v. *California* and *Times Mirror Co.* v. *Superior Court*, 314 U.S. 252 (1941).

The Supreme Court overturned the convictions, noting, "We are not willing to say under the circumstances of this case that these editorials are a clear and present danger to the fair administration of justice in Florida." Justice Stanley Reed wrote that although he could not precisely define clear and present danger, certainly the criticism of a judge's actions in a non-jury trial would not affect the legal process. What about the factual errors in the editorials? Justice Reed said the errors were quite immaterial. Free discussion, Reed said, is a cardinal principle of Americanism. Discussion after a trial ends might be inadequate and can endanger the public welfare. Freedom of discussion should be given the widest range compatible with the essential requirement of the fair and orderly administration of justice. "We conclude," Reed wrote, "that the danger under this record to fair judicial administration has not the clearness and immediacy necessary to close the door of permissible public comment. When that door is closed, it closes all doors behind it."[85]

The following year, the court once again reinforced the First Amendment barrier to the use of the contempt power in its decision in *Craig* v. *Harney,* the third case. In this case a Texas newspaper had been highly critical of a judge who directed a jury to return a verdict against a well-liked citizen in a civil suit. The Corpus Christi Caller-Times was found in contempt of court, and again the high court struck down the conviction. Justice William O. Douglas admitted that in the court's opinion the critical articles were unfair because they contained significant errors about what had actually occurred at the trial. "But inaccuracies in reporting," he wrote, "are commonplace. Certainly a reporter could not be laid by the heels for contempt because he missed the essential point in a trial or failed to summarize the issues to accord with the views of the judge who sat on the case."[86]

Douglas wrote that it took more imagination than the court possessed to find "in this sketchy and one-sided report of a case any imminent or serious threat to a judge of reasonable fortitude." Douglas added, "Where public matters are involved, the doubts should be resolved in favor of freedom of expression rather than against it."

The three cases just discussed—*Bridges, Pennekamp,* and *Craig*—represent three strong statements in favor of a broad discussion of judicial matters, of trials, and of the legal process. To some degree they also represent a limitation on the contempt power of the courts. The clear-and-present-danger test is a formidable hurdle for any judge to clear before punishing a newspaper or television station with a contempt citation. However, lest we get swept away by the court's rhetoric, it is important to look at what was involved in each of these cases, or rather what was not involved. In none of the cases did the judge first issue an order banning certain kinds of publicity about the case. In none of the cases could a jury have been influenced by the media publicity. In none of the cases did the press publish or broadcast evidence or statements prohibited at the trial. As a matter of fact, all three cases involved the same question—commentary or criticism directed toward a judge. From these cases it is clear that the Supreme Court expects the nation's judges to be strong, not to bend in the wind of public opinion, not to be influenced by journalistic commentary. But the court has never indicated that it has the same

85. *Pennekamp* v. *Florida,* 328 U.S. 331 (1946).
86. *Craig* v. *Harney,* 331 U.S. 367 (1947).

expectations with regard to juries. It has never said that a judge must allow the press free rein in its comments on a pending case with regard to material evidence or the credibility of witnesses. The caution, then, is not to read more into these decisions than is actually there. *Bridges, Pennekamp,* and *Craig* stand for almost unlimited discussion of pending nonjury cases. That is about as far as we dare go, however.

Interference with the trial process, on the other hand, especially in a jury trial, will usually not be tolerated, First Amendment or not. During a 1982 criminal trial in Boulder, Colo., the members of a venire—a panel of persons being examined to determine whether they will be seated as jurors—were instructed, in the presence of the press, not to talk with reporters or anyone else about the trial. But after many citizens complained that they thought that the venire members were being intimidated by attorneys during the examination process, two reporters for the Boulder Daily Camera contacted some prospective jurors to ask if they felt they were being intimidated. This contact was brought to the attention of the court, and 14 provisionally qualified jurors were dismissed. The examination procedure had to be started all over again. An angry judge, who said reporters were aware of his order to the venire, found the two reporters in contempt of court. An appellate court upheld the citation, and the reporters were forced to reimburse the state and the parties for the costs incurred because of the additional four days of trial during which the re-examination of the venire took place. The reporters also had to pay the costs for their own contempt trial.[87]

COLLATERAL BAR RULE

When a journalist violates a court order, a contempt citation is probably forthcoming. But what if the court order appears to be illegal or unconstitutional on its face? Can a reporter still be held in contempt for violating such an order? This problem is perhaps the most perplexing one the press faces today in relation to the contempt power. For there is no clear answer to these questions. The dilemma centers around what lawyers and judges call the collateral bar rule. This rule requires that court orders, even those that appear to be unconstitutional and are later deemed to be unconstitutional, must be obeyed. A person who violates a court order may not collaterally challenge the order's constitutionality as a defense to the contempt charge. Instead, that person must obey the order and then appeal the decision to a higher court. As legal scholar Richard Labunski notes, "The rule in effect, requires journalists to either accept almost certain conviction for contempt, or obey the order, seek review, and forfeit the First Amendment rights they seek to exercise."[88] A 1972 ruling, *U.S.* v. *Dickinson,*[89] demonstrates how this collateral bar rule works.

In November 1971 a hearing was under way in federal court in Baton Rouge, La. A VISTA worker had been indicted by the state on charges of conspiring to murder the mayor of Baton Rouge. The defendant complained that the state had no evidence in the case and that prosecution was merely an attempt to harass him. The hearing in federal court was to determine the motives of the state in the prosecution. Since it was possible that the charges would be sustained

87. in re *Stone,* 11 M.L.R. 2209 (1985).
88. Labunski, "The 'Collateral Bar' Rule," 323.
89. 465 F. 2d 496 (1972).

and that the VISTA worker would be tried later in criminal court, the federal judge ruled that there could be no publicity about what took place during the hearing. The press could report that such a hearing was taking place, but that was all. Reporters Gibbs Adams and Larry Dickinson of the Baton Rouge Morning Advocate and State Times ignored the order, published a story about the hearing, and were found in criminal contempt and fined $300 each.

Upon appeal, the U.S. Court of Appeals for the 5th Circuit struck down the trial court's no-publicity order but at the same time upheld the contempt convictions. The court cited a 1967 Supreme Court ruling—*Walker* v. *Birmingham*[90]—as precedent. In that case Martin Luther King and seven other clergymen were arrested and held in contempt for violating a Birmingham, Ala., court injunction banning all marches, parades, sit-ins, and so forth. The high court ruled that although the ban on marches and parades was unconstitutional, Dr. King and the other defendants should have challenged the ban in court rather than just violate it. The contempt citations stood.

The same logic was applied in the *Dickinson* case. Judge John R. Brown wrote:

> The conclusion that the district court's order was constitutionally invalid does not necessarily end the matter of the validity of the contempt convictions. There remains the very formidable question of whether a person may with impunity violate an order which turns out to be invalid. We hold that in the circumstances of this case he may not.[91]

This decision perplexes many persons who cannot understand why the press, or anyone else for that matter, should be punished for not obeying an order that is not legal in the first place. To most judges the answer to that question is simple: the court system would cease to operate as it is supposed to if people had a choice of whether or not to obey a court order. Court orders have to be obeyed until they are reversed, Judge Brown wrote. Disobedience to a court order directly affects the judiciary's ability to discharge its duties and responsibilities. Without the collateral bar rule, courts would become mere boards of arbitration whose judgments and decrees would be only advisory.

Journalists argue that while this rule makes good sense for most litigants, the press presents a special case because time is often a critical factor in publishing or broadcasting the news. Judge Brown said he understood this problem and hoped that appellate courts would grant a speedy review of court orders that blocked publication or broadcast of news. "But newsmen are citizens too," he wrote. "They too may sometimes have to wait."[92] The U.S. Supreme Court refused to hear an appeal by the journalists.

Only one important collateral bar case has occurred since the *Dickinson* ruling. In this case a federal judge in Rhode Island found the Providence Journal and its editor, Charles Hauser, in contempt of court for violating the judge's order forbidding the publication of any information that had been obtained by the government from an illegal FBI wiretap.[93] The 1st

This decision perplexes many persons who cannot understand why the press, or anyone else for that matter, should be punished for not obeying an order that is not legal in the first place.

90. 388 U.S. 307 (1967).
91. *U.S.* v. *Dickinson,* 465 F. 2d 496 (1972).
92. *U.S.* v. *Dickinson,* 465 F. 2d 496 (1972).
93. in re *Providence Journal,* 630 F. Supp. 993 (1986).

U.S. Circuit Court of Appeals ruled that the trial judge's order was transparently invalid and could not serve as a basis for a contempt citation. The appellate court added, however, that in the future publishers and broadcasters should first try to get an appellate review before violating a court order.[94] With the 5th Circuit and the 1st Circuit somewhat in disagreement about this matter, the Supreme Court agreed to hear an appeal. But after reading briefs and hearing arguments, the members of the high court dismissed the appeal because the special prosecutor who handled the appeal for the government had failed to obtain proper authorization from the Solicitor General of the United States to petition for a writ of certiorari.[95] At the federal level, then, the issue remains unresolved. But courts in Washington and Illinois have flatly rejected the rationale of the *Dickinson* case,[96] and courts in Arizona,[97] California,[98] Massachusetts,[99] and Alabama[100] have also considered the matter but have issued ambiguous rulings.

The power of a judge to punish for contempt of court is a remnant of the power of English royalty. Today, courts have broad powers to punish persons who offend the court, interfere with legal proceedings, or disobey court orders. Contempt is used both to protect the rights of private persons who are litigating matters in the courts and to punish a wrong committed against the court itself.

SUMMARY

Some limits have been placed on the contempt power. Legislatures often restrict the kinds of sentences judges may impose for contempt or require a jury trial before a contempt conviction. The Supreme Court has ruled that before criticism of a court may be punished by contempt, it must be shown that the criticism created a clear and present danger of the likelihood of interference with the administration of justice. In some jurisdictions appellate courts have ruled that persons must obey even unconstitutional contempt orders (the ***Dickinson* rule**).

BIBLIOGRAPHY

Agents of Discovery. Washington, D.C.: Reporters Committee for Freedom of the Press, 1995.

Alexander, Laurence B., and Leah Cooper. "Words That Shield: A Textual Analysis of the Journalist's Privilege." *Newspaper Research Journal* 18 (1997):51.

Berger, Robert G. "The 'No Source' Presumption: The Harshest Remedy." *American University Law Review* 36 (1987):603.

Chamberlain, Bill. "Protection of Confidential News Sources: An Unresolved Issue." *Popular Government* 44 (1978):18.

94. in re *Providence Journal*, 820 F. 2d 1354 (1987).
95. *U.S.* v. *Providence Journal*, 108 S. Ct. 1502 (1998).
96. *State ex rel Superior Court* v. *Sperry*, 483 P. 2d 609 (1971) and *Cooper* v. *Rockford Newspapers*, 365 N.E. 2d 746 (1977).
97. *Phoenix Newspapers* v. *Superior Court*, 418 P. 2d 594 (1966) and *State* v. *Chavez*, 601 P. 2d 301 (1979).
98. in re *Berry*, 493 P. 2d 273 (1968).
99. *Fitchburg* v. *707 Main Corp.*, 343 N.E. 2d 149 (1976).
100. ex parte *Purvis*, 382 So. 2d 512 (1980).

Confidential Sources and Information. Washington, D.C.: Reporters Committee for Freedom of the Press, 1993.

Denniston, Lyle. "Court: Leave the Press Alone." *Washington Journalism Review,* June 1988, 10.

Frazer, Douglas H. "The Newsperson's Privilege in Grand Jury Proceedings: An Argument for Uniform Recognition and Application." *Journal of Criminal Law and Criminology* 75 (1984):413.

Garry, Patrick. "The Trouble with Confidential Sources." *Hastings Communications and Entertainment Law Journal* 14 (1992):403.

Glaberson, William. "Wrestling Insults Fuel Free Speech Case." *The New York Times,* 24 October 1998, A10.

Goldfarb, Ronald. *The Contempt Power.* New York: Columbia University Press, 1963.

Kase, Kathryn. "When a Promise Is Not a Promise: The Legal Consequences for Journalists Who Break Promises of Confidentiality to Sources." *Hastings Comm/Ent Law Journal* 12 (1990):565.

Labunski, Richard. "The 'Collateral Bar' Rule and the First Amendment: The Constitutionality of Enforcing Unconstitutional Orders." *The American University Law Review* 37 (1988):323.

Langley, Monica, and Lee Levine. "*Branzburg* Revisited: Confidential Sources and First Amendment Values." *George Washington Law Review* 57 (1988):13.

Levin, Doron. "Police Raid of Reporter's Files Stirs Concern." *The New York Times,* 2 October 1990.

Malheiro, Sharon K. "The Journalist's Reportorial Privilege—What Does It Protect and What Are Its Limits?" *Drake Law Review* 38 (1988–89):79.

The Media Law Bulletin 1, no. 7 (1991):6.

Mullen, Lawrence J. "Developments in the News Media Privilege: The Qualified Constitutional Approach Becoming Common Law." *Maine Law Review* 33 (1981):401.

Newman, Craig A. "A Qualified Privilege for Journalists Branzburg v. Hayes: A Decade Later." *University of Detroit Journal of Urban Law* 61 (1984):463.

"The Newsman's Privilege: Government Investigations, Criminal Prosecutions, and Private Litigation." *California Law Review* 58 (1970):1198.

Osborn, John E. "The Reporter's Confidentiality Privilege: Updating the Empirical Evidence after a Decade of Subpoenas." *Columbia Human Rights Law Review* 17 (1985):57.

Parrell, Mark J. "Press/Confidential Source Relations: Protecting Sources and the First Amendment." *Communications and the Law* 47, March 1993.

Utevsky, David. "Protection of Sources and Unpublished Information." Paper presented at the meeting of Washington Volunteer Lawyers for the Arts, Seattle, Wash., 27 January 1989.

Wigmore, John H. *A Treatise on the Anglo-American System of Evidence in Trials at Common Law,* 2d ed. Boston: Little, Brown, 1934.

Free Press/Fair Trial
Trial Level Remedies and Restrictive Orders

Legal problems frequently arise as the press and the criminal justice system intersect in our society. These problems are usually cast as the result of two seemingly conflicting constitutional rights: the right to a free press guaranteed by the First Amendment, and the right to a fair trial guaranteed by the Sixth Amendment. If the press publishes and broadcasts anything it chooses about a crime or a criminal suspect, isn't it possible readers and viewers will make up their minds about the guilt or innocence of the accused? And if they do, won't the members of the jury (who are also readers and viewers) approach the case with prejudice either for or against the defendant? What will happen to the guarantee of a fair trial? But if the court moves to restrict this publicity by the mass media to protect the integrity of the trial process, won't this interfere with the rights of the press? What about the First Amendment? We explore these issues in Chapters 11 and 12. Included is a discussion of the kinds of publicity that may damage the right to a fair trial, and the various schemes adopted by the courts to try to minimize the impact of this publicity or restrict the flow of this kind of information.

PREJUDICIAL CRIME REPORTING

The American fascination with crime, especially violent crime, has never been greater. Stories about crimes are the prime fodder for local television news, with some stations devoting as much as half their broadcast time to reports of local, regional, and national crimes. Many newspapers seem poised to return to patterns of reporting that were more common in the early part of the last century, 1900 to 1930, when the police reporter was the most important person in the city room. Television programs about cops, bizarre crimes, and wanted criminals dot the landscape of prime-time television. It is not surprising, then, that some attorneys and judges express substantial fears that this press coverage might be endangering the constitutional rights of criminal defendants.

Not all reporting about criminal activities is a problem. The problem occurs with those instances in which media coverage saturates a community with stories about a particular criminal and a particular crime; the O.J. Simpson case, the Timothy McVeigh investigation, the killing of Matthew Shepard in Wyoming and JonBenet Ramsey in Colorado. What news reports cause the most problems? Here is a list of some of the more common kinds of stories, according to persons involved in the criminal justice system:

1. **Confessions or stories about the confession that a defendant is said to have made, which include even alluding to the fact that there may be a confession.** The Fifth Amendment says that a person does not have to testify against him- or herself. Therefore a confession given to police may be subsequently retracted and often cannot be used against the defendant at the trial.

2. **Stories about the defendant's performance on a test, such as a polygraph, lie detector, or similar device, and about the defendant's refusal to take such a test.** Most of this information will not be admitted as evidence at the trial.

3. **Stories about the defendant's past criminal record or that describe the defendant as a former convict**. This information is not permitted at the trial. It may seem entirely logical to some people that when someone has committed 99 robberies and is again arrested for robbery, the accused probably did commit the crime. As a matter of fact, past behavior is immaterial in the current trial for robbery. The state must prove that the defendant committed *this* robbery.

4. **Stories that question the credibility of witnesses and that contain the personal feelings of witnesses about prosecutors, police, victims, or even judges.**

5. **Stories about the defendant's character** (he or she hates children and dogs), **associates** (he or she hangs around with known syndicate mobsters), **and personality** (he or she attacks people on the slightest provocation).

6. **Stories that tend to inflame the public mood against the defendant.** Such stories include editorial campaigns that demand the arrest of a suspect before sufficient evidence has been collected; person-on-the-street interviews concerning the guilt of the defendant or the kind of punishment that should be meted out after the accused

is convicted; televised debates about the evidence of the guilt or innocence of the defendant. All of these kinds of stories put the jury in the hot seat as well as circulate vast quantities of misinformation.

Despite the stated fears of some attorneys and judges, it is fair to ask whether intensive publicity about a criminal case does in fact jeopardize the right of the defendant in the case to enjoy a fair trial. Is the pool of jurors poisoned in such a way as to undermine the impartiality of the judicial process? This tough question has not yet been answered satisfactorily. Let's look at what we do know.

IMPACT ON JURORS

The questions regarding the impact of pretrial publicity on jurors and even judges in a criminal case date to the early years of the republic. For almost two centuries, it has been assumed that intensive prejudicial publicity in a criminal case equals a biased jury and an unfair trial. For almost 55 years, social scientists have attempted to prove or disprove this assumption with less than great success. The law prohibits the use of real jurors in actual trials as subjects for this research. Consequently, researchers have tried to generate other means to gather the data that is needed. Some have attempted to replicate a trial in an experimental setting. Others have used survey research methods to poll members of a community about what they know and think about highly publicized criminal cases in the area. Neither technique has provided totally satisfactory results. Complicating the resolution of this problem is the fact that many social scientists are beginning to believe that people tend to remember far less about what they read or watch on television than has been traditionally assumed. Social science, then, has yet to prove the validity of the assumption that prejudicial publicity has a deleterious impact on the criminal justice system.

Some persons within the law are also beginning to express reservations about this traditional assumption. After a substantial study, University of Wisconsin researcher Robert E. Drechsel concluded that "the evidence also indicates that the magnitude of the fair trial–free press issue may be overblown. Most trial judges and other judicial sources do not seem to perceive frequent major problems with prejudicial publicity."[1] And the judges on at least two U.S. appeals courts have expressed a similar sentiment. "Pretrial publicity does not, however, lead in every criminal case to an unfair trial," noted judges on the 9th U.S. Circuit Court of Appeals in 1988.[2] And judges on the 4th U.S. Circuit Court of Appeals said that "it verges upon insult to depict all potential jurors as nothing more than malleable and mindless creations of pre-trial publicity." They added, "There is somewhat of a tendency to frequently overestimate the extent of the public's awareness of news."[3] So, perhaps prejudicial publicity is not the problem it has always been assumed to be, at least not in every case.

The next issue to focus on is the jury itself. Just what is an impartial juror?

"Most trial judges and other judicial sources do not seem to perceive frequent major problems with prejudicial publicity."

1. Drechsel, "Media-Judiciary Relations," 1.
2. *Seattle Times* v. *U.S. District Court,* 845 F. 2d 1243 (1988).
3. *The Washington Post Co.* v. *Hughes,* 923 F. 2d 324 (1991).

THE LAW AND PREJUDICIAL NEWS

The definition of an impartial juror used by the courts in the United States is more than 190 years old and stems from a ruling by Chief Justice John Marshall in the trial of Aaron Burr in 1807 for treason. Charges that the jurors were biased were made at the trial. Marshall proclaimed that an impartial juror was one free from the dominant influence of knowledge acquired outside the courtroom, free from strong and deep impressions that close the mind. "Light impressions," Marshall wrote, "which may fairly be supposed to yield to the testimony that may be offered, which leave the mind open to a fair consideration of that testimony, constitute no sufficient objection to a juror."[4]

In the last 50 years the U.S. Supreme Court has fashioned other tests to guide trial judges and appellate courts, tests constructed on Chief Justice Marshall's words. The high court has decided several cases relating to pretrial publicity, but three decisions stand out. The first stemmed from a series of brutal killings in Indiana. Leslie Irvin was arrested in connection with a series of sex murders. Statements that Irvin had confessed to all six killings received widespread publicity. At the trial, of 430 persons called as potential jurors, 375 told the judge that they believed Irvin was guilty. Of the 12 jurors finally selected, eight told the court they thought he was guilty before the trial started. The Supreme Court overturned the conviction, noting that in this case, in which so many persons so many times admitted prejudice, statements of impartiality could be given little weight.[5]

Fourteen years later Jack Murphy, the original "Murph the Surf," appealed his conviction for robbery and assault on the grounds that the jury had been prejudiced by extensive publicity about his previous criminal record and other extralegal exploits. The Supreme Court disagreed. Only 20 of the 78 potential jurors who were questioned told the Florida trial judge they believed Murphy was guilty. The high court said that this ratio was not comparable to the evidence of hostility or overwhelming prejudice toward the defendant that was found in the *Irvin* case. The Constitution requires that the defendant have a "panel of impartial, indifferent jurors," ruled Justice Thurgood Marshall; "they need not, however, be totally ignorant of the facts and issues involved."[6] It is sufficient that a juror can lay aside his or her impressions and personal opinions and render a considered opinion based on the evidence presented in court. Many people see this 1975 ruling in *Murphy* v. *Florida* as rejecting the often-asserted principle that publicity about a criminal case automatically results in bias toward the defendant.

The high court re-emphasized this point nine years later in the case of *Patton* v. *Yount*.[7] In this ruling the court said that "the relevant question is not whether the community remembered the case, but whether the jurors at Yount's trial had such a fixed opinion that they could not judge impartially the guilt of the defendant."

---

4. *U.S.* v. *Burr,* 24 Fed. Cas. 49 No. 14692 (1807).
5. *Irvin* v. *Dowd,* 366 U.S. 717 (1961).
6. *Murphy* v. *Florida,* 421 U.S. 784 (1975).
7. 467 U.S. 1025 (1984).

WHAT IS AN IMPARTIAL JUROR?

An impartial juror is one whose mind is free from the dominant influence of knowledge acquired outside the courtroom, free from strong and deep impressions that close the mind. *U.S.* v. *Burr,* 1807

"The constitution requires that the defendant have a panel of impartial, indifferent jurors. They need not, however, be totally ignorant of the facts and issues involved." *Murphy* v. *Florida,* 1975

"The relevant question is not whether the people in the community remember the case, but whether the jurors had such a fixed opinion they could not judge impartially the guilt of the defendant." *Patton* v. *Yount,* 1984.

On the basis of these rulings and others, two important generalizations emerge. The high court is willing to permit jury service by a person who possesses knowledge or has opinions about a case, so long as

1. The knowledge or opinions are not so closely held that they cannot reasonably be put aside in the face of evidence; and
2. The publicity surrounding the case is not so widespread and prejudicial as to render a potential juror's assurances of impartiality as unbelievable.[8]

SUMMARY

The First Amendment to the U.S. Constitution guarantees freedom of the press; the Sixth Amendment guarantees every criminal defendant a fair trial. Many people believe these two amendments are in conflict because, often, publicity about a criminal case can prejudice a community against a defendant and make it impossible to find a fair and impartial jury in the case. The kinds of publicity that can be most damaging to a defendant include material about confessions or alleged confessions, stories about a past criminal record, statements about the defendant's character, and comments about the defendant's performance on scientific tests or refusal to take such tests.

Social science has not yet proved that such publicity does in fact create prejudice or that persons cannot set aside their beliefs about a case and render a verdict based on the facts presented at the trial. An impartial juror is not required to be free of all knowledge or impressions about a case; the juror must be free of deep impressions and beliefs that will not yield to the evidence that is presented in court during the trial.

8. See Minow and Cate, "Who Is an Impartial Juror," 631.

TRADITIONAL JUDICIAL REMEDIES

For more than 200 years American judges have had tools at their disposal to try to mitigate or lessen the impact that pretrial publicity might have on a trial. These tools range from carefully examining potential jurors about their knowledge of the case, to moving the trial, to delaying a hearing while publicity abates. As a last resort a criminal conviction can be reversed if there is evidence that the trial was tainted by publicity. But this last resort is costly because it usually involves a retrial, resulting in added expense and inconvenience for all parties involved. These traditional judicial tools, sometimes called trial level remedies, permit the court to reduce the impact of the publicity on the trial without inhibiting the press in any way. As such, journalists tend to favor these means of ensuring the fair trial rights of the criminal defendant. Let's briefly explore the options a trial judge has to cope with heavy press coverage of a criminal case.

As a last resort a criminal conviction can be reversed if there is evidence that the trial was tainted by publicity.

TRIAL LEVEL REMEDIES FOR PRETRIAL PUBLICITY

1. Voir dire
2. Change of venue
3. Change of veniremen
4. Continuance
5. Admonition
6. Sequestration

VOIR DIRE

Before prospective jurors finally make it to the jury box, they must pass a series of hurdles erected both by the attorneys in the case and by the judge. These hurdles are designed to protect the judicial process from jurors who have already made up their minds about the case or who have strong biases toward one litigant or the other. In a process called **voir dire,** each prospective juror is questioned prior to being impaneled in an effort to discover bias. Pretrial publicity is only one source of juror prejudice. If the prospective juror is the mother of a police officer, she is likely to be biased if the defendant is on trial for shooting a police officer. Perhaps the juror is a business associate of the defendant. Possibly the juror has read extensively about the case in the newspapers and believes the police are trying to frame the defendant.

In some cases preliminary screening of jurors is accomplished by a questionnaire administered by the court. After this initial screening both sides in the case question the jurors, and both sides can ask the court to excuse a juror. This procedure is called challenging a juror. There are two kinds of challenges: **challenges for cause** and **peremptory challenges.** To challenge a juror for cause, an attorney must convince the court that there is a good reason for this person not to sit on the jury. Deep-seated prejudice is one good reason. Being an acquaintance of one of the parties in the case is also a good reason. Any reason can be used to challenge a potential juror. All the attorney must do is to convince the judge that the reason is proper. There is no limit on the number of challenges for cause that both prosecutor and defense attorney may exercise.

A peremptory challenge is somewhat different. This challenge can be exercised without cause, and the judge has no power to refuse such a challenge.* There is a limit, however, on the number of such challenges that may be exercised. Sometimes there are as few as two or three and sometimes as many as 10 or 20, depending on the case, the kind of crime involved, the state statute, and sometimes the judge. This kind of challenge is reserved for use against persons whom the defense or the prosecution does not want on the jury but whom the judge refuses to excuse for cause. An attorney may have an intuitive hunch about a potential juror and want that person eliminated from the final panel. Or the juror's social or ethnic background may suggest a problem to the attorney.

To select jury members for the typical criminal trial, attorneys rely on the answers to the questions they ask potential jurors and on their intuition. In the occasional high-profile trial it is not uncommon for attorneys on both sides to undertake a far deeper scrutiny of the panel of potential jurors. This examination could include doing background investigations on the people in the jury pool or hiring expensive jury consultants to help select a panel. The jury consultants use traditional investigative methods to screen the potential jurors but also advise attorneys by using body language experts and others who scrutinize the veniremen as they respond to questions from the attorneys. Some attorneys place a great deal of faith in such schemes; others regard them as pseudoscience.

Is voir dire a good way to screen prejudiced jurors? Seventy-nine percent of a large group of judges surveyed by Professor Emeritus Fred Siebert of Michigan State University said that the questioning process was either highly effective or moderately effective in screening biased jurors.[9] Most trial lawyers also agree, to a point. It is difficult, however, to argue with critics who say that voir dire uncovers only the prejudice that the prospective juror is aware of or is not too embarrassed to admit. Biased jurors can lie when questioned about their biases. They may not even know their mind is made up about the guilt or innocence of the defendant. And the prejudices may have nothing to do with pretrial news coverage of the crime. Potential jurors may be prejudiced against defendants because of their race, the kind of work they do, or the neighborhood in which they live.

Good lawyers walk a fine line in selecting jurors. A defense attorney certainly doesn't want a juror who knows all about the case and has already made up his or her mind regarding a defendant's guilt. On the other hand, a juror who doesn't know any thing about a widely publicized case might be just as bad. Mark Twain once facetiously suggested that "ignoramuses alone could mete out unsullied justice."** Few attorneys want the jury box filled with ignoramuses. The feelings of most good attorneys are reflected in remarks made by U.S. Attorney Jay B. Stephens, who suggested that the best jurors are intelligent jurors who listen

9. Bush, *Free Press and Fair Trial.*

*The Supreme Court has placed limits on the use of peremptory challenges by attorneys to exclude persons from a jury solely on the basis of their race or gender.
**Mark Twain, *Roughing It* (New York: New American Library Edition, 1962).

to the evidence, who evaluate the evidence, and who do not go off on extraneous kinds of issues. "That purpose is served, I think, by informed jurors, by jurors who are an integral part of the community, who participate in the community, who are aware of what is going on in the community and who stay informed."[10]

CHANGE OF VENUE

A serious crime that has been heavily publicized in one community might have received scant press coverage in another community in the state. The court can, in order to impanel a jury of citizens who know much less about the case, move the trial to the second community. This change of location of the trial is called a **change of venue.** If this relocation of the trial is ordered, all the participants in the trial—the prosecutor, defense attorney, judge, defendant, witnesses, and others—will go to this new location for the trial. The jury will be selected from citizens in the new community.

A trial in a state court can be moved to any other venue in the same state. A federal case can be moved to any other federal court, although keeping the trial as close as possible to the site of the crime is considered desirable. The federal trial of the defendants charged in the Oklahoma City bombing was moved to Denver, a city in the adjacent state of Colorado. In that case the move out of state rather than to another city in Oklahoma was prompted by the need to find courtroom facilities that could accommodate a trial of that magnitude.

Change of venue is costly. Witnesses, attorneys, and other persons must be transported and housed and fed while the trial takes place in a distant city. The defendant must surrender the constitutional right to a trial in the district in which the crime was committed. Publicity about the case could appear in the media located in the community in which the trial is scheduled to be held, defeating the purpose of the change of venue. Often the effectiveness of the change of venue depends on how far the trial is moved from the city in which the crime was committed. A trial judge in Washington state who was concerned about newspaper coverage of a local murder case granted a change of venue. But he moved the trial to an adjoining county, the only other county in the state in which the "offending" newspaper had significant circulation. The move accomplished very little, and the judge ultimately was forced to close portions of the proceedings to the press.[11] While a change of venue can reduce the risk of prejudicial publicity influencing a jury, other factors may be introduced into the trial which are equally problematic. The difference in the ethnic and racial composition of one community as opposed to another could possibly change the outcome of a trial. When the four white police officers accused of beating Rodney King, a black man, was moved to the largely white distant suburbs of Los Angeles in a change of venue, three of the officers were acquitted of the charges and the jury failed to reach a verdict regarding the fourth officer. This despite the fact that the beating was captured on videotape by a bystander. The officers' federal trial for violation of King's civil rights was held in the city of Los Angeles with a racially mixed jury, and all the officers were convicted.

Often the effectiveness of the change of venue depends on how far the trial is moved from the city in which the crime was committed.

10. U.S. Senate Subcommittee, *Federal Jury Selection*, 581.
11. *Federated Publications* v. *Kurtz*, 94 Wash. 2d 51 (1980).

In some states it is possible for the defense to seek a change of veniremen rather than a change of venue. Instead of moving the trial to another city, the court imports a jury panel from a distant community. The judge and attorneys visit the distant city, select a jury panel, and then transport the jurors to the community in which the trial will be held. This procedure costs the state less money, since all it must do is pay the expenses of the jurors for the duration of the trial.

CONTINUANCE

When a trial is continued, or a **continuance** is granted, the trial is delayed. By postponing a trial for weeks or even months, a judge expects that the people in the community will forget at least some of what has been written or broadcast about the case, and that expectation is probably legitimate. However, before a trial may be postponed, the defendant must sacrifice his or her right to a speedy trial, something guaranteed under the Constitution. Because the courtrooms in America are clogged, there are few truly speedy trials today, but a continuance delays a trial even longer. The defendant may spend this additional time in jail if bail has not been posted. It is also possible, even likely, that when the trial is finally set to begin, publicity about the case will reappear in the mass media.

But a continuance is a perfect solution in some cases. One judge told of how, just as he was scheduled to begin hearing a malpractice suit on a Monday morning, the Sunday paper, quite innocently, carried a long feature story on the skyrocketing costs of physicians' malpractice insurance because of the large judgments handed down in courts. The article pointed out that physicians passed the additional charges along to patients. The story was widely read. Jurors, who also pay doctors' bills, might hesitate to award a judgment to an injured patient knowing that it would raise insurance rates and ultimately cost patients more. The judge therefore continued the case for two months to let the story fade from the public mind.

ADMONITION TO THE JURY

Once a jury is impaneled, its members are instructed by the judge to render their verdict in the case solely on the basis of the evidence presented in the courtroom. Judges believe that most jurors take this **admonition** quite seriously. Jurors are also warned not to read newspaper stories or watch television broadcasts about the case while the trial is being held. Often jurors are excused from the courtroom while the trial judge hears arguments from the attorneys or even testimony from witnesses. In such instances the court usually wants to determine whether certain evidence is admissible in the case before the evidence is presented to the jury. The press may publish or broadcast reports about this evidence, whether or not it is admitted in the case. It would accomplish very little to keep such evidence from the jury during the trial if jurors could watch news stories about it during the evening television newscasts.

The following admonition, which is one used by King County, Wash., superior court judges, is typical:

> Do not discuss this case or any criminal case or any criminal matter among yourselves or with anyone else. Do not permit anyone to discuss such subjects with

you or in your presence. . . . Do not read, view, or listen to any report in a newspaper, radio, or television on the subject of this trial or any other criminal trial. Do not permit anyone to read about or comment on this trial or any criminal trial to you or in your presence.

Evidence shows that most jurors pay close attention to these instructions. In the single major study in which real jury deliberations were examined to determine the impact of mass media publicity on the trial process, researchers found that jurors listen carefully to the cautionary instructions given to them by judges. The coordinator of that research project, Harry Kalven, noted in a letter to the director of the American Law Institute:

We do . . . have evidence that the jurors take with surprising seriousness the admonition not to read the paper or discuss the case with other people. . . . Our overall impression . . . is that the jury is a pretty stubborn, healthy institution not likely to be overwhelmed either by a remark of counsel or a remark in the press.[12]

SEQUESTRATION OF THE JURY

Publicity during a trial can sometimes be as damaging to a defendant's fair trial rights as publicity before the trial. Often, significant portions of a criminal trial are played out while the jury is out of the courtroom. Arguments over the admissibility of a piece of evidence or the testimony of a witness are frequently conducted without the jury being present. It makes little sense for jurors to be exposed to such information if the judge then rules that it is not admissible as evidence. The substance of these arguments, however, can be reported in the press. Jurors might be exposed to this material via the mass media. It is just as likely that sensational or inflammatory information about the trial might be generated outside the courtroom, again to be printed in newspapers or broadcast by television. Judges have the prerogative of isolating the members of the jury during the duration of the trial to shield them from publicity about the case or other potentially harmful influences. This action is called **sequestration of the jury.** If a jury is sequestered, it is secluded from the community during the course of the trial. Jurors eat together, are housed at state expense at a hotel or motel, and are not permitted to visit with friends and relatives. Phone calls are screened, as is contact with the mass media. Jurors are allowed to read newspapers only after court officials delete stories that could be objectionable.

Sequestration is a costly process for both the state and the jurors. Sequestration for three or four days might be a lark, but the trials in which juries are normally sequestered are long trials, sometimes lasting six months. Life can be seriously disrupted. In extremely long trials, like the O.J. Simpson criminal trial, pressures on sequestered jurors often result in members of the panel asking to be excused. The number of people who can afford the loss of income involved in such a situation is limited.

Although sequestered jurors are free from prejudicial publicity, attorneys fear the long quarantine produces a different kind of prejudice—prejudice against one or the other of the

12. Bush, *Free Press and Fair Trial.*

two sides in the case—wrought from keeping jurors away from friends and family for so long. Defense attorneys express this fear most often, feeling that jurors will tend to hold the defendant responsible for the inconvenience and therefore vote for conviction.

COURT PROCEEDINGS AND THE SIMPSON TRIALS

The legal sagas of O.J. Simpson probably generated more media coverage than any other trials in the history of the nation. For months and months television viewers were glued to their sets during the criminal trial. The subsequent civil trial received comparable coverage except for actual pictures from the courtroom. There was considerable despair among many members of the legal community over the circuslike atmosphere that pervaded the trials and the media coverage. And this spectacle has had some impact on the way in which trial judges choose to deal with the press in high-profile cases.[13] Judge Hirashi Fujisaki, who presided at Simpson's civil trial, conducted the hearing with a tight fist and did his best to control the press, tactics that seemed to elude Judge Lance Ito during the criminal trial.

It is likely going to be harder for broadcasting stations to get their television cameras into the courtroom to cover a sensational trial. State trial judges have the final say on whether most criminal trials are televised (see pages 426–428), and most observers regard the existence of TV cameras in the courtroom as the reason for the posturing by most of the participants in the Simpson murder trial. Cameras were barred from the Simpson civil trial and from the trials of Timothy McVeigh and Terry L. Nichols, the so-called Oklahoma bombers. The California Supreme Court went so far as to adopt a new ethics rule that sharply limits what an attorney can say to reporters outside the courtroom as well. (See page 428 for more on lawyers' statements to the press.)

There was speculation that, in order to preserve faith in the jury system in the wake of the acquittal of Simpson and several other high-profile defendants, state courts would adopt rules to limit the number of peremptory challenges permitted in jury selection. This has not happened yet, but courts in some states are making it far more difficult for citizens to get out of jury duty. The more people who can get an exemption from serving on a jury, the less the jury is likely to mirror the citizenry in the community from which it is drawn. In some states jurors are now given the right to take notes during the trial and even ask questions of witnesses through the judge. Two states now permit a less-than-unanimous jury to convict in a criminal case. Other states have considered this policy as well.

Sequestration of the jury is likely to occur less often in future trials. The jurors in the second Simpson trial went home every night; they were not sequestered. Attorneys for Terry L. Nichols asked the court not to sequester the jurors in his trial. The fear that in a long trial a sequestered jury will punish one side or the other is the most likely reason for the resistance to sequestration.

In the end, the change in the conduct of criminal trials will probably be far less dramatic than many observers speculated in the immediate wake of the trial. And some say that is good, because the Simpson trial was an aberration. "The single most important thing to remember

13. Labaton, "Lessons of Simpson Case," A1.

about this case is that it involved a trial that is so vastly different from what criminal justice is in the United States," said Philip B. Heyman, a former deputy attorney general at the Justice Department and professor at the Harvard Law School. "It reveals an immense disparity in our criminal system, based on how much wealth a defendant has. In reality, the only reason our system works and does not grind to a standstill, the only reason most defendants reach plea agreements [plead guilty to lesser crimes rather than stand trial on the original charge] and do not fully exploit the benefits of the system, is because they can't afford it."[14]

SUMMARY

Trial courts have many ways to compensate for the prejudicial pretrial publicity in a criminal case. Each citizen is questioned by the attorneys and the judge before being accepted as a juror. During this voir dire examination, questions can be asked of the potential jurors about the kinds of information they already know about the case. Persons who have already made up their minds about the defendant's guilt or innocence can be excluded from the jury.

Courts have the power to move a trial to a distant county to find a jury that has not been exposed to the publicity about the case that has been generated by local mass media. While such a change of venue can be costly, it can also be an effective means of compensating for sensational publicity about a case.

A trial can be delayed until the publicity about the case dies down. The defendant must waive the right to a speedy trial, but, except in highly sensational cases, granting a continuance in a trial can thwart the impact of the massive publicity often generated in the wake of a serious crime.

Jurors are always admonished by the judge to base their decision on the facts presented in court and not to read or view any news stories about the case while they are on the jury. There is evidence that they take these warnings quite seriously.

In important cases it is always possible to seclude, or sequester, the jury after it is chosen to shield it from publicity about the trial.

RESTRICTIVE ORDERS TO CONTROL PUBLICITY

Judges have been trying for many, many years to compensate for prejudicial pretrial publicity using the remedies outlined in the previous section. Some jurists and lawyers feel that these schemes are badly out of date. It costs the state more money to try a defendant when there is a change of venue or when an extensive voir dire is needed. These remedies don't always work, it is contended. There is a better solution to the problem: The court should control the kind and amount of information that is published or broadcast about the case. If this is done, it won't be necessary later on to compensate for any prejudicial publicity.

14. Labaton, "Lessons of Simpson Case," A1.

In the late 1960s and early 1970s the tool of choice for trial judges who sought to control pretrial publicity in a criminal case was the **restrictive order.** These judicial orders are called **gag orders** by many journalists, and this is an apt description. They are designed to stop the parties, the attorneys, the witnesses, and sometimes even the press from making comments about specific aspects of a case. The growth in the use and popularity (among judges) of the restrictive order was primarily the result of a serious misunderstanding in the judiciary about what the U.S. Supreme Court said, or meant to say, about one of this century's most widely publicized murder cases: the prosecution of Dr. Sam Sheppard for the murder of his pregnant wife, Marilyn. Mrs. Sheppard was killed early in the morning on July 4, 1954. Her husband, Sam, claimed she was bludgeoned to death by an intruder who attacked her in her bedroom as she slept. From the very beginning of the investigation local police thought Sheppard was the killer. The case, which had all the elements of a good murder mystery, caught the fancy of the nation's press and was front-page news in all parts of the country. After three weeks of intense publicity, Sheppard was arrested and charged with murder. Publicity increased during the preliminary examination and trial, and few were surprised when the wealthy osteopath was convicted. Twelve years later, after several appeals had been denied, the U.S. Supreme Court reversed Sam Sheppard's conviction, ruling that he had been denied a fair trial because of pretrial and trial publicity about the case.[15]

Justice Tom Clark, who wrote the Supreme Court's opinion in the *Sheppard* case, came down hard on the press, noting that bedlam reigned during the trial and that "newsmen took

Headlines like these in the Cleveland Press pressured police to move against Sam Sheppard in 1951.
Special thanks to Cleveland State University Library

15. *Sheppard* v. *Maxwell*, 384 U.S. 333 (1966). Sheppard was retried by the state of Ohio after the Supreme Court ruling. He was acquitted in this second trial. But his life was in ruins, and he died several years later of a liver disease. And yes, this case was the inspiration for both the television series and the movie called "The Fugitive."

Chapter 11

over practically the entire courtroom, hounding most of the participants in the trial, especially Sheppard." Justice Clark saved his sharpest criticism for Judge Blythin, who conducted the trial, and the other officers of the court for allowing the publicity about the case and the coverage of the trial to get out of hand. Here are some excerpts from Clark's opinion:

> Bearing in mind the massive pretrial publicity, the judge should have adopted stricter rules governing the use of the courtroom by newsmen . . . the court should have insulated witnesses [from the media]. . . . The court should have made some effort to control the release of leads, information and gossip to the press by police officers, witnesses and the counsel for both sides. . . . And it is obvious that the judge should have further sought to alleviate this problem by imposing control over the statements made to the news media by counsel, witnesses, and especially the coroner and police officers. . . . The court might well have proscribed extra-judicial statements by any lawyer, party, witness or court official which divulged prejudicial matters . . . the court could also have requested the appropriate city and county officials to promulgate a regulation with respect to dissemination of information about the case by their employees. In addition, reporters who wrote or broadcast prejudicial stories could have been warned as to the impropriety of publishing material not introduced in the proceedings.[16]

The Supreme Court made it quite clear in the *Sheppard* decision that it holds the trial judge responsible for ensuring that the defendant's rights are not jeopardized by prejudicial press publicity. While the court was critical of the press's behavior, no suggestion was made that the judicial system launch an attack on the press. Nevertheless, at a meeting following the decision, a professor of law, in explaining the high court's opinion in *Sheppard,* suggested that the court had proposed that judges use restrictive orders and the contempt power to control the press. Justice Clark, who was at the same meeting, told the assembled trial lawyers that the professor misinterpreted the court's ruling:

> The Court never held up contempt and it may well be that it will never hold up contempt because the restraint is too stringent. . . . The Court's opinion never mentioned any guidelines for the press. . . . I am not proposing that you jerk a newspaper reporter into the courtroom and hold him in contempt. We do not have to jeopardize freedom of the press.[17]

"I am not proposing that you jerk a newspaper reporter into the courtroom and hold him in contempt."

As we will see shortly, the remarks by Justice Clark were soon forgotten.

Two years after the ruling in *Sheppard* v. *Maxwell,* the American Bar Association proposed that trial judges use court orders (restrictive orders) to control the public statements and activities of the many participants in a trial—the prosecutor, witnesses, defense attorneys, jurors, and others. (The document containing this proposal is known as the Reardon Report.) The bar association also recommended that judges use the contempt power against any persons who knowingly violated a valid judicial order not to disseminate information about the case. No state court system ever officially adopted the ABA recommendations, but the suggestions were taken to heart by many individual judges. Restrictive court orders became a common tool

16. *Sheppard* v. *Maxwell,* 384 U.S. 333 (1966).
17. Friendly and Goldfarb, *Crime and Publicity.*

420

for a judge who sought to control the publicity about a pending criminal trial. One observer estimated that in the 10 years between 1966 and 1976, trial courts issued almost 175 restrictive orders, 39 of which prohibited the press from reporting or commenting on some aspect of a pending criminal case. In addition, nearly all the federal courts adopted standing orders regarding publicity in criminal cases.

Court orders aimed at blocking the flow of information about a legal proceeding fall into one of two categories. First, there are orders aimed directly at the press, prohibiting newspapers, magazines, and radio and television stations from printing or broadcasting specific information about a case. The second kind of restrictive order is aimed at the participants in the trial. It endeavors to stop the attorneys or witnesses or police or whomever from making statements or releasing information regarding the case. If the information is not made public, the press will be unable to publish it. Or so the theory goes. The Supreme Court has sharply limited the application of the first type of restrictive order, the one aimed at the press.[18] Fewer limitations have been placed on restrictive orders directed at trial participants. Let's explore both kinds of orders.

RESTRICTIVE ORDERS AIMED AT THE PRESS

There is no such thing as a typical restrictive order; in fact, that is one of the virtues seen in them by judges. Each order can be fashioned to fit the case at hand. They are often quite comprehensive. Orders aimed at the press usually limit the press coverage of certain specific details about a case; a defendant's confession or prior criminal record, for example. Orders aimed at the participants in a trial are usually much broader, forbidding comments by attorneys, witnesses, and others about any aspect of the case. In 1975 another sensational murder case began, one that would ultimately bring the issue of pretrial publicity and gag orders before the Supreme Court.

Erwin Simants was arrested and charged in North Platte, Neb., with the murder of all six members of the Henry Kellie family. Like the *Sheppard* case, the arrest of Simants caught the eye of the national news media, and local judge Hugh Stuart had his hands full with scores of reporters from around the state and the nation. Stuart responded by issuing a restrictive order barring the publication or broadcast of a wide range of information that he said would be prejudicial to Simants. The order was later modified by the Nebraska Supreme Court to prohibit only the reporting of the existence and nature of any confessions or admissions Simants might have made to police or any third party and any other information "strongly implicative" of the accused. The order was to stand in effect until a jury was chosen.

The press in the state appealed the publication ban to the U.S. Supreme Court, and in June of 1976 the high court ruled that Judge Stuart's order was an unconstitutional prior restraint on the press. All nine members of the court agreed that Judge Stuart's court order was a violation of the First Amendment. But five members of the court ruled that such an order might be permissible in other circumstances, where the "gravity of the evil, discounted by its improbability, justifies such an invasion of free speech as is necessary to avoid the danger."[19]

18. *Nebraska Press Association* v. *Stuart,* 427 U.S. 539 (1976).
19. *Nebraska Press Association* v. *Stuart,* 427 U.S. 539 (1976).

Chief Justice Warren Burger, who wrote the majority opinion, outlined a three-part test to be used to evaluate whether a restrictive order that limited the press would pass First Amendment scrutiny. He said that such an order could only be constitutionally justified if:

1. Intense and pervasive publicity concerning the case is certain.
2. No other alternative measure might mitigate the effects of the pretrial publicity.
3. The restrictive order will in fact effectively prevent prejudicial material from reaching potential jurors.

Prior restraint is the exception, not the rule, Chief Justice Burger wrote. There must be a clear and present danger to the defendant's rights before such a restrictive order can be constitutionally permitted, he said. In Simants' case, Burger said, while there was heavy publicity about the matter, there was no evidence that Judge Stuart had considered the efficacy of other remedies to compensate for this publicity. Also, the small community was filled with rumors about Simants and what he had told the police. Burger expressed serious doubts whether the restrictive order would have in fact kept prejudicial information out of public hands.

NEBRASKA PRESS ASSOCIATION TEST FOR RESTRICTIVE ORDERS AIMED AT THE PRESS

1. There must be intense and pervasive publicity about the case.
2. No other alternative measure might mitigate the effects of the pretrial publicity.
3. The restrictive order will in fact effectively prevent prejudicial publicity from reaching potential jurors.

Of the remaining four members of the court, Justices Stewart, Brennan, and Marshall stated that such prior restraints against the press would not be constitutional under any circumstances. Justice White implied that he agreed with that notion, but since he was not compelled to answer that question in the case before the court, he would wait until another day to face the issue.

Please note, the Supreme Court did not declare restrictive orders aimed only at *trial participants* to be unconstitutional. This issue was not raised in the trial, but it is assumed that courts have much broader power to limit what attorneys, police, and other trial participants can say about a case out of court. "Guidelines on Fair Trial/Free Press," issued by the United States Judicial Conference, for example, specifically recommends that federal courts adopt rules that limit public discussion of criminal cases by attorneys and court personnel and suggests that courts issue special rules in sensational criminal cases to bar extrajudicial comments by all trial participants. But, in light of the ruling in *Nebraska Press Association* v. *Stuart,* the guidelines state:

> No rule of court or judicial order should be promulgated by a United States district court which would prohibit representatives of the news media from broadcasting or publishing any information in their possession relating to a criminal case.

In both 1978 and 1979 the Supreme Court issued opinions in cases that had the effect of reinforcing the rule from the *Nebraska Press Association* decision; that is, restrictions on what the press may publish are to be tolerated only in very rare circumstances. In 1978 the high court prohibited the state of Virginia from punishing the Virginian Pilot newspaper for publishing an accurate story regarding the confidential proceedings of a state judicial review commission.[20] A Virginia state statute authorized the commission to hear complaints of a judge's disability or misconduct, and because of the sensitive nature of such hearings, the Virginia law closed the proceedings to the public and the press. The state argued that confidentiality was necessary to encourage the filing of complaints and the testimony of witnesses, to protect the judge from the injury that might result from the publication of unwarranted or unexamined charges, and to maintain confidence in the judiciary that might be undermined by the publication of groundless charges. While acknowledging the desirability of confidentiality, the Supreme Court nevertheless ruled against the state. Chief Justice Burger, writing for a unanimous court, stated that the "publication Virginia seeks to punish under its statute lies near the core of the First Amendment, and the Commonwealth's interests advanced by the imposition of criminal sanctions are insufficient to justify the actual and potential encroachments on freedom of speech and of the press." The court did acknowledge that the state commission could certainly meet in secret and that its reports and materials could be kept confidential. But while the press has no right to gain access to such information, once it possesses the information, it cannot be punished for its publication. In this sense the court followed the *Nebraska Press Association* rule limiting restraints placed on the press's right to publish.

In 1979 the high court declared unconstitutional a West Virginia statute that made it a crime for a newspaper to publish, without the written approval of the juvenile court, the name of a youth charged as a juvenile offender.[21] Again Chief Justice Burger wrote the opinion for the court and stressed the fact that once the press has legally obtained truthful information, it cannot be stopped from its publication. In this case two Charleston, W.Va., newspapers published the name of a 14-year-old boy who was arrested for the shooting death of a 15-year-old student. Reporters for the newspapers got the name from persons who had witnessed the shooting. "If the information is lawfully obtained," the chief justice wrote, "the state may not punish its publication except when necessary to further an interest more substantial than is present here."

In the past two decades, in light of these three rulings, the number of restrictive orders aimed at the news media has dwindled substantially. If these orders are issued by a trial judge, they are typically overturned in rapid order on appeal. Here are examples of some cases.

The Utah Supreme Court struck down a gag order aimed at the Salt Lake City media that prohibited the media from referring to a defendant in a 1981 rape trial as the "Sugarhouse rapist." Ronald D. Easthope, the man on trial, had been convicted in the early 1970s for a

"If the information is lawfully obtained, the state may not punish its publication except when necessary to further an interest more substantial than is present here."

---

20. *Landmark Communications* v. *Virginia,* 435 U.S. 829 (1978).
21. *Smith* v. *Daily Mail Publishing Co.,* 443 U.S. 97 (1979).

series of rapes in the Sugarhouse area of Salt Lake City. He was arrested again for rape after he was paroled. The state's high court first outlined the three standards raised in the *Nebraska Press Association* case:

1. Did the publicity threaten his right to a fair trial?
2. Would measures short of the judge's restrictive order ensure the defendant a fair trial?
3. Will the restraint on the press achieve the desired results?

The state high court said the order was unconstitutional because the court had failed to consider any of these elements. The order was also invalid procedurally because the court had issued the order without notice or hearing. In addition, the state supreme court said, it was hard to see how the term "Sugarhouse rapist" could harm Easthope, since he had admitted his previous crimes in open court.[22]

The Supreme Court of Mississippi in December of 1998 threw out both a contempt citation and a gag order in a case involving the publication of material relating to a defendant's juvenile record.[23] The juvenile record was discussed by the prosecutor at an open sentencing hearing in an effort to convince the judge to impose a maximum sentence on a defendant who had been convicted of manslaughter. The judge told the reporter, Cynthia Jeffries of the Delta Democrat Times, not to include any material about the juvenile record in her story. Three days after the hearing the newspaper carried a story containing this information. Jeffries was arrested and brought before the judge, who found her in contempt for violating the order and sentenced her to three days in jail. The state's high court said the judge's action was improper in two ways. First, the judge treated this as a direct contempt—a contempt committed in the presence of the court (see page 396)—when in fact the contempt was committed outside the courtroom as the article was published. Jeffries should have had the benefit of procedural safeguards that accompany charges of an indirect or constructive contempt, the court ruled. Second, the court order regarding the juvenile record was invalid. The judge did not even consider the *Nebraska Press Association* test, the court ruled. The order should not have been issued had that test been applied, since it would not have been effective in protecting the defendant's rights. The courtroom was full of other people during the hearing, all of whom heard the same information the newspaper published. Also, the court could have used other means to avoid the problem in the first place, such as having the discussion about the juvenile record in the judge's chambers, away from the open courtroom.[24]

One case in which a restrictive order was upheld occurred in Utah, where that state's high court permitted a trial court to bar the news media from reporting that a defendant was allegedly associated with organized crime. The press had reported such matters both before and after the trial began, and the court had been forced to conduct a second voir dire of the impaneled jurors. The court had asked the press to voluntarily restrain the publication of such

---

22. *KUTV* v. *Conder*, 668 P. 2d 513 (1983).
23. *Jeffries* v. *Mississippi*, 724 So. 2d 897 (1998).
24. *Jeffries* v. *Mississippi*, 724 So. 2d 897 (1998).

material, but the news media had refused. The trial court said that waiver of a jury trial was too high a price for the defendant to pay and that sequestration of the jury during the long trial might prejudice the jury against the defendant. Strong admonitions to jurors might also result in such prejudice, the trial court concluded. The state supreme court ruled that the judge had met the burden of the *Nebraska Press Association* test and permitted the court order to stand.[25]

Although the law regarding gag orders issued against the press is generally unambiguous today, some trial judges still believe that circumstances exist in a case they are trying that justify issuing a restrictive order. Just such a case occurred in September of 1995 when U.S. District Judge John Feikens barred Business Week magazine from publishing an article it had prepared based on sealed court documents. The documents had been sealed by Feikens during litigation between Procter & Gamble Co. and Bankers Trust Co. Procter & Gamble was suing the bank for using improper sales tactics to sell the company derivative securities. The giant home products company said it suffered a $100 million loss on the securities.

A Business Week reporter, Linda Himelstein, was given copies of the sealed documents by one of the lawyers from the law firm representing Bankers Trust. The lawyer later said he did not realize the documents had been sealed. Upon discovering that the magazine was about to publish a story based on the documents, both litigants asked Judge Feikens to issue the restrictive order. He complied with this request and the order was issued three hours before the magazine was to go to press. Instead of asking Judge Feikens to reconsider the order or to hold a hearing on the matter, Business Week challenged the order at the U.S. Court of Appeals for the 6th Circuit. A three-judge panel dismissed the appeal.[26] Associate Justice John Paul Stevens of the U.S. Supreme Court also refused to grant relief in the case. The high court jurist said the magazine should have first asked Judge Feikens for a hearing so he could gather relevant facts in the case and consider the merits of the First Amendment arguments.[27]

Three weeks after the order was issued, Judge Feikens unsealed the relevant documents and permitted Business Week and other news media to publish stories related to the contents of these materials. Judge Feikens refused, however, to throw out his original order. He affirmed in court his right to issue the ban because of the confidential nature of the materials in question.[28] Six months later the U.S. Court of Appeals for the 6th Circuit ruled 2–1 that Judge Feikens had been wrong to bar the magazine from publishing the story. "At no time," the court ruled, "even to the point of entering a permanent injunction after two temporary restraining orders, did the District Court appear to realize that it was engaging in a practice that, under all but the most exceptional circumstances, violates the Constitution: preventing a news organization from publishing information in its possession on a matter of public concern." In the circumstances existing in this case, the appellate tribunal ruled, the court had no power to issue the restraining order.[29]

---

25. *KUTV* v. *Wilkinson,* 686 P. 2d 456 (1984).
26. Carmody, "Business Week Files Appeal."
27. *McGraw-Hill Cos.* v. *Procter & Gamble Co.,* 116 S. Ct. 6 (1995).
28. *Procter & Gamble Co.* v. *Bankers Trust Co.,* 900 F. Supp. 186 (1995).
29. *Procter & Gamble Co.* v. *Banker's Trust Co.,* 78 F. 3d 219 (1996). See also Peterson, "Court Voids Restraint."

RESTRICTIVE ORDERS AIMED AT TRIAL PARTICIPANTS

It is very difficult for judges to stop the press from publishing or broadcasting information about a case that has been legally obtained. As an alternative, many courts have sought to instead gag the participants in the trial. If the press has nothing to report, it can't publicize prejudicial material.

Typical of such orders are the ones handed down in the civil action brought against O.J. Simpson by the families of Ron Goldman and Nicole Brown Simpson, and the criminal trials of Timothy McVeigh and Terry L. Nichols for the bombing in Oklahoma City. In the Simpson trial Judge Hirashi Fujisaki cited the press coverage of Simpson's criminal trial when he issued his order barring the attorneys, parties, or witnesses under the control of the lawyers from discussing the wrongful death case in public or with members of the press. The order was also extended to employees and agents or representatives of the lawyers.[30] In the trials of McVeigh and Nichols the court barred attorneys and support personnel involved in the trial from releasing any information or opinions about the proceeding that could interfere with the defendants' right to a fair trial.[31] Judge Matsch's order contained a careful list of topics, including statements about

- the defendants' prior criminal records, character, reputation;
- the existence or content of any statements given to the police by the defendants;
- the defendants' performance on tests or refusal to take tests;
- the identity, testimony, or credibility of prospective witnesses;
- the possibility of a plea agreement; and
- any opinion as to guilt or innocence or as to the merits of the case or the quality or quantity of evidence in the case.

These kinds of restrictive orders are typically upheld by appellate courts. For example, the 4th U.S. Circuit Court of Appeals gave its approval to a restrictive order that stopped the witnesses in a highly publicized trial of members of the Ku Klux Klan and the Nazi party from discussing their testimony with reporters. The publication of the proposed testimony could endanger the fair trial rights of the defendants, the court ruled. But judges must be careful about the manner in which they shape these orders.[32] During the World Trade Center bombing trial in New York, Judge Kevin Duffy barred the lawyers for all parties from discussing any aspect of the case. "There will be no more statements [in the press, on TV, on radio, or in any other electronic media] issued by either side or their agents," Judge Duffy said. "The next time I pick up a paper and see a quotation from any of you, you had best be prepared to have some money. The first fine will be $200. Thereafter, the fines will be squared," he said. The threat of a $40,000 fine could certainly have a chilling effect on freedom of expression. The 2nd U.S. Circuit Court of Appeals, while sympathetic to Judge Duffy's problems, nevertheless ruled that the order was inappropriate. "The limitations on attorney speech should be no broader

---

30. *Rufo* v. *Simpson,* 24 M.L.R. 2213 (1996).
31. *U.S.* v. *McVeigh,* 931 F. Supp. 756 (1996).
32. in re *Russell,* 726 F. 2d 1007 (1984).

than necessary to protect the integrity of the judicial system and the defendant's right to a fair trial," the court ruled. This order was too broad. In addition, the judge made no finding that an alternative to this kind of blanket order would not work as well.[33]

Traditionally courts have barred third parties from intervening in a legal dispute. If your neighbor beats his wife, you cannot go to court and sue the husband for battery. You do not have an interest in the case; you lack what the courts call standing. This dispute has no effect on you. The rule regarding standing was a problem for the press for many years as newspapers and broadcasting stations attempted to challenge gag orders levied against the participants in the trial. Typically a court would rule that the press lacked standing; the restrictive order did not affect the reporters and editors. But lately, some judges have changed their minds, accepting the argument that if the participants are not permitted to talk about the case, this will limit the news that can be published. And this limitation does affect the press.[34] When the press is given the legal standing or right to challenge the restrictive order on First Amendment grounds, then the trial court must justify its court order under the standards applied in the *Nebraska Press Association* case: There is intense and pervasive publicity, nothing but the gag order will mitigate this publicity, and the order will in fact be effective.

The Ohio Supreme Court voided a restrictive order issued by a trial court that blocked all court personnel, attorneys, and law enforcement officials from commenting on matters relating to a sensational murder case. The state supreme court said the judge could set rules for the court personnel, but unless the lower court demonstrated that pervasive publicity endangered the right to a fair trial and that nothing short of a gag order would solve the problem, the restrictive order against the lawyers and police officials was not permissible.[35] In 1996 the 5th U.S. Circuit Court of Appeals vacated an unusual restrictive order issued by a U.S. district court judge in a case involving litigation to try to desegregate schools in the East Baton Rouge parish in Louisiana. Members of a newly elected school board indicated they were interested in working with the court in formulating a plan to end both the segregation and the litigation. Board members said they wanted to have private meetings with their attorneys and their staff to discuss these plans. Ostensibly to ensure the privacy of these sessions, the court issued an order prohibiting members of the board, its attorneys, school district employees, and other agents from discussing any parts of the new plan with persons other than the parties to the litigation. When the press challenged the order, the district court rejected its protests, noting that "there are some things better discussed and argued about in private." The Court of Appeals said the order was far broader than it needed to be to ensure the privacy of the discussions. It also interfered with the rights of the press to gather the news, rights that can be restricted only when justified by a strong governmental interest or individual rights. No such justification was present in this case, the court said.[36]

---

33. *U.S.* v. *Salameh,* 992 F. 2d 445 (1993).

34. See, for example, *Connecticut Magazine* v. *Moraghan,* 676 F. Supp. 38 (1987) and in re *Dow Jones,* 842 F. 2d 603 (1988).

35. *Ohio ex rel National Broadcasting Co., Inc.* v. *Lake County Court of Common Pleas,* 556 N.E. 2d 1120 (1990).

36. *Davis* v. *East Baton Rouge Parish School District,* 78 F. 3d 920 (1996).

These examples do not mean lawyers may not be barred from making comments about a pending court case. The U.S. Supreme Court made that clear in a 1991 ruling that focused not on a gag order but on an alleged violation of general court rules that applied to attorneys. A lawyer named Dominic Gentile, who represented a client charged with taking money and drugs from a safety deposit box rented by undercover police agents, held a press conference in which he claimed that police were using his client as a scapegoat. Gentile said his client was innocent, that a police officer was the likely thief who took the money and drugs, and described some of the witnesses for the prosecution in the case as drug dealers. Gentile's client was acquitted, but the Nevada Supreme Court ruled that the attorney's comments at the press conference violated a court rule that limits what an attorney can say about a pending case.

The rule prohibits attorneys in a criminal case from making prejudicial statements about the character, credibility, reputation, or criminal record of a party, suspect, or witness. The rule did provide a so-called safe haven for lawyers who were permitted to "elaborate the general nature" of the defense. The press joined in the defense of the attorney, seeing the Nevada rule as another impediment to gaining access to information about the judicial system.

In a 5–4 ruling, the high court ruled that states may prohibit out-of-court statements by attorneys if they have a substantial likelihood of materially prejudicing the proceeding. "Because lawyers have special access to information through discovery and client communications, their extrajudicial statements pose a threat to the fairness of a pending proceeding since lawyers' statements are likely to be received as especially authoritative," Chief Justice Rehnquist wrote for a five-person majority that included Justices White, O'Connor, Scalia, and Souter. However, Justice O'Connor joined the four dissenters in a separate opinion in the case, and these five justices ruled that the Nevada rule was unconstitutional because it was too vague. The so-called safe-haven provision, wrote Justice Kennedy for the five-person majority, contained terms that were so imprecise that they failed to give fair notice of what is permitted and what is forbidden, raising a real possibility of discriminatory enforcement. "The right to explain the general nature of the defense without elaboration provides insufficient guidance because 'general' and 'elaboration' are both classic terms of degree," Kennedy wrote.[37] Although the rule was struck down by the high court, Nevada (and other states with similar rules) can simply refashion the general exception or safe-haven clause with more precise language and continue to bar certain statements by attorneys in pending criminal cases.

Controlling comments to the press by jurors following a trial has grown as a judicial problem in recent years. A judge can certainly forbid any juror from talking with reporters during a trial, before jury deliberations are completed. But some reporters like to talk with jurors following a trial to try to uncover the reasons for a particular jury verdict. Today it is not unusual for tabloid television programs and tabloid newspapers to offer jurors in particularly sensational trials large fees for their comments. Many people believe such juror interviews are detrimental to the legal system. "It is now assumed that jurors must deliberate in secret so that they may communicate freely with one another, secure in the knowledge that what they say

Today it is not unusual for tabloid television programs and tabloid newspapers to offer jurors in particularly sensational trials large fees for their comments.

37. *Gentile v. Nevada State Bar,* 111 S. Ct. 2770 (1991).

will not be passed along to others," noted Yale law professor Abraham S. Goldstein.[38] If only a single juror reveals the comments or ideas of other jurors, the sanctity of the jury room has surely been breached.

Judges have tried a variety of schemes to protect juror privacy. Some judges have tried to solve this problem by denying the press and the public access to the names and addresses of the jurors (see pages 444–445). Courts have gone so far as to shield all identifying information about the jurors, such as names, addresses, professions, ages, and so on. The members of such an anonymous jury are referred to only by number. For example, before the so-called Unabomber, Ted Kaczynski, pleaded guilty, all identifying information about the 12 jurors and six alternates selected to hear his case was confidential. Anonymous juries were also used in both Oklahoma City bombing prosecutions and in the trials of the Branch Davidian survivors in Waco, Oliver North, and the World Trade Center bombers. First Amendment advocates note that the anonymous jury, once a rarity, seems to be becoming far more commonplace today.[39] But others note that this kind of jury was typically used in the past with very high-profile trials, and the nation has simply experienced a great many more such trials in recent years.

Other judges have issued restrictive orders barring the news media from questioning jurors about their deliberations. In November of 1997 the 5th U.S. Circuit Court of Appeals upheld such an order in a high-profile racketeering trial. Trial judge Sarah Vance told jurors they could not be interviewed "by anyone concerning the deliberations of the jury" unless she issued an order permitting it. The appellate court said the order was justified, considering the intense media scrutiny of the trial. The U.S. Supreme Court refused to review the decision.[40]

But judges have only limited discretion in this matter. For example, "The Handbook for Jurors," published by the Judicial Conference of the United States, specifically says that it should be up to each juror to decide whether he or she talks with the press following a trial. Some appellate courts have not permitted trial judges to ban such interviews. The 9th U.S. Circuit Court of Appeals struck down a lower court order that prohibited anyone from interviewing jurors after a trial. The order was issued by the trial court to minimize harassment of jurors, according to the trial judge, but the Court of Appeals ruled that not all jurors might regard media interviews as harassing.[41] And in 1989 the 11th U.S. Circuit Court of Appeals ruled that an order barring jurors who had been dismissed after a trial from speaking with anyone about the case was far too broad.[42] The jurors had failed to reach a verdict in a widely publicized trial that lasted eight months. A mistrial was declared, and the prosecution said it would reprosecute the seven defendants. The Court of Appeals said a narrow or specific ban on juror comments would be tolerated. For example, it would be permissible for the trial court to forbid jurors to talk about what other jurors said during the deliberations, or how other jurors voted during the discussions about the case. Given there was a mistrial, the court said,

38. Goldstein, "Jury Secrecy and the Media," 295.
30. Kirtley, *The Privacy Paradox.*
40. *U.S.* v. *Cleveland,* 128 F. 3d 267 (1997).
41. *United States* v. *Sherman,* 581 F. 2d 1358 (1978).
42. in re *Dallas Morning News Co.,* 916 F. 2d 205 (1989).

a somewhat broader than normal gag order was possible. But the instruction to the jurors in this case, "You simply are not to talk about this case," was too broad.

Finally, the U.S. Supreme Court ruled in 1990 that a Florida statute prohibiting witnesses who testified before a grand jury from revealing what they had said, even after the grand jury's term had expired, was unconstitutional.[43] Proceedings before grand juries are ultrasecret. Nothing but the true bill, or indictment, issued by a grand jury is a part of the public record. A reporter was working on a story when he uncovered information the prosecutor believed the grand jury should hear. The reporter was subpoenaed and testified before the grand jury. After he had given his testimony, he sought to write a news story about his investigation as well as his experiences before the grand jury. But the statute blocked his effort. So he sued in U.S. district court to have the law declared to be unconstitutional. Ultimately, the Supreme Court did just that.

Chief Justice William Rehnquist wrote that traditionally courts have taken very seriously the need for secrecy in grand jury proceedings. But, he said, "we have recognized that the invocation of grand jury interests is not some talisman that dissolves all constitutional protections." In this case, the chief justice said, the situation involved a reporter's right to divulge information of which he was in possession before he testified before the grand jury, not information he had gained as a result of his participation in the grand jury proceeding. Citing the ruling in *Smith* v. *Daily*[44] (see page 423), Rehnquist said the state could not punish a journalist for publishing information that he or she had legally obtained. While important interests were at stake in maintaining a veil around the activities of a grand jury, these interests in this case were insufficient to outweigh the First Amendment interests.

Restrictive orders that bar the press from publishing information about a criminal case have ceased to be a serious problem for journalists. Orders that limit what trial participants can say remain a nuisance, however, and probably do not serve the judicial system as well as many observers might imagine. Rumors tend to thrive in an atmosphere in which the release of accurate information is stifled. It would be better perhaps to provide journalists bound to publish something about a case with accurate and truthful statements rather than push them to report what is ground out by a rumor mill.

SUMMARY

In some instances trial courts have attempted to limit the publication of prejudicial information about a case by issuing court orders restricting what the press may publish or what the trial participants may publicly say about a case. These restrictive orders grew out of a famous U.S. Supreme Court decision in the mid-1960s that ruled a trial judge is responsible for controlling the publicity about a case.

In 1976 the Supreme Court ruled that the press may not be prohibited from publishing information it has legally obtained about a criminal case unless these conditions are met:

1. Intense and pervasive publicity about the case is certain.

43. *Butterworth* v. *Smith,* 110 S. Ct. 1376 (1990).
44. *Smith* v. *Daily Mail Publishing Co.,* 443 U.S. 97 (1979).

2. No other reasonable alternative is likely to mitigate the effects of the pretrial publicity.
3. The restrictive order will prevent prejudicial material from reaching the jurors.

In two subsequent rulings the high court reaffirmed its 1976 decision that confidential information legally obtained by the press may be published. These cases involved the name of a juvenile suspect in a murder case and the names of judges whose conduct had been reviewed by a confidential state judicial commission.

Although judges may still limit what trial participants say publicly about a case, even these restrictive orders have come under constitutional scrutiny in recent years.

BIBLIOGRAPHY

Buddenbaum, Judith M., et al. *Pretrial Publicity and Juries: A Review of Research.* Research Report no. 11. School of Journalism, Indiana University, 1981.

Bush, Chilton R., ed. *Free Press and Fair Trial: Some Dimensions of the Problem.* Athens: University of Georgia Press, 1971.

Carmody, Deirdre. "Business Week Files Appeal to Supreme Court." *The New York Times,* 20 September 1995, A10.

Drechsel, Robert E. "An Alternative View of Media-Judiciary Relations: What the Non-Legal Evidence Suggests about the Fair Trial–Free Press Issue." *Hofstra Law Review* 18 (1989):1.

Friendly, Alfred, and Ronald Goldfarb. *Crime and Publicity.* New York: Random House, Vintage Books, 1968.

Goldstein, Abraham S. "Jury Secrecy and the Media: The Problem of the Postverdict Interview." *University of Illinois Law Review* 1993 (1993):295.

Kirtley, Jane, ed. *The Privacy Paradox.* Arlington, Va.: The Reporters Committee for Freedom of the Press, 1998.

Labaton, Stephen. "Lessons of Simpson Case Are Reshaping the Law." *The New York Times,* 6 October 1995, A1.

Landau, Jack C. "The Challenge of the Communications Media." *American Bar Association Journal* 62 (1976):55.

Mansnerus, Laura. "Under Fire, Jury System Faces Overhaul." *The New York Times,* 4 November 1995, A7.

Minow, Newton, and Fred Cate. "Who Is an Impartial Juror in an Age of Mass Media?" *The American University Law Review* 40 (1991):631.

Pember, Don R. "Does Pretrial Publicity Really Hurt?" *Columbia Journalism Review,* September/October 1984, 16.

Peterson, Iver. "Court Voids Restraint on Business Week." *The New York Times,* 6 March 1996, C12.

U.S. Senate Subcommittee on Improvement in Judicial Machinery of the Senate Judiciary Committee. *Hearings on Federal Jury Selection.* 90th Cong., 1st sess., 1967, 581.

Free Press/Fair Trial
Closed Judicial Proceedings

Faced with Supreme Court rulings that blocked the use of restrictive orders to stop press coverage of the criminal justice system, judges in the 1980s began to close judicial proceedings to deny to reporters information that may be prejudicial to the defendant's fair trial rights. The press challenged these closures, and as with the restrictive orders, appellate courts found that such closures usually violated the First Amendment. This issue, as well as a discussion of voluntary press guidelines and the right to take photographic and electronic recording equipment into the courtroom, is the focus of this chapter.

CLOSED PROCEEDINGS AND SEALED DOCUMENTS

The closure of pretrial and even trial proceedings, which began as isolated events in the late 1970s, became commonplace in the early 1980s. Judges who lacked faith in the traditional trial level devices designed to mitigate the effects of pretrial publicity (i.e., change of venue, voir dire) had been frustrated in their efforts to control such publicity with restrictive orders. The Supreme Court said time and again that reporters could not be stopped from publishing or broadcasting information they had gathered about a case. But the high court had said little about whether reporters could be denied access to such information in the first place. Closure of judicial proceedings in particular seemed to be a simple solution to the problems faced by trial judges. Closure would keep prejudicial information out of the hands of reporters. The press quickly objected to these efforts by judges to close the courthouse doors. And appellate courts once again sustained these First Amendment challenges. In a series of important rulings the Supreme Court and lower federal courts have ruled that there is virtually an unqualified right for any citizen, including reporters, to attend a criminal or civil trial, and there is a strong but qualified right for the press to attend most other kinds of judicial proceedings and to inspect most court documents.

ACCESS TO TRIALS

In 1980 the Supreme Court of the United States ruled in a 7–1 decision (Justice Powell took no part in this case) that the right of the public and the press to attend a criminal trial is guaranteed by both the common law and the First Amendment to the U.S. Constitution. The ruling, *Richmond Newspapers* v. *Virginia*,[1] stemmed from a state court ruling in a Virginia criminal trial. In March 1976 John Stevenson was indicted for murder. He was tried and convicted of second-degree murder, but his conviction was reversed. A second trial ended in a mistrial when a juror asked to be excused in the midst of the hearing. A third trial also resulted in a mistrial because a prospective juror told other prospective jurors about Stevenson's earlier conviction on the same charges. This exchange was not revealed until after the trial had started. As proceedings were about to begin for the fourth time in late 1978, the defense asked that the trial be closed. The prosecution did not object and the court closed the trial. Richmond newspapers protested the closure to no avail. An appeal came before the U.S. Supreme Court in February 1980.

Chief Justice Burger wrote the court's opinion, noting that "through its evolution the trial has been open to all who cared to observe." A presumption of open hearings is the very nature of a criminal trial under our system of justice, the chief justice added. Although there is no specific provision in the Bill of Rights or the Constitution to support the open trial, the expressly guaranteed freedoms in the First Amendment "share a common core purpose of assuring freedom of communication on matters relating to the functioning of government," Burger wrote. "In guaranteeing freedoms such as those of speech and press the First Amendment can be read as protecting the right of everyone to attend trials so as to give meaning to

---

1. 448 U.S. 555 (1980).

those explicit guarantees," he added. The First Amendment, then, the chief justice noted, prohibits the government from summarily closing courtroom doors, which had been open to the public at the time that amendment was adopted.

But the chief justice refused to see the First Amendment as an absolute bar to closed trials. He noted that in some circumstances, which he explicitly declined to define at that time, a trial judge could bar the public and the press from a trial in the interest of the fair administration of justice. But, while the court did not outline such circumstances, it was clear from both the tone and the language of the chief justice's opinion that in his mind such circumstances would indeed be unusual. Justices White, Stevens, Brennan, Marshall, Stewart, and Blackmun all concurred with the chief justice in five separate opinions. All but Stewart went further in guaranteeing access to trials than did Chief Justice Burger. Justice Rehnquist dissented.

In 1984 the U.S. Court of Appeals for the 3rd Circuit ruled that civil proceedings are also presumptively open to the public and the press. In *Publicker Industries* v. *Cohen,*[2] a lawsuit involving a corporate proxy fight, the court noted that a "survey of authorities identifies as features of the civil justice system many of those attributes of the criminal justice system on which the Supreme Court relied in holding that the First Amendment guarantees to the public and to the press the right of access to criminal trials." The right is not absolute, the court said, but absent a clear showing that closing the trial serves an important governmental interest and that closing the trial is the only way to serve this interest, the civil proceeding should be open. In 1999 the California Supreme Court became the first state high court to make the same ruling, that the press and the public have a constitutional right of access to a civil proceeding.[3]

There are, of course, exceptions to the rule that trials are presumptively open to the press and the public. Juvenile hearings or trials traditionally have not been open to the public. Courts in many states continue to try to shield the identity of the juvenile offender. Important segments of the juvenile justice system are constructed on the principle of rehabilitating young offenders, and many juvenile authorities argue that revealing the name of the offender works against such rehabilitation efforts. Appellate courts continue to support this rationale. The Vermont Supreme Court supported a trial judge's decision to bar public access to a proceeding in which the judge was to consider the legal status (adult or juvenile) of a 15-year-old boy accused of murdering one girl and assaulting another. Publicity is often seen as a reward for hard-core juvenile offenders, the court noted.[4] The Ohio Supreme Court supported the closure of a juvenile custody hearing, saying there was no qualified right of access to juvenile court proceedings to determine if a child is abused, neglected, or dependent, or to determine custody of a minor child.[5]

The 8th U.S. Circuit Court of Appeals ruled that it was proper for a trial court to close a hearing set to determine whether a disabled student who threatened classmates with a pistol could be expelled from school. The appellate court cited the privacy rights of the student and his classmates guaranteed under federal law as justification for closing the hearing and sealing

The First Amendment, then, the chief justice noted, prohibits the government from summarily closing courtroom doors, which had been open to the public at the time that amendment was adopted.

2. 733 F. 2d 1059 (1984).
3. *NBC Subsidiary (KNBC-TV Inc.)* v. *Superior Court,* 980 P. 2d 337 (1999).
4. in re *J. S.,* 438 A. 2d 1125 (1981).
5. in re *T. R.,* 52 Ohio St. 3d 6 (1990).

the transcript.[6] Finally, the Court of Appeals for the District of Columbia Circuit ruled that all reporters should be barred from the trial of a 14-year-old charged with killing another juvenile. Reporters covering the case had previously agreed that they would not divulge the juvenile's name or other identifying information in return for permission to cover the court hearing. This agreement is a common one for the press to make in juvenile cases. But the Wall Street Journal published a story containing details that revealed the identity of the boy, defense lawyers charged. They sought to bar the press from the trial. The trial judge ruled that only reporters from the Journal would be barred, but on an appeal by the defense in the case, the District's high court said all reporters should be banned because readers and viewers would be able to determine the boy's name by simply referring back to the Wall Street Journal story.[7]

But while courts in many states continue to bar the press and public from juvenile hearings, courts in other states are opening the doors to such proceedings. At least 20 states now open most juvenile court proceedings to the public, although reporters are often asked not to publish the names of young offenders.[8] In Washington, for example, the state has divided the juvenile hearings into two groups: dependency and custody hearings, which are presumptively closed to press and public; and offender hearings, which are presumptively open. As juvenile crime becomes more of an issue in the United States, pressure mounts on state authorities to bring the juvenile justice system into the open. The 3rd U.S. Circuit Court of Appeals ruled in 1994 that the federal Juvenile Delinquency Act, the statute that governs the treatment of persons under the age of 18 who violate federal law, does not require that federal juvenile proceedings and records be closed. Rather, federal courts must make rulings regarding the closure of such hearings and records on a case-by-case basis, balancing the interests of all parties involved.[9]

The Supreme Court has ruled that it is permissible for a state to attempt to protect the victim of a sexual assault by permitting the closing of a trial during the victim's testimony. Laws exist in many states that provide for such closure. But these laws can only permit the court to close the proceeding during the testimony; they cannot require that such a closure take place. A Massachusetts statute required closure of a trial during the testimony of a juvenile sex offense victim. The U.S. Supreme Court ruled that the law was unconstitutional. Justice William Brennan agreed that the state has a strong interest to protect the victim in this kind of a case. The law was nevertheless flawed, he said, because it *required* closure of the proceeding. "As compelling as that interest is, it does not justify a mandatory closure rule, for it is clear that the circumstances of the particular case may affect the significance of the [state] interest," Brennan wrote. Under the statute, the trial judge is not permitted to allow testimony in open court, even if the victim desires it, the jurist noted.[10] A 1992 Washington state law that required courts to ensure that the identities of juvenile victims of sexual assault were not disclosed was ruled unconstitutional as well, since it would have required trial judges to close the courtroom during such hearings. The state's high court ruled that the identity of a juvenile victim can be

6. *Webster Groves School District* v. *Pulitzer Publishing Co.,* 898 F. 2d 1371 (1990).

7. in re *J.D.C.,* 594 A. 2d 70 (1991).

8. Eckholm, "A Young Offender," E4.

9. *U.S.* v. *A.D.,* 28 F. 3d 1353 (1994); see also *U.S.* v. *Three Juveniles,* 61 F. 3d 86 (1995).

10. *Globe Newspapers* v. *Superior Court,* 457 U.S. 596 (1982).

protected by a judge through a variety of tactics, but the legislature cannot mandate closure of the courtroom in all cases.[11] Finally, the 10th U.S. Circuit Court of Appeals ruled that before the press and public can be excluded from the courtroom during the testimony of a juvenile rape victim, the trial court must ascertain whether the victim's emotional and psychological condition warrants such an exclusion, as the prosecution asserted in arguments.[12]

Appellate courts usually permit the closure of those portions of a trial during which an undercover police officer testifies. The Appellate Division of the New York Supreme Court ruled in 1997 that a trial court acted properly when it closed the courtroom during the testimony of undercover officers because these police officers continued to work ongoing investigations in the specific area in which the defendant was arrested and they said they feared for their safety if the courtroom remained open during their testimony.[13] But such closure is not automatic. In a 1993 case the state's high court ruled that it was improper for a trial judge to close the court during an undercover officer's testimony based only on the showing that this officer continued to operate undercover in "the Bronx area." The Bronx encompasses 41 square miles and includes 2.1 million people, the court said. Closing a trial based on this interest would in effect require automatic closure every time any undercover officer testified.[14]

CLOSURE OF OTHER HEARINGS

One hundred years ago the criminal judicial process involved a trial, and that was about all. The defendant was brought to court to stand trial. The jury was selected and the trial began. The judge admonished jurors not to talk to anyone about the case and not to read about it in the newspapers or magazines. If there was a question that needed to be resolved and the jury was not supposed to hear this discussion, members of the jury would leave the courtroom until the matter was settled and then return. Today the judicial process involves myriad other kinds of hearings. Most of these hearings are the result of major changes in the manner in which the criminal justice system works, the tremendous expansion of the rights of criminal defendants, and attempts by the judicial system to work more closely with agencies in the state that operate the penal institutions. There are evidentiary or suppression hearings, pretrial detention hearings, plea hearings, presentence and postsentence hearings, and so on. Many of these hearings take place long before the trial begins, weeks before the jury is even selected. Many of these hearings focus on information that may be highly prejudicial to the defendant. At an evidentiary hearing, for example, the court may rule that a key piece of evidence, such as a weapon, is inadmissible at the trial because it was improperly seized by the police. The fact that the defendant had a weapon is certainly prejudicial. If this fact is publicized, some argue, it won't matter that the evidence is barred from trial because the members of the community, the jurors, will already know it exists.

11. *Allied Daily Newspapers* v. *Eikenberry,* 848 P. 2d 1258 (1993).
12. *Davis* v. *Reynolds,* 890 F. 2d 1105 (1989).
13. *New York* v. *Rivera,* 656 NYS 2d 884 (1997); see also *Ayala* v. *Speckard,* 131 F. 3d 62 (1997).
14. *New York* v. *Martinez,* 82 N.Y. 2d 436 (1993).

Before the ruling in *Nebraska Press Association* v. *Stuart*,[15] a judge could use a restrictive order to bar the press from publishing or broadcasting information about the evidence. With that option gone, judges began to close the pretrial hearings. Reporters were barred from these traditionally open proceedings. The press protested, but it was not until 1986, six years after the ruling in Richmond Newspapers, that the Supreme Court ruled that pretrial hearings are presumptively open. In a 7–2 ruling, the court declared that there exists a qualified privilege for the press and the public to attend a pretrial hearing, even in the face of opposition from the defendant. A California trial court had closed the pretrial hearing for Robert Diaz, a nurse accused of killing as many as 12 patients in a hospital in which he worked. The Riverside Press-Enterprise protested the closure, but the California appellate courts ruled that while there was a First Amendment right for the public and press to attend a trial, no corollary right existed to attend a pretrial hearing. The U.S. Supreme Court disagreed. The preliminary hearing may be closed "only if specific findings are made demonstrating that first, there is a substantial probability that the defendant's right to a fair trial will be prejudiced by publicity, and, second, reasonable alternatives to closure cannot adequately protect the defendant's fair trial rights," wrote Chief Justice Burger. Mere risk of prejudice does not automatically justify refusing public access to hearings, Burger stressed. If the judge makes specific findings that the probability of such prejudice does exist, the closure order must be tailored very narrowly to serve that interest. In other words, if only two hours' worth of testimony during a three-day pretrial hearing might cause the probability of prejudice, the hearing should be closed only during those two hours. Trial judges should use other means, where possible, to protect the defendant. "Through voir dire, cumbersome as it is in some circumstances, a court can identify those jurors whose prior knowledge of the case would disable them from rendering an impartial verdict," Burger added.[16] It should be noted that the requirement that the defendant or the state show there is a "substantial probability" of prejudice places a heavy burden on the party seeking closure.

PRESS-ENTERPRISE TEST FOR THE CLOSURE OF PRESUMPTIVELY OPEN JUDICIAL PROCEEDINGS AND DOCUMENTS

1. The party seeking closure, the defendant or the government or sometimes both, must advance an overriding interest that is likely to be harmed if the proceeding or document is open.

2. Whoever seeks the closure must demonstrate that there is a "substantial probability" that this interest will be harmed if the proceeding or document remains open.

3. The trial court must consider reasonable alternatives to closure.

15. 427 U.S. 539 (1976).
16. *Press-Enterprise* v. *Riverside Superior Court*, 478 U.S. 1 (1986).

4. If the judge decides that closure is the only reasonable solution, the closure must be narrowly tailored to restrict no more access than is absolutely necessary.
5. The trial court must make adequate findings to support the closure decision.

The Press-Enterprise *Test*

Before a pretrial hearing may be closed to the press and the public, a trial judge must apply a rather complex test to evaluate the situation at hand. These guidelines have emerged from the high court ruling in the *Press-Enterprise* case and other rulings. First the court must determine whether the kind of hearing involved—a bail hearing or an evidentiary hearing or whatever—is presumptively open or presumptively closed. The answer to this question will determine which party or parties will carry the burden of proof in this dispute. If the court rules that the hearing is presumptively open, then those seeking to close the hearing carry the burden of proving to the court it should be closed. If the hearing is presumptively closed, then those who seek to have it open must convince the court that it should be open. The judge will decide whether the hearing is presumptively open by determining

1. **whether this kind of hearing (or document, if access to a court record is involved) has traditionally and historically been open to the press and public, or**
2. **whether public and press access to this hearing will play a positive role in the functioning of the judicial process.**

If the court determines that this kind of hearing has traditionally been open, *or* that allowing the press and the public to attend the hearing will have a positive impact on the judicial process, then he or she must declare the hearing to be presumptively open. Then it is up to the persons seeking to close the hearing, the defendant or the state, to convince the court that there is a good reason to close it. In doing this, the advocates of closure must

1. **advance an overriding interest that is likely to be harmed if the proceeding remains open or the court permits access to the court document.** Examples of such interests include the right to a fair trial for the defendant, or protection of a witness's privacy. Then the advocate of closure must
2. **prove to the court that if the hearing or document is open to the press and public, there is a *substantial probability* that this interest will be harmed,** that the jury will be prejudiced or the privacy of the witness will be invaded, for example.

If the advocate of closure proves that there is a substantial probability that such harm may occur, then the judge must

3. **consider whether there are reasonable alternatives to closure that might solve the problem.** Perhaps a thorough voir dire or change of venue would reduce the probability of prejudice. Closure of the hearing or the sealing of the document should be a last option, not a first option, considered by the court.

If there are no alternatives, then it is the responsibility of the judge to

4. **narrowly tailor the closure so there is an absolute minimum of interference with the rights of the press and public to attend the hearing or see the document.** A pretrial hearing on evidence might include many issues beyond the single issue that could harm the defendant. The court must close only that portion of the hearing dealing with the single issue. Or, the court must exclude the press and public from only that portion of a witness's testimony that might cause embarrassment or humiliation, not the entire testimony.

Finally, the trial judge must

5. **make evidentiary findings to support this decision, and prepare a thorough factual record relating to the closure order, a record that can be evaluated by an appellate court.** This final element is important. Appellate courts want to be certain that the trial judge thoughtfully and carefully considered options other than closure as a solution to the problem. The Georgia Supreme Court voided an order closing the pretrial phase of a sensational murder trial because the judge had stated simply that alternatives to closure were considered and found to be insufficient. "A closure order must fully articulate the alternatives to closure and the reasons why the alternatives would not protect the movant's [the party seeking closure] rights," the court ruled.[17]

This test provides a difficult challenge for any advocate of closure. Consequently, it is quite unusual when a closure order is issued, or when one is upheld on appeal.

The *Press-Enterprise* test applies to documents as well as to hearings, and a decision by the 10th U.S. Circuit Court of Appeals is instructive in how the test is applied. Journalists covering the trials of Timothy McVeigh and Terry L. Nichols, who were charged with bombing the federal building in Oklahoma City, sought access to documents relating to the proceedings. They sought redacted (censored) portions of Nichol's motion to suppress certain evidence and exhibits, notes made by an FBI agent who initially interviewed Nichols, and redacted portions of McVeigh's and Nichol's motions for separate trials. The court said that while suppression motions are traditionally open, access has not been historically extended to evidence ruled inadmissible, and in this case only the inadmissible material has been sealed. Access to raw notes, such as those written by the FBI agent, is not supported by either tradition or logic, since it would provide exposure to hearsay and other unsupported and inadmissible matter. Finally, the court said it would assume, because of traditional practice, that there is a right of access to some portions of the documents relating to separate trials. With regard to the latter set of documents, the court said release of the material could endanger both defendants' right to a fair trial since these papers contained candid material needed by the court to assess whether separate trials were necessary. The appellate court said it would not second-guess this decision, since the trial judge had made adequate findings to support the closure order.[18]

17. *Rockdale Citizen Publishing Co.* v. *Georgia,* 463 S.E. 2d 864 (1995).
18. *U.S.* v. *McVeigh,* 119 F. 3d 806 (1997).

PRESUMPTIVELY OPEN HEARINGS

During the past 20 years, American courts have ruled that a wide variety of judicial proceedings are presumptively open to the press and the public. The Supreme Court has specifically ruled that both pretrial evidentiary hearings[19] and voir dire proceedings[20] are presumptively open. These rulings apply to all courts, everywhere. Other rulings on open hearings have come from U.S. courts of appeals and state appellate courts. Consequently, these rulings don't apply as broadly; they may, in fact, be confined to a single federal jurisdiction or a state. It is fair to say, however, that in most situations the following kinds of proceedings are regarded as open and can only be closed by a strong showing of the substantial probability of harm to some other compelling interest:

During the past 20 years, American courts have ruled that a wide variety of judicial proceedings are presumptively open to the press and the public.

- Pretrial detention hearings
- Bail hearings
- Plea hearings
- Sentencing hearings
- Attorney disciplinary hearings

This, of course, does not mean that all proceedings are now open. In some instances appellate courts have ruled that even a hearing that is presumptively open may be closed. For example, the 4th U.S. Circuit Court of Appeals ruled that it was proper for a trial court to close the voir dire proceedings at the highly sensational extortion trials of three members of the South Carolina General Assembly. The court said the trial court erred in not giving the press advance warning of the closures and in not giving the press an opportunity to oppose the closure. But the appellate court said it supported the judge's decision that closure of the process was necessary to get frank and candid responses from potential jurors. There were no reasonable alternatives to closure.[21] Federal courts in New York recently reached the same conclusion during the wire fraud trial of controversial boxing promoter Don King. The defense was concerned that because of a long stream of negative publicity about King, jurors who had a neutral or positive view of the fight promoter would not answer questions honestly during the voir dire. The trial judge agreed. "Prospective jurors, if made aware that their views will be publicly disseminated in the next day's newspapers or on radio or television broadcasts, will be under pressure not to express unpopular opinions relevant to their choice as trial jurors."[22] The 2nd U.S. Circuit Court of Appeals agreed.[23]

The 6th U.S. Circuit Court of Appeals has ruled that the press and public do not enjoy a presumptive right of access to what is called a summary jury trial, a rather unusual judicial proceeding sometimes used in civil cases. The **summary jury trial** is a device used by courts to attempt to get the parties in the case to settle their dispute before going to a full-blown jury trial. In such a case the attorneys present much-abbreviated arguments to jurors. There are no

19. *Press-Enterprise* v. *Riverside Superior Court,* 478 U.S. 1 (1986).
20. *Press-Enterprise* v. *Riverside Superior Court,* 464 U.S. 501 (1984).
21. in re *South Carolina Press Association,* 946 F. 2d 1037 (1991).
22. *U.S.* v. *King,* 26 M.L.R. 1464 (1998).
23. *U.S.* v. *King,* 140 F. 3d 76 (1998).

witnesses called, and objections to evidence or other matters are strongly discouraged. After hearing the arguments, the jurors issue an informal verdict that can then be used to settle the case. For example, if plaintiff Jones loses the verdict in the summary jury trial, she may be more willing to settle the case without a normal trial. The court said that there was no First Amendment right of access to such proceedings because such a right was not historically recognized and that permitting access might actually work against the purpose of the summary trial, that is, the settlement of the dispute.[24]

The U.S. Court of Appeals for the 5th Circuit ruled that it was permissible for a trial judge to question two jurors privately in his chambers about possible misconduct. This ruling came during the second trial of Edwin Edwards, who was then between his terms as governor of Louisiana. The first trial ended in a mistrial. During the second trial a juror reported to the marshal that another juror had remarked, "Did you know the last jury got paid for voting acquittal?" The judge questioned both jurors in chambers about the matter. He said he did so to keep the matter away from other jurors. The same thing happened a few days later and the judge responded in the same fashion. After the trial ended, the press sought a transcript and received an edited version with the jurors' names and other details stricken from the record. The court of appeals supported the judge. It noted that historically such questioning of jurors has been conducted in private. Additionally, opening up such a hearing could be extremely harmful in this case, turning what the court called a "tempest in a teapot" into a mistrial. The court also supported the judge's decision to edit the transcript in order to protect the jurors from embarrassment.[25]

The 3rd U.S. Circuit Court of Appeals responded somewhat differently when it had to review an unusual situation that developed in a racketeering and extortion trial in Philadelphia. After the trial ended, one of the jurors claimed that other members of the jury had watched television reports about the case, read newspaper accounts of the trial, and discussed the case with their spouses, all contrary to the instructions from the court. These allegations received considerable press coverage and the defendant, who had been convicted, requested that the jurors be examined by the judge regarding these charges. The judge proceeded to question the jurors in private, despite press requests that the examination be conducted in public. The Court of Appeals issued an order stopping the proceeding until a hearing could be held, but by that time the judge said there was no further need to question the jurors. The trial judge denied the defendant's motion for a new trial and released the transcript of the examination, from which the jurors' names had been deleted. He said he had conducted the inquiry in private because he feared that the presence of the press in the courtroom during the examination would be coercive and interfere with the expressions of candor of the jurors. In addition, the judge said that jurors might inadvertently talk about matters discussed in the jury room, and that the public should not hear about such matters.

The Court of Appeals, applying the *Press-Enterprise* test (see pages 439–440), found the district court's justification insufficient to support the closure. The appellate court said that there was little historical tradition regarding the posttrial examination of juror misconduct, but

---

24. *Cincinnati Gas and Electric Co. v. General Electric Co.,* 854 F. 2d 900 (1988).
25. *U.S. v. Edwards,* 823 F. 2d 111 (1987).

there were substantial societal interests that would be advanced if such a hearing was open. Included among these interests were the promotion of a public perception of fairness, a check on potentially corrupt judicial practices, and the discouragement of perjury. The hearing, then, is presumptively open and the court must strongly justify its closure. The district court failed to do this, the court said. How would the presence of the press in the courtroom coerce the jurors? the court asked. The judge could instruct the jurors not to talk about the deliberative process. The judge had failed, the Court of Appeals said, to articulate an overriding interest that would be jeopardized. The fact that the press was given a transcript of the hearing 10 days later is not sufficient, the court said. The argument that later release of a transcript makes everything OK "unduly minimizes, if not entirely overlooks, the value of 'openness' itself, a value which is threatened whenever immediate access to ongoing proceedings is denied, whatever provision is made for public disclosure," the court said. A transcript is not the same, the appellate judges ruled. It does not reflect the verbal and nonverbal cues that aid in the interpretation of meaning.[26]

Finally, rules that preserve the secrecy of grand jury proceedings apply equally to proceedings ancillary to grand jury proceedings. The press in 1998 sought access to proceedings that focused on whether "Monica Lewinsky or others suborned perjury, obstructed justice, intimidated witnesses, or otherwise violated federal law" in dealing with persons involved in Paula Jones' lawsuit against President Clinton. While these proceedings were related to Kenneth Starr's grand jury proceedings into Whitewater and the Clinton-Lewinsky affair, they were outside the scope of the primary focus of the proceedings. The District of Columbia Circuit of the U.S. Court of Appeals said there was no First Amendment right of access to such proceedings.[27]

PRESUMPTIVELY OPEN DOCUMENTS

A wide range of judicial documents have been ruled to be presumptively open as well. Documents filed in pretrial proceedings have been ruled to be open. The U.S. Court of Appeals for the 9th Circuit struck down a lower-court order that sealed a large number of court records filed when the government prosecuted automaker John DeLorean. Pretrial proceedings are open, the court said, and "there is no reason to distinguish between pretrial proceedings and the documents filed in regard to them." Such documents are often important to a full understanding of the way in which "the judicial process and the government as a whole are functioning," the court ruled.[28] The same court ruled in 1988 that presentencing and postsentencing reports are presumed to be open records. The records were sought after a convicted felon was put on probation for a subsequent crime, and then murdered an attorney. The court said the trial judge had shown no compelling need to keep the records secret.[29]

---

26. *U.S.* v. *Simone,* 14 F. 3d 833 (1994).
27. In re *Dow Jones & Co.,* 142 F. 3d 896 (1998).
28. *A.P.* v. *U.S. District Court,* 705 F. 2d 1143 (1983).
29. *U.S.* v. *Schlette,* 685 F. 2d 1574 (1988).

Many state and federal courts have ruled that written agreements between a defendant and a prosecutor in which the accused agrees to plead guilty, usually to a lesser charge than originally filed (so-called plea agreements), are open to public inspection. Information and indictments, search warrants, and supporting affidavits are also generally open to the press and public.

In their effort to protect the integrity of jury deliberations and shield jurors from unwanted harassment by the mass media, some judges have refused to reveal the names and addresses of jurors even after a trial has concluded. Courts have tended to split on whether there is a right of public access to such material. The 4th U.S. Circuit Court of Appeals has explicitly said there is such a right.[30] And in 1999 the Michigan Court of Appeals ruled that there was a qualified right of access when the press seeks postverdict names and addresses of jurors. The court said that trial courts have the discretion to impose appropriate restrictions on the manner and time of disclosure and, in some circumstances perhaps, to refuse disclosure when legitimate safety concerns of jurors are raised. Juror privacy concerns alone, the court said, are not sufficient to block disclosure.[31] But other courts, like the 5th U.S. Circuit Court of Appeals, have ruled that there is no such right of access.[32] As the activity in criminal courts increases, fewer Americans seem willing to serve as jurors. Judges have become increasingly protective of those citizens who are willing to perform this important public duty. For example, a U.S district court in Massachusetts ruled that a newspaper had the right of access to the names and addresses of jurors in a highly publicized civil trial, but not until 10 days after the verdict was returned. The judge wanted to give the jurors time to receive a court order he had prepared, which instructed the jurors that they could refuse any request to be interviewed and that once they had indicated they did not wish to be interviewed, no further requests need be tolerated.[33] In 1993 a U.S. district court in New Jersey sealed the transcript of a voir dire proceeding, barring reporters from getting the names and addresses of the jurors. The voir dire had been open, but reporters had voluntarily left the small courtroom in order to make room for a very large jury pool. After the voir dire proceeding and again when the trial ended, the reporters asked to see a transcript of the voir dire to identify the jurors. Five months later the judge unsealed the transcript, but imposed restrictions on juror contacts by the press. The judge told the long-dismissed jurors they were not under any obligation to talk with reporters, forbade reporters to make repeated requests for interviews, and barred reporters from asking the jurors about specific votes, statements, opinions, or other comments made by other jurors during the deliberations.[34] The 3rd U.S. Circuit Court of Appeals ruled that the trial judge had acted improperly. The court said there was no reason to seal the voir dire transcript in the first place. "Compounding the problem of the late release of the transcript was the nature of the restrictions placed upon the press's use of juror information in the absence of findings that jurors were being harassed or that a threat of undue harassment was impending," the court

30. in re *Baltimore Sun,* 14 M.L.R. 2379 (1988).
31. *People* v. *Mitchell,* 592 N.W. 2d 798 (1999).
32. *U.S.* v. *Edwards,* 823 F. 2d 111 (1987).
33. *Sullivan* v. *National Football League,* 839 F. Supp. 6 (1993).
34. *U.S.* v. *Antar,* 839 F. Supp. 293 (1993).

said.[35] The judge's concern, the appellate court said, was hypothetical, part of generalized social claims that should not bear on a decision about whether limitations should be placed on the press's posttrial access to jurors.

Publishing the names and addresses of jurors, whether permitted or not, is a decision that journalists have to study closely as an ethical issue. The knee-jerk reaction—"if we can get it, we'll publish it"—is inappropriate. In the wake of the first Rodney King trial in southern California in which the officers accused of the beating were exonerated, rioting broke out on the streets of Los Angeles by people protesting the verdict. One newspaper still published jurors' names, something that could have jeopardized the safety of each of these citizens. Key questions need to be asked: What is the purpose of publishing these names? Will publishing the names enlighten readers and viewers in an important way? Or will this action jeopardize the jurors' privacy or even safety? Responsible editors and broadcasters will take the high road.

There are some areas in which public and press access to court documents is routinely denied. Civil lawsuits often end with an out-of-court settlement; that is, both parties agree to a settlement without completing the trial. In the past cases involving defective gas tanks in Ford Pintos, the dangers of silicone breast implants, exploding cigarette lighters, and defective television receivers were all settled out of court and the terms and nature of the settlements were shrouded under confidentiality orders. Oftentimes judges play an important role in generating such settlements. These settlement agreements have traditionally been considered a private matter between the parties in the lawsuit.[36] Today more and more of these agreements contain provisions that the terms of the settlement are to remain confidential. Defendants often seek confidentiality to avoid the disclosure of sensitive or potentially damaging information. Plaintiffs are willing to agree to confidentiality in order to obtain a higher amount of money in the settlement. Therefore, the sealing of out-of-court settlements has become somewhat commonplace. At first glance there seems little difficulty with such sealed agreements; after all, these are private agreements between private parties. But the public interest can be harmed in some instances. The confidential settlement of a malpractice suit against a doctor, for example, will provide compensation to the injured patient. But such a settlement denies other patients knowledge of the doctor's wrongdoing. If an auto manufacturer obtains a confidential settlement with a customer who was injured because of a faulty part in the car, other owners of the same vehicle may not be warned of the danger. Journalists are increasingly seeking access to such sealed agreements. Their quest for information is somewhat compromised by the fact that newspapers and broadcasting stations sometimes will seek the confidential settlement of a libel or invasion of privacy action. Most judges have not been receptive to the arguments that the press and public should have access to sealed agreements. Many jurists believe that the secrecy clause in these agreements encourages the settlement of lawsuits, and with courts in America as crowded as they are, judges favor anything that will reduce their caseload.* In 1986 the 3rd U.S. Circuit Court of Appeals ruled that there is a right of public access to sealed

Many jurists believe that the secrecy clause in these agreements encourages the settlement of lawsuits, and with courts in America as crowded as they are, judges favor anything that will reduce their caseload.

---

35. *U.S.* v. *Antar,* 38 F. 3d 1348 (1994).
36. See Bechamps, "Sealed Out-of-Court Settlements," 117.

*In the spring of 1995 the Judicial Conference of the United States, a policy-making body for the federal courts, rejected a proposal that would have made the sealing of records almost automatic in civil cases.

settlement agreements, the first important court to make such a ruling.[37] Since then a few other courts have ordered that such agreements be open for inspection.[38] As a rule, however, these agreements remain beyond the reach of even First Amendment arguments. Reporters who expose the terms of such secret settlements can face severe consequences. A court clerk mistakenly gave reporter Kirsten Mitchell a file containing the details of a secret settlement between Conoco Inc. and residents of a trailer park who alleged that Conoco had contaminated their water supply. When the Wilmington (N.C.) Morning Star published a story about the settlement, the court held both the reporter and the newspaper in contempt. They were jointly fined $500,000.[39]

Other documents normally closed to inspection are records provided by litigants to the opposing party in a lawsuit that are covered by a protective court order. During the discovery process, both sides in a legal dispute are permitted to explore the records and witnesses and other material held by the opposing party. The court assists in the process by compelling disclosure of this information when necessary. Sometimes a party will refuse to disclose some material unless the court will guarantee that material will not be made public. The court then enters a protective order, shielding the material from public disclosure.

For example, a black couple filed a civil rights complaint against persons who had twice firebombed their home. In preliminary proceedings it was discovered that one of the defendants was an officer in the Ku Klux Klan. The plaintiffs sought from him a list of local Klan members, and the court issued a subpoena ordering the production of the names. The Klansman resisted, but finally provided the list when it was put under a protective order, meaning that only the attorneys involved in the case could see the names. The court later sealed all access to the list in an effort to protect the privacy and associational rights of those named. The court of appeals upheld the ruling, noting that the list would never have been generated if it had not been for the protective order.[40] The court in this case relied on a 1984 U.S. Supreme Court ruling in a somewhat similar issue. In that case, *Seattle Times Co.* v. *Rhinehart*,[41] the high court said that an order prohibiting the dissemination of information generated during the discovery process is not the classic kind of prior restraint that requires "exacting First Amendment scrutiny. . . . Where a protective order is entered on a showing of good cause . . . and does not restrict the dissemination of the information if gained from other sources, it does not offend the First Amendment." In all likelihood, courts will continue to resist the disclosure of those documents that are generated during the discovery process and protected from public scrutiny by a court order.

The qualified First Amendment right of access to judicial proceedings and documents has gone a long way to block attempts by courts to keep the public and the press out of the courtroom. Many trial judges, however, still see closure as a simple solution to the problem of publicity about a criminal case. And often the motion for closure is made totally unexpectedly.

37. *Bank of America* v. *Hotel Rittenhouse Assoc.,* 800 F. 2d 339 (1986).
38. See *EEOC* v. *The Erection Co.,* 900 F. 2d 168 (1990); *Pansy* v. *Stroudsburg,* 22 F. 3d 772 (1994); and *Des Moines School District* v. *Des Moines Register and Tribune Co.,* 487 N.W. 2d 667 (1992).
39. *Ashcraft* v. *Conoco Inc.,* 26 M.L.R. 1620 (1998).
40. *Courier-Journal* v. *Marshall,* 282 F. 2d 361 (1987).
41. 104 S. Ct. 2199 (1984).

What should a reporter do when faced with such a problem? Here are some tips for journalists from "The Seattle Times Newsroom Legal Guide," prepared by attorneys P. Cameron Devore, Marshall J. Nelson, and others at the Seattle law firm of Davis, Wright, and Jones.

Call the editor immediately so he or she can contact the company's lawyer. Try informally to remind the judge of the recent rulings and guidelines that provide for a presumptively open hearing. If that fails, the reporter should be prepared to make a formal objection to the closure, to try to hold the fort until legal help arrives. Reporters for The Seattle Times are prepared to read the following statement from a card they carry.

> Your honor, I am _____, a reporter for The Seattle Times, and I would like to object on behalf of my newspaper and the public to this proposed closing. Our attorney is prepared to make a number of arguments against closings such as this one, and we respectfully ask the court for a hearing on those issues. I believe our attorney can be here soon for the court's convenience and will be able to demonstrate that closure in this case will violate the First Amendment and article I, section 10, of the Washington state constitution. I cannot make the legal arguments myself, but our attorney can point out several issues for your consideration. If it pleases the court, we request the opportunity to be heard through counsel.

Such a statement would work in any court; simply cite the proper section of your own state constitution or any other relevant documents or guidelines. Reporters should be equipped to handle such an emergency.

**TIPS FOR REPORTERS WHEN
JUDICIAL HEARING IS CLOSED**

▮ Call the editor immediately to get a lawyer on the job
▮ Make a formal objection to closure
▮ Ask the judge to delay the closure until the lawyer arrives

---

ACCESS AND THE BROADCAST JOURNALIST

It is far easier for the courts to serve the needs of the print media than the broadcast media when it comes to providing access to judicial proceedings and documents. In many instances it suffices for the broadcast journalist to attend the hearing or inspect the document like colleagues who work for newspapers or magazines. But other times the broadcast journalist wants to show viewers the actual document, or allow listeners to hear the testimony, or view the proceeding. Courts have been much slower to respond to these needs than the simpler needs of the working print reporter.

It is far easier for the courts to serve the needs of the print media than the broadcast media when it comes to providing access to judicial proceedings and documents.

Two Supreme Court rulings initially loomed as major stumbling blocks for broadcast journalists: a 1965 ruling (*Estes* v. *Texas*[42]) that generally supported the ban on the telecast or

42. 381 U.S. 532 (1965).

broadcast of judicial proceedings, and a 1978 ruling (*Nixon* v. *Warner Communications*[43]) in which the high court refused to recognize the right of the journalists to make copies of audio-taped evidence for broadcast on the news. *Estes* will be discussed shortly. The second case involved tapes made by President Richard Nixon at the White House that were used as evidence in many of the Watergate trials of the 1970s. Broadcasters wanted to make copies of these tapes and play them for radio listeners and television viewers. The Supreme Court agreed that there is a generally recognized right of access to inspect evidentiary records in a case but said that this right was not an absolute right. "The decision as to access is one best left to the sound discretion of the trial court, a discretion to be exercised in light of the relevant facts and circumstances of the particular case," the court ruled. Courts have come a long way in granting press access to judicial evidence since 1978. But because the Nixon case focused specifically on the broadcast of taped evidence, those judges who wish to resist the broadcasters' efforts to use taped evidence in their newscasts have a fairly strong precedent on their side.[44] In this section we first discuss gaining access to audio- or videotape evidence. Then we discuss the recording or televising of judicial proceedings.

The courts have considered a variety of factors in reaching a decision on whether to permit the broadcast or telecast of audio- or videotape evidence. Whether transcripts of the recordings have already been published is an important factor. Courts have also considered whether the broadcast or telecast of the material would enhance public understanding of an important historical or public occurrence. The rights of the defendant are also considered: Would the broadcast of this material prejudice the right to a fair trial? In Maryland a television station sought to broadcast a home videotape that was introduced as evidence during a murder trial. The victim's husband had shot the video of his wife as she got into her car to take their daughter to nursery school. Appearing in the background of the videotape are two men whom police charged with the subsequent murder of the woman. The defendants were being tried separately. A television station asked permission to broadcast the tape after it was shown in court during the first trial. The trial court said the station could broadcast the tape, but not until after the second trial. The Maryland Court of Special Appeals affirmed this ruling. The appellate court rejected the argument that there was a First Amendment right to copy trial evidence, but conceded a limited common-law right did exist. Nevertheless, the court said that the trial judge was correct in balancing this limited right against the fair trial rights of the second defendant.[45]

Most courts will insist on clear evidence that the broadcast or telecast of the material will harm the rights of the defendant or someone or something else. The U.S. Court of Appeals for the 3rd Circuit ruled that there is a strong presumption favoring access and that this presumption is not outweighed by mere speculations on the potential impact the telecast of the material may have on related proceedings.[46] In Washington state the Supreme Court voided a contempt citation against a radio station that had broadcast, in violation of a court

43. 434 U.S. 591 (1978).
44. See, for example, *Group W Television Inc.* v. *Maryland,* 626 A. 2d 1032 (1993).
45. *Group W Television Inc.* v. *Maryland,* 626 A. 2d 1032 (1993).
46. *U.S.* v. *Martin,* 746 F. 2d 964 (1984).

order, tape-recorded testimony that had been placed into evidence because the trial court had "accepted the most superficial showing of justification and then shifted to KHQ [the radio station] the burden of proving that the prior restraint was not necessary."[47]

It is often important whether the tapes that are sought have been introduced into evidence. When John Hinckley was tried for the attempted assassination of Ronald Reagan, the television networks sought to televise the videotaped deposition given by actress Jodie Foster in the case. The court refused the request, noting that the testimony was never admitted into evidence. It was simply a statement from a witness; it just happened to be videotaped. No right existed to videotape and telecast the testimony of other witnesses. The videotaped deposition would not be an exception to that rule.[48] The New Mexico Supreme Court denied the press the right to copy and broadcast recordings of wiretaps that resulted in criminal indictments but were never played in open court or received into evidence.[49] Who has been videotaped is also an important consideration when a court examines a request to broadcast the material. Videotapes of defendants and police agents are more likely to be released than are recordings of innocent third parties. Jodie Foster was an "innocent witness" in the Hinckley case. She had been pulled into the case inadvertently. A U.S. district court in Minnesota rejected requests from broadcasters to air videotapes of a hostage recorded by her kidnapper. The court ruled that it would create serious hardship for the victim of the crime and would serve no proper purpose.[50] A good way to outline the dimensions of this problem is to look at two different cases, one where access was granted and one where it was denied.

The government presented a considerable amount of evidence on both videotape and audiotape on Congressman John Jenrette and John Stowe in the a trial that stemmed from an FBI sting operation that started in 1978 and resulted in the conviction of one U.S. senator and five congressmen. The tapes were recordings of the defendants in the case making what the government alleged were illegal deals with undercover FBI agents. The networks sought to copy and broadcast these tapes. The U.S. district court refused the request, fearing that if the tapes were televised it would be difficult to later impanel an impartial jury should a retrial be ordered by a higher court. The U.S. Court of Appeals for the District of Columbia Circuit disagreed and promulgated this test:

> Access may be denied only if the district court, after considering the relevant facts and circumstances of the particular case, and after weighing the interests advanced by the parties in light of the public interest and the duty of courts, concludes that justice so requires. . . . The court's discretion must clearly be informed by this country's strong tradition of access to judicial proceedings. In balancing the competing interests the court must also give appropriate weight and consideration *to the presumption—however gauged—in favor of public access to judicial records* [author emphasis].[51]

47. *Washington* v. *Coe,* 101 N.W. 2d 364 (1984).
48. in re *Application of ABC,* 537 F. Supp. 1168 (1982).
49. *New Mexico* v. *Brennan,* 645 P. 2d 982 (1982).
50. in re *Application of KSTP,* 504 F. Supp. 360 (1980).
51. in re *Application of NBC,* 653 F. 2d 609 (1981).

Several factors favored release of the tapes, the court concluded. They were admitted into evidence and played to a jury at a public trial. The tapes contained only admissible evidence. This was a trial in which the defendant was a high public official charged with betraying the public trust. The court admitted a retrial *might* be a problem, but there was no evidence that if there were a retrial, impartial jurors could not be found. What about protecting innocent third parties who were also pictured or heard in the tapes? There were only one or two instances of that, and the trial court can delete these sections, the court said. The tapes must be released.

The U.S. Court of Appeals for the 5th Circuit reached the opposite conclusion in another 1981 decision. The speaker of the Texas House of Representatives, two attorneys, and a labor leader were all indicted in an alleged bribery scheme. The speaker and the two attorneys were tried and acquitted. Broadcasters wanted to air audiotapes that had been made during the FBI sting operation that resulted in the indictments. These were discussions between the defendants and FBI undercover operatives that had been secretly recorded. The trial court refused on the grounds that the broadcast might make it difficult for the fourth defendant to have a trial by an impartial jury. The court of appeals supported this decision. The court noted that although there is a right in this country to inspect and copy judicial records and documents, it is not an absolute right.[52] The trial court may exercise considerable discretion in granting or refusing to grant access to material. Clearly, the concern that the fourth defendant's trial might be prejudiced if the tapes were broadcast is a legitimate concern, the court said. It is not the job of the appellate courts to second-guess the trial courts on these matters. The court said it could not agree with decisions by the District of Columbia U.S. Circuit Court of Appeals and other courts that there exists a strong presumption in favor of access to this kind of evidence. The court said it could not find a basis for that presumption.

Finally, the 8th U.S. Circuit Court of Appeals ruled in December of 1996 that neither the press nor the public had a First Amendment or common-law right of access to President Bill Clinton's videotaped deposition for a criminal trial in Arkansas. Transcripts of what was said in the deposition were made public and this satisfied the First Amendment requirements, the court ruled.[53]

RECORDING AND TELEVISING JUDICIAL PROCEEDINGS

In 1976 cameras and tape recorders were barred from the courtrooms in all but two states, Texas and Colorado. Today such equipment is banned only in the courtrooms in the District of Columbia, Mississippi, and South Dakota, according to the Radio-Television News Directors Association. In the other 48 states, cameras and other electronic recording equipment is permitted in appellate courts, trial courts, or both. The press must have consent from the judge or the parties involved or both before using cameras and tape recorders in 31 states. But in 15 states no consent of any kind is required. However, if circumstances exist that suggest the cameras in the courtroom would have a substantial detrimental impact on the proceeding, the judge can exclude them.

52. *Belo Broadcasting* v. *Clark,* 654 F. 2d 426 (1981).
53. *U.S.* v. *McDougal,* 103 F. 3d 651 (1996).

This swift reversal of the rules regarding the use of cameras in the courtroom climaxed a 40-year struggle by the press for relaxation of prohibitions that were instituted in the 1930s. At that time the press had conducted itself in an outrageous fashion in covering the trial of Bruno Hauptmann, who in 1934 was charged with kidnapping the baby of Charles and Anne Lindbergh. The trial judge, who had great difficulty in controlling the press, ordered that no pictures be taken during the court sessions. But photographers equipped with large, bulky, flash-equipped cameras moved freely about the courtroom, ignoring the judge's orders and taking pictures almost at will. As a result of this travesty, the American Bar Association adopted rules prohibiting the use of cameras and other electronic equipment in courtrooms. The rules, known as Canon 35, were adopted in most states and were followed in practice in those states that did not officially adopt the rules.[54]

After World War II, when the photographic equipment became smaller and less obtrusive and faster film permitted photography indoors without flash equipment, the press began to agitate for changes in the rules. The television industry especially chafed under the proscriptions (the ABA rules had been amended in 1952 to include television), as they put broadcast reporters, who depended on film to tell a story, at a distinct disadvantage in the competition with wordsmiths of the printed press. In the mid-1960s the U.S. Supreme Court had a chance to consider the constitutionality of the ban on cameras in the courtroom in a case that began in Texas, one of a handful of states that occasionally allowed photography and recording in the courtroom.

The defendant was Billie Sol Estes, who was accused of a swindle involving fertilizer tanks. The story was important in the Lone Star State; television was therefore permitted at the initial pretrial hearing, and still photographers were permitted throughout the trial. But there was disruption at the pretrial hearing. Twelve camera operators crowded into the tiny courtroom, cables and wires snaked across the floor, microphones were everywhere, and the distraction caused by this media invasion was significant. The situation improved during the trial when television and recording equipment was housed in a booth at the back of the courtroom. Estes appealed his conviction to the U.S. Supreme Court on the grounds that he had been denied a fair trial because of the presence of the cameras and recorders. The court agreed with the defendant. "While maximum freedom must be allowed the press in carrying out this important function [informing the public] in a democratic society, its exercise must necessarily be subject to the maintenance of absolute fairness in the judicial process," wrote Justice Tom Clark for the majority.[55] The photography and broadcasting equipment simply created too many impediments to a fair trial.

However, experimentation with cameras in the courtroom continued. Telecasting equipment improved. Journalists demonstrated to judges that they could act responsibly if they were permitted access to courtrooms with their cameras and recorders. More and more states began to permit telecasts and broadcasts of criminal and civil trials as well as of the oral arguments at appellate hearings. In the early 1980s two former Miami police officers challenged the new rules in Florida that permitted cameras in the courtroom. They argued that television

At that time the press had conducted itself in an outrageous fashion in covering the trial of Bruno Hauptmann, who in 1934 was charged with kidnapping the baby of Charles and Anne Lindbergh.

54. White, "Cameras in the Courtroom."
55. *Estes v. Texas,* 381 U.S. 532 (1965).

TABLE 12.1

Cameras in Court, State by State

State laws concerning photography, audiotape recording and television in courtrooms. All states allow coverage in criminal and civil courts at the trial and appellate levels except where indicated by (A), appellate courts only, or (T), trial courts only. Also, Maryland and Texas do not allow recordings of criminal trials except at the appellate level, and Pennsylvania allows recordings only of civil cases at the trial level.

STATE	CONSENT REQUIRED BY:		LIMITS ON COVERAGE OF:	
	JUDGE	PARTIES	PARTIES	JURORS
■ Alabama	Yes	Yes	Yes	Background only
■ Alaska	Yes	Yes[1]	No	No
■ Arizona	Yes	No	No	Background only
■ Arkansas	No	Yes	Yes	No
■ California	Yes	No	No	No
■ Colorado	Yes	No	No	Background only
■ Connecticut	Yes	No	Yes	Background only
□ Delaware (A)	No	No	No	
■ Florida	No	No	No	Yes
■ Georgia	Yes	No	Yes	Background only
■ Hawaii	Yes[2]	No	Yes	No
■ Idaho (A)	Yes[2]	No	No	No
■ Illinois (A)	No	No	No	
□ Indiana	Yes	No	No	
■ Iowa	Yes	Yes[1]	Yes	Background only
■ Kansas	No	No	Yes	Background only
■ Kentucky	Yes	No	No	Yes
■ Louisiana (A)	No	No	No	
■ Maine (A)	Yes	No	Yes	No
■ Maryland[3]	Yes	Yes[2]	Yes	Yes
■ Massachusetts	No	No	No	Background only
■ Michigan	Yes	No	Yes	No
■ Minnesota	Yes[2]	Yes[2]	Yes	No
Mississippi (no law)				
■ Missouri	Yes	No	Yes	No
■ Montana	No	No	No	Yes
■ Nebraska[4]	No	No	No	
■ Nevada	Yes	No	No	Background only
■ New Hampshire	Yes	No	No	Yes[5]
■ New Jersey	Yes	No	Yes	Background only
■ New Mexico	No	No	Yes	No
■ New York*				
■ North Carolina	No	No	Yes	No
■ North Dakota	Yes	No	Yes	No
■ Ohio	Yes	No	Yes	No
■ Oklahoma	Yes	Yes[1]	Yes	Yes[5]
■ Oregon	Yes[2]	No	Yes	No
□ Pennsylvania (T)	Yes	No	Yes	
■ Rhode Island	No	No	No	Background only
■ South Carolina	Yes	No	No	Background only
South Dakota (no law)				
■ Tennessee	Yes	Yes[1]	Yes	No
■ Texas[3]	Yes	Yes	No	
■ Utah[6]	Yes	No	No	No
■ Vermont	No	No	No	Background only
■ Virginia	No	No	Yes	No
■ Washington	Yes	No	Yes	Yes[5]
■ West Virginia	Yes	No	No	Yes
■ Wisconsin	No	No	Yes	Background only
■ Wyoming	Yes[2]	No	Yes	No

■ Permanent laws
■ Some permanent laws, some experimental
□ Experimental laws

[1]Certain types of cases only.
[2]No consent required for appellate courts.
[3]Criminal cases only at appellate level.

[4]Audio only for trials.
[5]Upon approval of judge, or unless a juror objects.
[6]Still photography only at trials.

*The situation in New York was somewhat confusing in the spring of 2000. New York adopted a law in 1987 that permitted cameras to photograph appellate court proceedings, but the law lapsed in 1997 and was not restored. Then, in January of 2000, the judge presiding at the criminal trial of four New York City police officers charged with killing Amadou Diallo ruled that the state statute barring cameras from New York courtrooms was unconstitutional. That trial was televised but the larger issue was unresolved.

SOURCE: *Radio-Television News Directors Association,* January 1999.

coverage of their trial in and of itself had deprived them of a fair trial. The Florida Supreme Court rejected their contention, and the U.S. Supreme Court agreed to hear the case. In a unanimous decision the high court ruled that the mere presence of cameras in the courtroom or simply televising or broadcasting portions of a trial does not in and of itself cause prejudice to the defendant or interfere with the right to a fair trial.[56] Chief Justice Burger wrote that at present "no one has been able to present empirical data sufficient to establish that the mere presence of the broadcast media inherently has an adverse effect on that [trial] process." It is true the presence of such equipment in the courtroom or the broadcast of a trial could endanger the defendant's right to a fair trial. But, Burger said, "an absolute constitutional ban on broadcast coverage of trials cannot be justified simply because there is a danger that, in some cases, prejudicial broadcast accounts of pretrial and trial events may impair the ability of jurors to decide the issue of guilt or innocence uninfluenced by extraneous matter." The chief justice said that in order to block the use of cameras and recorders at a trial, a defendant must demonstrate to the court how the trial will be adversely affected by the presence of this equipment. To overturn a conviction at a trial that has been televised, the defendant will need to show that the recording and photography equipment actually made a substantial difference in some material aspect of the trial. Proof that the jurors were aware of the cameras or that the presence of television cameras "told" jurors this was a big trial will not be sufficient to demonstrate prejudice, Burger wrote.

State courts have started to develop standards to assess complaints of prejudice from defendants who do not want their trials televised. In Florida, for example, the state supreme court has ruled that the trial court must hold an evidentiary hearing if a defendant or other participant in the trial protests the television coverage. Before cameras and recorders may be excluded, there must be a finding that electronic coverage of the trial would have an important "qualitatively different effect" on the trial than would other types of coverage.[57] Another Florida case demonstrates how such a difference might be shown. The defendant in the case had previously been found incompetent to stand trial. Treatment subsequently rendered her competent to proceed with the case. Her attorneys, armed with testimony from psychiatrists, asserted that television cameras in the courtroom would adversely affect the defendant's ability to communicate with her counsel and she might lapse into psychosis. The Florida Supreme Court ruled that this kind of evidence satisfied the standard for excluding television cameras.[58] Some states provide exemptions from coverage to certain classes of trial participants such as juvenile offenders, victims of sex crimes, or police informants.

State rules on the admission of cameras to the courtroom vary. In some states cameras will not be permitted unless various key trial participants agree. In more states the cameras are allowed on the discretion of the judge. If a participant objects to the admission of cameras to the courtroom, the press must honor this objection and refrain from photographing or recording this individual. And judges can and do require cameras to be turned off during the presentation of certain kinds of evidence, such as gory crime scene photos. Most states have adopted

56. *Chandler* v. *Florida,* 449 U.S. 560 (1981).
57. *Florida* v. *Palm Beach Newspapers,* 395 So. 2d 544 (1981).
58. *Florida* v. *Green,* 395 So. 2d 532 (1981).

guidelines that establish the number of still and motion picture cameras permitted in the courtroom at any one time. Rules often specify where the cameras may be placed, require that all pictures be taken with available light, and even set standards of dress for photographers and technicians. The press must often be willing to share the fruits of the photography through pooling agreements, since most states have guidelines limiting movement and placement of cameras to when the court is in recess only.

The matter of using cameras and recording equipment in federal courtrooms has yet to be resolved. A seemingly successful three-year experiment with the use of cameras in six federal district courts and two appellate circuits ended in 1994 with a vote by the U.S. Judicial Conference, the group of judges who make policy for the federal courts, to continue to ban cameras and recorders from the courtroom. According to observers, many judges were dismayed by what they called the "sound bite" problem, the tendency by most broadcasters to use 10-to-15-second snippets of video or audio rather than extended segments of coverage.[59] Eighteen months later the members of the conference reversed themselves and voted 14–12 to permit cameras in federal appellate courts. Cameras would continue to be barred from trial courts, and the policy does not affect the Supreme Court, which continues to ban the televising of its arguments. Under the terms of the vote, judges in each of the 13 federal circuits would decide whether to permit cameras in the appellate courtrooms of that particular circuit.[60] In April of 1996 judges for the U.S. Court of Appeals for the 9th Circuit announced they would permit electronic media coverage of most of the circuit appellate proceedings. The decision to allow cameras in the courtroom is made on a case-by-case basis by the judges in the panel presiding over each hearing. Cameras would only be automatically barred from hearings involving direct criminal appeals and from extradition proceedings.

A cautionary note should be included at this point. The fallout from the television coverage of the criminal trial of O.J. Simpson has caused a great many judges to reconsider their broad support for the use of cameras in the courtroom. Some members of the U.S. Judicial Conference who voted in 1994 to continue to bar cameras from the federal courts justified their votes by pointing specifically to the manner in which the Simpson trial was being covered by television. In California in 1996 rules regarding the use of television cameras in the courtroom were tightened and now include a ban on televising voir dire proceedings. Telecasting pictures of the spectators in the courtroom is also off-limits now. Judges were told to closely consider 18 different factors before deciding whether to permit cameras in the courtroom. And in Massachusetts a superior court judge refused to permit either television or still cameras in the courtroom during the trial of John C. Salvi III, who was being tried for murder and attempted murder after shootings at a Planned Parenthood office. The rules in the state require a judge to permit cameras in the courtroom unless the judge determines that such coverage would create a substantial likelihood of harm to any person or other serious consequences. The judge said he feared saturation coverage reminiscent of the Simpson criminal trial. "This constant replay and analysis of every aspect of the trial process, along with the

59. Greenhouse, "Federal Judges Banish TV," E3.
60. Greenhouse, "Panel Allows TV."

commentary upon and second-guessing of the strategy of the trial counsel, has greater potential to interfere with a juror's ability to render a verdict solely on his or her assessment of the evidence in court," the judge ruled.[61]

Photographic coverage of another aspect of the legal system became an issue in California when public television station KQED sought permission to televise an execution in the California gas chamber. The warden of San Quentin refused, and KQED petitioned the U.S. district court for relief. The station lawyers argued that it was appropriate in a democratic society for "citizens to be able to see virtually firsthand . . . the ultimate sanction of our criminal justice system. Accurate citizen awareness is especially important because the constitutionality of the sanction itself depends on the public's values, evolving standards and attitudes toward capital punishment." The federal court upheld the ban on photography during the execution, saying that prison officials reasonably feared that a televised execution might generate a violent reaction among other prisoners, which could endanger guards or cause a riot.[62]

SUMMARY

The public and the press have a right to attend trials and pretrial proceedings. This right is presumed when the proceeding has been historically or traditionally open, or when opening the hearing plays a significant positive role in the functioning of the judicial process. Although the right to attend a trial is not absolute, such a proceeding can be closed only in rare circumstances. Courts have permitted the closure of juvenile hearings as well as a portion of the public testimony of rape victims. The right of access to pretrial proceedings and documents is qualified. The presumption that these hearings are open can only be overcome by a showing that there is an overriding interest that must be protected, that there is a "substantial probability" that an open hearing will damage this right, that the closure is narrowly tailored to deny access to no more of the hearing than is necessary to protect this interest, that the court has considered reasonable alternatives to closure, that closure of the hearing would in fact protect the interest that has been raised, and that the trial judge has articulated findings—which may be reviewed by an appellate court—that support these four points.

Broadcast journalists are given somewhat less access when they seek to obtain copies of audio- or videotaped evidence or seek to record or televise a judicial proceeding. Access to the taped evidence is developing through a case-by-case approach, and courts have granted journalists increasing rights to make copies of this material for later broadcast. Cameras and recording devices are now permitted in courts in all but three states and the District of Columbia. The Supreme Court has ruled that the mere presence of such devices does not in and of itself prejudice a defendant's right to a fair trial. The federal courts refuse to permit cameras in the courtroom.

61. *Massachusetts* v. *Salvi,* 24 M.L.R. 1734 (1996).
62. *KQED, Inc.* v. *Vasquez,* 18 M.L.R. 2323 (1991). See also *Campbell* v. *Blodgett,* 982 F. 2d 1356 (1993) and *California First Amendment Coalition* v. *Calderon,* 130 F. 3d 976 (1998).

BENCH-BAR-PRESS GUIDELINES

Both restrictive orders and the closure of court proceedings are admittedly effective ways of stopping publicity from reaching the hands of potential jurors, but they are equally dangerous in a representative democracy where information about how well government is operating is fundamental to the success of the political system. The bench, the bar, and the press in many states have found that cooperation, restraint, and mutual trust can be equally effective in protecting the rights of a defendant, while at the same time far less damaging to rights of the people.

In more than two dozen states the members of the bench, the bar, and the press have tried to reach a common understanding of the problems of pretrial news coverage and have offered suggestions as to how most of these problems might be resolved. These suggestions are usually offered in the form of guidelines or recommendations to the press and to participants in the criminal justice system. **Bench-bar-press guidelines** normally suggest to law enforcement officers that certain kinds of information about a criminal suspect and a crime can be released and published with little danger of harm to the trial process. The guidelines also suggest to journalists that the publication of certain kinds of information about a case (see the list of damaging kinds of statements on pages 408–409) can be harmful to the defendant's chances for a fair trial without providing the public with useful or important information. The guidelines are often presented in a very brief form; at other times they encompass several pages of text.

Bench-bar-press guidelines have existed in some states for more than 40 years. In some communities these guidelines work very well in managing the problems surrounding the free press–fair trial dilemma. A spirit of cooperation exists between press, courts, attorneys, and law enforcement personnel. In such communities it is rare to find a restrictive order or a closed courtroom. But most communities and states have found it takes considerable effort to make the guidelines work. Drafting the guidelines is only the first step. If, after agreement is reached on the recommendations, the bench, the bar, and the press go their separate ways, the guidelines usually fail as a means of resolving the free press–fair trial problems.

Most communities and states have found it takes considerable effort to make the guidelines work.

A good deal of space has been devoted to the free press–fair trial problem because it is an important issue and because it continues to be a problem. Within both the press and the law, sharp divisions regarding solution of the problem remain. Many years ago, during a battle over a free press–fair trial issue in one southern state, the national office of the American Civil Liberties Union filed an amicus curiae (friend of the court) brief supporting a free and unfettered press, while the state chapter of the same civil liberties group filed a brief in favor of the court's position supporting a fair trial.

Most journalists probably agree that we need more, not less, reporting on the justice system in the United States. In "Crime and Publicity" Alfred Friendly and Ronald Goldfarb write:

> To shackle the press is to curtail the public watch over the administration of criminal justice. . . . The press serves at the gatehouse of justice. Additionally, it serves in the manorhouse itself, and all along the complicated route to it from the police station and the streets, to the purlieus of the prosecutor's office, to the courtroom corridors where the pressures mount and the deals are made.[63]

63. Friendly and Goldfarb, *Crime and Publicity.*

The two authors also point out that we do not want a press that is more or less free, just as we should not tolerate trials that are almost fair. "And to complicate the issue," they note, "it is evident that a free press is one of society's principal guarantors of fair trials, while fair trials provide a major assurance of the press's freedom."

Reporters dealing with the courts and the court system must be extremely sensitive to these issues. They should not be blinded to the sensitive mechanisms that operate in the courts to provide justice and fairness as they clamor for news. At the same time they should not let the authoritarian aspects of the judicial system block their efforts to provide the information essential to the functioning of democracy.

SUMMARY

In some states the press, attorneys, and judges have agreed to try to solve the problems surrounding the free press–fair trial controversy through voluntary bench-bar-press agreements. Such agreements usually contain suggestions to all parties as to what information should and should not be publicized about criminal cases. When the guidelines work, there is usually a cooperative, rather than a combative, spirit among the members of the press, the judiciary, and the bar. These guidelines often reduce or eliminate the need for restrictive orders or closed hearings.

BIBLIOGRAPHY

Bechamps, Anne T. "Sealed Out-of-Court Settlements: When Does the Public Have a Right to Know?" *Notre Dame Law Review* 66 (1990):117.

Bush, Chilton R., ed. *Free Press and Fair Trial: Some Dimensions of the Problem.* Athens: University of Georgia Press, 1971.

Eckholm, Erik. "When Does a Young Offender Lose the Right to Privacy?" *The New York Times,* 27 March 1994, E4.

Friendly, Alfred, and Ronald Goldfarb. *Crime and Publicity.* New York: Random House, Vintage Books, 1968.

Goldstein, Abraham S. "Jury Secrecy and the Media: The Problem of the Postverdict Interview." *University of Illinois Law Review* 1993 (1993):295.

Greenhouse, Linda. "Disdaining a Sound Bite, Federal Judges Banish TV." *The New York Times,* 25 September 1994, E3.

———. "Panel Allows TV in Appeals Courts." *The New York Times,* 13 March 1996, C6.

Judicial Records: A Guide to Access in State and Federal Courts. Washington, D.C.: Reporters Committee for Freedom of the Press, 1990.

Landau, Jack C. "The Challenge of the Communications Media." *American Bar Association Journal* 62 (1976):55.

Lindsey, Richard P. "An Assessment of the Use of Cameras in State and Federal Courts." *Georgia Law Review* 18 (1984):389.

Chapter 12

Minow, Newton, and Fred Cate. "Who Is an Impartial Juror in an Age of Mass Media?" *The American University Law Review* 40 (1991):631.
Raskopf, Robert. "A First Amendment Right of Access to a Juror's Identity: Toward a Fuller Understanding of the Jury's Deliberative Process." *Pepperdine Law Review* 17 (1990):357.
White, Frank W. "Cameras in the Courtroom: A U.S. Survey." *Journalism Monographs* 60 (1979).

Regulation of Obscene and Other Erotic Material

The regulation of obscene and other erotic material is surely at the periphery of the concerns of most professional communicators who work in the mass media. But this issue is at the heart of the struggle for freedom of expression today. Perhaps in no other area of the law is the First Amendment under such intense siege as factions on all sides of the political and cultural spectrum seek government assistance in censoring material they find offensive or distasteful. This chapter briefly explores the history of the regulation of obscenity, outlines current judicial definitions, and discusses the wide range of legal and quasi-legal strategies arrayed today against the publication or broadcast or electronic transmission of sexually oriented material.

THE LAW OF OBSCENITY

No First Amendment issue generates more emotion in Americans than does the regulation of the sale and distribution of obscene and other erotic materials. U.S. Judge H. Lee Sarokin noted more than 15 years ago that sexually explicit materials are supposed to arouse sexual passion.

> They also seem to arouse passions of an entirely different sort. If a merchant announced his intention to open a store dedicated to murder mysteries, no matter how violent or bloody, nary a picket or protestor would appear. But should one announce that sex is to be the main theme, then organized opposition is inevitable.[1]

IMPORTANT DATES IN OBSCENITY LAW

1791—Adoption of First Amendment

1815—First recorded obscenity prosecution

1842—First federal obscenity law

1873—Comstock Act adopted

1957—*Hicklin* rule abandoned
   Roth test emerges

1967—First presidential obscenity commission appointed

1973—*Miller* test enunciated

1985—Second presidential commission on obscenity appointed

1997—Communications Decency Act ruled unconstitutional

The Supreme Court of the United States has defined what is legally obscene (see pages 465–468). This particularly narrow range of material is considered beyond the ambit of First Amendment protection. Today, however, war is being waged against a far wider range of erotic material, much of it material that is not considered legally obscene. Song lyrics and music videos have been attacked. Public libraries have come under siege for owning admittedly frank but clinically sound sex education books. The Department of Justice with the support of various citizens groups successfully impaired the distribution of so-called men's magazines like Penthouse and Playboy during the 1980s. In a few states, efforts have been made to block the cablecasting of some R-rated movies. A rock musician was prosecuted in California for including a reproduction of an erotic painting inside an album jacket. And many state legislatures as well as the U.S. Congress made moves to ban the transmission of objectionable material over online networks like the Internet.

Those who seek to limit the flow of erotic material in the marketplace often raise legitimate concerns. Many women believe pornographic material fuels violence against women.

---

1. *E-Bru, Inc.* v. *Graves,* 566 F. Supp. 1476 (1983).

Parents express concern about what children may see and hear. Many individuals find such material antithetical to their religious beliefs. But there are compelling reasons to be concerned about the censorship of obscene and other erotic materials as well. The U.S. Supreme Court has declared with a bare minimum of justification that obscenity is outside the protection of the First Amendment. The high court has based this ruling largely on the dubious proposition that the Founding Fathers who drafted the First Amendment did not intend that it protect obscenity. It has been noted previously that there is little evidence to support any conclusions about the intent of the drafters of the First Amendment and the people who supported it. Colonial Americans often have been mistakenly described as a humorless, drab, sanctimonious people rooted in the strong Christian traditions that flowered in Puritan and other religious societies in the 17th century. In fact it was a lusty and often bawdy people who created this nation and who approved the constitutional guarantee of freedom of expression. What many today would call pornographic material was freely circulated in the late 18th century and people seemed unconcerned about it. The first civil prosecution for the distribution, sale, or display of erotic material was not recorded until 1815, nearly 25 years after the adoption of the First Amendment.* Contemporary American attitudes about sex and erotic material were shaped far more by the Victorian values of the middle-to-late 19th century than by the values of the people who first inhabited this continent and helped build this nation.

The Supreme Court has also attempted to justify the suppression of obscenity on the grounds that such books or magazines or movies are in some way detrimental to the community. But unassailable evidence to support this conclusion is also absent. Contemporary studies that suggest harmful consequences because of the circulation of obscenity are usually matched by equally persuasive studies that suggest the opposite conclusion. It is hardly a comforting proposition that the government can declare an entire category of speech and press to be outside the protection of the Bill of Rights with such limited justification. On this basis it may be obscenity that is banned today; it might be a religious dogma or political philosophy that is banned tomorrow. And that is an important reason to be concerned about the regulation of obscenity.

It is hardly a comforting proposition that the government can declare an entire category of speech and press to be outside the protection of the Bill of Rights with such limited justification.

There is another reason as well, however. Although the descriptions we use today to define obscenity are surely better than the ones used a half-century ago, they still lack sufficient precision to adequately warn booksellers or video retailers what it is they may or may not legally distribute. Consequently there is substantial self-censorship of nonobscene material. Record companies, magazine distributors, booksellers, and cable operators are often reluctant to take a chance and distribute material that might be illegal. The convenience store operator who drops the sale of Playboy to avoid a boycott or prosecution limits public access to the monthly centerfold pictures and other material some people regard as salacious or offensive. But also limited is public access to the not-infrequent news article or informative essay also contained in that magazine. Even the strongest proponents of the free flow of erotic material do not suggest that this kind of material should be thrust in the faces of those who are legitimately offended by erotic magazines or books or videos. Harm to the individual psyche

*Religious laws that governed some colonies in the 17th century forbade blasphemy, and blasphemous conduct could certainly involve sexually oriented books or pamphlets.

can be real even if undocumentable. All that advocates of freedom of expression seek is a society in which people can make up their own minds and have access to those materials that they want to read or watch.

COMMON TERMS

Obscenity—A narrow class of material defined by the Supreme Court in the *Miller* test (see pages 465–468). Material that is legally obscene is not protected by the First Amendment. Obscene material is sometimes referred to as hard-core pornography.

Indecent Material—Material that may be sexually graphic but is protected by the First Amendment. Indecent material is also referred to as adult material or sexually explicit material. Many laws ban the sale or distribution of indecent material to minors. Such material may, however, be freely distributed among adults.

EARLY OBSCENITY LAW

The first recorded obscenity prosecution in the United States occurred in 1815, when a man named Jesse Sharpless was fined for exhibiting a painting of a man "in an imprudent posture with a woman." There are on record earlier convictions for offenses tied to obscenity; these were prosecutions under common law for crimes against God, not for merely displaying erotic pictures. In 1821 Peter Holmes was convicted for publishing a spiced-up version of John Cleland's *Memoirs of a Woman of Pleasure.*

As the 19th century progressed, obscenity laws and prosecutions became more common, ebbing and flowing with major reform movements in the 1820s, 1830s, and in the wake of the Civil War. The first federal obscenity statute, a customs law regulating the importation of obscene articles, was adopted in 1842. The most comprehensive federal statute adopted during the century became law in 1873. Known as the Comstock Act because of the intense pressure applied on the Congress by a young man named Anthony Comstock, the law declared that all obscene books, pamphlets, pictures, and other materials were nonmailable. No definition of obscenity was provided by the Congress, however. The Comstock law, as amended, remains the federal law today.

Federal agencies such as the Bureau of Customs and the Post Office Department were the nation's most vigilant obscenity fighters during the late 19th and first half of the 20th centuries. Sometimes straying beyond what the law actually permitted, these agencies banned, burned, and confiscated huge amounts of erotic materials, including religious objects, pieces of art, books (including some of the best written during that era), magazines (including science and diving publications), and a wide array of material on birth control. When the motion picture industry began to grow in the early part of this century, local and state censors went after films that they believed to be obscene as well. The courts, especially the federal courts, became inundated with obscenity prosecutions and appeals. The Supreme Court of the United States seemed especially drawn to such litigation. Between 1957 and 1977, for example, the high court heard arguments in almost 90 obscenity cases and wrote opinions in nearly 40 of those cases. The remainder were decided by memoranda orders (see page 22 for a definition of this term).

DEFINING OBSCENITY

Outlawing obscenity is one thing. Defining it is something else. When American courts, in the wake of the adoption of the Comstock Act in 1873, first began considering what is and what is not obscenity they borrowed a British definition called the *Hicklin* rule.[2] Under this rule a work is obscene if **it has a tendency to deprave and corrupt those whose minds are open to such immoral influences and into whose hands it might fall.** Under this rule, then, if something might influence the mind of a child, it was regarded as obscene. In addition, if any part of the work, regardless of how small, met this definition, the entire work was regarded as obscene. This very broad and loose definition made it possible for both federal and state authorities to wage an aggressive and highly successful war against erotic materials in the first half of the 20th century.

In 1957 the Supreme Court abandoned the *Hicklin* rule, declaring that because of this rule American adults were permitted to read or watch only what was fit for children. "Surely this is to burn the house, to roast the pig," Justice Felix Frankfurter noted.[3] In abandoning the *Hicklin* rule, the high court was forced to fashion a new definition of obscenity, beginning with the case of *Roth* v. *U.S.*[4] in 1957. Over the next nine years, in a variety of obscenity rulings, what was called the *Roth-Memoirs* test was developed by the Supreme Court.[5] The test had three parts.

First, the dominant theme of the material taken as a whole must appeal to prurient interest in sex.

Second, a court must find that the material is patently offensive because it affronts contemporary community standards relating to the description or representation of sexual matters.

Third, before something can be found to be obscene, it must be utterly without redeeming social value.

While this entire test was far narrower than the *Hicklin* rule, it was the third part of the test that continually bedeviled government prosecutors. If a work had even the slightest social value, it could not be deemed to be obscene.

Prosecutions for obscenity did not occur in this nation until the early 19th century. In the 1820s and 1830s, many states adopted their first obscenity laws. The first federal law was passed in 1842. The government actively prosecuted obscenity in the wake of the Civil War,

SUMMARY

2. *Regina* v. *Hicklin*, L.R. 3 Q.B. 360 (1868).
3. *Butler* v. *Michigan*, 352 U.S. 380 (1957).
4. 354 U.S. 476 (1957).
5. See *Manual Enterprises, Inc.* v. *J. Edward Day*, 370 U.S. 478 (1962), *Jacobellis* v. *Ohio*, 378 U.S. 184 (1964), and *Memoirs of a Woman of Pleasure* v. *Massachusetts*, 383 U.S. 413 (1966).

and in 1873 the Congress adopted a strict new obscenity law. Obscenity was defined as being anything that had a tendency to deprave and corrupt those whose minds might be open to such immoral influences and into whose hands it might happen to fall. This was called the *Hicklin* rule. The rule meant that if any part of a book or other work had the tendency to deprave or corrupt any person (such as a child or overly sensitive individual) who might happen to see the work, the material was obscene and no person could buy it or see it. This definition facilitated government censorship of a wide range of materials.

In the 1950s and early 1960s, the Supreme Court adopted a new definition or test for obscenity, the *Roth-Memoirs* test. The test had three main parts:

1. The dominant theme of the material, taken as a whole, appeals to an average person's prurient interest in sex.
2. The material is patently offensive because it affronts contemporary community standards relating to sexual matters. It was assumed that there was a single, national standard that was applicable to all parts of the country.
3. The material is utterly without redeeming social value. It has no social value at all.

CONTEMPORARY OBSCENITY LAW

President Lyndon Johnson appointed a commission in 1967 to study the regulation of obscenity in the United States. Two years later a majority of the members of this blue-ribbon panel issued a report recommending the repeal of all laws that restricted the use of erotic materials by consenting adults.[6] But this was 1969 and Johnson was no longer president. Richard Nixon sat in the White House and flatly rejected the report. He vowed never to relax in the fight against obscenity, rejecting the commission's conclusion that the regular viewing or reading of obscenity produced no harmful effects in normal adults. The new president substantially changed the makeup of the Supreme Court as he made four appointments in three years.[*] By 1973, when the case of *Miller* v. *California*[7] was decided, a more conservative Supreme Court had its chance to redefine obscenity. This new test is the one courts must use today.

THE *MILLER* TEST

Marvin Miller was convicted of violating the California Penal Code for sending five unsolicited brochures to a restaurant in Newport Beach. The brochures, which advertised four erotic books and one film, contained pictures and drawings of men and women engaging in a variety of sexual activities. The recipient of the mailing complained to police, and Miller was prosecuted by state authorities.

6. *Report of the Commission on Obscenity and Pornography.*
7. 413 U.S. 15 (1973).

[*]President Nixon appointed Chief Justice Warren Burger and Associate Justices Harry Blackmun, Lewis Powell, and William Rehnquist.

In *Miller,* for the first time since 1957, a majority of the Supreme Court reached agreement on a definition of obscenity. Chief Justice Warren Burger and four other members of the high court agreed that material is obscene if the following standards are met:

In Miller, *for the first time since 1957, a majority of the Supreme Court reached agreement on a definition of obscenity.*

1. **An average person, applying contemporary local community standards, finds that the work, taken as a whole, appeals to prurient interest.**
2. **The work depicts in a patently offensive way sexual conduct specifically defined by applicable state law.**
3. **The work in question lacks serious literary, artistic, political, or scientific value.**

The implications and ambiguities in these three elements create the need for fuller explanation. As a result of the *Miller* ruling and subsequent obscenity decisions handed down by the court since 1973, some guidelines have emerged.

An Average Person

The first element of the *Miller* test asks if an average person, applying contemporary community standards, would find that the work, taken as a whole, appeals to prurient interest. It is the trier of fact who will make this determination. This can be the trial judge, but more commonly it is the jury. The Supreme Court expects the trier of fact to rely on knowledge of the standards of the residents of the community to decide whether the work appeals to a prurient interest. The juror is not supposed to use his or her own standards in this decision. The Supreme Court noted in 1974 that

> This Court has emphasized on more than one occasion that a principal concern in requiring that a judgment be made on the basis of contemporary community standards is to assure that the material is judged neither on the basis of each juror's personal opinion nor by its effect on a particular sensitive or insensitive person or group.[8]

Note the last phrase in this quote. The court expects the standards of an average person to be applied in making this critical determination. In California a trial judge told jurors to consider the effect of the material on all the members of the community, including children and highly sensitive persons. The Supreme Court ruled that these jury instructions were faulty.[9] "Children are not to be included for these purposes as part of the 'community,'" wrote Chief Justice Burger. However, instructing the jury to consider the impact of the material on sensitive or insensitive persons is permissible, so long as these persons are looked on as part of the entire community, Burger wrote. "The community includes all adults who comprise it, and a jury can consider them all in determining relevant community standards," Burger wrote. "The vice," he said, "is in focusing upon the most susceptible or sensitive members when judging the obscenity of the material."

8. *Hamling* v. *United States,* 418 U.S. 87 (1974).
9. *Pinkus* v. *U.S.,* 98 S. Ct.1808 (1978).

Community Standards

The definition of community standards is a key to the first part of the *Miller* test. The Supreme Court had failed to define which community standards governed a determination of obscenity under the *Roth-Memoirs* test; were these local, regional, or national standards? Two members of the court had declared in a plurality opinion that national standards were to be applied.[10] Chief Justice Burger made it clear in the *Miller* decision that local standards were to be applied. In most jurisdictions the term "local standards" has been translated to mean "state standards." All communities within the same state share the same standards. In fact, some state supreme courts have even ruled that local communities have no right to pass obscenity laws; the state has preempted this field.[11] The question of applicable community standards becomes an important factor in cases that involve the shipment of erotic material over long distances within the United States and in cases involving the importation of sexually explicit material from outside the United States.

In prosecutions initiated by the U.S. Postal Service, the government is free to choose the venue in which to try the case. This might be the city from which the material was sent; it might be the city in which it was received; or it might be any city through which the material passed during its transit. For example, a trial involving a magazine sent from Boston to Dallas might be held in Boston, Dallas, or anywhere in between. So Massachusetts standards might apply at the trial, or Texas standards, or even Pennsylvania or Kentucky standards if the publication passed through or over those states during its shipment. This government practice is called "venue shopping," or selecting a site where a conviction is most easily obtained. A postmaster in Oregon asked a postmaster in Wyoming to solicit (using a false name) erotic material distributed by an Oregon man. After the defendant sent material to Wyoming he was tried using Wyoming standards, not Oregon standards. The record shows that the defendant had never resided in, traveled through, or had any previous business contact in Wyoming. The 10th U.S. Circuit Court of Appeals upheld the conviction, noting that under the existing law "federal enforcement officers . . . are free to shop for venue from which juries with the most restrictive views are likely to be impanelled."[12] When imported erotic material is seized, the standards of the state in which the material is seized are applied at trial.

The application of local standards is causing increasing problems today as more and more of our mass media are distributed nationally, rather than locally or even regionally. The standards of one small community can at times effectively censor what is seen by the nation. In the late 1980s, Home Dish Satellite Corporation of New York City was beaming hard-core sex films to 30,000 subscribers across the nation and soft-core movies to 1.2 million other customers. Fifty persons in Montgomery County, Ala., subscribed to the service, and law enforcement officials there indicted the company on charges of violating the state obscenity statutes. Home Dish pleaded guilty to the charges and paid $150,000 in penalties. The grand jury also indicted GTE Corporation and its satellite subsidiaries. To escape the long arm of Alabama law, GTE dumped Home Dish off the satellite, which put the company out of business. Lawyers

10. *Jacobellis* v. *Ohio*, 378 U.S. 184 (1964).
11. *Spokane* v. *Portch*, 94 Wash. 2d 342 (1979).
12. *U.S.* v. *Blucher*, 581 F. 2d 244 (1978).

said that this case was the first time in the nation's history that local criminal laws were applied to programs carried nationwide by satellite technology. In 1994 a California couple was prosecuted for sending sexual images over a computer bulletin board carried on the Internet. Bulletin boards are generally small-scale information systems run out of someone's home and carried on a larger system like the Internet, a vast computer network that serves millions of computer users worldwide. The Amateur Action Computer Bulletin Board (AACBB) system featured e-mail, chat lines, public messages, and explicit sexual files that only paying bulletin board members could access, transfer, and download to their own computers. Robert and Carleen Thomas of Milipitas, Calif., were each convicted of 10 counts of transmitting obscenity through interstate telephone lines. Each count carries a penalty of up to five years in jail and a $250,000 fine. The Thomases had previously been investigated by the San Jose, Calif., police department, which ruled that the erotic material on the AACBB was not obscene under California standards. A postal inspector in Memphis joined the bulletin board under a false name and received the images through his computer in Tennessee. He initiated the complaint against the Thomases. Mike Godwin, a lawyer for the Electronic Frontier Foundation, said that the case had "one community attempting to dictate standards for the whole country."[13] The trial court's verdict was upheld by the 6th U.S. Circuit Court of Appeals in January of 1996, which noted that if the defendants didn't want to face a trial in Tennessee, they should not have enrolled a member from Tennessee.[14] The Supreme Court rejected an appeal by the California couple.

Patent Offensiveness

The second element of the *Miller* test says that a work is obscene if it depicts in a patently offensive way sexual conduct specifically defined by applicable state law. Patent offensiveness is also to be judged by the trier of fact, using contemporary community standards. But the Supreme Court has put limits on this judgment, ruling that only what it calls hard-core sexual material meets the patently offensive standard. Georgia courts ruled that the motion picture *Carnal Knowledge,* an R-rated film, was patently offensive. The Supreme Court reversed this ruling, saying that the Georgia courts misunderstood this second part of the *Miller* test.[15] Material that was patently offensive, Justice Rehnquist wrote, included "representations or descriptions of ultimate sexual acts, normal or perverted, actual or simulated" and "representations or descriptions of masturbation, excretory functions, and lewd exhibition of genitals." Rehnquist acknowledged that this catalog of descriptions was not exhaustive, but that only material like this qualifies as patently offensive material. The second part of the *Miller* test was "intended to fix substantive constitutional limitations . . . on the type of material . . . subject to a determination of obscenity," he added.

State laws are supposed to define the kinds of material or conduct that are prohibited as obscene. Many state obscenity statutes contain Rehnquist's descriptions noted above as their definition of obscenity. Other state laws are less precise. The Supreme Court has even given

State laws are supposed to define the kinds of material or conduct that are prohibited as obscene.

13. "Couple Guilty of Pornography," 12; see also Wallace and Mangan, *Sex, Laws, and Cyberspace.*
14. *U.S.* v. *Thomas,* 74 F. 3d 701 (1996).
15. *Jenkins* v. *Georgia,* 418 U.S. 153 (1974).

its approval to state laws that contain no descriptive phrases so long as the state supreme court has construed (or interpreted) the law to prohibit only the narrowly defined kind of material outlined by Justice Rehnquist.[16]

Serious Value

To be legally obscene a work must lack serious literary, artistic, political, or scientific value. While not as broad as the "utterly without redeeming social value" element in the *Roth-Memoirs* test, this third criterion in the *Miller* test nevertheless acts as a brake on judges and juries eager to convict on the basis of the first two parts of the test. The judge is supposed to play a pronounced role in deciding whether a work has serious value. The serious value element is not judged by the tastes or standards of the average person. The test is not whether an ordinary person in the community would find serious literary, artistic, political, or scientific value, but whether a reasonable person *could* find such value in the material.[17] Jurors are supposed to determine whether a reasonable person would see a serious value in the work. Both the state and the defense will frequently introduce expert testimony to try to "educate" the jury on the relative merit of the material in question.

The Supreme Court has not provided lower courts with specific guidelines regarding serious value; at least not as specific as the guidelines for patently offensive material. But the high court has continually warned lower courts "to remain sensitive to any infringement on genuinely serious literary, artistic, political, or scientific value."[18] The Supreme Court has also instructed lower appellate courts not to hesitate to scrutinize trial court judgments regarding serious value. The determination of whether a book or magazine or film lacks value "is particularly amenable to appellate review," wrote Justice Harry Blackmun.[19] So while a trial judge or an appellate court should be reluctant to second-guess a jury on a determination of contemporary community standards or patent offensiveness, the judge or court should not be hesitant in making an independent determination that a work has literary, artistic, political, or scientific value.

THE *MILLER* TEST

1. An average person, applying contemporary local community standards, finds that the work, taken as a whole, appeals to prurient interest.
2. The work depicts in a patently offensive way sexual conduct specifically defined by applicable state law.
3. The work in question lacks serious literary, artistic, political, or scientific value.

---

16. *Ward* v. *Illinois*, 431 U.S. 767 (1977).
17. *Pope* v. *Illinois*, 107 S. Ct. 1918 (1987).
18. *Miller* v. *California*, 413 U.S. 15 (1973).
19. *Smith* v. *U.S.*, 431 U.S. 291 (1977).

OTHER STANDARDS

The three-part test developed by the Supreme Court in *Miller* v. *California* is the legal test for obscenity in the United States today. But the Supreme Court, lower courts, and other elements of the government have with varying degrees of success attempted to raise additional standards by which to judge erotic material. Here is a brief outline of some of these standards.

Variable Obscenity

The Supreme Court has ruled it is permissible for states to adopt what are known as **variable obscenity statutes.** Material that may be legally distributed and sold to adults may be banned as obscene for distribution or sale to juveniles, usually persons under the age of 18. This is not a return to the old *Hicklin* rule in which if something is obscene to a child, it is obscene for everyone and its distribution or sale can be completely banned. Variable obscenity means a state can have two standards for obscenity, one for adults and one for minors. This concept emerged from the high court ruling in *Ginsberg* v. *New York* in 1968.[20] In *Ginsberg* the Supreme Court ruled that the First Amendment did not bar New York state from prosecuting the owner of a Long Island luncheonette who sold four so-called girlie magazines to a 16-year-old boy. The magazines, which contained female nudity, could have been legally sold to an adult. Justice Brennan said the state could maintain one definition of obscenity for adults and another for juveniles because the Supreme Court recognized the important state interest in protecting the welfare of children. But even variable obscenity statutes are not without constitutional limits. In 1975 the Supreme Court struck down such a law in *Erznoznik* v. *City of Jacksonville*[21] because the definition of material that could not be distributed to juveniles was not specific enough. A city ordinance barred drive-in theaters from showing films in which either female breasts or buttocks were exposed if the theater screen was visible from the street. The ordinance was justified as a means of protecting young people from exposure to such material. "Only in relatively narrow and well-defined circumstances may government bar dissemination of protected material to children," Justice Lewis Powell wrote. Banning the exhibition of nudity is simply not narrow enough; only materials that have significant erotic appeal to juveniles may be suppressed under such a statute, he added. A simple ban on all nudity, regardless of context, justification, or other factors, violates the First Amendment.

Although states and cities may adopt variable obscenity laws, these regulations cannot in any way interfere with the flow of constitutionally protected material to adults. Some communities have failed to meet this challenge. In 1992 the state of Washington adopted a statute that barred the sale of "erotic" recordings, tapes, and CDs to young people. Under the statute a county prosecutor would obtain a recording from a music store and then ask a local judge to declare the recording to be erotic in terms of the law.* This was called the stage one ruling. If

20. 390 U.S. 51 (1968).
21. 422 U.S. 205 (1975).

*The statute defined erotic material as material "the dominant theme of which taken as a whole, appeals to the prurient interest of minors in sex; which is patently offensive because it affronts contemporary community standards relating to the description or representation of sexual matters or sado-masochistic abuse; and is utterly without redeeming social value."

such a declaration was made, the store owner could either label the recording "Adults Only" and not sell it to anyone under 18 years old, or stop selling it to any person. Then, if that store owner, *or any other store owner in the state,* either failed to label the record or sold it to a minor, he or she could be prosecuted for violating the statute. Washington courts ruled that the law was unconstitutional for a variety of reasons. There was no provision in the law that required a local court that had declared a recording to be obscene to notify all record stores in the state of this determination.[22] Therefore another retailer could be prosecuted for selling to a minor a record that he or she did not know had been declared fit only for adults. The law was also overbroad, the courts ruled, because it regulated speech that is not obscene for adults by creating a massive chilling effect that would inhibit the legally permissible sale of material to record buyers over the age of 18. Finally, a record store owner was entitled under law to a jury trial on the matter of whether a record was erotic. The ruling by the judge was insufficient.[23]

Laws regulating the sale of books and magazines to young people are perhaps the toughest for legislatures to craft. How can you require a bookseller to limit juvenile access to books acceptable to adults without limiting adult access to these same books? A Virginia statute prohibited the commercial display of books and magazines that contained nudity and sexual conduct or described "sexual excitement," if such works were accessible to persons under the age of 18. But everything from steamy novels to classical art catalogs contain such material. It is not possible to simply keep such material behind the counter. Does the bookseller have to maintain a separate adults-only section for every category of books? Or does the bookseller ban juveniles from the store? A federal court found the statute seriously deficient.[24] The only way the state was able to salvage this law was for the state supreme court to first narrowly define the kind of material prohibited by the statute, and then rule that in order for the state to win a conviction under the law, it would have to show that the bookseller knowingly afforded juveniles an opportunity to peruse (study the cover or leaf through the pages) the material or took no reasonable steps to prevent such perusal.[25] One of the most difficult problems relating to variable obscenity is whether the government can restrict the flow of adult material on the Internet to shield children from this matter. This issue is discussed in depth on pages 487–493.

Child Pornography

For more than 20 years both the states and the federal government have had laws restricting the distribution and even the possession of material called child pornography. The previous section of this chapter discussed variable obscenity, the court doctrine that permits the state to stop the distribution and sale of certain kinds of nonobscene material to children, material that may be freely sold and distributed to adults. As such, variable obscenity focuses on the receiver of the material: Is it a child or an adult? Child pornography laws focus on content of

---

22. *Soundgarden* v. *Eikenberry,* 21 M.L.R. 1025 (1992).
23. *Soundgarden* v. *Eikenberry,* 871 P. 2d 1050 (1994).
24. *American Booksellers* v. *Strobel,* 617 F. Supp. 698 (1985).
25. *American Booksellers Association* v. *Virginia,* 12 M.L.R. 2271 (1986).

the suspect material. These laws prohibit the distribution and sale of material that depicts children in erotic poses or participating in erotic acts. In 1982 the U.S. Supreme Court unanimously upheld a New York child pornography statute.[26] The state law prohibits any person from knowingly promoting a sexual performance by a child under the age of 16 years by distributing material that photographically depicts such a performance. The statute explicitly defines sexual performance as sexual conduct and lists the kinds of conduct that are not permitted to be shown. Justice Byron White wrote that child pornography defined in the statute is unprotected speech and can be subject to content-based regulation. The state has a strong state interest in protecting the well-being of children. To help prevent the abuse of children who are made to engage in sexual conduct for commercial purposes, the state can prohibit the distribution of material that shows children engaged in such conduct, even if this material might not be obscene under the three-part *Miller* test. White said that when a judge considers photographic depictions of live sexual performances by children, the *Miller* formulation should be adjusted in the following respects: "A trier of fact need not find that the material appeals to the prurient interest of the average person; it is not required that sexual conduct portrayed be done so in a patently offensive manner; and the material at issue need not be considered as a whole." The value of permitting live performances and photographic reproductions of children engaged in lewd sexual conduct is exceedingly modest, the justice said. The law is aimed at stopping the sexual exploitation of children. One sure way to stop, or at least reduce, this exploitation is to ban the distribution of films in which children are depicted in sexual conduct.

The law is aimed at stopping the sexual exploitation of children.

When the Supreme Court gave its imprimatur to the child pornography laws in 1982, many of these laws were then amended to outlaw the mere possession of erotic images of children in addition to barring the sale and distribution of such material. Those who challenged these new laws argued that the high court had forbidden the government from punishing the mere possession of obscenity in a 1969 ruling, *Stanley* v. *Georgia*.[27] In that case the high court ruled that the Constitution protects the private possession of otherwise unprotected speech. "If the First Amendment means anything," Justice Thurgood Marshall wrote, "it means that the state has no business telling a man, sitting alone in his own house, what books he may read or what films he may watch." Nevertheless, in 1990, in a 6–3 ruling, the Supreme Court upheld the constitutionality of an Ohio law that permitted the prosecution of those who merely possess child pornography.[28] The *Stanley* precedent was not controlling, Justice Byron White wrote, because in that case Georgia had "sought to proscribe the private possession of obscenity because it was concerned that obscenity would poison the mind of its viewers." White said such a paternalistic motive was impermissible under the First Amendment. But the state of Ohio sought to ban the possession of child pornography to "destroy the market for the exploitation of children. It is reasonable," White said, "for the state to conclude that it will decrease the production of child pornography if it penalizes those who possess and view the product." The Ohio statute is written very broadly and bans the possession of depictions of a minor who is not the person's child or ward in a state of nudity. The Ohio Supreme Court, to

26. *New York* v. *Ferber*, 458 U.S. 747 (1982).
27. 394 U.S. 557 (1969).
28. *Osborne* v. *Ohio*, 110 S. Ct. 169 (1990).

save the statute from being ruled unconstitutionally broad, narrowed the meaning of the statute to apply only to "depictions of nudity involving a lewd exhibition or graphic focus on a minor's genitals." The Ohio court also said the state would have to prove criminal intent to convict someone under the law. A Florida court in 1997 ruled that storing images of children engaged in sexually explicit acts on the hard disk of a computer constituted possession of the material under terms of the Florida statute, which is similar to most state possession laws. The defendant argued that the material, which included photos from magazines and books scanned onto the hard drive, was not possessed until the images were viewed on the monitor or printed out. (The photos were discovered by a technician who was servicing the computer in a store.) The court disagreed.

> That pornographic images of children are scanned into a computer rather than pressed into the pages of a magazine, or that the images are stored on a hard drive rather than in a shoe box, does not change the fact that a defendant possesses pornographic representations of actual children.[29]

In 1996 the Congress adopted an amendment to the original federal child pornography law that bars the sale and distribution of any images that "appear" to depict minors performing sexually explicit acts. Under this statute child pornography is defined to include not only actual images (photos, videotapes, films) of children but also computer-generated images and other pictures that are generated by electronic, mechanical, or other means in which "such visual depiction is, or appears to be, a minor engaging in sexually explicit conduct." Drawings, cartoons, sculptures, and paintings are not included under the new law. Whereas the original child pornography laws were justified as a means to protect children from being exploited, the 1996 Child Pornography Prevention Act has been justified as a means to protect children from pedophiles and child molesters, people whose criminal behavior may be stimulated by such images. The law specifically states that no prosecution can be maintained if the material was produced by adults and was not advertised, promoted, described, or presented in such a way as to suggest children were in fact depicted in the images. Three U.S. courts of appeals have ruled on the constitutionality of this law. In 1999 the 1st U.S. Circuit Court of Appeals rejected a challenge to the statute by an appellant who argued that the phrase "appears to be minors" was too vague and resulted in the statute being overbroad. The court disagreed, ruling that ordinary persons can tell the difference between minors and adults pictured in the material.[30] In November of that same year the 11th U.S. Circuit Court of Appeals reached the same conclusion. The court, in ruling on the same argument—that the language "appears to be minors" was too vague—said that the statute only targets images that are virtually indistinguishable to unsuspecting viewers from unretouched photos of actual children.[31] One month later the 9th U.S. Circuit Court of Appeals ruled that the Child Pornography Protection Act of 1996 was unconstitutional. The law is overbroad, the court ruled. There is no explicit standard as to what the phrase "appears to be minors" means, the judges wrote. The phrase provides no measure to

29. *State* v. *Cohen,* Fla. Dist. Ct. App. 4th Dist. No. 96-2085, 7/2/97.
30. *U.S.* v. *Hilton,* 167 F. 3d 61 (1999).
31. *United States* v. *Acheson,* 28 M.L.R. 1219 (1999).

guide an ordinarily intelligent person about the prohibited conduct. "Because the 1996 Act attempts to criminalize disavowed impulses of the mind manifested in illicit creative acts, we determine that censorship through the enactment of criminal laws intended to control an evil idea cannot satisfy the constitutional requirements of the First Amendment," wrote Judge Donald Molloy.[32] With three circuit courts in disagreement regarding the statute, the odds are high that the Supreme Court will be forced to resolve this matter.

Pornography and Women

Some women have argued for many years that pornography both discriminates against women and provokes violence against women.[33] Several communities have considered adopting laws that revise the definition of obscenity to reflect this argument. Such a law was adopted in Indianapolis in 1984. The law declared that works that portrayed the graphic, sexually explicit subordination of women, whether in picture or in words, were pornographic if they also included scenes or pictures in which women were presented as sexual objects who enjoy pain or humiliation; who experience sexual pleasure in being raped; who are tied up, cut up, or mutilated; and who are presented as being dominated, violated, exploited, or possessed through postures or positions of servility or submission. U.S. District Judge Sarah Evans Barker ruled that the law was unconstitutionally vague and that the kind of expression it sought to bar was protected by the First Amendment. The 7th U.S. Circuit Court of Appeals sustained this ruling, noting that under the law, sexually explicit speech or expression is pornography or is not, depending on the perspective of the author. Speech that subordinates women is pornography, no matter how great the literary or political value of the work. Speech that portrays women in positions of equality is lawful, no matter how graphic the sexual conduct.[34] This ruling ended the movement to adopt such laws in the United States. But one of the proponents of this view, law professor Catherine McKinnon, was among a team of advocates to convince the Canadian Supreme Court to rule that erotic material that is harmful to women can be legally banned in that country.

The *Miller* test is used today by American courts to determine whether something is obscene. **SUMMARY** It has three parts. Material is legally obscene under the following conditions:

1. An average person, applying contemporary local community standards, finds that the work, taken as a whole, appeals to prurient interest. This test requires the fact finder to apply local (usually state) standards rather than a national standard. The jury (or the judge if there is not a jury) determines the standard, based on its knowledge of what is acceptable in the community.

32. *Free Speech Coalition* v. *Reno,* 28 M.L.R. 1225 (1999).
33. See "Pornography," 32, "First Amendment Under Fire," 40, and Strossen, *Defending Pornography* for a discussions of these issues.
34. *American Booksellers Association* v. *Hudnut,* 598 F. Supp. 1316 (1984); aff'd. 771 F. 2d 232 (1985).

2. The work depicts in a patently offensive way sexual conduct specifically defined by applicable state law. Again, the fact finder in the case determines patent offensiveness, based on local community standards. But the Supreme Court has ruled that only so-called hard-core pornography can be found to be patently offensive. Also, either the legislature or the state supreme court must specifically define the kind of offensive material that may be declared to be obscene.

3. The material lacks serious literary, artistic, political, or scientific value. This is a question of law, not of fact, to be decided in large part by the judge.

The three-part *Miller* test is the test that courts must use in defining obscenity in all cases except those involving juveniles. The Supreme Court has ruled that states may use a broader definition of obscenity when they attempt to block the sale or distribution of erotic material to children or when they attempt to stop the exploitation of children who are forced to engage in sexual conduct by pornographic filmmakers. But such laws must be careful so as not to unconstitutionally ban legal material as well. The federal courts blocked an attempt by the city of Indianapolis to outlaw written and visual material that might result in discrimination against women or provoke violence against women and children.

CONTROLLING OBSCENITY

For more than 100 years, the typical manner in which the state has attempted to control obscenity has been through a criminal prosecution. Such lawsuits are complicated, and to be successful in these cases, prosecutors must follow carefully prescribed paths in deciding whether material is obscene, in collecting and seizing evidence, and in making arrests. Often persons charged with exhibiting or selling obscene materials seek to plea-bargain with the state to reduce the charge. Booksellers, theater owners, and other merchants who deal in pornographic materials often do not want to fight the government in an obscenity prosecution. They are not in the business to crusade for the First Amendment. Their goal is to stay out of jail and to return to selling books or showing movies. If the state can be convinced to reduce the obscenity charge in exchange for a guilty plea, the defendant can often get by with paying a fine instead of going to jail and be back in business within a few days of the arrest. Prosecutors seem amenable to such plea bargaining because, as one noted, "our business is to stop public distribution of certain obscene materials, not put people in jail."

If a case goes to trial, the judge and the jury are the ones who must determine whether the material sold or exhibited is obscene. The fact finder in the trial—the jury or the judge if there is not a jury—determines parts one and two of the *Miller* test, prurient appeal and patent offensiveness. A jury can also rule on the serious value of a work, but since this determination is normally regarded as a matter of law, a judge plays a far greater role in this determination.

In addition to determining whether the material is obscene, jurors are also called on to answer the question of whether the defendant was knowledgeable about the contents of what was being sold, distributed, or published. This is called *scienter,* or guilty knowledge. In a

1959 case, *Smith v. California,*[35] the U.S. Supreme Court ruled that before a person can be convicted for selling obscene books or magazines or whatever, the state has to prove that the seller was aware of the contents of this material. "If the bookseller is criminally liable without knowledge of the contents . . . he will tend to restrict the books he sells to those he has inspected; and thus the state will have imposed a restriction upon the distribution of constitutionally protected as well as obscene literature," Justice Brennan wrote.

But what exactly must the state prove under the scienter requirement? Does the government have to produce evidence that the seller of the erotic material knew that it was legally obscene, but sold it anyway? No. The high court has ruled that it is sufficient that the government prove that the defendant had a general knowledge of the contents of the material, that a movie contains sadistic scenes, for example.[36] In the mid-1990s the prosecutor of Whatcom County, Wash., brought obscenity charges against two persons who operated a newsstand in the city of Bellingham for selling a publication called "Answer Me!", a magazine devoted to the discussion of rape. The newsstand operators insisted that the contents of the magazine, though sexually graphic, were nevertheless a satire. The prosecutor disagreed. But in the end that issue proved to be irrelevant. The jury acquitted the couple because, jurors said, the state had failed to prove that the newsstand operators were aware of the contents of the publication. There was insufficient evidence of scienter, or guilty knowledge.[37]

The criminal prosecution of obscenity in any community depends on whether the local prosecutor wants to be aggressive in this area of the law and on how the local courts have defined obscenity. Some prosecutors are militant foes of erotic material and continually prosecute purveyors of adult material. A great many more, however, find obscenity prosecutions far less important than the murder, rape, assault, robbery, and burglary cases that deluge their offices. At the same time, the citizens of some communities are far more tolerant of adult material than their counterparts in other regions. Within certain parameters, the people in a community can generally read the books they want to read, watch the films they want to watch, and buy the magazines they want to buy. What appellate courts and the Supreme Court say about obscenity is relevant in only an indirect way.

CIVIL NUISANCE LAWS

Some communities have attempted to use civil nuisance laws rather than criminal statutes to try to stop the flow of adult material. These statutes or ordinances define a public nuisance to include the sale or distribution of obscenity. Obscenity is defined by the three-part *Miller* test. Prosecutors can bring a nuisance suit against an adult bookstore or an adult theater, much as they can bring a nuisance suit against a factory that is polluting a nearby lake. A judge will first rule on whether or not obscene materials are being sold or distributed—if in fact a nuisance exists. If the court finds the material to be legally obscene, it issues an injunction to the defendant to abate or stop this nuisance. The defendant can no longer sell the books or magazines declared to be a nuisance. Case closed.

35. 361 U.S. 147 (1959).
36. *Hamling* v. *United States,* 418 U.S. 87 (1974).
37. Sheehan and Buller, "Jury Acquits."

Some communities have gone one step further in their laws and have given the court the option of issuing a second injunction as well, a so-called standards injunction. Under this second restraining order, the court forbids the defendant to sell material *comparable* to the items previously declared to be obscene. If the defendant violates this second ordinance, he or she can be held in contempt of court. Some persons have argued that the second injunction, which bans the future sale of comparable material, is an illegal prior restraint. Thus far most appellate courts have not agreed with this argument.[38] But the 6th U.S. Circuit Court of Appeals in 1986 struck down a Paducah, Ky., ordinance that was similar, but generally broader, than the typical civil nuisance statute.[39] Under this ordinance, once the board of commissioners ruled that the material in question was in fact obscene, the bookstore or theater was declared to be a public nuisance. Abatement proceedings were then initiated against the owner of the facility. If an abatement ruling was issued, the store owner had to forfeit all business licenses and permits. This action put the owner out of business and barred him or her from selling any books or magazines, not just obscene material. The Court of Appeals ruled that this ordinance was an unconstitutional prior restraint, one that was similar to the prior restraint placed against J.M. Near by government officials in Minnesota nearly 60 years earlier.[40] The application of this ordinance was a violation of the First Amendment, the court said.

RICO STATUTES

RICO stands for the Racketeering Influence and Corrupt Organizations Act, a law that was adopted by the U.S. Congress in 1970 as Title IX of the Organized Crime Control Act. The purpose of the law was to limit the influence of organized crime on legitimate business and labor unions. Congress specifically stated that the purpose of the statute was "to seek eradication of organized crime in the United States . . . by establishing new penal provisions, and by providing enhanced sanctions and new remedies to deal with the unlawful activities of those engaged in organized crime." The target of this law, and the similar laws in nearly 30 states, is organized crime—the mob, if you will.

Today, RICO statutes are used to fight a wide variety of illegal activities, including the production, sale, and distribution of obscenity. And although most experts believe organized crime plays some role in the pornography business, prosecutors are using the RICO laws to prosecute a wide range of defendants—most of whom have no connection with organized crime—from large-scale publishers and chain bookstore owners to mom-and-pop magazine stands.

The penalty for violating a RICO statute is a stiff fine and/or a 20-year jail sentence, fairly strong medicine. But the extraordinary aspect of these laws is that they permit the courts to order the guilty party to forfeit any property and proceeds derived from a RICO violation.[41] A bookstore owner, for example, could be required to give up his or her store, all the stock, and any money that was earned from the sale of the material. A typical criminal conviction for obscenity carries a small fine and a short jail term. Before the government may use the RICO

38. See, for example, *Fehlhaber* v. *North Carolina,* 675 F. 2d 1365 (1982).
39. *City of Paducah* v. *Investment Entertainment, Inc.,* 791 F. 2d 463 (1986).
40. *Near* v. *Minnesota,* 283 U.S. 697 (1931).
41. Bunker, Gates, and Splichal, "RICO and Obscenity Prosecutions," 692.

statutes in prosecuting anyone, it must demonstrate that there has been a pattern of illegal activity. This pattern is much easier to prove than it sounds, however, because all the government has to prove is that the defendant has committed two illegal acts (the nature of which are defined in the statute) in the past 10 years. These can even be acts for which the defendant was never charged, or at the federal level, acts for which the defendant has even been acquitted in a state court. When RICO laws are used to prosecute persons involved in the sale or distribution of printed matter or films, the government faces the additional problem of coping with the First Amendment. And while the few Supreme Court rulings on this matter are not regarded as satisfactory by most civil libertarians, they have helped a little.

The Indiana RICO statute received the first court test, and in 1989 the U.S. Supreme Court ruled that the First Amendment bars law enforcement authorities from seizing the inventory of an adult bookstore prior to a trial at which the material has been ruled to be obscene.[42] Three bookstores in Ft. Wayne were emptied and then padlocked after their owners were charged with, but not yet convicted of, engaging in a pattern of racketeering by repeatedly selling obscene books and films. Justice Byron White said the First Amendment's prohibition of prior restraint bars the state from confiscating material that has not yet been judged obscene. "The state cannot escape the constitutional safeguards of our prior cases by merely recategorizing a pattern of obscenity violations as racketeering," White said. The court was unanimous on this point.

But the high court did, with a 6–3 vote, sustain the use of the racketeering statutes to crack down on pornography, provided no confiscation takes place before a trial, even though the laws invoke a much harsher penalty. Four years later the high court sent a mixed message to federal prosecutors who sought to use the RICO statutes to prosecute purveyors of pornographic materials. In a 5–4 ruling in *Alexander* v. *U.S.*,[43] the Supreme Court said it was not a violation of the First Amendment for the government to seize a defendant's assets after he was convicted of racketeering by selling obscene material. In this case the owner of a chain of adult bookstores and movie houses was forced to forfeit his businesses and almost $9 million in profits. The defendant argued that the seizure violated his First Amendment rights by taking thousands of copies of books and other materials that were not obscene. Chief Justice Rehnquist called the forfeiture a permissible criminal punishment, not a prior restraint.

But in a second case decided the same day, *Austin* v. *United States*,[44] a case that involved illegal drugs, not obscenity, the high court unanimously ruled that a massive government seizure of any commodity as a punishment for violating a federal statute may violate the protection guaranteed by the Eighth Amendment that persons shall not be subject to excessive fines. Justice Harry Blackmun wrote that there must be some relationship between the gravity of an offense and the value of the property that is seized. The high court sent both cases back to lower courts to make a determination on whether the seizure of property was excessive and a violation of the Eighth Amendment. Even without the forfeiture provisions, however, the RICO statutes are a powerful weapon the government can use to try to reduce the flow of erotic adult material.

Justice Harry Blackmun wrote that there must be some relationship between the gravity of an offense and the value of the property that is seized.

42. *Ft. Wayne Books* v. *Indiana*, 109 S. Ct. 916 (1989).
43. 113 S. Ct. 2766 (1993).
44. 113 S. Ct. 2801 (1993).

POSTAL CENSORSHIP

No government agency is more diligent in policing obscenity in the United States than the U.S. Postal Service. The Post Office has been on the job for more than a century. In 1878 the U.S. Supreme Court ruled that the use of mail in the United States is a privilege, not a right.[45] This ruling has given the Postal Service substantial power to control the content of the mail. Although the government cannot legally tamper with first class mail, it is still illegal to send obscenity through the mail regardless of how it is delivered. Magazine sellers, book distributors, and others who use other postal classifications (2nd class, 4th class) to ship their goods face even more serious problems.

The 1873 Comstock Act (see page 462) provides the basic authority for the U.S. Postal Service to regulate the flow of erotic material in the mail. But many other laws are also applicable. For example, postal patrons who have received unwanted solicitations for what they define as obscene material can request the Postal Service to inform the mailer that they no longer wish to receive such material. Once this notice is sent by the Postal Service to the mailer, any subsequent mailing to that particular patron is a violation of the law. Because the mail patron decides whether the material is obscene, this law can affect a broad range of solicitations. The Supreme Court upheld the constitutionality of this law, Section 3008 of Title 39 of the U.S. Code, in a 1970 ruling.[46] Chief Justice Burger wrote that "It seems to us that a mailer's right to communicate must stop at the mailbox of an unreceptive addressee."

Section 3010 of Title 39 of the U.S. Code permits a mail patron to block the delivery of sexually oriented advertising, even if he or she has never received such a mailing. The mail patron simply informs the Postal Service that he or she does not wish to receive any advertising for sexually explicit material. The statute contains a definition of such material. The Postal Service periodically publishes a list of all mail patrons who have indicated they don't want to receive such advertisements and it is up to the mailers to buy a copy of this list or face the possibility of criminal and civil penalties if convicted of sending such material to a person whose name is on the list. The federal courts have upheld the constitutionality of this law as well.[47]

FILM CENSORSHIP

Censorship of motion pictures by cities and states is an infrequent occurrence today. The operators of so-called adult or X-rated theaters in most communities generally have a good idea of what kinds of films can be shown and what kinds of films will invite prosecution from local authorities, and they tend to operate within the permissible limits. As recently as the mid-1960s, however, there were active censorship boards in nearly 50 American cities. The application of a voluntary film rating system by the Motion Picture Association of America, or MPAA (G, PG, PG-13, R, and NC-17), has satisfied the concerns of most persons worried about the content of

Censorship of motion pictures by cities and states is an infrequent occurrence today.

45. ex parte *Jackson,* 96 U.S. 727 (1878).
46. *Rowan* v. *Post Office,* 397 U.S. 728 (1970).
47. *Pent-R-Books* v. *U.S. Postal Service,* 328 F. Supp. 297 (1971).

the movies. Recently, however, some people have called for theaters to tighten up the scrutiny of who is admitted to theaters in the wake of outbursts of violence at American schools.

Motion pictures were not granted First Amendment protection until 1952.[48] During the 1960s and 1970s courts scrutinized several local film censorship ordinances and established rigid guidelines to force local communities to conform to First Amendment principles.[49] Generally, censorship boards and the courts must make prompt rulings on whether a film may be exhibited, and the government bears the burden of proving that a film is not protected by the First Amendment.

Video dealers are not bound by the MPAA rating code and often stock films that would only be exhibited in so-called X-rated movie houses. The rules that apply to censoring movies in theaters apply in no small measure to video sales and rentals as well. Oklahoma City officials discovered this when they raided video stores and confiscated copies of the 20-year-old Academy Award–winning German film "The Tin Drum." The R-rated film was seized because authorities said it violated state child pornography laws. Police submitted a copy of the film to a judge, who later told them in his opinion the motion picture contained child pornography. No hearing was held, no written order was issued, and there was no evidence that the judge had watched any part of the film. Nevertheless, police confiscated all nine copies of the motion picture on the shelves of rental stores and in the home of at least one rental customer. A U.S. district court intervened and enjoined city officials from withholding the film until a proper hearing was conducted. "The admitted goal to remove the film from public access without a prior adversarial hearing runs afoul of the First Amendment," the judge ruled.[50]

Ten months later the same U.S. District Court ruled that distribution of the film did not violate the Oklahoma child pornography statute, which excludes from its purview material that does not have as its dominant theme an appeal to purient interests and that has literary, artistic, educational, or scientific value. The court said the film does not have a dominant sexual theme and has undisputed artistic merit.[51]

SUMMARY

Postal censorship has historically been an important means used by the U.S. government to control the flow of obscene material in the United States. Today the postal service is less aggressive and permits postal patrons themselves to block the delivery of solicitations for adult materials and other obscene publications. Communities may also censor films before they are shown, so long as the community follows strict procedures laid down by the U.S. Supreme Court.

48. *Burstyn* v. *Wilson,* 343 U.S. 495 (1952).
49. See, for example, *Freedman* v. *Maryland,* 380 U.S. 51 (1965); *Interstate Circuit* v. *Dallas,* 390 U.S. 676 (1968); and *Star* v. *Preller,* 95 S. Ct. 217 (1974).
50. *Video Software Dealers Assoc., Inc.* v. *Oklahoma City,* 6 F. Supp. 2d 1292 (1997).
51. *Oklahoma ex rel Macy* v. *Blockbuster Videos Inc.,* 27 M.L.R. 1248 (1998).

REGULATION OF NONOBSCENE EROTIC MATERIAL

Contemporary battles over sexually explicit material focus on material that doesn't meet the legal definition of obscenity. Magazines like Penthouse and Playboy, rap music, homoerotic art exhibits, adult films and the Internet are among a wide variety of mass media targeted for control and even censorship in various parts of the nation. Although this material is certainly offensive to some persons, it generally enjoys the full protection of the First Amendment because it does not qualify as obscenity under the *Miller* test. Here is an outline of some of these legal skirmishes.

ZONING LAWS

Many communities have attempted to use locational zoning ordinances to regulate businesses that sell or display sexually explicit but not legally obscene material. Seattle passed a law in 1977 that requires all adult theaters to be located within a small area downtown. City officials said that the character and quality of Seattle neighborhoods could be preserved and protected by isolating this adult activity to a small area downtown. Detroit took just the opposite approach. A city law passed in 1972 prohibits adult theaters from being located within 1,000 feet of other adult theaters, adult bookstores, cabarets, bars, taxi dance halls, hotels, pawnshops, pool halls, secondhand stores, and shoeshine parlors, or within 500 feet of areas zoned residential. The city did not want such businesses clustered together or near other types of "problem" businesses in the community. Both these statutes were upheld by the courts.[52]

The owners of these adult establishments have found that zoning, while perhaps inconvenient, provides them with a kind of safe haven from police harassment. They are normally permitted to operate their businesses without trouble unless they attempt to sell or exhibit material that is legally obscene (i.e., meets the definition of obscenity in the *Miller* test) or unless other criminal laws are violated as a result of the traffic frequenting the adult establishments.

LEGAL TEST FOR ZONING REGULATIONS

1. A community cannot, under the guise of zoning, completely bar or even significantly reduce the number of adult bookstores, movie theaters, or newsstands.
2. The ordinance must be justified by showing that it furthers a substantial state interest.
3. The ordinance must be narrowly drawn, so as not to restrict more speech than is necessary.

---

52. *Northend Cinema* v. *Seattle,* 585 P. 2d 1153 (1978) and *Young* v. *American Mini-Theaters, Inc.,* 427 U.S. 50 (1976).

Because these zoning laws are aimed at regulating constitutionally protected material, the government must follow strict rules in instituting and maintaining these rules. Courts have applied a three-part test to evaluate these zoning ordinances.

1. A community cannot, under the guise of zoning, completely bar or even significantly reduce the number of adult bookstores, movie theaters, or newsstands. The ordinance in Detroit that was approved by the Supreme Court in the *Young*[53] ruling did not substantially reduce the number of establishments selling adult material. And it left ample room for the introduction of new establishments. This point has been overlooked in some communities in which zoning regulations were used to try to close adult bookstores, theaters, and other businesses. In 1981 the Supreme Court struck down a Mount Ephraim, N.J., zoning regulation that effectively barred all live entertainment from the parts of the city zoned commercial. The high court called the ordinance unreasonable and said that it excluded from the city a wide range of protected expression. The high court also rejected Mount Ephraim's argument that its citizens had access to such entertainment, despite the zoning rules, because adult entertainment was readily available outside the city in nearby areas.[54] The U.S. Court of Appeals for the 6th Circuit threw out a Keego Harbor, Mich., zoning law that prohibited adult theaters within 500 feet of a tavern or bar, a church, or a school. There was no place in the small community that was not within 500 feet of such an establishment.[55] But a U.S. district court recently approved a zoning law in Brice, Ohio, that left only 27 percent of the town open for adult business.[56]

The federal courts have, however, shown a willingness to permit zoning laws that indirectly reduce the number of adult establishments in a community because of conditions in the real estate market. A Minneapolis ordinance was designed to force adult bookstores and theaters into the city's central business district. This was a small area in the city, and proprietors of some of the existing adult establishments said they simply could not afford to pay the very high cost of obtaining space in this area. One theater operator testified he could find only one suitable spot, and the owner wanted $3.5 million for the property. So although the zoning law did not physically or geographically reduce the number of adult businesses, the existing economic conditions and real estate market caused a substantial reduction in such establishments. A U.S. district court said the law was unconstitutional,[57] but this decision was overturned by the 8th U.S. Circuit Court of Appeals.[58] "The inquiry for First Amendment purposes is not concerned with economic impact," the court said, quoting a portion of a concurrence by Justice Lewis Powell in the 1976 *Young* v. *American Mini-Theaters, Inc.* Supreme Court ruling. The appellate court said that the adult theater owner must fend for himself in the real estate market. "That Alexander could not secure property meeting his economic or commercial criteria does not render Section 540.410 [the zoning ordinance] invalid," the court ruled. All the city must do is provide a reasonable opportunity for him to open and operate his theater.

---

53. *Young* v. *American Mini-Theaters, Inc.,* 427 U.S. 50 (1976).
54. *Schad* v. *Mount Ephraim,* 452 U.S. 61 (1981).
55. *Keego Harbor Company* v. *Keego Harbor,* 657 F. 2d 94 (1981).
56. *Wolfe* v. *Village of Brice, Ohio,* 37 F. Supp. 2d 1021 (1999).
57. *Alexander* v. *Minneapolis,* 713 F. Supp. 1296 (1989).
58. *Alexander* v. *Minneapolis,* 928 F. 2d 278 (1991).

2. The ordinance must be justified by showing that it furthers a substantial state interest. The state cannot justify these zoning laws by arguing that sexually explicit material is somehow bad, and therefore it should be segregated into one part of town or it should be spread out all over town. The state must show that the existence of these businesses generates undesirable "secondary effects" and it is for this reason that they must be regulated by zoning.* The city of Detroit provided a tremendous amount of data in defending its ordinance, data that demonstrated that concentrations of adult establishments caused neighborhood decay. The Detroit ordinance, then, was justified as preventing urban decay. Other communities have failed to do this, and their ordinances have been overturned. Keego Harbor, Mich., provided little data at all to support its argument that the adult movie theaters created traffic problems and therefore had to be regulated by zoning. "When a city effectively zones protected activities out of a political entity, the justification required is more substantial than when the First Amendment burden is merely incidental as it was in *Young* v. *American Mini-Theaters*," the court noted.[59] Of course the First Amendment burden was incidental in *Young* because the law did not diminish the number of adult establishments. The U.S. Court of Appeals for the 5th Circuit rejected a zoning ordinance adopted by the city of Galveston, Texas, modeled after the Detroit ordinance. The mayor and other city officials testified that they believed that the mere existence of adult theaters created crime and urban decay, but they offered no other evidence at the trial. "The paucity of evidence stands in sharp contrast to the facts of *American Mini-Theaters* v. *Young*," the court noted.[60] Although a community must produce evidence to support its zoning regulation, it doesn't necessarily have to generate fresh evidence that relates directly to that community. It can rely on the experience of other communities in the region. The city of Renton, Wash., a suburb of Seattle, relied on the experience of other area cities (most notably Seattle) to justify its zoning statute. The U.S. Supreme Court ruled in 1986 that this practice was acceptable. "The First Amendment does not require a city, before enacting such an ordinance to conduct new studies or produce evidence independent of that already generated by other cities," wrote Justice William Rehnquist, "so long as whatever evidence the city relies upon is reasonably believed to be relevant to the problem the city addresses."[61]

3. The ordinance must be narrowly drawn, so as not to restrict more speech than is necessary. This criterion applies to a variety of problems. For example, if the ordinance regulates "adult bookstores and theaters," the statute must define these terms. What is an adult bookstore? What is an adult motion picture? An Ann Arbor, Mich., zoning ordinance declared that any business whose "principal activity" was the sale of "adult material" had to locate in a specific area of the city. The law adequately defined adult material. Principal activity, however, was defined as involving 20 percent or more of the merchant's business. That is, if one out of five books sold by the merchant was an adult book, the merchant ran an adult bookstore, according to the law. The law was too restrictive, the U.S. Court of Appeals ruled. "A

The state must show that the existence of these businesses generates undesirable "secondary effects" and it is for this reason that they must be regulated by zoning.

59. *Keego Harbor Company* v. *Keego Harbor,* 657 F. 2d 94 (1981).
60. *Basiardanes* v. *City of Galveston,* 682 F. 2d 1203 (1982).
61. *Renton* v. *Playtime Theatres,* 475 U.S. 41 (1986).

*In March of 2000 the Supreme Court upheld an Erie, Pa., ordinance that banned nude dancing for the same reason: that such performances generated negative secondary effects.

limitation of adult materials up to twenty percent of a bookseller's wares conditions the constitutional right to speak in one way on the bookseller's willingness to speak in a different way eighty percent of the time," the court said.[62] In the *Mount Ephraim* case, the city had banned all forms of live entertainment, putting any sort of play or performance off-limits.[63] This restricted more speech than was needed to control adult entertainment. And the city of Galveston defined an adult theater as any theater that regularly screened films that the state of Texas prohibited minors from seeing. Of course, this description includes all R-rated films. Again, the city went too far and banned too much expression.[64] The city of Keego Harbor, on the other hand, might have used other methods—short of banning adult theaters—to handle its traffic problems. The court suggested that the increased ticketing of violators was a less intrusive means of serving the governmental interest involved.[65]

Zoning laws can be used to control the sale and exhibition of adult materials in a community, but only if they meet the three requirements just outlined: There can be no complete ban on such establishments or substantial reduction of the availability of such material in the community; a government must strongly justify—with evidence—such rules; and the laws must be narrowly drawn.

CLEANING UP THE POST EXCHANGE

The federal government, this time the Congress, launched another attack on the so-called adult magazines in 1996 when the Military Honor and Decency Act was adopted. The act prohibited the sale or rental of sexually explicit material in the post exchanges on military bases. The primary effect of the legislation was to bar the sale of magazines such as Playboy and Penthouse. In defending the law in court, government lawyers argued that a plain-meaning interpretation of the act leads to the conclusion that the purpose of the statute was to promote military core values and improve the public's perception of the nation's fighting men and women. A U.S. district court disagreed, saying that the "plain reading of the Act leads inevitably to the conclusion that it was drafted in an attempt to limit the sale and rental of nonobscene speech that Congress believed to be offensive and to penalize those who publish it by preventing its sale to military exchanges." The First Amendment prevents the government from taking such action, the court said.[66] On appeal the government argued that permitting the sale of such material in the exchanges sent the message that the military approved or endorsed the material. This implication will tarnish the military's image of honor, professionalism, and proper decency, the United States argued. Finally the government argued that the post exchanges were established to sell goods and articles necessary for the health, comfort, and convenience of military personnel. The 2nd U.S. Circuit Court of Appeals agreed with these arguments and overturned the lower-court ruling. Judge Jose Cabranes wrote that "Military exchanges are not public street corners; they are not available for everyone to 'speak'."

62. *Christy* v. *Ann Arbor,* 824 F. 2d 489 (1987).
63. *Schad* v. *Mount Ephraim,* 452 U.S. 61 (1981).
64. *Basiardanes* v. *City of Galveston,* 682 F. 2d 1203 (1982).
65. *Keego Harbor Company* v. *Keego Harbor,* 657 F. 2d 94 (1981).
66. *General Media Communications Inc.* v. *Perry,* 952 F. Supp. 1072 (1997).

Since military facilities are nonpublic forums, the government may reasonably restrict expressive activity as long as it does not discriminate against viewpoints. Congress could reasonably conclude, the court said, that sexually explicit material was not necessary for the health, comfort, or convenience of military personnel. A strong dissent argued that the regulation was not content neutral and that there was no evidence that the sale of such magazines would harm the military core values.[67] In June of 1998 the Supreme Court declined to review this decision.

ATTACKS ON THE ARTS

Elements of American popular culture came under attack in the late 1980s and 1990s. Charges were levied against popular music, especially rap and heavy metal music, art and art museums, and other mass media on the cutting edge of American art. There is no single explanation for the attack on the arts. Art is frequently misunderstood, and artists have historically been the object of public castigation and even censorship. Some contemporary artists, like their predecessors, have tested the boundaries of conventional taste and mainstream community standards. Sexually explicit or violent art, motion pictures, music, and reading matter are logical targets for many persons in the community who seek to explain what some of the mass media portray as an epidemic in this nation of incest, child abuse, spouse beating, drive-by shootings, and serial killings. Legislation was introduced in Congress in 1991 that would have given the victims of sex crimes the legal right to sue video retailers, booksellers, and even librarians for damages if the attacker had been provoked to violence by reading or viewing sexually explicit material or child pornography. The legislation died.

Attempts to censor popular music accelerated following the introduction of the cable television channel MTV. The music really didn't change, but until MTV most young people listened to the music they liked in the privacy of their bedrooms, in their automobiles, or at parties and dances. MTV brought popular music into the family room and living room, and parents (who seem genetically bound to hate the music their children enjoy) heard and saw performers like KISS, Judas Priest, Ozzy Osbourne, Culture Club, and later, various rap artists.

Attempts to censor popular music accelerated following the introduction of the cable television channel MTV.

"Protecting family values" became a shibboleth of many conservative Americans in the 1980s, a code word for censoring the mass media, controlling or eliminating sex education in the schools, getting tough on criminals and crime, and maintaining neighborhood schools. As such, censorship of the arts became a hot political issue with people like Susan Baker, the wife of Secretary of State James Baker, and Tipper Gore, the wife of then Senator Albert Gore, focusing the national spotlight on the entertainment industry.

Finally, one cannot ignore the public emergence of the so-called Christian Right when looking for ways to explain the censorship of the arts in the 1980s and 1990s. Membership in evangelical, fundamentalist, Pentecostal, and charismatic Christian groups rose rapidly in those two decades at the same time that membership in more mainstream Protestant churches (Lutheran, Methodist, etc.) decreased. Most observers agree that the members of the Christian Right have a political agenda as well as a religious one, and part of that agenda involves the censorship of cultural material they find in conflict with their religious teachings or that they find

67. *General Media Communications Inc. v. Cohen,* 131 F. 3d 273 (1997).

personally distasteful. In any case, these groups have become a dynamic political force, especially at the local level, where many of the battles over sexually explicit material are fought.

The results of these censorship efforts during the past 15 years have been notable.

- For the first time in the nation's history a record was declared to be obscene. In 1990 a U.S. district court ruled that the 2 Live Crew album "As Nasty As They Wanna Be" was obscene. The judge said the recording appealed to prurient interests, was patently offensive, and lacked any serious artistic merit.[68] Two years later the 11th U.S. Circuit Court of Appeals overturned this ruling. The court said the trial judge was unqualified to determine whether the recording lacked artistic merit. "We reject the argument that simply by listening to the musical work, the judge could determine that it had no serious artistic value."[69]

- For the first time in the nation's history a legitimate, public art museum was prosecuted for obscenity. The Cincinnati Contemporary Arts Center and its director, Dennis Barrie, were charged with violating Ohio obscenity laws for exhibiting homoerotic photographs taken by Robert Mapplethorpe. The state called the photos tasteless obscenity and relied on the shock value of the pictures on the members of the jury to win its case. The defense argued that while some of the photos were disturbing, they were art. Several experts supported this position. The members of the jury, only three of whom said they had ever been in an art museum, took only two hours to find the defendants not guilty.

- Record labeling became a staple of the music industry. A campaign began in the mid-1980s when a group of highly influential Washington, D.C., women (Parents Music Resource Committee), many of whom were married to U.S. senators and high administration officials, succeeded in convincing the U.S. Senate Commerce Committee to hold hearings on whether popular music was undermining the values of the nation's youth. The widely publicized hearings ultimately focused on the notion that record companies should place stickers on recordings containing lyrics that are sexually explicit or promote violence. The final resolution of the matter came in 1990 when the recording industry, faced with mounting pressure from conservatives in government and a growing array of state labeling laws, agreed to put labels on albums, CDs, and tapes.

- The Congress adopted the Communications Decency Act (CDA), which barred the transmission of indecent (but constitutionally protected) material via the Internet. The law also resurrected long-abandoned provisions of the 19th-century Comstock law and forbade the transmission of birth control information over the Internet as well. (See pages 487–491 for a full discussion of the CDA.)

Less visible results of this labeling agreement include a substantial amount of self-censorship within the recording industry and the difficulty record distributors have in placing all but the most heavily publicized stickered recordings in many record stores. Giant retailers

68. *Skywalker Records, Inc. v. Navarro,* 739 F. Supp. 578 (1990).
69. *Luke Records, Inc. v. Navarro,* 960 F. 2d 134 (1992).

1" × 1/2"
For cassette box and CD jewel box

1" × 1/2"
For cassette box and CD jewel box

1-1/2" × 1"
For album cover and CD long box

1-1/2" × 1"
For album cover and CD long box

Warning label on CDs, tapes, and albums. "Parental Advisory– Explicit Lyrics" is a certification mark of the Recording Industry Association of America, Inc. Permission to reproduce such mark has been granted thereby. Courtesy, Recording Industry Association of America, Inc.

like Wal-Mart and Kmart, which account for a large percentage of CD and tape sales, have refused to stock albums with lyrics or cover art that they find objectionable, including any recording that carries a warning label. Because of the clout of these retailers, record labels and bands will actually produce a second version of the recording—in which they omit objectionable songs, design different covers and CD and tape insert booklets, electronically mask objectionable words, and even change lyrics—just to gain a spot on the shelves of Wal-Mart, Kmart, and other family-oriented retailers.

Censorship of material by retailers is a little like an avalanche. It starts small but can quickly take on much larger proportions. Oftentimes it is sloppily done without much rhyme or reason. After selling more than 150,000 copies of a recording by Prodigy, Wal-Mart, without saying why, suddenly banned the album from its stores. Ten years ago the Fred Meyer chain of variety stores put a warning sticker on Frank Zappa's album, "Jazz from Hell." The label warned prospective buyers of sexually explicit lyrics on the totally instrumental recording. Finally, the operators of Wal-Mart apparently believe they need to protect their customers from more than simply erotic recordings. The chain refused to sell a nonerotic recording by popular performer Sheryl Crow because one song on the album was critical of Wal-Mart for selling firearms.

CONGRESS AND ARTS FUNDING

Most of the battles involving the arts have been fought outside the courtroom. Congress has been the site of a continuing struggle over whether the government should be able to control the content of art that is even partially generated by grants from the National Endowment for the Arts. The NEA was created by Congress in 1965 and since that time has made nearly 90,000 grants to artists and arts organizations, funding everything from symphony orchestras to painters and writers to contemporary alternative art spaces. The current annual NEA budget is under $200 million. Few recipients receive more than a small portion of the total cost of their endeavor. Still, to an artist or arts organization, every dollar counts. The flap over the NEA grants began in 1989 when some members of Congress professed extreme shock and distaste that the work of artists Robert Mapplethorpe and Andres Serrano was partially funded by these federal grants. Some of Mapplethorpe's homoerotic photographs focused on human genitalia and Serrano's portfolio included a picture of a crucifix submerged in the artist's urine. Starting in 1989 the Congress attempted to place restrictions on the NEA grants, forcing artists who accept the grants to agree beforehand to produce only acceptable art. In 1990 federal legislators passed a law that required NEA administrators to "take into consideration general standards of decency" when awarding NEA grants. Both a U.S. district court and the 9th U.S. Court of Appeals ruled that the law was unconstitutional.[70] In the summer of 1998 the Supreme Court reversed these lower-court rulings, but only after a majority of the justices interpreted the 1990 law as containing only advisory language, not a congressional mandate. In other words, the court said the NEA administrators could take general standards of decency into account when grants are awarded, but they are not required to do so. The majority opinion, written by Justice Sandra Day O'Connor, contained strong implications that if the law in fact required consideration of standards of decency it would be unconstitutional.[71] Congress has been routinely approving NEA budgets since this ruling.

EROTIC MATERIALS IN CYBERSPACE

The subject of sex on the Web was commonly discussed before 1995. But after the Georgetown Law Review published a lengthy article on the subject that year, these discussions became more intense.[72] It is fair to regard this law review article as the genesis of two federal statutes banning the transmission of adult material via the Internet: the Communications Decency Act of 1996 and the Child Online Protection Act of 1998.

The law review article was based on a study that concluded that the exchange of sex-related images was one of the largest recreational applications by Internet users. The study was undertaken by Marty Rimm when he was an undergraduate in electrical and computer engineering at Carnegie-Mellon University in Pittsburgh. Most observers with greater skills in this type of research than those possessed by Rimm labeled the study as bogus, noting that Rimm had serious problems with his data, his definitions, and his methodology. Indeed, subsequent studies have found substantially less than 1 percent of the content of the Web to be focused on sex. But Rimm's findings were quickly embraced by conservative Christians like Ralph Reed of the Christian Coalition, some members of Congress, and prominent anti-pornography feminists like Catherine MacKinnon. The findings in the study became the impetus for the adoption of many laws.

The transmission of legally obscene material via a computer network is clearly banned by federal law. U.S. statutes banning the transporting of obscene material in interstate commerce,

---

70. *Finley v. NEA,* 795 F. Supp. 1457 (1992), affd. 100 F. 3d 671 (1996).
71. *National Endowment for the Arts v. Finley,* 66 *Law week,* 4586 (1998).
72. Rimm, "Marketing Pornography," 1849.

whether in a private car or via a common carrier like United Parcel Service or the U.S. Postal Service, also prohibit the transmission of this material electronically by computer. In 1999 the Supreme Court upheld portions of a federal law that forbids the transmission of obscene e-mail.[73] Computer transmission of child pornography is also banned under federal law. Virtually all U.S. statutes related to obscenity have been amended to include computer transmission of this material. The reactions to sex on the Internet sometimes have amounted to what many would describe as overkill. In 1996 University of Oklahoma president David Boren blocked certain newsgroups with an "alt.sex" address from the university's news server. The order was so loosely defined that it initially denied students access to a newsgroup that offered support to victims of assault and abuse (alt.sexual.abuse.recovery) and a newsgroup that focused on the "Star Trek" captain Jean-Luc Picard, played by Patrick Stewart (alt.sexy.bald.captains).[74]

In 1996 Congress adopted the Communications Decency Act as part of the massive restructuring of telecommunications regulations. Among other things, the act made it a crime to transmit indecent material or allow it to be transmitted over public computer networks to which minors have access. The measure covered both public online forums and interactive computer services. Fines of up to $250,000 and a jail sentence of up to five years were possible for persons convicted of violating this measure. The law defined indecency as "any comment, request, suggestion, proposal, image or other communication that, in context, depicts or describes in terms patently offensive as measured by contemporary community standards, sexual or excretory activities or organs." The act also resurrected language from the Comstock Act, passed more than 123 years earlier, that barred the dissemination of information about birth control over the Internet.

Shortly after the law was adopted Attorney General Janet Reno announced that the Justice Department would not enforce this last provision of the law, stating that it would be unconstitutional to bar the dissemination of information about abortion via computer-mediated communication. The Communications Decency Act was a last-minute Senate amendment to the Telecommunications Act of 1996. It was adopted without hearings and, as New York Times reporter Linda Greenhouse wrote, amid substantial doubts about its constitutionality.[75] For that reason, Greenhouse said, its sponsors agreed to add a provision guaranteeing a quick Supreme Court review after a hearing by a single three-judge court, a shortcut through the normal appellate process.

Two lawsuits were quickly filed against the new law. A three-judge panel in Philadelphia declared the law unconstitutional in June of 1996. By attempting to limit the access of children to indecent or offensive material the Congress placed unacceptable restrictions on what adults can publish or see, the court said. Two of the three federal judges also found the definitions of the terms "indecent" and "patently offensive" to be insufficient. The CDA was unconstitutionally vague, they said.[76] About one and a half months later a second three-judge

73. *ApolloMedia* v. *Reno*, U.S. 98-933, 4/1/99.
74. "Constitutional Attack on University's Block of Sex Newsgroups Raises Important Issues," 1 E.P.L.R. 674 (1996).
75. Greenhouse, "Decency Act Fails."
76. *American Civil Liberties Union* v. *Reno*, 929 F. Supp. 824 (1996) and Lewis, "Judges Turn Back Law."

panel, this one in New York, also declared the CDA a violation of the First Amendment. This panel said the law was overbroad because it prohibited the creation and distribution of constitutionally protected speech among adults.[77]

The CDA contained what are called affirmative defenses for those accused of violating the statute. If a defendant could show that he or she attempted to discern whether minors were accessing the indecent material, they could escape conviction. Credit card verification was one such defense. Providers who required a credit card number from the receiver could assume an adult was on the other end of the transmission. Kids don't have credit cards. The law also excused the transmission of indecent material if the content provider took reasonable, effective, and appropriate actions under the circumstances to prevent minors from accessing indecent communications. The court said that for noncommercial providers and even some commercial providers the maintenance of a credit card verification scheme would be too costly. The providers would be forced to simply refrain from engaging in constitutionally protected indecent speech. The good faith defense is equally lame, the court said. "There is no persuasive evidence that a substantial number of Internet content providers can make material available potentially within the scope of the CDA, without fear of prosecution and criminal liability," the judges added. The court also rejected the oft-cited scenario of an innocent child stumbling upon indecent material by accident as he or she used the Internet. It takes several affirmative steps for a user to gain access to material through an interactive communication service, the judges wrote.

In June of 1997 the Supreme Court, hearing an appeal of the ruling in Philadelphia, agreed that the Communications Decency Act was unconstitutional.[78] The court stressed that its ruling did not in any way limit the government in prosecuting those who disseminate obscenity or child pornography over the Internet. Its ruling was aimed exclusively at provisions in the law that barred the transmission of indecency. As noted earlier (see pages 119–123), the court rejected the government's argument that the Internet should be regulated like a broadcasting station. And like the three-judge panel in New York, the high court also found the so-called affirmative defenses in the statute to be insufficient to save the law.

Justice John Paul Stevens, writing for the 7–2 majority, agreed with the lower court that the law was plagued by vagueness. Without a definition of either indecency or patent offensiveness, "could a speaker confidently assume that a serious discussion about birth control practices, homosexuality . . . or the consequences of prison rape would not violate the CDA?" he asked. "This uncertainty undermines the likelihood that the CDA has been carefully tailored to the congressional goal of protecting minors from potentially harmful materials." The high court said just because the term "patently offensive" was accepted by the court as a part of the definition of obscenity in the 1973 *Miller* ruling does not mean that the term standing alone is not vague. "We are persuaded," Stevens wrote, "that the CDA lacks the precision that the First Amendment requires when a statute regulates the content of speech." Justice Stevens added that by attempting to deny minors access to potentially harmful speech, the Communications

---

77. *Shea* v. *Reno,* 930 F. Supp. 916 (1996); see also 1 E.P.L.R. 415 (1996).
78. *Reno* v. *American Civil Liberties Union,* 117 S. Ct. 2329 (1997).

Decency Act effectively suppresses a large amount of speech that adults have a constitutional right to receive and to address to one another. "It is true," Stevens wrote, "that we have repeatedly recognized the governmental interest in protecting children from harmful materials. But that interest does not justify an unnecessarily broad suppression of speech addressed to adults."

In 1998 the Congress tried again to rid the Web of adult material. It adopted the Child Online Protection Act, which prohibits commercial Web sites from knowingly transmitting to minors (under 17 years of age) material that is harmful to minors. Generally speaking, material that, with respect to minors, is specifically created to appeal to prurient interests, that graphically depicts lewd or sexual behavior, and that lacks serious literary, artistic, or scientific value is regarded as harmful to minors. A fine of $50,000 and a six-month jail sentence may be imposed for each violation. Like the CDA, this law, dubbed the "son of CDA," also contained affirmative defenses. There can be no prosecution if the defendant has restricted access to the site to persons with credit cards, debit accounts, adult access codes, or adult personal ID numbers (whatever these are).

What are the differences between the CDA and the Child Online Protection Act? The Congress thinks it has overcome the Supreme Court's objections to the language in the CDA. The American Civil Liberties Union and 16 other plaintiffs say they disagree. The ACLU contends that this act is old wine in a new bottle. The new law, the organization argues, still will deny access by adults to constitutionally protected material in an effort to shield minors from this material. The term "harmful to minors" is both narrower and less vague than "indecent." The government argues that for the past 30 years courts have upheld laws regulating the access of young persons to material that is harmful to minors, laws, for example, that prohibit retailers from displaying merchandise (such as books) that are harmful to minors in areas that are generally accessible to minors. These restrictions fall under the heading of variable obscenity laws (see pages 469–470). The CDA regulated all communication on the Internet, including e-mail. The Child Online Protection Act only regulates commercial Web sites. But the ACLU says the loose wording in the statute regarding commercial Web sites means that not only will businesses that sell pornography over the Internet for a profit face potential sanctions, but the operator of any site that is supported by advertising could also be in jeopardy. The law threatens free Internet publications, such as Salon Magazine or The New York Times on the Web, that posted special prosecutor Kenneth Starr's report on the Clinton-Lewinsky scandal on the Web, the ACLU argues. The plaintiffs argue that filtering software is the answer, not federal laws. The government argues that a law is much more effective than filtering software, since children have access to computers in public places and at the homes of friends or relatives that might not have filters installed.

In February of 1999 U.S. District Judge Lowell Reed Jr. in Philadelphia issued a restraining order barring enforcement of the Child Online Protection Act. Judge Reed said that while the new law differed from the CDA in many respects, it nevertheless suffered from the same defects as the old one. In its attempt to pass a law to keep minors away from commercial sex sites, the Congress has again passed a law that interferes with the receipt by adults of constitutionally protected material, Reed said. Web publishers, fearful that they might be posting material that is harmful to minors, would be forced to censor themselves or put up credit card gates, which would interfere with rights of adults. Reed said that Congress's goal was certainly legitimate, but that the new law did not represent the least restrictive means to reach this goal. Private blocking software might be an equally effective alternative that did not impose a burden on Web site operators or adult users. Reed said he personally regretted his decision because it would interfere with the efforts of the government to carefully protect children. But, he added, "perhaps we do the minors of this country harm if the First Amendment protections, which they will with age inherit fully, are chipped away in the name of their protection."[79] On June 22, 2000, a three-judge panel on the 3rd U.S. Court of Appeals affirmed Judge Reed's ruling, noting that the federal indecency law falls well short of meeting First Amendment standards. In addition to the federal government, many states have tried to pass statutes regulating adult-oriented Internet content. As of late spring 2000, laws in four states—New York, Michigan, New Mexico, and California—were struck down. A lawsuit was filed against a similar Virginia law in late 1999.[80]

SOFTWARE FILTERS AND THE FIRST AMENDMENT

Judges, civil libertarians, and others argue that technology will solve the problems related to adult material on the Internet. Software filters already exist that can be installed on computers to block access to sites that the user might find objectionable. Parents, for example, can buy software that will block a child's access to Web sites containing sexually explicit matter. Most such programs use search engines that block access to sites with certain words in their addresses, words like "sex" or "breast." A problem common to these programs is their inability to distinguish between a site that may be obscene or indecent (www.bigbreasts.com) and one that is not (www.symofbreastcancer.org). Inevitably the software blocks access to much more material than is intended. But parents who use such software realize they must live with these problems.[*]

Civil libertarians acknowledge that parents have the right to control what their children may access on the Internet, just as parents have the right to control what books their kids read or television programs they watch. But the installation of such filtering software on computers in the public sphere is another matter, they argue. In February of 2000, according to a report in The New York Times, the American Library Association estimated that 15 percent of the nation's public libraries have already installed filtering software to prevent patrons from visiting various kinds of sites, especially ones with erotic content.[81] Currently the courts are beginning to hear lawsuits from library patrons who object to the installation of such screening devices on computers in public libraries. They argue that by trying to protect children, the libraries are denying access to material that adults have every right to see and hear. Typical of these lawsuits is a Virginia case that was decided in late 1998.

The trustees of the Loudoun County (Va.) Public Library in November of 1997 installed X-Stop rating software in all the computers in its branches. This program is a somewhat more

---

79. *ACLU* v. *Reno,* 31 F. Supp. 2d 473 (1999); see also Mendels, "Setback for a Law."
80. Mendels, "States Just Won't Give Up."
81. Bradsher, "Town Rejects Bid to Curb."

*In addition to the filters, several Internet entrepreneurs now offer "reverse-filtering" systems. Parents allow children to log on to these kid-friendly sites (YOW, Apple KidSafe, JuniorNet, and others), which will permit the youngsters to access only preapproved additional sites.

sophisticated filter. The search program, called Mudcrawler, uses a word search to locate potentially offensive sites and then a human operator makes the decision whether to block the site. But opponents of the installation of this software said the filter still lacked precision. The software blocked most obscene or erotic material, but still allowed access to some graphic sexual images. The filter also blocked sites on sex education, breast cancer, and gay and lesbian rights as well as access to a site generated by the Quaker religious sect and the home page of the Yale University biology department.[82] Arguments were heard in a U.S. district court on the defendant library's motion for summary judgment. Trustees of the library denied that use of the filtering software amounted to censorship, saying that clicking on a Web site is like requesting the library to order a book through interlibrary loan. The library has no First Amendment obligation to fulfill every such request. Opponents disagreed and argued that by applying the software it was as if the library purchased a new set of encyclopedias and then cut out all the articles in the books that didn't meet with the library's approval.

In April of 1998 the U.S. District Court rejected the library's motion for a summary judgment. The court said application of the filter constituted a removal decision, not a decision not to buy. "Unlike an interlibrary loan or outright book purchase, no appreciable expenditures of library time or resources is required to make a particular Internet publication available to a library patron," the court said. In effect, the judge ruled, by purchasing one such publication [buying Internet access], the library has purchased them all.[83]

In November of 1998, following a trial on the issue, Judge Leonie M. Brinkema ruled that the installation of filtering software on all the computers in the library was a violation of the First Amendment. "Such a policy offends the guarantee of free speech in the First Amendment and is, therefore, unconstitutional," she wrote. The library had argued that it was not doing the censoring; the software makers were the ones limiting access to the Web. Brinkema dismissed this argument, noting that "a defendant cannot avoid its constitutional obligation by contracting out its decision making to a private entity." The court, however, did not consider the matter of whether the library could install filtering software on only those computers set aside for use by children. This restriction is a typical practice among the 15 percent of libraries in the nation that use the filters on at least some of their computers.[84]

In January of 1999 a California Superior Court dismissed another filtering suit, this one brought by a women who sought to have filters installed on all the computers in the Livermore Public Library. She alleged that her 12-year-old son was able to view and download pornography at the public library. The judge wrote no opinion in the case. The library took the position that it would provide open access to the Internet to all users. "We don't want to be in the position to decide what people see or hear," said the library director. "This is not the library's responsibility, it's the parents."[85]

One additional problem relates to the regulation of erotic material on computer networks. The Internet is a worldwide communications medium. Laws relating to publication or

82. Harmon, "Library Suit Becomes."
83. *Mainstream Loudoun* v. *Board of Trustees of the Loudoun County Library,* 2 F. Supp. 2d 783 (1998).
84. *Mainstream Loudoun* v. *Board of Trustees of the Loudoun County Library,* 24 F. Supp. 2d 552 (1998).
85. Richtel, "Library Filtering."

transmission of erotic material vary significantly from nation to nation. In 1999 the Bertelsmann Foundation, a nonprofit social policy organization associated with the giant German media corporation Bertelsmann, sponsored a three-day symposium on Internet self-regulation in Munich, Germany. The thrust of the meeting was to outline an international filtering plan that would be applicable in all nations.[86] This notion is in its earliest stages, and should something develop, it will probably not occur for several years.

In August of 1997, The American Civil Liberties Union expressed concern over the push toward ratings in a policy paper it released on the topic entitled "Fahrenheit 451.2: Is Cyberspace Burning?" The title of the paper is a reference to the classic anticensorship novel by author Ray Bradbury. The theme of the paper was that ratings and blocking programs "limit the free marketplace of ideas." The authors of the paper continued:

> The administration's push for content ratings and blocking mechanisms is leading to a situation where the free market is not deciding what people want. The industry is moving in large part because it feels under the gun from the government. Moreover, by giving the government the tools with which to try to control speech on the Internet, labeling and blocking regimes will lead to the creation of an Internet infrastructure that will empower government censorship.[87]

SUMMARY

Significant efforts were made on many fronts during the '80s to control the flow of nonobscene, sexually explicit material. Many communities attempted to use zoning ordinances to regulate such material. These laws are permissible so long as they are strongly justified, don't exclude or substantially reduce the number of such businesses, and are drawn in a narrow fashion to limit only the narrowest possible range of speech. Conservative groups applied considerable pressure to music and the arts in the past two decades. Rock groups like 2 Live Crew were tried (but acquitted) of obscenity. Pressure on the record industry resulted in a labeling scheme that troubles many civil libertarians. Controversies surrounding art erupted in the Congress, and one gallery director was charged with obscenity for displaying a photographic exhibit. In the end there were few legal victories for the conservative critics. But some fear that intimidation and the threat of lawsuits will result in a growing conservatism in the arts community. Government efforts at censorship today are increasingly aimed at computer networks. In 1997 the Supreme Court ruled that the Communications Decency Act violated the First Amendment. Congress adopted the Child Online Protection Act in 1998 in an attempt to overcome the objections to the CDA voiced by the Supreme Court but this too was deemed a violation of the First Amendment. A federal court in Virginia ruled that public libraries cannot install on all the computers in the library filtering software that denies users access to certain Web sites.

86. Kaplan, "Yale Law Professor."
87. Drolte, "Net Ratings Chill Speech."

BIBLIOGRAPHY ⟶

Above the Law: The Justice Department's War Against the First Amendment. Medford, N.Y.: The American Civil Liberties Union, 1991.

Attorney General's Commission on Pornography. *Final Report.* Washington, D.C.: U.S. Department of Justice, 1986.

Blakely, C. "Is One Woman's Sexuality Another Woman's Pornography?" *Ms.,* April 1985, 37.

Bradsher, Keith. "Town Rejects Bid to Curb Library's Internet Access." *The New York Times,* 24 February 2000, A12.

Bunker, Matthew D., Paul H. Gates Jr., and Sigman L. Splichal. "RICO and Obscenity Prosecutions: Racketeering Laws Threaten Free Expression." *Journalism Quarterly* 70 (1993):692.

Catlett, Steven T. "Enjoining Obscenity as Public Nuisance and the Prior Restraint Doctrine." *Columbia Law Review* 84 (1984):1616.

Caughlin, Susan G. "Private Possession of Child Pornography: The Tensions Between *Stanley* v. *Georgia* and *New York* v. *Ferber.*" *William and Mary Law Review* 29 (1987):187.

"Couple Guilty of Pornography Offered on Computer Network." *The New York Times,* 31 July 1994, 12.

"Court Upholds Conviction in Child Pornography Case." *The New York Times,* 12 June 1994, 16.

Courtler, Ann H. "Restricting Adult Access to Material Obscene as to Juveniles." *Michigan Law Review* 85 (1987):1681.

de Grazia, Edward. *Girls Lean Back Everywhere: The Law of Obscenity and the Assault on Genius.* New York: Random House, 1992.

Drolte, Angela. "ACLU Says Net Ratings Chill Speech." *Electronic Information Policy & Law Report* 2 (15 August 1997): 858.

Eggenberger, Tod R. "RICO vs. Dealers in Obscene Matter: The First Amendment Battle." *Columbia Journal of Law and Social Problems* 22 (1988):71.

Elkins, Susan. "Taking Serious Value Seriously: Obscenity, *Pope* v. *Illinois,* and an Objective Standard." *University of Miami Law Review* 41 (1987):855.

"The First Amendment Under Fire From the Left." *The New York Times,* 13 March 1994, 40.

Garber, Marjorie. "Maximum Exposure." *The New York Times,* 3 December 1993, 15.

Gates, Henry Louis, Jr. "2 Live Crew Decoded." *The New York Times,* 19 June 1990.

Golden, Tim. "Court Bars Decency Standards in Awarding of U.S. Arts Grants." *The New York Times,* 6 November 1996, A10.

Goodchild, Seth. "Twisted Sister, Washington Wives, and The First Amendment: The Movement to Clamp Down on Rock Music." *Entertainment and Sports Law Journal* 3 (1986):131.

Greenhouse, Linda. "Decency Act Fails." *The New York Times,* 27 June 1997, A1.

———. "Justices Uphold Decency Test in Awarding Arts Grants, Backing Subjective Judgments." *The New York Times,* 26 June 1998, A17.

Harmon, Amy. "Library Suit Becomes Key Test of Freedom to Use the Internet." *The New York Times,* 2 March 1998, C1.

Kaplan, Carl S. "Yale Law Professor Is Main Architect of Global Filtering Plan." *The New York Times* on the Web, 10 September 1999.

Lewis, Peter. "Judge Temporarily Blocks Law That Bans Indecency on Internet." *The New York Times,* 16 February 1996, A1.

———. "Judges Turn Back Law to Regulate Internet Decency." *The New York Times,* 13 June 1996, A1.

———. "On-Line Service Ending Its Ban of Sexual Materials on Internet." *The New York Times,* 14 February 1996, A1.

"Library Can't Filter Internet, Judge Rules." *The New York Times,* 24 November 1998, A19.

Maag, Marilyn J. "The Indianapolis Pornography Ordinance: Does the Right to Free Speech Outweigh Pornography's Harm to Women?" *Cincinnati Law Review* 54 (1985):249.

McCormick, Jim. "Protecting Children From Music Lyrics: Sound Recordings Harmful to Minors Statutes." *Golden Gate University Law Review* 23 (1993):679.

Mendels, Pamela. "Child Pornography Issue Raised in Budget." *The New York Times,* 3 October 1996, A11.

———. "Setback for a Law Shielding Minors From Smut Web Sites." *The New York Times,* 2 February 1999, A10.

———. "States Just Won't Give up on Online Pornography Laws." *The New York Times* on the Web, 8 October 1999.

Pareles, Jon. "A Rap Group's Lyrics Venture to the Edge of Obscenity." *The New York Times,* 14 June 1990.

———. "Lyrics, the Law, and Louisiana's Musical Tradition." *The New York Times,* 19 July 1990.

"Pornography." *Ms.,* January/February 1994, 32.

Report of the Commission on Obscenity and Pornography. New York: Bantam Books, 1978.

Rimer, Sara. "In 2 Live Crew Trial, Cultures Didn't Clash." *The New York Times,* 22 October 1990.

Rimm, Marty. "Marketing Pornography on the Information Superhighway." *Georgetown Law Journal* 83 (1995):1849.

Richtel, Matt. "Library Filtering Case Dismissed." *The New York Times* on the Web, 14 January 1999.

Sheehan, Kathy, and Helen Buller. "Jury Acquits Newsstand Operators." *The Bellingham Herald,* 2 February 1996, A1.

Stein, Ronald M. "Regulation of Adult Businesses Through Zoning After *Renton.*" *Pacific Law Journal* 18 (1987):351.

Stern, Ronald M. "Sex, Lies, and Prior Restraints: 'Sexually Oriented Business'—The New Obscenity." *University of Detroit Law Review* 68 (1991):253.

Strossen, Nadine. *Defending Pornography, Free Speech, Sex, and the Fight for Women's Rights.* New York: Scribner, 1994.

"U.S. Shifts to Conservative Stance in Child Pornography Case." *The New York Times,* 11 November 1994, A14.

Van Dyke, Michael S. "Regulation of Pornography: Is Erotica Self-Expression Deserving of Protection?" *Loyola Law Review* 33 (1987):445.

Wallace, Jonathan, and Mark Mangan. *Sex, Laws, and Cyberspace.* New York: Henry Holt, 1996.

Weiser, Benjamin. "Sex-Magazine Ban on Military Bases Is Upheld." *The New York Times,* 22 November 1997, A10.

Copyright

The law of copyright is almost 500 years old. British King Henry VIII issued the first royal grant of printing privilege, the forerunner of copyright law, in 1518. American copyright law springs from the U.S. Constitution and protects a wide variety of intellectual creations. While case law today still focuses on the rights of authors and artists who generate traditional creative compositions like books, photographs, and poetry, the courtroom battles also involve the protection of computer programs, videotapes, audiotapes, and even more exotic materials. The rapid growth of the Internet has generated myriad new copyright problems. In this chapter we explore what the law of copyright protects, the important defense of fair use, infringement, and how creators can protect their work from thievery.

IMMATERIAL PROPERTY LAW

Copyright is an area of the law that deals with intangible property—property that a person cannot touch or hold or lock away for safekeeping. This concept is sometimes confusing to people; how can the law protect something you can't hold or touch? One good way to explain this concept is to think for a moment about a personal letter you have written to your friend. After the letter has been received by your friend, who owns it? Your friend owns the piece of paper that contains the words. That is his or her personal property now and is protected by property law. But you retain ownership of the words and the words are protected by copyright law. Your friend could not publish the letter without your permission. But he or she could throw it away or set fire to it and destroy the paper. In such a case, your friend is not using your words, your property, but merely destroying the letter.

Copyright is a close cousin to the law regulating patents and trademarks and to plagiarism, which also affects intangible property. But all four of these areas protect something different.

PATENTS

There are at least three different kinds of patent protections. One variety protects inventions that have utility, such as a machine or a process. A typewriter can be patented; so can a specific way of reducing the hiss or noise on an audiotape. Patent law also protects designs—the appearance of an article of manufacture. The design of a piece of furniture or a tire tread or a belt buckle can be patented. A variety of patents also protect plants, but only those kinds that can be reproduced asexually through means other than seeds, like cuttings or grafting. Patent rights do not exist until the patent is issued by the U.S. government. Hence, the famous abbreviation on many items, "pat. pending," which means the patent has been applied for and is pending.

TRADEMARKS

A trademark is any word, symbol, or device—or combination of the three—that differentiates an individual's or company's goods and services from the products or services of competitors. The trademark on a particular item assures the buyer that he or she is getting the real item and protects the manufacturer or service provider from the unfair business practices of others. The function of trademark law is to stop confusion in the marketplace, to clearly identify the products and services created by specific businesses. Popsicles, Q-Tips, Jell-O, Super Glue, Velcro, Walkman, and thousands of other brand names are protected by trademark. Anyone can manufacture and sell a portable or pocket-size cassette tape player, but only Sony can call its player aWalkman. But it is possible to get trademark protection for more than simply a trade name. The hourglass shape of the classic Coca-Cola bottle is a registered mark. So is the art deco spire of the Chrysler Building in New York and the neoclassic facade of the New York Stock Exchange Building in the same city. In 1998 the stock exchange sued New York–New York Hotel and Casino in Las Vegas for constructing a one-third scale model of the building at its gambling and entertainment complex. A growing number of landlords are seeking to control the ways in which images and likenesses of their distinctive buildings are used by others, claiming that this protection is no different than a celebrity protecting the property value of his

or her name or image.[1] Slogans such as "Don't Leave Home Without It," "All the News That's Fit to Print," and even "Uh-huh!" (Pepsi Cola) are registered trademarks. Some telephone numbers can be protected as trademarks (e.g. 1-800-FLOWERS). In 1985 a federal court overruled a decision by the Patent and Trademark Office and granted trademark registration to a color for the first time. The Owens-Corning Fiberglas Corporation won protection for the color pink, the hue of its popular home insulation. The company showed the court it was the only manufacturer to use the color pink on insulation, it had been selling this pink product since 1956, the color pink was a basic part of its advertising and marketing strategy for the product, and that consumers, questioned in a sample survey, recognized the color pink as identifying a specific brand. In 1995 the Supreme Court reinforced this concept when it ruled unanimously that the Qualitex Company, which since the 1950s used a particular shade of green-gold on the pads it makes for use on dry-cleaning presses, can register that color as a trademark.

This area of the law also provides protection for what are called service marks for businesses such as Holiday Inn and McDonald's and certification marks for goods and services, such as Dolby for cassette decks and Real (real cheese) for food products. Finally, what are called collective marks identify and protect members of organizations, such as the National Association of Realtors. There is also protection for something called trade dress, the way a product is packaged. Merriam-Webster, which published the Webster's Ninth New Collegiate Dictionary, collected more than $4 million in damages in 1991 when it successfully sued Random House for trademark infringement. When Random House published its Webster's College

The New York Stock Exchange alleged in 1998 that when the New York–NewYork Hotel and Casino was built in the mid-1990s its model of the stock exchange building (right) infringed on the trademark on the real stock exchange facade (left). Stone/Greg Pease (left), Eric Sander/Liaison Agency, Inc. (right).

---

1. Dunlap, "What Next?"

Dictionary it copied the look of the Merriam-Webster volume. The color, the design of the dust jacket, and the placement of the word Webster's on the spine of the book were all intended to fool potential customers, the plaintiffs argued. The jury agreed. In 1999 the U.S. Supreme Court agreed to hear an appeal by Wal-Mart Stores, which had been found guilty of infringing on the trade dress of a line of children's clothing manufactured by Samara Brothers. Wal-Mart argued that the design of the clothing was not distinctive enough to enjoy trade dress protection, but the 2nd U.S. Circuit Court of Appeals disagreed and sustained a jury award of more than $1 million against the chain store.[2] Once registered, a trademark must be renewed after five years. Renewal is then required at 10-year intervals. But as long as it is properly renewed, a trademark can be maintained indefinitely. Some of the earliest American trademarks still in use date to the 18th and 19th centuries. Colgate dates to 1806; Gordon's (Gin) was first used in 1769. Chiquita bananas were first sold in 1876; Kodak cameras and film, 1886; and Tabasco pepper sauce, 1868.

THE FOUR MAIN FUNCTIONS OF
TRADEMARKS AND SERVICE MARKS

▪ They identify one seller's goods and distinguish them from goods sold by others.
▪ They signify that all goods bearing the trademark or service mark come from a single source.
▪ They signify that all goods bearing the mark are of an equal level of quality.
▪ They serve as a prime instrument in advertising and selling goods.

While personal ownership of a trademark may exist perpetually, the ownership of a trademark or trade name can also be lost. Failure to use a trademark for two years carries with it the presumption under the law that the trademark has been abandoned, and another can then use it. It is also possible that trademark protection can be lost if the owner of the mark allows others to use the mark in a generic way. For example, if the makers of Super Glue (a trade name) adhesive failed to try to stop other adhesive makers from referring to their products as super glues, the trademark protection could be lost. These generic words—nylon, dry ice, escalator, toasted corn flakes, raisin bran, aspirin, lanolin, mimeograph, cellophane, linoleum, shredded wheat, zipper, yo-yo, and brassiere—were all at one time registered trademarks that slipped away from owners who failed to protect these names. Angry letters, threats of lawsuits, even legal action must be initiated to stop others from illegally using the name or phrase or mark. This responsibility falls on the owner of the mark; no government agency polices such misbehavior.

The United States Trademark Association, a trade group that works to protect the value of trademarks, reminds journalists and others in a variety of ways that trademarks are proper

While personal ownership of a trademark may exist perpetually, the ownership of a trademark or trade name can also be lost.

2. "High Court Will Hear Wal-Mart Case."

adjectives and should be capitalized; they are not nouns or verbs. Hence, you can use a Xerox photocopier to duplicate a letter, but you can't make a xerox, or xerox a letter. Printed or broadcast references of the latter variety will usually earn journalists a stern letter from the trademark holder reminding them of the law. Simple innocent infractions like these rarely cause serious problems for the offender. Calculated trademark infringement can be costly. A federal court in Chicago ordered the Quaker Oats Co., the maker of Gatorade, to pay a small company in Vermont nearly $43 million in damages for infringing on the trademark Thirst-Aid.

As previously noted, trademark law is designed to reduce the likelihood of confusion in the marketplace. As such, U.S. trademark law only forbade the use of a registered trademark or trade name on a product that was similar to the product produced by the owner of the trademark or trade name. A competitor to Sony could not call its portable cassette player a Walkman, but the manufacturer of exercise equipment could call its treadmill a Walkman. In January of 1996 the Congress, following the lead of the legislatures in 27 states, added more muscle to trademark protection when it adopted the Federal Dilution Trademark Act. This law gives the owners of trademarks and trade names legal recourse against anyone who uses the same or similar trademarks on even dissimilar products. In other words, in the past Maytag could only block the use of its trademark and name on home appliances made by its competitors. Under the new law Maytag could block the use of its name and registered trademark on an automobile or a camera as well. And Sony could stop the exercise equipment manufacturer from calling its treadmill a Walkman. Supporters of this new legislation argued that any use of another's name or mark weakened or diluted its value and distinctiveness, even in the absence of confusion as to the source of the goods. The statute prohibits the use of the mark by another in commerce, but only if the use is likely to cause confusion or to cause a purchasing mistake by a consumer, or if the use is intended to deceive a buyer as to the affiliation, origin, or sponsorship of the product. This law does not apply to the use of a registered name or mark in news reports or news commentary, or in parody, satire, or other such forms of expression.

It is not difficult to legally establish a trademark. The applicant should first undertake a search to determine whether someone else has already registered the mark. This can be done by computer today at the Patent and Trademark Office search library in Arlington, Va., or at about 60 regional sites (libraries) around the nation. A registration application is then sent to the Patent and Trademark Office, where an examiner reviews the application and determines whether the mark may be registered. A registration fee of $245 must accompany the application. Although it is not necessary to precede the application with a search, it is advisable. If the examiner discovers in his or her search that the mark has been previously registered, the application fee is forfeited. Anyone who claims the right to a trademark can use the ™ designation with the mark to alert the public to the claim. It is not necessary to have registration or even a pending application to use this designation. And under the law, it is the person who first uses the mark, not the person who first registers the mark, who holds the rights to the symbol or word or phrase.[*]

---

[*]Persons seeking more information about trademarks should send for the booklet *Basic Facts About Registering a Trademark,* U.S. Department of Commerce, Patent and Trademark Office, Washington, D.C., 20231.

PLAGIARISM

Plagiarism is the act of taking ideas, thoughts, or words from another and passing them off as your own. The notion of passing off someone else's work as your own is critical in a plagiarism case. Plagiarism is probably far more common in the American mass media than copyright or trademark infringement is. Film and television producers seem especially vulnerable to plagiarism suits. For example, writer-director Amy Heckerling and TriStar Pictures were sued in 1991 by other writers who claimed that the script from the 1989 hit film "Look Who's Talking" had been plagiarized. The case was settled out of court after the trial judge issued an opinion that he saw substantial similarity between the movie script and the plaintiffs' work. In 1997, one month before the release of the film "Amistad," Steven Spielberg's Dreamworks was sued for plagiarism/copyright infringement by author Barbara Chase-Riboud. The novelist claimed that the filmmaker had stolen important parts from her historical novel "Echo of Lions." Spielberg's lawyers denied the charges, saying the portions of the film Chase-Riboud cited in her complaint were based on history, which cannot be owned by any person, and on another novel, "Black Mutiny," a book published 36 years before "Echo of Lions." The producers of the film "Amistad" bought the rights to "Black Mutiny" in 1989. Lawyers for the film producers argued that extensive passages in Chase-Riboud's book had been in fact lifted from "Black Mutiny," and that she was the plagiarist. Judge Audrey Collins of U.S. District Court in Los Angeles rejected Chase-Riboud's request for an injunction to halt the release of the film, but allowed the plaintiff to continue her $10 million lawsuit against Dreamworks, the producer of the picture. This was the second time in 10 years that Chase-Riboud had sued, complaining that someone had stolen her work for a play or a film[3] (see page 536).

It would be absurd to say that plagiarism doesn't occur in journalism. Reporters and editors often use a variety of sources when preparing their stories, and it is not unusual that the original source for the material is uncredited. But many in the craft were surprised by a 1995 article published in the highly regarded Columbia Journalism Review in which contributing editor Trudy Lieberman outlined 20 cases of plagiarism that surfaced since 1988 at some of the nation's leading newspapers and magazines.[4] Eight reporters were fired and three were suspended for varying lengths of time. The publications included the Chicago Sun-Times, Washington Post, Denver Post, Los Angeles Times, and The New York Times. For example, the Washington Post fired its Miami bureau chief, claiming she had included too much material from an Associated Press story and a story in the Miami Herald in a piece she wrote on mosquito and grasshopper infestation in Florida. The New York Times suspended its Boston bureau chief for including in one of his stories several paragraphs that closely resembled paragraphs previously published in The Boston Globe. It may seem ironic that Lieberman's account seemed to focus on some of the most distinguished members of the American journalism community. But it is not. These are cases in which the newspapers actually took public actions in light of the supposed plagiarism. Such behavior undoubtedly goes unchecked or at least is not publicly noted in scores of other publications.

3. Weinraub, "'Amistad' Plagiarism Charge Rebutted."
4. Lieberman, "Plagiarize, Plagiarize, Plagiarize."

Many observers have noted that very little material is new and original; most writers in one way or another borrow from their predecessors. This is an especially evident problem in journalism, where reporters are always trying to cover what the competition has published or broadcast. Giving credit to others for work that is borrowed will surely reduce the plagiarism problem, since passing off the work of others as your own is a critical element in the tort. Doing as much original work as possible is an even better strategy.

Copyright law protects "all works of authorship fixed in a tangible medium of expression." This description includes writings, paintings, music, drama, and other similar works. Ideas are protected by the law relating to patents and plagiarism. Copyright does not protect ideas, but the specific expression of those ideas. Trademark protection is based on marketplace use; patents and copyright are statutory creations. Trademark protection can last forever; copyright and patent protection is limited by law. This chapter focuses exclusively on copyright. Persons who work in the mass media do not need to become copyright attorneys to avoid lawsuits in the 1990s. But news writers, broadcasters, advertising copywriters, and public relations specialists should know both how to protect their own work from theft and how to avoid illegally taking the work of someone else.

PROTECTING LITERARY PROPERTY

Protecting the rights of authors and other creators was not a problem prior to the development of mechanical printing. Each hand-copied manuscript was the result of the intensive labor of a copyist. Each book was an individual entity and could be protected by the law of personal property. The time and effort it took to reproduce even one book made the theft of a book through duplication an unattractive prospect. But the printing press changed all this, for it became possible to quickly and easily mass-produce exact copies of a written work. Through the printing process, two separate yet combined pieces of property emerged. The first was the book itself—a piece of physical property. The second was the arrangement and organization of the words or ideas in the book—a piece of intangible property.

The printing press was the first technological development that provided the inexpensive means of copying the work of others. As each new mass communications form has developed, the problem of protecting intangible property has arisen anew. Today the pirating of tapes, both video and audio, is causing serious harm to the creators of motion pictures and musical performances. The film industry estimates that it loses as much as a billion dollars a year because of film and videotape piracy. The Motion Picture Association of America spends tens of millions of dollars each year trying to catch the pirates. And the recording industry has been seriously hurt for years as copies of CDs and cassettes are made legally by individuals for personal use and illegally by well-organized gangs of pirates for resale.

The growth of digital interactive computer technology has complicated matters considerably. Early transmission technology made it awkward to transmit sound recordings over the Internet because it took so long to move the data. But data compression technology changed all that by reducing the time it takes to transfer the data. A song of near-CD quality that is 50 megabytes in size when saved in traditional digital format can be compressed into about 4.5 megabytes. It is now possible to download an entire CD's worth of music from the Web to a computer hard drive in less than 12 minutes. Today copies of CDs commonly move on the Internet. New technology also generated an inexpensive way to move the contents of CDs from computer hard drives to portable replay units. The MPEG-1 Layer 3, popularly known as the MP3 or the Rio, is a portable audio player that costs less than $200 and is about the size of a pack of cigarettes. The MP3 has two parts, a player and accompanying software. Once a file—the contents of a CD, for example—is downloaded to a computer hard drive, the software allows the user to transfer those files to the MP3. The device cannot receive audio files from any source other than a computer equipped with the Rio software. The user can then access the music through headphones. The MP3 cannot make copies of files stored on it or transfer those files to another device.

Lawyers for the Recording Industry Association of America went to court to try to block the distribution of the MP3, arguing that it would make a bad music piracy situation even worse. RIAA represents more than 90 percent of all offline sellers and distributors of music in the United States and has been battling Web sites that allow downloading of unlicensed music files. The court dismissed the RIAA suit, saying that the device is merely a space shifter, not an audio recording device.[5] The MP3 merely "makes copies in order to render portable . . . files that already reside on a user's hard drive. Such copying, as with time shifting [home video recording of television programs], is paradigmatic non-commercial personal use," the court said, something that is entirely consistent with copyright law. Under the ruling consumers will be able to make copies of digital recordings that they own or have acquired properly. Users can transfer audio CDs to their hard drives and then download them into the Rio. Or they may download authorized files, like noncopyrighted works or freebies, from the Internet and then transfer them to the MP3.[6]

In the wake of this court ruling new copyright disputes arose between the music industry and companies that attempt to distribute recorded music on line. MP3.com, which is affiliated with the maker of the MP3 player, collected and stored vast numbers of recordings and then allowed its customers to download the music via their MP3 players. Napster, another online music distribution service, allows Internet users to share their private music collections with others. In both cases the music industry charged copyright infringement. And the problem was not a small one. A study of Internet users published in June of 2000 estimated that 13 million Americans have paid these companies to download music files without any payment of royalties to the music industry. A federal court declared the MP3.com system a copyright infringement in April of 2000 and two months later the online music distributor began signing licensing agreements with recording companies. Napster argued that it had done nothing wrong, since it did not collect or store the recordings, but merely provided a pathway for one Internet user to gain access to music files stored by another user. RIAA and musical groups like Metallica brought legal action against Napster, but the issue was unresolved in early summer of 2000. At the same time RIAA was attempting to devise a technological solution to

---

5. *Recording Industry Association of America* v. *Diamond Multimedia Systems,* 9th Cir., No. 98-56727, 6/15/99.

6. Kaplan, "In Court's View."

protect its members' works. The industry hoped to be able to attach a kind of "watermark" to each recorded song. This watermark would tell a player device whether it is authorized to play the music. It was hoped this system would be in place by the summer of 2001.[7]

ROOTS OF THE LAW

Copyright law developed in Great Britain in the 16th century as the government sanctioned and supported the grant of printing privileges to certain master printers in exchange for their loyalty and assistance in ferreting out anti-government writers and publishers. But the rights of authors, as opposed to printers, were not protected until the early 18th century when the British Parliament passed the nation's first copyright law. The 1710 statute was called "An Act for the Encouragement of Learning, by Vesting the Copies of Printed Books in the Authors or Purchasers of Such Copies, during the Time Therein Mentioned." The law was passed in the eighth year of the reign of Queen Anne and hence became known as the "Statute of Eight Anne." The law gave the legal claim of ownership of a piece of literary property to the person who created the work or to a person who acquired the rights to the work from the author. The statute was a recognition by the Crown that in order to encourage the creation of books, plays, and art, the creators of these works had to be assured that they would be rewarded for their labor. And that is the real logic behind copyright law, the fostering of the creative spirit. If a dramatist knew, for example, that as soon as her play was published she would lose control of the work because others could freely copy it, there would be little stimulation for the creation of plays.

And that is the real logic behind copyright law, the fostering of the creative spirit.

British copyright law was applied in the colonies until American independence. American copyright law derives directly from the U.S. Constitution. In Article I, Section 8, of that document lies the basic authority for modern United States copyright law:

> The Congress shall have Power . . . To promote the Progress of Science and useful Arts, by securing for limited Times to Authors and Inventors the exclusive Right to their respective Writings and Discoveries.

This provision gives the Congress the power to legislate on both copyright and patent. The Congress did just that in 1790 by adopting a statute similar to that of Eight Anne. The law gave authors who were U.S. citizens the right to protect their books, maps, and charts for a total of 28 years—a 14-year original grant plus a 14-year renewal. In 1802 the law was amended to include prints as well as books, maps, and charts. In 1831 the period of protection was expanded by 14 years. The original grant became 28 years with a 14-year renewal. Also, musical compositions were granted protection. Photography was given protection in 1865, and works of fine art were included five years later. Translation rights were added in 1870.

A major revision of the law was enacted in 1909, and our current law was adopted in 1976. The 1976 federal law preempted virtually all state laws regarding the protection of writing, music, and works of art. Hence, copyright law is essentially federal law and is governed by the federal statute and by court decisions interpreting this statute. Parenthetically, it might

7. Robinson, "3 Copyright Lawsuits"; see also Richtel and Robinson, "Ear Training."

be noted that in 1988 the Congress finally approved U.S. participation in the 102-year-old Berne Convention, the world's pre-eminent international copyright treaty. The United States had been hesitant in the past to join the treaty because of significant differences between United States and international law, but after the 1976 revision of U.S. copyright law, the differences were minimal. American media companies, anxious to expand their international business, sought to improve trade relations and strengthen U.S. influence on matters relating to international copyright law and therefore put pressure on the government to join the convention.

WHAT MAY BE COPYRIGHTED

The law of copyright gives to the author, or the owner of the copyright, the sole and exclusive right to reproduce the copyrighted work in any form for any reason. There are actually six exclusive rights recognized under the law:

- **The right of reproduction of the work**
- **The right of preparation of derivative works**
- **The right of public distribution of the work**
- **The right of public performance of the work**
- **The right of public display of the work**
- **The right of public digital performance of a sound recording**

These rights are fairly clear with regard to traditional mass media. If Bogus Publishing prints 1,000 copies of a copyrighted Stephen King novel and distributes them to bookstores, this is a violation of King's exclusive distribution rights under the law. But the rights are less clear when it comes to computers and the Internet. Is storing a copyrighted document on a hard disk or a diskette or even in the computer's RAM a violation of the exclusive right to reproduce a copyrighted item? Probably, the courts seem to indicate. Does transmitting a copyrighted work via the Internet constitute a public performance of the work? Possibly. The courts are just now sorting out these questions. Several lower courts have ruled that it can be an infringement of copyright to download material off the Internet for unauthorized use or upload copyrighted material onto a Web site or bulletin board without the permission of the copyright holder.[8] A federal court in Texas ruled in December of 1997 that an online service provider that provided subscribers unauthorized copies of copyrighted images infringed on the copyright holder's rights of reproduction, distribution, and display and was liable for direct copyright infringement. The provider argued that it was merely a conduit between the subscription service that scanned the photos into the system and the subscribers who downloaded them. The defendant said that all it sold was access to the subscription service, not images. The court disagreed, ruling that "Webbworld didn't sell access—it sold images."[9] However, under a federal statute adopted in 1998 an online service provider that acts as merely a *conduit* during the infringement of copyrighted works will not be held liable for the illegal act in most instances (see page 538). A U.S. district court in Nevada ruled in 1999 that scanning a copyrighted photo into a computer for graphic manipulation and insertion into a new work constitutes a

---

8. See, for example, *Playboy Enterprises Inc.* v. *Starware Publishers Corp.,* 900 F. Supp. 433 (1995).
9. *Playboy Enterprises Inc.* v. *Webbworld Inc.,* D.C.N. Texas Civil No. 3196-CV-3222-H, 12/11/97.

copyright infringement. The court said that digitizing any copyrighted material may support an infringement finding—even if it has only the briefest existence in a computer's memory.

Before a copyrighted work may be printed, broadcast, dramatized, or translated, the consent of the copyright owner must first be obtained. The law grants this individual exclusive monopoly over the use of that material. To quote the statute specifically, copyright extends to "original works of authorship fixed in any tangible medium of expression." The Congress has defined *fixed in a tangible medium* as that work which is "sufficiently permanent or stable to permit it to be perceived, reproduced, or otherwise communicated for a period of more than a transitory duration." Under these standards such things as newspaper stories or entire newspapers, magazine articles, advertisements, and almost anything else created for the mass media can be copyrighted. Material that is created in digital form and stored or transmitted electronically via computer diskettes or CD-ROM can also be protected by copyright, although some experts believe that existing copyright law needs to be modified to make this point more explicit. Extemporaneous performances and speeches, and improvised sketches are examples of materials that are not fixed in a tangible medium and are not protected by the federal copyright statute. But this does not mean that someone can film or record a performer's act, for example, without the performer's permission. A federal law criminalizes the unauthorized recording of a live musical performance.[10] This action would also be forbidden by other laws, such as the right to publicity (see Chapter 7) and common-law copyright.*

The federal statute lists a wide variety of items that can be copyrighted, but this list is only illustrative. It includes:

1. Literary works (including computer software)
2. Musical works, including any accompanying words
3. Dramatic works, including any accompanying music
4. Pantomimes and choreographic works
5. Pictorial, graphic, and sculptural works
6. Motion pictures and other audiovisual works
7. Sound recordings

10. *United States* v. *Moghadam,* 11th Cir., No. 98-2180, 5/19/99.

*Under the 1909 law the United States had two kinds of copyright protection: common-law copyright and statutory copyright. Much as it did in 18th-century England, the common law protected any work that had not been published. Common-law protection was automatic; that is, the work was protected from the point of its creation. And it lasted forever—or until the work was published. In order to protect published works, the author, photographer, or composer had to register the book or picture or song with the U.S. government and place a copyright notice on the work. The 1976 statute does away with common-law copyright for all practical purposes. The only kinds of works protected by the common law are works like extemporaneous speeches and sketches that have not been fixed in a tangible medium. They are still protected from the point of their creation by common-law copyright. Once they are written down, recorded, filmed, or fixed in a tangible medium in any way, they come under the protection of the new law.

Copyright law is equally specific about what cannot be copyrighted:

1. Trivial materials cannot be copyrighted. Such things as titles, slogans, and minor variations on works in the public domain are not protected by the law of literary property. (But these items might be protected by other laws, such as unfair competition, for example.)

2. Ideas are not copyrightable. The law protects the literary or dramatic expression of an idea, such as a script, but does not protect the idea itself. "This long established principle is easier to state than to apply," notes law professor David E. Shipley. It is often difficult to separate expression from the ideas being expressed.

3. Utilitarian goods—things that exist to produce other things—are not protected by copyright law, according to William Strong in *The Copyright Book*. A lamp is a utilitarian object that exists to produce light. One cannot copyright the basic design of a lamp. But the design of any element that can be identified separately from the useful article can be copyrighted, according to Strong. The design of a Tiffany lamp can be copyrighted. The unique aspects of a Tiffany lamp have nothing to do with the utilitarian purpose of producing light; these aspects are purely decorative.

4. Methods, systems, and mathematical principles, formulas, and equations cannot be copyrighted. But a description, an explanation, or an illustration of an idea or system can be copyrighted. In such an instance the law is protecting the particular literary or pictorial form in which an author chooses to express herself or himself, not the idea or plan or method itself. For example, an individual writes and publishes a book in which she outlines a new mathematical formula. Although the book itself may be protected by copyright, the formula cannot be, and others may use it freely. In other words, the copyright on an article or a book does not preclude the public from making use of what the book teaches.

Can all books and other creative works be copyrighted? No. The law specifically says that only "original" works can be copyrighted. What is an original work? In interpreting this term in the 1909 law, courts ruled that the word "original " means that the work must owe its origin to the author. In 1973 a court reporter (an employee of the court who transcribes the proceedings) attempted to claim copyright over a transcript he had made of some of the proceedings during the investigation of the death of Mary Jo Kopechne. This young woman drowned when a car driven by Senator Edward Kennedy went off a bridge and into a creek near Chappaquiddick, Mass. In *Lipman* v. *Commonwealth*,[11] a federal judge ruled that the transcript could not be copyrighted. "Since transcription is by very definition a verbatim recording of other persons' statements, there can be no originality in the reporter's product."

In 1985 an organization called Production Contractors Inc., or PCI, tried to block Chicago television station WGN from televising a Christmas parade on Thanksgiving Sunday.

---

11. 475 F. 2d 565 (1973).

PCI, which put on the parade, sold the exclusive right to televise it to WLS. It claimed the parade was copyrighted, and WGN would be in violation of the law by televising it. A federal district court disagreed and ruled that a Christmas parade is not something that can be copyrighted; it is a common idea, not an event of original authorship.[12]

The work must be original. Must it be of high quality or be new or novel? The answer to both questions is no. Even common and mundane works are copyrightable. Courts have consistently ruled that it is not the function of the legal system to act as literary or art critic when applying copyright law. In 1903 Justice Oliver Wendell Holmes wrote in *Bleistein* v. *Donaldson Lithographing Co.,* "It would be a dangerous undertaking for persons trained only to the law to constitute themselves final judges of the worth of pictorial illustrations, outside of the narrowest and most obvious limits."[13] Even the least pretentious picture can be an original, Holmes noted in reference to the posters involved in this case.

The 9th U.S. Circuit Court of Appeals echoed this statement in 1992 when it ruled that raw, unedited video footage of news events was sufficiently original to be protected by copyright.[14] The case involved the Los Angeles News Service and Audio Video Reporting Service. LANS records live news events on video and then sells the unedited but copyrighted footage to television stations. The TV stations take the raw footage, edit it any way they want, and use it in newscasts. Audio Video Reporting Services videotapes newscasts and then sells clips of the newscasts to interested parties. A businesswoman who has been interviewed for a news story, for example, may want to buy a copy of the story from Audio Video. Or the parents of children featured in a news story on a school project might want to have a copy of that story.

LANS sued Audio Visual, claiming that in selling these video clips, which were taken from the copyrighted raw footage LANS had provided to local television stations, Audio Video was infringing on the copyright LANS held on the videotape. Audio Visual attempted to defend the suits on several bases, including the argument that raw, unedited videotape was not sufficiently original to be protected by copyright; all the photographer did was switch on the camera and point it at the news event. No creativity or intellectual input was required. The Court of Appeals disagreed, noting that there were several creative decisions involved in producing a photograph. The photographer must select the subject, the background, the perspective, consider the lighting and the action, and so on. The "requisite level of creativity [to qualify as an original work] is extremely low; even a slight amount will suffice," the court said. Likewise, novelty is not important to copyright: The author does not have to be the first person to say something in order to copyright it. "All that is needed to satisfy both the Constitution and the statute is that the 'author' contributed something more than a merely trivial variation, something recognizably his own," one court ruled.[15]

12. *Production Contractors* v. *WGN Continental Broadcasting,* 622 F. Supp. 1500 (1985).
13. 188 U.S. 239 (1903).
14. *Los Angeles News Service* v. *Tullo,* 973 F. 2d 791 (1992).
15. *Amsterdam* v. *Triangle Publishing Co.,* 189 F. 2d 104 (1951).

TELEPHONE BOOKS AND DATABASES

In 1991 the Supreme Court decided a seemingly innocuous case involving copyright protection for white-pages telephone directories. Is the alphabetical list of names, addresses, and telephone numbers in a telephone book an original document? The law had long held that facts are not copyrightable. The finder of a fact is not granted the right to own that fact. Names, addresses, and telephone numbers are facts. Seemingly then, the telephone directory cannot be copyrighted.

The plaintiff in this case was Rural Telephone Service, a small, rural telephone company that issued a white-pages directory listing the names, addresses, and phone numbers of its 1,309 subscribers. The defendant was Feist Publications, a business that specializes in publishing telephone directories. Feist will publish a single directory that includes the names and telephone numbers contained in several small directories, creating a kind of regional phone book that includes the subscribers of several small telephone companies. When Feist asked Rural for permission to take the 1,309 names from its telephone book for use in its regional directory, Rural refused to grant permission. Feist used the names anyway and Rural sued for copyright infringement. The plaintiff proved to the court that four of the 1,309 names in the directory were fictitious, planted there to snare a thief who reproduced the directory without permission.

Rural made two arguments to try to overcome the difficulty in establishing copyright protection for facts. First, the plaintiff argued that the directory was more than just facts, it was a compilation or collection of facts. The law has recognized limited protection for compilations of facts. Second, Rural raised what was known in copyright law as the "sweat of the brow" doctrine. This is a legal proposition recognized in the past by some courts that even though facts are not copyrightable, a man or woman who invests great energy and hard work in amassing these facts deserves some reward for this hard work. Hence, the law should protect a directory or a road map not because it is necessarily original, but because it took a lot of work to create.

In a unanimous decision the Supreme Court rejected both arguments. With regard to the latter, Justice Sandra Day O'Connor said the "sweat of the brow" doctrine was a bogus argument. Quoting former justice William Brennan, she said, "The primary objective of copyright law is not to reward the labor of authors, but to promote the process of science and the arts." O'Connor agreed that some compilations of facts can be protected by copyright. The key to determining whether protection is merited is whether there is some novelty or originality in the manner in which the facts are organized or selected or coordinated. An alphabetical listing of names—the organization of the Rural directory and indeed all white pages—is not novel enough to generate copyright protection for the directory.[16]

The high court ruling was important, but seemingly narrow in its reach. How many cases involving copyright protection for white-pages directories emerge each year? Yet in recent years the importance of the *Feist* ruling has expanded exponentially. What can be said about the originality of an alphabetical list of names in a telephone book can be said as well about any alphabetically ordered list of facts. And the creation of alphabetically ordered lists of facts, which are also called databases, is among the fastest growing uses for CD-ROM computer software and

"The primary objective of copyright law is not to reward the labor of authors, but to promote the process of science and the arts."

16. *Feist Publications, Inc.* v. *Rural Telephone Service Co., Inc.,* 111 S. Ct. 1282 (1991).

interactive Web sites on the Internet. Because of the *Feist* ruling, most of these databases do not qualify for copyright protection.* Hence there is no way to protect the compiler's investment of time, money, and effort in gathering the data. Many states have misappropriation laws (see pages 513–514) that can be used to bar database piracy, but most database owners want a federal law to restore the protection of their property that seemingly existed before the *Feist* decision. In early 2000 the Congress was considering at least two measures to reinstate this protection. One rather broad bill would prohibit the user of someone else's database from sharing the information in the database with a third party, if that sharing would harm the original database publisher. Another, less draconian measure would merely prohibit the wholesale duplication and sale of a database, but would allow reuse of factual information.

NEWS EVENTS

Facts cannot be copyrighted. What about a news event? Can one journalist claim the exclusive right to report on a story? Suppose a TV reporter gets an exclusive interview with a reclusive public figure and then broadcasts the copyrighted interview on the evening news. Does the law of copyright prevent other journalists from relating the substance of what was revealed in that interview? The answer is no. Other stations cannot replay the same interview. Newspapers cannot publish a transcript of the interview. But both broadcast and print journalists can tell their viewers and readers what the public figure said in the interview. Copyright law doesn't even require the competitors to credit the TV journalist for the interview. However, failing to give proper credit to the TV journalist who got the interview could result in a lawsuit for misappropriation or plagiarism and is certainly grossly unethical.

Copyright law protects the expression of the story—the way it is told, the style and manner in which the facts are presented—but not the facts in the story. For many writers this concept is a difficult one to understand and to accept. After all, if one reporter works hard to uncover a story, shouldn't he or she have the exclusive right to tell that story? Even some courts have had a hard time acknowledging this notion. The so-called sweat-of-the-brow doctrine rejected by the Supreme Court in the *Feist* ruling (see page 510) is evidence that some judges believe hard work should be rewarded. But whether it is fair or not, the law is clear. Hard work must be its own reward. Copyright only protects the way the story is told, not the story itself. A copyright case that evolved from a brutal kidnapping graphically demonstrates this point.

Gene Miller, a Pulitzer Prize–winning reporter for the Miami Herald, wrote a book entitled "83 Hours Till Dawn", an account of the kidnapping of Barbara Mackle. Miller said he had spent more than 2,500 hours on the book, and many aspects of the kidnapping case were uncovered by the journalist and reported only in his book. Universal Studios wanted to

---

*The same year the *Feist* case was decided the 2nd U.S. Circuit Court of Appeals ruled that the creator of a directory of businesses in New York City had demonstrated novelty by arranging and selecting the businesses to be included in the directory in a creative fashion. See *Key Publications, Inc.* v. *Chinatown Today,* 945 F. 2d 509 (1991). And in 1997 the 7th U.S. Circuit Court of Appeals ruled that a taxonomy (a way of describing items in a body of knowledge or practice) of dental procedures was a creative work, far different from a simple compilation. *American Dental Association* v. *Delta Dental Plan Association,* CA 7, 96-4140, 9/30/97. See also *Warren Publishing Co.* v. *Microdos Data Corp.* CA 11 en banc, No. 93-8474, 6/10/97.

film a dramatization of the 1971 incident but was unable to come to terms with Miller on payment for the rights. The studio produced the so-called docudrama anyway, and Miller sued for infringement of copyright. The similarities between Miller's book and the Universal script were striking—even some of the errors Miller had made in preparing the book were found in the film. But Universal argued that it was simply telling a story of a news event, and as such the research that Miller had done in digging out the facts regarding the story was not protected by copyright law. A U.S. district court agreed with Miller's contention. "The court views the labor and expense of the research involved in the obtaining of those uncopyrightable facts to be intellectually distinct from those facts, and more similar to the expression of the facts than the facts themselves," the court said. The judge ruled that it was necessary to reward the effort and ingenuity involved in giving expression to a fact.[17] But the U.S. Court of Appeals for the 5th Circuit reversed the lower-court ruling. "The valuable distinction in copyright law between facts and the expression of facts cannot be maintained if research is held to be copyrightable. There is no rational basis for distinguishing between facts and the research involved in obtaining the facts," the court said. To hold research copyrightable, the court said, is no more or less than to hold that the facts discovered as a result of research are entitled to copyright protection.[18] The court added: "A fact does not originate with the author of a book describing the fact. Neither does it originate with the one who 'discovers' the fact. The discoverer merely finds and records. He may not claim that the facts are 'original' with him, although there may be originality and hence authorship in the manner of reporting, i.e. the 'expression' of the facts."

The 7th U.S. Circuit Court of Appeals handed down a similar ruling in 1990 in a case involving the infamous John Dillinger, the subject of a widely publicized manhunt by local police and the FBI during the 1930s. Most historians believe that Dillinger was killed on July 22, 1934, when he was shot by government agents who ensnared him in an ambush when he left the Biograph movie theater in Chicago. Jay Robert Nash has written at least two books that dispute this conclusion. Nash argues that Dillinger learned about the ambush and sent a look-alike to the theater instead. The FBI, embarrassed that its setup failed, kept quiet. And Dillinger retired from a life of crime and lived the rest of his life on the West Coast.

A 1984 episode of the CBS television series "Simon and Simon" involved a story that suggested that Dillinger was still alive, living in California. Nash sued the network, claiming copyright infringement. The officials at the network admitted that they had seen Nash's books and said they had used some of his ideas. But, they argued, Nash claimed to be writing history, and history is a collection of facts. Such material cannot be copyrighted. The court agreed. The network might be liable if Nash portrayed his work as a novel, as fiction. But he didn't. "The inventor of Sherlock Holmes controls that character's fate while the copyright lasts; the first person to conclude that Dillinger survives does not get his dibs on the history," Judge Easterbrook wrote. Nash's rights lie in his expression, not in the naked truth.[19]

---

17. *Miller* v. *Universal City Studios,* 460 F. Supp. 984 (1978).
18. *Miller* v. *Universal City Studios,* 650 F. 2d 1365 (1981).
19. *Nash* v. *CBS,* 899 F. 2d 1537 (1990). Also see *Burgess* v. *Chase-Riboud,* 765 F. Supp. 233 (1991) on page 000.

MISAPPROPRIATION

Although this chapter focuses on copyright, an ancillary area of the law needs to be briefly mentioned, as it too guards against the theft of intangible property. **Misappropriation,** or **unfair competition,** is sometimes invoked as an additional legal remedy in suits for copyright infringement. Unlike copyright, which springs largely from federal statute today, misappropriation, or unfair competition, remains largely a creature of the common law. One of the most important media-oriented misappropriation cases was decided by the Supreme Court more than 80 years ago and stemmed from a dispute between the Associated Press (AP) and the International News Service (INS), a rival press association owned by William Randolph Hearst. (INS merged with the United Press in 1958 and today represents the *I* in UPI.)

The Associated Press charged that the International News Service pirated its news, saying that INS bribed AP employees to gain access to news before it was sent to AP member newspapers. The press agency also charged that the Hearst wire service copied news from bulletin boards and early editions of newspapers that carried AP dispatches. Sometimes INS editors rewrote the news, and other times they sent the news out on the wire just as it had been written by AP reporters. Copyright was not the question, because AP did not copyright its material. The agency said it could not copyright all its dispatches because there were too many and they had to be transmitted too fast. The International News Service argued that because the material was not copyrighted, it was in the public domain and could be used by anyone.

Justice Mahlon Pitney wrote the opinion in the 7–1 decision. He said there can be no property right in the news itself, the events, the happenings, which are publici juris, the common property of all, the history of the day. However, the jurist went on to say:

> Although we may and do assume that neither party [AP or INS] has any remaining property interest as against the public in uncopyrighted matter after the moment of its first publication, it by no means follows that there is no remaining property interest in it as between themselves.[20]

Pitney said there was a distinct difference between taking the news collected by AP and publishing it for use by readers and taking the news and transmitting that news for commercial use, in competition with the plaintiff. This action is unfair competition, he said—interference with the business of the AP precisely at the point where profit is to be reaped.

In 1963 a Pennsylvania broadcasting station was found guilty of pirating the news from a local newspaper and reading it over the air as if it were the fruits of its own news-gathering efforts.[21] In 1994 the Reading (Pa.) Eagle Co., which publishes the morning Times and the afternoon Eagle, sued another Pennsylvania radio station, WIOV in Reading, charging copyright infringement, misappropriation, and unfair competition. The publisher claimed the station was lifting its news stories and sought $50,000 in damages.[22]

20. *Associated Press* v. *International News Service,* 248 U.S. 215 (1919).
21. *Pottstown Daily News Publishing* v. *Pottstown Broadcasting,* 192 A. 2d 657 (1963).
22. Shepard, "Does Radio News Rip Off Newspapers?" 15.

The law of misappropriation, or unfair competition, is intended to stop

- **A person trying to pass his or her work off as the work of someone else, and**
- **A person trying to pass off the work of someone else as his or her own work.**

Imagine that a new magazine is published with the title News-Week. The cover design mirrors that of Newsweek. The design and title would be an attempt to confuse readers and pass off the new magazine as the well-established original, a publisher trying to pass his or her work off as the work of someone else. Or, imagine a daily newspaper reporter picking up a story that was published in a small weekly paper, rewriting the story, and then passing it off as his or her original reporting. Such an action would be trying to pass off the work done by someone else as the daily reporter's own work.

The critical legal issue in an unfair competition or misappropriation suit is whether there is a *likelihood* that an appreciable number of ordinarily prudent purchasers are likely to be misled, or simply confused, as to the source of the goods in question.

DURATION OF COPYRIGHT PROTECTION

The length of time that a copyright will protect a given work depends on when the work was created. The major revision of the copyright law in 1976 included a significant extension of the duration of copyright protection. In 1998 Congress adopted the Sonny Bono Copyright Extension Act, adding 20 more years to the protection of a copyrighted work. Any work created after January 1, 1978, will be protected for the life of the creator, plus 70 years.[*] This rule allows creators to enjoy the fruits of their labor until death and then allows the heirs to profit from the work of their fathers, mothers, sisters, or brothers for an additional length of time. After 70 years the work goes into what is called public domain. At that point it may be copied by any person for any reason without the payment of royalty to the original owner. The copyright on a work created by two or more authors extends through the life of the last author to die plus 70 years. What is called a "work for hire" is protected for 95 years after publication. Works for hire include books written by an author for a publisher, which then holds the copyright. Also included are most motion pictures, sound recordings, television programs, and so on that are created through a collaborative effort.

What about works created before 1978? Prior to the revision of copyright law in 1976, works were protected for a term of 28 years. The owner could renew the copyright and add a second 28-year term for a total of 56 years. Under terms of the 1976 law, works created before that date are protected for a total of 95 years. If a work is in its initial 28-year term, it is protected for the remainder of that 28-year term plus 67 more years. Imagine that a book was copyrighted in 1970. It was protected until 1998 under its original 28-year term, plus 67 more

---

[*]Additional information concerning duration of copyright is available in circulars *RI5A* and *RI5T,* which are published by the Copyright Office, Library of Congress, Washington, D.C., 20559.

years, until 2065. But to gain the additional 67 years, the copyright holder will have to renew the copyright as was required under the previous statute.

If the copyrighted work is already in its renewal term—the second 28 years under the old law—it will be protected for a total of 95 years. Imagine, for example, that a song was originally copyrighted in 1940. The copyright was renewed in 1968, the end of the first 28-year term. It will be protected for an additional 67 years from 1968, or until 2035. No renewal request is needed in this case.

SUMMARY

American copyright law derives from rules and regulations established by the British government in the 16th and 17th centuries. The contemporary basis for the protection of intangible property is contained in the U.S. Constitution, and since 1789 the nation has had numerous federal copyright statutes. The current law, adopted in 1976, gives to the author or owner of a work the sole and exclusive right to reproduce the copyrighted work in any form for any reason. The statute protects all original works of authorship fixed in any tangible medium. Included are such creations as literary works, newspaper stories, magazine articles, television programs, films, and even advertisements. Trivial items, utilitarian goods, ideas, and methods or systems cannot be copyrighted.

News events cannot be copyrighted, but stories or broadcasts that endeavor to describe or explain these events can be copyrighted. What is being protected is the author's style or manner of presentation of the news. Similarly, facts cannot be copyrighted, but works that relate these facts can be protected as expression. While news and facts cannot be copyrighted, anyone who attempts to present news or facts gathered by someone else as his or her own work may be guilty of breaking other laws, such as misappropriation, or unfair competition. In most cases copyrighted works are protected for the life of the author or creator plus 70 years. Different rules apply for works created before 1978 and for works made for hire.

FAIR USE

Owners of a copyright are granted almost exclusive monopoly over the use of their creations. The word *almost* must be used, for there are really four limitations on this monopoly. Three of the limitations have been discussed already. First, the work must be something that can be copyrighted. There can be no legal monopoly on the use of something that cannot be protected by the law. Second, the monopoly only protects original authorship or creation. If the creation is not original, it cannot be protected. Third, copyright protection does not last forever. At some point the protection ceases and the work falls into the public domain.

The fourth limitation on exclusive monopoly is broader than the other three, is certainly more controversial, and is concerned with limited copying of copyrighted material. This is the doctrine of fair use, which has been defined by one court as:

Owners of a copyright are granted almost exclusive monopoly over the use of their creations.

> A rule of reason . . . to balance the author's right to compensation for his work,
> on the one hand, against the public's interest in the widest possible dissemination
> of ideas and information on the other.[23]

This doctrine, then, permits limited copying of an original creation that has been properly copyrighted and has not yet fallen into the public domain.

One hundred and twenty-five years ago all copying of a copyrighted work was against the law. This absolute prohibition on copying constituted a hardship for scholars, critics, and teachers seeking to use small parts of copyrighted materials in their work. A judicial remedy for this problem was sought. It was argued that since the purpose of the original copyright statute was to promote art and science, the copyright law should not be administered in such a way as to frustrate artists and scientists who publish scholarly materials. In 1879 the U.S. Supreme Court ruled in *Baker* v. *Selden:*

> The very object of publishing a book on science or the useful arts is to commu-
> nicate to the world the useful knowledge which it contains. But this object would
> be frustrated if the useful knowledge could not be used without incurring the
> guilt of piracy of the book.[24]

The doctrine of **fair use** emerged from the courts, and under this judicial doctrine small amounts of copying were permitted so long as the publication of the material advanced science, the arts, criticism, and so forth.

The 1976 copyright law contains the common-law doctrine of fair use. Section 107 of the measure declares, "The fair use of a copyrighted work . . . for purposes such as criticism, comment, news reporting, teaching (including multiple copies for classroom use), scholarship or research is not an infringement of copyright."

In determining whether the use of a particular work is a fair use, the statute says that courts should consider the following factors.

1. **The purpose and character of the use**
2. **The nature of the copyrighted work**
3. **The amount and substantiality of the portion used in relation to the copyrighted work as a whole**
4. **The effect of the use on the potential market for or value of the copyrighted work**

Each factor on this list will be considered separately as the doctrine of fair use is explored. Interestingly, the fair-use criteria included in the statute and just listed here (1 through 4) are very close to the criteria that courts used under the old common-law fair-use doctrine. This similarity is no accident. In a report issued by committees in the House and the Senate on Section 107, the legislators said that the new law "endorses the purpose and general scope of the judicial doctrine of fair use" but did not intend that the law be frozen as it existed in 1976. "The courts must be free to adapt the doctrine to particular situations on a case-by-case basis. Section 107 is intended to restate the present judicial doctrine of fair use, not to change, narrow, or enlarge it in any way."

23. *Triangle Publications* v. *Knight-Ridder,* 626 F. 2d 1171 (1980).
24. *Baker* v. *Selden,*101 U.S. 99 (1879).

PURPOSE AND CHARACTER OF USE

The purpose and character of the use of a work is the initial factor to be considered. A use is more likely to be considered a fair use if it is a noncommercial or nonprofit use. But simply because material is used in a commercial venture doesn't disqualify it as a fair use. The U.S. Court of Appeals for the 2nd Circuit noted that according to committee reports compiled when the new copyright law was adopted, the Congress did not intend that only nonprofit educational uses of copyrighted works would qualify as fair use. The reports, said the court, are "an express recognition that . . . the commercial or nonprofit character of an activity, while not conclusive with respect to fair use, can and should be weighed along with other factors in fair-use decisions."[25]

The law lists several categories of use that normally fall under fair use: criticism, comment, news reports, teaching, scholarship, and research. A weekly newspaper in Minneapolis republished a short copyrighted article that had been written by a police officer and first published in a police federation magazine. The article, which was written as a fable, was followed by commentary in the weekly. The editor said he ran the entire piece because he believed it was racist and should not have been published in the police federation magazine. The U.S. district court ruled that this use was a fair use since the weekly had published the piece to criticize it, not to capitalize on it.[26] A book reviewer is clearly protected when quoting even long passages from a work being evaluated. A journalist could undoubtedly publish one or two stanzas from a poem by a poet who was named the winner of a Pulitzer Prize. Yet if a poster publisher took the same two stanzas of poetry, printed them in large type on 11-by-14-inch stock, and tried to sell them for $10 each, the publisher would be guilty of an infringement of copyright. The purpose of the use in the case of the journalist was to give readers an example of the poet's work, but the poster publisher simply wanted to make a few bucks.

Copyright law has traditionally regarded the limited use of copyrighted material for educational purposes as a fair use. The teacher who makes copies of a short article from Newsweek and distributes them to class members is normally considered an innocent infringer. But more substantial copying may not receive the same protection, especially when commercial interests are involved. In 1991 U.S. District Judge Constance B. Motley ruled that businesses that commercially copy collections of articles and excerpts from books without first gaining permission from copyright holders are violating the copyright laws, even if the copies are designed for classroom use.[27] This suit was launched by eight U.S. publishers against Kinko's, a national chain of copy shops based in California. Many college instructors collect magazine and journal articles, chapters from books, and other written material and create a kind of instant anthology for use in a class. Kinko's would copy this material, put it together into course packets or course resource books, and then sell it to the students enrolled in the course for $10 or $20, considerably less than the cost of a published anthology or a textbook. Teachers liked the scheme because they could fashion an individual collection of materials for each class. Students liked it as well because the resource books cost less than a published book. And, of course, Kinko's

---

25. *Maxtone-Graham* v. *Burtchaell,* 803 F. 2d 1253 (1986).
26. *Belmore* v. *City Pages, Inc.* 880 F. Supp. 673 (1995).
27. *Basic Books Inc.* v. *Kinko's Graphics Corp.,* 758 F. Supp. 1552 (1991).

liked it because it was a very profitable endeavor. But the copyright holders did not appreciate the scheme and went to court to block it. Kinko's argued that the fair-use standard permits photocopying of material for educational use. Judge Motley agreed, but ruled that the nature and extent of the copying and Kinko's profit-making intent had clearly exceeded fair use. Citing the photocopier's "historic willful blindness to the copyright laws," Judge Motley ordered Kinko's to stop copying this material without first getting permission from the copyright holder. Most publishers will require Kinko's to pay a licensing fee or royalty to do such copying. In addition, the court ordered the copy shop to pay the publishers more than a half-million dollars in damages plus court costs and attorneys' fees.

The decision in the Kinko's case was reinforced five years later when the 6th U.S. Circuit Court of Appeals, sitting en banc, also ruled that the creation of anthologies of copyrighted material for classroom use was a violation of the law. In this case the defendant argued that, because the professors who required the students to buy the anthologies had placed the same material on reserve in the library where students were free to copy it on their own, selling the same materials in a course pack was not a copyright infringement. The court said the copying of the material by the Michigan Document Service was a commercial use, regardless of how the copying would be regarded if a student did it on his or her own. The court noted that when the 1976 Copyright Act was approved, the Congress had accepted guidelines for educational use copying that would be regarded as a fair use. The copying must

- **be brief—under 1,000 words;**
- **be spontaneous—there would be no time to get permission;**
- **not occur more than 9 times a term, with a limited number of copies from a single author;**
- **carry a copyright notice;**
- **not be a substitute for purchase of the original work and not cost the student more than the actual copying cost.**

These guidelines also make clear, the court said, that the kind of anthologies created by the Michigan Document Service could not be regarded as a fair use.[28] The Supreme Court declined to review the Court of Appeals ruling.

At times defendants have argued that the use of copyrighted material serves a public interest and hence should be protected. In 1966 the 2nd U.S. Circuit Court of Appeals ruled that the use by Random House of copyrighted material in a biography of, at that time, America's best-known recluse, multimillionaire Howard Hughes, was a fair use. In an attempt to thwart the publication of the biography, a Hughes company called Rosemont had purchased the rights to a series of articles published in Look magazine that were heavily quoted in the book. The court ruled that the purpose of copyright law was not to stop the dissemination of information about publicity-shy public figures. It would be contrary to the public interest to permit individuals to buy up the rights to anything published about them to stop authors from using the material, the court ruled.[29] The public interest criteria came to the fore again two

---

28. "Copying of Materials for Coursepack Does Not Constitute Fair Use, CA6 Rules," 1 E.P.L.R. 809 (1996).
29. *Rosemont* v. *Random House,* 366 F. 2d 303 (1966).

years later when a federal court permitted the author of a book to use copyrighted frames of 8mm motion picture film to illustrate his theory regarding the assassination of John F. Kennedy. The motion picture, taken by a spectator named Abraham Zapruder, was then owned by Time, Inc., which had bought the film shortly after the killing.[30]

Today judges talk about transformative uses in a manner similar to the earlier discussions about public interest. For example, when ABC broadcast a television news report about how the advocates of the legalization of marijuana have changed the image of the typical user from the long-haired hippie to a seriously ill medical patient, it used both the cover and a photo from a recent issue of Newsweek. The magazine's story focused on the medical uses of marijuana. The federal court said the use of the photo was transformative, or the use of a news photo to talk about the news. This use was permissible under fair use, the court said in dismissing the lawsuit brought by photographer Richard Morgenstein.[31] The public interest dimension of the purpose and character of use criterion is certainly available to a defendant, but it has not been widely cited by U.S. courts.

NATURE OF THE COPYRIGHTED WORK

Courts look at several considerations when applying this criterion in a copyright infringement action.

- **Is the copyrighted work still available?** Using a part of a work that is out of print is far less serious than using a segment of a book that can be readily purchased at the local bookstore.
- **Is the copyrighted work what is called a consumable work?** A consumable work is something that is intended to be used just once: a workbook that accompanies a text, or a book of crossword puzzles. These are usually cheaply priced and are intended to be used and then discarded. It would not be a fair use for a teacher to purchase a single copy of a biology workbook, make 30 photocopies of each page, and then pass out the photocopies for use by the students. But it would very likely be a fair use for the same teacher to make 30 copies of an article in Science magazine for class distribution.
- **Is the work an informational work or a creative work?** It is more likely to be a fair use if the copying involves a work like a newspaper or news magazine or encyclopedia than a novel or play or poem. This doesn't mean that copying an informational work is always a fair use; just that it is more likely to be.
- **Is the work published or unpublished?** This factor is critical. As will be noted in the discussion of the cases to follow, the courts tend to passionately protect the author's right of first publication.

This story begins in the backwash of the seminal mid-20th-century political event, the Watergate scandal, and involves the unpublished memoirs of Richard Nixon's successor, Gerald

30. *Time, Inc. v. Bernard Geis Associates,* 239 F. Supp. 130 (1968).
31. *Morgenstein v. ABC Inc.,* 27 M.L.R. 1350 (1998).

Ford. Weeks prior to the publication of the Ford book, The Nation magazine published a 2,250-word article containing paraphrases and quotes from the unpublished manuscript. An unnamed source had given a copy of the 200,000-word manuscript to the magazine, and although the article contained only about 300 words that were legitimately protected by copyright (the remainder of the article was uncopyrightable accounts of news and history), the Nation piece contained the heart of Ford's work—his discussion of the pardon he gave to former president Nixon. A U.S. district court said the publication amounted to copyright infringement, but a U.S. court of appeals disagreed, saying the publication of the material was a fair use.[32] The U.S. Supreme Court rejected the fair-use claim and reversed the lower appellate court ruling. "In using generous verbatim excerpts of Mr. Ford's unpublished manuscript to lend authenticity to its account of the forthcoming memoirs, The Nation effectively arrogated to itself the right of first publication, an important marketable subsidiary right," Justice Sandra Day O'Connor wrote. The 1976 Copyright Act clearly recognizes the right of first publication for an author, O'Connor said. The scope of fair use is narrowed where unpublished works are concerned. The Senate report that accompanied the 1976 law specifically states: "The applicability of the fair-use doctrine to unpublished works is narrowly limited since, although the work is unavailable, this is the result of a deliberate choice on the part of the copyright owner. Under ordinary circumstances the copyright owner's 'right of first publication' would outweigh any needs of reproduction." Justice O'Connor concluded that "the unpublished nature of a work is a key, though not necessarily determinative, factor, tending to negate a defense of fair use."[33]

Justice O'Connor concluded that "the unpublished nature of a work is a key, though not necessarily determinative, factor, tending to negate a defense of fair use."

Mark Twain once noted that it is possible to get more out of a lesson than the teacher intended. A cat that sits on a hot stove will likely never sit on another hot stove, he noted. It is just as likely, he added, the cat won't sit on a cold stove either. Such was the case when some lower courts interpreted Justice O'Connor's opinion in the Nation decision. When they read the sentence, "We conclude that the unpublished nature of a work is a key, *though not necessarily determinative,* [author emphasis] factor, tending to negate a defense of fair use," they ignored the italicized phrase. In a series of increasingly restrictive rulings, judges on the 2nd U.S. Circuit Court of Appeals, a court with considerable national authority, ruled that the copying of an unpublished work *can never* be a fair use.[34] The impact of these rulings especially affected scholars who frequently use unpublished letters, diaries, and other materials in preparing serious biographies of important public persons. Many in the publishing industry panicked. Editors at Harper & Row made author James Reston Jr. remove sections of a biography he had prepared of former Texas governor John Connally. Reston had quoted from unpublished letters Connally had sent to President Lyndon Johnson. And former New York

---

32. *Harper & Row Publishers* v. *Nation Enterprises,* 557 F. Supp. 1067 (1983), rev'd. 723 F. 2d 195 (1983).
33. *Harper & Row Publishers* v. *Nation Enterprises,* 471 U.S. 539 (1985). Newsweek magazine in 1995 did something akin to what The Nation had done 16 years earlier when it ran a long cover story on the memoirs of Gen. Colin Powell a week before an excerpt from the not-yet-published book was to be printed in Time magazine. But Newsweek was careful not to quote from the book and instead ran analyses of the autobiography based on an advance copy of the book it had somehow obtained.
34. See *Salinger* v. *Random House,* 811 F. 2d 90 (1987) and *New Era Publications* v. *Henry Holt & Co., Inc.,* 873 F. 2d 576 (1990).

THE FORD MEMOIRS

BEHIND THE NIXON PARDON

In his memoirs, *A Time to Heal*, which Harper & Row will publish in late May or early June, former President Gerald R. Ford says that the idea of giving a blanket pardon to Richard M. Nixon was raised before Nixon resigned from the Presidency by Gen. Alexander Haig, who was then the White House chief of staff.

Ford also writes that, but for a misunderstanding, he might have selected Ronald Reagan as his 1976 running mate, that Washington lawyer Edward Bennett Williams, a Democrat, was his choice for head of the Central Intelligence Agency, that Nixon was the one who first proposed Nelson Rockefeller for Vice President, and that he regretted his "cowardice" in allowing Rockefeller to remove himself from Vice Presidential contention. Ford also describes his often prickly relations with Henry Kissinger.

The Nation obtained the 655-page typescript before publication. Advance excerpts from the book will appear in *Time* in mid-April and in *The Reader's Digest* thereafter. Although the initial print order has not been decided, the figure is tentatively set at 50,000; it could change, depending upon the public reaction to the serialization.

Ford's account of the Nixon pardon contains significant new detail on the negotiations and considerations that surrounded it. According to Ford's version, the subject was first broached to him by General Haig on August 1, 1974, a week before Nixon resigned. General Haig revealed that the newly transcribed White House tapes were the equivalent of the "smoking gun" and that Ford should prepare himself to become President.

Ford was deeply hurt by Haig's revela-

(Continued on Page 363)

City Mayor Ed Koch substantially altered a book he was preparing that contained letters he had written to New Yorkers while he was mayor. He chose to not publish segments of the letters that had been written to him that prompted his written responses.

Congress came to the rescue in the autumn of 1992 when it amended the federal copyright statute. The law now states that "the fact that a work is unpublished shall not itself bar a finding of fair use," if such a finding is justified based on the application of all four fair-use criteria. President George Bush signed this amendment to the statute in late October 1992. This change puts the law back to where it was after the ruling in *Harper & Row Publishers* v. *Nation Enterprises.* It remains exceedingly dangerous, though not necessarily fatal, to publish or broadcast material that has never before been published. Such a use will likely only be sustained provided the user can make a strong case under the other three fair-use criteria.

AMOUNT OF A WORK USED

The amount of a work used is not as important as the relative proportion of a work used. Word counts, for example, really don't mean as much as percentages. The use of 500 words from a 450-page book is far less damaging than the use of 20 words from a 40-word poem. How much of the work, in relation to the whole, was used? Courts will consider exact copying when looking at this question; but they will also often consider paraphrasing. Pirates will find little refuge in a dictionary of synonyms. For example, in the mid-1980s respected writer Ian Hamilton sought to publish a biography of reclusive novelist J.D. Salinger, the author of "Catcher in the Rye." Salinger didn't want his biography written and challenged Hamilton in court on the grounds that the biographer was using portions of unpublished letters written by Salinger in violation of the novelist's copyright. Hamilton reworked portions of his manuscript so that in the end he was only using about 200 words copied directly from the letters. But in a great many other instances Hamilton closely paraphrased what Salinger had written in the letters. The 2nd U.S. Circuit Court of Appeals ruled that this use was an infringement of copyright, not a fair use. Paraphrasing Salinger's words did not protect Hamilton. "What is protected is the manner of expression, the author's analysis or interpretation of events—the way he structures his material and marshalls facts, his choice of words and the emphasis he gives to particular developments," wrote Judge Jon O. Newman.[35] The paraphrasing was too close to Salinger's own choice of words, to his creativity. There were 44 letters involved, and Hamilton had copied or paraphrased one-third or more of 17 letters and more than 10 percent of 42 letters. Such material is on 40 percent of the pages of Hamilton's manuscript, Judge Newman noted. The biographer had taken the "heart of the material" from the letters. Hamilton abandoned his initial effort and instead wrote "In Search of J.D. Salinger," a book about Salinger's literary life (without the material from the letters) and his unsuccessful efforts to publish a biography of the reclusive author.

One of the toughest tasks facing a judge is measuring fair use when someone presents a parody of a copyrighted work. A parody is a critical and usually humorous effort to lampoon

---

35. *Salinger* v. *Random House,* 811 F. 2d 90 (1987).

a creation. To qualify as a parody the work must reflect the content of the original work, not just the style or method of presentation. In 1995 two authors wrote a poetic account of O.J. Simpson's double murder trial using a rhyming scheme like that used in the famous Dr. Seuss book, "The Cat in the Hat." The parody was called "The Cat NOT in the Hat! A Parody by Dr. Juice." When sued by Dr. Seuss Enterprises the authors claimed fair use, among other defenses, saying their book was a parody of the original Dr. Seuss book. The court rejected this argument, ruling that the "NOT in the Hat" book had nothing to do with the Seuss original; the authors simply used Seuss's style to ridicule Simpson.[36]

To be both a successful legal and an artistic parody the new work must conjure up in the viewers' or listeners' minds the original work; hence, it must use some aspects of the original work. But how much of the original can be used? "Saturday Night Live," an NBC television program, presented a parody of a New York City public relations campaign. The city had even commissioned the writing of a song—"I Love New York"—as a theme for the campaign. The NBC "Saturday Night Live" parody ended with the singing of "I Love Sodom" to the tune of "I Love New York." The city claimed use of the song was a copyright infringement, but the court disagreed. "A parody is entitled to conjure up the original. Even more extensive use would still be fair use, provided the parody builds upon the original, using the original as a known element of modern culture and contributing something new for humorous effect or commentary," the U.S. Court of Appeals for the 2nd Circuit ruled.[37] The U.S. Court of Appeals for the 9th Circuit ruled that it was a fair use for disc jockey Rick Dees to use the melody and some of the words from the first six bars of the song, "When Sunny Gets Blue," in his comic parody, "When Sonny Sniffs Glue." The lyrics in the original song are: "When Sunny gets blue, her eyes get gray and cloudy, then the rain begins to fall;" in Dees' version: "When Sonny sniffs glue, her eyes get red and bulgy, then her hair begins to fall." The court noted that "like a speech, a song is difficult to parody effectively without exact or near-exact copying. If the would-be parodist varies the music or the meter of the original substantially, it simply will not be recognizable to the general audience." It is this special need for accuracy that gives the parodist some license in these cases, the court added.[38]

In one of the most celebrated copyright cases in years, the U.S. Supreme Court in 1994 focused on the question of whether a commercial parody could ever be considered a fair use. The case involves one of the most recognizable pop/country songs of the 20th century, "Pretty Woman," written by Roy Orbison and William Dees in 1964. Acuff-Rose Music now owns the rights to the song. In the late 1980s Luther Campbell and 2 Live Crew, a rap group, asked Acuff-Rose Music for permission to record a parody of the song. Campbell said Acuff-Rose would be given full credit for the ownership of the original song and that he was willing to pay a fee for using the material. Acuff-Rose refused. The recorded parody was made anyway and included on 2 Live Crew's 1989 album, "As Clean As They Wanna Be." Acuff-Rose Music was given proper credit on the album, which sold more than 250,000 copies in the year after

36. *Dr. Seuss Enterprises L.P.* v *Penguin Books USA, Inc.,* 109 F. 3d 1394 (1997).
37. *Elsmere Music* v. *NBC,* 623 F. 2d 252 (1980).
38. *Fisher* v. *Dees,* 794 F. 2d 432 (1986).

it was released. Acuff-Rose sued for copyright infringement. A trial court ruled that the song was a parody protected by the defense of fair use. But the 6th U.S. Circuit Court of Appeals reversed and remanded the case, stating that a commercial parody could never be a fair use.[39]

The Supreme Court reversed and sent the case back for a trial.[40] Justice David Souter wrote the court's opinion and said a jury trial was needed to determine whether the parody was indeed a fair use. But the language of the opinion showed strong support for the notion of parody as a fair use, commercial or otherwise. "The language of the statute," he said, "makes it clear that the commercial or nonprofit educational purpose of a work is only one element of the first factor enquiry into its purpose and character. . . . Accordingly, the mere fact that a use is educational and not for profit does not insulate it from a finding of infringement, any more than the commercial character of a use bars a finding of fairness. If indeed, commerciality carried presumptive force against a finding of fairness, the presumption would swallow nearly all of the illustrative uses listed [in the statute] . . . including news reporting, comment, criticism, teaching, scholarship and research since these activities are generally conducted for profit in this country."

The Court of Appeals also had held that Luther Campbell had taken the heart of the original song in his parody, a factor, the Supreme Court said in its 1985 *Harper & Row* ruling,[41] that weighed against a fair-use finding. Campbell used the first line of the song, the melody, and the signature bass riff, which is a kind of musical theme throughout the original song. Souter acknowledged that it is important for the court to consider not only how much but the importance of the material taken in a use. But he said that a parody presents a difficult problem. Parody, he said, springs from its allusion to the original. "Its art lies in the tension between a known original and its parodic twin," he said. It is true the parody here took the opening lines and the musical signature. "But if quotation of the opening riff and the first line may be said to go to the 'heart' of the original, the heart is also what most readily conjures up the song for parody, and it is the heart at which parody takes aim. Copying does not become excessive in relation to parodic purpose merely because the portion taken was the original's heart." It was significant, Souter said, that after taking the first line, 2 Live Crew added its own lyrics. And while the bass riff was copied, other original sounds were added as well. A trial is needed, Souter said, to make a better factual determination on just how much of the original was taken and whether the parody version has or will hurt the sale of the original recording, the critical fourth factor in a fair-use evaluation.

A parody presents a difficult problem.

But the would-be parodist must be careful. Not all attempts to spoof another artistic work will necessarily be regarded as protected parody. In the late 1970s, Showcase Atlanta presented what it called a parody of the film "Gone With the Wind." MGM, which holds the copyright on the film, sued for infringement. The U.S. district court found that the locale, settings, characters, situations, and relationships were basically the same in the so-called parody, "Scarlett Fever," and the original "Gone With the Wind." The theme and characterizations

39. *Campbell* v. *Acuff-Rose Music, Inc.,* 92 F. 2d 1429 (1992).
40. *Campbell* v. *Acuff-Rose Music, Inc.,* 114 S. Ct. 1164 (1994).
41. *Harper & Row Publishers* v. *Nation Enterprises,* 471 U.S. 539 (1985).

were also the same, although somewhat more comical in "Scarlett Fever." The story line was the same in both, and some of the dialogue in "Scarlett Fever" followed the dialogue in the classic motion picture almost verbatim. "Scarlett Fever" certainly looks like a version of "Gone With the Wind," the court said. But "Scarlett Fever" was a spoof, a funny version. Doesn't that make a difference? In this case the court said no. In order for a parody to qualify as a fair use, it must do more than simply achieve a comic effect. "It must also make some critical comment or statement about the original work which reflects the *original perspective* [author emphasis] of the parodist—thereby giving the parody social value beyond its entertainment function." "Scarlett Fever" failed on two counts to meet the test of fair use. It lacked the critical edge required, and the parodist had taken too much from the original film. In a parody, the court said, copying is limited to that amount needed for the audience to recall or conjure up the original.[42] This case is a conservative statement of what is or is not a legal parody. But it is certainly not outside the mainstream of judicial thinking on this matter and must be regarded as a viable precedent.

EFFECT OF USE ON MARKET

The effect of the use on the potential market for, or value of, the copyrighted work is the fourth criterion. While a cautionary note should be sounded against assigning relative weight to the four criteria, this final one—harm to the plaintiff—is given greater weight by most courts than any of the other three. In a congressional committee report on the 1976 law, the legislators noted that "with certain special exceptions . . . a use that supplants any part of the normal market for a copyrighted work would ordinarily be considered an infringement." And in the action by Harper & Row against The Nation, Justice Sandra Day O'Connor noted that "this last factor is undoubtedly the single most important element of fair use."[43] "More important," Justice O'Connor wrote, "to negate fair use one need only show that if the challenged use should become widespread, it would adversely affect the potential market for the copyright work."

Conversely, the inability to demonstrate an adverse economic impact from the copying can frequently in and of itself sustain a fair-use ruling. The 5th U.S. Circuit Court of Appeals ruled in 1980 that it was a fair use when the Miami Herald used the copyrighted covers of TV Guide magazine in advertising for the newspaper's new television magazine. This commercial use of the entire cover would hardly seem to be a fair use except that it had absolutely no economic impact on the market value of TV Guide. The advertising might hurt the sale of the portable TV magazine, the court noted, but the advertising did this, not the use of the copyrighted covers. The court added that the fourth factor "is widely accepted as the most important factor."[44] In 1998 a federal judge in Washington state threw out a nearly $700,000 jury award to author Wade Cook after a trial where Cook asserted that motivational writer and speaker Tony Robbins had copied two phrases originated by Cook. The jury decided that Robbins had

42. *MGM* v. *Showcase Atlanta,* 479 F. Supp. 351 (1979).
43. *Harper & Row Publishers* v. *Nation Enterprises,* 471 U.S. 539 (1985).
44. *Triangle Publications* v. *Knight-Ridder,* 626 F. 2d 1171 (1980).

used the two phrases, "meter drop" and "rolling stocks," as many as 12 times in a workbook he (Robbins) distributed at financial seminars. But Judge Jack Tanner said there was not a scintilla of evidence that the use of these phrases caused any harm at all to plaintiff Cook.[45]

In evaluating economic impact the court considers not only direct impact, but also the impact that using the copyrighted material might have on some derivative creation. Imagine the hypothetical situation in which a screenwriter, Virginia Miller, uses a Stephen King novel as the basis of a screenplay she prepares. The screenplay contains a great deal of material from the book. In a copyright action King would have difficulty maintaining the argument that Miller's screenplay had any direct economic impact on his novel. A novel and a screenplay are two different commodities. But should Miller sell her screenplay to Paramount Pictures, King could certainly argue this sale had an adverse economic impact on his work. The sale of Miller's screenplay deprives King of the opportunity to create and sell his own screenplay of his novel. This situation illustrates the loss of a derivative right, a creation derived from the original work. Let's look at a couple of actual cases to further explore this point.

In the mid-1990s the Carol Publishing Group published "The Seinfeld Aptitude Test," a trivia book based on material contained in various episodes of the "Seinfeld" TV program. When sued by Castle Rock Entertainment for copyright infringement Carol Publishing raised fair use as a defense, arguing first, that the book just contained a collection of uncopyrightable facts from the TV program, and second, that the publication of the book had no impact on the market value of the television show. Judge Sonia Sotomayor rejected the first argument by noting that "Seinfeld is fiction. Both the 'facts' in various Seinfeld episodes and the expression of those facts, are the plaintiff's creation." The only unprotected facts in the show were the actors' real names, the names of the director and producer, and the number of seasons the show has run, she added. With regard to impact on the market value of the work, the judge reminded the defendants that the book was a derivative work and its publication deprived the plaintiffs of the opportunity to sell a similar work. The plaintiff controls these rights, she said.[46]

Another case involved professional photographer Art Rogers, who took a picture of a man, his wife, and their eight German Shepherd puppies. He displayed the photo and ultimately had it published as a postcard that was sold in card shops. Artist Jeff Koons bought a copy of the postcard, tore off the copyright notice, and sent it to an Italian art studio with instructions to make four exact polychromed wood sculptures of the scene depicted in the photo. The lab complied and Koons sold three of the four sculptures for more than $350,000. Rogers sued, but Koons claimed his work was a parody of the original photo, an attempt to point out the banality of contemporary American society. The 2nd U.S. Circuit Court of Appeals rejected this argument as well as Koons' assertion that his sculpture would not have an impact on the market for Rogers' photograph. Although the two pieces of art are not in direct competition, Koons' unauthorized use of the photo deprived Rogers of the potential income he could earn by selling the right to reproduce the photo to another sculptor, the court ruled.[47] He lost the opportunity of the sale of a derivative right.

45. "Jury Award for Wade Cook Overruled."
46. *Castle Rock Entertainment* v. *Carol Publishing Group Inc.,* DC SNY 95 Civ. 0775 (SS), 2/27/97.
47. *Rogers* v. *Koons,* 960 F. 2d 301 (1992).

> **FACTORS TO BE CONSIDERED**
> **IN DETERMINING FAIR USE**
>
> 1. The purpose and character of the use
> 2. The nature of the copyrighted work
> 3. The amount and substantiality of the portion used in relation to the copyrighted work as a whole
> 4. The effect of the use on the potential market for or value of the copyrighted work

APPLICATION OF THE CRITERIA

When a court is faced with a defendant who claims fair use, it must apply the four criteria to the facts in the case. A decision by a U.S. district court in Virginia is a good example of how the court will do this. The case involved a long-running dispute between the Church of Scientology and Arnold Lerma, a former member of the church who for many years has sought to expose what he claims is the fraudulent nature of the cult religion. Lerma gained access to what the church considers its sacred texts, and he has posted excerpts at various times on the Internet. The Church of Scientology regards these texts as its property. (The texts are physically protected in locked vaults that are guarded 24 hours each day. They are accessible only by church members, who must sign nondisclosure agreements before they can see them.) Lerma was sued by the Religious Technology Center, an arm of the church, after he scanned portions of the printed texts into his computer for posting on the Internet. The RTC claimed this use was a copyright infringement; Lerma said it was a fair use.

Judge Leonie Brinkema applied the four fair-use criteria to evaluate the defendant's claim. Brinkema rejected Lerma's contention that his posting constituted criticism, comment, news reporting, or scholarship as defined by the law. His motives were not neutral and his postings were not done primarily for public benefit. Although his posting was not commercially motivated, it certainly did not fall into those categories that favor the defendant in making a claim of fair use. The first factor favors the RTC, Brinkema said.

In applying the second factor, Judge Brinkema said although the factual (rather than fictional) nature of the work favors Lerma, the fact that the materials were previously unpublished favors RTC. The third factor clearly favors RTC because Lerma copied entire portions of certain discrete subparts of the texts. The fourth factor—the effect on the market for the copyrighted work—favors the defendant; there was little evidence that the posting harmed the church or that Lerma was operating as a competitor to the church. Putting all four together, the court ruled that Lerma's posting of the material was not a fair use.[48]

---

48. *Religious Technology Center v. Lerma,* 1 E.P.L.R. 729 (1996); 24 M.L.R. 2473 (1996).

While the copyright statute gives the author or owner of a copyrighted work an exclusive monopoly over the use of that work, the law recognizes that in some instances other persons ought to be able to copy portions of a protected work. No liability will attach to such copying if the use is what the law calls a "fair use."

SUMMARY

A court will consider four factors when determining whether a specific use is fair use:

1. What is the purpose of the use? Why was the material copied? Was it a commercial use or for nonprofit educational purpose? Was the use intended to further the public interest in some way?

2. What is the nature of the copyrighted work? Is it a consumable item such as a workbook, or is it a work more likely to be borrowed from, such as a newspaper or magazine article? Is the copyrighted work in print and available for sale? Has the work been previously published or is it unpublished?

3. How much of the copyrighted work was used in relation to the entire copyrighted work? Was it a small amount of a large work? Or was it a large portion of a small work?

4. What impact does the use have on the potential market or value of the copyrighted work? Has the use of the material diminished the chances for sale of the original work? Or is the use unrelated to the value or sale of the copyrighted material?

Although a court considers each of these items closely, most courts tend to give extra weight to item 4. In a close ruling the impact on the market or value of the copyrighted work often becomes the most crucial question.

COPYRIGHT PROTECTION AND INFRINGEMENT

Until 1989 when the provisions of the Berne Convention (see page 506) became applicable to American copyright law, a work would not be protected from infringement unless it contained a **copyright notice.** Failure to affix a notice meant the automatic loss of most copyright protection. Under international law, however, the affixing of a copyright notice is not required to protect a work. Once a work is created it is protected. American law now states that a copyright notice "may" be placed on works that are publicly distributed. The U.S. Copyright office, however, still strongly urges creators to include notice on all their works. Copyright law protects the "innocent infringer" from liability for infringement. Someone who copies a work that does not contain a notice could claim an innocent infringement, that is, could argue that she did not realize the work she copied was actually protected by copyright. If the court agreed, the creator would lose the ability to collect any damages as a result of the infringement. Placing a proper notice on the work is simply prudent behavior.

When the question arises of whether a creator intended his or her work to be protected by copyright, regardless of whether notice was placed on the work, the court will often look to the initial distribution or publication of the work. In 1998 a federal court in Georgia was forced to take this tack to resolve a long-simmering dispute between the estate of Martin Luther King Jr. and CBS. On August 28, 1963, Martin Luther King gave his now-famous "I have a dream" speech in front of the Lincoln Memorial in Washington, D.C., before about 200,000 people. The speech was also broadcast live on CBS and other major radio and television networks. Copies of the speech were freely distributed, and the event organizers worked diligently to obtain maximum press coverage of the oration. There was no copyright notice on the speech and at no time did anyone in King's organization say anything to the press about copyright. On September 30, 1963, King applied for copyright protection for the speech. In 1984 CBS produced a documentary series for the Arts & Entertainment cable television network called "The 20th Century With Mike Wallace." One segment was dedicated to King's march on Washington and his speech. About 60 percent of the speech was included in the program. The King estate sued for copyright infringement.

The speech was given before the new copyright law was adopted in 1976, so the court had to resolve the issues using old law, in this case, state common-law copyright. The question was, Had King published the speech in August of 1963, before he had applied for copyright protection? If the speech had been published, it pushed the oration into the public domain where anyone was free to use it. The court said the test was whether the work was "made available to members of the public at large without regard to their identity or what they intend to do with the work." In this case the organizers of the march, who were aware of and encouraged press coverage, made a studied effort to secure as wide a dissemination of King's speech as possible, the court ruled. This behavior epitomizes the definition of publication. The dissemination justified the belief by CBS officials that the speech had been dedicated to the public. When the speech was copyrighted more than a month later, it was too late to put the horse back in the barn. It was long gone. There was no copyright protection for the historic presentation.[49] Late in 1999 the 11th U.S. Circuit Court of Appeals reversed the lower court's dismissal of the lawsuit and sent the case back to U.S. District Court Judge William C. O'Kelley for a more thorough hearing. The appellate court did not make a ruling based on the legal arguments in the case, but simply ruled that there were issues to be decided about whether the delivery of the speech constituted a general publication, issues that should be explored at a trial.[50]

COPYRIGHT NOTICE

A copyright notice should contain the word *Copyright,* the abbreviation *Copr.,* or the symbol © (the letter *C* within a circle; the symbol Ⓟ is used on phonorecords). The year of publication must also be included in the notice. For periodicals the date supplied is the date of publication. For books the date is the year in which the book is first offered for sale (e.g., a book printed in November or December 2000 to go on sale January 2001 should carry a 2001 copyright). The notice must also contain the name of the copyright holder or owner. Most authorities recommend that both the word *Copyright* and the symbol © be used, since the use of the symbol is

---

49. *Estate of Martin Luther King Jr. Inc.* v. *CBS Inc.,* 13 F. Supp. 1347 (1998).
50. *Estate of Martin Luther King, Jr. Inc.* v. *CBS, Inc.,* 194 F. 3d 1211 (1999); see also Sack, "Appeals Panel Revives Suit."

required to meet the standards of the international copyright agreements. The symbol © protects the work from piracy in most foreign countries. A copyright notice should look something like this:

> Copyright © 2001 by Jane Adams

The copyright notice can be placed anywhere that it "can be visually perceived" on all publicly distributed copies. (The rules are different for sound recordings, which by nature cannot be visually perceived.) The Copyright Office of the Library of Congress has issued rules that implement the statutory description that the notice be visually perceptible. For example, the rules list eight different places where a copyright notice might be put in a book, including the title page, the page immediately following the title page, either side of the front cover, and so forth. For photographs, a copyright notice label can be affixed to the back or front of a picture or on any mounting or framing to which the photographs are *permanently* attached.[*]

The copyright notice can be placed anywhere that it "can be visually perceived" on all publicly distributed copies.

The law also provides that omission of the proper notice does not destroy copyright protection for the work if the notice is omitted from only a relatively small number of copies, if an effort is made within five years to correct the omission, or if the notice is omitted in violation of the copyright holder's express requirement that as a condition of publication the work carry a copyright notice.

At the same time, the law protects persons who copy a work on which the copyright notice was inadvertently omitted. Such an innocent infringer incurs no liability—cannot be sued—unless this infringement continues beyond the time notice is received that the work has been copyrighted.

REGISTRATION

Proper notice is the only requirement that an author must fulfill to copyright a work. The work is then protected from the moment of creation for the life of the author plus 70 years. However, before a copyright holder can sue for infringement under the law, the copyrighted work must be registered with the federal government. To register a work the author or owner must do three things:

1. Fill out the proper registration form. The type of form varies, depending on the kind of work being registered. The forms are available from the Information and Publications Section, Copyright Office, Library of Congress, Washington, D.C. 20559.
2. Pay a $20 fee.

---

[*]Additional information is available in the bulletin *Methods of Affixation and Position of the Copyright,* published by the Copyright Office, and in the *Federal Register,* vol. 42, no. 247, for 23 December 1977, pp. 64374–78.

3. Deposit two complete copies of the work with the Copyright Office. (One complete copy is all that is required for unpublished works.)

The statute gives an author or owner 90 days to register a work. What happens if the work is still not registered after 90 days and an infringement takes place? The owner can still register the work and bring suit. But a successful plaintiff in such a suit cannot win statutory damages (see page 541) or win compensation for attorney fees. It is best to get into the habit of registering a work as soon as it is published or broadcast.

Affixing a notice on a work is an important last step in the creative process. It allows all the works that no one wants to copyright to fall into the public domain immediately. It also tells the reader whether a work is copyrighted, was ever copyrighted, or is still copyrighted. It also identifies the owner of the work and the date of publication.

INFRINGEMENT

Persons who believe their exclusive right to control the use of a copyrighted work has been violated will sue for infringement. The federal copyright statute does not actually define infringement. The law simply states that anyone who violates any of the "exclusive rights" of the copyright holder is guilty of an infringement of copyright. Courts that litigate copyright cases seem to focus most often on three criteria to determine whether a particular use is an infringement (see following boxed text). A brief outline of each of these three points follows.

■ Is the copyright on the plaintiff's work valid? While this inquiry will look at matters such as the proper registration of the work, the heart of this examination is to determine whether the copyrighted work is an original work that can be protected by copyright.

■ Did the defendant have access to the plaintiff's work prior to the alleged infringement?

■ Are the two works the same or substantially similar?

Originality

The copyright on the plaintiff's work must be valid before a successful infringement suit can be maintained. As has been previously noted, a work that is not original cannot be protected by copyright. A central question, then, in many infringement suits is whether the plaintiff's work is original, or is the plaintiff attempting to bring suit on the basis of the theft of material that cannot be legally copyrighted because it lacks originality or novelty?

History, for example, exists for all to use in a book or a story. Margaret Alexander brought an infringement suit against Alex Haley, claiming that he had copied portions of her novel "Jubilee" and her pamphlet "How I Wrote Jubilee" when he wrote and published his successful novel "Roots." But the court noted that most of what Alexander claimed Haley had stolen was history—the story of the slave culture in the United States—or material in the public domain, such as folktales about early American black culture. "Where common sources exist for the alleged similarities, or the material that is similar is not original with the plaintiff, there is no infringement," the court ruled.[51]

An NBC employee tried to sue the network, arguing that he had originally proposed the concept for the highly successful "Bill Cosby Show" in 1980, some four years before the television program premiered. At that time NBC said it was not interested in the idea, the plaintiff said. But the court said that there was really nothing original in the concept proposed by plaintiff Hwesu Murray or in the Cosby show itself, for that matter. It merely combined two ideas that had been circulating for years: a family situation comedy, and the casting of blacks in nonstereotypical roles. The portrayal of a nonstereotypical black family in a half-hour show was a breakthrough in television broadcasting, the court noted, comparing the Cosby program with shows like "The Jeffersons," "Good Times," "Diff'rent Strokes," and "Sanford and Son," all of which featured blacks in fairly stereotypical roles. But the fact that such a show had never before been broadcast does not necessarily mean that the idea for the program itself was novel. "Whereas here, an idea consists in essence of nothing more than a variation on a basic theme—in this case the family situation comedy—novelty cannot be found."[52]

Judith Rossner, the author of the successful book "Looking for Mr. Goodbar," sued CBS for copyright infringement in 1985 when the network produced the film "Trackdown: Finding Mr. Goodbar." Both Rossner's book and the TV movie are based on the murder in 1973 of Roseann Quinn by John W. Wilson. Rossner's book leads readers up to the point of the murder; the CBS movie purportedly tells the story of the capture of the killer. Rossner claimed the use of the term "Mr. Goodbar" in the title of the movie violated her copyright. But a U.S. district court disagreed, noting that the term "Mr. Goodbar" had been used in newspaper stories about the killing before Rossner wrote her book. An author can't build a story around a historical incident and then claim exclusive right to the use of that incident, the court said. "To the extent that Rossner's characters were inspired by actual persons, she cannot prevent the future depiction of these characters through the individual creative efforts of others," the court ruled. "Since the Mr. Goodbar concept was not original with Rossner, she could not claim it under copyright."[53]

The author of a book entitled "Fort Apache" sued the producers of the film "Fort Apache—The Bronx" for copyright infringement. Both the book and the movie focused on the 41st Precinct of the New York City Police Department. Police officers had dubbed the South Bronx precinct Fort Apache because of the high incidence of violent crime in the area. Thomas Walker, a former police officer who was assigned to the 41st Precinct for 15 months, wrote and published his book in 1976. The book was a series of stories about his work in the precinct, a narrative moving from one anecdote to the next with no real plot. The film, on the other hand, was intensely plotted, with several interrelated story lines all taking place at once. Walker claimed the producers of the film had stolen his material, but a court of appeals disagreed. "To

51. *Alexander* v. *Haley*, 460 F. Supp. 40 (1978).
52. *Murray* v. *NBC*, 844 F. 2d 988 (1988).
53. *Rossner* v. *CBS*, 612 F. Supp. 334 (1985).

be sure, the book and the film share an identical setting, and police officers are central characters in both works," the court noted. "But the South Bronx and the 41st Precinct are real places known to the public through media coverage. Accordingly, the notion of telling a police story that takes place there cannot be copyrightable," the court ruled. The parts of the film that were similar to the book were not original with the book's author.[54]

Access

The second dimension of an infringement suit is access: the plaintiff must convince the court that the defendant had access to the copyrighted work. An opportunity to copy has to exist. If plaintiffs cannot prove that the so-called literary pirate had a chance to see and read the work, they are hard-pressed to prove piracy. As Judge Learned Hand once wrote:

> If by some magic a man who had never known it were to compose anew Keats's, "Ode on a Grecian Urn," he would be an 'author' and if he copyrighted it, others might not copy that poem, though they might of course copy Keats's.[55]

Here, in contemporary terms, is what Judge Hand said. If, through some incredible coincidence, a young composer were to write and publish a song called "Born in the U.S.A." that was an exact duplicate of the song by Bruce Springsteen, it would not be an infringement of copyright. Publishing a song exactly like a copyrighted song is not an infringement; copying a copyrighted song is infringement. Moreover, if the young composer could prove that he had lived in a cave since birth, had never listened to the radio or tapes, and had never watched television or gone to the movies, and if Springsteen could not prove that the defendant had access to "Born in the U.S.A.," he would lose his suit. It is obvious that such a coincidence can never occur, but this illustration nevertheless makes the point. The *plaintiff* must prove that the defendant had access to the stolen work. The smaller the circulation of the copyrighted matter, the harder it is to prove access.

In 1998 Marion Leon Bea sued Home Box Office, claiming it had infringed on his script for a film called "N and Out" when it made the HBO motion picture "First Time Felon." The similarities between the two scripts were thin, the court noted. But what killed the suit was the plaintiff's inability to prove that HBO had access to his script before "First Time Felon" was produced.[56] Failure to prove that the defendant had access to a copyrighted book was also fatal to a lawsuit brought by Sonya Jason against the writers and producers of the film "Coming Home." Defendants Jane Fonda and others stated that their film was conceived in the late 1960s, that a first draft of the screenplay was completed by late 1973 and was revised in 1977. Jason's book, "Concomitant Soldier," was first printed in April 1974. Only 1,100 copies were printed. About 500 copies were sold in New Jersey, 100 were sold through the plaintiff's church, 200 copies were returned to the printer because they were defective, and the remaining copies were sold in southern California. Jason claimed that a copy of the book might have been given to Nancy Dowd, a screenwriter for the film, but there was no evidence that Dowd

The plaintiff must prove that the defendant had access to the stolen work.

54. *Walker* v. *Time-Life Films,* 784 F. 2d 44 (1986).
55. *Sheldon* v. *Metro-Goldwyn-Mayer Pictures,* 81 F. 2d 49 (1939).
56. *Bea* v. *Home Box Office,* 26 M.L.R. 2373 (1998).

or anyone else connected with the film had seen the book. Jason was only able to prove that several hundred copies of "Concomitant Soldier" were sold in southern California where Fonda, Dowd, and others associated with the film lived and worked. "That level of availability creates no more than a 'bare possibility' that defendants may have had access to plaintiff's book," the court said. "In and of itself, such a bare possibility is insufficient to create a genuine issue of whether defendants copied plaintiff's book."[57]

Copying and Substantial Similarity

The final factor the court will consider is evidence that the defendant copied the plaintiff's work or evidence that the two works are substantially similar. In some cases an infringer will take the exact work in question—dub copies of a videocassette, reprint a short story, or use a song lyric on a poster. This action is direct copying—sometimes called literal similarity—and is simple to prove. Slight changes in the work will not protect the infringer. A group aptly named Air Pirates copied Walt Disney characters for posters and T-shirts, but portrayed the lovable Disney creations in a hideous manner. This use was copying and an infringement, the court said, despite the change in the nature of Mickey, Pluto, and the rest of the gang.[58] But more often than not, direct or literal copying is not an issue. The story was not copied word for word, the character was not an exact duplicate of the defendant's character. In such a case the defendant is not accused of taking a particular line or segment of a work, but of appropriating "the fundamental essence or structure of the work." There must be more than minor similarities between the two works; they must be substantially similar. But this is another instance in which it is easier to state a rule than to apply it. How can you determine whether two works are substantially similar? Courts use a variety of tests to determine substantial similarity, but virtually all the tests focus on two aspects of the work.[59] The courts will first ask whether the general idea or general theme of the works is the same. If the general idea of the two works is not similar, there is no infringement. But if the general idea is substantially similar, then the court looks at how the idea is expressed, how the theme is carried out. For example, the themes of the 1953 Alan Ladd film "Shane" and the 1985 Clint Eastwood movie "Pale Rider" are quite similar. Good people in a western town are being pushed around by bad men. Mysterious stranger comes to town and cleans out the villains. Good gunfighter rides off into the sunset. End of movie. But is this theme expressed in the same way in both films? Not really. The townspeople are different; the villains are different; the slight romantic subplot is different; even the leading characters are different. The expression of the common theme is not substantially similar. Let's examine how these criteria were applied in some actual copyright cases.

Warner Brothers, which owns the film rights to "Superman," sued ABC in the early 1980s for broadcast of the network series, "The Greatest American Hero." The general idea of both the "Superman" films and the ABC series is similar—a character, who wears a red and

---

57. *Jason* v. *Fonda et al.,* 526 F. Supp. 774 (1981).
58. See *Walt Disney Productions* v. *Air Pirates,* 345 F. Supp. 180 (1972).
59. See, for example, *Sid and Marty Krofft Television Productions* v. *McDonald's Corporation,* 562 F. 2d 1157 (1977) and *Apple Computer Inc.* v. *Microsoft Corp.,* 35 F. 3d 1435 (1994).

blue suit with a cape and is able to fly, battles the forces of evil. But the court ruled that Warner Brothers could not "claim a protected interest in the theme of a man dressed in a cape and tights who has the power to fly, resist bullets, crash through walls, break handcuffs, etc." The plaintiff must show that the concrete expression of the Superman idea has been appropriated. Warner Brothers could not do this. The characters in "Superman" and "The Greatest American Hero" are quite different. The hero of the ABC program is Ralph Hinckley, an ordinary man who reluctantly takes on abnormal abilities through a magic costume and is comically inept. Superman is naturally endowed with these powers, which he wields with grace and confidence. As a person Hinckley is the antithesis of the strong Superman character, the court said. In some ways the ABC show is a parody of Superman. "As a comedy that parodies American superheroes," Judge Motley wrote, "'The Greatest American Hero' has a very different appeal from Superman, a real superhero, and plaintiffs have not sufficiently proven that it will reduce demand for movies and programs about Superman, and products bearing the Superman image."[60]

The U.S. Court of Appeals for the 9th Circuit was asked to determine whether writer/director Michael Crichton had stolen a screen treatment for his film called "Coma," which was based on a book by Robin Cook. Plaintiff Ted Berkik in 1968 wrote a 54-page screen treatment for a story he called "Reincarnation, Inc." Crichton apparently saw the screen treatment but did not use it 10 years later when he wrote the screenplay for "Coma." Berkik alleged that both the film and Robin Cook's book were taken from his screen treatment.

The stories have certain similarities, the court noted. Both deal with criminal organizations that murder healthy young people and then remove and sell their vital organs to wealthy people in need of organ transplants. And in both stories, courageous young medical professionals investigate and finally expose the criminal organization. But these similarities are at a high level of generality. When one looks at the manner in which these similar ideas are expressed in the two works, the similarity ends. The plots of the two stories develop differently; the settings are different. "Coma" is replete with medical terminology and is an old-fashioned detective story; "Reincarnation, Inc." is more of a romance. Yes, there are some similarities, but general ideas are not protected. Nor are situations and incidents that flow naturally from a basic plot premise, so-called *scènes à faire.* "These familiar scenes [depictions of the small miseries of domestic life or romantic frolics at the beach] and themes are among the very staples of modern American literature and film. The common use of such stock material cannot raise a trial issue of fact on the plaintiff's copyright claim," the appellate court ruled. "It merely reminds us that in Hollywood, as in the life of real men generally, there is only rarely anything new under the sun."[61]

Is it impossible to win a suit based on substantial similarity? Of course not. But the works have to be similar in many respects. There must be strong parallels. Universal City Studios successfully sued Film Ventures for copyright infringement when the company released a film called "Great White," which was very similar to the movie "Jaws." In this case the general idea of both films was obvious to an average filmgoer. But the similarities in the two pictures

60. *Warner Bros.* v. *ABC,* 523 F. Supp. 611 (1981).
61. *Berkik* v. *Crichton,* 761 F. 2d 1289 (1985).

became even more apparent when the court objectively looked at the manner in which the ideas were expressed. Major characters were the same, the sequence of incidents was the same, the development and interplay of the major characters were the same, and even minor story points were the same. The court said the films were not identical but that "defendants have captured the total concept and feel of plaintiff's motion picture."

The court pointed to the following similarities in the films. In both films a local politician plays down the news of a great white shark in the interest of local tourism. Both films featured a salty English sea captain and a shark expert who go out to hunt the shark. The opening scenes of both films show innocent teenagers swimming on a beach who become the first victims of the shark. In both films a local fisherman's empty boat is found. In both films the shark approaches a small boat, bumps it hard, and causes a child to fall into the water. Finally, in both films the shark devours the English sea captain during the hunt but is finally killed when it swallows something that explodes in its stomach. "In light of the great similarity in expression, it would seem fair to conclude that the creators of 'Great White' [which was titled 'The Last Jaws' when it was released overseas] wished to be as closely connected with the plaintiff's motion picture 'Jaws' as possible." The court issued an injunction to stop the exhibition of "Great White" and set a hearing to consider the award of damage.[62]

More recently, a U.S. district court in Pennsylvania ruled that a playwright had infringed on a copyrighted novel when he wrote a drama about Thomas Jefferson and his alleged romantic relationship with a slave he owned. Allegations that Jefferson was romantically involved with a woman named Sally Hemings were first aired by his political opponents in 1802. Biographers of the third U.S. president have variously rejected and accepted these charges. In 1974 author Fawn Brodie published a sensational biography of Jefferson, which she subtitled "An Intimate History," and gave a full airing to the allegations, which she suggested she believed. Five years later Barbara Chase-Riboud wrote "Sally Hemings: A Novel," a work of fiction that explored in considerable detail the woman's supposed love affair with the man from Monticello. Three years later Granville Burgess wrote a play based on the same subject, "Dusky Sally." The play was about to be produced when Chase-Riboud sent letters to Burgess threatening a copyright suit. The playwright went to court seeking a declaratory judgment that "Dusky Sally" did not infringe upon the copyrighted novel.

Burgess argued that both works were based on history, and history cannot be copyrighted. But Chase-Riboud disagreed, noting that little historical data about the Jefferson-Hemings relationship existed and that the play was instead based largely on her work of fiction. Both works did use the few historical facts known about the supposed relationship, but Judge Robert Kelly said that beyond that there was a substantial similarity in the two works. "Chase-Riboud's assertion that other than the few facts which are known, practically everything about Sally Hemings, which appears in both works, was 'invented' by Chase-Riboud is not much of an overstatement," the jurist said. In both works, for example, Jefferson initiates the sexual relationship while in Europe on the night before he is to leave on a trip. In both works Sally Hemings seems somewhat resigned to his romantic advances. In the novel she says a prayer to herself in this scene. Stage directions for the play tell the character playing Sally Hemings to

---

62. *Universal City Studios* v. *Film Ventures,* 543 F. Supp. 1134 (1982).

close her eyes, perhaps in prayer. It is known that Jefferson did injure his wrist while in Paris in 1787. But both works contain a scene where the slave is massaging the future president's wrist, a kind of prologue to the sexual relationship. Many other similarities existed as well, the court ruled.[63]

It is not easy to prove infringement of copyright; yet surprisingly, a large number of suits are settled each year in favor of plaintiffs. Most of these cases are settled out of court. In such instances the obvious theft of the material would generally appall an honest person. An individual who works to be creative in fashioning a story or a play or a piece of art usually has little to fear. The best and simplest way to avoid a suit for infringement is simply to do your own work, to be original.

COPYRIGHT INFRINGEMENT AND THE INTERNET

Just as the so-called road agents and highwaymen preyed on innocent travelers along country roads a century ago, so too do their descendants stalk unwary wayfarers and commuters along the information superhighway today. As software analyst Andy Johnson-Laird told conferees at a meeting of the Electronic Information Law Institute in San Francisco in 1995,

> Digitized information can be copied quickly, easily and cheaply, and the copy is quite literally every bit as good as the original. Add to that the notion that by standing on an electronic street corner, millions of passersby can make identical copies for themselves in an instant, and one can easily see why the Internet, both physically and psychologically, is on a collision course with conventional copyright law.[64]

Johnson-Laird said the Internet should be called the National Copy Machine, adding that people who either do not know or do not care about copyright laws freely infringe.

Part of the problem is that it is so easy to steal copyrighted material on the information superhighway. But another part of the problem is that many Internet users simply don't believe in copyright law. When cartoonist Gary Larson sent online fans across the world a plea to stop duplicating "The Far Side" on the Internet, many operators honored his wishes. But typical of the philosophy of many Internet users accustomed to a free flow of information was this response posted on the same site as Larson's plea: "All this copyright infringement enforcing ticks me off. What is the Net for if we can't view a Far Side cartoon, or listen to a sound file from the Simpsons, or perhaps, dare I say it, look at a picture from a scanned magazine!"

The infringement problems include stealing software and other digitized material created for the electronic computer networks; copying material originally in other forms, like photos in a magazine, onto the Internet and transmitting it without authorization; and downloading copyrighted material from the Internet for use in other formats, again without permission.

Some persons accused of copyright infringement after they pirated copyrighted material off the Internet or uploaded works owned by others argued that traditional copyright law did not apply to computer-mediated communications. The technology was so new and different,

---

63. *Burgess* v. *Chase-Riboud,* 765 F. Supp. 233 (1991).
64. Johnson-Laird, "Exploring the Information Superhighway."

they said, that fresh laws would have to be adopted to protect the copyright of works transmitted in cyberspace. The courts have rejected this notion. "New technologies—from television, to video cassette recorders, to digitized transmissions—have been made to fit within the overall scheme of copyright law and to serve the ends which copyright was intended to promote," wrote U.S. District Judge Leonie Brinkema in 1996. "The Internet is no exception."[65]

Others agree with the judge for the most part, but still think new laws are needed to clarify and stabilize the existing law. To that end the representatives of 160 nations gathered in 1996 to consider adoption of new regulations that would help protect intellectual property in the digital age. Delegates to the World Intellectual Property Organization conference adopted two new treaties in December of 1996 that grant copyright owners protection for the distribution of their work in digital form.[66] One treaty covers artistic and literary work, including films and computer software. The other covers recorded music. The treaties also provide that the fair-use defense applies in cyberspace. The treaties must be approved by at least 30 nations before they become international law.

The U.S. Congress signed on to these treaties when it passed the Digital Millennium Copyright Act in late 1998. Much of this legislation simply implemented language in the WIPO treaties. The new law prohibits the circumvention of technological measures that control access to copyrighted work on computer networks and outlaws the manufacture, importation, or sale of devices used to circumvent such technological protections. The act contains other protections for copyrighted digital matter and exempts Internet service providers from copyright liability for simply transmitting information others have put onto the Internet. Finally, the 1998 statute imposes a compulsory licensing and royalty distribution scheme for the transmission of music on the Internet, a scheme similar to those provided for the traditional air play of music on the radio or television. President Clinton signed the new law in late 1998.

The growth of the Internet has created other problems as well. Historically, when a broadcast station plays a record or tape or CD on the air, it is obligated to pay a licensing fee or a royalty to the owners of the copyright on the music. These fees are collected by two organizations, BMI and ASCAP. The Digital Millennium Copyright Act of 1998 contains provisions that require so-called Internet radio stations to pay similar royalties to the copyright owners of the music when recordings are transmitted over the Web. But because digital distribution involves additional intellectual property issues, such as the ability to make high-quality digital copies of recordings taken off the Internet, the 1998 law requires Webcasters to pay an additional licensing fee to the record labels. But the law did not set a royalty rate, and Internet companies and the recording industry failed to agree on an acceptable rate. Royalty percentages sought by the recording industry ranged as high as 15 percent of the site's gross revenue, while the Webcasters argued for fees as low as 1 or 2 percent. A three-person arbitration panel was appointed in early 2000, as provided for by the 1998 law, and the matter was expected to be resolved sometime in the first year of the new millennium.[67]

65. *Religious Technology Center* v. *Lerma,* 1 E.P.L.R. 729 (1996), 24 M.L.R. 2473 (1996).
66. Schiesel, "Global Agreement Reached," A1.
67. Richtel, "Web Sites and Recording Labels."

While Congress attempts to deal with some copyright issues, the courts must face other issues unassisted by new legislation. Emerging decisions seem to indicate that judges are attempting with substantial success to apply traditional copyright remedies to cases of infringement in cyberspace. For example, the Church of Scientology has used basic copyright law to protect its interests in certain documents that were infringed upon (see page 527).[68] And Playboy magazine has been successful in copyright actions against parties who had illegally used photos from the magazine. The publisher won a $1.1 million judgment in a copyright suit against Starware Publishing Corp., which distributed a CD-ROM disk containing images owned by Playboy. The defendant in the case urged those who bought the disk to load the images onto the electronic network so the pictures would be permanent travelers on the information superhighway.[69] In another case Playboy won a judgment against George Frena, the operator of a subscription computer bulletin board service, Techs Warehouse BBS, who distributed copyrighted Playboy photos. For a fee, customers could download high-quality digitized copies of the photos and store them in their home computers.[70]

SUMMARY

To protect the copyright of a work, the author or owner should give proper notice and register the work with the government. A proper copyright notice looks like this:

Copyright © 2001 by Jane Adams (use the letter Ⓟ for phonorecords)

Notice must be placed where it can be visually perceived. To gain the full benefits of the law, a work must be registered with the Copyright Office in the Library of Congress as well. The proper registration form along with $20 and two complete copies of the work must be sent to the Register of Copyrights.

When a plaintiff sues for infringement of copyright, the court will consider three important criteria. First, is the plaintiff's work original? If the plaintiff has attempted to copyright material that legitimately belongs in the public domain, the plaintiff cannot sue for infringement of copyright. Second, did the defendant have access to the plaintiff's work? There must be some evidence that the defendant viewed or heard the copyrighted work before the alleged infringement took place. Finally, is there evidence that the defendant actually copied the plaintiff's work? If no such evidence exists, are the two works substantially similar? In examining this last issue, the court seeks to determine whether the ideas in the two works are similar. If the general idea of the two works is similar, is the expression of these ideas similar as well? Transmission of copyrighted documents via the Internet is regarded as an infringement.

68. *Religious Technology Center* v. *Lerma,* 1 E.P.L.R. 729 (1996), *Religious Technology Center* v. *Lerma,* 879 F. Supp. 260 (1995). See also Lewis, "A Posting on Internet."
69. *Playboy Enterprises Inc.* v. *Starware Publishing Corp.,* 900 F. Supp. 433 (1995).
70. *Playboy Enterprises Inc.* v. *George Frena et al.,* 839 F. Supp. 1552 (1993).

FREE-LANCING AND COPYRIGHT

What rights does a free-lance journalist, author, or photographer hold with regard to stories or pictures that are sold to publishers? The writer or photographer is the creator of the work; he or she owns the story or the photograph. Consequently, as many rights as such free-lancers choose to relinquish can be sold or given to a publisher. Beginning writers and photographers often do not have much choice but to follow the policy of the book or magazine publisher. Authors whose works are in demand, however, can retain most rights to the material for their future benefit. Most publishers have established policies on exactly what rights they purchase when they decide to buy a story or photograph or drawing. "The Writer's Market" is the best reference guide for the free-lancer. The boxed text lists some of the rights that publishers might buy.

1. All rights: The creator sells complete ownership of the story or photograph.
2. First serial rights: The buyer has the right to use the piece of writing or picture for the first time in a periodical published anywhere in the world. But the publisher can use it only once, and then the creator can sell it to someone else.
3. First North American serial rights: The rights are the same as those provided in number 2, except the publisher buys the right to publish the material first in North America, not anywhere in the world.
4. Simultaneous rights: The publisher buys the right to print the material at the same time other periodicals print the material. All the publishers, however, must be aware that simultaneous publication will occur.
5. One-time rights: The publisher purchases the right to use a piece just one time, and there is no guarantee that it has not been published elsewhere first.

It is a common practice for publishers to buy all rights to a story or photograph but to agree to reassign the rights to the creator after publication. In such cases the burden of initiating the reassignment rests with the writer or photographer, who must request reassignment immediately following publication. The publisher signs a transfer of rights to the creator, and the creator should record this transfer of rights with the Copyright Office within two or three weeks. When this transaction has taken place, the creator can then resell the material.

A critical question for free-lancers today is whether—without a clear, contractual agreement—a publisher who buys a story for publication in a magazine or newspaper also owns the electronic publishing rights to that material. In other words, after the material appears in The New York Times or Sports Illustrated, can this publisher sell this material for use in a CD-ROM compilation of stories or in a database accessible through the Internet? Six writers who sold work to The New York Times, Newsday, Sports Illustrated, and other publications objected when these publications sold the contents of the newspapers and magazines to the Mead Corp., which operates the Lexis/Nexis database, and to University Microfilms, which produces The New York Times on Disc. The writers argued they deserved at least a royalty payment. But a U.S. district court ruled in favor of publishers in a lawsuit initiated by the free-lance writers. U.S. copyright law, the court said, gave the owners of a collective work (like a newspaper or magazine) the right to reproduce and distribute any "revision" of that collective work without the permission of the contributors to that work. So when a free-lance writer sold an article to a newspaper, the writer was also in effect giving the publisher of the paper the right to resell the article for inclusion on a CD-ROM or a database.[71] Two years later the 2nd U.S. Circuit Court of Appeals disagreed. The judges said that while a newspaper or magazine publisher did have the right to sell a revised edition of such a publication, the law was intended to apply to later editions of the newspaper or reissues of the magazine. Databases and CD-ROMs are not revised editions of the original publications. Databases contain many articles, the court noted, that may be retrieved according to criteria unrelated to the particular edition of the magazine or newspaper in which the articles first appear. The court remanded the case to the trial court with instructions to enter the judgment for free-lance writers.[72]

Although other court rulings have revised a long-held tradition in the law that gave publishers virtually unbridled rights of republishing a free-lancer's work,[73] a writer or photographer has no good excuse for failing to specify exactly what rights are being sold when submitting free-lance work. These terms should be spelled out in the query letter to the publisher, which, in the absence of a formal agreement, will be material in any future dispute. Freelancers are also urged to beware of endorsements on payment checks from publishers. It is not uncommon for a publisher to include a statement on a royalty check to the effect that "the endorsement of this check constitutes a grant of reprint rights to the publisher." In order to cash the check, the writer must agree to grant the reprint rights. In such cases writers should quickly notify the publisher that such an agreement is unacceptable and demand immediate payment for the single use of the story. Other pitfalls too numerous to mention await the inexperienced free-lancer. The best advice is to understand exactly what you are doing at all times during the negotiation of rights. Take nothing for granted; just because you are honest and ethical does not mean everyone else is. And if questions come up, consult a qualified attorney. Legal advice is costly, but it can save a writer or photographer money in the long run.

DAMAGES

Plaintiffs in a copyright suit can ask the court to assess the defendant for any damage they have suffered, plus the profits made by the infringer from pirating the protected work. Damages can be a little bit or a lot. In each case the plaintiff must prove to the court the amount of the loss or the amount of the defendant's profit. But, rather than prove actual damage, the plaintiff can

71. *Tasini* v. *The New York Times,* 972 F. Supp. 804 (1997).
72. *Tasini* v. *The New York Times,* 192 F. 3d 356 (1999).
73. *Community for Creative Non-Violence* v. *Reid,* 109 S. Ct. 2166 (1989).

ask the court to assess what are called statutory damages, or damage amounts prescribed by the statute. The smallest statutory award is $750, although in the case of an innocent infringement, the court may use its discretion and lower the damage amount. The highest statutory award is $30,000. However, if the plaintiff can prove that the infringement was committed willfully and repeatedly, the maximum damage award can be as much as $150,000.

In addition, the courts have other powers in a copyright suit. A judge can restrain a defendant from continued infringement, can impound the material that contains the infringement, and can order the destruction of these works. Impoundment and destruction are rare today. A defendant might also be charged with a criminal offense in a copyright infringement case. If the defendant infringed on a copyright "willfully and for purposes of commercial advantage or private financial gain," he or she could be fined and jailed for not more than one year.

The law of copyright is not difficult to understand and should not be a threat to most creative persons in the mass media. The law simply says to do your own work and not to steal from the work of other persons. Some authorities argue that copyright is an infringement on freedom of the press. In a small way it probably is. Nevertheless most writers, most authors, and most reporters—persons who most often take advantage of freedom of the press—support copyright laws that protect their rights to property that they create. Judge Jerome Frank once attempted to explain this apparent contradiction by arguing that we are adept at concealing from ourselves the fact that we maintain and support "side by side as it were, beliefs which are inherently incompatible." Frank suggested that we keep these separate antagonistic beliefs in separate "logic-tight compartments."

The courts have recognized the needs of society, as well as the needs of authors, and have hence allowed considerable latitude for copying material that serves some public function. Because of this attitude, copyright law has little, or should have little, impact on the information-oriented mass media.

BIBLIOGRAPHY ⟶

Ames, E. Kenly. "Beyond *Rogers* v. *Koons:* A Fair Use Standard for Appropriation." *Columbia Law Review* 93 (1993):1473.

Bilder, Mary Sarah. "The Shrinking Back: The Law of Biography." *Stanford Law Review* 43 (1991):299.

Cambridge Research Institute. *Omnibus Copyright Revision.* Washington, D.C.: American Society for Information Science, 1973.

Chervokas, Jason. "Internet CD Copying Tests Music Industry." *The New York Times,* 6 April 1998, C3.

"Copyright: Hollywood Versus Substantial Similarity." *Oklahoma Law Review* 32 (1979):177.

Dunlap, David W. "What Next? A Fee for Looking?" *The New York Times,* 22 August 1998, B1.

Finn, Michael. "From Tarzan to Threepeat." *American Journalism Review,* April 1994, 41.

Ginsburg, Jane C. "No Sweat? Copyright and Other Protection of Works of Information After *Feist* v. *Rural Telephone.*" *Columbia Law Review* 92 (1992):339.

Hays, Constance. "Two Dictionaries in a Legal War Over Words." *The New York Times,* 23 October 1991.

Helfand, Michael T. "When Mickey Mouse Is as Strong as Superman: The Convergence of Intellectual Property Laws to Protect Fictional Literary and Pictorial Characters." *Stanford Law Review* 44 (1992):623.

"High Court Will Hear Wal-Mart Case." *The New York Times,* 5 October 1999, C15.

Holusha, John. "A Clash Over Course Work and Copyrights." *The New York Times,* 25 April 1996, C7.

Johnson-Laird, Andy. "Exploring the Information Superhighway: The Good, the Bad, and the Ugly." Paper presented at the Electronic Information Law Institute meeting, San Francisco, March 2–3, 1995.

"Jury Award for Wade Cook Overruled." *Seattle Post-Intelligencer,* 18 December 1998, E4.

Kaplan, Benjamin, and Ralph S. Brown Jr. *Cases on Copyright.* 2d ed. Mineola, N.Y.: Foundation Press, 1974.

Kaplan, Carl S. "In Court's View, MP3 Player Is Just a 'Space Shifter.'" *The New York Times* on the Web, 9 July 1999.

Kramer, David H. "Who Can Use Yesterday's News? Video Monitoring and the Fair Use Doctrine." *The Georgetown Law Journal* 81 (1993):2345.

Kurtz, Leslie A. "The Independent Legal Lives of Fictional Characters." *1986 Wisconsin Law Review,* 429.

Lewis, Peter. "A Posting on Internet Is Ruled Illegal." *The New York Times,* 26 January 1996.

Lieberman, Trudy. "Plagiarize, Plagiarize, Plagiarize." *Columbia Journalism Review,* July/August 1995, 21.

Muchnick, Irvin. "Protecting Writers' Rights Online." *Macworld,* July 1996, 236.

Richtel, Matt. "Web Sites and Recording Labels at Impasse on Fees." *The New York Times,* 29 November 1999, C19.

Richtel, Matt, and Sara Robinson. "Ear Training: A Digital Music Primer." *The New York Times,* 19 July 1999, C6.

Riordan, Teresa. "Writing Copyright Law for an Information Age." *The New York Times,* 7 July 1994, C1.

Robinson, Sara. "3 Copyright Lawsuits Test Limits of New Digital Media." *The New York Times,* 24 January 2000, C8.

Sack, Kevin. "Appeals Panel Revives Suit on Use of Dr. King Speech." *The New York Times,* 7 November 1999, A18.

Schiesel, Seth. "Global Agreement Reached to Widen Law on Copyright." *The New York Times,* 21 December 1996, A1.

Shaw, David. "Plagiarism: A Taint in Journalism." *The Los Angeles Times,* 5 July 1984.

Shepard, Alicia. "Does Radio News Rip Off Newspapers?" *American Journalism Review,* September 1994, 15.

Strauss, Neil, and Matt Richtel. "Pact Reached on Downloading of Digital Music." *The New York Times,* 29 June 1999, C1.

Strong, William. *The Copyright Book.* Cambridge, Mass.: The M.I.T. Press, 1981.

Tatum, Kevin. "Demonstration on Internet Piracy of Copyright Properties Reinforces the Need for Legislation." *Journal of Copyright Information,* May 1996, 6.

"Textbook Anthologies on Campuses Are Curbed by Rulings on Copyrights." *The New York Times,* 16 April 1991.

"Trademarks and the Press." *American Journalism Review,* October 1993, 43.

Weinraub, Bernard. "'Amistad' Plagiarism Charge Rebutted." *The New York Times,* 4 December 1997, B9.

Yen, Alfred C. "When Authors Won't Sell: Parody, Fair Use, and Efficiency in Copyright Law." *University of Colorado Law Review* 62 (1991):79.

Regulation of Advertising

Advertising is the dominant cultural icon of 21st-century America. More than $180 billion was spent on advertising in the United States in 2000, an amount that exceeds the annual state budget for all but the largest of the 50 United States. Each of us is exposed to hundreds of advertisements each week. Many Americans have become walking advertisements themselves, strolling through shopping malls or the city square wearing Corona beer T-shirts or Ralph Lauren Polo sweaters, carrying gym bags with Nike or Reebok stenciled on the side. Advertising today is a critical component of our economic system, and most economists, even those who detest advertising excesses, agree that capitalism as we know it in this nation could not continue to function without modern advertising.

Advertising messages are regulated by the government; in fact, advertising is probably the most heavily regulated form of modern speech and press. Laws at every level—federal, state, and local—have been adopted to control what businesses and institutions may claim about their products and services. This chapter is an outline of the most common kinds of regulations that affect advertising. It is not comprehensive. There are thousands of laws that regulate advertising messages, far too many to cover in a single chapter. Persons in advertising, especially copywriters, need to have a comprehensive understanding of the law and should use this material only as a starting point.

ADVERTISING AND THE FIRST AMENDMENT

From 1791, the year the Bill of Rights became the law of this land, until 1942, the Supreme Court of the United States never even considered the question, Is advertising protected by the First Amendment? In 1942, in an unusual case involving a man named Chrestensen who sought to pass out handbills on the streets of New York City urging recipients to make a paid visit to a submarine he had moored at a nearby wharf, the high court ruled that "the Constitution imposes . . . no restraint on government as respects purely commercial advertising." What the Supreme Court called commercial speech, advertising, is not shielded by the Constitutional guarantee of freedom of expression.[1]

In 1964 the Supreme Court implicitly rejected this precedent in the landmark case of *The New York Times* v. *Sullivan*[2] (see pages 162–164). The cause of that libel suit against The Times was a paid advertisement, albeit an ad containing a political message, not a commercial one. Therein lies the explanation, many said. Nine years later, however, the high court explicitly rejected the *Chrestensen* ruling. The case involved a small newspaper, the Virginia Weekly, which was published in Charlottesville and widely distributed on the University of Virginia campus. In February of 1971, two years before the Supreme Court ruling in *Roe* v. *Wade*[3] that legalized abortion in the United States, the newspaper published a small ad for the Women's Pavilion of New York City. The ad announced that the Pavilion would help women with unwanted pregnancies to obtain "immediate placement in accredited hospitals and clinics at low cost," and would make all arrangements on a strictly confidential basis. When the advertisement was published, abortion was legal in New York but not in Virginia. Jeffrey Bigelow, a director and managing editor of the Weekly, was charged with violating a Virginia state law that made it a misdemeanor for "any person by publication, lecture, advertisement, or by the sale or circulation of any publication, or in any other manner," to encourage or prompt the procuring of abortion or miscarriage. Four years later Bigelow's appeal ended up before the Supreme Court of the United States. Authorities in Virginia argued that because the offending material was a newspaper advertisement, there was no First Amendment prohibition against punishing Bigelow for this publication. The high court disagreed. "The existence of commercial activity in itself, is not justification for narrowing the protection merely because it appears as a commercial advertisement," wrote Justice Harry Blackmun for the seven-person majority on the court.[4]

Since 1975 the Supreme Court and lower federal courts have built upon the *Bigelow* ruling in a number of cases, fashioning what legal experts now call the **commercial speech doctrine.**

∎ In 1976 the Supreme Court ruled that a Virginia statute that forbade the advertising of the price of prescription drugs violated the First Amendment.[5]

---

1. *Valentine* v. *Chrestensen,* 316 U.S. 52 (1942).
2. 376 U.S. 254 (1964).
3. 410 U.S. 113 (1973).
4. *Bigelow* v. *Virginia,* 421 U.S. 809 (1975).
5. *Virginia State Board of Pharmacy* v. *Virginia Citizens Consumer Council, Inc.,* 425 U.S. 748 (1976).

- In 1977 the high court invalidated a township ordinance in New Jersey that banned the placement of "for sale" and "sold" signs on front lawns. Township authorities said the law was needed because such signs contributed to panic selling by white homeowners who feared that property values would decline because the township was becoming populated by black families. The Supreme Court rejected this argument and ruled that the placement of such signs was protected by the First Amendment.[6]

- In 1980 a New York Public Service Commission rule that forbade utilities from publishing or broadcasting advertising that promoted the use of electricity was ruled to be an infringement on the First Amendment rights of these businesses.[7]

Not all decisions involving advertising and freedom of expression resulted in First Amendment victories. The Supreme Court permitted the state of Texas to ban the practice of optometry under a trade name (i.e., Acme Optometrists),[8] and allowed the Commonwealth of Puerto Rico to prohibit the owners of legal gambling casinos to advertise these establishments to the local population, the people of Puerto Rico.[9] (Commonwealth officials said the gambling casinos were for the tourists who came to the island.) In addition, the high court has granted states fairly extensive authority to regulate advertising for professional services by individuals like doctors, lawyers, dentists, and others. For example, while the Supreme Court would surely rule that advertising claims by plumbers or electricians or piano teachers that extol the quality of their services are completely permissible, the states may restrict these claims and many other kinds of advertising messages generated by doctors or lawyers.[10]

Why did the Supreme Court change its mind and decide that advertising enjoyed the protection of the First Amendment? Undoubtedly there are many reasons. But at the core of the rationale in most rulings by the high court is the assertion that advertising frequently transmits important information. Justice Harry Blackmun probably best stated this argument in the 1976 ruling that struck down a Virginia statute that forbade the advertising of prescription drug prices by pharmacies:

Why did the Supreme Court change its mind and decide that advertising enjoyed the protection of the First Amendment?

> Advertising, however tasteless and excessive it sometimes may seem, is nonetheless dissemination of information as to who is producing and selling what product, for what reason, and at what price. So long as we preserve a predominantly free enterprise economy, the allocation of our resources in large measure will be made through numerous private economic decisions. It is a matter of public interest that those decisions in the aggregate be intelligent and well informed. To this end, the free flow of commercial information is indispensable.[11]

6. *Linmark Associates* v. *Township of Willingboro,* 431 U.S. 85 (1977).
7. *Central Hudson* v. *Public Service Commission,* 447 U.S. 557 (1980).
8. *Friedman* v. *Rogers,* 440 U.S. 1 (1979).
9. *Posadas de Puerto Rico Assoc.* v. *Tourism Co.,* 478 U.S. 328 (1986). However, the high court rejected the rationale of this ruling in 1996.
10. See, for example, *Bates and Van O'Steen* v. *Arizona,* 433 U.S. 350 (1977); *Zauderer* v. *Office of Disciplinary Council,* 471 U.S. 626 (1985); *Ohralik* v. *Ohio State Bar Association,* 98 S. Ct. 1912 (1978); and *Florida Bar* v. *Went For It, Inc.,* 115 S.Ct. 2371 (1995).
11. *Virginia State Board of Pharmacy* v. *Virginia Citizens Consumer Council, Inc.,* 425 U.S. 748 (1976).

COMMERCIAL SPEECH DOCTRINE

Government may regulate advertising that is false or misleading, and advertising for unlawful goods and services.

Government may regulate truthful advertising for legal goods and services if:

    a. There is a substantial state interest to justify the regulation.

    b. There is evidence that the regulation directly advances this interest.

    c. There is a reasonable fit between the state interest and the government regulation.

COMMERCIAL SPEECH DOCTRINE

While advertising enjoys First Amendment protection, it does not enjoy the broad range of protection that shields political speech, for example. The constitutional protection for advertising is limited.

- **The government may regulate advertising that is false, misleading, or deceptive.** Much of the rest of this chapter is devoted to defining and explaining such regulation.

- **The government may regulate advertising for unlawful goods and services.** This broad exception to the protection of the First Amendment was established primarily to permit the government to bar discriminatory employment advertising. It is illegal for an employer to discriminate on the basis of race or religion or ancestry or even gender when hiring employees. Help wanted ads that offer employment to "whites" or "men only" or whatever are also illegal.[12] The government can also bar discriminatory housing advertising or advertising for products that may not be legally sold (e.g., if the federal government has banned the sale of certain kinds of weapons, advertising the sale of these kinds of weapons could also be banned).

Even truthful advertising for legal goods and services can be regulated, provided that the government can satisfy the three requirements outlined here.

- **The government must assert a substantial state interest to justify the regulation.** States that seek to limit advertising by doctors and lawyers will argue that the public is not sophisticated enough to evaluate many claims that might be made by these professionals, and even perfectly truthful claims could be deceptive. Protecting the public from such deception is a substantial state interest.[13] The state

---

12. *Pittsburgh Press Co.* v. *Pittsburgh Commission on Human Relations,* 413 U.S. 376 (1973).
13. *Bates and Van O'Steen* v. *Arizona,* 433 U.S. 350 (1977).

of New York justified its ban on advertising by electrical utilities as part of the state effort to conserve energy.[14] But the interest must be a valid one in the eyes of the court. A statute in the state of Washington forbade the publication or broadcast of lies in political advertising for initiative and referenda issues. In 1998 the Washington Supreme Court said the state had failed to assert a substantial state interest in its defense of this 13-year-old statute. Justice Richard Sanders wrote that the state's interest, to shield the public from falsehoods during a political campaign, "is patronizing and paternalistic. It assumes the people of this state are too ignorant or disinterested to investigate, learn, and determine for themselves the truth or falsity in political debate."[15] Government has a wide range of interests that it seeks to protect; any one of these might be an acceptable reason for a ban on certain kinds of advertising.

■ **Next, the government must demonstrate that the ban on advertising it has instituted will directly advance the interest outlined in the previous paragraph.** Think of the interest as a kind of goal the state is seeking to reach. Will the ban on advertising help the state reach this goal? Will limiting advertising claims by doctors and lawyers protect the public from confusion and deception? Will a prohibition on advertising by electrical utilities result in the conservation of energy? Will a law against advertising by the casinos result in a reduction in gambling by the local population of Puerto Rico? A Baltimore ordinance that banned outdoor advertising for alcoholic beverages in areas in which children walk to school or neighborhoods in which children play was ruled permissible because it directly and materially advanced the city's interest in promoting the welfare and temperance of minors.[16] There should be some evidence to support any conclusion that the court might reach, evidence beyond simple speculation that this ban may work.

■ **Finally, the state must show that there is a "reasonable fit" between the state interest being asserted and the government regulation.** All the parts of this test except this last requirement were generated in the *Central Hudson* case noted previously, a 1980 ruling.[17] In the *Central Hudson* decision the court said the government regulation must be the "least restrictive means" of accomplishing the goal established by the state. That is, the regulation could prohibit no more communication than absolutely necessary to satisfy this state interest. But in a 1989 ruling, *Board of Trustees of the State University of New York* v. *Fox,* the high court abandoned this "least restrictive means" test and substituted the "reasonable fit" test. What does reasonable fit mean? Justice Scalia, in writing the decision, said "What our decisions require is a 'fit' between the legislature's ends and the means chosen to accomplish those ends."[18] A reasonable fit means the regulation must be narrowly tailored to achieve the desired objective, but it doesn't have to be

A reasonable fit means the regulation must be narrowly tailored to achieve the desired objective, but it doesn't have to be the least restrictive means available.

14. *Central Hudson* v. *Public Service Commission,* 447 U.S. 557 (1980).
15. "Election Ad Law Struck Down."
16. *Anheuser-Busch Inc.* v. *Schmoke,* 101 F. 3d 325 (1996).
17. *Central Hudson* v. *Public Service Commission,* 447 U.S. 557 (1980).
18. *Board of Trustees of the State University of New York* v. *Fox,* 492 U.S. 469 (1989).

the least restrictive means available. The 10th U.S. Circuit Court of Appeals, for example, ruled that reasonable fit means that "the governmental goal must be substantial and the cost carefully calculated. The possibility of less extensive means or regulations does not require the conclusion that the chosen means are impermissible."[19]

Several recent commercial speech cases are good illustrations of how the Supreme Court applies this test that it has developed. None of these cases involved advertising that was deceptive or for unlawful goods and services.

In 1995 the Supreme Court struck down a federal rule that forbade brewers from listing the alcohol content on labels attached to bottles and cans of beer and malt liquor. The government justified the rule by arguing that it sought to discourage young drinkers from buying a particular beer or malt liquor simply because it had the highest alcohol content. It is certainly legitimate for the government to try to dissuade young people from drinking too much and this rule assists the state in this role, U.S. attorneys argued. The government's interest in reducing the amount of alcohol consumed by young people is a laudable goal, a unanimous Supreme Court said, but added that there is really no evidence this rule advances that goal. There was no government ban on the disclosure of the alcohol content in advertising for these brews, Justice Clarence Thomas wrote. Nor were there limits on the words a brewer could use to describe these products. "To be sure," Thomas wrote, "the Government's interest in combating strength wars is a valid goal. But the irrationality of this unique and puzzling framework ensures that the labeling ban will fail to achieve that end."[20]

In 1996 the Supreme Court ruled that a Rhode Island statute that barred liquor stores from advertising the price of distilled spirits ran afoul of the First Amendment. The state attempted to justify the law by arguing that the ban on advertising reduced competition in the sale of liquor, which resulted in higher liquor prices that in turn led to reduced consumption. But in his principal opinion for the badly splintered Supreme Court, Justice John Paul Stevens referred to the state's assertions that the ban would significantly reduce liquor consumption as speculation and conjecture. He said the court was not prepared to restrict truthful speech about a legal product on such flimsy justification and that the state had not even considered other means that did not restrict speech to accomplish its clearly valid goals. The justice added that raising liquor prices through taxation would have the same impact. He also noted that the state could limit per capita sales of spirits, as it does with prescription medicine, and that educational campaigns about the problems associated with alcohol consumption might also be used. None of these measures limited truthful speech protected by the First Amendment, Stevens noted. "Precisely because bans against truthful, nonmisleading commercial speech rarely seek to protect consumers from either deception or overreaching, they usually rest solely on the offensive assumption that the public will respond 'irrationally' to the truth," Justice Stevens wrote. "The First Amendment directs us to be especially skeptical of regulations that seek to keep people in the dark for what the government perceives to be their own good."[21]

19. *Adolph Coors Co.* v. *Brady,* 944 F. 2d 1543 (1991).
20. *Rubin* v. *Coors Brewing Co.,* 115 S. Ct. 1585 (1995).
21. *44 Liquormart, Inc.* v. *Rhode Island,* 116 S. Ct. 1495 (1996).

In the late 1990s the federal courts were asked to consider the constitutionality of a ban on broadcast advertising for casino gambling in states where such gambling was legal. Restrictions on the broadcast of advertising for lotteries and other gambling had been in place since the 1930s. But beginning in 1950 the government began to permit exceptions to what had always been an absolute ban. The government permitted broadcasting stations in states with state-run lotteries to advertise these contests. Exceptions were also granted to broadcast advertising for gambling casinos on Indian reservations, for fishing contests, for not-for-profit lotteries, and for lotteries conducted as promotional activities by commercial organizations.

Broadcasters and casino owners in Nevada, New Jersey, Louisiana, and Mississippi challenged the federal prohibition. The 9th U.S. Circuit Court of Appeals[22] and a U.S. district court in New Jersey[23] ruled that the ban failed the three-part test for commercial speech. These courts ruled that the myriad exceptions to the anti-gambling advertising rule made it highly unlikely that this censorship would directly advance the state interest in reducing gambling among the citizenry. The 5th U.S. Circuit Court of Appeals, which heard the case that came from Louisiana and Mississippi broadcasters, rejected the challenge to the law and upheld the ban.[24]

The Supreme Court weighed into the fray and in 1999 unanimously ruled that the ban on broadcast advertising was a violation of the First Amendment because it "sacrifices an intolerable amount of truthful speech about lawful conduct." Justice John Paul Stevens wrote that the government failed to prove that the ban on such advertising will reduce either gambling or the social costs of gambling. While the government's interest in reducing the demand for gambling is valid, Stevens said, the law as it exists "is so pierced by exemptions and inconsistencies" that this valid state interest could not salvage the regulation or overcome the presumption "that the speaker and the audience, not the government, should be left to assess the value of accurate and nonmisleading information about lawful conduct."[25] In August of 1999 the federal government announced it would no longer enforce the ban on such broadcast advertising, even when the ads originate from stations in states that do not permit casino gambling.

TOBACCO ADVERTISING AND THE FIRST AMENDMENT

Whether or not the government can ban all advertising for tobacco products is one of the most contentious issues in the commercial speech area. Tobacco advertising can be regulated. A Baltimore city ordinance that prohibits stationary, outdoor advertisements for cigarettes in certain areas of the city has been upheld by a U.S. court of appeals.[26] The Food and Drug Administration adopted a comprehensive series of rules regarding the marketing and advertising of tobacco products. But federal courts sustained a challenge to these rules by the tobacco industry, agreeing that the Congress had never given the FDA the power to regulate

22. *Valley Broadcasting Co.* v. *U.S.,* 107 F. 3d 1328 (1997).
23. *Players International Inc.* v. *U.S.,* 986 F. Supp. 497 (1997).
24. *Greater New Orleans Broadcasting Association* v. *U.S.,* 149 F. 3d 334 (1998).
25. *Greater New Orleans Broadcasting Association* v. *U.S.,* 119 S. Ct. 1923 (1999).
26. *Penn Advertising of Baltimore Inc.* v. *Mayor and City Council of Baltimore City et al.,* 63 F. 3d 1318 (1995).

tobacco. The FTC could impose such regulations, or the Congress could expand the authority of the FDA to provide it the power to adopt such regulations.[27] But even strict regulation of tobacco advertising does not go far enough for many people in the anti-smoking movement, and proposals have been advanced that all such promotion be banned. The prospects that such a total ban on advertising for a legal product would be sustained in a First Amendment challenge have always been somewhat dim. In 1996 these prospects got even dimmer.

Proponents of a ban on tobacco advertising were sustained for 10 years by a Supreme Court ruling that involved the regulation of advertising for gambling instituted by Puerto Rico. In the ruling the high court said it was permissible for the Commonwealth of Puerto Rico to prohibit the owners of gambling casinos on the island from advertising their casinos to the citizens of Puerto Rico. Advertising these clubs to tourists was permitted. The Supreme Court upheld Puerto Rico's advertising ban by ruling that since the commonwealth could certainly ban all gambling on the island and close the casinos, it could certainly ban advertising for these gaming establishments. If a government can constitutionally ban an activity, it can then ban the advertising for that activity, even if it chooses not to ban the activity. This was the message sent in *Posadas de Puerto Rico Assoc.* v. *Tourism Co.*[28] Anti-tobacco advertising supporters argued that if the government could ban the sale of tobacco products—and many authorities believe it could because of the health risk that is posed—the government could ban advertising for tobacco products, even if it permitted the sale of cigarettes, cigars, and pipe tobacco.

Justice John Paul Stevens completely undercut this argument in 1996 when, in his opinion in the *44 Liquormart* case, he wrote that the *Posadas* case had been wrongly decided. "Given our long-standing hostility to commercial speech regulation of this type," he wrote, "*Posadas* clearly erred in concluding that it was up to the legislature to choose suppression over a less restrictive policy." The majority opinion in that case cannot be reconciled with the unbroken line of prior cases striking down similarly broad regulations on truthful, nonmisleading advertising when alternative solutions that do not impact speech are available, Stevens said. The argument that if the state can ban the activity it can ban the advertising for the activity does not take into account the long-established recognition of the distinction between an activity or conduct and truthful speech about that activity. Under the First Amendment, attempts to regulate speech are much more dangerous than attempts to regulate conduct, the justice concluded.[29]

The push to regulate tobacco advertising slowed considerably in 2000. The tobacco industry and most of the states agreed on a multi-billion-dollar settlement that contained substantial regulations relating to advertising of tobacco products. Anti-smoking advocates seeking laws to further regulate the industry paused to determine the impact of these agreements.

One other dimension of the relationship between the First Amendment and advertising needs to be briefly explored. Is it a violation of the First Amendment for a newspaper or

27. See, for example, *Coyne Beahm Inc. et al.* v. *U.S. Food and Drug Administration et al.,* DC MNC No. 2:95CV00591, 4/25/97.
28. 478 U.S. 328 (1986).
29. *44 LiquorMart, Inc.* v. *Rhode Island,* 116 S. Ct. 1495 (1996).

magazine or broadcasting station to refuse to carry an advertisement? No. The long-standing legal doctrine is that the First Amendment is not even implicated; such a situation is one private entity, the mass medium, refusing to do business with another private entity.* In 1996 a U.S. district court extended this doctrine to the Internet when it ruled that a private company called Cyber Promotions had no right under the First Amendment to e-mail unsolicited promotional advertisements to America Online subscribers. The court ruled that although the Internet provides the opportunity to disseminate vast amounts of information, the Internet does not have at the present time the means to police the dissemination of that information. "We therefore find that . . . the private online service has a right to prevent unsolicited e-mail solicitations from reaching its subscribers over the Internet," Judge Weiner wrote.[30]

American advertising is regulated by scores of laws adopted by all levels of government. Persons in advertising must be aware of such rules as well as all other regulations (libel, invasion of privacy, obscenity, etc.) that restrict the content and flow of printed and broadcast material. Since the mid-1970s, commercial advertising has been given the qualified protection of the First Amendment because much advertising contains information that is valuable to consumers. The government may regulate or prohibit advertising (1) that promotes an unlawful activity or (2) that is misleading or untruthful. The state may also regulate truthful advertising for lawful activities and goods if it can prove (1) that there is a substantial state interest to justify the regulation, (2) that such regulation directly advances this state interest, and (3) that there is a "reasonable fit" between the state interest being asserted and the governmental regulation. Advertising by professionals such as attorneys and physicians may be regulated in a somewhat more restrictive fashion.

SUMMARY

THE REGULATION OF ADVERTISING

The regulation of deceptive or untruthful advertising is a large and difficult task policed by the advertising industry itself, the mass media, and various governmental agencies. Advertising in the past two decades became especially problematic because of the growth of comparative advertising, advertising in which the attributes of one product are placed squarely alongside those of another. There was also more advertising for more products than ever before. During the 1980s, a time when advertising claims were increasing in intensity and in number, the federal government, a primary player in the regulation of advertising, pulled back from the aggressive stance it had taken during the 1970s. New means to control the content of commercial messages were explored. Let's briefly examine this process of regulation today.

30. *Cyber Promotions, Inc. v. America Online, Inc.,* 1 E.P.L.R. 756 (1996), 24 M.L.R. 2505 (1996).

*Broadcasters do have certain obligations related to carrying political advertising. See Chapter 17.

SELF-REGULATION

Newspapers, magazines, broadcasting stations, online service providers, and other mass media all have rules that more or less regulate the kind of advertising they will carry. These guidelines may reflect matters of taste (no ads for NC-17 movies or certain sex-related products like condoms), economic protectionism (a newspaper with its own Web site may not permit others to advertise their competing Web sites), or the acceptability of advertising matter. Ads that promote illegal goods or services, that contain claims that appear to be deceptive of unfounded, or that unfairly trash competing products may be rejected. In 1996, for example, the ABC television network said it would no longer accept any drug advertising that made safety claims about rival products. Remember, a mass medium is permitted to reject any content it chooses.

But the screening of advertising by the mass media does not present an unbreachable wall. Misleading, unfair, false, and deceptive advertising is published and broadcast, and because of this the advertising industry has constructed a self-regulatory scheme to try to resolve as many problems as possible. The Better Business Bureau has two divisions available to advertisers who believe a competitor's claims are hurting the sale of their own products. The **National Advertising Division** and the National Advertising Review Board have been hearing advertiser complaints for several decades. While decisions by these components of the Better Business Bureau are not binding on advertisers, the mass media tend to take findings of false or misleading claims quite seriously and usually bar such advertisements from newspapers, magazines, or broadcast stations. And usually advertisers will pay heed as well. In 1993 Wal-Mart Stores changed its corporate slogan from "Always the low price, always," to "Always Low Prices, Always" after the Better Business Bureau found that the first slogan could mislead some shoppers. In rare instances an advertiser's complaint about a competitor's practices will be referred to the Federal Trade Commission.

But the screening of advertising by the mass media does not present an unbreachable wall.

Sometimes an advertiser will not believe that a complaint to the Better Business Bureau is sufficient and instead will take more formal action such as filing a lawsuit in federal court. This is another level of self-regulation.

LAWSUITS BY COMPETITORS AND CONSUMERS

In 1999 a federal judge did what virtually nobody else had been able to do in myriad television ads: He stopped the Energizer Bunny. A U.S. district court ruled that Energizer's manufacturer, the Ralston Purina Company, must stop advertising that its batteries are superior to competing batteries, including Duracell's Ultra. Gillette, which makes Duracell batteries, initiated the lawsuit. The court said the Energizer claims were based on a study that was flawed and could not be used to substantiate a claim of superiority. Gillette won another lawsuit in 1999 when it convinced a jury that the Optiva Co., maker of the Sonicare electric toothbrush, made false and misleading claims about its product, claims that hurt the sales of a Gillette electric toothbrush, the Braun Oral-B. The jury awarded Gillette $2.5 million in damages.

Lawsuits for false advertising claims were relatively rare until the last quarter of the 20th century. With the rapid growth of comparative advertising (in which the advertised product is compared to a competitor's product), more and more advertisers have taken competitors to court over what they claim is deceptive and false advertising. In 1995 Hershey Foods, which makes several brands of pasta, sued two importers of Turkish pasta, charging that the packages were mislabeled. Statements on the packaging claimed the two pastas were made from 100 percent durum wheat; Hershey's said these statements were untrue. The suit was settled out of court. And in the fall of 1996 Gillette sued Norelco, charging that a Norelco campaign for electric shavers was false because it included exaggerated and distorted statements about wet shaving in an attempt to sell electric shavers. One of the longest running legal battles was waged between American Home Products, the maker of Anacin and Advil, and Johnson & Johnson, the manufacturer of Tylenol, who were in court for more than a decade fighting over claims of the relative effectiveness of the two pain relievers.[31] Neither pharmaceutical manufacturer wanted to give the other any competitive edge while fighting for market share in the sale of over-the-counter pain relievers, a $3-billion-a-year business in the mid-1990s.

These lawsuits were filed under provisions of the federal Lanham Act, which was adopted more than 50 years ago by the Congress to stop unfair competition in the marketplace. Section 43(a) creates a legal cause of action for false advertising. The statute provides that a person who generates "any false designation of origin, false or misleading description of fact, or false or misleading representation of fact, which . . . in commercial advertising or promotion, misrepresents the nature, characteristics, qualities, or geographical origin of his or another person's goods or services, or commercial activities" is liable for civil damages. As originally written, the law only prevented one advertiser from making false statements about his or her own goods. But Congress amended the act in 1989 and now the law also prohibits an advertiser from making false statements about a competitor's product. This section of the law was rarely used until the 1970s. In fact, between the time the law was adopted in 1946, and 1968, courts heard fewer than 30 false advertising cases.[32] The growth of comparative advertising in the 1970s certainly generated more Lanham Act suits. Also, advertising increased in importance in the past 25 years as a part of general marketing strategies for retail goods. In 1974 a U.S. district court established for the first time a test that defined the requirements that must be met by a plaintiff to win a false advertising case under this statute.[33] The plaintiff must show (a) that the defendant, in its advertising, makes false statements of fact, (b) that this advertising actually deceives or has a tendency to deceive a substantial segment of the audience, (c) that this deception is likely to influence a purchasing decision, (d) that the defendant's falsely advertised goods are in interstate commerce, and (e) that the plaintiff has been or is likely to be injured as the result of the foregoing either by direct diversion of sales from itself to the defendant, or by a lessening of the goodwill that the products enjoy with the buying public.

This standard evolved in the subsequent case law and has now become more favorable to a prospective plaintiff.[34] The Lanham Act false advertising test has been reduced to three parts (see following boxed text).

31. See Mann and Plummer, "The Big Headache," 39.
32. Pompeo, "To Tell the Truth," 565.
33. *Skil Corp.* v. *Rockwell Int'l Corp.,* 375 F. Supp. 77 (1974).
34. Singdahlsen, "The Risk of Chill," 339.

> ## LANHAM ACT FALSE ADVERTISING TEST
> ▪ What message the ad conveys, either explicitly or implicitly
> ▪ Whether the message is false or misleading
> ▪ Whether that message is likely to injure the plaintiff

A plaintiff in a Lanham Act case will try either to obtain equitable relief—that is, ask the court to force the defendant to stop or change the deceptive advertising—or to recover damages. Plaintiffs in the past almost always sought to have the court eliminate the advertisements or force the defendant to modify them. For example, in 1976 American Brands won an injunction that forced R.J. Reynolds to remove the words "The lowest tar of all cigarettes" from advertising for Now cigarettes.[35] And 10 years later Maybelline won a court order forcing the Noxell Corporation to halt the distribution of its Clear Lash mascara, which it had falsely claimed was waterproof.[36] Plaintiffs sought equitable relief rather than damages because it was far easier to win an injunction. All the plaintiff had to show to win an injunction was that it was *likely* that the defendant's advertising caused or will cause the plaintiff to lose sales. To win damages the plaintiff had to show a specific monetary loss *caused* by the defendant's advertising. But some courts have begun to ease this latter standard, awarding damages on the same proof that in the past had only justified the award of an injunction.[37]

If money damages can be won, a plaintiff can pocket not only actual damages and court costs but the profits made by the defendant through the use of the false claim. And a judge may double or triple this amount in cases of flagrant falsity. For example, in the mid-1980s U-Haul, which rents trucks and trailers, sued a competitor, Jartran, claiming false advertising. U-Haul had pretty much had its own way in this business, even in the face of new competition. But the Jartran advertising campaign (which won a prestigious marketing award) hurt U-Haul badly. The advertising featured price comparisons between the two companies that were computed in a manner unfair to U-Haul. The campaign also asserted that Jartran trucks were better. The size of the trucks pictured in the print advertising had been altered photographically to make the Jartran trucks appear larger. And nice, shiny new Jartran trucks were compared with less desirable-looking U-Haul models. U-Haul presented several consumer-perception surveys to the court that showed considerable consumer confusion regarding the advertising and charted a direct link between its lost sales and the Jartran campaign. During the year of the campaign, Jartran experienced a $92 million revenue increase; U-Haul, a $49 million revenue decline. The court computed the damages by adding Jartran's advertising expense for the

---

35. *American Brands, Inc.* v. *R.J. Reynolds Tobacco Co.*, 413 F. Supp. 1352 (1976).
36. *Maybelline* v. *Noxell Corporation*, 643 F. Supp. 294 (1986).
37. See *PPX Enterprises* v. *Audiofidelity Enterprises*, 818 F. 2d 266 (1987) and *U-Haul International* v. *Jartran, Inc.*, 793 F. 2d 1034 (1986).

misleading campaign, about $6 million, to the money spent by U-Haul to counteract the Jar-tran campaigning, close to $14 million. The judge then doubled this total and awarded U-Haul $40 million in damages, the largest award by far ever given in a Section 43(a) case.[38]

Consumers, as opposed to competitors, have a much more difficult time in maintaining an action for false advertising. There is no common-law tort for deceptive advertising. As George and Peter Rosden point out in their massive compendium "The Law of Advertising," historically, common-law courts have not been receptive to protecting consumers. "During the most formative period of common law," they write, "only a few goods in the marketplace were manufactured products so that the buyer was in an excellent position to judge for himself goods offered to him."[39] Dairy products could be judged by their smell and texture; vegetables, meat, and fruit, by their looks. Judgments about wine, beer, and cloth were also easy to make. Protection was really necessary only in case of fraud, such as watered beer. The basic slogan in those days was caveat emptor—buyer beware.

Consumers, as opposed to competitors, have a much more difficult time in maintaining an action for false advertising.

While today consumers are far better protected—they must be because of the thousands of consumer products about which they know little or nothing—there is little consumers can do themselves to attack the dishonest advertiser, short of reporting the advertisement to the proper authorities. The Rosdens point out that it is possible for a consumer to sue under product liability laws, but in such cases the advertisement must contain a commitment about the product that is not fulfilled after purchase by the consumer. For example, an advertisement for a carpet cleaning product states that it will not damage carpets, but after a consumer uses the product, a large hole appears in the rug. The consumer would be able to sue for a new carpet.

Federal courts are currently divided over whether a consumer has standing to sue for false advertising claims under the Lanham Act. The 2nd, 3rd, and 7th U.S. Circuit Courts of Appeals have said consumers do not have the right to sue under the federal law,[40] but the 9th U.S. Circuit Court of Appeals ruled that any person damaged by an advertising misrepresentation may file an action under the Lanham Act.[41] If given standing to sue, it is hard for a consumer to mount a successful false advertising suit. The amount of damage to an individual or even group of consumers is small compared to the damage to a competing business.

STATE AND LOCAL LAWS

State regulation of advertising predates federal regulation by several years. This fact is not surprising when you consider that at the time the public became interested in advertising regulation—around the turn of the century—the federal government was a minuscule creature relative to its present size. Harry Nims, a New York lawyer, drafted a model law called the **Printers' Ink statute** (it was Printers' Ink magazine that urged passage of the law) in 1911.

38. *U-Haul International* v. *Jartran,* 793 F. 2d 1034 (1986).
39. Rosden and Rosden, *The Law of Advertising.*
40. See *Colligan* v. *Activities Club of New York,* 442 F. 2d 686 (1971) and *Serbin* v. *Ziebert Int'l Corp.,* 11 F. 3d 1163 (1994).
41. *Thorn* v. *Reliance Van Co.,* 736 F. 2d 929 (1984).

Most states today have such laws. In addition, many states have what are called unfair and deceptive acts and practices statutes, which give consumers the right to seek a judicial remedy in false advertising cases. These acts are often called "Little FTC Acts," and the guidelines developed by the FTC in applying federal advertising law (discussed shortly) are used by the state courts in administering these state regulations.[42] In addition, many local governments have consumer protection laws that apply broadly to false advertising.

Enforcement of state and local regulations is in the hands of attorneys general and local prosecutors. The intensity of such enforcement varies dramatically from one jurisdiction to another. Local prosecutors often find it difficult to devote staff time to consumer problems when faced with growing amounts of violent crimes, drug cases, and other seemingly more serious threats to the public safety and welfare.

At times local enforcement of consumer protection laws is aggressive. During the late 1980s and early 1990s the federal government tended to relax its policing of false advertising claims. The Reagan administration mandate to "get government off the back of business" dictated a tempering of advertising regulation. At this time the states tried to pick up some of the slack. For example, Texas sued Volvo for false advertising for a television commercial that showed a giant pickup truck with huge tires drive over the tops of a line of cars, including a Volvo 240 station wagon. All the cars except the Volvo are flattened. Texas asserted, and Volvo admitted, that the ad was a phony. The roof of the Volvo station wagon was reinforced with lumber and steel, while structural roof pillars in the other cars had been cut or weakened. The company paid a $316,250 settlement to the state, an additional $150,000 fine to the Federal Trade Commission, and fired the agency that had handled its $40 million advertising account for the past 23 years. In 1991 the California attorney general brought a false advertising suit against Life Alert Emergency Response, a company that used television advertising to promote a medical alert system for the sick and the elderly ("Help! I've fallen and I can't get up"). And New York state accused the makers of Perrier of falsely claiming that its bottled mineral water is naturally sparkling and of ancient origins. Perrier paid a $40,000 fine and agreed to stop making the claim. In the late 1990s, Connecticut, West Virginia, Florida, New York, and several other states aggressively pursued American Family Publishers, the magazine sweepstakes company, charging that the firm's promotions were blatantly false. New York won an $800,000 settlement from the company in August of 1998.[43]

FEDERAL REGULATION

A variety of federal agencies are empowered to enforce consumer protection laws. The **Federal Trade Commission,** or **FTC,** is the primary agent of the government, but clearly not the only agent. Beginning in the 1990s the Food and Drug Administration began an aggressive campaign against a variety of companies to force them to change their labeling and promotional practices. For example, the FDA

---

42. Kertz and Ohanian, "Recent Trends," 603.
43. Rohde, "Sweepstakes in Agreement."

- told Procter & Gamble to stop calling its Citrus Hill Fresh Choice orange juice "fresh-squeezed," because it was made from concentrate, not fresh-squeezed oranges.
- ordered Ragu to stop promoting its bottled pasta sauces as "fresh" when they weren't.
- barred the maker of Mrs. Fields cookies from advertising its Chocolite and Semi-Sweet Classic brands as "low-fat," because the snacks contained almost twice the fat allowed by the law in "low-fat" cookies.
- began more closely scrutinizing video news releases and advertising prepared by pharmaceutical companies and broadcast by many networks and local television stations. A 1999 study by the FDA revealed that several drug companies made false or misleading statements in the releases and in TV advertising for prescription drugs.
- forced the makers of Relenza, a flu medication, to stop exaggerating the effectiveness of the drug. The agency said the product does not cure the flu, as the ads implied, but cuts the duration of the symptoms of the illness.

The FTC was created by Congress in 1914 to police unfair methods of business competition. The agency was to make certain that Company A did not engage in practices that gave it an unfair advantage over its competitor, Company B. And, of course, an unfair advantage may be gained through the use of false or misleading advertising. As originally conceived, the FTC was not supposed to worry about the impact of advertising on consumers, only competitors. During the 1920s, however, the FTC perceptively enlarged its mission in an effort to try to protect consumers as well. This effort was suddenly stopped in 1931 when the Supreme Court ruled the FTC had illegally enlarged its jurisdiction and that it could only attempt to regulate advertising that unfairly affected the advertiser's competitor.[44]

In 1938 Congress adopted the Wheeler-Lea Amendment to the Trade Commission Act, which gave the FTC the power to proceed against all unfair and deceptive acts or practices in commerce, regardless of whether they affect competition. Since that time the commission has developed into one of the nation's largest independent regulatory agencies. In addition to policing false advertising, the FTC is charged with enforcing the nation's antitrust laws and several federal statutes such as the Truth in Lending Law and the Fair Credit Reporting Act. The five members of the commission are appointed by the president and confirmed by the Senate for a term of seven years. No more than three of the commissioners can be from the same political party. A chairperson, one of the five commissioners, is appointed by the president. Although the agency is located in Washington, D.C., it has 11 regional offices throughout the nation.

The history of the agency reveals that it has often been swept by the political winds of the time. For years it was known as the "Little Gray Lady on Pennsylvania Avenue" because of its timid performance. During the late '60s and '70s, in an era of consumer concern, the FTC showed new muscle and attacked some of the nation's largest advertisers, such as Coca-Cola and ITT Continental Baking. In the '80s the FTC reflected the spirit of deregulation that ran throughout Washington, D.C., as Ronald Reagan entered the White House.

44. *FTC v. Raladam,* 283 U.S. 643 (1931).

The "hands off" policies of the previous decade began to be modified in the early 1990s. In fact, in fiscal year 1994 the FTC's consumer protection arm brought or completed 233 enforcement actions, one of the highest totals since the early 1980s. The agency publicly announced that it was going to be more vigilant about policing advertising. To emphasize this point, the FTC instituted false advertising actions against several national advertisers, including Kraft General Foods, which the agency claimed misrepresented the amount of calcium in its Kraft Singles cheese slices. In addition, the agency brought charges against a group of companies that were using program-length commercials, or infomercials, to sell a variety of goods and services, including diet plans and treatments for cellulite buildup and baldness. In the spring of 1996 President Clinton named Robert Pitofsky to head the FTC, yet another indication that the agency was awakening from its slumber during the Reagan years. Pitofsky had been an aggressive chief of the consumer protection arm of the FTC from 1970 to 1973 and later served as an FTC commissioner during the Carter administration.

Self-regulation by the advertising industry has increased in recent years, especially with the growth of comparative advertising. The National Advertising Division and the National Advertising Review Board, divisions within the Better Business Bureau, are the primary agents for this self-regulation. Such regulation is geared toward satisfying the interests of advertisers rather than consumers, however. There has also been a rapid increase in lawsuits brought by advertisers against one another under Section 43(a) of the Lanham Act. An advertiser seeking redress under this 50-year-old federal law can seek to either stop the misleading practice and/or win money damages. Again, this law provides little relief for consumers. Laws banning false advertising exist at both the state and local levels, but tend to be applied half-heartedly. The Federal Trade Commission remains the nation's most potent weapon against false or misleading advertising, but in the 1980s reflected the national political mood of getting government "off the backs of business" and took a passive approach to problems in advertising. The FTC became more vigorous in consumer protection in the late 1990s. **SUMMARY**

FEDERAL TRADE COMMISSION

One of the FTC's most important responsibilities is to ensure that consumers are not victimized by unfair, misleading, or deceptive advertising. Through custom and practice, the agency has defined advertising as any action, method, or device intended to draw the attention of the public to merchandise, to services, to persons, and to organizations. Trading stamps, contests, freebies, premiums, and even product labels are included in this definition, in addition to the more common categories of product and service advertising. At times a business has challenged a ruling by the agency that its particular exposition is an advertisement rather than an essay about science or a statement of company philosophy. Rarely have these challenges been successful. Normally, what the FTC says is an advertisement is considered to be an advertisement for purposes of regulation.*

Does the FTC regulate all advertising? Legally, no, it cannot. But practically, it can regulate almost all advertising. Because the agency was created under the authority of Congress to regulate interstate commerce, products or services must be sold in interstate commerce or the advertising medium must be somehow affected by interstate commerce before the FTC can intervene. Although many products and services are sold locally only, nearly every conceivable advertising medium is somehow affected by or affects interstate commerce. All broadcasting stations are considered to affect interstate commerce. Most newspapers ship at least a few copies across state lines. Even when a newspaper is not mailed across state lines, it is very likely that some of the news in the newspaper comes across state lines or that the paper on which the news is printed, the ink and type used to print the news, or parts of the printing machinery travel across state lines.

The FTC has also asserted jurisdiction over misleading or unfair practices on the Internet. Between 1996 and 2000 the agency has brought more than 100 Internet-related enforcement actions against nearly 300 businesses. For example, in early 1998 the FTC won a lawsuit against Internet Business Broadcasting Inc., a company that used unsolicited e-mails to try to convince Web users to buy billboards and banners on Web sites. This space could be rented to advertisers, and the original buyers could realize a return of more than 100 percent on their investment, Internet Business Broadcasting claimed. The FTC said the claim was false and misleading. "The rules for advertising by e-mail are the same as the rules for advertising through regular mail; don't mislead or lie to consumers or the FTC will come after you," said Jodie Bernstein, director of the agency's Bureau of Consumer Protection.[45] Later that year the agency reached a settlement with GeoCities. The Web site operator had created a kind of virtual community by offering both free and fee-based home pages to its 2-million-plus subscribers. The company, the FTC said, misrepresented the purpose for which it was collecting personal identifying information from both adults and children. The information, which GeoCities said would be used only to provide members specific advertising offers they requested, was released to third parties who used it to target GeoCities members for solicitations. GeoCities agreed in its settlement with the FTC not only to stop this practice but to post a notice on

Normally, what the FTC says is an advertisement is considered to be an advertisement for purposes of regulation.

---

45. *Federal Trade Commission* v. *Maher*, DC Md, No. WMN 98-495, 3/4/98.

*The courts are not quite this consistent in defining advertising. Judges in both New York and California were asked recently whether statements contained on the cover of a book were ads for the book or part of the text of the book. The publication involved was the "Beardstown Ladies' Common-Sense Investment Guide," a volume which contained highly exaggerated claims for the success of a particular investing scheme. All sides agreed that the false claims in the book were fully protected by the First Amendment, but the plaintiffs in both cases argued that when the claims were reprinted on the cover of the book (and the outside of a videotape cassette box) they were advertising or commercial speech, and did not enjoy the full protection of the First Amendment. The court in California said the comments were commercial speech and not fully protected. The court in New York came to the opposite conclusion. See *Keimer* v. *Buena Vista Books,* 28 M.L.R. 1050 (1999) and *Lacoff* v. *Buena Vista Publishing Inc.,* N.Y. Sup. Ct. No. 606005/98, 1/28/00.

its site explaining to members what data was being collected, for what purposes, to whom it will be disclosed, and how customers can both access the data collected about themselves and remove such data from GeoCities files.[46]

Some other requirements must be met before the FTC can act. It must be shown that the agency is acting in the public interest, which is really not too difficult since false advertising generally has an impact on the public. If the FTC says it is acting in the public interest, courts usually take its word for it.

Once it has been shown that the action meets the agency definition of "advertisement" and that it affects interstate commerce in some way, one final element must be present before FTC powers are invoked—the advertisement must be deceptive or untruthful. The standards currently used by the FTC to define deceptive advertising were outlined in 1983.[47] As cases proceed through the agency, minor tinkering with these standards can and does occur.[48] It is an evolving policy. There are three parts to this deception policy.

**FTC DEFINITION OF FALSE
OR DECEPTIVE ADVERTISING**

1. There must be a representation, omission, or practice that is likely to mislead the consumer.
2. The act or practice must be considered from the perspective of a consumer who is acting reasonably.
3. The representation, omission, or practice must be material.

FALSE ADVERTISING DEFINED

1. **There must be a representation, omission, or practice that is likely to mislead the consumer.** The commission will consider the entire advertisement as well as all other elements of a transaction when making this determination. The issue is whether the act or practice is likely to mislead rather than whether it causes actual deception. In 1994, for example, the FTC ruled that health claims made by Häagen-Dazs about its frozen yogurts were false and misleading because many of the flavors were anything but "low fat" or "98 percent fat free." The commission also said that the company falsely claimed that its yogurt bars contained 100 calories and one gram of fat. Seven of the nine Häagen-Dazs flavors had 4 to 12 grams of fat per serving, while the Food and Drug Administration says "low fat" means 3 grams of fat or less. In addition, three of the eight frozen-bar flavors had more than 200 calories. The company said that each ad contained a disclaimer, in tiny print, that said the "98 percent fat free" referred only to certain flavors.[49]

---

46. *in re GeoCities Inc.,* FTC File No. 9823015.
47. FTC Policy Statement on Deceptive Acts and Practices, 4 Trade Reg. Rep. ¶ 13,205 at 20,919 (Oct. 4, 1983).
48. in re *Southwest Sunsites, Inc.,* 105 F.T.C. 7 (1985).
49. Burros, "Minding the Store," B8.

A deceptive statement may be made expressly, such as "Wellrite Aspirin will cure the common cold," or the claim may simply be implied. Thompson Medical advertised its Aspercreme as an effective pain reliever for the symptoms of arthritis. The substance was to be applied directly to the body, and its effectiveness was compared with the effectiveness of aspirin in the advertising. There was a clear implication that the creme contained aspirin, which is known as an effective pain reliever, but it did not. The FTC ruled that it was deceptive to imply that it did because a consumer could be easily misled.[50]

The omission of important or material information in an advertisement can also be deceptive. For example, Beneficial Corporation, a finance company, advertised that it would provide a customer with an "instant tax refund" if the individual's tax return entitled him or her to a refund. But actually, what was unstated was that the customer had to first qualify for a loan, and there was nothing instant about the loan procedures. This omission was ruled to be deceptive by the FTC, and the agency ruling was upheld by a court of appeals.[51] A claim by an advertiser that 93 percent of all its watches that have been sold since 1952 still keep perfect time would be deceptive if the advertiser did not reveal that the watches have only been on the market for the last five years. The FTC ruled that a claim by the makers of Wonder Bread that its bread is fortified with vitamins and minerals to help children grow up to be big and strong was deceptive because it did not reveal that nearly all commercially baked bread is fortified with vitamins and minerals. The FTC argued that by not disclosing that Wonder Bread is really no different from other bread, the baking company omitted an important element; it told only half the story.[52]

2. **The act or practice must be considered from the perspective of a consumer who is acting reasonably.** The test is whether the consumer's interpretation or reaction is reasonable. When advertisements or sales practices are targeted to a specific audience, such as those aimed at children, the elderly, or the terminally ill, they will be viewed from the perspective of a reasonable member of that group. "For instance, if a company markets a cure to the terminally ill, the practice will be evaluated from the perspective of how it affects the ordinary member of that group," the commission noted in the 1983 policy statement. The terminally ill consumer is likely to be far more susceptible to exaggerated cure claims than is a healthy person. Also, advertising aimed at a special vocational group, such as physicians, will be evaluated from the perspective of a reasonable member of that group. A well-educated physician might be better able to understand a complicated pharmaceutical ad than the average individual can.

One problem that some commentators have noted with this second criterion relates to infomercials, the 30-minute product advertisements that have rapidly grown in popularity on local television in the past several years. Many of these programs feature the most improbable kinds of items like miracle diets, impotence remedies, and baldness cures. It is at least arguable that no reasonable person would take these promotions seriously, and hence some of the more outrageous of these product pitches could escape FTC sanctions because of this second deception standard.[53]

---

50. in re *Thompson Medical Co.,* 104 F.T.C. 313 (1984).
51. *Beneficial Corporation* v. *FTC,* 542 F. 2d 611 (1976).
52. in re *ITT Continental Baking Co.,* 79 F.T.C. 248 (1971).
53. See Kertz and Ohanian, "Recent Trends."

The advertiser is not responsible for every interpretation or behavior by a consumer. The law is not designed to protect the foolish or the "feeble minded," the commission has noted. "Some people, because of ignorance or incomprehension, may be misled by even a scrupulously honest claim," one commissioner noted. "Perhaps a few misguided souls believe, for example, that all Danish pastry is made in Denmark. Is it therefore an actionable deception to advertise Danish pastry when it is made in this country? Of course not," the commissioner noted.[54] When an advertisement conveys more than one meaning to a reasonable consumer, one of which is false, the seller is liable for the misleading interpretation. Here is a classic example: "Jones Garage will put a new motor in your car for only $350." What does this claim mean? One meaning is that the garage will sell you a new motor and install it for only $350. But an equally reasonable meaning is that the garage will install a motor that you already own for only $350. If the second meaning is intended, the seller may very well be held responsible for the first meaning—which is false—as well.

The commission will evaluate the entire advertisement when examining it for misrepresentation. Accurate information in the text may not remedy a false headline, because a reasonable consumer may only glance at the headline. If a television announcer proclaims that a watch is 100 percent waterproof, the advertiser cannot qualify this claim in a long printed message in small type that crawls across the bottom of the TV screen while the announcer tries to sell the product.[55] Nissan Motor Corporation agreed to stop its "Nissan Challenge" promotional advertising campaign. On its face the advertising said that Nissan would give consumers $100 if they bought a Honda Accord or Toyota Camry after test-driving a Nissan Stanza. But in order to get the $100 consumers had to meet several conditions, which were not prominently noted in the advertising. Consumers had to actually buy a Honda or Toyota, take delivery of it, and submit proof of purchase to Nissan within seven days of the test drive—but not on the same day as the test drive.[56] Similarly, an advertiser cannot correct a misrepresentation in an advertisement with point-of-sale information. A seller cannot advertise a vacuum cleaner as having a 100 percent money-back guarantee and then expect to qualify that claim in a tag that is attached to the product as it is displayed for sale in a store. Qualifying disclosures must be legible and understandable, the FTC has ruled.

"The commission generally will not bring advertising cases based on subjective claims (taste, feel, appearance, smell)," according to the 1983 guidelines. The agency says it believes the typical reasonable consumer does not take such claims seriously and thus they are unlikely to be deceptive. Such claims are referred to as **puffery** and include representations that a store sells "the most fashionable shoes in town" or a cola drink is "the most refreshing drink around."

Finally, the commission has stated that when consumers can easily evaluate the product or service, when it is inexpensive, and when it is frequently purchased, the commission will scrutinize the advertisement or representation in a less critical manner. "There is little incentive for sellers to misrepresent . . . in these circumstances since they normally would seek to

---

54. in re *Kirchner,* 63 F.T.C. 1282 (1963), aff'd. 337 F. 2d 751 (1964).
55. *Giant Food, Inc.* v. *FTC,* 322 F. 2d 977 (1963).
56. "Nissan Unit Will Pull Ads."

encourage repeat purchases," a 1983 statement proclaims. That means the advertiser of small, dry cell batteries, a relatively inexpensive product purchased often by most consumers, will be given a bit more leeway in advertising than the advertiser of a $600 home generator.

   3. **The representation, omission, or practice must be material.** A material misrepresentation or practice is one that is likely to affect a consumer's choice of a product. In other words, according to the commission policy statement, "it is information that is important to the consumer." The FTC considers certain categories of information to be more important than others when deciding whether a claim is material. Express claims as to the attributes of a product are always considered material. Advertising claims that significantly involve health and safety are usually presumed to be material. Information pertaining to the "central characteristics of the product or service" are usually considered to be material. Information has also been found to be material where it concerns the purpose, efficacy, or cost of the product or service. Claims about durability, performance, warranties, or quality have also been considered material. An example of a claim that was not considered material is a statement made by Chevron in the advertising of a gasoline additive, F-310. In both television and print advertising, a company spokesman claimed to be standing in front of the Chevron research laboratories while he made the pitch for the product. In fact, he was standing in front of a county courthouse. The statement was false, but was it material? An administrative law judge said it was not. The location of the spokesperson is immaterial to a consumer judging the product.[57]

   Demonstrations or mock-ups often become the subject of FTC inquiries, and the question of materiality is often raised. For many years a shaving cream manufacturer claimed that its product was so good that it could be used to shave sandpaper. In a TV demonstration, Rapid Shave was spread on sandpaper and then, a few moments later, the sand was shaved off. The demonstration was phony. What the demonstrator shaved was not sandpaper, but sand sprinkled on glass. The FTC argued that this advertisement was deceptive and that the claim that Rapid Shave could be used to shave sandpaper was a material representation. The Supreme Court agreed, despite the plea from Colgate-Palmolive that the product really could shave sandpaper if it was left on the paper long enough, but because the sand and the paper were the same color, a TV demonstration did not work. Hence the company had to use sand on glass.[58] More recently, the FTC found that two demonstrations used to advertise an immersion-style kitchen mixer in a 30-minute infomercial called "Amazing Discoveries: Magic Wand" were phony and hence misleading. The advertiser used a pineapple with the center core removed and precrushed to create the impression that Magic Wand could crush a whole fresh pineapple. The marketers also claimed Magic Wand would whip up skim milk, but they actually used a commercial dairy topping in their demonstration, the FTC said.[59]

   But not all mock-ups or fake demonstrations are necessarily deceptive. Only those that are used to support a material product claim must be restricted. For example, plastic ice cubes may be substituted for the real thing in an advertisement for a soft drink because no claim

---

57. *Standard Oil Co.* v. *FTC,* 577 F. 2d 653 (1978).
58. *FTC* v. *Colgate-Palmolive Co.,* 380 U.S. 374 (1965).
59. Tewkesbury, "FTC Restricts Claims."

about the quality of the ice cubes is involved. But plastic ice cubes cannot be used in a television commercial aimed at selling ice cubes if the advertisement extols the attributes of these marvelous, uniform-sized, crystal clear ice cubes. The phony ice cubes are then being used to demonstrate a material claim for the product.

Some lawyers who represent advertisers take the cynical view that an advertisement is deceptive when the FTC says it is, regardless of the content of policy statements or other official pronouncements. There is undoubtedly some truth to this argument. If an ad is ruled to be deceptive, what happens next? Let's now look at the means the FTC has at its disposal to control or correct false and deceptive advertising.

MEANS TO POLICE DECEPTIVE ADVERTISING

In dealing with false advertising, the FTC's greatest enemy is the time needed to bring an action against an advertiser. Since advertising campaigns are ephemeral, the FTC often has difficulty in catching up with the advertiser before the short-lived campaign has been replaced with something else. But if time is the greatest enemy, publicity is the FTC's strongest ally. Advertisers don't like the publicity that accompanies a charge of false advertising. A study by the commission of 122 false advertising cases acted upon between 1962 and 1985 revealed that the stock of companies charged usually dropped sharply after the charges were published. Bad publicity can cost a company millions of dollars. In addition, consumer reaction to the charges often results in lost sales as well.

In addition to the informal sanction of publicity, the FTC has a wide range of remedies to deal with advertising. Let's briefly look at this arsenal.

FTC TOOLS OR REMEDIES TO STOP FALSE ADVERTISING

- Guides
- Voluntary compliance
- Consent agreement
- Litigated orders
- Substantiation
- Corrective advertising
- Injunctions
- Trade regulation rules

Guides

The FTC issues industry guides for a variety of products, services, and marketing practices. These guides are policy statements that alert businesses to what the agency believes are permissible advertising claims or practices. Hundreds of such guides have been issued, including a guide on when the word "free" can and cannot be used in advertising, and guides for advertising private vocational schools, home study courses, and environmental claims. In July of

1997 the FTC issued a statement that laid down principles by which it would evaluate the propriety of information collection and endorsement practices on Web sites used by children. The statement says, for example, that it is deceptive for a Web site operator to represent that the personally identifiable information it collects from a child will be used for one purpose if the information will really be used for another purpose. The guide also says it is improper for Web site operators to collect personally identifiable information about children and sell or disclose this information to third parties without the consent of the parents. In November of 1998 the agency issued a 26-page set of guidelines for advertising claims about dietary supplements. The guidelines address not only advertising claims made by the companies, but also claims that may be implied by advertising. The booklet contains 36 hypothetical advertising claims and explains how the law would apply to them. The dietary supplement industry earned nearly $12 billion in 1997, and many manufacturers have been accused of making extravagant claims about the efficacy of their products.[60]

The guides don't have the force of law; in other words, a business that violates a provision of a guide is not automatically guilty of false advertising. The FTC will usually require an advertiser to substantiate claims that go beyond those permitted by the guides or may even bring a false advertising action against the business. The guides are of great benefit, however, to honest advertisers who seek to stay within the boundaries of what is allowable under the law.

Voluntary Compliance

Industry guides apply only to prospective advertising campaigns, events that have not yet occurred. The next remedy on the ladder is voluntary compliance and is used for advertising campaigns that are over or nearly over. Imagine that a company is nearing the end of an advertising campaign in which it has advertised that its mouthwash can prevent a consumer from getting a common cold. The FTC believes that the claim is deceptive. If the advertiser has had a good record in the past and if the offense is not too great, the company can voluntarily agree to terminate the advertisement and never use the claim again. In doing this, the advertiser makes no admission and the agency no determination that the claim is deceptive. There is just an agreement not to repeat that particular claim in future advertising campaigns. Such an agreement saves the advertiser considerable legal hassle, publicity, and money, all especially desirable since the advertising campaign is over or almost over. This remedy is infrequently used.

Consent Agreement

The most commonly used FTC remedy is the consent agreement, or **consent order.** This is a written agreement between the commission and the advertiser in which the advertiser agrees to refrain from making specific product claims in future advertising. The advertiser admits no wrongdoing by signing such an order, so there is no liability involved. The consent agreement is merely a promise not to do something in the future. Sometimes the misleading statements are minor errors, but other times they represent a major attempt at deception. In 1996 the FTC won a consent agreement with the Remco Toys division of Azrak-Hamway International for

---

60. Grady, "F.T.C. Guidelines Restrict Ad Claims."

the television advertising of its Steel Tec toy vehicle kits. The FTC said that the company misrepresented the number of toys that could be constructed from the kits and the kinds of things the toys could do. The toys, which cost between $9 and $40, were manipulated off-screen in the advertisements by hidden wires or tubes. Children who tried to play with the vehicles discovered that the toys did not perform as they had in the advertisements. Although the toy company continued to deny that its advertising was misleading, it nevertheless agreed to give customers who bought the toys a complete refund to avoid long and costly litigation with the FTC.[61] Here are some other examples of recent consent agreement settlements:[*]

- Abbott Laboratories agreed that it would not make any claims about the extent to which doctors and other professionals recommended the consumption of Ensure nutritional beverage without competent and reliable scientific evidence to substantiate the claim.
- The makers of Promise margarine agreed to stop making false health claims for its product, including statements that eating this spread helps reduce the risk of heart disease and advertising that promoted Promise as having no cholesterol but did not reveal that the margarine still contained a significant amount of fat.
- Jenny Craig Inc. agreed to terminate advertising that featured testimonial claims from customers who succeeded in losing weight unless these advertisements actually reflect the common results of Jenny Craig clients or explicitly state that the results portrayed are not typical.
- Subsidiaries of Quaker State Corp. agreed not to make certain claims about the performance, benefits, efficacy, or attributes of Quaker State's Slick 50 engine treatment.
- Gerber Products Company agreed to stop claiming that four out of five pediatricians recommended Gerber baby food, since the study on which the company relied showed that only 12 percent of the pediatricians surveyed recommended Gerber.
- Liberty Financial Companies agreed to stop using false and deceptive practices in gathering information from youngsters who used its Young Investor Web site. The company said it would post a privacy notice on the site and obtain verifiable parental consent before obtaining personal data.

Considerable pressure is placed on the advertiser to agree to a consent order. Refusing to sign the agreement will result in litigation and publicity. The publicity can do more harm to the advertiser than a monetary fine. Also, the time factor works in the advertiser's favor. Typically the advertising campaign is already over. A spokesperson for Häagen-Dazs said the company signed the consent agreement promising not to misrepresent the calorie or fat content of any of its products in the future "because we pulled the ads a year ago."[62]

Considerable pressure is placed on the advertiser to agree to a consent order.

61. Collins, "Toy Maker to Give Refunds," C5.
62. Burros, "Minding the Store," B8.

*FTC News Notes 96, no. 52 (30 December 1996); 97, no. 21 (26 May 1997); 97, no. 28 (21 July 1997); and 97, no. 10 (10 March 1997).

What happens to an advertiser who signs a consent decree, then violates the provisions of the decree? In 1997 Mazda Motors of America signed an agreement to disclose far more clearly in its advertising important terms and conditions it imposed in leasing automobiles, including the up-front costs and the number, amount, and timing of scheduled lease payments. While the company did improve disclosure in its advertising, it still spent too much time and space highlighting low monthly payments and insufficient time and space outlining the total lease cost, the government said. In October of 1999 the FTC, working in conjunction with 24 states, levied a $5.25-million fine against the auto maker for failing to follow the stipulations it agreed to in the consent decree.[63]

Litigated Order

Sometimes an advertiser doesn't want to sign a consent agreement. He or she may believe that the advertising claim is truthful or may simply want to hold off any FTC ban on certain kinds of product claims. In this case the Federal Trade Commission can issue an order, usually called a **litigated order,** to stop the particular advertising claim. Staff attorneys at the FTC will issue a complaint against the advertiser and a hearing will be held before an administrative law judge. The judge can uphold the complaint or reject it. In either case, the losing side can appeal to the federal trade commissioners for a final ruling. If the advertiser loses this final appeal before the commissioners, he or she can appeal the litigated order in federal court. Failure to abide by the provisions of a litigated order can result in the advertiser facing a severe civil penalty, as much as $10,000 per day. In the long-running (11 years) Geritol case, for example, the commission issued an order in 1965 prohibiting the J.B. Williams Company from implying in its advertising for Geritol that its product could be helpful to persons who were tired and run-down.[64] The commission contended that medical evidence demonstrated that Geritol, a vitamin-and-iron tonic, helps only a small percentage of persons who are tired and that in most persons tiredness is a symptom of ailments for which Geritol has no therapeutic value. The J.B. Williams Company violated the cease and desist order (at least, that is what the commission alleged) and in 1973 was fined more than $800,000. A court of appeals threw out the fine in 1974 and sent the case back to district court for a jury trial, which the advertisers had been denied the first time around.[65] The jury was to decide whether the Geritol advertisements did in fact violate the cease and desist order. At a second hearing in 1976, the FTC won a $280,000 judgment against the patent medicine manufacturer.

In 2000 the manufacturers of Bayer Aspirin agreed to pay a $1 million fine after the FTC charged that the company was falsely advertising that nearly all adults could prevent heart attacks and strokes by taking Bayer Aspirin. While aspirin can be a potent heart protector for some people, the agency said, it is not recommended for just anyone. There is little evidence that aspirin prevents a heart attack in someone who does not already have vascular disease, said a spokesperson for the American Heart Association. The drugmaker agreed to spend the $1

63. "Mazda Gets Hit With $5.25 Million in Fines."
64. *J.B. Williams* v. *FTC,* 381 F. 2d 884 (1967).
65. *U.S.* v. *Williams Co.,* 498 F. 2d 414 (1974).

million to settle the case. The money was to be used for consumer education—including newspaper advertising and a consumer brochure—that was designed to clear up any misunderstanding about the effectiveness of the drug in preventing heart attacks and strokes.[66]

Substantiation

Advertising **substantiation** has been an important part of the FTC regulatory scheme since 1972. The basis of the program is simple: The commission asks advertisers to substantiate claims made in their advertisements. The FTC does not presume that the claims are false or misleading. The advertiser is simply asked to prove the claims are truthful. In 1999 the FTC did an extensive review of health claims in advertising and promotional material on the Internet and identified 400 sites and usenet groups making questionable claims. The agency notified the operators of the Web sites via e-mail that their claims required scientific substantiation and forced four advertisers to sign consent orders in which they agreed to stop making certain claims. Included were a purveyor of a beef tallow derivative who claimed it would cure arthritis, a promoter of shark cartilage as a cancer treatment, and two peddlers of magnetic therapy devices who claimed they could cure cancer and other diseases.[67] The substantiation process has been modified at least three times since it was initiated. Initially, the commission demanded that all advertisers in a particular industry—such as soap and detergent makers— provide documentation for all their claims. This demand resulted in tremendous grumbling from advertisers, as well as mountains of studies and reports for the FTC. The agency was drowned in documentation. The process is therefore streamlined today. Panels of experts scrutinize advertisements and target for documentation those claims that seem most suspect. The most recent commission policy statement on substantiation was issued in 1984. Under this policy, express substantiation claims, such as "doctors recommend" and "specific tests prove," require the level of proof advertised. Otherwise, advertisers will be expected to have at least a "reasonable basis" for claims in their advertising, wrote attorney Thomas J. McGrew in a 1985 article in the Los Angeles Daily Journal.[68] The degree of substantiation that will be deemed reasonable varies with "the type of claim, the product, the consequences of a false claim, the benefits of a truthful claim, the cost of developing substantiation . . . and the amount of substantiation experts in the field believe is reasonable," the policy statement said.

Corrective Advertising

Corrective advertising is a highly controversial scheme based on the premise that to merely stop an advertisement is in some instances insufficient. If the advertising campaign is successful and long running, a residue of misleading information remains in the mind of the public after the offensive advertisements have been removed. Under the corrective advertising scheme, the FTC forces the advertiser to inform the public that in the past it has not been honest or has been misleading. One commentator called the scheme "commercial hara-kiri."

66. Neergaard, "Bayer Rolls Back Ad Claims."
67. "FTC Goes After Fraudulent Health Claims on World Wide Web," 4 E.C.L.R. 582 (1999).
68. McGrew, "Advertising Law."

Under what circumstances will the FTC ask for corrective advertising sanctions? The commission has resisted issuing a specific policy regarding this question. For example, it responded to a request for such a policy from the Institute for Public Representation in Washington, D.C., by saying it would continue to deal with corrective advertising problems on a case-by-case basis. In the past, however, the agency has adopted this rather vague standard for the imposition of corrective advertising:

> If a deceptive advertisement has played a substantial role in creating or reinforcing in the public's mind a false and material belief which lives on after the false advertising ceases, there is clear and continuing injury to competition and to the consuming public as consumers continue to make purchasing decisions based on the false belief.

In such a case, corrective advertising is appropriate, according to the FTC.

The FTC first attempted to force what it calls affirmative or corrective disclosures in 1950, but a court of appeals ruled that it lacked the power to do so under the Federal Trade Commission Act. The court ruled in *Alberty* v. *FTC*[69] that the agency lacked the authority to encourage or require informative advertising. Ten years later, however, in *Feil* v. *FTC,*[70] the courts reversed the *Alberty* decision. The FTC threatened to use the remedy against the Campbell Soup Company to correct the misperception created when the company put clear marbles in the bottom of a bowl of vegetable soup to force the vegetables to the top.[71] The first corrective advertisement did not appear until 1971. It was the result of a consent order signed by the ITT Continental Baking Company with regard to its advertising for Profile Bread. For years the bread maker had been making two claims the government contended were misleading. First, ads touted a slice of Profile as having fewer calories than a slice of other breads. This claim was true only because Profile slices were thinner, the government said. In addition, advertisements asserted that someone who ate two slices of Profile Bread before a meal would lose weight. The company presumed that someone who ate two slices of bread before a meal would eat a reduced amount of breakfast, lunch, or dinner. But the advertising didn't say that. The FTC forced the baking company to reveal these falsehoods in 25 percent of its advertising during the 12 months following the signing of the agreement.

Corrective advertising was a popular FTC remedy during those years in the 1970s when the FTC was aggressively responding to a vocal consumer movement in the United States. It has been applied sparingly since that time. In May of 1999 the FTC ordered a giant pharmaceutical company, Novartis A.G., to run advertising correcting earlier statements that called its Doan's back-pain relievers superior to other analgesics. The agency said the company must spend $8 million on advertising messages that include the words, "Although Doan's is an effective pain reliever, there is no evidence that Doan's is more effective than other pain relievers for back pain." The company must make similar disclosures on its packaging for one year.[72]

---

69. 182 F. 2d 36 (1950).
70. 285 F. 2d 879 (1960).
71. *Campbell Soup Co.,* 71 F.T.C. 664 (1970).
72. "Novartis Is Ordered to Fix Doan's Ads."

Injunctions

When Congress passed the Trans-Alaska Pipeline Authorization Act in 1973, attached to that piece of legislation was a bill that authorized the FTC to seek an injunction to stop advertisements that it believed violated the law. Attorneys for the FTC can seek these restraining orders in federal court. An injunction is clearly a drastic remedy and one that the agency has said it will not use often. Spokespersons for the FTC have said that the agency will use the power only in those instances in which the advertising can cause harm, in those cases that contain a clear law violation, and in those cases in which there is no prospect that the advertising practice will end soon.

Attorneys for the FTC can seek these restraining orders in federal court.

For example, the FTC won a preliminary injunction against the National Commission on Egg Nutrition to block advertising claims that no scientific evidence exists linking egg consumption to a higher risk of heart disease. A lower court ruled that an injunction was too severe because it limited public debate on the cholesterol issue and damaged the advertisers financially. But a court of appeals reversed the lower-court ruling and granted the injunction.[73]

Trade Regulation Rules

In January 1975, President Ford signed the Magnuson-Moss Warranty–Federal Trade Commission Improvement Act, the most significant piece of trade regulation legislation since the Wheeler-Lea Amendment in 1938. The new law did many things, but basically it greatly enlarged both the power and the jurisdiction of the FTC. Until the bill was signed, the FTC was limited to dealing with unfair and deceptive practices that were "in commerce." The new law expanded the jurisdiction to practices "affecting commerce." The change of a single word gave the FTC broad new areas to regulate. The law also gave the agency important new power.

Three sections of the act expanded the remedies the FTC can use against deceptive advertising. First, the agency was given the power to issue trade regulation rules defining and outlawing unfair and deceptive acts or practices. The importance of this power alone cannot be overestimated. In the past the agency had to pursue deceptive advertisements one at a time. Imagine, for example, that four or five different breakfast cereals all advertise that they are good for children because they contain nine times the recommended daily allowance of vitamins and minerals. Medical experts argue that any vitamins in excess of 100 percent of the recommended daily allowance are useless; therefore, these advertisements are probably deceptive or misleading. In the past the FTC would have had to issue a complaint against each advertiser and in each case prove that the statement was a violation of the law. Under the new rules, the agency can issue a trade regulation rule—as it had done for nutritional claims— which declares that claims of product superiority based on excessive dosage of vitamins and minerals are false and misleading. If advertisers make such claims, they are in violation of the law. All the commission must prove is that the advertiser had actual knowledge of the trade regulation rule, or "knowledge fairly implied from the objective circumstances."

The advantages of the **trade regulation rules,** or TRRs as they are called, are numerous. They speed up and simplify the process of enforcement. Advertisers can still litigate the

---

73. *FTC* v. *National Commission on Egg Nutrition,* 570 F. 2d 158 (1977).

question, challenge the trade regulation rule, seek an appeal in court, and so forth. In most cases they probably will not go to that expense. Trade regulation rules have had a great deterrent effect, as they comprehensively delimit what constitutes an illegal practice. In the past, after the commission issued a cease and desist order, businesses frequently attempted to undertake practices that fell just outside the narrow boundaries of the order. The TRRs are much broader and make it much harder for advertisers to skirt the limitations. Finally, via TRRs the FTC is able to deal with problems more evenhandedly. An entire industry can be treated similarly, and just one or two businesses are not picked out for complaint.

The second aspect of the law that improved FTC remedies allowed the FTC to seek civil penalties against anyone who knowingly violates the provisions of a litigated order, even if that person was not originally the subject of the order. To wit: Chemical company A sells a spray paint that is toxic if used in a closed area, but the product is advertised as being completely harmless. The FTC moves against the company and issues a cease and desist order stating that in the future the firm must not advertise the product as being completely harmless. Chemical company B also sells a spray paint that has the same toxicity and is advertised the same way. If it can be shown that company B was aware of the provisions of the order against company A and continued to advertise its product as being completely safe, B can be fined up to $10,000 per day for violating the order, even though the order is not directed against B.

The third section of the law gave the FTC the right to sue in federal court on behalf of consumers who have been victimized by practices that are in violation of a cease and desist order or by practices that are in violation of a TRR, a right that the agency has been reluctant to use.

SUMMARY

The Federal Trade Commission has the power to regulate virtually all advertising that is deceptive or misleading. To be deceptive an advertisement must contain a representation, omission, or practice that is likely to mislead the consumer; the advertisement or practice must be considered from the perspective of a reasonable consumer; and the representation, omission, or practice must be material. The FTC has many remedies to regulate deceptive or untruthful advertising:

1. Guides or advisory opinions that attempt to outline in advance what advertisers may say about a product
2. Voluntary agreements by advertisers to terminate a deceptive advertisement
3. Consent agreements or consent orders signed by advertisers promising to terminate a deceptive advertisement
4. Litigated orders to advertisers to terminate a particular advertising claim, failure to comply with which can result in severe penalty
5. Substantiation of advertisements in which the advertiser must prove all claims made in an advertisement
6. Corrective advertising in which an advertiser must admit in future advertisements that past advertisements have been incorrect

7. Injunctive power to immediately halt advertising campaigns that could cause harm to consumers

8. Trade regulation rules that can be issued to regulate advertising throughout an entire industry

THE REGULATORY PROCESS

To understand the importance of the regulatory process, students should be familiar with procedures followed in a deceptive advertising case, be aware of the kinds of advertising that can be considered deceptive, and be familiar with the defenses to a charge of deceptive advertising.

PROCEDURES

The FTC does not attempt to scrutinize every advertisement that is published or broadcast. Most cases come to the attention of the agency from letters written by either consumers or competitors. When a complaint is received, FTC staff attorneys examine it to see if it has merit. If they can find none, the case ends. If the staff members believe there is a provable violation, then a proposed complaint, a proposed consent agreement, and a memorandum are prepared for the commissioners. The commissioners then vote on whether to issue a complaint.

If the commissioners agree that the advertisement is in violation of the law, the advertiser is notified and given the opportunity to either sign the consent agreement that has been drafted or negotiate with the agency for a more favorable order. At this point one of three things can happen:

1. The advertiser can agree to sign the agreement, and the commissioners vote to accept this agreement. If this happens the order is published and made final in 60 days.

2. The advertiser can agree to sign the agreement, but the commissioners reject it.

3. The advertiser can refuse to sign the agreement.

If either of the latter two events occurs, a complaint is issued against the advertiser, and a hearing is scheduled before an administrative law judge. The judge works within the FTC and officiates at these hearings. The hearing is a lot like a trial, only more informal. If the judge believes that there is substantial evidence that the advertisement violates the law, he or she will issue an order telling the advertiser to stop this illegal practice (this is the litigated order). The judge also has the authority to dismiss the case. At this point either side can appeal to the commissioners to overturn the ruling of the judge.

If the commissioners agree that the advertisement is not misleading or deceptive, the case ends. But if the commissioners support an administrative law judge's ruling against an advertiser, the order becomes law after it is finalized by an appellate court. The advertiser may appeal this decision in a federal court.

It is difficult for courts to reverse an FTC ruling. There are only a handful of reasons that a judge can use to overturn the commission decision. The case goes to the court of appeals,

There are only a handful of reasons that a judge can use to overturn the commission decision.

and there is no new finding of fact: What the FTC says is fact, is fact. The following are all instances in which a court can overturn an FTC ruling: (1) "convincing evidence" that the agency made an error in the proceedings, (2) no evidence to support the commission's findings, (3) violation of the Constitution—for example, the agency did not provide due process of law, (4) the action goes beyond the agency's powers, (5) facts relied on in making the ruling are not supported by sufficient evidence, and (6) arbitrary or capricious acts by the commission. An appeal of an adverse ruling by a circuit court can be taken to the Supreme Court, but only if certiorari is granted.

SPECIAL CASES OF DECEPTIVE ADVERTISING

A few special problems regarding deceptive advertising deserve special mention before we leave this topic.

Testimonials

The publication and broadcast of advertising of all kinds has escalated in recent years, but none faster than the growth of testimonial advertising. Whether the testimony comes from a celebrity like Bill Cosby, a race car driver, an organization like the National Football League, or simply an average consumer, product endorsements have grown dramatically in popularity. A dramatic increase in the broadcast of the 30-minute infomercials, which often feature celebrities, has resulted in even more testimonial advertising. For whatever reasons, advertisers believe (and they might be right) that for many people, a recommendation to buy a product by either a celebrity or a common person is highly persuasive. The Federal Trade Commission has issued "Guides Concerning Use of Endorsements and Testimonials in Advertising."[74] (See page 566 for more about FTC guides.) These guides don't have the force of law; the FTC would have to prove that an advertiser who failed to follow one of the guidelines violated the federal false advertising statute. But they do clearly outline the parameters that guide the agency in scrutinizing testimonial advertising.

The FTC defines an endorsement or testimonial as an advertising message that consumers are likely to believe reflects the opinions, beliefs, findings, or experience of a party other than the sponsoring advertiser. The endorsement can be communicated by a verbal message, demonstration, picture or likeness, signature, or other identifying personal characteristic or the seal of an organization.

The question of what is or is not an endorsement becomes more complicated each day, especially when an entertainer or celebrity is involved. An unknown announcer who reads a pitch for an automobile is not an endorser. But when a fashion model like Cindy Crawford touts a particular line of cosmetics, it is an endorsement. Is it an endorsement when an actor like Jack Lemmon does the voice-over in a television commercial for Honda? No, it is not. He is simply reading a script as a narrator. Anonymous actors and actresses reading lines in a commercial are not regarded as endorsing the product, even when they are pretending to be

74. 16 C.F.R. § 25 (1990).

typical consumers talking about the product in a supermarket. What about the advertisements Don Rickles has done for Fidelity investments? Is he an endorser? No, he is an actor playing a series of roles in advertisements. But the question becomes more complicated when actor Edward Hermann acts as a spokesperson for Dodge cars and trucks. Is his appearance an endorsement, or is he simply acting as a spokesman for the company?

Prior to 1932, when an individual received money for giving a testimonial, that fact had to be clearly stated in the advertisement. That is no longer the law. The government today believes that when a celebrity or expert endorses a product, consumers expect that person to have been paid for that testimony. But payment to a nonexpert or noncelebrity, the so-called average consumer, must be revealed if the promise of payment was made prior to the endorsement, or the consumer/endorser had reason to believe that a favorable endorsement might later result in payment, through the appearance in an advertisement for the product. Let's look at a hypothetical situation. Dr Pepper is seeking consumer endorsements for a new soda it has marketed. It takes these endorsements from letters it has received from satisfied customers. The soda drinkers gave the endorsement without any promise or hope of getting something in return. They can be paid for the use of their endorsements in advertising, and this payment does not have to be revealed. But if Dr Pepper seeks favorable consumer reactions at an in-store tasting of the new product and promises people who have not yet tasted the drink that if they give a good review to the new soda they may be paid to be in a television commercial, the fact that the endorsers were paid must be revealed in the advertisement. Even if the soda maker doesn't make a promise of payment but has a video camera recording customer reactions, this situation would meet the government standard that the consumer had reason to believe that a favorable review of the product could result in some future benefit. The entire thrust of these "Guides on Endorsements" is to assure the consumer that he or she is getting the honest opinions and beliefs of the endorser.

Experts who endorse products must have the expertise to evaluate the products. The government is especially concerned about endorsements of health and safety products. The identification of the expert must be accurate. The endorser of an automobile identified as an "engineer" must be an automotive engineer, not a chemical engineer. The FTC ruled that an expert endorsement by former astronaut Gordon Cooper of a product that supposedly increased automobile performance, reduced smog emission, and cleaned an engine was improper. Cooper's skill related to space missions; he did not have the education or training to qualify as an "expert" in the field of automobile engineering.[75]

A celebrity or expert endorser must be a bona fide user of a product at the time of the endorsement. This rule means the individual must use the product more than "now and then" or "once in a while." And endorsers must use a product because they like it and approve of it. The advertiser can continue to use the endorsement only so long as there is good reason to believe that the endorser still uses the product.

When an organization—like the National Football League—endorses a product, there must be evidence that the endorsement represents the collective judgment of the members of the organization, not just the judgment of the executive director or the management council of the group.

75. in re *Leroy Gordon Cooper,* 94 F.T.C. 674 (1979).

Celebrity endorsements must also reveal a material connection between endorsers and products if one exists. Singer Pat Boone was fined by the FTC for failing to meet this rule in his endorsements of Acne-Statin, a skin-blemish medication. Cooga Mooga Corporation, owned and operated by Boone for the purpose of promoting the performer's business interests, was one of several companies marketing and promoting the skin medication. Boone received 25 cents for each $9 bottle sold. In this case Boone also implied that his four daughters had used the preparation successfully, which was not completely true, and that Acne-Statin was superior to other similar products, an expert evaluation he was not qualified to make.[76] This case was the first time a celebrity had been held directly responsible for deceptive endorsement. The singer paid a large fine and was ordered to pay partial restitution to persons who had bought the product. The link between a product and a celebrity endorser does not have to be as direct as the connection between Boone and Acne-Statin to require disclosure. Former astronaut Gordon Cooper was paid for his endorsement of the previously noted automotive product on the basis of the number of devices sold. The more products sold, the more money he received. The FTC ruled that this arrangement was a material connection between the product and the endorser and should have been revealed in the endorsements.[77]

Celebrity endorsements must also reveal a material connection between endorsers and products if one exists.

An endorser cannot make any statement about a product that an advertiser cannot make. An advertiser cannot state that a cough syrup cures a cold; an endorser cannot say that either, even if he or she truly believes it. Satisfied users of the Ball-Matic Gas Saver Valve testified that the product resulted in gas savings. The FTC said this statement was deceptive advertising because there was no evidence to support this proposition and the claims made by users were not verifiable.[78]

Endorsements that claim to be from typical consumers must be made by consumers, not by actors playing the part of consumers. Note that most "man/woman on the street" testimonials never make the claim that the endorsers—who are normally actors—are typical consumers. That conclusion is one that advertisers hope we as viewers reach, but since no such claim is made, the ads are permissible. Finally, an endorsement concerning the efficacy of a product must represent the experience of a typical user. If a so-called baldness cure works on only one man in 500, the endorsement of the product by this person as a representative user would be clearly misleading.

Bait-and-Switch Advertising

One of the classic false advertising games is what is called **bait-and-switch advertising.** Here is the general idea. An appliance store advertises in the newspaper that it is selling a brand-new washing machine for $57. The advertisement is the bait to get customers into the store. When customers come to the store to grab up this bargain, the salespeople are very honest about the advertised washer and say that it is a pile of junk (and it probably is!): it has no dials, it tears fine fabrics, it tends to leak, its motor is loud, and so forth. However, over in a

---

76. in re *Cooga Mooga, Inc. and Charles E. Boone,* 92 F.T.C. 310 (1978).
77. in re *Leroy Gordon Cooper,* 94 F.T.C. 674 (1979).
78. in re *Cliffdale Associates,* 103 F.T.C. 110 (1984).

corner is a really good buy, a snappy model that is on sale for $595. This high-pressure sell-ing is the switch. If customers insist on buying the bait, chances are they will be told the machines have all been sold. The merchant had never intended to sell that model. The whole idea is to use the bait to lure into the store people who are in the market for washing machines, and then skillful, if not honest, salespersons switch customers to a more costly model via high-pressure selling—convenient monthly payments and so forth.

Bait-and-switch advertising is illegal. Technically, the law says that it is deceptive to advertise goods or services with the intent not to sell them as advertised or to advertise goods and services with the intent not to supply reasonably expected public demand, unless limita-tion on the quantity is noted in the advertisement.

Bait-and-switch advertising is not the same as loss-leader advertising, legal in many places, in which a merchant offers to sell one item at below cost (the leader) in order to get cus-tomers into the store in the hope that they will then buy additional merchandise at regular cost. Supermarkets use this scheme and so do other retail outlets. Those states that outlawed this practice did so because of pressure from small merchants who cannot afford to sell anything at a loss and do not want to be put at a marketing disadvantage with high-volume sellers.

DEFENSES

The basic defense against any false advertising complaint is truth, that is, proving that a prod-uct does what the advertiser claims it does, that it is made where the advertiser says it is made, or that it is as beneficial as it is advertised to be. Although the burden is on the government to disprove the advertiser's claim, it is always helpful for an advertiser to offer proof to substan-tiate advertising copy.

Another angle that advertisers can pursue is to attack a different aspect of the government's case rather than try to prove the statement true. For example, an advertiser can argue that the deceptive statement is not material to the advertisement as a whole (that is, it will not influence the purchasing decision) or that the advertisement does not imply what the government thinks it implies. For example, to say, as Dry Ban did, that a deodorant "goes on dry" does not mean that it is dry when it is applied, merely that its application is drier than that of other antiperspirants.

The success rate in defending false advertising cases is not high. As with most legal problems, it is best to consult legal counsel before a problem arises and not after a complaint has been issued.

ADVERTISING AGENCY/PUBLISHER LIABILITY

What is the liability of the advertising agency that generates the ad or the medium that publishes or broadcasts it? The law in both regards is slowly changing. At one time neither the agency nor the publisher had much to fear. That is not the case now. Let's look at ad agency liability first.

At one time the ad agency could likely have avoided liability if it could show that it acted at all times under the direction and control of the client.[79] But today an agency might be held responsible if it can be shown that the agency was an active participant in the production

---

79. Kertz and Ohanian, "Recent Trends."

of a false or misleading ad, and that it knew or *should have known* that the advertisement was false and misleading.[80] This liability could result if the agency uses false and misleading data provided by the client or if it creates a false impression in the advertisement based on truthful data provided by the client.[81] It is the extent and nature of the agency's participation in the false campaign that will ultimately determine liability.

The liability of publishers is also changing. Traditionally publishers have not been held responsible for the contents of their advertising. Courts, however, have re-examined this principle. In 1988 a U.S. district court ruled that Soldier of Fortune magazine was liable in a wrongful death action because it had published an advertisement that led indirectly to a murder. In 1984 a man named John W. Hearn placed this advertisement in the personal services section of the magazine's classified advertising:

The liability of publishers is also changing.

> Ex-Marine—67–69 Nam Vets—ex D.I.—weapons specialist—jungle warfare, pilot, M.E. high risk assignments U.S. or overseas.

A phone number accompanied the advertisement. Robert Black Jr. contacted Hearn and paid him $10,000 to kill his wife, Sandra Black. Hearn was caught and convicted of the crime and is now serving three life sentences in Florida for that murder and two other contract killings. Robert Black was convicted as well and was sentenced to die for his part in the slaying.

Sandra Black's mother and son sued the magazine and in March of 1988 a jury awarded the pair $9.4 million. The federal court ruled in this case that the First Amendment protection of commercial speech did not foreclose a simple negligence action by the survivors against the magazine.[82] But the 5th U.S. Circuit Court of Appeals threw out the decision, asserting that the ad placed by Hearn was simply too innocuous to punish the magazine for publishing it. "Given the pervasiveness of advertising in our society, and the important role it plays, we decline to impose on publishers the obligation to reject all ambiguous advertising for products or services that might pose a threat of harm," the court said.[83]

Two years later, however, another federal trial court, looking at another classified ad in Soldier of Fortune, again found the magazine responsible. A gunman who killed one man and wounded another was hired on the basis of a classified ad in the magazine. This time the advertisement said:

> Gun for Hire: 37-year-old mercenary desires jobs. Vietnam Veteran. Discreet and very private. Bodyguard, courier, and other special skills. All jobs considered.

---

80. in re *American Home Products Corp.,* 98 F.T.C. 136 (1981).
81. in re *Merck & Co.,* 69 F.T.C. 526 (1966).
82. *Eimann v. Soldier of Fortune,* 680 F. Supp. 863 (1988).
83. *Eimann v. Soldier of Fortune,* 880 F. 2d 830 (1989).

A telephone number and address followed. The U.S. district judge noted that in *Eimann,* the appellate court had ruled that the magazine was not liable because the advertisement was too innocuous or vague. Here, however, the ad was different: much less vague, according to the court. The phrases "Gun for Hire," "Discreet and very private," and "All jobs considered" certainly raise issues not found in the earlier ruling, the judge said. Whether a magazine should be held liable in this wrongful death action is a question properly left with the jury, the court said. The jury awarded the plaintiff $12.4 million, but the court reduced that amount to $2.4 million.[84]

In 1992 the 11th U.S. Circuit Court of Appeals upheld the lower-court ruling, saying that a publisher could be found liable for publishing "a commercial advertisement where the ad, on its face, and without the need for investigation, makes it apparent that there is a substantial danger of harm to the public."[85] The court granted $4.3 million in damages to the plaintiff. There have been no subsequent adverse decisions, but these rulings are a warning to publishers and broadcasters that it is always prudent to exercise care when accepting advertising.

SUMMARY

Complaints against advertisers are prepared by the FTC staff and approved by a vote of the commission. Administrative law judges can hold hearings, which are somewhat like trials, to determine whether the FTC charges are valid. A U.S. court of appeals can review all commission orders. Advertisers need to take special care when dealing with testimonials and endorsements. The law outlaws bait-and-switch advertising in which customers are lured to a store with promises of low prices but then are pushed by salespersons to buy more expensive products. Although ad agencies and publishers/broadcasters are generally not held liable in cases of false or harmful advertising, there are signs that the law is changing.

BIBLIOGRAPHY ⟶

Berman, Jeffrey A. "Constitutional Realism: Legislative Bans on Tobacco Advertisements and the First Amendment." *University of Illinois Law Review* 1986 (1986):1193.

Broder, John. "F.T.C. Charges 'Joe Camel' Ad Illegally Takes Aim at Minors." *The New York Times,* 29 May 1997, A1.

———. "Cigarette Makers in a $368 Billion Accord to Curb Lawsuits and Curb Marketing." *The New York Times,* 21 June 1997, A1.

Burros, Marian. "Minding the Store on Food Claims." *The New York Times,* 23 November 1994, B8.

Collins, Glenn. " In Settlement, Toy Maker to Give Refunds." *The New York Times,* 13 February 1996, C5.

"Coors, CPC to Fight RICO Ad Charges." *Advertising Age,* 22 October 1990, 3.

84. *Braun* v. *Soldier of Fortune,* 757 F. Supp. 1325 (1991).
85. *Braun* v. *Soldier of Fortune,* 968 F. 2d 110 (1992).

Cornell, Arthur B., Jr. "Federal Trade Commission Permanent Injunction Actions Against Unfair and Deceptive Practices: The Proper Case and the Proper Proof." *St. John's Law Review* 61 (1987):503.

Cushman, John, Jr. "Judge Rules F.D.A. Has Right to Curb Tobacco as Drug." *The New York Times,* 26 April 1997, A1.

DeVore, P. Cameron. "Commercial Speech: 1988." Remarks to Communications Law 1988 Practicing Law Institute, New York City, 10 November 1988.

———. "Supreme Court Boots Commercial Speech." *First Amendment Law Letter,* Fall 1990, 5.

Edwards, Krista L. "First Amendment Values and the Constitutional Protection of Tobacco Advertising." *Northwestern University Law Review* 82 (1987):145.

"Election Ad Law Struck Down." *The Washington Newspaper,* July 1998, 1.

Grady, Denise. "F.T.C. Guidelines Restrict Ad Claims for Supplements." *The New York Times,* 18 November 1998, A20.

Greenhouse, Linda. "Justices Strike Down Ban on Casino Gambling Ads." *The New York Times,* 15 June 1999, A1.

Howard, John A., and James Hulbert. *A Staff Report to the Federal Trade Commission.* Washington, D.C.: Federal Trade Commission, 1974.

Karns, Jack E. "The Federal Trade Commission's Evolving Deception Policy." *University of Richmond Law Review* 22 (1988):399.

Kertz, Consuelo L., and Roobina Ohanian. "Recent Trends in the Law of Endorsement Advertising." *Hofstra Law Review* 19 (1991):603.

Kilborn, Peter. "Sweeping Limits Put on Tobacco." *Seattle Post-Intelligencer,* 24 August 1996, A1.

Kogan, Jay S. "Celebrity Endorsement: Recognition of a Duty." *The John Marshall Law Review* 21 (1987):47.

Mann, Charles C., and Mark L. Plummer. "The Big Headache." *The Atlantic Monthly,* October 1988, 39.

"Mazda Gets Hit With $5.25 Million in Fines." *The Seattle Post-Intelligencer,* 1 October 1999, B2.

McGrew, Thomas J. "Advertising Law: Inactive FTC, Activism in Courts." *Los Angeles Daily Journal,* 17 January 1985.

Morris, Brian. "Consumer Standing to Sue for False and Misleading Advertising under Section 43(a) of the Lanham Trademark Act." *Memphis State University Law Review* 17 (1987):417.

Neergaard, Lauran. "Bayer rolls back ad claims of benefits from aspirin use." *Seattle Post-Intelligencer,* 12 January 2000, A3.

"A Nissan Unit Will Pull Ads." *The New York Times,* 10 March 1993.

"Novartis Is Ordered to Fix Doan's Ads." *The New York Times,* 28 May 1999, C16.

Pompeo, Paul E. "To Tell the Truth: Comparative Advertising and Lanham Act Section 43(a)." *Catholic University Law Review* 36 (1987):565.

Rohde, David. "Sweepstakes in Agreement to Reimburse New Yorkers." *The New York Times,* 25 August 1998, A16.

Rohrer, Daniel M., ed. *Mass Media, Freedom of Speech, and Advertising.* Dubuque: Kendall/Hunt, 1979.

Rosden, George E., and Peter E. Rosden. *The Law of Advertising.* New York: Matthew Bender, 1986.

Singdahlsen, Jeffrey P. "The Risk of Chill: A Cost of the Standards Governing the Regulation of False Advertising Under Section 43(a) of the Lanham Act." *Virginia Law Review* 77 (1991):339.

Tepper, Maury. "False Advertising Claims and the Revision of the Lanham Act: A Step in Which Direction?" *Cincinnati Law Review* 59 (1991):957.

Tewkesbury, Don. "FTC Restricts Claims by Infomercial Producers." *Seattle Post-Intelligencer,* 8 July 1993.

Tyler, Marcella A. "Federal Trade Commission Regulation of Advertising Today." Institute for Communication Law Studies, *Catholic University School of Law,* 1984.

Waltzer, Garrett J. "Monetary Relief for False Advertising Claims Arising Under Section 43(a) of the Lanham Act." *UCLA Law Review* 34 (1987):953.

Weber, Matthew G. "Media Liability for Publication of Advertising: When to Kill the Messenger." *Denver University Law Review* 68 (1991):57.

Whelan, Margaret. "Common Sense and Commercial Speech." *University of Pittsburgh Law Review* 48 (1987):1121.

Telecommunications Regulation
History and Licensing

The telecommunications industry in the United States is in the midst of a revolution as technologies emerge, merge, and dissipate. What began as radio and developed into television now encompasses a broad spectrum of technologies that includes not only traditional broadcasting stations but also cable television, satellite television, computer networks, and even telephone companies. The word "telecommunications" has become the current shibboleth in the marketplace as a variety of entrepreneurs race to cash in on the developing age of information.

The regulation of telecommunications is also experiencing revolutionary change. Since the beginning of the 1980s, long-standing rules have been abandoned, new rules have been put into place, and important parts of the fundamental philosophy that has guided the regulation of electronic communication for more than 70 years have been discarded. Ensuring service to the public through competition, not regulation, is the mantra of the 21st century. This chapter briefly outlines the past, highlights important changes that have occurred in the past two decades, and presents the basic structure of how the law currently regulates broadcasting. Chapter 17 outlines the current regulation of the content of broadcasting as well as the regulation of cable television and other telecommunications technologies.

HISTORY OF REGULATION

Radio is not the invention of a single individual. Rather, it represents an accumulation of many ideas that emerged during the last years of the 19th century. At first only simple radio signals were transmitted. But gradually, transmission of more complicated voice signals became possible. The basic hardware of radio had been developed by 1910, but the medium grew far differently than did the print medium. Remember, printing came at a time when people were groping for a means of spreading information and propaganda, and the printing press became a major weapon in the battle for democracy and religious freedom in England. The press was used as a means of spreading information and ideas. Radio has never really been dedicated to those ends. Initially, it was a gadget that tinkerers built as a plaything for talking with friends and neighbors and for listening to strangers in distant places. The military was first to see the practical value of radio. The Navy used radio as a means of keeping track of its ships out of port and for transmitting messages to captains on the high seas. The Army, too, saw radio as an effective device for improving military communications. After World War I the armed forces made one concerted push to have the government take control of all radio communication, but the effort failed.

The regulation of telecommunications in the United States dates from 1910, when Congress ruled that all U.S. passenger ships must carry a radio. Two years later the lawmakers passed the **Radio Act of 1912** in response to considerable pressure from the Army and Navy, which asserted that increasing numbers of amateur broadcasters interfered with military transmissions. The 1912 law required that all radio transmitters be licensed by the federal government and that operators of the transmitters be required to have a license. The secretary of labor and commerce, who was delegated the job of administering the law, was given authority to assign specific broadcast wavelengths to specific kinds of broadcasting (military wavelength, ship-to-shore wavelength, etc.). The secretary also had the power to determine the time periods during which broadcasts could be carried, but he had no discretionary power to license. Anyone walking in the door and filling out an application could get a license.

By the 1920s the popularity of radio propelled the growth of the new medium beyond even the wildest dreams of its supporters, and this growth outstripped the ability of the government to manage the orderly development of broadcasting. Secretary of Labor and Commerce Herbert Hoover fought diligently to protect the listeners' interests during this period. "We hear a great deal about freedom of the air, but there are two parties to freedom of the air, and to freedom of speech for that matter," he said at one of the annual national radio conferences he convened. "Certainly in radio I believe in freedom of the listener." But Hoover's best efforts were doomed by aggressive and competitive broadcasters who fought among each other and with the government over frequencies and broadcast times and often used radio broadcasting for a wide range of scams and hokum. Hoover used the limited powers he had under the Radio Act of 1912 in an expansive way and brought some semblance of order to radio broadcasting. It wasn't long before he was challenged in court. In 1926 Eugene F. McDonald, who operated station WJAZ in Chicago on an unauthorized wavelength and during times not authorized by his license, took the government to court when Hoover tried to rein him in, and the government lost. "There is no express grant of power in the [1912] act to

The regulation of telecommunications in the United States dates from 1910, when Congress ruled that all U.S. passenger ships must carry a radio.

the secretary of commerce to establish regulations," the court ruled.[1] Attorney General William J. Donovan refused Hoover's request that the United States appeal the ruling,[2] and chaos and cacophony once again ruled the airwaves. Congress, which for nearly a decade had been reluctant to join the fray, was forced to act and adopted the nation's first comprehensive set of broadcasting regulations, the **Radio Act of 1927.** The new law governed programming, licensing, license renewal, assignment of broadcast frequencies, hours of operation, and a multitude of other matters.

The philosophical foundation of the new regulation was the simple notion that the radio spectrum, the airwaves, was a scarce resource that belonged to the people of the United States. Congress gave selected individuals permission to use this valuable public resource for a limited time as long as they served the interests of the people. The legal standard was and still is that the broadcaster must serve "the public interest, convenience and necessity" at all times. The conduct of those given broadcast licenses would be measured against this standard by an independent government agency, the Federal Radio Commission, which was established by the new law to supervise the regulation of broadcasting. In 1934 the Congress substantially revised the seven-year-old radio act and adopted the **Federal Communications Act** of 1934, which regulated the telephone and telegraph industries as well as broadcasting. This law, which has been substantially amended in the past 60-odd years, stands as the basic regulation of the broadcast industry today.

It is certainly legitimate to ask the question, What about the First Amendment? How can such a comprehensive system of broadcast regulation, which includes provisions under which broadcasters are licensed by the government, be reconciled with freedom of expression? Some First Amendment concerns were raised as the government contemplated comprehensive broadcast regulation, but these concerns were most often raised by educators, labor and religious leaders, and others who saw broadcasting primarily as a noncommercial vehicle for educating and informing the public. The so-called commercial broadcasters, people who saw the new medium as an important money-making device, were more interested in seeing Congress clear up the chaos on the airwaves through regulation than they were concerned about hypothetical First Amendment problems.[3] Two other factors help explain the lack at that time of a serious discussion about government censorship. First, the meaning of the First Amendment was somewhat limited even in 1934. The courts had added little flesh to the bare bones of this constitutional guarantee. The First Amendment certainly meant far less in the mid-1930s than it does today. Just as important, however, is the fact that radio broadcasting was perceived far differently 75 years ago than it is today. Modern American radio and television offers listeners and viewers a mixture of information, education, and entertainment. Radio was primarily an entertainment and propaganda medium in the 1920s and early 1930s. Broadcast news as we now know it did not develop until several years after the 1934 Federal Communications Act was adopted. Radio in the 1930s more closely resembled motion pictures than newspapers, and the movies did not enjoy the protection of the First Amendment.

1. *U.S.* v. *Zenith Radio Corp.,* 12 F. 2d 616 (1926).
2. 35 Op. Attys. Gen. 126 (1926).
3. McChesney, "The Battle for the U.S. Airwaves."

CHANGES IN PHILOSOPHY, CHANGES IN RULES

By 1980 a comprehensive and multilayered set of rules governed American broadcasting. Wrought by a fundamental change in philosophy, these rules began to change. The Congress and the Federal Communications Commission (which replaced the Federal Radio Commission in 1934) still profess the belief that service to the public interest is fundamental to the operation of a broadcasting station in the United States. But the government has more recently adopted the notion that the public interest can be best served through spirited competition among broadcasters and others who seek to use the valuable airwaves. Regulation by the forces inherent in the marketplace is far more effective than regulation by Congress or the FCC, according to advocates of this regulatory (or deregulatory) philosophy. The best measure of serving the public interest is success in business. A popular radio or television station must be serving the needs of its listeners and viewers.

The history of broadcast regulation since the early 1980s, with rare exception, has been marked by the abandonment of one rule after another that regulated the behavior of broadcasters. This entire wave of deregulation was capped with the adoption of the Telecommunications Act of 1996, described by most observers as the most comprehensive revision of the Federal Communications Act ever enacted.

DEREGULATION BY THE FCC

On its own the Federal Communications Commission made the following changes in broadcast regulation in the past 20 years:

- Rules that restricted the three major television networks from owning and syndicating television programs were abandoned. These so-called fin-syn rules effectively kept the networks out of the lucrative television rerun business.
- Rules that forced broadcasters to formally ascertain from listeners and viewers the kinds of needs and interests that existed in the community were dropped. It was through this **ascertainment** procedure that broadcasters were supposed to learn what kinds of programming would best serve their community. Also abandoned were rules requiring the broadcaster to maintain extensive records relating to the operation of the station.
- An anti-trafficking rule was abandoned that forced an individual to own a radio or television station for three years before selling it. This change resulted in a hectic scramble in the marketplace as some radio and television stations were bought and sold like antiques at a rummage sale, with little regard to the impact that the sale might have on listeners and viewers.
- The FCC abolished the Fairness Doctrine, a rule that required broadcasters to include programming on their schedules that discussed important community issues. In these discussions the broadcaster carried the responsibility of ensuring that all significant viewpoints represented in the community on these issues were aired.
- Rules that indirectly limited the number of commercial minutes that could be broadcast each hour were dropped, resulting in the tremendous growth on

television of so-called infomercials, 30-minute commercials for a variety of products and services. The Federal Communications Commission attempted to abolish limits on the number of minutes of commercials permitted in children's television programs, but intense public pressure forced the Congress to overrule the agency on this matter (see pages 600–601).

- Rules that prohibited a single individual or company from owning more than one television station in a single market were dropped. It is now possible for a single license holder to own two television stations in the nation's largest markets.

THE TELECOMMUNICATIONS ACT OF 1996

In one fell swoop in 1996, Congress enacted a broad package of changes that in many ways went well beyond anything the FCC had done in 16 years of deregulation. Many of these rule changes have been and will be discussed elsewhere in this book, but here is a brief outline of the key parts of the legislation:

- Until 1984 the maximum number of broadcast properties any single individual or company could own was 21; seven television, seven AM radio, and seven FM radio. No limit exists on the number of television stations that may be owned by a single party today, so long as the total audience served by those stations does not exceed 35 percent of the population of the United States. No limit exists on the number of radio stations that may be owned by a single entity (see pages 591–592).
- A rule that barred one party from owning both a radio and television station in the same market was dropped for broadcasters who operate in one of the largest 50 broadcasting markets (see pages 591–592).
- In 1980 broadcast licenses were granted for terms of three years. The licensing period was extended incrementally over the next 16 years. Under the Telecommunications Act, the licensing period for both radio and television stations was extended to eight years.
- The regulation of rates for most cable services was eliminated (see pages 623–624).
- The partial ban on broadcasting networks owning cable television systems was abolished.
- A rule that prohibited a television station from owning a cable system in the same market, or vice versa, was dropped.
- Rules that kept cable TV companies and telephone companies from competing in each other's businesses were eliminated.

The new Telecommunications Act did more, however, than simply deregulate. It added regulation in two important areas. The bill sought to restrict the flow of erotic material on electronic communication networks (see pages 487–491) and imposed regulations that will force television set manufacturers to insert microchip circuitry into TV sets to allow parents to block out objectionable programming (see pages 605–607).

Despite the significant deregulation of the telecommunications industry, broadcasting remains heavily regulated. The next section contains an outline of this regulatory scheme and how it has been modified by the Telecommunications Act of 1996.

Radio, the original electronic medium, was regulated almost from its inception. But until 1927 the regulation was minimal and failed to control the growing number of competitive broadcasters in a way that served the needs of the listeners. Congress passed comprehensive broadcasting rules in 1927, rules based on the assumption that because broadcasters used a valuable public resource, the radio spectrum or airwaves, they should be required to serve the public interest. This philosophy engendered the growth of broadcast regulation until the 1980s, when a competing philosophy constructed on free market economic theory began to dominate the Congress and government regulatory agencies. Under the new scheme, traditional market forces are seen as the best regulator of any industry. In the past 20 years, broadcasting and the telecommunications industry have seen a period of substantial deregulation, topped off by the adoption of the Telecommunications Act of 1996.

SUMMARY

BASIC BROADCAST REGULATION

FEDERAL COMMUNICATIONS COMMISSION

The 1934 Federal Communications Act provided that a seven-member **Federal Communications Commission** regulate the broadcast industry. In 1982 Congress reduced the size of the commission to five members as an economy measure. Members of the FCC are appointed by the president, with the approval of the Senate, to serve a five-year term. One member is selected by the president to be chairperson. No more than a simple majority of the commission (three members) can be from the same political party.

Like all administrative agencies, the FCC is guided by broad congressional mandate—in this case the Federal Communications Act. The agency has the power to make rules and regulations within the broad framework of the act, and these regulations carry the force of the law. With regard to some matters, the 1934 law is very specific. For example, Section 315—the equal opportunity provision (or equal time rule)—details regulations concerning the use of the broadcast media by political candidates. But in other areas, Congress was eloquently vague. The mandate that broadcasters operate their stations in "the public interest, convenience or necessity" can mean almost anything a person wants it to mean. Consequently, the FCC developed a great many rules and policies in its effort to implement the public-interest requirement.

Powers

Congress approved the 1934 law under the authority of the commerce clause of the U.S. Constitution, which gives the federal legislature the exclusive power to regulate interstate commerce. This means that states, counties, and cities have no regulatory power over broadcasting stations. The federal government has *pre-empted* the law in this area (state and local authorities have retained some jurisdiction to regulate cable television and other telecommunication industries such as common carriers). Under the 1927 act, the question had arisen whether this clause

States, counties, and cities have no regulatory power over broadcasting stations.

meant that the federal government lacked power to regulate broadcasters whose signals did not cross state lines, stations that were not engaged in interstate commerce. In 1933 in *FRC* v. *Nelson Brothers,*[4] the U.S. Supreme Court ruled that state lines did not divide radio waves and that national regulation of broadcasting was not only appropriate but also essential to the efficient use of radio facilities.

Some communications businesses—telephone and telegraph companies, for example—have been designated common carriers by the government. A common carrier must do business with any customer who wishes to use its service. Broadcasting stations are not common carriers. They may refuse to do business with whomever they please. Broadcasters do not have to make their facilities available to all members of the public. In addition, the commission lacks the power to set rates for the sale of broadcasting time. Broadcasting is founded on the basis of free competition among holders of broadcast licenses.

The act makes it clear that although broadcasters may freely compete, they in no way assume ownership of a frequency or wavelength by virtue of using it for three years or for 300 years. When a license is granted, the broadcaster must sign a form in which any claim to the perpetual use of a particular frequency is waived.

Censorship Powers

Technically, the FCC lacks the power to censor broadcasters. Section 326 of the act states:

> Nothing in this act shall be understood or construed to give the commission the power of censorship over radio communications or signals transmitted by any radio station, or condition shall be promulgated or fixed by the commission which shall interfere with the right of free speech by means of radio communication.

No censorship, then. At least that is what Section 326 states. But that is not the way this section has been interpreted. The FCC has chosen to interpret Section 326 (with the approval of the courts) to mean that it may not censor specific programs, that is, forbid a broadcaster to carry programs on radical politicians or programs that picture members of a minority group in a derogatory fashion. However, at license renewal time, the agency can consider the kind of programming the licensee broadcasts, and if the agency finds the programming objectionable, this finding can be held against the licensee. The U.S. Supreme Court adopted this understanding of Section 326 in its 1978 ruling in *FCC* v. *Pacifica Foundation*[5] when the court sustained the agency's censure of WBAI-FM for broadcasting George Carlin's monologue "Seven Dirty Words" (see page 604). Most people would call this censorship. Section 326, then, has limited meaning and is of limited value to broadcasters.

The commission has broad-ranging powers in dealing with American broadcasters. (These include the power to regulate the activities of the American broadcast networks. See *National Broadcasting Co.* v. *U.S.*[6]) Section 303 of the act outlines some of the basic responsibilities of the agency, which include classification of stations, determination of the power

4. 289 U.S. 266 (1933).
5. 438 U.S. 726 (1978).
6. 319 U.S. 190 (1943).

and technical facilities licensees must use, and specification of hours during the day and night that stations can broadcast. The FCC also regulates the location of stations, the area each station can serve, the assignment of frequency or wavelength, and even the designation of call letters. There are not many things that broadcasters can do without first seeking the approval or consent of the FCC.

The key powers held by the FCC, however, focus on licensing and renewal of licenses and the authority to regulate programming and program content. It is toward these powers that primary consideration is directed in the remainder of this chapter.

LICENSING

Issuing and renewing broadcast licenses are perhaps the most important functions of the FCC. These functions are very important to broadcasters as well, for without a license there can be no broadcasting. Virtually everything the broadcaster does is tied in some way to having the license renewed. In addition to getting a license for a new station, the broadcaster must also seek FCC approval for most operational changes, such as increasing power, changing the antenna height or location, selling the station, transferring ownership, and so forth. Broadcasting licenses are granted to radio and television stations for eight years.

An applicant for a broadcast license may seek a license to operate a new station or an existing station that he or she wishes to purchase. In either case the process is extremely complicated. Attorneys familiar with FCC rules guide the applicant throughout the process. Someone seeking a license for a new station, more and more a rarity as the broadcast spectrum is being filled up, must first obtain what is called a construction permit. Obtaining this permit is actually the biggest hurdle. If the permit is granted, if construction of the station conforms to technical requirements, and if the work is completed within the time specified by the permit, the license is routinely issued.

The prospective licensee must meet several qualifications:

1. The applicant must be a citizen of the United States. Companies with less than 25 percent foreign ownership also qualify.[*]
2. The applicant must have sufficient funds to build and operate the station for at least three months without earning any advertising revenue.
3. The applicant must either possess or be able to hire people who possess the technical qualifications to operate a broadcasting station.
4. The applicant must be honest and open in dealing with the commission and must have good character. Making fraudulent statements on the application can doom the applicant to failure. The character matter relates to violation of FCC rules and regulations as well as felony convictions of the owners or managers.

---

[*]The FCC in 1995 granted Rupert Murdoch, owner of the Fox Network and eight television stations, a waiver of this rule. While Murdoch is a naturalized U.S. citizen, News Corporation, Murdoch's parent company, which owns a 99 percent share in the broadcast properties, is an Australian company.

Multiple Ownership Rules

For nearly 55 years the government sharply limited the number of broadcasting properties any single individual or company could own. These rules were founded on the notion that diversity in broadcast programming is a good thing, and one way to gain such diversity is to have as many different people as possible operating the nation's broadcasting stations. In recent years the rules regarding the multiple ownership of broadcast properties have been sharply trimmed. The important rules are as follows:

- No limit is placed on the number of television stations a single individual or company can own. However, the television stations owned by a single party cannot reach more than 35 percent of all TV households in the United States.
- A single individual can own two television stations in the nation's largest markets, but only one in other markets.
- No limit exists on the number of radio stations a single individual or company can own.
- A single entity can own in a single market as many as six radio stations and two television stations or seven radio stations and one television station if that single market has at least 20 media outlets (newspapers and television and radio stations).
- As of the spring of 2000, rules still existed that prohibited license applicants from owning a broadcasting station and a daily newspaper in the same market. But under pressure from large media owners and some members of Congress, the FCC announced it was examining whether this rule was still viable.

The FCC can and sometimes does waive these rules if it deems a waiver will serve the public interest, convenience, or necessity. However, in some circumstances the Justice Department will bar a merger or acquisition it believes will be harmful to station owners or the public. Since the passage of the 1996 Telecommunication Act more than 4,000 of the nation's 11,000 radio stations have changed hands. The Justice Department objected to eight of these deals. In five cases a settlement was reached between the government and the parties that resolved competitive concerns. Three other deals were restructured or abandoned.

More than most rules of government, broadcast regulations are sensitive to the winds of politics or what public officials perceive to be the nation's political mood. For a time in the recent past the government gave minority group members special preferences when applying for broadcast licenses. The Supreme Court upheld the constitutionality of these programs in 1990. Justice William Brennan, writing his last important Supreme Court decision, declared that under the Constitution the federal government has the power to devise what he called "benign race conscious" measures "to the extent they serve important governmental objectives."[7] The interest in enhancing broadcast diversity is, at the very least, Brennan wrote, an important governmental objective and is therefore a sufficient basis for the commission's minority-ownership policies. In 1995, however, affirmative action programs designed to give minorities preferential treatment in many areas were under attack. Not surprisingly, then, in a

7. *Metro Broadcasting, Inc.* v. *FCC,* 497 U.S. 547 (1990).

5–4 ruling the high court repudiated its 1990 decision and ruled that the minority preference programs administered by the FCC were overbroad. The ruling came from a case involving a government set-aside program that benefited minority businesses in the awarding of construction contracts. The opinion, written by Justice Sandra Day O'Connor, contained numerous comments that disparaged the 1990 opinion written by Brennan.[8] Earlier in 1995 Congress had killed a tax certificate program designed by the FCC to help spur minority ownership in broadcasting. In 1998 the District of Columbia U.S. Circuit Court of Appeals struck down the FCC affirmative action guidelines aimed at the hiring practices of radio and TV stations. The court said the rules did not serve a compelling public interest.[9] Two years later the FCC announced a new set of rules relating to the hiring of women and minorities. The old rules required broadcasters to hire a certain number of women and minorities. Failure to meet these quotas could have an impact on license renewal. The new rules require broadcasters to broadly advertise jobs and make them available to women and minorities, but there is no requirement that minorities and women actually be hired or promoted.[10]

Competing Applicants

The FCC may use a number of strategies to select a license holder when there is competition for a frequency. Lotteries have been used to select licensees for some kinds of nonbroadcast services, such as multichannel multipoint distribution services, cellular telephones, paging services, and low-power television station licenses. When a lottery is used, all applicants are prescreened to ensure that they meet government requirements. In 1994 an auction was used for the first time to award licenses for advanced paging networks and interactive TV. The government took in more than $2 billion in bids for these licenses. And in March of 1995, the government auctioned off 99 (geographically) large licenses for personal communications services, a catch-all phrase that includes advanced cellular phones, wireless links for personal computers, and other new information services. This auction generated $7 billion for the federal government. Until 1997 the FCC never considered using an auction to decide the ownership of full-service radio and television stations. When two or more parties sought the same license—either a new frequency or an existing one that was being sold—the FCC held what was called a **comparative license hearing.** This hearing was an equitable process designed to award the frequency to the most qualified applicant. But it was time-consuming and costly for the applicants. Competitors were measured on a variety of criteria:

The FCC may use a number of strategies to select a license holder when there is competition for a frequency.

1. Diversification of control of the media: Applicants holding existing media (like a newspaper or a second broadcasting station) in the area or having significant media holdings elsewhere were not considered as favorably as those without or with fewer media holdings.
2. Full-time participation in station operation by the owners: The FCC favored working owners over absentee owners.

8. *Adarand Constructors Inc. v. Pena,* 515 U.S. 200 (1995).
9. Holmes, "Broadcasters Vow."
10. Lewis, "FCC Revises Rule."

3. Proposed program service: What does the applicant propose to do with the frequency? Supposedly, applicants who planned to devote more time to programs on public affairs and education and information were favored over those who planned to program heavily with entertainment. Overall service to the public was the key factor.

4. The past broadcast record of all the applicants, if one exists. If the past record was average, it was disregarded; if it was exceptional, with unusual attention to public needs and interests, or if it was especially poor with regard to serving the public interest, the past record then became a factor.

5. Efficient use of the frequency: This technical question had to do with judicious use of the spectrum.

6. Character of applicant: Did the applicant have a record free of criminal prosecution? Was the applicant considered honest and trustworthy? and so forth.

7. Other factors: Any relevant and substantial factor, according to the commission.

The U.S. Court of Appeals for the District of Columbia Circuit invalidated the second criterion, which was called the integration factor, in 1993. The court said the policy was capricious and arbitrary and hence unenforceable. The court said there was no evidence to support the notion that full-time participation by owners in the operation of the broadcasting station will improve performance and make the station more responsive to community needs.[11] At that point the FCC put the comparative license renewal policy on hold while it attempted to generate a new plan. Competing applicants were told to wait and a massive logjam resulted. In 1997 the Congress entered the picture and told the FCC to abandon the comparative hearing process and instead use auctions to decide mutually exclusive broadcast cases. Whichever applicant is willing to pay the most money will get the license.[12]

How much does a license cost? Remarkably little when compared to the profitability of most broadcasting stations. An annual fee of $41,225 is assessed the owner of a VHF television station in one of the 10 largest U.S. markets. Only $2,775 a year is assessed for a similar license in the smallest markets. The most powerful AM and FM radio stations pay $4,400 per year.

License Renewal

Broadcasting licenses must be renewed every eight years. Renewal is typically a routine matter, but for decades many broadcasters have argued vigorously that renewal should be more than just routine, it should be automatic. For a time in the 1960s and 1970s, when a license came up for renewal the broadcaster might face challenges from other applicants for that license, all of whom promised the FCC that if they were given the license they would surely do a better job. The current renewal process is certainly not automatic, but under provisions of the 1996 Telecommunications Act, it is very close. Unless the license holder has seriously fouled up in the preceding eight years, the FCC will not even consider other applicants for the license. Under provisions of the law, Congress has instructed the FCC to renew a broadcaster's license as long as

11. *Bechtel* v. *Federal Communications Commission,* 10 F. 3d 875 (1993).
12. Cys, "Broadcaster License Auctions."

1. the station has served the public interest, convenience, and necessity;
2. the licensee has not committed any *serious* violations of the Communications Act or commission rules and regulations; and
3. the licensee has not committed any other violations of the Communications Act or the rules and regulations of the commission that, taken together, would constitute a pattern of abuse.

The act specifically states that the commission cannot even consider whether the public interest might be better served by granting the license to someone other than the license holder. If the commission determines that the license holder has in fact failed to meet the requirements listed here, the license renewal must be denied. Only after the renewal is denied can the commission consider other applicants for the license.

Only after the renewal is denied can the commission consider other applicants for the license.

What kinds of law violations is the FCC sensitive about? Stations that broadcast fraudulent advertising have been denied the renewal of their licenses.[13] The renewal of a license for a station that was used solely to promote the causes of its owner was denied.[14] If a station does not adequately supervise the programming it carries, its license may not be renewed.[15] Today, most nonrenewals result from the applicant lying on the renewal application. Federal courts have ruled that denial of a license renewal does not violate the First Amendment. Acknowledging that a First Amendment issue might arise when a licensee is stripped of the power to broadcast, the U.S. Court of Appeals for the District of Columbia Circuit nevertheless ruled 70 years ago:

> This does not mean that the government, through agencies established by Congress, may not refuse a renewal of license to one who has abused it to broadcast defamatory or untrue matter. In that case there is not a denial of freedom of speech, but merely the application of the regulatory power of Congress in a field within the scope of its legislative authority.[16]

The previous year another U.S. court of appeals judge had ruled that the commission had a perfect right to look at past programming practices of a renewal applicant to determine whether the license should be renewed. Invoking the biblical injunction "By their fruits ye shall know them," the court affirmed that past programming is a central issue in consideration of service in the public interest.[17]

The Public's Role

Although it is rare, a renewal applicant can also face a challenge from listeners and viewers. These persons aren't seeking the license for themselves; they simply don't want the incumbent license holder to be able to keep on operating his or her station. If the license is ultimately stripped from the incumbent, then other applicants may seek the license as if it were a new license.

---

13. *May Seed and Nursery,* 2 F.C.C. 559 (1936).
14. *Young People's Association for the Propagation of the Gospel,* 6 F.C.C. 178 (1936).
15. *Cosmopolitan Broadcasting Corp.,* 59 F.C.C. 2d 558 (1976).
16. *Trinity Methodist Church, South* v. *FRC,* 62 F. 2d 650 (1932).
17. *KFKB Broadcasting Association* v. *FRC,* 47 F. 2d 670 (1931).

Public challenges to the renewal of a license are a relatively modern phenomenon and today are quite rare. It wasn't until 1966 that citizens were even permitted to take part in the renewal process, and then only after a U.S. court of appeals ordered the FCC to change its policies. A group of persons from Mississippi were blocked by the FCC in their attempt to stop the renewal of a television license for a station in Jackson, Miss., that citizens accused of racist policies. The FCC said the group lacked "standing" to take part in the hearing. "Standing" is a legal word that means a direct and substantial interest in the outcome of the hearing. Judge Warren Burger (who became the nation's chief justice) wrote in *Office of Communication, United Church of Christ* v. *FCC* that the action of the FCC

> denies standing to spokesmen for the listeners, who are often most directly concerned with and intimately affected by the performance of the licensee. . . . The theory that the commission can always effectively represent the listener interests in a renewal proceeding without the aid and participation of legitimate listener representatives . . . is one of the assumptions we collectively try to work with so long as they are reasonable and adequate. When it becomes clear, as it does to us now, that it is no longer a valid assumption which stands up under the realities of actual experience, neither we nor the commission can continue to rely upon it.[18]

Recent FCC rulings have made it far more difficult for a citizen to challenge the renewal of a license. Because a station no longer is forced to keep many records that were at one time routine, it is often hard for a citizens' group to document its charges against the broadcaster. More important, however, the FCC has substantially lowered performance standards for radio and television stations. This move has sharply reduced the number of issues that a citizens' group might raise in challenging the renewal of the license.

SUMMARY

The five-member Federal Communications Commission has been established by law to regulate the broadcasting industry. The agency has the responsibility to supervise all over-the-air broadcasting as well as any other electronic communication that has an impact on over-the-air communications. Although the FCC is forbidden by law from censoring the content of broadcast programming, the agency nevertheless has considerable control over what is broadcast by radio and television. By licensing and relicensing broadcasting stations, the FCC can ensure that broadcasters meet certain standards, including programming standards.

Broadcast stations are licensed for eight years. To gain a license to broadcast, an applicant must meet several important criteria that have been established by the Congress and by the FCC. When two or more persons seek the same license, the FCC uses an auction process to select who will get the license. The auction process replaces a comparative hearing process that was based on applicant merit. This latter process was costly and time consuming, and courts ruled that at least one criterion used in the process was unenforceable. Listeners and viewers can challenge a renewal. Public participation in this process is relatively rare, and recent rule changes have made it even harder for citizens to mount an effective license challenge.

18. *Office of Communication, United Church of Christ* v. *FCC*, 359 F. 2d 994 (1966).

BIBLIOGRAPHY ⟶

American Enterprise Institute. *Broadcast Deregulation.* Washington, D.C.: American
 Enterprise Institute for Public Policy Research, 1985.

Brinkley, Joel. "Warning to Broadcasters That Renege on Running HDTV." *The New York
 Times,* 15 September 1997, C1.

Creech, Kenneth C. *Electronic Media Law and Regulation.* Boston: Focal Press, 1993.

Cys, Richard L. "Broadcaster License Auctions: A Replacement for Comparative Hearings."
 WSAB Bulletin, January 1998, 4.

Fields, Howard. "Congress All Fed Up With Runaway FCC; Full-Time Parent Now."
 Television/Radio Age, 6 July 1987, 40.

Ginsberg, Douglas, Michael Botein, and Mark Director. *Regulation of the Electronic Media.*
 St. Paul, Minn.: West Publishing, 1991.

Holmes, Steven. "Broadcasters Vow to Keep Affirmative Action." *The New York Times,*
 30 August 1998, A12.

Johnston, David. "U.S. Acts to Bar Chancellor Media's L.I. Radio Deal." *The New York
 Times,* 7 November 1997, C10.

Lewis, Neil. "FCC Revises Rule on Hiring Women and Minorities." *The New York Times,*
 21 January 2000, A16.

McChesney, Robert W. "The Battle for the U.S. Airwaves, 1928–1935." *Journal of Communication* 40 (autumn 1990):29.

Pember, Don R. *Mass Media in America.* 6th ed. New York: Macmillan, 1992.

Powe, Lucas A., Jr. *American Broadcasting and the First Amendment.* Berkeley: University
 of California Press, 1982.

Robinson, Glen O., and Ernest Gelhorn. *The Administrative Process.* St. Paul, Minn.: West
 Publishing, 1974.

Wharton, Dennis. "Court Axes FCC Minority Role." *Variety,* 15 June 1995, 22.

Telecommunications Regulation
Content Controls and Cable

CHAPTER

17

F ederal statutes and FCC rules that focus on the content of broadcast programming are among the most controversial aspects of the regulation of radio and television. Those who find all broadcast regulation wrong regard rules dictating the content of programming to be the most onerous aspect of this regulation. Yet many others who normally oppose government censorship argue that even more rules are needed—rules limiting violence on television, for example. The government itself has been inconsistent in this area, eliminating some rules like the fairness doctrine in the name of the First Amendment, while at the same time proposing more restrictions on the broadcast of adult programming. This chapter focuses on several current problem areas of content regulation, including rules related to children's programming, so-called indecent programming, violent content, and political broadcasting. In the second section of the chapter, the changing regulation of cable television and other, newer broadcast technologies is outlined.

REGULATION OF PROGRAM CONTENT

Obtaining a license to broadcast is no easy task, as was noted in the preceding chapter. But the subsequent operation of a station is no simple matter either. Aside from the day-to-day problems that plague any business, broadcasters are responsible for knowing and following hundreds of rules relating to their broadcasts. Among these rules are content regulations that range from fairly specific federal statutes, like Section 315 of the Communications Act, which tells a broadcaster how to deal with appearances on the station by political candidates, to vague FCC policy pronouncements, such as the agency's statement regarding broadcasters' responsibility for the lyrics of recordings and tapes that are played over the air. The Communications Act contains some rules relating to programming. The FCC has itself generated rules relating to other matters.

SANCTIONS

Failure to abide by programming rules can cost a broadcast license at renewal time. But this sanction is rarely imposed by the FCC. The agency has a wide range of other kinds of sanctions, however, which are frequently levied against those who transgress the regulations (see boxed text). Sometimes the commission will simply write a letter to a broadcaster inquiring about a programming practice. This letter alerts station management that the FCC is aware of the practice or even concerned about the practice. Often the letter of inquiry results in the station changing the programming practice. Some people call this "regulation by raised eyebrow."

FCC SANCTIONS

(Listed in reverse order of magnitude)

1. A letter of reprimand that is put in a licensee's file and may be material at renewal time
2. Cease and desist order, which is rarely issued but can be used to stop a broadcaster from doing something the commission does not believe should be done
3. Forfeiture or fine, which can range from a few thousand dollars into the millions. Infinity Broadcasting Corporation, which produces Howard Stern's syndicated program, was fined $1.7 million because of multiple violations by Stern of the government regulations regarding the broadcast of indecency.
4. Short-term renewal, from six months to two years, while the FCC studies the broadcaster's record to determine whether the license should be renewed at all
5. Nonrenewal or revocation of the license, the nuclear bomb of broadcast regulation (rarely used as a sanction)

Broadcasters have many programming responsibilities that are supervised by the FCC. In the broadest sense the radio or television station owner must carry programming that serves the needs of the community as they have been determined by the station. There was a time when the FCC required each and every broadcaster to carry a wide variety of programming: religious, educational, agricultural, news, sports, weather, and many other kinds. At renewal time a checklist was prepared to be certain the broadcaster fulfilled the station's responsibilities in all these areas. Such rules are no longer applied, but a broadcaster is still expected to meet these kinds of needs if they exist in the community.

In a narrower sense, many simple little program rules have been promulgated by both the Congress and the commission. Stations, for example, are required to identify themselves periodically. Broadcasters must announce when the station or program receives a gratuity in return for an advertising plug on the air. A station may not knowingly broadcast fraudulent advertisements. Many of these rules have remained unchanged over more than half a century. Some, however, evolved as changing social circumstances dictated alteration of the rules. For many years, for example, it was illegal for a station to broadcast information about a lottery, a contest in which a person trades something of value for a chance to win a prize.[1] But lotteries became very popular in the United States during the past 25 years. States began raising money through lotteries; casino gambling was permitted on American Indian reservations; and later many other communities joined the state of Nevada and permitted privately operated gambling establishments. Incrementally the FCC diluted the absolute ban on the broadcast of advertising and information about lotteries. In 1999 the Supreme Court ruled that the restriction had been so heavily diluted that it was no longer constitutional under the First Amendment[2] (see page 551).

Can the FCC control a broadcast station's format as part of its regulation of programming content? For many years the FCC resisted efforts by citizens' groups to force the agency to get involved when a radio station dropped one kind of music format—classical, for example—and adopted another format, such as rock. But listeners went to federal court, and the FCC was ordered in 1970 to *review* a format change by a station when the abandonment of a unique format produced community protests.[3] The U.S. Court of Appeals for the District of Columbia Circuit went one step further in 1974 and ordered the FCC to *hold a hearing* whenever a unique format was being abandoned by a radio station and persons in the community objected.[4] A unique format would be one that no other station in the market used. The loss of this format would deny the citizens in the community access to a particular kind of music or programming. Normally it has been supporters of classical music who have protested when a local station drops the classical format. But in Seattle in 1981, New Wave rock fans mounted a protest when the community's only (at that time) New Wave music station abandoned that format. Despite the earlier court rulings, the FCC continued to argue through the late '70s that the marketplace should determine the broadcaster's format; the government should not get involved. And in

Can the FCC control a broadcast station's format as part of its regulation of programming content?

1. See *FCC v. American Broadcasting Co. et al.,* 347 U.S. 284 (1954).
2. *Greater New Orleans Broadcasting Ass'n. v. United States,* 119 S. Ct. 1923 (1999).
3. *Citizens' Committee to Preserve the Voice of the Arts in Atlanta v. FCC,* 436 F. 2d 263 (1970).
4. *Citizens' Committee to Save WEFM v. FCC,* 506 F. 2d 246 (1974).

1981 the Supreme Court of the United States supported the agency and overturned a lower federal court decision calling for a hearing on a format change. Justice Byron White, writing for the seven-person majority, stated, "We decline to overturn the commission's policy statement which prefers reliance on market forces to its own attempt to oversee format changes at the behest of disaffected listeners." Justice White warned the agency, however, to be alert to the consequences of its policies and stand ready to change its rules if necessary to serve the public interest more fully.[5]

REGULATION OF CHILDREN'S PROGRAMMING

Government institutions have always regarded children as special and treated them differently than adults. There is a juvenile justice system, for example, that runs parallel to the system of justice for adults. A crime against a child usually carries a far greater penalty than a similar crime against an adult. The FCC and the Congress have traditionally treated young listeners and viewers in a special way in the regulation of broadcasting. For decades broadcasters were evaluated on the manner in which they provided appropriate programming for children. Commercials on children's programs were limited in number and clearly separated from the programming itself.[*] In 1984, as a part of its deregulation of broadcasting, the FCC abruptly abandoned some of these rules. Thus began a legal odyssey that would last for 10 years.

FCC Changes

Until the mid-1980s, the number of commercial minutes permitted during the broadcast of children's programming was 9.5 minutes per hour on weekends and 12 minutes per hour on weekdays. In addition, television stations were required to broadcast a minimum amount of educational and informational programming for children. But these rules were dropped in 1984. FCC commissioners noted that there were lots of over-the-air and cable channels that carried children's programming, and so long as the informational and educational needs of young people were in some way being met by one station in a community, it was unnecessary for all broadcasters to carry such programming. The limit on commercial minutes fell as part of the agency's attempt to abandon "quantified" standards of programming service (i.e., rules relating to the number of minutes or number of programs). In a terse, two-sentence statement, the FCC attempted to justify its decision:

> Elimination of the policy [on children's programming] is consistent with the commission's general deemphasis regarding quantitative guidelines. . . . Moreover, the commission has consistently noted the importance of advertising as a support mechanism for the presentation of children's programming.

---

5. *FCC* v. *WNCN Listeners Guild,* 101 S. Ct. 1266 (1981).

[*]There must be some kind of visual or oral indication of the switch from program to commercial, such as an announcement ("Bucky Beaver will be right back after these messages") or a substantial pause with a fade to black on the screen.

The result of this and other FCC actions on children's television was immediate. Many stations increased the number of commercial minutes in their children's programming. More important, the FCC action paved the way for what are really program-length commercials, cartoon shows built around popular toys like "GI Joe" and "Smurfs." In many instances, toy companies actually subsidized the production of these programs from their promotion budgets and offered them to television stations at rates far below what the station would have to pay for a non-toy-oriented program. Some broadcasters even partook in revenue sharing with the toy companies, earning a percentage of the profits from the toys. In 1987 Peggy Charren, the head of Action for Children's Television, or ACT, estimated that 75 such programs were on the air.

ACT went to court and won a technical victory. The U.S. Court of Appeals for the District of Columbia Circuit ruled that the FCC had failed to justify changing its policies regarding children's television. "Far be it from us to demand long-winded, tiresome explanations. But the commission's barebones incantations of two abbreviated rationales cannot do service as the requisite 'reasoned basis' for altering its long-established policy," the court ruled. The court noted that for the past 15 years the FCC had justified its policy regarding television for children on the assumption that the marketplace doesn't work when children are in the audience. Now, the agency embraces a conclusion that the marketplace did work. This conclusion has to be more fully explained, the court ruled.[6]

While the FCC was rethinking its assumptions regarding children's television, Congress decided to act. A bill limiting the number of commercial minutes on children's television was adopted by the Congress in 1988 but vetoed by President Ronald Reagan. In 1991 the Congress repassed the measure despite a threat from President George Bush that he too would veto such a law. In the end Bush didn't sign the law, but he didn't veto it either. It became law without his signature.

The new statute limits the number of commercial minutes permitted in each hour of children's programming: 10.5 on weekends, 12 minutes on weekdays. The new law also orders broadcasters to serve the educational and information needs of children as well. Specifically, broadcasters must present programming that furthers the positive development of the child in any respect, including a child's cognitive and intellectual or emotional and social needs.

Whereas the Children's Television Act did not mandate a minimum number of hours of "quality" children's programming, in 1996 the FCC did. In August of that year the federal agency ruled that television broadcasters must air three hours per week of educational programming targeting viewers 16 years and younger. The agency added, however, that broadcasters had some flexibility in abiding by this rule and could in some circumstances telecast slightly less than the three hours required. But as a practice, the FCC will renew the licenses of broadcasters more quickly if they conform to the three-hour rule.

The 1996 regulations also outlaw program-length commercials. The FCC has said that a program is a program-length commercial if a product associated with the program appears in commercial spots within the program, or if those spots are not separated from the start or close of a program by intervening and unrelated program material. Even the slightest reference can result in a program being deemed a program-length commercial. A shoe decorated

6. *Action for Children's Television* v. *FCC*, 821 F. 2d 741 (1987).

with the Teenage Mutant Ninja Turtles was briefly displayed during a commercial for a shoe store that was broadcast during the "Teenage Mutant Ninja Turtles" program. The FCC said this display resulted in the program being a program-length commercial.

Passage of these rules did not totally resolve the problem. Many broadcasters were reluctant to give up the inexpensive and popular cartoon shows and tried to convince the FCC that programs like "GI Joe" and "Super Mario Brothers" could fulfill their obligation to further the intellectual, emotional, and social development of their young viewers. The FCC told broadcasters that such programs would not suffice to meet the new programming requirements and delayed the renewal of several television station licenses to emphasize this point. In June of 1999 the Annenberg Public Policy Center at the University of Pennsylvania released the results of a study that found that 20 percent of all so-called educational programs telecast by broadcasters have little or no educational value. The study also revealed that many broadcasters were confused about what constitutes educational programming. Research fellow Kelly Schmitt said that shows such as "Duck Tails" and "Hercules" were being offered by stations to satisfy the educational needs of children even though the creators and distributors of these programs claimed they were not designed for that purpose.[7] In the late 1990s the FCC reported that as many as 26 percent of all commercial television stations were unable to show they had not exceeded commercial limits in children's programs. Substantial fines were levied against more than 50 stations in the summer of 1998 alone. Finally, despite the good intent of public interest groups, the Congress, and the FCC, other studies reveal that children tend to spend more time viewing noneducational programs than the better-quality shows. In the spring of 1999 the highest-rated (the show with the most viewers) educational program was "Hang Time," which aired on Saturday mornings and had a rating of 2.8 (it was viewed in 2.8 percent of the households with television). Noneducational cartoon programs normally pull in twice as many viewers.[8]

OBSCENE OR INDECENT MATERIAL

The FCC and Congress spent much of their time during the past two decades cloaked in the mantle of the First Amendment, abandoning rules that restricted broadcasters' programming practices. But there is one exception: They have materially attempted to tighten the screws that limit the broadcast of obscene or indecent material. Section 1464 of the United States Code gives the FCC the power to revoke any broadcast license if the licensee transmits obscene or indecent material over the airwaves. As noted previously in this book, having the power to ban obscenity and indecency is one thing; defining obscenity and indecency is another.

The broadcast of obscenity on over-the-air television or radio stations has rarely been a problem. Courts have defined obscenity, broadcasters know what it is (as much as anyone can know what it is based on these definitions), and radio and television stations simply don't program such material. Indecency is a different matter. The legal definition of indecency has traditionally lacked precision. A tremendous amount of material that might be indecent to some

---

7. McQueen, "Educational Value Lacking."
8. Cys, "Learn a Lesson," and Sterngold, "Lessons Not Quite Ready."

people is perfectly acceptable to others. And the context in which the material is presented has added to the difficulty of regulating such broadcasts. With the tremendous audience segmentation in radio in the 1990s, a single station can survive and even prosper using so-called shock jockeys like Howard Stern. These stations are interested in serving only a small segment of the listening audience, a segment that can live with programming that contains occasional profanity, scatological humor, and other elements that most listeners would find offensive. If there are no complaints, the station can generally operate without a problem.

Television is a different matter, however, because most over-the-air television stations strive to reach the largest possible audience. Television broadcasters are usually fearful of offending even a small segment of viewers and, until recently, have set programming standards that are more conservative than those imposed by the government. In 1975, for example, the three commercial television networks (ABC, CBS, and NBC), with the cooperation of the National Association of Broadcasters, an industry trade group, and the FCC, instituted what was called "the family hour." Stations that subscribed to the NAB Code of Good Practices were told that the hours from 7 to 9 each evening were to be set aside for family viewing and that programs with sexual overtones and excessive violence were taboo in this period. The censorship undertaken by the networks was heavy-handed. The word "virgin" was cut from one program ("innocent" was substituted). Censors began to look anew at Cher's navel, and a braless guest on the "Phyllis" show was re-dressed before filming began. Programs that had been broadcast in the 8 p.m. time slot for several years were either moved or toned down to meet the new family-hour standards. But the rule was challenged by the creators of television programs. Writers and directors in Hollywood, where most television programs are produced, went to court, and in 1976 federal judge Warren J. Ferguson of the District Court for Southern California ruled that the "adoption of the family viewing policy by each of the three networks constituted a violation of the First Amendment." The judge ruled that the policy had been motivated by informal statements from the FCC, which threatened government action against the industry should not the family hour or something like it be adopted.[9] The judge's conclusion is more than substantiated in Geoffrey Cowan's fascinating book "See No Evil," the story of the genesis of the family hour.[10]

Because of the general conservatism of the broadcasting industry, the FCC has had few problems with regard to indecent broadcasting. There are but a few recorded instances of FCC action during the past 40 years. In 1962 the commission refused to renew the license of radio station WDKD at least partially because a disc jockey at the station habitually told "off-color" or "indecent" jokes on the air.[11] A college radio station was fined $100 for broadcasting "indecent" four-letter words over the air in 1970.[12] A $2,000 fine was levied against an Illinois radio

Television is a different matter, however, because most over-the-air television stations strive to reach the largest possible audience.

---

9. *Writers Guild* v. *FCC,* 423 F. Supp. 1064 (1976). A U.S. court of appeals later overturned the lower-court ruling on the grounds that the U.S. district court lacked jurisdiction in the case, that the issue should have first gone to the FCC for resolution. See *Writers Guild* v. *ABC,* 609 F. 2d 355 (1979). The networks made no effort to re-establish the policy.
10. Cowan, *See No Evil.*
11. in re *Palmetto Broadcasting Co.,* 33 F.C.C. 250 (1962).
12. in re *WUHY-FM, Eastern Educational Radio,* 24 F.C.C. 2d 408 (1970).

station in 1973 for broadcasting a discussion between an announcer and a listener about oral sexual practices.[13] The discussion stemmed from the station's call-in "topless radio" format. A federal court of appeals upheld the judgment two years later.[14]

The most recent battle over indecent programming began more than 20 years ago when the Supreme Court of the United States upheld an FCC ruling that radio station WBAI in New York City had violated the law when it broadcast a recorded monologue by comedian George Carlin.[15] The monologue, called "Seven Dirty Words," was broadcast on the listener-supported station during a long discussion on the English language. The FCC said it was impermissible to broadcast "language that describes in terms patently offensive as measured by contemporary community standards for the broadcast medium, sexual or excretory activities and organs, *at times when there is a reasonable risk children may be in the audience*" [author emphasis]. The agency said it was unlikely children would be listening or watching after 10 p.m. and before 6 a.m., and designated this eight-hour block of time a safe harbor for the broadcast of adult material.

During the next 13 years the issue of indecent broadcasting on radio and television consumed a considerable amount of time for members of Congress, the FCC, and the federal courts. Some in Congress thought that indecent material should be completely banned; there should be no safe harbor. The FCC took action against numerous stations that it believed violated the rules and along the way broadened its definition of adult programming. In 1987 indecency was defined as "exposure of children to language that describes in terms patently offensive as measured by contemporary community standards for the broadcast media, sexual or excretory activities and organs." The agency also shrunk its safe harbor to midnight to 6 a.m. The courts were again drawn into the matter in the early 1990s when nearly half a dozen lawsuits were litigated. The FCC rules were finally upheld after an en banc hearing of the U.S. Court of Appeals for the District of Columbia Circuit in 1995.[16] The following year the Supreme Court declined to review this decision.[17]

Under current law it is illegal for a radio or television station to broadcast indecent material between 6 a.m. and 10 p.m. Indecent material is defined as material, in context, that depicts or describes sexual or excretory activities or organs in terms patently offensive as measured by contemporary community standards for the broadcast medium. The FCC is vigorous in enforcement of this rule. In late 1996 the former owner of a Richmond, Va., radio station was fined $10,000 for airing two indecent Howard Stern broadcasts. At about the same time a radio station in San Antonio, Texas, was fined $7,500 for broadcasting an unedited version of the song "Erotic City" by the Artist Formerly Known as Prince. In 1997 the FCC reportedly had 90 pending indecency complaints against radio and television stations.

13. *Sonderling Broadcasting Corp.,* 27 P & F Rad. Regs. 287 (1973).

14. *Illinois Citizens Committee for Broadcasting* v. *FCC,* 515 F. 2d 197 (1975).

15. *FCC* v. *Pacifica Foundation,* 438 U.S. 726 (1978).

16. *Action for Children's Television* v. *F.C.C.,* 58 F. 3d 654 (1995).

17. *Action for Children's Television* v. *F.C.C. et al.,* U.S. Sup. Ct. No. 95-520, cert. den.; *Pacifica Foundation* v. *F.C.C,* U.S. Sup. Ct. No. 95-509, cert. den.

VIOLENCE ON TELEVISION

After years of hand wringing and hearings, Congress finally took steps in early 1996 to try to control the amount of violence American children watch on television. A provision in the Telecommunications Act of 1996 mandates that the manufacturers of television sets must install a microchip—nicknamed a V-chip—in the receivers that they make that will permit parents to block out violent programming.

The V-chip in a television set will be activated by a signal contained in each program broadcast. The signal tells the receiver that a program with a certain rating is being transmitted. If the receiver is programmed to reject a show with that rating, reception of the program will be blocked. The key to the technology is the program rating system. Under the 1996 law, the industry was given a year to adopt such a rating system. If the industry failed to adopt such a system, one would be imposed by the government.

In March of 1998 the broadcast industry, parent advocacy groups, the Motion Picture Association of America, and the FCC finally announced agreement on a rating system. The system has two tiers. One is age-based and is designed to inform a viewer whether a particular program is suitable for children of a certain age. There are two ratings for children's programs:

TV-Y—approved for all children

TV-Y7—approved for children 7 or older

All other entertainment programs are rated at one of four levels (news programs and news magazine shows are exempt from the ratings):

TV-G—suitable for all ages; little or no violence, no strong language, and little or no sexual dialogue

TV-PG—parental guidance; may contain material that many parents would find unsuitable for younger children

TV-14—parent strongly cautioned; may contain material that many parents would find unsuitable for children 14 years of age

TV-M—mature audience only; programs for adults, may be unsuitable for children under 17 years of age

The second tier of the system provides viewers with reasons for the age-based ratings. The descriptive letters attempt to summarize the content:

V—violence

S—sexual situations

L—coarse language

D—suggestive dialogue

FV—fantasy violence

Some broadcast and cable channels have refused to use the descriptive letters. A 1998 study by the Kaiser Family Foundation, an organization devoted to public health, revealed that one year after the new lettering system was added, 92 percent of programs that carry some sexual content did not carry the S label; 79 percent of shows with some violence did not carry the V

label; and 81 percent of programs that contained some fantasy violence did not carry the FV designation. But the group noted it found nearly 96 percent compliance with the age-based ratings.[18] Resistance to use the descriptive letters was defended by many in television's creative community. John Wells, executive producer of one of TV's most popular shows, "E.R.," said he feared that labels would cause many families to tar all similarly rated shows with the same brush. "It will make it much more difficult to get a show like 'E.R.' on the air," Wells said. "We have violence, but it's in the context of showing the terrible effect of violence—it's exactly the sort we should see. Violence is part of our society and as artists we are right to chronicle it."[19]

All television sets manufactured after January 1, 2000, with screens larger than 13 inches must contain the V-chip.

The Federal Communications Commission in the spring of 1998 adopted television program ratings to work with the V-chips scheduled to be built into new TV receivers. Vice President Al Gore, a strong proponent of the system, discusses the new guidelines. AP/Wide World Photos

18. Mifflin, "Study Finds TV Networks Fail."
19. Mifflin, "TV Ratings Accord Comes Under Fire."

The ratings were being telecast even before sets with V-chips came on the market. Many observers said they felt the whole scheme would fail. Some people have hypothesized that the content of television may become even more violent in the future. Producers who have been wary about putting too much violence in a program for fear of alienating some viewers may now rationalize that those viewers who don't want to watch violent programming will have ample warning because of the rating system and the V-chip. Even more violent content may be added to attract those viewers who seem to thrive on such action programs. And the ratings could inadvertently advertise violent programs to young people who seem attracted to such programs.

SUMMARY

The FCC has broad control over the content of broadcast programming. To enforce this control, the agency has a wide variety of sanctions, which include letters of reprimand, fine or forfeiture, and nonrenewal or revocation of broadcast licenses. Content regulations involve a wide range of broadcast programming. In the broadest sense, the broadcaster must program to meet the needs of the community. But programming rules also involve simple regulations, such as the requirement to present station identification at various times of the broadcast day.

The FCC has chosen not to attempt to control the selection of format by a broadcaster. Citizens' groups have urged the FCC to hold hearings when a radio station drops one program format and adopts a new one. In the early 1970s federal courts supported these citizen protests, but in 1981 the U.S. Supreme Court ruled that the government need not get involved when a broadcaster decides to switch from one format to another. In the mid-1980s the FCC attempted to remove rules dictating programming standards for children's broadcasting. The Congress resisted these changes and forced the agency to reinstate rules regarding both the number of commercial minutes permitted per hour in children's programming and minimum service standards for the younger viewers.

Federal law prohibits the broadcast of any obscene or indecent material. In 1978 the Supreme Court ruled that a radio or television station could be punished for broadcasting material that is not obscene but merely indecent. The court based its ruling on the premise that children might be present during the broadcast. Since the mid-1980s, the FCC and the Congress have attempted to establish a policy governing the broadcast of indecent or adult material. A federal court finally approved such a policy in 1995. In 1996 Congress mandated that microchip circuitry be added to all new television sets that would allow parents to block the reception of programs rated as violent.

REGULATION OF POLITICAL PROGRAMMING

The guarantees of freedom of speech and freedom of the press were added to the Constitution in large measure to protect the political debate in this nation from interference by the government. Yet the government is permitted to regulate some aspects of this kind of broadcasting. Opponents of such regulation argue that these regulations fly directly in the face of the First Amendment and are dangerous to the political process. Those who support such regulation argue that it is because political and public affairs broadcasting is so important that it must be regulated. The broadcaster, proponents say, doesn't take his or her public service responsibility seriously enough and must be prodded by the government; without regulation, broadcasters—who tend to be of a like mind—will favor one political adversary over another, or will completely ignore the political process. Let's examine briefly the kind of regulation that exists.

CANDIDATE ACCESS RULE

Broadcasters cannot completely block candidates for *federal* office from buying airtime on the station to promote their candidacies because of the existence of the **candidate access rule. Section 312** (a) (7) of the Federal Communications Act, adopted in 1971 by the Congress, states that a broadcast license can be revoked for willful and repeated failure "to allow reasonable access to or to permit the purchase of reasonable amounts of time for the use of a broadcasting station by a legally qualified candidate for federal elective office on behalf of his candidacy." This statute applies only to candidates for federal office: presidents and vice presidents and U.S. senators and representatives.

Federal courts have provided two important interpretations of this statute. Both cases stemmed from the 1980 presidential election campaign. The Carter-Mondale presidential committee sought to buy 30 minutes of time on all three networks in early December 1979 for President Jimmy Carter to announce that he would be a candidate for re-election and to present a film outlining Carter's record as president. The request was made in October 1979. NBC refused. ABC said it could not reach a decision on the question. CBS offered two five-minute segments, one at 10:55 p.m. and one during the day. Privately, all three networks were fearful of breaking into their prime-time entertainment schedules for a political broadcast. But publicly, the broadcasters argued that the political campaign had not yet started; it was too early (the election was scheduled for November 1980) to begin to carry political programming.

The FCC ruled against the networks, the U.S. Court of Appeals for the District of Columbia Circuit ruled against the networks, and the Supreme Court of the United States ruled against the networks. The high court ruled in its 6–3 decision that a broadcaster could not institute an across-the-board policy rejecting all requests from federal candidates for airtime.[20] Chief Justice Burger wrote that once a political campaign begins, a broadcaster must give reasonable and good faith attention to access requests from legally qualified candidates.

> Such requests must be considered on an individualized basis, and broadcasters are required to tailor their responses to accommodate, as much as reasonably possible, a candidate's stated purpose in seeking air time. In responding to access requests, however, broadcasters may also give weight to such factors as the amount of time previously sold to the candidate, the disruptive impact on regular programming, and the likelihood of requests for time by rival candidates under the equal opportunities provision of Section 315 (a). These considerations may not be invoked as pretexts for denying access; to justify a negative response, broadcasters must cite

20. *CBS* v. *FCC,* 453 U.S. 567 (1981).

a realistic danger of substantial program disruption—perhaps caused by insufficient notice to allow adjustments in the schedule—or of an excessive number of equal time requests.

Burger added that broadcasters must explain their reasons for refusing airtime or making limited counteroffers so the FCC can review these decisions if needed. Each of the networks had argued, however, that the 1980 presidential campaign had not really started. After all, the time period sought by Carter was 11 months prior to the election. In this case the networks should not be bound by Section 312, they asserted. The majority of the Supreme Court rejected this argument, noting the following evidence that the campaign had started:

1. Ten Republican candidates and two Democratic candidates had announced they were running for president.
2. The selection of delegates to the national political conventions had started in many states.
3. Many candidates were making speeches in an effort to raise money.
4. The Iowa caucuses to select convention delegates were scheduled for January, one month after the broadcast time sought by Carter.
5. Newspapers had been covering the national political campaign for at least two months.

Burger rejected the notion that Section 312 created a right of access to the media. None is created by this decision, he added. But a licensed broadcaster is "granted the free and exclusive use of a limited and valuable part of the public domain; when he accepts that franchise, it is burdened by enforceable public obligations."[21]

The Supreme Court's ruling means that a broadcaster cannot adopt an across-the-board policy of rejecting all requests for airtime. Each request must be considered individually and can be rejected only if the broadcaster can demonstrate good cause.

The Supreme Court's ruling means that a broadcaster cannot adopt an across-the-board policy of rejecting all requests for airtime.

Section 312 implies that the candidate can seek to buy time on a station or ask for free time. Does this mean a broadcast station must *give* a candidate for federal office free time if fulfilling such a request would not interfere substantially with the broadcast schedule or would not prompt requests for equal time from other candidates? The U.S. Court of Appeals for the District of Columbia Circuit answered no when that question was asked. On March 14, 1980, President Carter delivered a 30-minute speech on the economic condition of the nation. The speech was carried on all three networks. This was four days before the presidential primary in Illinois. Senator Ted Kennedy, who was also seeking the Democratic nomination for president, requested that the networks *give* him 30 minutes of airtime to respond to the president's speech. The networks said they would sell Kennedy the time but would not give it to him. Kennedy argued that they were obliged to provide him 30 minutes at no cost because of Section 312. The court of appeals supported the FCC's denial of Kennedy's request. The law does not confer upon a candidate the privilege of using a broadcaster's facilities without charge.

21. *CBS* v. *FCC,* 453 U.S. 567 (1981).

Broadcasters may meet the demands of Section 312 by either giving the candidate free time or making time available for purchase, the court said. The networks had already given Kennedy's campaign considerable free time through its news coverage of the candidate.[22]

In September of 1999 the FCC reversed a decision it had made five years earlier and ruled that federal candidates who seek to buy broadcasting time cannot be limited to buying only 30- and 60-second spots. In 1994, the FCC had ruled that broadcasters could refuse to sell the longer spots. The 1999 ruling did not specify a length of time the candidates could buy, but the agency did note that five-minute spots might be better for the candidates.

Supporters of Section 312 see it as a means to permit candidates for federal office to use the important broadcast communication channels in this nation to talk to prospective voters. Opponents say Section 312 is government interference in broadcasters' operation of their business, and it can cause severe financial hardship if programming schedules are disrupted to facilitate political broadcasts.

When Congress adopted Section 312 in 1971, it also specified the highest rates that a broadcaster can charge a candidate for federal office for using station facilities. The general rule is that 45 days before a primary election and 60 days before a general election, the charge to a candidate cannot exceed the lowest rate the station charges its local advertisers for that particular time slot. At other times the rate must be "comparable" to what the station charges other advertisers. These rules contain other considerable details that are important but are too involved to outline here. Students who intend to enter broadcast sales should closely study Section 312 (a) (7) of 47 *United States Code.*

Although Section 312 applies only to candidates for federal office, a station that routinely denied candidates for state and local office reasonable access to communicate with voters would undoubtedly be sanctioned by the government. The FCC has interpreted Section 307 of the Communications Act, which outlines a licensee's public interest responsibilities, to bar any station from denying any candidate reasonable access simply to avoid obligations under the equal opportunity rules, which will be outlined next.

EQUAL OPPORTUNITY/EQUAL TIME RULE

Section 315 of the Communications Act outlines what are called the equal opportunity or **equal time rules.** These rules have been a part of the law since it was passed in 1934, although this section was substantially amended in 1959. The rules are quite simple. If a broadcasting station permits one legally qualified candidate for any elective public office to use its facilities, it must afford an equal opportunity for all other legally qualified candidates for the same office.

What does equal opportunity mean? It means equal time, equal facilities, and comparable costs. If John Smith buys one-half hour of television time on station WKTL to campaign for the office of mayor, other legally qualified candidates for that office must be allowed to purchase one-half hour of time as well. If Smith is able to use the station's equipment to prerecord his talk, other candidates must have the same opportunity. If the station charges Smith $100 for the one-half hour of time, the station must charge his opponents $100.

22. *Kennedy for President Committee* v. *FCC,* 636 F. 2d 417 (1980).

The station does not have to solicit appearances by the other candidates; it merely must give them the opportunity to use the facilities if they request such use within one week of Smith's appearance. Finally, Section 315 does not provide a right of access to any candidate to use a station's facilities. Section 315 only applies if the station first chooses to permit one candidate to appear on the station. However, remember the earlier discussion about requirements that exist under Section 312 and the general public interest standards that govern station operation.

Section 315 specifically bars the station from censoring material in broadcasts made by political candidates. And the courts interpret this provision quite strictly. In 1992 an Atlanta television station received many complaints when it aired a conservative congressional candidate's graphic anti-abortion spot in the early evening. So when Daniel Becker tried to buy an additional 30 minutes of airtime to show the video "Abortion in America—The Real Story" between 4 p.m. and 5 p.m. on Sunday following an NFL football telecast, the station claimed the highly graphic video was indecent and refused to show it in the afternoon. The station said it would broadcast the video after midnight when children were less likely to be in the audience. Becker claimed this violated both the candidate access rule (Section 312; see pages 608–610) and the equal opportunity rule as well as his First Amendment rights.

Both the FCC and a U.S. district court sided with the station in the dispute,[23] but the District of Columbia U.S. Circuit Court of Appeals reversed these rulings. In September of 1996 the court said that permitting a broadcaster to schedule the airing of political spots based on the content of the spot violates both Section 312 and the no censorship provisions of Section 315. A rigid policy of refusing to provide access during prime-time hours would be "unreasonable," the court said, and would deny the candidate access to time periods with the greatest audience potential. This policy forces the candidate to choose between the content in the advertisement and the composition of the audience, the court added. "This self-censorship must surely frustrate the full and unrestricted discussion of political issues envisioned by Congress."[24]

Use of the Airwaves

Under Section 315 if one candidate gets the use of a broadcast facility, his or her opponents get to use the facility as well. What is a "use" under the law? Any presentation or appearance that features a candidate's voice or image is regarded as a "use" by the FCC. It is not a use if, for example, in a political advertisement an announcer simply recites the candidate's record or his or her position on an issue. Similarly, it is not a use if the candidate's voice or image is used by an opponent in one of his or her ads. But short of these exceptions most other appearances count, including appearances on TV entertainment programs like a situation comedy, guest shots on an entertainment talk show like the David Letterman program, and even appearances in televised feature films, sometimes made years earlier when the candidate was a professional performer.

23. *Gillett Communications of Atlanta, Inc.* v. *Becker,* 807 F. Supp. 757 (1992).
24. *Becker* v. *FCC,* 1 E.P.L.R. 580 (1996).

In 1959 the Congress amended Section 315 and carved out four rather broad exceptions to the meaning of the term "use." Since 1959 the FCC has liberally interpreted these exceptions to broaden them even more. The following appearances by a candidate do not constitute a use under the law. That is, an opponent cannot use one of these appearances as a justification for equal time from the station.

APPEARANCES BY A POLITICAL CANDIDATE THAT ARE NOT GOVERNED BY EQUAL OPPORTUNITY RULE

▪ Appearance in a bona fide newscast
▪ Appearance in a bona fide news interview show
▪ Appearance in the spot news coverage of a bona fide news event
▪ Incidental appearance in a news documentary

---

1. **The appearance by a candidate in a bona fide or legitimate newscast does not constitute use of the facility in the eyes of the law.** Section 315 will not be triggered. The FCC has ruled that appearances by political candidates on ABC's "Good Morning America," NBC's "Today," and CBS's "This Morning" are exempt from provisions of Section 315, as are interview shows such as "Oprah Winfrey," "Rosie O'Donnell," and "Sally Jessy Raphael." The agency considers all programs bona fide newscasts. The FCC ruled that an appearance in a news clip broadcast as a part of the program "McLaughlin Group" constitutes an appearance in a newscast.[25] But a candidate appearance during the panel discussion part of the program would not fall under the newscast exemption. If the newscaster or reporter who reads the news is a candidate for public office, this exemption does not apply to that candidacy. In an unusual case, TV reporter William Branch, a general assignment reporter for KVOR-TV in Sacramento, announced he was a candidate for town council in a nearby community. The station told him he would have to take an unpaid leave of absence if he chose to run for office because it could not afford to give his opponent free time equal to the time Branch appeared in the newscasts. Branch sought help from the FCC, arguing that his appearances in a bona fide newscast would not trigger Section 315. The FCC disagreed and a U.S. court of appeals supported the regulatory agency. "When a broadcaster's employees are sent out to cover a news story involving other persons . . . the bona fide news event is the activity engaged in by those other persons, not the work done by the employees covering the event," the three-judge panel ruled. Branch argued that this ruling extinguished his right to hold public office. The court disagreed; the ruling simply says the station will have to provide equal time for opposing candidates if the reporter is a candidate.[26]

25. *Telecommunications Research and Action Center* v. *FCC,* 26 F. 3d 185 (1994).
26. *Branch* v. *FCC,* 824 F. 2d 37 (1987).

2. **The appearance of a candidate in a bona fide news interview program does not constitute a use.** The key words are "bona fide." An appearance on "Meet the Press," which is a bona fide regularly scheduled news interview show, is not use of a broadcasting facility. But an appearance on "Meet the Candidates," a public affairs show created by a television station for the express purpose of interviewing candidates prior to an election, is use because it is not a bona fide news interview show. The show was created especially for the election campaign by the station and is not broadcast when electioneering is not in progress. Independent presidential candidate Lenora Fulani challenged a 1992 FCC ruling that an appearance by another independent candidate, Ross Perot, on ABC's "Nightline" was exempt from the equal time rule because this show was a bona fide news interview program. The ABC news program is typically broadcast each weeknight from 11:35 p.m. to 12:05 a.m. But the Perot broadcast was longer. It started with a one-hour documentary about Perot from 10 to 11 p.m. Then from 11:35 p.m. until 1:10 a.m. the network presented a live town meeting broadcast, a meeting in which Perot participated. ABC anchor Peter Jennings hosted this second program. When Fulani asked ABC for equal time the network refused, saying the Perot program was simply a longer version of the regularly scheduled "Nightline." Fulani appealed this rejection to the FCC, claiming that the 90-minute town meeting was much longer than a typical "Nightline" and that the network did not use the "Nightline" logo during the broadcast. However, ABC had used the town meeting format in previous "Nightline" programs. The FCC supported ABC, and Fulani challenged this ruling, claiming the agency's decision was arbitrary, capricious, and lacking any rational basis. But the U.S. Court of Appeals for the 2nd Circuit supported the FCC, noting that the agency had wide discretion to make such rulings.[27] Congress has given the agency broad authority to carry out the law, the court said. "This explicit delegation for the equal time provision in particular constitutes something more than the normal grant of authority permitting an agency to make ordinary rules and regulations, and counsels exceptional deference to FCC dispositions of equal opportunity claims," the court ruled.

3. **The appearance of a candidate in the spot news coverage of a bona fide news event is not use.** When candidate Smith is interviewed at the scene of a bad fire about the problems of arson in the city, this is not use in terms of Section 315. Political conventions are considered bona fide news events; therefore an appearance by a candidate at the convention can be broadcast without invoking Section 315.

4. **The appearance of a candidate in a news documentary is not a use if the appearance is incidental to the presentation of the subject of the program.** Imagine that during January 2000, Turner Sports decided to telecast a documentary on the great NBA teams of the last half of the 20th century. Included among the teams covered are the New York Knicks of the late 1960s and early 1970s. Bill

---

27. *Fulani* v. *FCC*, 49 F. 3d 904 (1995).

Bradley, a presidential candidate in 2000, was a member of the Knicks and is interviewed about the team. Would this appearance trigger Section 315? No, because Bradley is being interviewed because of his career as an NBA player, not his political candidacy. His appearance is incidental because the program is about basketball.

Debates between political candidates are considered bona fide news events, and the broadcast of these events will not initiate use of Section 315. This is true even if the broadcaster sponsors the debate, according to a 1984 ruling by the FCC. Prior to this ruling, an outside third party had to sponsor the debate before it was considered a news event. In both 1976 and 1980, for example, the League of Women Voters sponsored presidential debates that included only the candidates from the Democratic and Republican parties. Feminist Sonia Johnson, who ran for president with the Citizens Party in 1984, challenged this FCC policy after she was not permitted to take part in the nationally televised debates. She argued that exclusion from the debates effectively excluded her from winning the election and denied voters who were sympathetic to her cause, but who were unacquainted with her, the opportunity to vote for her. A U.S. court of appeals disagreed, ruling that Johnson did not enjoy a right under any federal law to be included in the televised debates.[28] By 1988 there was little pretense of outside sponsorship of the debates.

In 1996 the major television networks gave free time to Bill Clinton and Bob Dole to air their statements about major issues in the campaign. CBS and NBC did this within the scope of their evening newscasts and were not required to give time to other presidential candidates. ABC, PBS, and Fox aired the short statements at other times, and the FCC declared that such telecasts were on-the-spot coverage of bona fide news events and exempted the three networks from obligations under Section 315.

Press conferences held by political candidates are also normally considered bona fide news events and are exempt from the provisions of Section 315. A press conference held by President Jimmy Carter in February 1980, several months after he announced he was a candidate for re-election, was broadcast live by all the television networks. Carter's opponent for the Democratic nomination, Ted Kennedy, sought time from the television networks under the equal opportunity rule. The networks said no. The FCC agreed with the broadcasters; the press conference was a bona fide news event. The agency had ruled in 1975 that all press conferences featuring political candidates were exempt from Section 315 as news events. Kennedy appealed the ruling to the U.S. Court of Appeals for the District of Columbia Circuit and lost. The court said that to determine if the coverage of a news conference can be considered spot coverage of a bona fide news event, three criteria must be examined:

1. Was the press conference broadcast live? Coverage of spot news should be live coverage.
2. Was there any evidence of favoritism on the part of the broadcaster? Did the station just carry Carter's press conferences and ignore his opponent's conferences?

---

28. *Johnson* v. *FCC,* 829 F. 2d 157 (1987).

3. Finally, did the broadcaster make a good-faith judgment that the news conference was a bona fide news event?

In this case the press conference was carried live, the networks had covered Kennedy press conferences, and it was obvious that a determination had been made by the broadcasters that this was an important news event.[29]

Legally Qualified Candidates

The FCC has attempted to define who is and who is not a legally qualified candidate as precisely as possible (see boxed text).

A LEGALLY QUALIFIED CANDIDATE IS ANY PERSON

■ who publicly announces that he or she is a candidate for nomination or election to any local, county, state, or federal office, *and*

■ who meets the qualifications prescribed by law for that office, *and*

■ who qualifies for a place on the ballot or is eligible to be voted for by sticker or write-in methods, *and*

■ who was duly nominated by a political party that is commonly known and regarded as such or makes a substantial showing that he or she is a bona fide candidate.

The first requirement is clear; the candidate must say he or she is a candidate. The second requirement means that the individual must be qualified to hold the office. There is an age requirement for most elective offices. Residency requirements usually apply to legislative offices: A woman can't run for Congress in Arkansas' 1st District if she lives in the 2nd District. Only natural-born citizens qualify as candidates for president. The third requirement speaks for itself; the person's name must either appear on the ballot, or the individual must be an eligible write-in or sticker candidate. The last requirement is the most confusing. What is a substantial showing? What is a political party, "commonly known and regarded as such"? The FCC will answer a broadcaster's inquiries regarding matters such as these.

In primary elections, Section 315 applies to intraparty elections, not interparty elections. In a primary election Democrats run against Democrats, Republicans run against Republicans, Libertarians run against Libertarians. If there is an appearance by a Democrat, the other Democratic candidates for the same office must be afforded an equal opportunity. The station does not have to give Republicans or Libertarians or even independents the opportunity to make an appearance. During general elections, Section 315 applies across party lines since at this point all candidates are running against each other for the same office.

In primary elections, Section 315 applies to intraparty elections, not interparty elections.

---

29. *Kennedy for President Committee* v. *FCC,* 636 F. 2d 432 (1980).

Whereas only an appearance by the candidate himself or herself can trigger Section 315, appearances by supporters of the candidate trigger another regulation called the **Zapple Rule.** This rule was formulated by the FCC in response to a letter from Nicholas Zapple, who was a staff member on the Senate Subcommittee on Communications. This rule states that if a broadcaster permits the supporter of a candidate to make an appearance on the station, then the station must provide an equal opportunity for an appearance by supporters of other legally qualified candidates for the same office. In the FCC's 1972 "Report Regarding the Handling of Political Broadcasts," the agency outlined the Zapple Rule in this way:

> The commission held in "Zapple" that when a licensee sells time to supporters or spokesmen of a candidate during an election campaign who urge the candidate's election, discuss the campaign issues, or criticize an opponent then the licensee must afford comparable time to the spokesmen for an opponent. Known as the quasi-equal opportunity or political party corollary to the fairness doctrine, the "Zapple" doctrine is based on the equal opportunity requirement of Section 315 of the Communications Act; accordingly, free reply time need not be afforded to respond to a paid program.

Three last points need to be made about Section 315. First, since broadcasters are not permitted to censor the remarks of a political candidate, they are immune from libel suits based on those remarks. In 1959 the Supreme Court ruled that because stations cannot control what candidates say over the air, they should not be held responsible for the remarks. The candidate, however, can still be sued.[30] Second, ballot issues like school bond levies, initiatives, and referendums do not fall under Section 315. Finally, in 1986 a U.S. court of appeals ruled that the provisions of the equal opportunity rule do apply to electronic data transmission processes, such as teletext. Teletext is a system whereby the sender encodes data on the unused portion of a standard television signal and sends it through the airwaves. With proper decoding equipment, the receiver sees that data as text on the television screen. The FCC had ruled previously that none of the political affairs content regulations—Section 315, Section 312, or the fairness doctrine—applied to such data transmission services. The court of appeals agreed that neither Section 312 nor the fairness doctrine was applicable to teletext. But it said that the FCC could not exclude the application of Section 315, at least not without a rational reason. The court noted that teletext was capable of generating high-resolution graphics. It would seem, the court ruled, that if a pictorial representation of the candidate were transmitted via teletext with a message, this would satisfy the statutory definition of use under the federal statute.[31]

SUMMARY

Several rules govern political broadcasts carried by radio and television broadcasters. Section 312 of the Federal Communications Act states that broadcasters cannot have an across-the-board policy rejecting all paid and nonpaid appearances by candidates for federal office. A candidate's request must be evaluated and can be rejected only if it could cause serious disruption

30. *Farmers Educational and Cooperative Union of America* v. *WDAY,* 360 U.S. 525 (1959).

31. *Telecommunications Research and Action Center* v. *FCC,* 801 F. 2d 654 (1986), rehearing den. 806 F. 2d 1115 (1986).

of program schedules or might prompt an excessive number of equal-time requests. Although this rule applies only to requests from candidates for federal office, the government's mandate that broadcasters operate their stations in the public interest may very well include similar standards for the treatment by broadcasters of requests for access to air time from state and local candidates.

Section 315 states that if a broadcaster provides one candidate for office with the opportunity to use a station's broadcast facilities, all other legally qualified candidates for the same office must be given the same opportunity. The use of the station's facilities includes all appearances on the station with the exception of the following:

1. Bona fide newscasts
2. Bona fide news interview programs
3. Spot news coverage
4. Incidental appearance in a news documentary

Candidate press conferences and debates between candidates are considered spot news events. During primary elections, Section 315 applies only to candidates from the same political party running against each other to win the party's nomination to run in the general election.

NEWS AND PUBLIC AFFAIRS

While the FCC has been quite willing to impose content regulations on entertainment programming, the agency has purposely steered away from making similar rules regarding broadcast news. The violence ratings do not apply to television news, for example. The agency reinforced this position in May of 1998 when it rejected a petition to strip four Denver television station licenses on the grounds that the news programs on the stations are heavily saturated with violent content. A group called Media Watch asked the FCC to deny the station's license renewals because the news programming contained "toxic" levels of television violence, which in turn leads to "fear, disrespect, imitative behavior, desensitization and increased violent behavior." The agency responded by saying that "journalistic or editorial discretion in the presentation of news and public information is the core concept of the First Amendment free press guarantee."[32]

The agency has treated claims of the falsification of broadcast news in a similar fashion. It is common today to see reenactments of news events on the so-called infotainment programs like "Cops" or "Hard Copy." These programs are usually labeled as such, albeit in small letters in a rush of credits. Distortion or falsification in real news programs is a fairly rare occurrence and involves a good deal more than simply a disagreement between a news source and a producer with the way a story has been reported. The FCC's deliberate distortion rule is quite specific and states that the distortion or staging must be deliberately intended to slant or mislead—and this allegation must be supported by extrinsic evidence. For example,

32. Brooke, "F.C.C. Supports TV News."

independent witnesses must testify that they saw the staging. Also, the distortion or staging must involve a significant part of the news event, not a minor or incidental part of the news report. The FCC has refused to investigate "inaccurate embellishments concerning peripheral aspects of news reports or attempts at window dressing which concerned the manner of presenting the news, as long as the essential facts of the news stories to which these presentational devices were related were broadcast in an accurate manner."[33]

Complaints were made to the commission about such programs as "The Selling of the Pentagon" and "Hunger in America." CBS was accused of careless editing in the program on the Pentagon, editing that took quotations from various parts of a speech and made it appear that these separate statements were actually one statement. There were other questionable editing practices as well. In "Hunger in America" the same network showed viewers a baby that it claimed had died of malnutrition. Although many babies do die each week of malnutrition, the one photographed by the network had, in fact, died of other causes. The response of the FCC in "The Selling of the Pentagon" case is typical of how that agency handles such complaints. "Lacking evidence or documents that on their face reflect deliberate distortion, we believe that this government licensing agency cannot properly intervene," the commission ruled. "As we stated in the 'Hunger in America' ruling, the commission is not the national arbiter of truth." While taking a hands-off action itself, the agency reminded broadcasters, "The licensee must have a policy of requiring honesty of its news staff and must take reasonable precautions to see that news is fairly handled. The licensee's investigation of substantial complaints . . . must be a thorough, conscientious one, resulting in remedial action where appropriate." From this statement one can presume that obvious and blatant staging of news will be considered a disservice to the public interest but that the FCC is not capable of evaluating or monitoring the editing techniques of thousands of news departments. Errors will have to be serious and well documented before the commission will intervene. The agency took no action, for example, when ABC broadcast faked video footage of an alleged transfer of documents between a U.S. government official and a foreign agent. Embarrassment to the network was probably regarded as a sufficient penalty.

The FCC usually has the last word in such falsification matters, but in August of 1998 the U.S. Court of Appeals for the District of Columbia Circuit overturned an FCC decision exonerating CBS in a charge of news distortion and told the agency to re-examine the complaint. In 1994 the CBS news magazine show "60 Minutes" broadcast a segment highly critical of life in the post-communist Ukraine entitled "The Ugly Face of Freedom." Complaints were filed by Alexander Serafyn, an American of Ukrainian ancestry. Among other charges, Serafyn claimed that the program had broadcast quotes out of context, mistranslated words to paint a dark picture of life in the former Soviet republic, and refused the help of a Ukrainian professor of history who could have given the report needed context and perspective. Other viewers complained about the program as well. When the FCC rejected his complaints, Serafyn appealed. A unanimous ruling by a three-judge panel reversed the FCC decision, finding that the agency had acted arbitrarily and capriciously when it denied Serafyn's claims. The

33. *Galloway* v. *FCC,* 7878 F. 2d 16 (1985).

judges acknowledged that each complaint taken separately might not be sufficient to prove a claim of distortion, but the FCC must reconsider all the claims taken as a whole in determining whether the broadcast had distorted the news.[34]

OTHER CONTENT REGULATIONS

The fairness doctrine and two ancillary rules relating to political editorials and personal attacks have been the most controversial of all federal broadcast regulations. Supporters of these rules regard them as a lifeline to fairness and responsibility in broadcasting; opponents regard them as serious infringements on the broadcaster's First Amendment rights. In the 1980s the FCC announced it would no longer enforce the fairness doctrine and this decision was upheld in two separate appellate court rulings.[35] Broadcasters were unsatisfied for two reasons. The FCC left rules regarding personal attacks and political editorials intact, and the agency refused to totally abandon the fairness doctrine, even though it refused to enforce it. The National Association of Broadcasters has sought the repeal of all three restrictions, but the FCC has failed to act on this request. In 1998 the agency issued a public notice that the commissioners were deadlocked 2–2 on the issue, the chairman not taking part in the matter. In 1999 the District of Columbia U.S. Circuit Court of Appeals ordered the FCC to resolve this issue by either abandoning the rules or explaining in detail why it has not repealed or modified them. No timetable was set by the court.[36] What follows are brief outlines of all three rules.

The Fairness Doctrine

The fairness doctrine has two parts:

- Broadcasters must provide adequate time on their station for the discussion of important and controversial public issues.
- The broadcaster must ensure that in this coverage all significant viewpoints on these issues are represented in some way.

This doctrine grew from an FCC ruling in 1949 that permitted broadcasters to editorialize on important public matters.[37] Such editorialization was possible, the agency ruled, so long as the broadcaster made certain that other points of view in the particular issue were aired as well. Only rarely were stations sanctioned for violating the fairness doctrine. In 1969 the Supreme Court upheld the constitutionality of the fairness doctrine.[38] The fairness doctrine applies to news and public affairs broadcasts. It does not apply to entertainment programming, even though such programs often focus on controversial issues.[39] Only one time was the doctrine

---

34. Kirtley, "Second Guessing News Judgment."
35 *Syracuse Peace Council* v. *FCC*, 867 F. 2d 654 (1989) and *Arkansas AFL-CIO* v. *FCC*, 11 F. 3d 1430 (1993).
36. Cys, "The Fairness Doctrine."
37. *In the Matter of Editorializing by Broadcast Licensees*, 13 F.C.C. 1246 (1949).
38. *Red Lion Broadcasting Co.* v. *FCC*, 395 U.S. 367 (1969).
39. *Diocesan Union of Holy Name Societies of Rockville Center and Long Island Coalition for Life*, 41 F.C.C. 2d 497 (1973).

applied to advertising—in this case cigarette advertising[40]—and the FCC subsequently said this ruling had been a mistake and would not be repeated.[41]

PERSONAL ATTACKS AND POLITICAL EDITORIALS

Rules regarding personal attacks and political editorials are a separate part of the fairness doctrine.

PERSONAL ATTACKS

(a) When, during the presentation of views on a controversial issue of public importance, an attack is made upon the honesty, character, integrity or like personal qualities of an identified person or group, the licensee shall, within a reasonable time and in no event later than one week after the attack, transmit to the person or group attacked (1) notification of the date, time and identification of the broadcast; (2) a script or tape (or an accurate summary if a script or tape is not available) of the attack; and (3) an offer of a reasonable opportunity to respond over the licensee's facilities. (b) The provisions of paragraph (a) of this section shall not be applicable (1) to attacks on foreign groups or foreign public figures; (2) to personal attacks which are made by legally qualified candidates, their authorized spokesmen, or those associated with them in the campaign, or other such candidates, their authorized spokesmen, or persons associated with the candidates in the campaign; and (3) to bona fide newscasts, bona fide news interviews, and on-the-spot coverage of a bona fide news event (including commentary or analysis contained in the foregoing programs, but the provisions of paragraph (a) of this section shall be applicable to editorials of the licensee).

POLITICAL EDITORIALS

(c) Where a licensee, in an editorial, (i) endorses or (ii) opposes a legally qualified candidate or candidates, the licensee shall, within twenty-four hours after the editorial, transmit to respectively (i) the other qualified candidate or candidates for the same office or (ii) the candidate opposed in the editorial (1) notification of the date and time of the editorial; (2) a script or tape of the editorial; and (3) an offer of a reasonable opportunity for a candidate or a spokesman of the candidate to respond over the licensee's facilities: *Provided, however,* that where such editorials are broadcast within seventy-two hours prior to the day of the election, the licensee shall comply with the provisions of this paragraph sufficiently far in advance of the broadcast to enable the candidate or candidates to have a reasonable opportunity to prepare a response and to present it in a timely fashion.

---

40. *WCBS-TV: Applicability of the Fairness Doctrine to Cigarette Advertising,* 8 F.C.C. 2d 381 (1967), aff. 9 F.C.C. 2d 921 (1967).

41. *In the Matter of the Handling of Public Issues Under the Fairness Doctrine and the Public Interest Standards of the Communications Act,* 48 F.C.C. 2d 1 (1974).

The **personal attack rules** stem from FCC rulings in 1962 stating that when licensees broadcast what amounts to a personal attack on an individual or group within the community, they have an affirmative obligation to notify the target of the attack of the broadcast and offer the target an opportunity to respond. In 1967 these earlier decisions were clarified and made more specific with the publication of the personal attack rules.

As you can see from the rules, the licensee's obligations are quite specific. It is important to remember that just naming someone in an editorial or commentary does not necessarily constitute a personal attack. On the other hand, the rules apply to attacks made by everyone, not just by the station itself.

Paragraph (b) of the rules exempts attacks made by candidates and their followers on other candidates and their followers. Newscasts, news interviews, and on-the-spot news coverage are also exempted from the personal attack. Paragraph (c) outlines licensee obligations with regard to editorial endorsements of candidates.

THE FIRST AMENDMENT

Broadcasting stations are not common carriers; that is, they have the right to refuse to do business with anyone they choose. During 1969 and 1970 two groups, the Democratic National Committee and a Washington, D.C., organization known as Business Executives Movement for Peace, sought to buy time from television stations and networks to solicit funds for their protest of the Vietnam War and to voice their objections to the way the war was being waged by the government. Broadcasters rebuffed these groups on the grounds that airing such controversial advertisements and programming would evoke the fairness doctrine, and they would then be obligated to ensure that all sides of the controversy were aired. Such action was a nuisance and could be costly. The broadcasters told the Democratic committee and the business executives that one of their basic policies was not to sell time to any individual or group seeking to set forth views on controversial issues.

When this policy was challenged before the FCC, the commission sided with the broadcasters, noting that it was up to each individual licensee to determine how best to fulfill fairness doctrine obligations. But the U.S. Court of Appeals for the District of Columbia Circuit reversed the FCC ruling, stating that the right of the public to receive information is deeply rooted in the First Amendment. A ban on editorial advertising, the court ruled, "leaves a paternalistic structure in which licensees and bureaucrats decide what issues are important, whether to fully cover them, and the format, time and style of coverage." This kind of system, the court ruled, is inimical to the First Amendment.[42]

> It may unsettle some of us to see an antiwar message or a political party message in the accustomed place of a soap or beer commercial. . . . We must not equate what is habitual with what is right or what is constitutional. A society already so saturated with commercialism can well afford another outlet for speech on public issues. All that we may lose is some of our apathy.

---

42. in re *Business Executives Movement for Peace* v. *FCC,* 450 F. 2d 642 (1971).

The victory of the business organization and the Democrats was short-lived, for by a 7–2 vote, the U.S. Supreme Court overturned the appellate court ruling. Stations have an absolute right to refuse to sell time for advertising dealing with political campaigns and controversial issues, the court ruled. To give the FCC the power over such advertising runs the risk of enlarging government control over the content of broadcast discussion of public issues.

In response to the argument that by permitting broadcasters to refuse such advertising, we place in their hands the power to decide what the people shall see or hear on important public issues, Justice Burger wrote:

> For better or worse, editing is what editors are for; and editing is the selection and choice of material. That editors—newspaper or broadcast—can and do abuse this power is beyond doubt, but that is no reason to deny the discretion Congress provided. Calculated risks of abuse are taken in order to preserve high values.[43]

"For better or worse, editing is what editors are for."

The court was badly fractured on this case, and Justices Brennan and Marshall dissented. Only two other justices—Stewart and Rehnquist—joined the chief justice in his opinion. The remainder joined in overturning the court of appeals ruling, but for their own reasons.

Finally, the high court used the First Amendment to strike down a congressional statute forbidding all noncommercial educational broadcasting stations that receive money from the Corporation for Public Broadcasting from editorializing on any subject at all.[44] The government attempted to justify the law on two grounds. It argued that a ban on editorials was needed to prevent noncommercial broadcasting stations from being coerced, as a result of getting money from the federal government, into becoming vehicles for government propaganda. Also, it said the law was needed to keep stations from becoming convenient targets for capture by private interest groups wishing to express their own partisan viewpoints. These justifications were insufficient, wrote Justice William Brennan for the five-member majority. The ban on all editorials by every station that receives CPB funds is too broad and far exceeds what is necessary to protect against the risk of governmental interference or to prevent the public from assuming that editorials by public broadcasting stations represent the official views of government. "The regulation impermissibly sweeps within its prohibition a wide range of speech by wholly private stations on topics that do not take a directly partisan stand or that have nothing whatever to do with federal, state or local government," Brennan wrote. And the ban really isn't effective, since the very same opinions that cannot be expressed by the station's management may be aired by someone appearing on a program as a guest. Chief Justice Burger and Justices Rehnquist, White, and Stevens dissented. Public broadcasting stations are still prohibited from endorsing political candidates, however.

SUMMARY

The government exercises limited control over the content of public affairs broad-casts. The FCC has thus far rejected all complaints that television news coverage was slanted or staged and has made it difficult for those who seek to pursue this cause with the agency. The most

43. *CBS v. Democratic National Committee,* 412 U.S. 94 (1973).
44. *FCC v. League of Women Voters,* 468 U.S. 912 (1984).

serious imposition on public affairs programming, the fairness doctrine, has not been enforced since the mid-1980s. The agency does enforce specific rules regarding personal attacks and political editorials. The Supreme Court has given broadcasters the right to determine whether to air specific editorial advertising and has struck down a statute that forbade public broadcasting stations from telecasting editorial opinions.

REGULATION OF NEW TECHNOLOGY

One of the most perplexing aspects of contemporary mass media law is the attempt by the government to regulate or control the bewildering array of new electronic information-transmitting technology that has burst on the scene in recent years. In the pages that follow, we focus on the regulation of the newer broadcast services, especially cable television. We will also briefly consider some aspects of the regulation of low-power television (LPTV), multipoint distribution services (MDS), satellite master antenna television (SMATV), and private earth stations, or dish antennas. Attempts to regulate the new mass media are coming at every level and occur at a pace equal to the introduction of the new technology. Comprehensive rules regarding such technology will take a long time to develop. Cable television has been around since the late 1940s, yet it was not until 1984 that the Congress finally adopted what might be called comprehensive cable television regulations.

CABLE TELEVISION

Cable television, the oldest of the new technologies, first appeared in the late 1940s. At that time it was called community antenna television (CATV). In rural communities where television reception was poor because of distance or topography, entrepreneurs installed large antennas on hilltops to receive the incoming television signals and then transmitted these signals (for a small price) to local homeowners via coaxial cable. The FCC first asserted its jurisdiction of cable or CATV in the early 1960s. But the agency had to move tenuously at first because its right to regulate cable television was not clearly established. Cable is not broadcast; signals travel through wires, not the airwaves. There is no scarcity of spectrum space, that important factor that justifies government regulation of broadcasting. Cable is not a common carrier, as are telephone and telegraph. The FCC authority to regulate these point-to-point services does not establish its right to regulate cable. It took more than 20 years, with the adoption of the Cable Communications Policy Act of 1984, before FCC jurisdiction over cable was firmly established.

FEDERAL LEGISLATION REGULATING CABLE TELEVISION

Two federal laws provide the foundation of the regulation of cable television. The first measure, the comprehensive Cable Communications Policy Act of 1984, was a cable-friendly measure designed to foster the orderly growth of this new medium. Cable flourished under this law. By the 1990s nearly all American homes had access to cable television, and more than 60 percent of all Americans received their television via cable. But viewers, and then members of Congress, became angry at many heavy-handed policies adopted by the cable industry using the freedom it had been granted under the 1984 legislation. Viewers complained about escalating cable rates among other things. In 1992 the Congress adopted the Cable Television Consumer Protection and Competition Act, a decidedly not cable-friendly measure that imposed rate regulations on most cable systems, directed the FCC to develop mandatory service standards for cable television, and greatly strengthened the competitive position of local, over-the-air television stations vis-à-vis cable. The 1984 law remains the basic regulatory measure. Its most important provisions are outlined on the following pages. It will be noted where the 1992 law has modified this legislation.

Viewers complained about escalating cable rates among other things.

The Cable Communications Policy Act of 1984 (hereafter Cable Act) was adopted after decades of crazy-quilt regulation at the federal, state, and local levels. The act was needed because some state and local governments were attempting to assert increased control over an industry that had become increasingly national in scope. In the summer of 1988, in a decision regarding the right of the FCC to establish certain technical standards for cable television, the Supreme Court read the new Cable Act in an expansive fashion, giving the FCC assurances that its regulation of the medium would be supported under the law.[45] Attorney Michael Meyerson points out in the Georgia Law Review that to understand the law, it is important to recognize that it is a compromise.[46] Representatives of the cable industry and the cities—the government units that award cable franchises—negotiated for three years before a bill was drafted that both could find acceptable.

Purpose of the Law

The purposes of this legislation are enumerated in Section 601 of the Cable Act itself. They are as follows:

1. To establish a national policy concerning cable communications
2. To establish franchise procedures and standards that encourage the growth and development of cable systems and that ensure that cable systems are responsive to the needs and interests of the local community
3. To establish guidelines for the exercise of federal, state, and local authority with respect to the regulation of cable systems
4. To ensure and encourage that cable communications provide the widest possible diversity of information sources and services to the public
5. To establish a process that protects cable operators against unfair denials of renewal by franchising authorities and that provides for an orderly process for consideration of renewal proposals

45. *New York City* v. *FCC,* 108 S. Ct. 1637 (1988).
46. Myerson, "Cable Communications Policy Act," 543.

Jurisdiction and Franchises

The federal government has jurisdiction to regulate cable television, but has given local governments the power to impose a variety of obligations on cable operators. The local government is what is called the "franchising authority"; it is given the power to grant the cable system the right to operate in a particular area. The local government awards a franchise agreement to the cable system operator. Throughout the history of cable television, local governments typically awarded cable operators an exclusive franchise to operate in an area. Cable companies were forced to bid against each other for what was in effect a monopoly. The policy of awarding exclusive franchises was questioned, but not outlawed in a 1986 Supreme Court ruling, *Los Angeles* v. *Preferred Communications.*[47] The case involved a challenge to the city of Los Angeles' policy of granting exclusive franchises. While the high court did not make a direct ruling on this matter, language in the unanimous decision suggested that cable television enjoyed a fuller First Amendment protection than did broadcast television. "Cable television partakes of some of the aspects of speech and the communication of ideas as do the traditional enterprises of newspaper and book publishers, public speakers and pamphleteers," wrote Justice Rehnquist. Granting cable television a full measure of First Amendment protection, of course, would make exclusive franchise agreements unconstitutional. Congress resolved the matter in 1992 when it barred the awarding of exclusive franchises. Practically, only one cable system per (most) neighborhood(s) or area(s) is economically feasible at this time. But real competition is not unlikely in the future as the telephone companies and other enterprises enter the picture. The 1984 statute speaks of "services" and "facilities and equipment." "Services" generally means programming. "Facilities and equipment" refers to hardware of the system and the physical capabilities of the system, such as channel capacity, two-way or one-way, and so on. Local governments are generally barred from establishing requirements for service or programming but are given a wide latitude to establish standards for equipment and facilities. The local government can insist that a cable operator provide broad categories of programming to meet the needs of children, different ethnic groups, or others and can insist that the cable operator provide public access channels for citizens to use.

Both the 1984 and the 1992 cable laws contained provisions that gave the FCC substantial power to control the rates that cable television systems charge their customers. Congress changed its mind on this matter. The 1996 Telecommunications Act immediately abolished rate regulation for small cable systems, that is, systems serving less than 1 percent of all subscribers in the United States and unaffiliated with a larger system. Regulation of the rates for other cable systems ceased in March of 1999. Regulation would no longer be needed, the Congress presumed, because two alternative systems—the delivery of television signals through local telephone lines and the 18-inch direct broadcast satellite (DBS) dishes—would compete with cable, and this competition would lower prices. But that did not happen. The presumed competition failed to materialize, and cable rates continued to climb, by 22 percent between early 1996 and early 1999.[48] The competition fizzled because the alternative delivery systems

47. 476 U.S. 488 (1986).
48. Gomery, "Cable TV Rates"and Labaton, "Cable Rates Rising."

failed to live up to their early promise. Telephone companies that were expected to scoop up cable companies and offer expanded service through telephone lines were seduced instead by the Internet. And while DBS was attractive to many viewers who wanted more movie choices and a fuller sports programming menu, it had drawbacks that tended to stifle its growth. Federal regulations prohibited the satellite systems from carrying local stations, so viewers still had to use an antenna or a cable system to watch the local news and other local programs. And viewers with more than one set who wanted to watch different channels at the same time had to have two or more decoder boxes, which added extra cost to the system. Cable companies generally do not charge extra for additional cable drops for multiple receivers. In 1999 Congress passed and President Clinton signed legislation permitting DBS services to transmit programming broadcast by local television stations. Provisions in the law do require satellite operators to cut off subscriber access to network (ABC, CBS, NBC, Fox, etc.) programming carried on distant stations that might compete with local broadcasts of the same network programming.[49] The measure also provides that DBS operators may introduce the local stations in a piecemeal fashion, but by 2002 if a DBS service carries any local stations in a community, it must carry all local stations.

Cable Operators and Local Broadcasters

Historically the government required all cable operators to retransmit the signals of all local television stations. These were called the "must-carry rules" and were instituted to protect local broadcasters. By the 1980s, when cable networks proliferated, many cable operators found the rules to be onerous because they required operators to carry local over-the-air stations in preference to the more attractive (and lucrative) cable networks. Despite the so-called lack of scarcity in cable, most systems were limited to 36 channels. The must-carry rules were challenged, and in 1985 a U.S. court of appeals ruled them to be a violation of the First Amendment.[50] By forcing a cable operator to carry a local station, the government denied the cable operator his or her First Amendment rights to communicate some other kind of programming. In other words, the court saw the must-carry rules as a content-based regulation. Attempts by the government to recast the rules failed to win court approval as well.[51] The 1992 cable law attempted to strengthen the position of the local broadcaster and contained substantially modified must-carry rules. Under this law the local broadcaster could either insist that the cable operator retransmit the station's signal to subscribers or forbid the cable operator from retransmitting the signal unless he or she paid what is called a retransmission fee. The application of the must-carry provisions varied with the channel capacity of the cable system. Small systems with less than 12 channels, for example, only had to carry three local commercial stations and one noncommercial station. Larger cable systems had to carry most or all local stations. Independent local stations with limited popularity insisted on cable carriage; popular network-affiliated stations often sought the retransmission fee.

---

49. Clausing, "Satellite TV Is Poised."
50. *Quincy Cable* v. *FCC*, 768 F. 2d 1434 (1985).
51. *Century Communications* v. *FCC*, 835 F. 2d 292 (1987).

Congress justified the new rules with the argument that 60 percent of Americans receive their television signals via cable. The heart of the American broadcasting system has consistently been local broadcasting. If cable operators are free to refuse to carry local broadcasters on their cable systems, this action could cause serious harm to the local stations. Cable operators said this fear was groundless, that it would be imprudent of them to drop the retransmission of popular local stations. But many local stations are not that popular, the broadcasters said, and the cable operator earns substantially more revenue by carrying a cable channel than by retransmitting a local broadcast signal. Many of the less popular channels could be abandoned and ultimately die.

Turner Broadcasting, which operates several cable channels that might be displaced on cable systems if the must-carry rules were applied, challenged the new rules. Four substantive federal court rulings were handed down before the matter was finally settled. A U.S. district court upheld the new rules in 1993.[52] In 1994 the U.S. Supreme Court upheld the rules in principle, but ordered the lower court to take testimony to see if the arguments put forth by the government to sustain the rules could in fact be supported by facts.[53] The lower court supervised more than 18 months of fact finding and in 1995, in a 2–1 vote, once again upheld the constitutionality of the rules.[54]

In the spring of 1997 the U.S. Supreme Court finally ended the long-running legal saga when it affirmed the lower court ruling in a 5–4 vote.[55] The high court in 1994 had rejected the argument of Turner Broadcasting and others who challenged the law that it was a violation of the First Amendment because it was not "content neutral." In other words, opponents of the legislation asserted that the congressional rule favored one kind of programming (local-over-the-air broadcasts) over another (cable-channels) based on the content of the programs. "It is true," Justice Kennedy wrote in the 1994 ruling, "that the must-carry provisions distinguish between speakers in the television programming market. But they do so based only upon the manner in which the speakers transmit their messages to viewers, not upon the messages they carry."[56] Because the court had found the rule to be content neutral, the government merely had to show that the policy furthered an important governmental interest without burdening speech more than necessary. The government argued that the rule was justified in order to preserve the benefits of free, over-the-air programming; that it promoted the widespread dissemination of information from a multiplicity of sources; and that it promoted fair competition in the TV programming market. Four of the five justices who supported the must-carry rules were satisfied that the government had evidence to support all three interests. Justice Stephen Breyer, the fifth vote, said he did not agree that the rules were needed to promote fair competition in the market. In the end, the case was decided less on free speech grounds and more on the high court's determination that Congress had done its homework in passing these rules and it would be improper for the court to "substitute its judgment for the reasonable conclusion of a legislative body."[57]

52. *Turner Broadcasting System, Inc. v. FCC,* 819 F. Supp. 32 (1993).
53. *Turner Broadcasting System, Inc. v. FCC,* 114 S. Ct. 2445 (1994).
54. *Turner Broadcasting System, Inc. v. F.C.C.,* D.C.D.C. No. 92-2247 (1995).
55. *Turner Broadcasting System, Inc. v. FCC,* 117 S. Ct. 1174 (1997).
56. *Turner Broadcasting System, Inc. v. FCC,* 114 S. Ct. 2445 (1994).
57. *Turner Broadcasting System, Inc. v. FCC,* 117 S. Ct. 1174 (1997).

Programming and Freedom of Expression

The FCC has imposed on cable systems that originate programming many of the same content rules that govern over-the-air television. The equal time rules, the "lowest unit rate" rule for political advertising, the candidate access rules, the sponsor identification rule, the personal attack and political editorial rules, and many others apply to cable-originated programs. Federal rules prohibit the broadcast of obscenity on over-the-air television; similar rules apply to cable. The FCC has also ruled that broadcasters must limit their broadcast of indecent material to those hours when children are not likely to be in the television viewing audience, between 10 p.m. and 6 a.m. (see page 604). But the Congress and the courts have, in the past, given cable television operators far greater leeway in the broadcast of indecency. Federal courts, for example, have consistently struck down attempts by the states to bar cable companies from transmitting indecent or adult programming but denied cable operators any right to censor programming.[58] The 1984 Cable Act required that every cable operator provide, on request from a subscriber, a lock box device that permits the subscriber to block out the reception of specific channels. The 1992 law contained hastily drafted provisions that *permitted* cable operators to prohibit indecent programming on the commercial leased-access channels and on the public access channels available to government and public schools. If the operator decided to permit indecent programming on the commercially leased channels, these signals had to be scrambled and subscribers could only view these channels by requesting access in writing 30 days in advance of the viewing. In 1993 these provisions were declared to be unconstitutional by the U.S. Court of Appeals for the District of Columbia Circuit because they restricted speech protected by the First Amendment.[59] But two years later the full court sitting en banc reversed this earlier ruling. Then the court ruled that the provisions that *permitted* the cable operator to ban indecent programming from the access channels didn't involve any action by the government. The censorship is the result of an action by the cable system operator, a private party. Hence there were no First Amendment implications to these provisions.[60] In June of 1996 a badly splintered Supreme Court voided some of these new cable rules but sustained other portions of the law. The court sustained the portion of the law that allowed the cable operator to ban patently offensive programming from the leased-access channels but struck down the regulation that required cable operators to scramble such programming and force subscribers to ask for access in writing. This latter rule limited what subscribers could see and constituted an invasion of their privacy by forcing them to acknowledge in writing that they wanted to see such programming, the court said. At the same time, the high court struck down that portion of the law that gave cable operators the right to ban indecent programming from the government access channels. The court said there was no history of problems of the transmission of indecency on such channels and indicated a concern that conservative cable operators might try to control the kind of programming telecast on public access channels, traditionally the haven of nonprofit organizations

---

58. See, for example, *Home Box Office* v. *Wilkinson,* 531 F. Supp. 987 (1982) and *Jones* v. *Wilkinson,* 800 F. 2d 989 (1986), aff'd 480 U.S. 926 (1987).
59. *Alliance for Community Media* v. *FCC,* 10 F. 3d 812 (1993).
60. *Alliance for Community Media* v. *FCC,* 56 F. 3d 105 (1995).

who seek to communicate with the larger audience.[61] Several opinions were written in the case, with members of the court shifting from majority to minority status depending on the particular rule under consideration.

In December of 1998 a special three-judge panel of the U.S. District Court for Delaware struck down Section 505 of the 1996 Communications Decency Act, which required the distributors of adult programming over cable television to completely scramble both the video and audio signals, regardless of whether customers requested the programming to be scrambled. The law was aimed at protecting children from what is called "signal bleed," or incomplete scrambling. When signal bleed occurs viewers can see and hear portions of the scrambled program. Programming distributors who could not fulfill this obligation were told to confine the transmission of this adult programming to the hours between 10 p.m. and 6 a.m. Playboy Entertainment challenged the provision, arguing that cable operators who could not afford the expensive scrambling technology would simply stop carrying this kind of programming rather than risk violating the law. The court ruled that while the government had a legitimate interest in attempting to shield young people from the adult programming, Section 505 was not the least restrictive means to fulfill this interest. The court said another provision in the CDA, which requires cable operators to supply blocking devices to subscribers who want them to screen out such channels, accomplishes the same goal without substantially interfering with the program distributors' First Amendment rights. In May of 2000 the Supreme Court affirmed this ruling, noting that cable television, unlike over-the-air television, enjoys the highest level of First Amendment protection.[62]

The Cable Act has established that third parties—that is, persons other than the cable operator or the local government—must have access to the cable system. Several means are provided for such access. The local franchising authorities are permitted to require that the cable operator provide public access and government and educational access channels. A public access channel is set aside for free public use on a nondiscriminatory, first-come, first-served basis. Neither the cable operator nor the government can censor what appears on such a channel. The franchising authority can prescribe limited (content-neutral) time, place, and manner rules for the public access channel, such as deciding that the access channel will give each user 30 minutes of time or that persons must sign up three days before the date they wish to use the channel. But these are about the only limits. The government and educational channels are used either by schools or to broadcast public hearings or city council meetings. These channels are to be programmed as the government sees fit.

Commercial access channels must also be provided by the cable operator. The law provides that a certain number of channels must be set aside for use by "unaffiliated programmers" at reasonable rates. The cable operator cannot control the content of these programs. The number of channels that must be set aside for commercial access depends on the number of activated channels in the cable system. An activated channel is one that is being used or is

Commercial access channels must also be provided by the cable operator.

---

61. *Denver Area Educational Telecommunications Consortium Inc.* v. *FCC; Alliance for Community Media* v. *FCC,* 1 E.P.L.R. 331 (1996); see also Greenhouse, "High Court Splits," A1.

62. *Playboy Entertainment Group, Inc.* v. *U.S.,* 30 F. Supp. 2d 702 (1998); *U.S* v *Playboy Entertainment Group,* No.98-1682.

available for use. Systems with fewer than 36 channels need not have any commercial access channels; those with 36 to 54 channels must set aside 10 percent of the channels for commercial access. Systems with more than 54 channels must reserve 15 percent of these channels for commercial access. The cable operator can set the price and conditions of use for these channels, so long as they are "reasonable." Costs cannot have anything to do with content; that is, a cable operator cannot charge someone who puts on a conservative talk show $100 per hour and someone who puts on a liberal talk show $500. However, the cable operator can set different rates for different categories of program; i.e., news programs cost $50 per hour, movies $100 per hour.

Whoever runs the public access channels can ask a user to sign an agreement that he or she will not broadcast obscenity while on the air, and of course any programmer who does broadcast obscenity can be punished after the telecast. But the public access channels are supposed to be free from close government scrutiny. That is why the law relieves the cable operator of any liability for the broadcast of any obscenity, libel, false advertising, or invasion of privacy that appears on the access channels.

Access to Information and Privacy

Cable operators are not permitted to redline, that is, refuse to wire one portion of a franchise area because the citizens are poor or because most persons would not subscribe to the cable. Protection of subscribers' right to privacy is a special concern. The prospect of widespread use of two-way cable television—something that hasn't happened yet—gives the cable company the opportunity to gather an immense amount of data on subscribers. Products that are ordered via television, films that are watched, votes on public referendums would be recorded by the system's computer for legitimate reasons. But the use of this kind of data by the cable company for other purposes would surely violate the privacy of the subscriber. Even users of one-way cable provide the cable company with some kinds of information subscribers might not like to have widely known. The names of persons who subscribe to adult movie channels is one example. The Cable Act states that a cable company can collect "personally identifiable information" for only two purposes: (1) to obtain the information that is necessary to serve the subscriber and (2) to search for unauthorized reception of the cable signal. All personally identifiable information must be destroyed once it has been used for the purpose it was gathered for, and the cable operator cannot disclose such information, even to the government, unless the government can establish a compelling reason to have this data that outweighs the subscriber's right to privacy. The subscriber must be told at least once a year what kind of data is being collected and is permitted to see this information and correct it if it is in error.

OTHER TELECOMMUNICATIONS SERVICES

The FCC maintains the right to regulate other new broadcast services. Multipoint distribution services have the configuration of traditional over-the-air broadcasting stations and are controlled by the FCC rather than local government. An MDS is wireless cable; the operator transmits television signals via microwave signals to subscribers who are equipped with a special antenna and a device that converts the microwave signal to one that can be received through a television set. Operation of such systems is regulated by federal law. In 1983 the FCC decided to allocate eight microwave channels per market for commercial use, setting off a stampede for the MDS licenses. The FCC scheduled lotteries to determine which of the 16,000 applicants would get the thousand licenses, but it took two years for the lotteries to occur. Even then they were held under a legal cloud as minority and female applicants challenged the FCC licensing process.

The Cable Act has given the local governments some control over the regulation of satellite master antenna television. The SMATVs are really private cable companies that service large apartment and condominium complexes. The complex owner sets up antennas and provides residents with television services. Congress was concerned that these television viewers receive as many of the benefits of cable television as regular cable subscribers do and gave local government limited power to franchise such operations and establish levels of performance, as they can with cable operators.

In 1982 the FCC authorized the development of what is called low-power television, or LPTV. LPTV stations broadcast no more than 10 miles in one direction. They are really neighborhood stations. The process of licensing these stations through lotteries has gone very slowly.

SUMMARY

The power of the FCC to regulate cable television was a clouded issue for many years. Slowly but surely, the commission, with the permission of the courts, moved to regulate this new technology. In 1984 both the Supreme Court and the Congress gave the FCC what seemed to be clear jurisdiction to set broad rules for government cable casting. But a subsequent court of appeals ruling has cast some doubt on all government regulation of cable.

The Cable Communications Policy Act of 1984 is a comprehensive measure setting policies and standards for the regulation of cable television. The 1992 Cable Television Consumer Protection and Competition Act made some modifications in the earlier law. Local governments are given the primary responsibility under this measure to regulate the cable systems in their communities. They may issue franchises, collect franchise fees, and renew franchises. The Cable Act also provides for the inclusion of public, government, and commercial access channels. It also makes provisions to protect subscribers' right to privacy. The FCC does retain the power to regulate other forms of communications technology, however, including MDSs and low-power television.

BIBLIOGRAPHY ⟶

Andrews, Edmund. "Court Upholds a Ban on 'Indecent' Broadcast Programming." *The New York Times,* 1 July 1995, A9.

Bernstein, Andrew A. "Access to Cable, Natural Monopoly, and the First Amendment." *Columbia Law Review* 86 (1986):1663.

Botein, Michael. "Who Came Out Ahead in the Cable Act?" *Channels,* March/April 1985, 14.

Brooke, James. "The F.C.C. Supports TV News as Free Speech." *The New York Times,* 3 May 1998, A13.

Brown, Rhonda. "Ad Hoc Access: The Regulation of Editorial Advertising on Television and Radio." *Yale Law and Policy Review* 6 (1988):449.

Clausing, Jeri. "Satellite TV Is Poised for New Growth." *The New York Times,* 26 November 1999, C1.

Cowan, Geoffrey. *See No Evil.* New York: Simon & Schuster, 1979.

Cys, Richard L. "The Fairness Doctrine—Still Waiting After All These Years." *Washington State Association of Broadcasters Bulletin,* August 1999, 5.

———. "Learn a Lesson From Other Broadcasters' Mistakes." *WSAB Bulletin,* June 1998, 4.

"FCC Launches Attack in Indecency." *Broadcasting,* 20 April 1987, 35.

Fogarty, Joseph R., and Marcia Spielholz. "FCC Cable Jurisdiction: From Zero to Plenary in Twenty-Five Years." *Federal Communications Law Journal* 37 (1979):361.

Gomery, Douglas. "Cable TV Rates: Not a Pretty Picture." *American Journalism Review,* July/August 1998, 66.

Greenhouse, Linda. "High Court Splits on Indecency Law Cable TV." *The New York Times,* 29 June 1996, A1.

Gregory, Robert S. "Regulating Cable Television: Quincy Cable's Unnatural Approach to Cable's Natural Monopoly." *New York School Law Review* 31 (1986):591.

Kirtley, Jane. "Second Guessing News Judgment." *American Journalism Review,* October 1998, 86.

Labaton, Stephen. "Cable Rates Rising As Industry Nears End of Regulation." *The New York Times,* 3 March 1999, A1.

Levi, Lili. "The Hard Case of Broadcast Indecency." *New York University Review of Law and Social Change* 20 (1992–93):49.

McQueen, Anjelta. "Educational Value Lacking in Children's TV." *Seattle Post-Intelligencer,* 28 June 1999, A3.

Meyerson, Michael. "The Cable Communications Policy Act of 1984: A Balancing Act on the Coaxial Wires." *Georgia Law Review* 19 (1985):543.

Mifflin, Lawrie. "Fight Looms Over an Age-Based TV Ratings Plan." *The New York Times,* 11 December 1996, A1.

———. "Revisions in TV Ratings Called Imminent." *The New York Times,* 16 June 1997, B1.

———. "Study Finds TV Networks Fail in Alerts to Sex and Violence." *The New York Times,* 25 September 1998, A17.

———. "TV Ratings Accord Comes Under Fire From Both Flanks," *The New York Times,* 11 July 1997, A1.

Pember, Don R. *Mass Media in America.* 6th ed. New York: Macmillan, 1992.

Robbins, Vicky H. "Indecency on Cable Television—A Barren Battleground for Regulation of Programming Content." *St. Mary's Law Journal* 15 (1985):417.

Robinson, Glen O., and Ernest Gelhorn. *The Administrative Process.* St. Paul, Minn.: West Publishing, 1974.

Sterngold, James. "Lessons Not Quite Ready for Prime Time." *The New York Times,* 28 March 1999, D5.

GLOSSARY

A

absolute privilege An immunity from libel suits granted to government officials and others based on remarks uttered or written as part of their official duties.

absolutist theory The proposition that the First Amendment is an absolute, and that government may adopt no laws whatsoever that abridge freedom of expression.

actual damages Damages awarded to a plaintiff in a lawsuit based on proof of actual harm to the plaintiff.

actual malice A fault standard in libel law: knowledge before publication that the libelous material was false or reckless disregard of the truth or falsity of the libelous matter.

administrative agency An agency, created and funded by the Congress, whose members are appointed by the president and whose function is to administer specific legislation, such as law regulating broadcasting and advertising.

admonition to a jury Instructions from a judge to a trial jury to avoid talking to other persons about the trial they are hearing and to avoid news broadcasts and newspaper or magazine stories that discuss the case or issues in the case.

Alien and Sedition Acts of 1798 Laws adopted by the Federalist Congress aimed at stopping criticism of the national government by Republican or Jeffersonian editors and politicians.

amici curiae "Friends of the court"; persons who have no specific legal stake in a lawsuit but are allowed to appear on behalf of one of the parties in a case.

appellant The party who initiates or takes the appeal of a case from one court to another.

appellate court(s) A court that has both original and appellate jurisdiction; a court to which cases are removed for an appeal.

appellee The person in a case against whom the appeal is taken; that is, the party in the suit who is not making the appeal.

appropriation In the law of privacy, use of a person's name or likeness without consent for advertising or trade purposes.

arraignment The first official court appearance made by a criminal defendant at which he or she is formally charged with an offense and called on to plead guilty or not guilty to the charges contained in the state's indictment or information.

ascertainment A procedure established by the Federal Communications Commission that instructs broadcast licensees in the manner in which they are to determine important problems and issues in a community.

B

bait-and-switch advertising An illegal advertising strategy in which the seller baits customers by an advertisement with a low-priced model of a product but then switches customers who seek to buy the product to a much higher-priced model by telling them that the cheaper model does not work well or is no longer in stock.

bench-bar-press guidelines Informal agreements among lawyers, judges, police officials, and journalists about what should and should not be published or broadcast about a criminal suspect or criminal case before a trial is held.

bond; bonding A large sum of money given by a publisher to a government to be held to ensure good behavior. Should the publisher violate a government rule, the bond is forfeited to the government, and the newspaper or magazine cannot be published again until a new bond is posted.

C

California Plan See Missouri Plan.

candidate access rule Section 312 of the Federal Communications Act, which forbids a broadcaster from instituting an across-the-board policy that denies all candidates for federal office the opportunity to use the station to further a political campaign.

case reporter(s) A book (or books) containing a chronological collection of the opinions rendered by a particular court for cases that were decided by the court.

challenge for cause The request by a litigant in a criminal or civil case that a juror be dismissed for a specific reason.

change of venue Moving a trial to a distant community in order to find jurors who have not read or viewed prejudicial publicity about the defendant.

citation The reference to a legal opinion contained in a case reporter that gives the name, volume number, and page number where the opinion can be found. The year the opinion was rendered is also included in the citation.

civil complaint A written statement of the plaintiff's legal grievance, which normally initiates a civil suit.

commercial speech doctrine The legal doctrine that states that truthful advertising for products and services that are not illegal is normally protected by the First Amendment to the U.S. Constitution.

common law Principles and rules of law that derive their authority not from legislation but from community usage and custom.

comparative license hearing A hearing to evaluate potential licensees when two or more persons seek the same broadcast license, as required by a Federal Communications Commission rule. Auctions have replaced this process.

concurring opinion A written opinion by an appellate judge or justice in which the author agrees with the decision of the court but normally states reasons different from those in the court opinion as the basis for his or her decision.

consent A defense in both libel and invasion of privacy cases that provides that individuals who agree to the publication of a libelous story or the appropriation of their name cannot then maintain a lawsuit based on the libel or the appropriation.

consent order or decree A document in which an individual agrees to terminate a specific behavior, such as an advertising campaign, or to refrain from a specific action, such as making a certain advertising claim.

constitution A written outline of the organization of a government that provides for both the rights and responsibilities of various branches of the government and the limits of the power of the government.

contempt of court An act of disobedience or disrespect to a judge, which may be punished by a fine or jail sentence.

continuance The delay of a trial or hearing; that is, the trial is postponed.

copyright That body of law which protects the works created by writers, painters, photographers, performing artists, inventors, and other persons who create intangible property.

copyright notice The words "Copyright ©2001 by Don R. Pember," for example, which indicate to a user that a work is copyrighted by the author or creator.

corrective advertising Rules established by the Federal Trade Commission that require an advertiser to correct the false impressions left by deceptive advertising in a certain percentage of future advertisements.

court's opinion The official opinion of an appellate court that states the reasons or rationale for a decision.

criminal history privacy laws State laws that limit the access of non–law enforcement personnel to criminal records maintained by states.

criminal libel A libel against the state, against the dead, or against a large, ill-defined group (such as a race) in which the state prosecutes the libel on behalf of the injured parties.

criminal prosecution; criminal action A legal action brought by the state against an individual or group of individuals for violating state criminal laws.

criminal syndicalism laws Laws that outlaw advocacy, planning, or processes aimed at establishing the control over industry by workers or trade unions.

D

damages Money awarded to the winning party in a civil lawsuit.

defamation Any communication that holds a person up to contempt, hatred, ridicule, or scorn and lowers the reputation of the individual defamed.

defendant The person against whom relief or recovery is sought in a civil lawsuit; the individual against whom a state criminal action is brought.

demurrer An allegation made by the defendant in a lawsuit that even if the facts as stated by the plaintiff are true, they do not state a sufficient cause for action.

de novo New or fresh. In some instances a court of general jurisdiction will hear an appeal from a case from a lower court and simply retry the case. This is a de novo hearing.

Dickinson **rule** A rule emanating from a decision by the U.S. Court of Appeals for the 5th Circuit stating that even a patently unconstitutional court order must be obeyed until it is overturned by an appellate court.

dicta Remarks in a court opinion that do not speak directly to the legal point in question.

direct appeal The statutorily granted right of an aggrieved party to carry the appeal of a case to the Supreme Court of the United States. The high court can deny this right if the appeal lacks a substantial federal question.

dissenting opinion A written opinion by a judge or justice who disagrees with the appellate court's decision in a case.

E

en banc; sitting en banc A French term to describe all or most of the justices or judges of an appellate court sitting together to hear a case. This situation is the opposite of the more typical situation in which a small group (called a panel) of judges or justices in a particular court hears a case.

equal time rule Section 315 of the Federal Communications Act, which states that when broadcasters permit a legally qualified candidate for elective office to use their broadcasting facilities, all other legally qualified candidates for the same elective office must be given similar opportunity.

equity A system of jurisprudence, distinct from the common law, in which courts are empowered to decide cases on the basis of equity or fairness and are not bound by the rigid precedents that often exist in the common law.

Espionage Act A law adopted by the Congress in 1917 that outlawed criticism of the U.S. government and its participation in World War I in Europe.

executive privilege An asserted common-law privilege of the president and other executives to keep presidential papers, records, and other documents secret, even from the Congress.

executive session A popular euphemism for a closed meeting held by a government body such as a city council or school board.

F

fair comment A libel defense that protects the publication of libelous opinion that focuses on the public activities of a person acting in a public sphere.

fairness doctrine A Federal Communications Commission rule (abandoned in 1987) that requires that broadcasters devote a reasonable portion of broadcast time to the discussion of important public issues and that the coverage of these issues be fair in the sense that all important contrasting views on the issues are presented.

fair use A provision of the copyright law that permits a limited amount of copying of material that has been properly copyrighted.

false light That portion of privacy law which prohibits all publications or broadcasts that falsely portray an individual in an offensive manner.

Federal Communications Act The law, adopted in 1934, that is the foundation for the regulation of broadcasting in the United States.

Federal Communications Commission (FCC) A five-member body appointed by the president whose function is to administer the federal broadcasting and communications laws.

federal open-meetings law (Government in Sunshine Act) A federal law that requires approximately 50 federal agencies and bureaus to hold all their meetings in public, unless a subject under discussion is included within one of the 10 exemptions contained in the statute.

Federal Trade Commission A five-member body appointed by the president whose function is to administer the federal laws relating to advertising, antitrust, and many other business matters.

Fighting Words Doctrine A legal doctrine that permits prior censorship of words that create a clear and present danger of inciting an audience to disorder or violence.

FOIA See Freedom of Information Act.

Freedom of Information Act A federal law that mandates that all the records created and kept by federal agencies in the executive branch of government must be open for public inspection and copying, except those records that fall into one of nine exempted categories listed in the statute.

FTC See Federal Trade Commission.

G

gag order(s) A restrictive court order that prohibits all or some participants in a trial from speaking about a case or that stops publications and broadcasting stations from reporting on certain aspects of a case.

Government in Sunshine Act See federal open-meetings law.

grand jury A jury whose function is to determine whether sufficient evidence exists to issue an indictment or true bill charging an individual or individuals with a crime and to take such persons to trial. It is called a grand jury because it has more members than a petit, or trial, jury.

I

identification As used in a libel suit, the requirement that the plaintiff prove that at least one person believes that the subject of the libelous remarks is the plaintiff and not some other person.

impeachment A criminal proceeding against a public officer that is started by written "articles of impeachment" and followed by a trial. The House of Representatives, for example, can issue articles of impeachment against the president, who is then tried by the Senate.

indictment A written accusation issued by a grand jury charging that an individual or individuals have committed a specific crime and should be taken to trial.

information A written accusation issued by a public officer rather than by a grand jury charging that an individual or individuals have committed a specific crime and should be taken to trial.

intrusion An invasion of privacy committed when one individual intrudes upon or invades the solitude of another individual.

invasion of privacy A civil tort that emerged in the early 20th century and contains four distinct categories of legal wrongs: appropriation, intrusion, publication of private facts, and false light.

J

judgment of the court The final ruling of a court, which determines the outcome of a lawsuit. It is different from the verdict, which is the decision of the jury in a trial.

judicial decree A judgment of a court of equity; a declaration of the court announcing the legal consequences of the facts found to be true by the court.

judicial instructions A statement (often written) made by a judge to the members of a jury informing them about the law (as distinguished from the facts) in a case.

judicial review The power of a court to declare void and unenforceable any statute, rule, or executive order that conflicts with an appropriate state constitution or the federal constitution.

jury A group of men and women called together in a trial court to determine the facts in a civil or criminal lawsuit. It is sometimes called a petit jury to distinguish it from a grand jury.

L

legal brief(s); brief Written legal argument presented to the court by one or both parties in a lawsuit.

libel Published or broadcast communication that lowers the reputation of an individual by holding him or her up to contempt, ridicule, or scorn.

licensing process The process by which a government gives a publisher or a broadcaster prior permission to print a newspaper or operate a broadcasting station. Revocation of a license can be used as punishment for failing to comply with the law or the wishes of the government. Licensing of the printed press in the United States ended in the 1720s.

litigant A party in a lawsuit; a participant in litigation.

litigated order An order issued by a government agency, like the FTC, requiring that a particular practice, such as a certain advertisement, be stopped.

M

memorandum order The announcement by an appellate court of a decision in a case that does not include a written opinion containing the rationale or reasons for the ruling.

misappropriation Taking what belongs to someone else and using it unfairly for one's own gain; for example, attempting to pass off a novel as part of a popular series of novels written and published by someone else. It is often called unfair competition.

Missouri Plan A system used in some states by which judges are appointed to the bench initially and then must stand for re-election on a ballot that permits citizens to vote to retain or not retain the judge.

N

NAD See next entry.

National Advertising Division (NAD) of the Council of Better Business Bureaus An industry organization that evaluates and rules on the truthfulness of advertising claims. Complaints are normally brought to the NAD by competing advertisers.

negligence A fault standard in libel and other tort law. Negligent behavior is normally described as an act or action that a reasonably prudent person or a reasonable individual would not have committed. In libel law, courts often measure negligence by asking whether the allegedly libelous material was the work of a person who exercised reasonable care in preparation of the story.

neutral reportage An emerging libel defense or privilege that states that it is permissible to publish or broadcast an accurate account of information about a public figure from a reliable source even when the reporter doubts the truth of the libelous assertion. The defense is not widely accepted.

nonjusticiable matter An issue that is inappropriate for a court to decide because the jurists lack the knowledge to make the ruling,

because another branch of government has the responsibility to answer such questions, or because a court order in the matter would not likely be enforceable or enforced.

O

open-meetings laws State and federal statutes that require that certain meetings of public agencies—normally in the executive branch of government—be open to the public and the press.

open-records laws State and federal statutes that require that certain records of public agencies—normally in the executive branch of government—be open for inspection and copying by the public and the press.

opinion The written statement issued by a court that explains the reasons for a judgment and states the rule of law in the case.

oral argument An oral presentation made to a judge or justices in which the litigants argue the merits of their case.

original jurisdiction Jurisdiction in the first instance, as distinguished from appellate jurisdiction. A court exercising original jurisdiction determines both the facts and the law in the case; courts exercising appellate jurisdiction may only rule on the law and the sufficiency of the facts as determined by a trial court.

P

per curiam opinion An unsigned court opinion. The author of the opinion is not known outside the court.

peremptory challenge A challenge without stated cause to remove a juror from a panel. Litigants are given a small number of such challenges in a lawsuit.

personal attack rules Specific rules issued by the Federal Communications Commission that outline the responsibilities of a broadcast licensee if and when an attack on an individual or identifiable group is made during a radio or television broadcast. The licensee must inform the individual or group of the attack and provide an opportunity for a reply, among other requirements.

petitioner One who petitions a court to take an action; someone who starts a lawsuit, or carries an appeal to a higher court (appellant). This person is the opposite of a respondent, one who responds to a petition.

plaintiff An individual who initiates a civil lawsuit.

pleadings The written statements of the parties in a lawsuit that contain their allegations, denials, and defenses.

precedent An established rule of law set by a previous case. Courts should follow precedent when it is advisable and possible.

preferred position balancing theory A theory on how the First Amendment should be interpreted that states that when the guarantees of freedom of speech and freedom of the press are balanced against other important rights, the rights of freedom of expression are to be given extra weight, to be preferred. Legally, this proposition requires that persons who would restrict freedom of expression bear the burden of proving that such restrictions are justified and not a violation of the First Amendment.

presumed damages Damages a plaintiff can get without proof of injury or harm.

pretrial hearing A meeting prior to a criminal trial at which attorneys for the state and for the defense make arguments before a judge on evidentiary questions; that is, whether a confession made by the defendant should be admitted as evidence at the trial. This type of hearing is sometimes called a suppression hearing.

Printers' Ink statute A model law drafted in 1911 to control false or misleading advertising. Most states adopted some version of this model in the early 20th century. Such laws are largely ineffective because they are not normally enforced.

prior restraint Prepublication censorship that forbids publication or broadcast of certain objectionable material, as opposed to punishment of a perpetrator after the material has been published or broadcast.

Privacy Act A federal statute that forbids the disclosure of specific material held by federal agencies on the grounds that its release could invade the privacy of the subject of the report or document.

publication In libel law, exposing an allegedly libelous statement to one person in addition to the subject of the libel.

publication of private information In privacy law, publicizing embarrassing private information about an individual that is not of legitimate public concern.

puffery Often expansive hyperbole about a product that does not contain factual claims of merit. Normally, puffery is permitted by the law (e.g., "This is the best-looking automobile on the market today").

punitive damages Money damages awarded to a plaintiff in a lawsuit aimed not to compensate for harm to the injured party but to punish the defendant for his or her illegal conduct.

Q

qualified privilege In libel law, the privilege of the reporter (or any person) to publish a fair and accurate report of the proceedings of a public meeting or public document and be immune from lawsuit for the publication of libel uttered at the meeting or contained in the document.

R

Radio Act of 1912 The first federal broadcast law, which imposed only minimal regulation on the fledgling broadcast industry. Radio operators were required to have a license under this statute.

Radio Act of 1927 The first comprehensive national broadcast law, which provided the basic framework for the regulation of broadcast that was later adopted in the Federal Communications Act of 1934.

respondent The person who responds to a petition placed before a court by another person; the opposite of the petitioner. At the appellate level, the respondent is often called the appellee.

restrictive order A court order limiting the discussion of the facts in a criminal case both by participants in the case and by the press. See also gag order.

retraction In libel law, a statement published or broadcast that attempts to retract or correct previously published or broadcast libelous matter. A timely retraction will usually mitigate damages, and in some states that have retraction laws, plaintiffs must seek a retraction before beginning a lawsuit or they lose the opportunity to collect anything but special damages.

right of publicity An offshoot of privacy law that protects the right of persons to capitalize on their fame or notoriety for commercial or advertising purposes.

right of reply A little-used libel defense that declares as immune from a lawsuit a libelous remark made against an individual in reply to a previously published libelous remark made by that individual.

S

scienter Guilty knowledge. In many criminal prosecutions, the state must prove that the accused was aware of the nature of his or her behavior. In an obscenity case, for example, the state must normally show that the defendant was aware of the contents of the book he or she sold.

Section 312 See candidate access rule.

Section 315 See equal time rule.

Sedition Act of 1918 An amendment to the Espionage Act adopted in the midst of World War I that severely limited criticism of the government and criticism of U.S. participation in the European war.

seditious libel Libeling the government; criticizing the government or government officers. It is sometimes called sedition.

sequestration of the jury Separating the jury from the community during a trial. Usually a jury is lodged at a hotel and members are required to eat together. In general, sequestration means to keep jurors away from other persons. Exposure to news reports is also screened to shield jurors from information about the trial.

shield laws State statutes that permit reporters in some circumstances to shield the name of a confidential news source when questioned by a grand jury or in another legal forum.

single mistake rule In libel law, a rule that states that it is not libelous to accuse a professional person or business person of making a single mistake (e.g., "Dr. Pat Jones incorrectly diagnosed the patient's illness").

slander Oral defamation.

Smith Act A federal law adopted in 1940 that makes it illegal to advocate the violent overthrow of the government.

special damages Damages that can be awarded to a plaintiff in a lawsuit upon proof of specific monetary loss.

stare decisis "Let the decision stand." This concept is the operating principle in the common-law system and requires that judges follow precedent case law when making judgments.

statute of limitations A law that requires that a legal action must begin within a specified period of time (usually one to three years for a civil case) after the legal wrong was committed.

statutes Laws adopted by legislative bodies.

statutory construction The process undertaken by courts to interpret or construe the meaning of statutes.

subpoena A court document that requires a witness to appear and testify or to produce documents or papers pertinent to a pending controversy.

substantiation A Federal Trade Commission rule that requires an advertiser to prove the truth of advertising claims made about a product or service.

summary contempt power The power of a judge to find an individual guilty of a contempt of court and impose a sentence without giving the individual the benefit of a jury trial.

summary judgment A judgment granted to a party in a lawsuit when the pleadings and other materials in the case disclose no material issue of fact between the parties, making it possible for the case to be decided on the basis of the law by the court. A summary judgment avoids a costly jury trial.

summary jury trial An abbreviated jury trial where jurors hear arguments but no witnesses are called and little evidence is presented. The jurors can issue an informal verdict, which can be used as the basis for a settlement of the case, thus avoiding a full-blown and costly trial.

survival statute A statute that permits an heir to continue to maintain a lawsuit if the plaintiff died after the suit was filed but before it was resolved.

Glossary

T

time, place, and manner restrictions or rules Rules, when justified by a substantial government interest, that can regulate the time, place, and manner of speaking or publishing and the distribution of printed material.

trade libel Product disparagement, and not considered true libel; disparaging a product as opposed to the manufacturer or maker of the product.

trade regulation rules Rules adopted by the Federal Trade Commission that prohibit specific advertising claims about an entire class of products. For example, makers of fruit drinks that contain less than 10 percent fruit juice cannot advertise these products as fruit juice.

trespass Unlawful entry on another person's land or property.

trial court(s) Normally the first court to hear a lawsuit. This court is the forum in which the facts are determined and the law is initially applied, as opposed to an appellate court, to which decisions are appealed.

U

unfair competition See misappropriation.

V

variable obscenity statutes A Supreme Court doctrine that permits states to prohibit the sale, distribution, or exhibition of certain kinds of nonobscene matter to children, so long as these laws do not interfere with the accessibility of this material to adults.

verdict The decision of a trial jury based on the instructions given to it by the judge.

voir dire A preliminary examination the court makes of persons chosen to serve as jurors in a trial. Persons can be challenged for cause or on the basis of a peremptory challenge by either side in the legal dispute.

W

writ of certiorari A writ by which an appellant seeks the review of a case by the Supreme Court of the United States. When the writ is granted, the court will order the lower court to send up the record of the case for review.

Z

Zapple Rule A corollary to the equal time rule that states that when the supporters of a legally qualified candidate are given time on a radio or television broadcast, the supporters of all other legally qualified candidates for the same office must also be given equal opportunity.

TABLE OF CASES

Table of Cases

Table of Cases

INDEX

Index

Index

Index